Texas Modern Chemistry

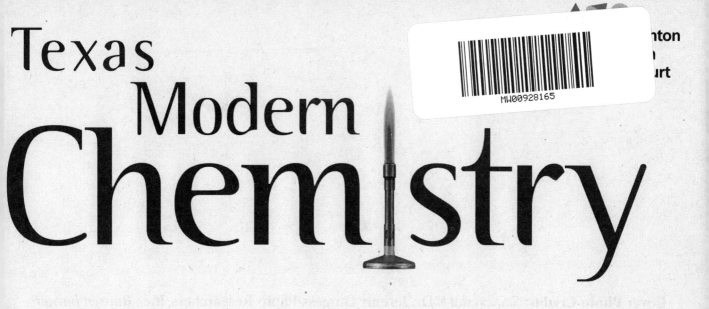

Interactive Reader

Printed in the U.S.A.

ISBN 978-0-544-03401-3

7 8 9 10 0928 21 20 19 18

4500697283   A B C D E F G

CONTENTS

Modern Chemistry
Interactive Reader

Texas Essential Knowledge and Skills

The **Holt McDougal Texas Modern Chemistry** program provides a full year of interactive experiences structured around the Texas Essential Knowledge and Skills (TEKS) for Chemistry. This Interactive Reader features all the essential content from your textbook but with additional learning support to help you complete your chemistry course.

The full language of the TEKS is given here for your convenience. Look for TEKS codes on the opening pages of each section. You can refer to these pages to see the full text for each TEKS.

TEKS 1 Scientific Processes

The student, for at least 40% of instructional time, conducts laboratory and field investigations using safe, environmentally appropriate, and ethical practices.

The student is expected to:

A demonstrate safe practices during laboratory and field investigations, including the appropriate use of safety showers, eyewash fountains, safety goggles, and fire extinguishers;

B know specific hazards of chemical substances such as flammability, corrosiveness, and radioactivity as summarized on the Material Safety Data Sheets (MSDS); and

C demonstrate an understanding of the use and conservation of resources and the proper disposal or recycling of materials.

TEKS 2 Scientific Processes

The student uses scientific methods to solve investigative questions.

The student is expected to:

A know the definition of science and understand that it has limitations, as specified in subsection **b.2** of this section;

b.2 Nature of Science. Science, as defined by the National Academy of Sciences, is the "use of evidence to construct testable explanations and predictions of natural phenomena, as well as the knowledge generated through this process." This vast body of changing and increasing knowledge is described by physical, mathematical, and conceptual models. Students should know that some questions are outside the realm of science because they deal with phenomena that are not scientifically testable.

B know that scientific hypotheses are tentative and testable statements that must be capable of being supported or not supported by observational evidence. Hypotheses of durable explanatory power which have been tested over a wide variety of conditions are incorporated into theories;

C know that scientific theories are based on natural and physical phenomena and are capable of being tested by multiple independent researchers. Unlike hypotheses, scientific theories are well-established and highly-reliable explanations, but may be subject to change as new areas of science and new technologies are developed;

D distinguish between scientific hypotheses and scientific theories;

E plan and implement investigative procedures, including asking questions, formulating testable hypotheses, and selecting equipment and technology, including graphing calculators, computers and probes, sufficient scientific glassware such as beakers, Erlenmeyer flasks, pipettes, graduated cylinders, volumetric flasks, safety goggles, and burettes, electronic balances, and an adequate supply of consumable chemicals;

F collect data and make measurements with accuracy and precision;

G express and manipulate chemical quantities using scientific conventions and mathematical procedures, including dimensional analysis, scientific notation, and significant figures;

H organize, analyze, evaluate, make inferences, and predict trends from data; and

I communicate valid conclusions supported by the data through methods such as lab reports, labeled drawings, graphs, journals, summaries, oral reports, and technology-based reports.

TEKS 3 Scientific Processes

The student uses critical thinking, scientific reasoning, and problem solving to make informed decisions within and outside the classroom.

The student is expected to:

A in all fields of science, analyze, evaluate, and critique scientific explanations by using empirical evidence, logical reasoning, and experimental and observational testing, including examining all sides of scientific evidence of those scientific explanations, so as to encourage critical thinking by the student;

B communicate and apply scientific information extracted from various sources such as current events, news reports, published journal articles, and marketing materials;

C draw inferences based on data related to promotional materials for products and services;

D evaluate the impact of research on scientific thought, society, and the environment;

E describe the connection between chemistry and future careers; and

F research and describe the history of chemistry and contributions of scientists.

TEKS 4 Science Concepts

The student knows the characteristics of matter and can analyze the relationships between chemical and physical changes and properties.

The student is expected to:

A differentiate between physical and chemical changes and properties;

B identify extensive and intensive properties;

C compare solids, liquids, and gases in terms of compressibility, structure, shape, and volume; and

D classify matter as pure substances or mixtures through investigation of their properties.

TEKS 5 Science Concepts

The student understands the historical development of the Periodic Table and can apply its predictive power.

The student is expected to:

A explain the use of chemical and physical properties in the historical development of the Periodic Table;

B use the Periodic Table to identify and explain the properties of chemical families, including alkali metals, alkaline earth metals, halogens, noble gases, and transition metals; and

C use the Periodic Table to identify and explain periodic trends, including atomic and ionic radii, electronegativity, and ionization energy.

TEKS 6 Science Concepts

The student knows and understands the historical development of atomic theory.

The student is expected to:

A understand the experimental design and conclusions used in the development of modern atomic theory, including Dalton's Postulates, Thomson's discovery of electron properties, Rutherford's nuclear atom, and Bohr's nuclear atom;

B understand the electromagnetic spectrum and the mathematical relationships between energy, frequency, and wavelength of light;

C calculate the wavelength, frequency, and energy of light using Planck's constant and the speed of light;

D use isotopic composition to calculate average atomic mass of an element; and

E express the arrangement of electrons in atoms through electron configurations and Lewis valence electron dot structures.

TEKS 7 Science Concepts

The student knows how atoms form ionic, metallic, and covalent bonds.

The student is expected to:

A name ionic compounds containing main group or transition metals, covalent compounds, acids, and bases, using International Union of Pure and Applied Chemistry (IUPAC) nomenclature rules;

B write the chemical formulas of common polyatomic ions, ionic compounds containing main group or transition metals, covalent compounds, acids, and bases;

C construct electron dot formulas to illustrate ionic and covalent bonds;

D describe the nature of metallic bonding and apply the theory to explain metallic properties such as thermal and electrical conductivity, malleability, and ductility; and

E predict molecular structure for molecules with linear, trigonal planar, or tetrahedral electron pair geometries using Valence Shell Electron Pair Repulsion (VSEPR) theory.

TEKS 8 Science Concepts

The student can quantify the changes that occur during chemical reactions.

The student is expected to:

A define and use the concept of a mole;

B use the mole concept to calculate the number of atoms, ions, or molecules in a sample of material;

C calculate percent composition and empirical and molecular formulas;

D use the law of conservation of mass to write and balance chemical equations; and

E perform stoichiometric calculations, including determination of mass relationships between reactants and products, calculation of limiting reagents, and percent yield.

TEKS 9 Science Concepts

The student understands the principles of ideal gas behavior, kinetic molecular theory, and the conditions that influence the behavior of gases.

The student is expected to:

A describe and calculate the relations between volume, pressure, number of moles, and temperature for an ideal gas as described by Boyle's law, Charles' law, Avogadro's law, Dalton's law of partial pressure, and the ideal gas law;

B perform stoichiometric calculations, including determination of mass and volume relationships between reactants and products for reactions involving gases; and

C describe the postulates of kinetic molecular theory.

TEKS 10 Science Concepts

The student understands and can apply the factors that influence the behavior of solutions.

The student is expected to:

A describe the unique role of water in chemical and biological systems;

B develop and use general rules regarding solubility through investigations with aqueous solutions;

C calculate the concentration of solutions in units of molarity;

D use molarity to calculate the dilutions of solutions;

E distinguish between types of solutions such as electrolytes and nonelectrolytes and unsaturated, saturated, and supersaturated solutions;

F investigate factors that influence solubilities and rates of dissolution such as temperature, agitation, and surface area;

G define acids and bases and distinguish between Arrhenius and Bronsted-Lowry definitions and predict products in acid base reactions that form water;

H understand and differentiate among acid-base reactions, precipitation reactions, and oxidation-reduction reactions;

I define pH and use the hydrogen or hydroxide ion concentrations to calculate the pH of a solution; and

J distinguish between degrees of dissociation for strong and weak acids and bases.

TEKS 11 Science Concepts

The student understands the energy changes that occur in chemical reactions.

The student is expected to:

A understand energy and its forms, including kinetic, potential, chemical, and thermal energies;

B understand the law of conservation of energy and the processes of heat transfer;

C use thermochemical equations to calculate energy changes that occur in chemical reactions and classify reactions as exothermic or endothermic;

D perform calculations involving heat, mass, temperature change, and specific heat; and

E use calorimetry to calculate the heat of a chemical process.

TEKS 12 Science Concepts

The student understands the basic processes of nuclear chemistry.

The student is expected to:

A describe the characteristics of alpha, beta, and gamma radiation;

B describe radioactive decay process in terms of balanced nuclear equations; and

C compare fission and fusion reactions.

Matter and Change

Key Concepts

Review Previous Concepts

1. Compare and contrast the properties of a metal spoon and a plastic spoon. Name at least three properties that are similar and three properties that are different.

_____

_____

_____

_____

_____

_____

_____

_____

SECTION 1.1

Chemistry Is a Physical Science

Science is many things. We might define **science** as the knowledge obtained by observing natural events and conditions in order to discover facts and formulate laws or principles that can be verified or tested.

Physical science is the study of nonliving objects and materials. Physics, astronomy, and geology are examples of physical sciences. Chemistry is another physical science. **Chemistry** is the study of the composition, structure, and properties of matter, the processes that matter undergoes, and the energy changes that accompany these processes. A chemist studies matter and tries to answer such questions as "What makes up this material?", "How does this material change when heated or cooled?", "What happens when I mix this material with another material?", and "What rules determine how materials change in different situations?"

The materials with which chemists work are called chemicals. A **chemical** is any substance with a definite composition. For example, sucrose is a chemical that is also called cane sugar. One unit of sucrose found in a sugar cane plant is exactly the same as one unit of sucrose found anywhere else, whether in another plant, in the ground, or in your body.

Chemistry is the study of matter and its processes.

Chemists divide their areas of study into many different branches. Six major branches are shown in the table at the right. These branches often overlap, depending on what process or material the chemist is studying. Projects in each branch can be classified as basic research, applied research, or technological development.

KEY TERMS

science   chemistry   chemical

READING CHECK

1. Write two questions that a chemist could try to answer about a material called "Chemical X."

_____

_____

_____

Branches of Chemistry

1. Organic chemistry—the study of materials with carbon

2. Inorganic chemistry—the study of non-organic materials

3. Physical chemistry—the study of the properties of matter

4. Analytical chemistry—the identification of materials

5. Biochemistry—the study of the chemistry of living things

6. Theoretical chemistry—predicting the properties of new materials

Basic Research

The goal of basic research is to increase knowledge. In chemistry, basic research includes the study of the properties of a chemical. It also includes the study of what happens when two chemicals are mixed.

Sometimes, scientists do basic research simply to satisfy their curiosity about a chemical and its qualities. Sometimes basic research results in a new product or technology, though such results are not the scientists' goal.

Applied Research

The goal of applied research is to solve problems. In chemistry, applied research includes finding materials with certain properties. For example, a chemist might want to develop a new cooling fluid for a refrigerator that is not dangerous to the environment. Sometimes applied research in chemistry has the goal of learning how to prevent a certain reaction from occurring, or how to control the reaction, or how to speed up the reaction.

Technological Development

The goal of technological development is to come up with new products and processes that improve the quality of life. Sometimes new technologies are the result of determined efforts to create a certain product. New technologies can also result from knowledge gained in basic and applied research, or can build on other technologies. For example, lasers were developed from basic research on crystals and light. Scientists looking for new ways to transmit information found that laser pulses could be sent through plastic fibers. This led to the technology of fiber optic cables that carry television, telephone, and computer signals.

 CONNECT

Basic research can lead to chance discoveries. For example, Roy Plunkett discovered the properties of Teflon® by accident. After removing the gas from a container, the container was still heavier than expected. Inside, he found a white solid with nonstick properties.

Sometimes the uses of a material or chemical are not realized at first. It was many years later before Teflon® was used in nonstick cookware.

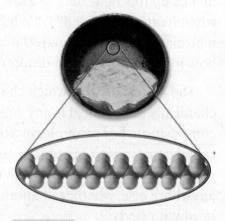

The nonstick coating on this frying pan is new technology that makes use of the unique properties of Teflon®.

🔍 Critical Thinking

2. **Connect** Why is basic research important to technological development?

_____

_____

_____

_____

Chemistry helps us understand our world.

Chemistry can help you better understand the world around you. Each day, you can find many news reports, magazine articles, and advertisements containing scientific claims. Each scientific claim is meant to be undeniable evidence supporting a viewpoint. But scientific claims may or may not be valid. Knowing some chemistry can help you assess the validity of the claims.

TIP The word *valid* means logically correct, well-grounded, and justifiable.

Current Events: Radon Gas

You may have read a news article or heard a news report about health risks caused by radon gas in homes. So if you found out that granite countertops contain radon gas, you might decide to avoid granite. However, think further about the claim. Do you know what it means for a substance to be radioactive?

A substance is radioactive if its atoms break apart, or decay. When the atoms decay, they emit radiation in the form of subatomic particles and energy. This radiation can cause damage to living tissues by interfering with cellular functions. It is important to note that radioactivity is a natural part of the environment. In most places, the level of radioactivity is too low to cause harm.

Radioactive radon gas can be a serious danger. Sometimes the gas seeps into basements through openings in houses' foundations. The radon gas rises and is inhaled by people, becoming a health threat. Keeping the gas out of homes or keeping them well ventilated is the way to eliminate the risk.

How dangerous are granite countertops? It is possible that any piece of granite is radioactive, as are most rocks. The Environmental Protection Agency has stated that the amount of radioactive material in most granite is not enough to be dangerous.

You should take any potential health risk seriously. You should not, however, simply believe any warning you read or hear about.

Critical Thinking

3. **Analyze** Suggest a way that chemistry knowledge could help you make decisions about a claim.

_____

_____

Products and Services

Science is used to sell products and services. Companies commonly use the words "laboratory tested" or "special formula" on product labels. This happens because science as proof of quality is appealing to consumers. Companies hope that their scientific claims become strong selling points.

Critical Thinking

4. **Infer Conclusions** Why do you think some consumers believe that laboratory testing of a product serves as proof of quality?

_____

_____

_____

_____

An example of a company using scientific claims to sell its products follows. A label on a shampoo bottle (as shown) might use the words:

"New and improved foaming agents"
"No-tears formula"
"Scientifically proven to rejuvenate hair!"

All of those phrases make the product seem to be a very good choice when you are shopping for a shampoo. However, use what you know about science to question what those words really mean. You may want to find out:

- Which chemicals are used as foaming agents, and what is new and improved about them?
- Are the ingredients really non-irritants to eyes?
- Hair is made up of dead cells, so how is it possible to rejuvenate it?
- What makes one shampoo more effective than another? Does "more foam" mean it's a more effective shampoo?
- What do the chemicals listed on the bottle actually do in the shampoo? Could they be in the shampoo for reasons other than cleaning hair?

Product Labels Hair shampoos make many claims and may even list chemicals to influence the consumer.

Chemistry helps us change and improve our world.

Chemists are, and have always been, concerned with the study of the substances around them and the changes those substances undergo. The knowledge they've gained has helped them change and improve our world.

Chemists of the Past

Alchemy is an ancient field of study from which the field of chemistry eventually developed. The word *chemistry* comes from the word *alchemy*.

The study of alchemy was more a philosophical tradition than a science. Alchemists believed that, in studying changes in matter, they were unlocking fundamental secrets about the world. Alchemists hoped that these powerful secrets could help them gain great wealth or eternal youth.

One goal of alchemists was to discover a way to turn base metals into precious metals, such as gold and silver. The alchemists used experimentation to explore, as today's chemists do. Alchemists tested, heated, mixed, crushed, and burned all kinds of substances in their efforts to unravel the mysteries of those substances.

Advances in chemical knowledge have had profound impacts on societies throughout history. Chemists have made it possible to have:

- medications for healing illnesses
- purified metals for constructing machines
- gunpowder
- fertilizers for improving crop quality
- cleansers for improving sanitary conditions
- inks for writing

The list of chemical innovations that have improved or changed our world goes on and on.

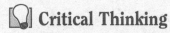 Critical Thinking

5. **Apply** List at least three chemical innovations that improve or change your everyday life.

_____

_____

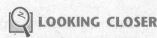 LOOKING CLOSER

Alchemists may seem to have been all fakes and mystics, but they did do a lot of experimentation. Many pieces of equipment used in modern chemistry labs date back to the alchemists. Alchemists may never have achieved the dream of turning base metals into gold, but they did leave their mark on the chemists of today.

Chemists Today

In the world today, those working in the chemical sciences are doing some exciting things. Examples of these things include advances in the fields of pharmaceuticals, forensics, and green chemistry.

Pharmaceutical chemists currently use highly advanced computer modeling techniques to build molecules with desired properties. With computer visualization, chemists can rotate the molecule to view it in any orientation. It is even possible to view how the molecule reacts under different conditions. Chemists are becoming more reliant on computer models as they make more complex molecules.

Forensic chemists analyze evidence such as hair samples, bloodstains, fingerprints, and paint chips from crime scenes. Chemical analysis of this evidence can help tell the story of what happened and who was involved with the crime. As expert witnesses during criminal trials, forensic chemists give objective conclusions about their findings. Forensic chemists can also help with crime prevention. For example, counterfeiting of money can be made difficult by designing hard-to-reproduce dyes for printed money.

Green chemists develop products and processes that minimize the production of substances harmful to society. The goal of green chemistry is to prevent waste. This is achieved by designing processes that have very small amounts of by-products, or by making products that break down after their intended use.

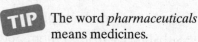

TIP The word *pharmaceuticals* means medicines.

(a) Modeling Computers can help design complex molecules.

(b) Forensic Chemistry The new U.S. currency owes much to forensic chemistry.

(c) Green Chemistry This cup is made from 100% recycled material.

✓ READING CHECK

6. Give one example of each: (a) how today's pharmaceutical chemists can build molecules, (b) how today's forensic chemists can help solve crimes, and (c) how today's green chemists can lessen the harmful substances in our environment.

_____

_____

_____

_____

VOCABULARY

1. Define science.

_____

_____

2. Define chemistry.

_____

_____

3. What types of substances do chemists work with?

_____

REVIEW

4. Name six branches in the study of chemistry.

_____

_____

_____

5. Compare and contrast basic research, applied research, and technological development.

_____

_____

_____

_____

Critical Thinking

6. **INFERRING RELATIONSHIPS** Scientific and technological advances are constantly changing how people live and work. Discuss a change that you have observed in your lifetime that has made life easier or more enjoyable for you.

_____

_____

_____

_____

SECTION 1.2

Matter and Its Properties

Everything around you is made of matter. Books, desks, computers, trees, and buildings are all made of matter, as are water and even air. **Matter** has two properties: it takes up space and it has mass.

Mass is a measure of the amount of material that makes up an object or substance. You can measure mass by using a balance. The mass of matter will always measure at greater than zero, because mass is a necessary property of matter.

The second property of matter is that it takes up space. Another way to describe this property is to say that all matter has volume. An object such as a book or a tree takes up space that you can see with your eyes. Air also takes up space, so air is also considered matter.

KEY TERMS	
matter	gas
mass	plasma
element	chemical property
atom	chemical change
compound	chemical reaction
extensive property	reactant
intensive property	product
physical property	mixture
physical change	homogeneous
change of state	solution
solid	heterogeneous
liquid	pure substance

Atoms are the building blocks of matter.

All the matter that people have observed is made of certain building blocks called elements. An **element** is a pure substance that cannot be broken down into simpler, stable substances. Carbon and gold are elements. An element is always made of only one type of atom.

An **atom** is the smallest unit of an element that maintains the chemical identity of that element. For example, an atom of carbon can be separated from other carbon atoms and combined with other types of atoms such as oxygen. However, it can still be identified as a carbon atom.

A **compound** can be broken down into simpler, stable substances. Each compound contains atoms of two or more elements that are chemically bonded. For example, water is a compound made of two elements. Two atoms of hydrogen and one atom of oxygen are bonded in a water molecule. A *molecule* is the smallest unit of a compound or element that retains all the properties of the compound or element.

LOOKING CLOSER

1. Read the underlined definitions for matter, element, and compound and give an example of each.

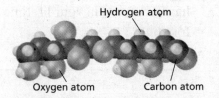

Hydrogen atom

Oxygen atom   Carbon atom

A compound, such as sucrose (table sugar), is made up of two or more types of atoms.

All substances have characteristic properties.

Every substance has characteristic properties. Chemists use properties to distinguish between different substances. Properties can help reveal the identity of an unknown substance. Comparisons of several properties can be used together to establish the identity of the unknown.

Chemists also use properties to separate different substances that are mixed together. For example, a mixture of iron and aluminum shavings can be separated using the magnetic property of iron. The iron shavings are attracted to a magnet and the aluminum shavings are not.

Extensive properties depend on the amount of matter that is present. The volume of an object is an extensive property because it changes when material is added to, or taken away from, an object. Extensive properties include the volume, mass, and amount of energy in an object.

In contrast, **intensive properties** do not depend on the amount of matter present. Such properties include melting point, boiling point, and density. Intensive properties are the same for two samples of a substance even if the samples are different in size.

✓ READING CHECK

2. A copper wire can conduct electricity whether the wire is very thin or very thick. Is electrical conductivity an extensive property or an intensive property?

Physical Properties and Physical Changes

A **physical property** can be observed or measured without changing the identity of the substance. Physical properties describe the substance itself, rather than describing how it can change into other substances. One physical property of a substance is its boiling point. Liquid water boils into water vapor at 100°C (373 K or 212°F).

A change in a substance that does not involve a change in the identity of the substance is called a **physical change.** Examples of physical changes include grinding, cutting, melting, and boiling. These types of changes do not change the identity of the substance present.

The boiling point of water is a physical property and an intensive property.

Changes of State The three common states of matter are solid, liquid, and gas. One type of physical change is a change from one of these states to another, such as when ice melts into liquid water. The change of matter from one state to another is called a **change of state.**

Another example of a change of state is freezing, the opposite of melting, in which a substance changes from a liquid to a solid state. When matter changes state, the movement of and distance between the particles in the matter change, but the matter itself stays the same.

☑ READING CHECK

3. Why is boiling a pot of water an example of a physical change?

_____

_____

_____

Solids A **solid** has a definite volume and a definite shape. For example, a piece of coal keeps its size and its shape, regardless of the container it is in. Particles in solids are packed together. The particles can vibrate back and forth, but they cannot change position. The particles are held together because they are attracted to each other.

Liquids A **liquid** has a definite volume but a shape that can change. Liquids assume the shape of their containers. For example, when a thin glass of water is poured into a pot, it takes up the same amount of space in the pot. But the water spreads out to take the shape of the pot. The particles in liquids are close together but they can slide past one another. Because particles in a liquid move more rapidly than the particles in a solid, attractive forces cannot hold the particles in place.

Gases A **gas** has neither a definite volume nor a definite shape. For example, a given quantity of oxygen gas expands to fill any size container and takes the shape of the container. Gas particles move much more rapidly and are farther away from one another compared with the particles of liquids and solids. The attractive forces between gas particles are unable to keep the fast-moving particles close together.

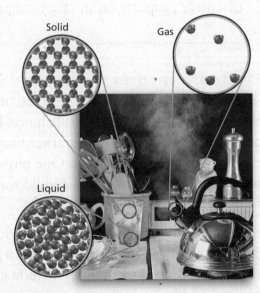

The circles show particle models for water as a solid, a liquid, and a gas.

A fourth state of matter, plasma, is found in fluorescent bulbs and stars. A **plasma** has a high temperature and its matter is made up of charged particles. Like a gas, a plasma takes the shape of its container. Unlike a gas, its particles can be influenced by electrical charges. A lightning bolt is made of air particles that have been converted into plasma.

Most of the material in the sun is in the form of a plasma.

Chemical Properties and Chemical Changes

Physical properties can be observed without changing the identity of the substance. However, the chemical properties of a substance cannot be observed without changing its identity. A **chemical property** relates to a substance's ability to undergo changes that transform it into different substances.

A **chemical change** is a change in which one or more substances are converted into different substances. The substances are said to react with one another to form the new substance or substances. Therefore, a change in which at least one new substance is formed is called a **chemical reaction.**

The chemical properties of a substance are easiest to see when the substance is involved in a chemical reaction. For example, the rusting of iron when combined with the oxygen in air is a chemical property.

READING CHECK

4. List the three common states of matter in order from the state with the fastest-moving particles to the state with the slowest-moving particles.

_____

_____

5. Give an example of a physical change involving iron and a chemical change involving iron.

_____

_____

_____

_____

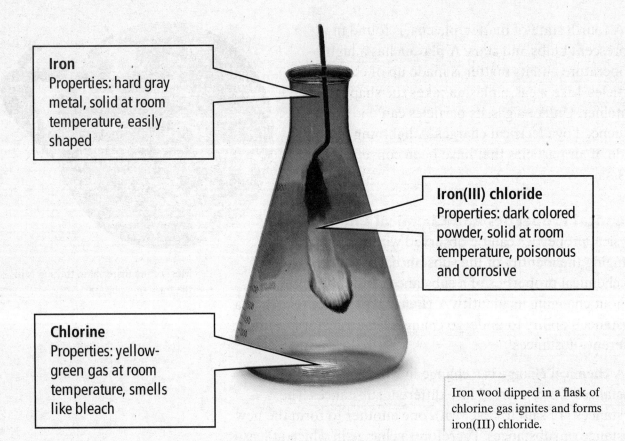

Iron
Properties: hard gray metal, solid at room temperature, easily shaped

Iron(III) chloride
Properties: dark colored powder, solid at room temperature, poisonous and corrosive

Chlorine
Properties: yellow-green gas at room temperature, smells like bleach

Iron wool dipped in a flask of chlorine gas ignites and forms iron(III) chloride.

The substances that react in a chemical change are called the **reactants.** The substances formed by the chemical change are called the **products.** A chemical reaction is often represented as an equation similar to a mathematical statement. For example, the chemical reaction in the diagram above can be described as follows:

$$\text{iron} + \text{chlorine} \longrightarrow \text{iron(III) chloride}$$

In this reaction, iron and chlorine are the reactants and iron(III) chloride are the products.

Chemical reactions form products whose properties can differ greatly from the properties of the reactants. The diagram above shows that the properties of iron and chlorine are different from the properties of iron(III) chloride. However, chemical reactions do not affect the total amount of matter present before and after the change. The amount of matter, and therefore the total mass, remains the same.

Critical Thinking

6. Compare and Contrast When charcoal is burned, carbon in the charcoal combines with oxygen to form carbon dioxide. Compare and contrast the properties of charcoal and carbon dioxide.

_____

_____

_____

_____

_____

Energy and Changes in Matter

Every physical change and chemical change requires energy. This energy can take several forms, such as heat or light. The amount of energy helps to determine what type of change takes place. For example, heat can cause the change of state in which water boils and becomes water vapor. But heat can also cause water vapor to break down into oxygen gas and hydrogen gas. This decomposition of water vapor is a chemical change.

Scientists keep track of the energy present before and after a physical or chemical change. In every case, they have found that the total amount of energy present before the change is also present after the change. Energy can be absorbed or released by one of the substances involved in the change. However, even if some of the energy has changed form, the total energy in the system remains the same. This concept is called the *law of conservation of energy*.

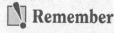 **Remember**

A scientific law is a statement that summarizes how the natural world works.

Matter can be a pure substance or a mixture.

Any sample of matter can be classified as either a pure substance or as a mixture. The composition of a pure substance is the same throughout, with no variation from sample to sample. A pure substance can be either an element or a compound.

Mixtures, in contrast, contain more than one substance. The properties within a mixture can vary from sample to sample. Sometimes two samples from the same mixture will be different depending on the composition of the mixture at each location. For example, samples from different places on a block of gold will have the same composition and properties because gold is a pure substance. But, samples from different places on a large rock may be completely different because a rock is usually a mixture of smaller minerals.

Two samples from this mixture of salt, sand, poppy seeds, and iron would not be identical.

✓ READING CHECK

7. What is the difference between a compound and a mixture?

_____

_____

Mixtures

Nearly every object around you, including most things you eat and drink, and even the air you breathe, is a mixture. A **mixture** is a blend of two or more kinds of matter, each of which keeps its own identity and properties. As a result, the properties of a mixture are a combination of the properties of its components.

A mixture is called **homogeneous** if it is uniform in composition. In other words, a homogeneous mixture looks the same throughout the entire mixture. Often it is hard to tell that a homogeneous mixture contains more than one substance. An example of a homogeneous mixture is salt water. Homogeneous mixtures are also called **solutions.**

A mixture is called **heterogeneous** if it is not uniform throughout. For example, in a mixture of clay and water, heavier clay particles concentrate near the bottom of the container. A sample from the bottom of the container will be different from a sample from the top of the container.

 **TIP** Knowing the meanings of the prefixes *homo-* and *hetero-* can help you remember the meanings of homogeneous and heterogeneous. *Homo-* means "same." *Hetero-* means "other" or "different."

LOOKING CLOSER

8. Use the chart below to classify chocolate milk as a homogeneous mixture, a heterogeneous mixture, a compound, or an element.

_____

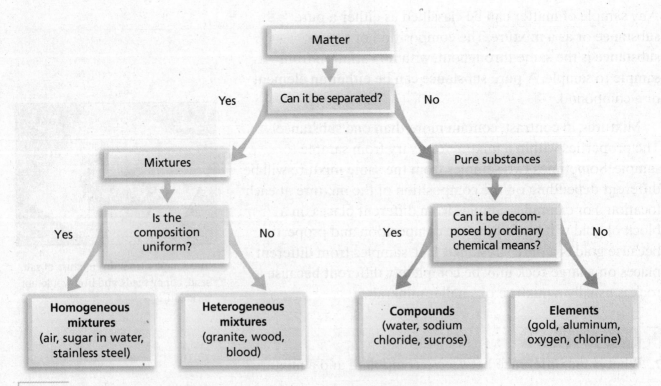

This classification scheme shows the relationships among mixtures, compounds, and elements.

Separating Mixtures The parts of a mixture can usually be separated. Using differences in properties of the substances making up the mixture enables their separation. For example, passing some mixtures through a filter or sieve will separate the components. Filters separate parts of a mixture using the property of particle size.

Other methods of separating mixtures include using centrifuges and chromatography. When a centrifuge spins really fast, the solid particles tend to accumulate at the bottom of the test tube. A centrifuge separates substances using density. Paper chromatography can separate mixtures of dyes or pigments. Different substances are absorbed and flow up through the fibers of the paper at different rates.

Barium chromate can be separated from the solution in the beaker using filtration.

Pure Substances

Though mixtures can be either homogeneous or heterogeneous, any sample of a pure substance is homogeneous. A **pure substance** has a fixed composition and differs from a mixture in the following ways:

1. Every sample of a pure substance has the same physical and chemical properties. These properties are so specific they can be used to identify the substance. In contrast, the properties of a mixture depend on the relative amounts of the mixture's components. They represent a blend of the properties of each component.

2. Every sample of a pure substance has exactly the same composition as every other sample. For example, pure water is always 11.2% hydrogen and 88.8% oxygen by mass.

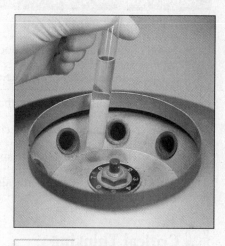

A centrifuge spins rapidly to separate components of a solution.

✓ **READING CHECK**

9. Is every mixture also a solution? Is every solution also a mixture? Explain.

_____

_____

10. Is a substance that a filter can separate into two parts a mixture or a pure substance? Explain.

_____

_____

Breaking Down Compounds Pure substances are either compounds or elements. A compound can only be broken down into two or more simpler compounds or elements by a chemical change. In contrast, a mixture can be separated by the use of its physical properties.

Laboratory Chemicals and Purity

The chemicals in laboratories are treated as if they are pure. However, all chemicals are at least a little impure. Different government agencies have different standards as to whether a chemical is pure enough. The table below lists several agencies' chemical grades of purity. The strictest standards are listed toward the top of the table, and the least strict standards are listed toward the bottom.

Chemists need to be aware of the kinds of impurities present because these impurities could affect the results of a reaction. Companies that make chemicals must ensure that the American Chemical Society's standards are met.

When sucrose is heated to a high enough temperature, it breaks down completely into carbon and water.

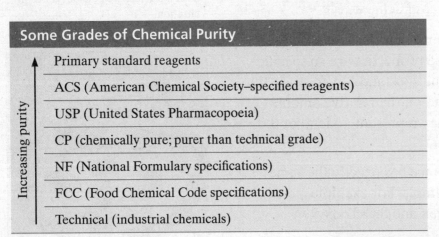

Some Grades of Chemical Purity

Increasing purity →

- Primary standard reagents
- ACS (American Chemical Society–specified reagents)
- USP (United States Pharmacopoeia)
- CP (chemically pure; purer than technical grade)
- NF (National Formulary specifications)
- FCC (Food Chemical Code specifications)
- Technical (industrial chemicals)

💡 Critical Thinking

11. Identify Look at the two photographs of zinc nitrate, and the list of chemical grades. What grade is this chemical?

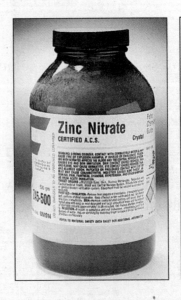

Zn(NO$_3$)$_2$•6H$_2$O   F.W. 297.47

Certificate of Actual Lot Analysis

Acidity (as HNO$_3$)	0.008%
Alkalies and Earths	0.02%
Chloride (Cl)	0.005%
Insoluble Matter	0.001%
Iron (Fe)	0.0002%
Lead (Pb)	0.001%
Phosphate (PO$_4$)	0.0002%
Sulfate (SO$_4$)	0.002%

Store separately from and avoid contact with combustible materials. Keep container closed and in a cool, dry place. Avoid contact with skin, eyes and clothing.

LOT NO. 917356

FL-02-0588   CAS 10196-18-6

VOCABULARY

1. Classify each of the following as either a physical change or a chemical change.

   a. tearing a sheet of paper: _____

   b. melting a piece of wax: _____

   c. burning a log: _____

REVIEW

2. What is the main difference between physical properties and chemical properties?

   _____

   _____

3. Give an example of a physical change and a chemical change.

   _____

   _____

4. How do you decide whether a sample of matter is a solid, liquid, or gas?

   _____

   _____

   _____

5. Contrast mixtures with pure substances.

   _____

   _____

   _____

Critical Thinking

6. **ANALYZING INFORMATION** Compare the composition of sucrose purified from sugar cane with the composition of sucrose purified from sugar beets. Explain your answer.

   _____

   _____

   _____

SECTION 1.3

Elements

As you have read, elements are pure substances that cannot be broken down by chemical changes. Each element has characteristic properties. Chemists have organized the elements into groups based on these properties. This organization of the elements is called the *periodic table*. The periodic table on the next page uses the chemical symbol for each element to show its position. The complete periodic table that includes the names for all of the elements can be found in the chapter "The Periodic Law."

KEY TERMS

group

family

period

metal

nonmetal

metalloid

The periodic table organizes elements by their chemical properties.

Each small square of the periodic table shows the symbol for an element and its atomic number. For example, the first square, at the upper left, represents element 1. This element has the symbol H, and is called hydrogen. As you look through the table, you will see many familiar elements, including iron, Fe; sodium, Na; neon, Ne; silver, Ag; copper, Cu; aluminum, Al; sulfur, S; and lead, Pb.

As you can see, sometimes the symbol for an element, such as those for neon and sulfur, is directly related to its name. Other symbols have arisen from the element's name in other modern languages, or from ancient Latin or German names. For example, the symbol for iron, Fe, comes from the Latin word *ferrum*.

The vertical columns of the periodic table are called **groups.** The elements in a group are referred to as a **family.** Notice that the groups are numbered from 1 to 18 from left to right. Each group contains elements with similar chemical properties. For example, the elements in Group 2 are beryllium, Be; magnesium, Mg; calcium, Ca; strontium, Sr; barium, Ba; and radium, Ra. All of these elements are metals, tend to react quickly with other elements, and bond to other kinds of atoms in similar ways.

READING CHECK

1. Write the symbols of the elements in Group 13.

The periodic table:

	Group 1	Group 2												Group 13	Group 14	Group 15	Group 16	Group 17	Group 18
1 H																			2 He
	3 Li	4 Be												5 B	6 C	7 N	8 O	9 F	10 Ne
	11 Na	12 Mg	Group 3	Group 4	Group 5	Group 6	Group 7	Group 8	Group 9	Group 10	Group 11	Group 12		13 Al	14 Si	15 P	16 S	17 Cl	18 Ar
	19 K	20 Ca	21 Sc	22 Ti	23 V	24 Cr	25 Mn	26 Fe	27 Co	28 Ni	29 Cu	30 Zn		31 Ga	32 Ge	33 As	34 Se	35 Br	36 Kr
	37 Rb	38 Sr	39 Y	40 Zr	41 Nb	42 Mo	43 Tc	44 Ru	45 Rh	46 Pd	47 Ag	48 Cd		49 In	50 Sn	51 Sb	52 Te	53 I	54 Xe
	55 Cs	56 Ba	57 La	72 Hf	73 Ta	74 W	75 Re	76 Os	77 Ir	78 Pt	79 Au	80 Hg		81 Tl	82 Pb	83 Bi	84 Po	85 At	86 Rn
	87 Fr	88 Ra	89 Ac	104 Rf	105 Db	106 Sg	107 Bh	108 Hs	109 Mt	110 Ds	111 Rg	112 Cn		114 Fl		116 Lv			

Legend: Metals / Metalloids / Nonmetals

58 Ce	59 Pr	60 Nd	61 Pm	62 Sm	63 Eu	64 Gd	65 Tb	66 Dy	67 Ho	68 Er	69 Tm	70 Yb	71 Lu
90 Th	91 Pa	92 U	93 Np	94 Pu	95 Am	96 Cm	97 Bk	98 Cf	99 Es	100 Fm	101 Md	102 No	103 Lr

The periodic table of the elements. The names of the elements can be found on the expanded periodic table in the chapter "The Periodic Law."

The horizontal rows of elements in the periodic table are called **periods**. Physical and chemical properties change in a somewhat regular pattern as you move from left to right across a period. Elements that are close to each other in the same period tend to be more similar than elements that are farther apart. For example, the Period-2 elements lithium, Li, and beryllium, Be, in Groups 1 and 2, respectively, have somewhat similar properties. However, their properties are very different from the properties of fluorine, F, the Period-2 element in Group 17.

The two sets of elements placed below the periodic table make up what are called the lanthanide series and the actinide series. These metallic elements fit into the table just after elements 57 and 89. They are placed below the table to keep the table from being too wide.

TIP The elements in the bottom two rows belong to none of the 18 groups. The elements in the first of these rows are called lanthanides, and the elements in the second of these rows are called the actinides.

✓ READING CHECK

2. What is the group and period number for the element with the chemical symbol O, called oxygen?

_____

Some elements are metals.

The periodic table is broadly divided into two main sections: metals and nonmetals. The metals are at the left and in the center of the table. The nonmetals are toward the right. Some elements, such as boron, B, and silicon, Si, show characteristics of both metals and nonmetals.

A **metal** is an element that is a good electrical conductor and a good heat conductor. At room temperature, most metals are solids. Most metals are also malleable, meaning that they can be hammered or rolled into thin sheets. Metals also tend to be ductile, making it possible for them to be drawn into a fine wire. Metals behave this way because they have high tensile strength, the ability to resist breaking when pulled. Most metals also have a silvery or grayish white luster, or shine.

Though metals generally share these properties, they are diverse. Mercury is a liquid at room temperature. The metals in Group 1 are soft enough that they can be cut with a knife. Some metals, such as manganese, are brittle. Instead of being silvery, gold and copper shine yellow and reddish brown, respectively.

🔍 LOOKING CLOSER

3. List below all of the words that indicate the typical properties of metals.

_____

_____

_____

_____

🔗 CONNECT

Any metal becomes a better conductor of electricity as its temperature decreases. In 1911, scientists discovered that when mercury is cooled to about −269°C, it loses all resistance and becomes a superconductor. Today, scientists can make superconducting materials that only need to be cooled to −183°C.

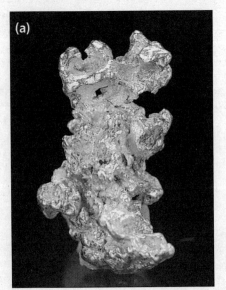

(a) Gold has low reactivity and is usually found in a pure form.
(b) Aluminum is malleable and can be made into a thin foil for wrapping.

Copper: A Typical Metal

Copper has a characteristic reddish color and a metallic luster. It is found naturally in minerals such as chalcopyrite and malachite. Pure copper melts at 1083°C and boils at 2567°C. It can be readily drawn into fine wire, pressed into thin sheets, and formed into tubing. Copper conducts electricity with little loss of energy.

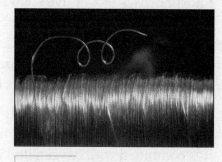

Copper is used in electrical wiring because of its high electrical conductivity.

Copper remains unchanged in pure, dry air at room temperature. When heated, it reacts with oxygen in air. It also reacts with sulfur and the elements in Group 17 of the periodic table. The green coating on a piece of weathered copper comes from the reaction of copper with oxygen, carbon dioxide, and sulfur compounds. Copper is an essential mineral in the human diet.

 READING CHECK

4. Which groups in the periodic table are composed entirely of metals?

_____

Some elements are nonmetals or metalloids.

A **nonmetal** is an element that is a poor conductor of heat and electricity. The periodic table includes many more metals than nonmetals. Many nonmetals are gases at room temperature. These include nitrogen, oxygen, fluorine, and chlorine. One nonmetal, bromine, is a liquid. The solid nonmetals include carbon, phosphorus, selenium, sulfur, and iodine. These solids tend to be brittle rather than malleable and ductile.

(a) (b) (c) (d)

Some nonmetallic elements: (a) carbon, (b) sulfur, (c) phosphorus, and (d) iodine

Phosphorus: A Typical Nonmetal

Phosphorus is one of five solid nonmetals. Pure phosphorus is known in two common forms. Red phosphorus is a dark red powder that melts at 597°C. White phosphorus is a waxy solid that melts at 44°C. Because it ignites in air at room temperature, white phosphorus is stored underwater.

Phosphorus is too reactive to exist in pure form in nature. It is present in huge quantities in phosphate rock, where it is combined with oxygen and calcium. All living things contain phosphorus.

White phosphorus is kept underwater to keep it from catching fire.

Noble Gases

The elements in Group 18 of the periodic table are the noble gases. These elements are generally unreactive. Low reactivity makes the noble gases very different from the other families of elements. Group 18 elements are gases at room temperature. Neon, argon, krypton, and xenon are all used in lighting. Helium is used in party balloons and weather balloons because it is less dense than air.

Metalloids

A **metalloid** is an element that has some characteristics of metals and some characteristics of nonmetals. As you look from left to right on the periodic table, you can see that the metalloids are found between the metals and the nonmetals. All metalloids are solids at room temperature. They tend to be less malleable than metals but not as brittle as nonmetals. Some metalloids, such as antimony, have a somewhat metallic luster.

Phosphorus is often found in match heads.

Metalloids tend to be semiconductors of electricity. That is, their ability to conduct electricity is intermediate between that of metals and that of nonmetals. Metalloids are used in the solid state circuitry found in desktop computers, digital watches, televisions, and radios.

Critical Thinking

5. **Draw Conclusions** To what group of elements do the noble gases belong: metals, nonmetals, or metalloids? Explain.

_____

_____

_____

VOCABULARY

1. Describe the main differences among metals, nonmetals, and metalloids.

_____

_____

_____

_____

REVIEW

2. Use the periodic table in the chapter "The Periodic Law" to write the names
for the following elements:

a. O _____

b. S _____

c. Cu _____

d. Ag _____

3. Use the periodic table to write the symbols for the following elements:

a. iron _____

b. nitrogen _____

c. calcium _____

d. mercury _____

4. Which elements are most likely to undergo the same kinds of reactions,
those in a group or those in a period?

_____

Critical Thinking

5. INFERRING CONCLUSIONS If you find an element in nature in its pure
elemental state, what can you infer about the element's chemical reactivity?
How can you tell whether that element is a metal or a nonmetal?

_____

_____

_____

_____

_____

Math Tutor   CONVERTING SI UNITS

SI units of measurement are based on multiples of 10, making them much easier to work with mathematically than the unrelated units of the U.S. standard measurements like ounces, pounds, feet, and gallons. Most calculations with SI units can be converted from one unit to another simply by moving the decimal point.

For example, look at the illustration below.

10^3 m	10^2 m	10^1 m	10^0 m	10^{-1} m	10^{-2} m	10^{-3} m
kilo	hecto	deka	**Base Unit**	deci	centi	milli
king	harry	drools	ugly	dark	chocolate	milk

To convert the SI base unit for distance, meters, to centimeters, the decimal point is simply moved 2 spaces to the right. One meter is equal to 100 centimeters.

Problem-Solving TIPS

- Make note of the unit that is given at the beginning of the problem and check to see if the answer you are seeking is given in the same or a different unit.
- Is the unit given at the beginning an SI base unit, or does it have a prefix?
- If you are converting from a smaller unit to a larger unit, the decimal point will move to the left.
- If you are converting from a larger unit to a smaller unit, the decimal point will move to the right.
- The number of places you move the decimal point is equal to the power of 10 that is indicated by the prefix.
- If you are converting from a unit with a prefix back to a base unit, start with the prefix unit. Make note of the power of 10 of that prefix in the table in your text.
- Check your final unit to see if it makes sense in terms of the answer sought. For example, if you are measuring the length of a tabletop, an answer in tens of kilometers would not be appropriate.

SAMPLE

How many liters are there in 9.844 mL?

The prefix *milli* has a power of 10 of −3. It is therefore smaller than the base unit of liters. Because you are converting from a smaller unit (mL) to a larger unit (L), move the decimal point 3 places to the left:

9.844 mL = 0.009844 L

Convert 0.35543 km into meters.

The power of 10 for the prefix *kilo* is 3. It is therefore a larger value than the base unit of meters. To convert from a larger unit (km) to a smaller unit (m), move the decimal point 3 places to the right:
0.35543 km = 355.43 m

1. What is meant by the word *chemical*, as used by scientists?

_____

_____

2. In which of the six branches of chemistry would a scientist be working if he or she were doing the following?

   a. the study of carbon compounds _____

   b. investigating energy relationships for various reactions _____

   c. comparing properties of alcohols with those of sugars _____

   d. studying reactions that occur during the digestion of food _____

3. Identify each of the following as an example of either basic research, applied research, or technological development.

   a. A new type of environmentally friendly refrigerant is developed. _____

   b. A new element is synthesized in a particle accelerator. _____

   c. A computer chip is redesigned to increase a computer's speed. _____

4. How is science used as a selling point for products and services?

_____

_____

5. a. What is mass? _____

   b. What is volume? _____

6. How does the composition of a pure compound differ from that of a mixture?

_____

_____

7. Define property. _____

_____

8. What is the difference between extensive properties and intensive properties?

_____

_____

9. Define chemical property. List two examples of chemical properties.

_____

_____

10. Distinguish between a physical change and a chemical change.

_____

_____

11. a. Is breaking an egg an example of a physical change or chemical change?
Explain your answer.

_____

_____

b. Is cooking an egg an example of a physical change or chemical change?
Explain your answer.

_____

_____

12. a. How does a solid differ from a liquid? _____

_____

b. How does a liquid differ from a gas? _____

_____

c. How is a liquid similar to a gas? _____

_____

13. What is meant by a change of state?

_____

_____

14. Identify the reactants and products in the following reaction:

potassium + water → potassium hydroxide + hydrogen

reactants: _____ products: _____

15. Suppose different parts of a sample material have different compositions.
What can you conclude about the material?

_____

16. a. What is the significance of the vertical columns of the periodic table? _____

_____

b. What is the significance of the horizontal rows of the periodic table? _____

_____

17. Compare the physical properties of metals, nonmetals, metalloids, and noble gases, and describe where in the periodic table each of these kinds of elements is located.

_____

_____

_____

_____

18. Suppose element X is a poor conductor of electricity and breaks when hit with a hammer. Element Z is a good conductor of electricity and heat. In what area of the periodic table does each element most likely belong?

a. Element X: _____   **b.** Element Z: _____

19. Use the periodic table to write the names of the elements that have the following symbols, and identify each as a metal, nonmetal, metalloid, or noble gas.

a. K _____   **d.** Na _____

b. Ag _____   **e.** Hg _____

c. Si _____   **f.** He _____

20. An unknown element is shiny and is found to be a good conductor of electricity. What other properties would you predict for it?

_____

21. Use the periodic table to identify the group numbers and period numbers of the following elements:

a. carbon, C _____   **c.** chromium, Cr _____

b. argon, Ar _____   **d.** barium, Ba _____

22. Determine the number of significant figures.

a. 42.200 L _____   **b.** 0.055 00 mol _____

23. Perform the following calculations and apply the rules for significant figures.

a. 56.05 g ÷ 13.3 cm^3 _____   **b.** 1.057 g + 3.02 g + 12.4 g _____

CHAPTER 2

Measurements and Calculations

Key Concepts

Section 1 *Scientific Method*

What is the purpose of the scientific method?

What types of observations does a scientist make?

How do hypotheses, theories, and models differ?

Section 2 *Units of Measurement*

What measurement system do scientists use?

What is density and how is it calculated?

How are conversion factors determined?

Section 3 *Using Scientific Measurements*

How are significant figures in measurements determined?

What is scientific notation?

What are the two types of proportional relationships?

Review Previous Concepts

1. What is chemistry and what types of questions do chemists try to answer?

2. What is a unit of measurement? Name some units of measurement for length and time.

SECTION 2.1

Scientific Method

Sometimes progress in science results from an accidental discovery. However, scientific discoveries usually result from carefully planned investigations. The process scientists use to carry out an investigation is called the scientific method. The **scientific method** is a logical approach to solving problems by collecting data, formulating hypotheses, testing hypotheses, and coming up with theories that are supported by the data. The stages in the scientific method are summarized in the flowchart in this section.

Observation includes making measurements and collecting data.

When you use one of the five senses—sight, hearing, touch, taste, or smell—to obtain information, you are making an observation. Observations in science usually involve making measurements and collecting data. Descriptive data, such as the fact that the sky is blue, are *qualitative* observations. Numerical data, such as the fact that a sample has a mass of 25.7 grams, are *quantitative* observations. Numerical data are often summarized in graphs. Graphs show the relationship between different measurements or how the measurements have varied with time.

A scientific experiment involves carrying out a procedure under controlled conditions to make observations and collect data. To learn more about the nature of matter, chemists study systems. A **system** is a specific portion of matter in a given region of space that has been selected for study. For example, when you observe a chemical reaction in a test tube, the test tube and its contents form a system. In a closed system, in which nothing can enter or leave, the energy in the system remains constant.

KEY TERMS

scientific method	theory
system	model
hypothesis	

Critical Thinking

1. Describe A scientist is studying the different rates at which different parts of a car rust in a humid garage. Describe the system the scientist is studying.

_____

_____

_____

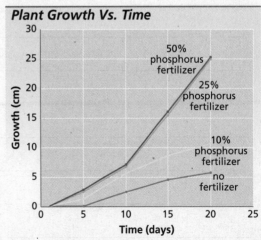

The graph shows data collected during an experiment on the effect of phosphorus on plant growth.

Hypotheses are testable statements.

Scientists attempt to find relationships and patterns in the observations and data they collect by studying systems. Besides graphs, scientists use a wide array of tools and techniques to help them analyze their data. For example, they can organize data into tables or perform a statistical analysis on data using a computer.

These students have designed an experiment to determine how to get the largest volume of popcorn from a fixed number of kernels.

After scientists have collected and analyzed enough data to find a relationship or pattern, they want to determine the reason the relationship exists. Scientists construct a **hypothesis,** or testable statement. The hypothesis serves as a basis for making predictions and for carrying out further experiments. A hypothesis is often written as an "if-then" statement. The "then" part of the hypothesis is a prediction. The scientist can design and conduct an experiment to see if the prediction is correct.

To test a hypothesis, a scientist must make measurements to determine if the prediction in the hypothesis was correct. If testing reveals that the prediction was not correct, the scientist must reject or modify the hypothesis.

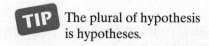 **TIP** The plural of hypothesis is hypotheses.

Critical Thinking

2. **Predict** Create your own hypothesis about what might happen if you began a new exercise program. Make sure you can test your hypothesis. Use the following structure for your hypothesis:

If I _____, **then** _____, **because**
_____

_____

_____

_____

_____

_____

_____

Controls and Variables

A scientist must also design an experiment that eliminates all the other factors besides the factor mentioned in the "if" part of the hypothesis. This allows the scientist to state that the result was a direct consequence of the factor being tested. During testing, the conditions that remain constant, and therefore are not factors in the result, are called *controls*. Any conditions that change during the experiment are called *variables*. The outcome of the experiment should rely on the effect of the variables and not of the controls.

Here is an example. When some products are shipped, packets of silica gel are included in the shipping boxes. Silica gel is a desiccant—a material that removes moisture from the air. The silica gel packets can help ensure that conditions inside the shipping box don't change from dry to moist, because moisture might damage the product being shipped.

READING CHECK

3. A condition that does not change during an experiment is a

_____,

and a condition that does change during an experiment is a

_____.

Silica gel packets are placed in packages in order to absorb excess moisture that could harm the content of the package.

🎧 Critical Thinking

4. Apply Concepts In the example above, is a silica gel packet a control or a variable? Are the conditions inside the shipping box controls or variables?

_____

_____

_____

Repetition and Replication

One correct prediction does not prove a hypothesis is correct. It is important that the same experiment gets the same results when it is repeated many times. This consideration is known as repetition.

Another important part of testing one person's hypothesis is the idea that any other scientist could perform the same experiment and get the same results. This consideration is known as replication.

🎧 Critical Thinking

5. Apply Concepts Explain how using a recipe to make a cake is an example of replication.

_____

_____

Exact measurements and instructions allow recipes to be replicated many times.

Scientific theories are well-established and highly reliable explanations.

When a hypothesis or group of related hypotheses have been thoroughly tested and survived repetition and replication, they can form the basis for a scientific theory. A **theory** is a broad generalization that explains a body of facts or phenomena. Theories are bigger and more general than hypotheses, including more observations, information, and general terms.

Theories in Chemistry

Here is an example of a recent hypothesis and theory.

A radiation hypothesis about chemical reactions was made about a hundred years ago. The idea was that chemical reactions that happen at low pressures could only be caused by background radiation that "energized" the molecules. Since this radiation hypothesis was thought of, no experiments have provided conclusive evidence for it. The idea that radiation energizes molecules has been overshadowed by a more widely accepted collision theory.

The collision theory holds that reactions occur when reacting atoms and molecules collide in the right orientation and with sufficient energy. Experiments have been able to provide evidence for the collision theory. The following details of this theory have consistent evidence to back them up:

- Ground-up substances react more vigorously than those that are whole, because the greater surface area of the ground-up material means more of the reactant molecules can come into contact (collide) with one another. That creates a greater opportunity for them to react.

- Heated substances also react more vigorously than cooler ones, because the increased energy causes molecules to move faster. The faster movement results in increased collisions with greater energy. That creates a greater opportunity for them to react.

When tested, the collision theory was considered to be superior to the radiation hypothesis because it had consistent results and explained a variety of observations. The radiation hypothesis did not explain these observations as well.

READING CHECK

6. Why is the collision theory considered to be well-established and highly reliable?

_____

_____

_____

_____

_____

For centuries, the mortar and pestle has been used to grind up substances to encourage a faster reaction, even before chemists had formulated the collision theory.

Theories and Models

After a hypothesis is tested and is believed to be correct, the next step is often to construct a model. A **model** is an explanation of why an event occurs and how data and events are related. In science, a model is more than just a physical object. Models may be visual, verbal, or mathematical. One important model in chemistry is the atomic model of matter, which states that matter is composed of tiny particles called atoms.

If a model successfully explains many observable facts, it may become part of a theory. Theories are considered successful if they can predict the results of many new experiments. The flowchart below shows where scientific theories fit in the scheme of the scientific method. The ability to contribute to the development of new theories is often the reason people become scientists.

Critical Thinking

7. **Infer** In the diagram below, communication is listed under every stage. Why is communication important at every stage in the scientific method?

_____

_____

_____

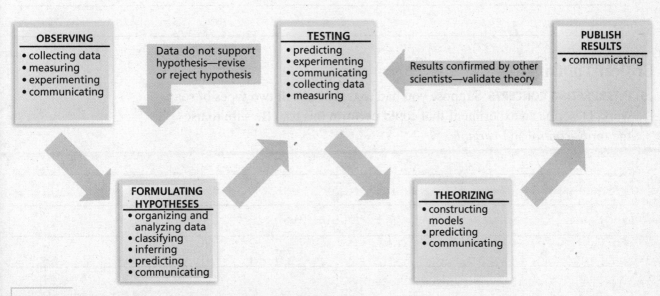

The scientific method is not a single, fixed process. Each stage represents a number of different activities, and stages are often repeated several times.

VOCABULARY

1. How do hypotheses and theories differ?

_____

_____

_____

REVIEW

2. What is the scientific method?

_____

_____

_____

3. Once scientists have agreed upon a theory, will that theory ever change?
   Explain.

_____

_____

4. How are models related to theories and hypotheses?

_____

_____

_____

_____

Critical Thinking.

5. **INTERPRETING CONCEPTS** Suppose you had to test how well two types of soap
   work. Describe an experiment that could perform this test. Be sure to use
   the terms *control* and *variable*.

_____

_____

_____

_____

_____

SECTION 2.2

Units of Measurement

Suppose a book has a recipe listing amounts such as 1 salt, 3 sugar, and 2 flour. You cannot use the recipe without more information. You need to know whether the number 3 represents teaspoons, tablespoons, cups, ounces, grams, or some other unit for sugar. For the measurements in the recipe to be useful, the units must be specified.

Nearly every measurement is a number plus a unit. The choice of unit depends on the quantity being measured. A quantity is not the same as a measurement. A **quantity** is something that has magnitude, size, or amount. For example, the quantity represented by a teaspoon is volume. The teaspoon is a unit of measurement, while volume is a quantity.

Units of measurement compare what is measured with a previously defined amount. Many centuries ago, people sometimes marked off distances using the length of a foot. But people can have feet of different lengths, and different people could measure different distances between the same two points. Therefore, a standard length for a foot was agreed upon. It no longer mattered who made the measurement, as long as the standard measuring unit was correctly applied.

KEY TERMS	
quantity	volume
SI	density
weight	conversion factor
derived unit	dimensional analysis

When iced tea is ordered, the amount of sugar added is specified with a unit.

Scientists worldwide use SI measurements.

Scientists have agreed on a single measurement system called Le Système International d'Unités, or **SI**. The system has seven base units, which are shown in the table on the next page. Each unit is defined in terms of a standard of measurement. Some standards are specific objects used for comparison. Others are amounts that do not vary and can be reproduced easily.

TIP Numbers in this book appear without commas to separate groups of digits because the comma is often used as a decimal point in other countries. For example, in Europe the number seventy-five thousand might be written as 75.000. In this book, therefore, the number seventy-five thousand will appear as 75 000.

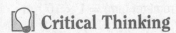 Critical Thinking

1. **Apply** What quantity is being measured when you measure the duration of an event in seconds?

SI Base Units

Quantity	Symbol	Name	Abbreviation	Defined standard
Length	l	meter	m	the distance light travels in 1/299 792 458 s
Mass	m	kilogram	kg	the mass of the international prototype
Time	t	second	s	the time it takes cesium-133 to transition between two levels of its ground state a total of 9 192 631 770 times
Temperature	T	kelvin	K	1/273.16 of the temperature at which water can exist as a solid, liquid, and gas at the same time
Amount of substance	n	mole	mol	the number of atoms in 0.012 kg of carbon-12
Electric current	I	ampere	A	the current that would produce 2×10^{-7} N/m of force per unit length between two parallel conducting plates
Luminous intensity	I_v	candela	cd	the luminous intensity of light from a 540×10^{12} Hz source that has radiant intensity of 1/683 watt per steradian

Critical Thinking

2. **Analyze** Fill in the missing information in the table.

SI Prefixes

Prefix	Unit abbreviation	Exponential factor	Meaning	Example
giga	G	10^9	1 000 000 000	1 gigameter (Gm) = 1×10^9 m
mega	M	10^6	1 000 000	
kilo	k	10^3		1 kilometer (km) = 1000 m
hecto	h		100	1 hectometer (hm) = 100 m
deka	da	10^1	10	
—	—	10^0	1	1 meter (m)
deci	d		1/10	1 decimeter (dm) = 0.1 m
centi	c	10^{-2}	1/100	
milli	m	10^{-3}		1 millimeter (mm) = 0.001 m
micro	µ	10^{-6}	1/1 000 000	1 micrometer (µm) = 1×10^{-6} m
nano	n		1/1 000 000 000	1 nanometer (nm) = 1×10^{-9} m
pico	p	10^{-12}	1/1 000 000 000 000	
femto	f	10^{-15}		1 femtometer (fm) = 1×10^{-15} m

Prefixes added to SI base units indicate larger or smaller quantities.

The seven base units in the SI system are listed at the top of the previous page. All of the other SI units can be derived from these seven units. The prefixes listed in the bottom table on the previous page are often added to the names of the base units to represent quantities that are much larger or much smaller than the base units. For example, the prefix *kilo-*, abbreviated *k*, represents a factor of 10^3. Therefore, a kilogram is 1000 grams. Similarly, the prefix *centi-* represents a factor of 1/100. A centimeter is 1/100 of a meter, or 0.01 meter.

Mass Versus Weight

As you learned in the chapter "Matter and Change," mass is a measure of the quantity of matter. The SI standard unit of mass is the kilogram, which is about the weight of a small textbook. The kilogram is the only base unit with a prefix.

Mass is often confused with weight because people often express the weight of an object in kilograms. Mass is determined by comparing the mass of an object with a set of standard masses. **Weight** is a measure of the force with which gravity pulls on matter. Weight depends on the strength of the force of gravity, while mass does not. For example, the weight of an object on the moon is about one-sixth of its weight on Earth. But the object has the same mass whether it is on the moon or on Earth. Mass is measured on instruments such as a balance, and weight is typically measured on a spring scale.

TIP When a mass is given as a unit with a prefix, the prefix compares the amount to grams, not kilograms. For example, a milligram is 1/1000 of a gram, not 1/1000 of a kilogram, the SI base unit.

Length

The standard unit for length is the meter. A distance of 1 m is about the width of an average doorway. Longer distances are often expressed in kilometers. Kilometers are used for highway distances in most countries other than the United States. A kilometer is about six-tenths of a mile.

The base unit of length is the meter, but the centimeter is often used to measure smaller distances.

PRACTICE

A. How long is the piece of aluminum foil shown above?

_____

B. Name an appropriate unit for measuring the length of the period at the end of this sentence.

_____

SI base units combine to form derived units.

Many SI units are combinations of the seven base units. For example, speed is measured in meters per second, which is a combination of the base units for length and time. **Derived units** are formed by multiplying or dividing standard units.

For example, area is a derived unit formed by multiplying length times width. If both length and width are expressed in meters, then the area is expressed in meters times meters, or square meters, abbreviated m^2. Prefixes can also be added to derived units. For example, area can be expressed in cm^2, square centimeters, or mm^2, square millimeters.

Some combination units are given their own names. For example, the unit for force is a combination of the units for mass, length, and time, given by kg•m/s^2. The name *newton*, N, is given to this combination. A joule is another combined unit used to measure the quantity of energy in a system or object. A *joule* is a newton times a meter.

A speedometer measures distance traveled per unit of time. This speedometer shows speed in miles per hour and kilometers per hour.

✓ READING CHECK

3. Fill in the missing information in the table below using the information given in the other columns.

Derived SI Units

Quantity	Quantity symbol	Unit	Unit abbreviation	Derivation
Area	A	square meter	m^2	length × width
Volume	V	cubic meter		length × width × height
Density	D	kilograms per cubic meter	$\dfrac{kg}{m^3}$	$\dfrac{mass}{volume}$
Molar mass	M		$\dfrac{kg}{mol}$	$\dfrac{mass}{amount\ of\ substance}$
Molar volume	V_m	cubic meters per mole		$\dfrac{volume}{amount\ of\ substance}$
Energy	E	joule	J	force × length

Volume

Volume is the amount of space occupied by an object. The derived SI unit of volume is cubic meters, m^3. One cubic meter is equal to the volume of a cube whose edges are 1 m long. Such a large unit is inconvenient for expressing the volume of materials in a chemistry laboratory. Instead, a smaller unit, the cubic centimeter, cm^3, is often used. There are 100 centimeters in a meter, so a cubic meter contains 1 000 000 cm^3.

$$1m^3 \times \frac{100\ cm}{1\ m} \times \frac{100\ cm}{1\ m} \times \frac{100\ cm}{1\ m} = 1\ 000\ 000\ cm^3$$

When chemists measure the volumes of liquids and gases, they often use a non-SI unit called the liter. The liter, L, is equivalent to one cubic decimeter. Because there are 10 centimeters in a decimeter, a cube with sides one decimeter long has a volume of 10 cm times 10 cm times 10 cm, or 1000 cm^3. Thus, 1 L is also equivalent to 1000 cm^3.

Another non-SI unit used for smaller volumes is the milliliter, mL. There are 1000 mL in 1 L. Because there are also 1000 cm^3 in 1 L, the two units—milliliter and cubic centimeter—are interchangeable.

✓ READING CHECK

4. Explain why volume is measured by a derived unit and not a base unit in the SI system of measurement.

_____

_____

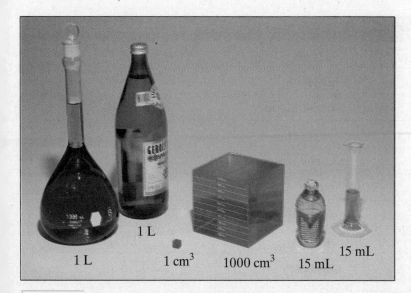

1 L   1 cm^3 1000 cm^3 15 mL

The relationships between various volumes are shown here.

Density

Density is the mass of a substance divided by its volume. Mathematically, density is written as:

$$\text{density} = \frac{\text{mass}}{\text{volume}} \text{ or } D = \frac{m}{V}$$

The quantity m is mass, V is volume, and D is density. The SI unit for density is derived from the base units for mass and length. Since volume is length cubed, density is mass divided by length cubed. The SI unit for density is expressed as kilograms per cubic meter, or kg/m^3.

Density is an intensive property, which means it is a characteristic property of a substance. It does not depend on the size of a sample. If a more massive sample is taken, the volume would increase by the same proportion. Therefore, density is a property that can be used to identify substances. An object or substance will float on a liquid if it has a density less than that of the liquid.

The density of water is often used as a reference because its density is so close to 1 when expressed in grams per cubic centimeter. Mercury is a liquid that is much denser than water. The photograph above shows that water floats on mercury. Copper is a metal that has a density between those of water and mercury. The copper in the photograph floats between the water and the mercury. Cork has a density that is much less than that of water. If a cork cylinder were added to the graduated cylinder above, it would float on top of the water.

Density is the ratio of mass to volume. Both water and copper shot float on mercury because mercury is so dense.

READING CHECK

5. How many of these objects would float on water: an ice cube, a bone dog toy, a sugar cube?

_____

_____

Densities of Some Familiar Materials			
Solids	**Density at 20°C (g/cm³)**	**Liquids**	**Density at 20°C (g/mL)**
cork	0.24*	gasoline	0.67*
butter	0.86	ethyl alcohol	0.791
ice	0.92†	kerosene	0.82
sucrose	1.59	turpentine	0.87
bone	1.85*	water	0.998
diamond	3.26*	sea water	1.025**
copper	8.92	milk	1.031*
lead	11.35	mercury	13.6

† measured at 0°C   * typical density   ** measured at 15°C

A sample of aluminum metal has a mass of 8.4 g. The volume of the sample is 3.1 cm³. Calculate the density of aluminum.

SOLUTION		
1 ANALYZE	*Determine what information is given and unknown.*
	Given: mass (m) = 8.4 g; volume (V) = 3.1 cm³
	Unknown: density (D)
2 PLAN	*Write an equation for the unknown in terms of what is given.*
	$\text{density} = \dfrac{\text{mass}}{\text{volume}}$ or $D = \dfrac{m}{V}$
3 SOLVE	*Substitute the known values and calculate.*
	$D = \dfrac{m}{V} = \dfrac{8.4 \text{ g}}{3.1 \text{ cm}^3} = 2.7 \text{ g/cm}^3$
4 CHECK YOUR WORK	*Determine if the answer makes sense.*
	The answer is given in the correct units. Also, the mass is close to 9 g, the volume is close to 3 cm³, and 9 ÷ 3 = 3.

PRACTICE

C. What is the density of a block of marble that occupies 311 cm³ and has a mass of 853 g?

Given:	$D = \dfrac{m}{V} =$
Unknown:	

D. Diamond has a density of 3.26 g/cm³. What is the mass of a diamond that has a volume of 0.351 cm³?

E. What is the volume of a sample of liquid mercury that has a mass of 76.2 g, given that the density of mercury is 13.6 g/cm³?

Conversion factors change one unit to another.

A **conversion factor** is a ratio derived from a relationship between two different units that can be used to convert from one unit to the other. For example, suppose you want to know how many quarters there are in 12 dollars. To figure out the answer, you need to know how quarters and dollars are related. There are four quarters in a dollar. This fact can be expressed in many ratios, such as those shown below.

$$\frac{4 \text{ quarters}}{1 \text{ dollar}} = 1 \qquad \frac{1 \text{ dollar}}{4 \text{ quarters}} = 1$$

$$\frac{0.25 \text{ dollar}}{1 \text{ quarter}} = 1 \qquad \frac{1 \text{ quarter}}{0.25 \text{ dollar}} = 1$$

Notice that each conversion factor, or ratio, equals 1. That is because the two quantities in any conversion factor are equivalent to each other. This is important because any number that is multiplied by 1 remains the same. Therefore, a measurement can be multiplied by a conversion factor equal to 1 and result in an equivalent measurement.

Dimensional analysis is a mathematical technique that allows you to use units to solve problems involving measurements. Dimensional analysis helps you determine what conversion factor to use to solve a problem.

For example, to determine the number of quarters in 12 dollars, you want the conversion factor that changes a quantity from dollars to quarters. To eliminate dollars, you must divide the quantity by dollars. Therefore, the correct conversion factor must have dollars in the denominator. The first conversion factor listed above has dollars in the denominator.

number of quarters

$= 12 \text{ dollars} \times \text{conversion factor}$

$= 12 \text{ dollars} \times \dfrac{4 \text{ quarters}}{1 \text{ dollar}}$

$= 48 \text{ quarters}$

🔍 **LOOKING CLOSER**

6. What does the term *analysis* mean?

_____

_____

_____

_____

F. How many quarters are there in 73 dollars?

G. How many dollars are there in 182 quarters? Write your answer as a decimal.

Deriving Conversion Factors

You can derive conversion factors if you know the relationship between the unit you have and the unit you want. For example, from the fact that the prefix *deci-* means "one-tenth," you know that there is one-tenth of a meter in a decimeter. In other words, there are 10 decimeters in a meter. One conversion factor for decimeters and meters is shown.

$$\frac{10 \text{ dm}}{\text{m}}$$

TIP In a conversion factor, if there is no digit given in the denominator, then the value is assumed to be 1.

H. Write at least two more conversion factors for meters and decimeters.

I. Write at least three conversion factors for seconds and minutes.

Express a mass of 5.712 grams in milligrams and kilograms.

	SOLUTION	
1	ANALYZE	*Determine what information is given and unknown.*

        Given: mass = 5.712 g

        Unknown: mass in mg
                           mass in kg

2 PLAN   *Derive conversion factors.*

The expressions that relate grams to milligrams and grams to kilograms are the following.

$$1 \text{ g} = 1000 \text{ mg}$$

$$1000 \text{ g} = 1 \text{ kg}$$

The two conversion factors that can be formed from each expression are

$$\frac{1000 \text{ mg}}{\text{g}} = 1 \text{ and } \frac{1 \text{ g}}{1000 \text{ mg}} = 1$$

$$\frac{1000 \text{ g}}{\text{kg}} = 1 \text{ and } \frac{1 \text{ kg}}{1000 \text{ g}} = 1$$

3 SOLVE   *Determine the correct conversion factor and multiply.*

To convert from grams to another unit, the conversion factor should result in division by grams. Choose the conversion factor that has grams in the denominator.

$$5.712 \text{ g} = 5.712 \text{ g} \times \frac{1000 \text{ mg}}{\text{g}} = 5712 \text{ mg}$$

$$5.712 \text{ g} = 5.712 \text{ g} \times \frac{1 \text{ kg}}{1000 \text{ g}} = 0.005\ 712 \text{ kg}$$

4 CHECK YOUR WORK   *Determine if the answer makes sense.*

Milligrams are smaller than grams, so there should be more milligrams than grams. Kilograms are larger than grams, so there should be fewer kilograms than grams. Both of the answers above agree with these statements.

J. Express a length of 16.45 m in centimeters.

Given:

Unknown:

The expression relating meters to centimeters
is 1 m = _____ cm.

Write two conversion factors for centimeters and meters.

_____	_____

Circle the conversion factor for converting from meters
to centimeters. Then use the space below to multiply.

16.45 m = 16.45 m ×

K. Express a length of 16.45 m in kilometers.

L. Express a mass of 0.014 mg in grams.

VOCABULARY

1. How does a quantity differ from a unit? Use examples to explain the difference between the two terms.

_____

_____

REVIEW

2. Label each of the following measurements by the quantity each represents. For instance, 10.6 kg/m^3 represents a density.

a. 5.0 g/mL_____   **c.** 47 J_____   **e.** 25.3 cm^3 _____

b. 37 s_____   **d.** 39.56 g_____   **f.** 30.23 mL_____

3. Complete the following conversions.

a. 3.5 mol = _____ μmol

b. 358 cm^3 = _____ m^3

4. Write a conversion factor for each equality.

a. 1 m^3 = 1 000 000 cm^3

b. 1 in. = 2.54 cm

5. What is the density of an 84.7 g sample of an unknown substance if the sample occupies 49.6 cm^3?

Critical Thinking

6. INFERRING CONCLUSIONS A student converts grams to milligrams by multiplying by the conversion factor $\frac{1 \text{ g}}{1000 \text{ mg}}$. Is the student performing this calculation correctly? Explain.

_____

_____

SECTION 2.3

Using Scientific Measurements

When a scientist makes the same measurement twice, the result is often different the second time. This does not mean that the scientist has made a mistake. The reliability of a measurement is often limited by the tool used. For example, it is hard to measure the length of a highway with a meterstick. When reporting a measurement, a scientist must give an indication of the measurement's uncertainty.

KEY TERMS

accuracy
precision
percentage error
significant figure
scientific notation
directly proportional
inversely proportional

Accuracy is different from precision.

The terms accuracy and precision mean the same thing to many people. However, in science they have very specific meanings. **Accuracy** refers to how close the measurement is to the correct or accepted value. **Precision** refers to how close a set of measurements made in the same way are to each other. Measured values that are accurate are close to the accepted value. Measured values that are precise are close to one another.

Imagine that four darts are thrown at the center, or bull's-eye, of a dartboard. The accuracy of the throws is determined by how close the darts land to the bull's-eye. The precision of the throws is determined by how close the four darts land to each other.

High Precision Examine the two dartboards at the right. In both cases, the darts landed close to each other, so the dart thrower was precise. However, because the thrower was attempting to hit the bull's-eye, the thrower only threw accurately at the dartboard on the left.

(a)   (b)

Dardos en un área pequeña = Gran precisión
Dardos en un área pequeña = Gran precisión

Área centrada en el blanco = Gran exactitud
Área alejada del blanco = Poca exactitud

Both of these dartboards show high precision, but only dartboard (a) shows high accuracy.

✓ READING CHECK

1. What is the difference between accuracy and precision?

_____

_____

High Accuracy In the set of dartboards shown at the right, the region covered by the throws is centered on the bull's-eye. Both dartboards show that the thrower was accurate. However, only the left dartboard shows that the thrower was both accurate and precise.

In scientific experiments, it is important to be both accurate and precise. The second dartboard shown in each of these pairs of dartboards illustrate the problems that can occur if one of the two qualities is missing.

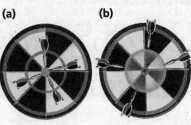

(a)   (b)

Darts within small area = High precision | Darts within large area = Low precision

Area centered on bull's-eye = High accuracy | Area centered around bull's-eye = High accuracy (on average)

Both of these dartboards show high accuracy, but only dartboard (a) shows high precision.

⚗ Critical Thinking

2. **Apply** Imagine that you throw four darts at the dartboard below. Your throws are both imprecise and inaccurate. Draw four X's on the dartboard that show a set of darts that you have thrown imprecisely and inaccurately.

Percentage Error

The accuracy of an experimental value can be compared with the correct or accepted value by calculating its percentage error. To calculate the **percentage error,** subtract the accepted value from the experimental value, dividing the difference by the accepted value, and then multiply by 100.

$$\text{Percentage error} = \frac{\text{Value}_{\text{experimental}} - \text{Value}_{\text{accepted}}}{\text{Value}_{\text{accepted}}} \times 100$$

Percentage error is positive if the accepted value is less than the experimental value. Percentage error is negative if the accepted value is greater than the experimental value.

⚗ Critical Thinking

3. **Reasoning** What is the percentage error if the experimental value is equal to the accepted value?

A student measures the mass and volume of a substance and calculates its density as 1.40 g/mL. The correct, or accepted, value of the density is 1.30 g/mL. What is the percentage error of the student's measurement?

SOLUTION

1 ANALYZE

Determine what information is given and unknown.

Given: $Value_{experimental} = 1.40$ g/mL, $Value_{accepted} = 1.30$ g/mL

Unknown: Percentage error

2 PLAN

Write an equation for the unknown in terms of what is given.

$$Percentage\ error = \frac{Value_{experimental} - Value_{accepted}}{Value_{accepted}} \times 100$$

3 SOLVE

Substitute the known values and calculate.

$$Percentage\ error = \frac{1.40\ gm/L - 1.30\ gm/L}{1.30\ g/mL} \times 100 = 7.69\%$$

4 CHECK YOUR WORK

Determine if the answer makes sense.

The percentage error should be positive because the experimental value is larger than the actual value. The error should be small because the value is close to correct.

PRACTICE

A. What is the percentage error for a mass measurement of 17.7 g, given that the correct value is 21.2 g?

$$Percentage\ error = \frac{\boxed{} - \boxed{}}{\boxed{}} \times 100 = \boxed{}$$

B. A volume is measured experimentally as 4.26 mL. What is the percentage error, given that the correct value is 4.15 mL?

Error in Measurement

Some error or uncertainty always exists in any measurement. For example, the skill of the measurer places limits on reliability. The measuring instruments limit how precisely a value can be determined. In addition, the readings from balances, rulers, and graduated cylinders are controlled by how fine the markings are on the instruments.

As an example, look at the ruler above. This ruler can be used to determine the length of an object precisely to the tenths digit. You can tell that the nail is definitely between 6.3 cm and 6.4 cm long. However, it is hard to tell whether the value should be read as 6.35 cm or 6.36 cm. The hundredths place is somewhat uncertain, but a reasonable estimate of the digit can be made. You might include a plus-or-minus value to express the range, such as 6.36 cm ± 0.01 cm.

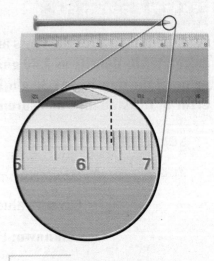

A nail's length is measured by a centimeter ruler.

> **Significant figures are those measured precisely, plus one estimated digit.**

In science, measured values are reported in terms of significant figures. **Significant figures** are all of the digits known with certainty plus one final digit that is estimated.

For example, the length of the nail in the photograph above was given as 6.36 cm. All three of these digits are significant, even the uncertain one. All contain information and are included in the value.

The term *significant* does not mean *certain*. In any correctly reported measurement, the final digit is significant but not certain. Insignificant digits are never reported.

Determining the Number of Significant Figures

If a measurement does not have any digits that are zero, then all of the digits are significant. For example, the nail's length of 6.36 cm has three non-zero digits, and therefore three significant figures. However, the digit zero can be significant or not depending on how it is used. The rules in the table on the next page summarize how to determine if a zero is a significant digit.

Critical Thinking

4. Explain Why would 6.4 cm not be an appropriate measurement for the nail in the diagram above?

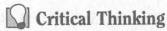

_____

_____

_____

_____

_____

Rules for Determining Significant Zeros

Rule	Examples
1. Zeros appearing between nonzero digits are significant.	**a.** 40.7 L has three significant figures. **b.** 87 009 km has five significant figures.
2. Zeros appearing in front of all nonzero digits arc not significant.	**a.** 0.095 897 m has five significant figures. **b.** 0.0009 kg has one significant figure.
3. Zeros at the end of a number and to the right of a decimal point are significant.	**a.** 85.00 g has four significant figures. **b.** 9.000 000 000 mm has 10 significant figures.
4. Zeros at the end of a number but to the left of a decimal point may or may not be significant. If a zero has not been measured or estimated but is just a placeholder, it is not significant. A decimal point placed after zeros indicates that they are significant.	**a.** 2000 m may contain from one to four significant figures, depending on how many zeros are placeholders. **For measurements given in this book, assume that 2000 m has one significant figure.** **b.** 2000. m contains four significant figures due to the presence of the decimal point.

PRACTICE

C. Determine the number of significant figures in each of the following measurements.

a. 28.6 g _____

b. 3440. cm _____ (see Rule 4)

c. 910 m _____ (see Rule 4)

d. 0.046 04 L _____ (see Rule 2)

e. 0.006 700 0 kg _____ (see Rules 2 and 3)

D. Determine the number of significant figures in each of the following measurements.

a. 804.05 g _____   **d.** 400 mL _____

b. 0.014 403 0 km _____   **e.** 30 000. cm _____

c. 1002 m _____   **f.** 0.000 625 000 kg _____

E. Suppose the value "seven thousand centimeters" is reported to you. How should the number be expressed if it is intended to contain the following numbers of significant figures?

a. 1 significant figure _____

b. 4 significant figures _____

c. 6 significant figures _____

Rounding

When you add, subtract, multiply, or divide two measurements, the reliability of the result should be reflected by its significant figures. How the result should be rounded is determined partly by the rules given at the bottom of the page. A measurement's rounding is also determined by the operation (addition, subtraction, multiplication, or division) that is used.

Addition or Subtraction with Significant Figures

Consider two mass measurements, 25.1 g and 2.03 g. The first measurement has one digit to the right of the decimal point in the tenths place. There is no information on possible values for the hundredths digit.

If you add 25.1 g and 2.03 g without considering significant figures, the result is 27.13 g. However, it doesn't make sense that the sum is more precise than one of the individual measurements. Therefore, when two measurements are added or subtracted, the final digit of the result should be significant in both of the original measurements.

Multiplication and Division with Significant Figures

A calculator often gives many more digits than are justified by the measurements. For example, suppose you use a calculator to divide 3.05 g by 8.47 mL. The calculator would show a numerical answer of 0.360094451. The answer contains digits that are not justified by the measurements used to calculate it. For multiplication and division, the answer can have no more significant figures than the measurement with the fewest significant figures.

 **TIP** When adding or subtracting, aligning the values vertically can often help you determine the correct number of significant figures in the answer. For example,

```
  25.1  g
+  2.03 g
  27.1  g
```

✓ READING CHECK

5. According to the table below, how would the value 3.245 g be rounded to the nearest hundredths place?

Rules for Rounding Numbers		
If the digit following the last digit to be retained is:	**then the last digit should:**	**Example (rounded to three significant figures)**
greater than 5	be increased by 1	42.68 g → 42.7 g
less than 5	stay the same	17.32 m → 17.3 m
5, followed by nonzero digit(s)	be increased by 1	2.7851 cm → 2.79 cm
5, not followed by nonzero digit(s), and preceded by an odd digit	be increased by 1	4.635 kg → 4.64 kg (because 3 is odd)
5, not followed by nonzero digit(s), and the preceding significant digit is even	stay the same	78.65 mL → 78.6 mL (because 6 is even)

Rules for Addition and Subtraction	Examples
1. For decimals, the sum or difference should have the same number of significant figures after the decimal point as the measurement with the fewest digits to the right of the decimal point.	25.1 g + 2.03 g = 27.1 g 3.70 mL – 0.493 mL = 3.21 mL 17 cm + 5.7 cm = 23 cm
2. For whole numbers, the final significant digit of the sum or difference should be the same as the final significant digit of the least precise measurement.	5400 g + 365 g = 5800 g 2710 mL – 1000 mL = 2000 mL

Rule for Multiplication and Division	Examples
1. The product or quotient should have no more significant figures than the given measurement with the fewest significant figures.	3.05 g ÷ 8.47 mL = 0.360 g/mL 3.7 m × 16.5 m = 61 m^2 18 g ÷ 2.34 cm^3 = 7.7 g/cm^3

Conversion Factors and Significant Figures

Earlier in this chapter, you learned how conversion factors are used to change one unit to another. These conversion factors usually do not have any uncertainty. For example, there are exactly 100 centimeters in a meter. If you were to use the conversion factor 100 cm/m to change meters to centimeters, the 100 would not limit the degree of certainty in the answer.

A counting measurement is also exact. For example, suppose you have 10 test tubes, each containing 5.67 mL of a liquid. The number 10 is exact. It should not be a limit to the significant figures in a calculation. You can safely report that you have 10 times 5.67 mL, or a total of 56.7 mL of liquid.

> **PRACTICE**

F. Carry out the following calculations. Express each answer to the correct number of significant figures.

a. 5.44 m – 2.6103 m _____

c. 2.099 g + 0.05681 g _____

b. 2.4 g/mL × 15.82 mL _____

d. 87.3 cm – 1.655 cm _____

G. Calculate the area of a rectangular crystal surface that measures 1.34 μm by 0.7488 μm. _____

H. A certain plastic has a density of 1.2 g/cm^3. A photo frame is constructed from two sheets of plastic that measure 28 cm by 22 cm by 3.0 mm. What is the mass of the photo frame? _____

Scientific notation is used to express very large or very small numbers.

Sometimes measurements are very small or very large. It is often awkward to give measurements with a lot of zeros, such as 23 000 000 000 000 or 0.000 000 000 000 001 79. Instead, measurements are often given in scientific notation.

In **scientific notation,** numbers are written in the form $M \times 10^n$, where M is greater than or equal to 1 and less than 10 and n is a whole number. When numbers are written in scientific notation, only the significant figures are shown.

For example, to write 65 000 km in scientific notation and show that the first two digits are significant, you would write 6.5×10^4 km. If you wanted to show that the first three digits were significant, you would write 6.50×10^4 km.

To write a number in scientific notation, use the following two steps.

1. Determine M by moving the decimal point in the original number to the left or the right so that only one nonzero digit remains to the left of the decimal point. Delete all zeros that are not significant.

2. Determine n by counting the number of places that you moved the decimal point. If you moved it to the left, n is positive. If you moved it to the right, n is negative.

This scientific calculator shows the most common format for displaying scientific notation. The number shown is 5.44×10^7.

PRACTICE

i. Write the following measurements in scientific notation.

a. 0.000 12 mm _____

b. 560 000 cm _____

c. 33 400 kg _____

d. 0.000 4120 s _____

J. The following measurements are in scientific notation. Write them in ordinary notation.

a. 7.050×10^3 g _____

b. $4.000\ 05 \times 10^7$ mg _____

c. 2.3500×10^4 mL _____

Mathematical Operations Using Scientific Notation

Numbers in scientific notation can be added, subtracted, multiplied, and divided just as any number can. The rules for adding, subtracting, multiplying, and dividing two numbers in scientific notation are given below.

Addition and Subtraction

1. If the exponents of the two numbers differ, rewrite one number so that both numbers have the same exponent.

2. To find the new value of M, find the sum or difference of the M values of the two numbers. Keep the same value of n.

   Example: 5.93×10^6 kg $- 4.2 \times 10^5$ kg
   $$= 5.93 \times 10^6 \text{ kg} - 0.42 \times 10^6 \text{ kg}$$
   $$= 5.51 \times 10^6 \text{ kg}$$

Multiplication and Division

1. To find the value of M in a product, multiply the two values of M. To find the value of M in a quotient, divide the first value of M by the second value of M.

2. To find the new value of n in a product, add the two values of n. To find the value of n in a quotient, subtract the value second value of n from the first value of n.

   Example: $(2.6 \times 10^8 \text{ s})(4.7 \times 10^4 \text{ s}) = (2.6)(4.7) \times 10^{8+4}$ s
   $$= 12 \times 10^{12} \text{ s}$$
   $$= 1.2 \times 10^{13} \text{ s}$$

Remember that a calculator does not display the correct number of significant figures after performing an operation.

Often, the result of these calculations is not in scientific notation. If M is less than 1 or greater than or equal to 10, the decimal point must be moved. If the decimal point is moved one spot to the left, increase n by 1. If the decimal point is moved one spot to the right, decrease n by 1.

PRACTICE

K. Perform the following calculations and express the answers in scientific notation.

a. 4.2×10^4 kg $+ 7.9 \times 10^3$ kg _____

b. $(5.23 \times 10^6 \text{ μm})(7.1 \times 10^{-2} \text{ μm})$ _____

c. 5.44×10^7 g $\div 8.1 \times 10^4$ mol _____

d. 8.40×10^5 km $- 3.1 \times 10^5$ km _____

Learning to analyze and solve such problems requires practice and a logical approach. In this section, you will review a process that can help you analyze problems effectively.

Step 1 Analyze

The first step is to read the problem carefully at least twice and to analyze the information in it. Identify and list the data in the problem and identify what you are being asked to find.

Step 2 Plan

The second step is to develop a plan for solving the problem. The plan should show how the information given is to be used to find the unknown. It is often helpful to draw a picture that represents the problem to help you visualize the problem.

Decide which conversion factors, mathematical formulas, or chemical principles you will need to solve the problem. Your plan might suggest a single calculation or a series of them involving different conversion factors. Once you understand how you need to proceed, you may wish to sketch out the stages of your solution in a table or a flowchart.

Step 3 Solve

The third step is using the data and conversion factors to carry out your plan. Make sure to keep track of the units and to round the result to the correct number of significant figures.

Step 4 Check Your Work

Examine your answer to determine if it is reasonable. Make sure that the units in the answer are what you would expect. Use simpler, rounded numbers and repeat the calculations to check the order of magnitude of your answer.

Remember

A problem may not always give you all the data you need for a solution. For example, you may need to look up a value on the periodic table.

☑ READING CHECK

6. Which stage of this problem-solving process involves substituting values into an equation and solving for the unknown value?

Calculate the volume of a sample of aluminum that has a mass of 3.057 kg. The density of aluminum is 2.70 g/cm^3.

	SOLUTION	
1	**ANALYZE**	*Determine what information is given and unknown.*

        Given: mass = 3.057 kg, density = 2.70 g/cm^3

        Unknown: volume of aluminum

2 PLAN *Determine the equations and conversion factors needed.*

Because density is given in g/cm^3 and mass in kg, a conversion between g and kg is necessary. The relationship between g and kg is 1000 g = 1 kg.

The equation for density is needed to complete the problem. It should be rearranged to solve for volume.

$$D = \frac{m}{V} \quad \Rightarrow \quad V = \frac{m}{D}$$

3 SOLVE *Substitute the known values and calculate.*

The answer should be rounded to three significant figures because the least precise measurement, density, has three significant figures.

$$V = \frac{3.057 \text{ kg}}{2.70 \text{ g/cm}^3} \times \frac{1000 \text{ g}}{\text{kg}}$$

$$= 1.13 \times 10^3 \text{ cm}^3$$

4 CHECK YOUR WORK *Determine if the answer makes sense.*

The unit of the answer is a cubic length, and the problem asked for a volume. An order-of-magnitude estimate suggests that the right answer should be around 1000 cm^3.

$$\frac{3}{3} \times 1000 = 1000$$

L. A clock gains 0.020 second per minute. How many seconds will the clock gain in exactly six months, assuming exactly 30 days per month?

SOLUTION

1 ANALYZE

What information is given and unknown?

Given: clock gains _____ seconds per minute

Unknown: _____

2 PLAN

What equations and conversion factors are needed?

The final answer is given in seconds. The given time gain is in seconds per minute. Three conversion factors are necessary. Complete the relationships between the units.

_____ minutes = 1 hour

_____ hours = 1 day

_____ days = 1 month

The final answer will be the number of seconds the clock gains per month multiplied by _____ months.

3 SOLVE

What is the correct answer?

Write the three conversion factors into the equation below. Then perform the calculation and cancel all of the units.

$$t = \frac{0.020 \text{ second}}{\text{minute}} \times \text{\underline{\hspace{2cm}}} \times \text{\underline{\hspace{2cm}}} \times \text{\underline{\hspace{2cm}}} \times 6 \text{ months}$$

$$= \text{\underline{\hspace{5cm}}}$$

4 CHECK YOUR WORK

Does the answer make sense?

Does the answer have the correct units? _____

Explain how you could estimate your answer to determine if it is the correct order of magnitude.

_____

_____

> **Variables that are directly proportional increase or decrease by the same factor.**

Two quantities are **directly proportional** to each other if dividing one by the other gives a constant value. For example, the quantities mass and volume are proportional. The table below shows the measured mass and volume of five separate samples of aluminum. As the masses of the samples increase, their volumes increase by the same factor.

When two variables, x and y, are directly proportional to each other, the relationship can be expressed as $y \propto x$, which is read as "y is proportional to x." The relationship can be shown in these two forms using a proportionality constant k:

$$\frac{y}{x} = k \quad \text{or} \quad y = kx$$

The first equation shows that there is a constant ratio between the values of two quantities that are directly proportional. Note that the data in the table have ratios that are nearly equal, indicating a relationship that is directly proportional.

The second equation shows that a directly proportional relationship is a straight line with a slope of k. The graph of every directly proportional relationship also passes through the origin, or the data point (0,0). Both the values in the third column of the table below and the graph demonstrate that the data in the table are directly proportional.

 Remember

A variable is a quantity that can take on many values.

 LOOKING CLOSER

7. What is the constant of proportionality for the data in the table and what does it represent?

_____

_____

_____

Mass-Volume Data for Aluminum at 20°C		
Mass (g)	Volume (cm³)	$\frac{m}{V}$ (g/cm³)
54.7	20.1	2.72
65.7	24.4	2.69
83.5	30.9	2.70
96.3	35.8	2.69
105.7	39.1	2.70

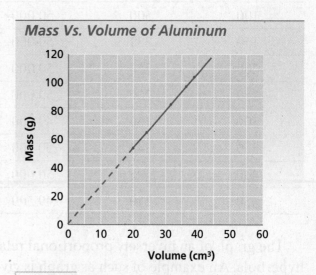

Mass Vs. Volume of Aluminum

The graph shows a relationship that is directly proportional. Notice that the line is extended to pass through the origin.

> **Quantities are inversely proportional if one decreases in value when the other increases.**

Two quantities are **inversely proportional** to each other if multiplying them gives a constant value. For example, the amount of time it takes to travel a certain distance is inversely proportional to the speed of travel. The greater the speed, the less time is needed to go a certain distance.

When two variables, x and y, are inversely proportional to each other, the relationship can be expressed as

$$y \propto \frac{1}{x}$$

This is read as "y is proportional to 1 divided by x." The relationship can be expressed in this form using a proportionality constant k:

$$xy = k$$

This equation shows that the product of the two variables will yield a constant value. The table below shows that the pressure and volume of a sample of nitrogen gas are inversely proportional. The product of the pressure and volume at any particular time is almost exactly the same.

> ✔ **READING CHECK**
>
> **8.** Two quantities are
>
> _____ proportional if their product is constant.
>
> Two quantities are
>
> _____ proportional if their quotient is constant.

Pressure-Volume Data for Nitrogen at Constant Temperature		
Pressure (kPa)	Volume (cm³)	P × V
100	500	50 000
150	333	50 000
200	250	50 000
250	200	50 000
300	166	49 800
350	143	50 100
400	125	50 000
450	110	49 500

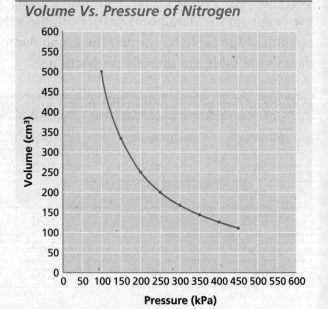

Volume Vs. Pressure of Nitrogen

The graph of an inversely proportional relationship is a hyperbola. An example of such as graph is given at the right, showing the data in the table. The ends of the graph approach the x-axis and y-axis because as one value moves away from zero, the other value must approach zero.

The graph shows a relationship that is inversely proportional.

VOCABULARY

1. What is the difference between a graph representing data that are directly proportional and a graph of data that are inversely proportional?

_____

_____

_____

REVIEW

2. The density of copper is 8.94 g/cm^3. Two students each measure the density of three samples of the substance. Student A's results are 7.3 g/mL, 9.4 g/mL, and 8.3 g/mL. Student B's results are 8.4 g/cm^3, 8.8 g/cm^3, and 8.0 g/cm^3. Compare the two sets of results in terms of precision and accuracy.

_____

_____

_____

3. Carry out the following calculations.

   a. 52.13 g + 1.7502 g _____ b. 16.25 g ÷ 5.1442 mL _____

4. Perform the following operations. Express each answer in scientific notation.

   a. 7.023×10^9 g $- 6.62 \times 10^7$ g _____

   b. $(8.99 \times 10^{-4}$ m$)(3.57 \times 10^4$ m$)$ _____

   c. 2.17×10^{-3} g $\div 5.022 \times 10^4$ mL _____

5. A student measures the mass of a beaker filled with corn oil. The mass reading averages 215.6 g. The mass of the beaker is 110.4 g. What is the density of the corn oil if its volume is 114 cm^3.

   _____

Critical Thinking

6. **APPLYING CONCEPTS** The mass of a liquid is 11.50 g and its volume is 9.03 mL. How many significant figures should its density value have? Explain the reason for your answer.

_____

_____

Any value expressed in scientific notation has two parts. The first part, the *first factor*, consists of a number greater than or equal to 1 but less than 10. The second part consists of a power of 10. To write the first part, move the decimal to the right or the left so that there is only one nonzero digit to the left of the decimal point. To write the second part, count how many places the decimal point was moved. The exponent is positive if the decimal point moved to the left and negative if the decimal point moved to the right.

$$6.02 \times 10^{23}$$

first factor   power of ten

exponent

Problem-Solving TIPS

- In addition and subtraction, all values must first be converted to numbers that have the same exponent of 10. The result is the sum or the difference of the first factors, multiplied by the same exponent of 10. The result should be rounded to the correct number of significant figures and expressed in scientific notation.
- In multiplication, the first factors are multiplied and the exponents of 10 are added.
- In division, the first factors of the numbers are divided and the exponent of 10 in the denominator is subtracted from the exponent of 10 in the numerator.

SAMPLE

Write 299 800 000 in scientific notation.

The decimal must move to the left 8 places, which indicates a positive exponent. The value in scientific notation is 2.998×10^8 m/s.

$$299\ 800\ 000.\ \text{m/s}$$
$$8\ 7\ 6\ 5\ 4\ 3\ 2\ 1$$

Write $(3.1 \times 10^3)(5.21 \times 10^4)$ in scientific notation.

Multiply the first factors, and then add the exponents of 10.

$$(3.1 \times 10^3)(5.21 \times 10^4) = (3.1 \times 5.21) \times 10^{(3+4)}$$
$$= 16 \times 10^7$$
$$= 1.6 \times 10^8$$

Practice Problems: Chapter Review practice problems 18 and 19

1. How does quantitative information differ from qualitative information?

_____

_____

2. What is the difference between hypotheses and theories?

_____

_____

3. What are the five stages in the scientific method?

_____

_____

_____

4. What is a derived unit, and what is the SI-derived unit for area?

_____

_____

_____

5. Explain how conversion factors are used.

_____

_____

6. What is meant by a mass measurement expressed in the form 4.6 g $\pm$ 0.2 g?

_____

7. Round each of the following measurements to the number of significant figures indicated.

   a. 67.029 g to three significant figures _____

   b. 0.15 L to one significant figure _____

   c. 52.8005 mg to five significant figures _____

8. Arrange in the correct order the following four basic steps for finding the solution to a problem: check your work, plan, solve, and analyze.

_____

9. What is the volume, in cubic meters, of a rectangular solid that is 0.25 m long, 6.1 m wide, and 4.9 m high?

10. Find the density of a material, given that a 5.03 g sample occupies 3.24 mL.

11. A sample of a substance that has a density of 0.824 g/mL has a mass of 0.451 g. Calculate the volume of the sample.

12. How many grams are in 882 µg? _____

13. The density of gold is 19.3 g/cm^3. What is the volume, in cubic centimeters, of a sample of gold that has a mass of 0.715 kg? If this sample of gold is a cube, what is the length of each edge in centimeters?

14. A student measures the mass of a sample as 9.67 g. Calculate the percentage error, given that the correct mass is 9.82 g.

15. A handbook gives the density of calcium as 1.54 g/cm^3. Based on lab measurements, what is the percentage error of a density calculation of 1.25 g/cm^3?

16. How many significant figures are in each of the following measurements?

a. 0.4004 mL _____   **c.** 1.000 30 km _____

b. 6000 g _____   **d.** 400. nm _____

17. Perform the following calculations. Express the answers with the correct number of significant digits.

a. 6.078 g + 0.3329 g _____   **c.** (0.8102 m)(3.44 m) _____

b. 8.2 cm − 7.11 cm _____   **d.** 94.20 g ÷ 3.167 22 mL _____

18. Calculate the product of 0.002 115 m and 0.000 040 5 m. Express the answer in scientific notation and with the correct number of significant figures.

_____

19. A sample of a certain material has a mass of 2.03 × 10^{-3} g. Calculate the volume of the sample, given that the density is 9.133 × 10^{-1} g/cm^3. Use the four-step method to solve the problem.

ANALYZE:

PLAN:

SOLVE:

CHECK YOUR WORK:

CHAPTER 3

Atoms: The Building Blocks of Matter

Key Concepts

Review Previous Concepts

1. What is the relationship between an atom and an element?

_____

_____

_____

2. How are conversion factors used to solve problems in chemistry?

_____

_____

_____

SECTION 3.1

The Atom: From Philosophical Idea to Scientific Theory

When you crush a lump of sugar, you can see that it is made up of many smaller sugar particles. You may grind these particles into a very fine powder, but each tiny piece is still sugar. Now suppose you mix the sugar powder into water. The tiny particles seem to disappear. Yet if you were to taste the solution, you'd know that the sugar is still there.

Observations like these led people to wonder about the nature of matter. Can matter be divided into pieces forever or is it made of miniature pieces that cannot be divided at all?

The particle theory of matter was supported as early as 400 B.C. by certain Greek thinkers, such as Democritus. He called nature's basic particle an *atom*, based on the Greek word meaning "indivisible." On the other hand, Aristotle did not believe in atoms. He thought that all matter was continuous. He lived in the generation after Democritus, and his opinion was accepted for nearly 2000 years.

The opinions of Aristotle and Democritus were not based on experimental evidence. The discussion remained a philosophical one until the eighteenth century. Then scientists began to gather evidence favoring the atomic theory of matter.

KEY TERMS

law of conservation of mass
law of definite proportions
law of multiple proportions

Sugar seems to disappear when it is mixed with water.

Three basic laws describe how matter behaves in chemical reactions.

By the late 1700s, chemists agreed that elements cannot be broken down further by ordinary chemical means. They also agreed that elements combine to form compounds that have different properties from the elements that form them. They did not agree on what makes up elements, or if a compound always has the same ratio of elements in it.

Critical Thinking

1. Interpret Why are the opinions of Aristotle and Democritus not considered scientific theories?

_____

_____

_____

Evidence for Atomic Theory

Law of conservation of mass	Mass is neither created nor destroyed during ordinary chemical reactions or physical changes.
Law of definite proportions	A compound contains the same elements in exactly the same proportions regardless of sample size or source of the compound.
Law of multiple proportions	If two or more compounds are composed of the same two elements, then the ratio of the masses of the second element combined with a certain mass of the first element is a ratio of small whole numbers.

Toward the end of the eighteenth century scientists made several discoveries about chemical reactions. A *chemical reaction* is the change of a substance or substances into one or more new substances. Using improved equipment, scientists made more exact measurements before and after reactions than ever before. In the process, they discovered some basic principles, which are summarized in the table.

Law of Conservation of Mass Chemists measured the mass of substances before and after a reaction. The total mass of the products was always equal to the total mass of the reactants. From this evidence, chemists deduced that matter cannot be created or destroyed during a reaction, a scientific law known as the **law of conservation of mass.**

Law of Definite Proportions Chemists measured the mass of two elements before forming a compound with the elements. They discovered that the compound always contained the same ratio of the elements, no matter how the compound was formed. From this evidence, chemists deduced that all compounds have a fixed composition that does not vary from sample to sample, a law known as the **law of definite proportions.**

Law of Multiple Proportions Chemists also worked with multiple compounds made from the same two elements. For example, carbon and oxygen form carbon monoxide and carbon dioxide. In carbon monoxide, there is 1.00 g of carbon for every 1.33 g of oxygen. In carbon dioxide, there is 1.00 g of carbon for every 2.66 g of oxygen. The ratio of the mass of the oxygen in the two compounds is 1 to 2. For any two such compounds made of the same two elements, chemists found a simple ratio relating the masses of the variable element via this **law of multiple proportions.**

Each of these salt crystals contains exactly 39.34% sodium and 60.66% chlorine by mass.

READING CHECK

2. Complete this sentence. The total mass of the products in any chemical reaction is equal to

_____

_____

_____

_____

Compounds contain atoms in whole-number ratios.

In 1808, an English schoolteacher named John Dalton proposed an explanation for the three newly discovered laws. He reasoned that elements were composed of atoms and that only whole numbers of atoms can combine to form compounds. His theory is summarized in the table below.

Dalton's Atomic Theory
1. All matter is composed of extremely small particles called atoms.
2. Atoms of a given element are identical in size, mass, and other properties. Atoms of different elements differ in these properties.
3. Atoms cannot be subdivided, created, or destroyed.
4. Atoms of different elements combine in simple whole-number ratios to form chemical compounds.
5. In chemical reactions, atoms are combined, separated, or rearranged.

This theory provides an explanation for the law of conservation of mass during a chemical reaction. According to Statement 3, atoms cannot be divided, created, or destroyed. According to Statement 4, atoms form compounds in simple whole-number ratios. The same number of atoms is present before and after a compound forms or breaks apart.

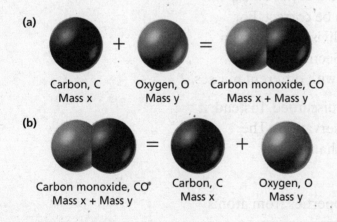

(a) Carbon, C Mass x + Oxygen, O Mass y = Carbon monoxide, CO Mass x + Mass y

(b) Carbon monoxide, CO Mass x + Mass y = Carbon, C Mass x + Oxygen, O Mass y

In both reactions shown here, the total mass stays the same during the reaction because the mass of a carbon atom and the mass of an oxygen atom are fixed.

READING CHECK

3. Which statement in Dalton's atomic theory implies that an atom of gold is exactly the same as any other atom of gold?

_____

_____

(a)

Carbon, C   Oxygen, O   Carbon monoxide, CO

(b)

Carbon, C   Oxygen, O   Oxygen, O   Carbon dioxide, CO2

(a) CO is always composed of one C atom and one O atom. (b) CO_2 molecules are always composed of one C atom and two O atoms. The same number of CO_2 molecules contain twice as many O atoms.

Dalton's theory also provides an explanation for the law of definite proportions and the law of multiple proportions. Statement 4 implies that a compound is always formed using atoms in the same whole-number ratio. Because an atom has a fixed mass, it also follows that using twice as many atoms of an element will result in a compound containing twice the mass of that element. For example, carbon dioxide molecules always contain two oxygen atoms for every atom of carbon. Carbon monoxide always contains one oxygen atom for every atom of carbon. So carbon dioxide will always have twice as many oxygen atoms as carbon monoxide for every atom of carbon.

Atoms can be subdivided into smaller particles.

Dalton turned Democritus's *idea* about atoms into a *scientific theory* that could be tested by experiment. But not all aspects of Dalton's atomic theory have proven to be correct. For example, today we know that atoms are divisible into even smaller particles. And, as you will see in Section 3 of this chapter, a given element can have atoms with different masses.

However, atomic theory has not been discarded. Instead, it has been modified to explain the new observations. The following important concepts remain unchanged.

- All matter is composed of atoms.
- Atoms of any one element differ in properties from atoms of another element.

Critical Thinking

4. **Infer** When scientists discovered that atoms are composed of smaller particles, why didn't they reject atomic theory?

_____

_____

VOCABULARY

1. What chemical laws can be explained by Dalton's atomic theory?

_____

_____

_____

REVIEW

2. List the five main points of Dalton's atomic theory.

1. _____

_____

2. _____

_____

3. _____

_____

4. _____

_____

5. _____

_____

Critical Thinking

3. ANALYZING INFORMATION Three compounds containing potassium and oxygen are compared. Analysis shows that for each 1.00 g of O, the compounds have 1.22 g, 2.44 g, and 4.89 g of K, respectively. Show how these data support the law of multiple proportions.

_____

_____

_____

_____

_____

_____

_____

SECTION 3.2

The Structure of the Atom

The atomic theory proposed by John Dalton stated that atoms are indivisible. This idea was proven incorrect by the end of the nineteenth century. It became clear that atoms are actually composed of several basic types of particles. The number and arrangement of these particles determine the properties of the atom.

The **atom** is now defined as the smallest particle of an element that retains the chemical properties of the element. Atoms consist of two regions. Each region contains different types of particles, called *subatomic* particles.

- The *nucleus* is a very small region located at the center of the atom. The nucleus includes at least one positively charged particle called a *proton* and usually one or more neutral particles called *neutrons*.
- Surrounding the nucleus is a much larger region that contains negatively charged particles called *electrons*.

Atoms contain positive and negative particles.

The electron was the first subatomic particle to be discovered. In the late 1800s, many experiments were performed in which electric current was passed through various gases. A gas with the same pressure as the air at Earth's surface is a poor conductor of electricity. For that reason, the scientists made sure to keep the gases in their experiments at very low pressures.

For their experiments, scientists made glass tubes called *cathode-ray tubes*, and filled them with low-pressure gas. Metal disks were placed on either side of the tube. One disk, the cathode, was given a positive charge. The other disk, the anode, was given a negative charge.

KEY TERMS

atom   nuclear forces

READING CHECK

1. Draw a model showing the two regions of an atom in the space below. Label the nucleus and the electron region.

Cathode Rays and Electrons

Scientists discovered that the surface of a cathode-ray tube glowed when electric current was passed through the tube. They hypothesized that the glow was caused by a stream of particles, called a cathode ray, that traveled from the cathode to the anode. They also found that cathode rays could be deflected by a magnet or away from a negatively charged object. This led to the hypothesis that the particles in a cathode ray are negatively charged.

Experiments carried out by English physicist Joseph John Thomson in 1897 supported this hypothesis. He was able to calculate the ratio of the charge of the particles to the mass of the particles in a cathode ray. He found that this ratio was the same, no matter what metals were used in the cathode and anode. The ratio also stayed the same if the gas in the tube changed.

Thomson concluded that all cathode rays are composed of identical negatively charged particles called electrons. The atoms in the cathode-ray experiments above were releasing electrons. This was evidence that atoms are divisible and that electrons are present in different types of atoms.

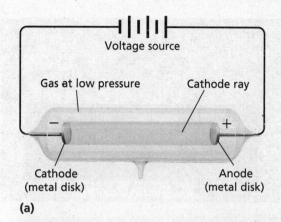

Voltage source
Gas at low pressure
Cathode ray
Cathode (metal disk)
Anode (metal disk)

(a)

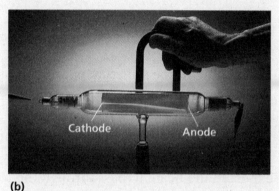

Cathode
Anode

(b)

(a) A simple cathode-ray tube. (b) A magnet above a cathode-ray tube deflects the beam downward, showing that the particles in the beam must have a negative charge.

Charge and Mass of the Electron

Thomson's experiments also revealed that the electron has a very large charge-to-mass ratio. In 1909, the American physicist Robert A. Millikan was able to measure the charge of the electron. Scientists used this information to determine the mass of an electron. They found that an electron has about one two-thousandth the mass of the smallest known atom.

Thomson proposed a *plum pudding model* to explain the properties of the atom known at the time. Because atoms are electrically neutral, he proposed that the electrons were balanced by a "pudding" of positive charge. The electrons were embedded within this positively-charged material. The region of positive charge was also thought to contain most of the mass of the atom, since the electron has so little mass.

CONNECT

Today, experiments have determined that the electron has a mass of 9.109×10^{-31} kg. This is 1/1837 the mass of the smallest type of hydrogen atom.

READING CHECK

2. Sketch the plum pudding model proposed by Thomson. Label the electrons and the region of positive charge.

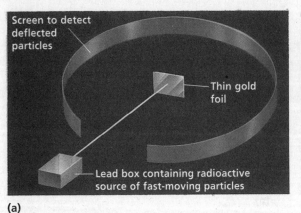

Screen to detect deflected particles

Thin gold foil

Lead box containing radioactive source of fast-moving particles

(a)

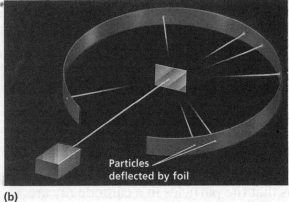

Particles deflected by foil

(b)

Atoms have small, dense, positively-charged nuclei.

More detail of the structure of atoms was discovered by New Zealander Ernest Rutherford and his associates Hans Geiger and Ernest Marsden. They bombarded a piece of gold foil with fast-moving *alpha particles*, which are positively charged particles with four times the mass of a hydrogen atom. They expected the beam to pass through the foil with a very slight deflection because the mass and charge were evenly distributed in the gold foil. They were surprised when about 1 in 8000 particles deflected backwards toward the source.

Rutherford hypothesized that small, densely packed bundles of matter with a positive charge must have caused the backwards deflections. The bundles had to be small because so few of the particles bounced backwards. Rutherford used the term nucleus to describe each bundle of matter.

Rutherford had discovered that the volume of the nucleus was very small compared to the total volume of an atom. The source of the positive charge of an atom had been discovered. Rutherford's student, Niels Bohr, later discovered the location of the electrons in an atom.

(a) Geiger and Marsden bombarded a thin piece of gold foil with a beam of alpha particles. (b) Some of the particles were deflected back toward their source.

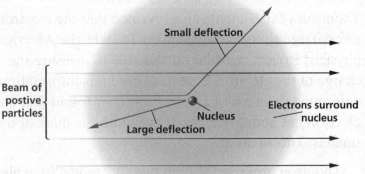

Beam of postive particles

Small deflection

Large deflection

Nucleus

Electrons surround nucleus

READING CHECK

3. What is the nucleus of an atom?

Most particles passed through the gold foil undisturbed. A small number were deflected by the nucleus.

A nucleus contains protons and neutrons.

With one exception, all atomic nuclei are made of two kinds of particles, protons and neutrons. A proton has a positive charge equal in magnitude to the negative charge of an electron. Atoms are electrically neutral because they contain equal numbers of protons and electrons. A neutron has no charge, and, like an atom, is electrically neutral.

The one atomic nucleus that lacks a neutron is that of the simplest hydrogen atom. Its nucleus is a single proton with a single electron moving around it. A proton has a mass of 1.673×10^{-27} kg, which is 1836 times greater than the mass of an electron. Therefore, a proton has nearly all of the mass in the simplest hydrogen atom. The mass of a neutron is 1.675×10^{-27} kg, which is slightly larger than the mass of a proton.

The nuclei of atoms of different elements differ in the number of protons they possess. Therefore, the number of protons determines an atom's identity. For every proton an atom has in its nucleus, the same number of electrons surrounds the nucleus. Physicists have discovered other subatomic particles, but they have little effect on the chemical properties of matter. The properties of electrons, protons, and neutrons, are summarized in the table below.

TIP Many words derived from Latin that end with -us form plurals by changing the ending to -i. Thus, the plural of nucleus is nuclei and the plural of radius is radii.

✓ READING CHECK

4. What quantity determines the identity of an atom?

_____

Properties of Subatomic Particles					
Particle	Symbols	Relative electric charge	Mass number	Relative mass (u*)	Actual mass (kg)
Electron	e^-, $_{-1}^{0}e$	−1	0	0.000 5486	9.109×10^{-31}
Proton	p^+, $_{1}^{1}H$	+1	1	1.007 276	1.673×10^{-27}
Neutron	$n°$, $_{0}^{1}n$	0	1	1.008 665	1.675×10^{-27}

*1 u (unified atomic mass unit) = $1.660\ 540 \times 10^{-27}$ kg

Forces in the Nucleus

Generally, particles that have the same electric charge repel one another. Therefore, you might expect a nucleus with more than one proton in it to be unstable. However, a force exists between two protons that overcomes the electric force trying to push them apart. This force only acts when two protons are very close to one another.

A similar force acts when two neutrons are very close together, or when a neutron and a proton are very close together. Together, these short-range proton-proton, neutron-neutron, and proton-neutron forces are called **nuclear forces.** These forces allow atoms with up to 83 positively-charged protons in the same nucleus to be stable.

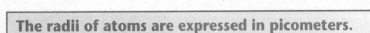
The radii of atoms are expressed in picometers.

Because the nucleus is so small, the size of an atom is determined by the size of the region in which electrons are present. This region is sometimes thought of as an electron cloud—a cloud of negative charge. The radius of an atom is the distance from the center of the nucleus to the outer edge of the electron cloud.

Because atomic radii are so small, they are expressed in a unit that is more convenient for the sizes of atoms. This unit is called the *picometer.* Another unit, called the *unified atomic mass unit,* or u, is used to express the mass of atoms.

$$1 \text{ pm} = 10^{-12} \text{ m} = 10^{-10} \text{ cm}$$

$$1 \text{ u} = 1.660\ 540 \times 10^{-27} \text{ kg}$$

To get an idea of how small a picometer is, consider that 1 cm is the same fractional part of 1000 km (about 600 mi) as 100 pm is of 1 cm. Atomic radii range from 40 pm to 270 pm across. Atomic nuclei have a much smaller radius, about 0.001 pm. Atomic nuclei are also incredibly dense, with a density of about 2×10^{14} g/cm^3.

Critical Thinking

5. **Calculate** Verify the value for the density of an atomic nucleus given above for a spherical atom with a mass of 1 u. Recall that the volume of a sphere is given by $V = \frac{4}{3}\pi r^3$.

 CONNECT

In physics, there are four known fundamental forces that describe how matter interacts. These forces are the electromagnetic force, the gravitational force, the strong nuclear force, and the weak nuclear force.

VOCABULARY

1. Define each of the following:

a. atom _____

_____

b. neutron _____

_____

REVIEW

2. Describe one conclusion made by each scientist that led to the development of the current atomic theory.

a. Thomson _____

_____

b. Millikan _____

_____

c. Rutherford _____

_____

3. Compare the three subatomic particles in terms of location in the atom, mass, and relative charge.

_____

_____

4. Why is the cathode-ray tube shown earlier in this section connected to a vacuum pump?

_____

_____

Critical Thinking

5. **EVALUATING IDEAS** Nuclear forces are said to hold protons and neutrons together. What is it about the composition of the nucleus that requires the concept of nuclear forces?

_____

_____

_____

SECTION 3.3

Counting Atoms

Neon gas only makes up 0.002% of the air you breathe. Yet there are 5×10^{17} atoms of neon in each breath you take. In most experiments, atoms are too small and numerous to track individually. Instead, chemists make calculations that take into account the properties of large groups of atoms.

> **All atoms of an element must have the same number of protons, but not neutrons.**

All atoms are composed of the same basic particles. Yet all atoms are not the same. Atoms of different elements have different numbers of protons. Atoms of the same element all have the same number of protons. The **atomic number** (Z) of an element is the number of protons of each atom of that element.

Turn to the large periodic table in Section 2 of the chapter "The Periodic Law." The periodic table square for lithium is also shown at the right. An element's atomic number is indicated above its symbol. Notice that the elements are placed in order in the periodic table according to the atomic number. At the top left is hydrogen, H, with an atomic number of 1. Next in order is helium, He, with an atomic number of 2. The next row of the periodic table includes the elements with the atomic numbers 3, 4, 5, and so on.

The atomic numbers give the number of protons in an element. So all atoms of hydrogen have one proton, all atoms of helium have two protons, and so on.

The atomic number also identifies an element. If you want to know which element has atomic number 47, you can look at the periodic table for the box with a "47" at the top. Silver, Ag, is the correct element. You then know that all silver atoms have 47 protons. Since atoms are electrically neutral, you also know that all silver atoms must also have 47 electrons.

3
Li
Lithium
6.941
$[He]2 s^1$

This periodic table entry shows that the atomic number of lithium is 3.

READING CHECK

1. How many protons does every atom of hydrogen have?

_____

2. How many protons does every atom of lithium have?

_____

Isotopes

The simplest atoms are those of hydrogen. All hydrogen atoms have only one proton. However, like many naturally occurring elements, hydrogen atoms can have different numbers of neutrons.

Three types of hydrogen atoms are known. The most common type of hydrogen is sometimes called *protium*. It accounts for 99.9885% of the hydrogen atoms found on Earth. A protium atom has one electron and a nucleus with one proton. Another form of hydrogen is called *deuterium*. A deuterium atom has one electron and a nucleus with two particles: a neutron and a proton. Finally, a *tritium* atom is a hydrogen atom with one electron and a nucleus of one proton and two neutrons.

Protium, deuterium, and tritium are isotopes of hydrogen. **Isotopes** are atoms of the same element that have different masses. Isotopes of an element have the same number of protons and electrons but a different number of neutrons. All isotopes of an atom are electrically neutral. A sample of an element usually consists of a mixture of its isotopes. Tin has 10 stable isotopes, more than any other element.

Mass Number

An isotope is identified by its name, such as protium, or its atomic number and mass. The **mass number** of an isotope is the total number of protons and neutrons that make up its nucleus. For example, the mass number of protium is one because there is one particle, a proton, in its nucleus.

READING CHECK

3. Use the definition of mass number to complete the table.

TIP The names for the types of hydrogen atoms are derived from the number of particles in the nucleus. The prefix *proto-* means "first," *deutero-* means "second," and *trito-* means "third." The "o" is dropped before the ending *-ium* in the names of the hydrogen atoms.

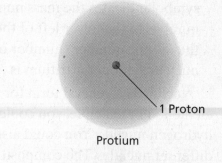

1 Proton

Protium

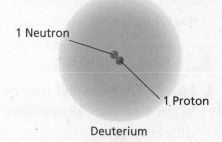

1 Neutron

1 Proton

Deuterium

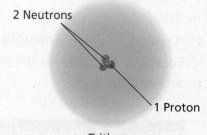

2 Neutrons

1 Proton

Tritium

The three hydrogen isotopes are shown.

Mass Numbers of Hydrogen Isotopes			
	Atomic number (number of protons)	Number of neutrons	Mass number (protons + neutrons)
protium	1	0	1
deuterium	1	1	
tritium	1	2	

Identifying Isotopes

That the isotopes of hydrogen have their own names is unusual. An isotope is usually identified by specifying its mass number. There are two methods for specifying isotopes.

- In *hyphen notation*, the mass number is written with a hyphen after the name of the element. For example, in hyphen notation, tritium would be written as hydrogen-3.

- A *nuclear symbol* is used to show the composition of an isotope's nucleus. A number to the upper left of the element symbol indicates the mass number (protons + neutrons). A number to the lower left of the element symbol indicates the atomic number (number of protons). For example, the nuclear symbol for tritium is $^3_1$H.

  Nuclide is a general term for the specific isotope of an element. For example, you could say that deuterium is a hydrogen nuclide. You could also say that hydrogen has three different nuclides. The composition of the three isotopes, or nuclides, of hydrogen and the two isotopes of helium are given in the table below.

Critical Thinking

4. **Identify** A particular isotope of uranium has a nucleus with 92 protons and 143 neutrons. Identify this isotope in two different ways.

---

5. **Apply** Use the information in the other columns to complete the table on the five nuclides of hydrogen and helium.

Isotopes of Hydrogen and Helium				
Isotope	Nuclear symbol	Number of protons	Number of electrons	Number of neutrons
hydrogen-1 (protium)	$^1_1$H	1	1	0
hydrogen-2 (deuterium)	$^2_1$H	1	1	
hydrogen-3 (tritium)	$^3_1$H	1		2
helium-3	$^3_2$He		2	1
helium-4	$^4_2$He	2		

How many protons, electrons, and neutrons are there in an atom of chlorine-37?

	SOLUTION	
1	**ANALYZE**	*Determine what information is given and unknown.*
		Given: name of isotope is chlorine-37
		Unknown: number of protons, electrons, and neutrons
2	**PLAN**	*Write equations for the unknowns in terms of what is given.*
		number of protons = number of electrons = atomic number
		mass number = number of neutrons + number of protons, so
		number of neutrons = mass number − number of protons
3	**SOLVE**	*Substitute the known values and calculate.*
		Because the name of the isotope is chlorine-37, its mass number is 37. The element chlorine is element 17 on the periodic table, so its atomic number is 17.
		number of protons = number of electrons = 17
		number of neutrons = 37 − 17 = 20
		An atom of chlorine-37 has 17 electrons, 17 protons, and 20 neutrons.
4	**CHECK YOUR WORK**	*Determine if the answer makes sense.*
		The number of protons in a neutral atom equals the number of electrons. The number of protons plus the number of neutrons equals the mass number because 17 + 20 = 37.

PRACTICE

    A. How many protons, electrons, and neutrons make up an atom of bromine-80?

Mass number of bromine-80: _____

Atomic number of bromine: _____

Number of protons: _____ Number of electrons: _____

Number of neutrons = _____ − _____ = _____

Atomic mass is a relative measure.

Masses of atoms expressed in grams are very small. For example, an atom of oxygen-16 has a mass of 2.656×10^{-23} g. It is usually more convenient to talk about the *relative* mass of an atom. The relative atomic mass of an atom is the mass of the atom as compared to the mass of a defined standard.

Scientists use a standard measurement for comparing atomic mass. One **unified atomic mass unit,** or u, is exactly 1/12 the mass of a carbon-12 atom. In other words, one u is the average mass of a particle in the nucleus of a carbon-12 atom. The value of u in grams is $1.660\ 540 \times 10^{-24}$ g.

The mass of a hydrogen-1 atom is slightly more than one unified atomic mass unit—1.007 825 u. An oxygen-16 atom has a precise mass of 15.994 915 u. Additional atomic masses for the isotopes of certain elements are given in the table below.

Isotopes of an element do not differ significantly in their chemical behavior from the other isotopes of the element. So the three isotopes of oxygen all have the same chemical properties despite varying in mass.

The table below shows some isotopes that can be found in nature. The *natural abundance*, or relative amount of each isotope in a sample of an element, is also given in the table. *Artificial isotopes* can only be created in the laboratory. They have a natural abundance of zero.

LOOKING CLOSER

6. Define the two parts of the term *unified atomic mass unit* separately in your own words:

unified atomic mass

_____

_____

_____

unit

_____

_____

Atomic Masses and Abundances of Several Naturally Occurring Isotopes

Isotope	Mass number	Percentage natural abundance	Unified atomic mass unit (u)	Average atomic mass of element (u)
Hydrogen-1	1	99.9885	1.007 825	1.007 94
Hydrogen-2	2	0.0115	2.014 102	
Carbon-12	12	98.93	12 (by definition)	12.0107
Carbon-13	13	1.07	13.003 355	
Oxygen-16	16	99.757	15.994 915	15.9994
Oxygen-17	17	0.038	16.999 132	
Oxygen-18	18	0.205	17.999 160	
Copper-63	63	69.15	62.929 601	63.546
Copper-65	65	30.85	64.927 794	
Cesium-133	133	100	132.905 447	132.905

Average atomic mass is a weighted value.

Chemists have found that a sample of an element will contain the same percentage of each isotope no matter where on Earth the sample is obtained. This percentage is taken into account when calculating the average atomic mass that is reported on the periodic table. The **average atomic mass** is the weighted average of the atomic masses of the isotopes of an element found in nature. The table on the bottom of the previous page also includes the average atomic mass for each element in the table.

Calculating Average Atomic Mass

The average atomic mass of an element is a *weighted average*. It depends on both the mass of each isotope and the natural abundance of each isotope of the element.

For example, 69.15% of the copper atoms in a sample are copper-63 atoms. This isotope has an atomic mass of 62.93 u. The remaining 30.85% of the sample is copper-65, which has an atomic mass of 64.93 u. The weighted average is the sum of the proportions of the mass that are taken up by each type of atom.

69.15% × 62.93 u = 43.52 u of copper-63

30.85% × 64.93 u = 20.03 u of copper-65

43.52 u + 20.03 u = 63.55 u

The value is reasonable because the average atomic mass is closer to the atomic mass of copper-63 than the mass of copper-65, because copper-63 takes up the largest proportion of a natural sample of copper. The value also matches the average atomic mass in the periodic table to four significant figures.

Critical Thinking

8. **Reasoning** Why is the average atomic mass usually a decimal number and not a whole number like the mass number?

_____

_____

_____

READING CHECK

7. Define the two parts of the term *average atomic mass* separately in your own words:

average

_____

_____

_____

atomic mass

_____

_____

_____

TIP In this book, an element's atomic mass is usually rounded to two decimal places before it is used in a calculation.

A relative mass scale makes counting atoms possible.

The unified atomic mass unit allows scientists to compare the mass of an atom to the mass of a standard atom. The average atomic mass gives scientists a value for the average mass of an atom in a sample. Another quantity that scientists also need to determine is the number of atoms in a sample.

The Mole

The mole is the SI unit for the amount of a substance. The abbreviation for a mole is mol. A **mole** is the amount of a substance that contains as many particles as there are atoms in exactly 12 g of carbon-12. The mole is a counting unit, just like a dozen. If you buy two dozen ears of corn at a farm stand, you are purchasing 2 times 12, or 24 ears of corn. Similarly, a chemist might desire 1 mol of carbon or 2.567 mol of calcium.

A penny contains about 1/20 mol of copper atoms, or 2.964×10^{22} atoms. A sample of 20 copper pennies is a little less than one mole of copper.

Avogadro's Number

Chemists have determined that 12 g of carbon-12 contains $6.022\ 141\ 79 \times 10^{23}$ atoms. This means that one mole of any substance contains $6.022\ 141\ 79 \times 10^{23}$ atoms. This number is called Avogadro's number after Amedeo Avogadro. A nineteenth-century Italian scientist, Avogadro helped explain the relationship between mass and numbers of atoms.

For most calculations, the number given above is rounded to four significant figures. So, **Avogadro's number** is the number of particles in exactly one mole of a pure substance, and is given by 6.022×10^{23}. To get a sense of how large this number is, consider this: If every one of the 7 billion people on Earth counted one atom per second, it would take the 7 billion people about 7 million years to count all of the atoms in one mole.

✓ READING CHECK

9. What is the SI unit for the number of particles in a sample?

10. How many particles does the SI unit for the number of particles represent?

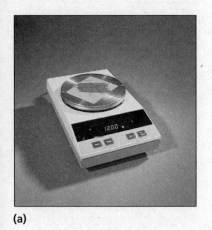

(a)

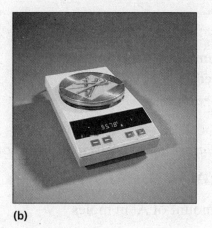

(b)

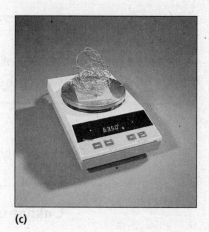

(c)

About one molar mass of (a) carbon (graphite), (b) iron (nails), and (c) copper (wire) is shown on each balance.

Molar Mass

The number of particles in one mole of a substance is given by Avogadro's number. The mass of one mole of a substance is called the **molar mass** of that substance. Molar mass is usually written in units of g/mol. The molar mass of an element in g/mol is equivalent to the atomic mass of the element as given on the periodic table in u. For example, the molar mass of carbon is 12.01 g/mol, the molar mass of iron is 55.84 g/mol, and the molar mass of copper is 63.55 g/mol.

Gram/Mole Conversions

Chemists use molar mass as a conversion factor in chemical calculations. For example, to find the mass of 2 mol of a substance, you would multiply 2 mol by the molar mass of the substance (in grams per mole) to obtain a value in grams.

Conversions with Avogadro's Number

The diagram below can be used to convert between the mass of a sample, the moles in a sample, and the number of atoms in a sample. The conversion between moles and number of atoms is performed using Avogadro's number. The following sample problems explain how to convert between all three of these quantities.

✓ READING CHECK

11. The periodic table gives the average atomic mass of mercury as 200.59 u. What is the mass of one mole of mercury?

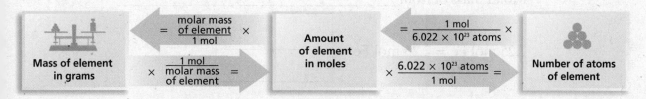

Mass of element in grams	$= \dfrac{\text{molar mass of element}}{1 \text{ mol}} \times$	Amount of element in moles	$= \dfrac{1 \text{ mol}}{6.022 \times 10^{23} \text{ atoms}} \times$	Number of atoms of element
	$\times \dfrac{1 \text{ mol}}{\text{molar mass of element}} =$		$\times \dfrac{6.022 \times 10^{23} \text{ atoms}}{1 \text{ mol}} =$	

The diagram shows the relationship among mass, moles, and number of atoms.

A chemist produced 11.9 g of aluminum, Al. How many moles of aluminum were produced?

	SOLUTION	
1	ANALYZE	*Determine what information is given and unknown.*

Given: 11.9 g Al

Unknown: amount of Al in moles

2 PLAN — *Determine the equation and conversion factor needed.*

To convert from mass to number of moles, divide by the molar mass. This is the same as using the reciprocal of molar mass as a conversion factor, as shown below.

$$\text{gram Al} = \text{grams Al} \times \frac{\text{moles Al}}{\text{grams Al}}$$

$$= \text{moles Al}$$

3 SOLVE — *Substitute the known values and calculate.*

The molar mass of aluminum from the periodic table, rounded to four significant figures, is 26.98 g/mol.

$$11.9 \text{ g Al} = 11.9 \text{ g Al} \times \frac{\text{mol Al}}{26.98 \text{ g Al}}$$

$$= 0.441 \text{ mol Al}$$

4 CHECK YOUR WORK — *Determine if the answer makes sense.*

The answer and the original value have three significant figures. The answer is reasonable because 11.9 g is a little less than half of 26.98 g.

PRACTICE

B. What is the mass in grams of 2.25 mol of iron, Fe?

Molar mass of iron: _____

$$2.25 \text{ mol Fe} = 2.25 \text{ mol Fe} \times \boxed{}$$

$$\doteq \underline{\hspace{2cm}} \text{ g Fe}$$

SAMPLE PROBLEM

How many moles of silver, Ag, are in 3.01×10^{23} atoms of silver?

SOLUTION

1 ANALYZE *Determine what information is given and unknown.*

Given: 3.01×10^{23} atoms Ag

Unknown: amount of Ag in moles

2 PLAN *Determine the equation and conversion factor needed.*

To convert from number of atoms to number of moles, divide by Avogadro's number. This is the same as using the reciprocal of Avogadro's number as a conversion factor, as shown below.

$$\text{Ag atoms} = \text{Ag atoms} \times \frac{\text{moles Ag}}{\text{Avogadro's number of Ag atoms}}$$

$$= \text{moles Ag}$$

3 SOLVE *Substitute the known values and calculate.*

$$3.10 \times 10^{23}\ \text{Ag atoms} = 3.01 \times 10^{23}\ \cancel{\text{Ag atoms}} \times \frac{\text{mol Ag}}{6.022 \times 10^{23}\ \cancel{\text{Ag atoms}}}$$

$$= 0.500\ \text{mol Ag}$$

4 CHECK YOUR WORK *Determine if the answer makes sense.*

The answer and the original value have three significant figures. The units cancel correctly and the number of atoms is half of Avogadro's number.

PRACTICE

C. How many atoms of aluminum, Al, are in 2.75 mol of aluminum?

Molar mass of aluminum: ______________________

$$2.75\ \text{mol Al} = 2.75\ \text{mol Al} \times \frac{\boxed{}}{\boxed{}}$$

= __________ atoms Al

What is the mass in grams of 1.20×10^8 atoms of copper, Cu?

SOLUTION		
1	ANALYZE	*Determine what information is given and unknown.*

Given: $1.20 \text{ g} \times 10^8$ atoms of Cu

Unknown: mass of Cu in grams

2 PLAN   *Determine the equation and conversion factors needed.*

As shown in the diagram earlier in this section, converting from number of atoms to mass is a two-step process. To convert from number of atoms to moles, divide by Avogadro's number. To convert from moles to mass, multiply by the molar mass.

$$\text{Cu atoms} = \text{Cu atoms} \times \frac{\text{moles Cu}}{\text{Avogadro's number of Cu atoms}}$$

$$\times \frac{\text{grams Cu}}{\text{moles Cu}}$$

$$= \text{grams Cu}$$

3 SOLVE   *Substitute the known values and calculate.*

The molar mass of copper from the periodic table, rounded to four significant figures, is 63.55 g/mol.

$$1.20 \times 10^8 \text{ Cu atoms} \times \frac{1 \text{ mol Cu}}{6.022 \times 10^{23} \text{ Cu atoms}} \times \frac{63.55 \text{ g Cu}}{\text{mol Cu}}$$

$$= 1.27 \times 10^{-14} \text{ g Cu}$$

4 CHECK YOUR WORK   *Determine if the answer makes sense.*

The units cancel correctly to give the answer in grams. The order of magnitude of the answer is also reasonable because 10^8 divided by 10^{24} and then multiplied by 10^2 is 10^{-14}.

PRACTICE

D. How many atoms of sulfur, S, are in 4.00 g of sulfur?

Molar mass of sulfur: _____

$$4.00 \text{ g S} = 4.00 \text{ g S} \times \boxed{} \times \boxed{}$$

$$= \text{_____ S atoms}$$

VOCABULARY

1. Define the term *molar mass*.

_____

_____

REVIEW

2. Complete the table at the right.

3. Write the nuclear symbol and hyphen notation for each of the following isotopes.

    a. mass number of 28, atomic number of 14

    _____

    b. 26 protons and 30 neutrons

    _____

Isotope	Number of protons	Number of electrons	Number of neutrons
sodium-23			
calcium-40			
$^{64}_{29}$Cu			
$^{108}_{47}$Ag			

4. To two decimal places, what is the relative atomic mass and the molar mass of the element potassium, K?

_____

5. Determine the mass in grams of the following:

    a. 2.00 mol N

    b. 3.01×10^{23} atoms Cl

6. Determine the amount in moles of the following:

    a. 12.15 g mol Mg

    b. 1.50×10^{23} atoms F

Critical Thinking

7. ANALYZING DATA Beaker A contains 2.06 mol of copper, and Beaker B contains 222 g of silver.

    a. Which beaker contains the larger mass? _____

    b. Which beaker has the larger number of atoms? _____

Math Tutor CONVERSION FACTORS

Most calculations in chemistry require that all measurements of the same quantity (mass, length, volume, temperature, and so on) be expressed in the same unit. To change the units of a quantity, you can multiply the quantity by a conversion factor. With SI units, such conversions are easy because units of the same quantity are related by multiples of 10, 100, 1000, or 1 million.

Suppose you want to convert a given amount in milliliters to liters. You can use the relationship 1 L = 1000 mL. From this relationship, you can. derive the conversion factors shown at the right.

$$\frac{1000\ mL}{1\ L} \text{ and } \frac{1\ L}{1000\ mL}$$

Problem-Solving TIPS

- Multiply the given amount by the conversion factor that allows the units from which you are converting to cancel out and the new units to remain.
- Most conversion factors are based on exact definitions, so significant figures do not apply to these factors. The number of significant figures in a converted measurement depends on the certainty of the measurement you start with.

SAMPLE

A sample of aluminum has a mass of 0.087 g. What is the sample's mass in milligrams?

Based on SI prefixes, you know that 1 g = 1000 mg. The possible conversion factors are

$$\frac{1000\ mg}{1\ g} \text{ and } \frac{1\ g}{1000\ mg}$$

The first conversion factor cancels grams, leaving milligrams.

$$0.087\ g = 0.087\ \cancel{g} \times \frac{1000\ mg}{1\ \cancel{g}} = 87\ g$$

A sample of a mineral has 4.08×10^{-5} mol of vanadium per kilogram of mass. How many micromoles of vanadium per kilogram does the mineral contain?

$1\ \mu mol = 1 \times 10^{-6}$ mol. The possible conversion factors are

$$\frac{1 \times 10^{-6}\ mol}{1\ \mu mol} \text{ and } \frac{1\ \mu mol}{1 \times 10^{-6}\ mol}$$

The second conversion factor cancels moles, leaving micromoles.

$$4.08 \times 10^{-5}\ mol = 4.08 \times 10^{-5}\ \cancel{mol} \times \frac{1\ \mu mol}{1 \times 10^{-6}\ \cancel{mol}} = 40.8\ \mu mol$$

Practice Problems: Chapter Review practice problems 8–10 and 13–14

1. Explain each law in terms of Dalton's atomic theory.

    a. the law of conservation of mass _____

    _____

    b. the law of definite proportions _____

    _____

    c. the law of multiple proportions _____

    _____

2. According to the law of conservation of mass, if element A has an atomic mass of 2 units and element B has an atomic mass of 3 units, what mass would be expected for each compound?

    a. AB _____   **b.** A_2B_3 _____

3. What is an atom? What two regions make up all atoms?

    _____

    _____

4. Summarize Rutherford's model of the atom and explain how he developed his model based on the results of his famous gold-foil experiment.

    _____

    _____

5. What are isotopes? How are the isotopes of a particular element alike and how are they different?

    _____

    _____

6. Complete the table at the right concerning the three isotopes of silicon, Si.

7. What is the definition of a mole? How many particles are in one mole, and what is that number called?

Isotope	Number of protons	Number of electrons	Number of neutrons
silicon-28			
silicon-29			
silicon-30			

_____

_____

8. What is the mass in grams of each of the following?

   a. 1.00 mol Li _____

   b. 1.00 mol Al _____

   c. 1.00 molar mass Ca _____

   d. 1.00 molar mass Fe _____

   e. 6.022×10^{23} atoms C _____

   f. 6.022×10^{23} atoms Ag _____

9. How many moles of atoms are there in each of the following?

   a. 6.022×10^{23} atoms Ne _____

   b. 3.011×10^{23} atoms Mg _____

10. How many moles of atoms are there in each of the following?

    a. 3.25×10^{5} g Pb   b. 4.50×10^{-12} g O

11. Three isotopes of argon occur in nature: $^{36}_{18}$Ar, $^{38}_{18}$Ar, and $^{40}_{18}$Ar. Calculate the average atomic mass of argon to two decimal places, given the following relative atomic masses and abundances of each of the isotopes: argon-36 (35.97 u; 0.337%), argon 38 (37.96 u; 0.063%), and argon-40 (39.96 u; 99.600%).

12. Naturally occurring boron is 80.20% boron-11 (atomic mass of 11.01 u) and 19.80% of some other isotopic form of boron. What must the atomic mass of this second isotope be in order to account for the 10.81 u average atomic mass of boron? (Write the answer to two decimal places.)

13. What is the mass in grams of each of the following?

    a. 3.011×10^{23} atoms F

    d. 8.42×10^{18} atoms Br

    b. 1.50×10^{23} atoms Mg

    e. 25 atoms W

    c. 4.50×10^{12} atoms Cl

    f. 1 atom Au

14. Determine the number of atoms in each of the following.

    a. 5.40 g B

    e. 1.00×10^{-10} g Au

    b. 0.250 mol S

    f. 1.50 mol Na

    c. 0.0384 mol K

    g. 6.755 mol Pb

    d. 0.025 50 g Pt

    h. 7.02 g Si

CHAPTER 4

Arrangement of Electrons in Atoms

Key Concepts

Review Previous Concepts

1. What subatomic particles make up an atom and how do their properties compare with each other?

_____

_____

_____

_____

2. How did Ernest Rutherford describe the characteristics and properties of an atom after the gold-foil experiment?

_____

_____

_____

SECTION 4.1

The Development of a New Atomic Model

The Rutherford model of the atom was an improvement over previous models, but it was still incomplete. Scientists were able to revise the atomic model when they discovered a connection between light and atomic structure.

Light has characteristics of both particles and waves.

Before 1900, scientists thought that light behaved only as a wave. A wave is a disturbance of a medium that transmits energy without changing position. The medium can vibrate but its particles do not move forward with the wave. An ocean wave moving toward a beach is one example.

The Wave Description of Light

Waves have a repeating, or periodic, nature. The **wavelength** (λ) of a wave is the distance between corresponding points on two consecutive waves. Wavelength is commonly measured in meters, centimeters, or nanometers. The **frequency** (ν) of a wave is the number of waves that pass a point in a given amount of time. Frequency is expressed in waves per second. One wave/second is also called a hertz.

READING CHECK

1. Which wave in the figure to the left, (a) or (b), has a longer wavelength?

_____

2. Which wave in the figure to the left, (a) or (b), has a higher frequency?

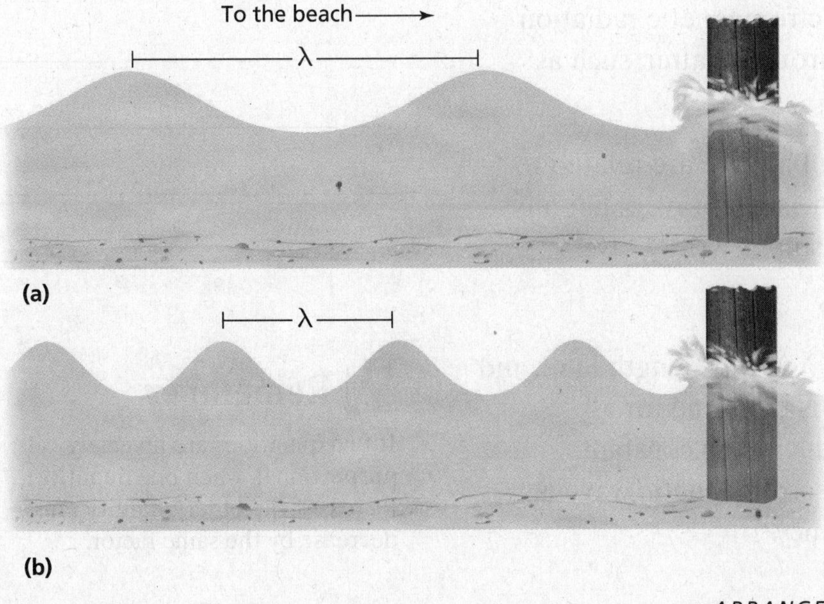

_____

To the beach ⟶

λ

(a)

λ

(b)

The wavelength, λ, of these two waves is the distance between two wave crests. The frequency, ν, is the time it takes for the water to rise and fall at the wave post.

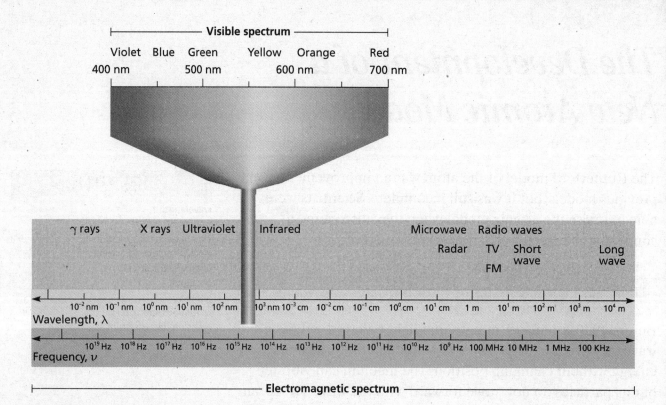

Visible light is another type of wave. It is a form of **electromagnetic radiation,** which is energy that travels through space in the form of a wave. Electromagnetic radiation does not need a medium to travel. X-rays, ultraviolet light, infrared light, microwaves, and radio waves are forms of electromagnetic radiation. Together, all forms of electromagnetic radiation make up a band called the **electromagnetic spectrum,** as shown in the diagram above.

All forms of electromagnetic radiation travel at 3.00×10^8 m/s through a vacuum. This number is also called the speed of light. The speed of electromagnetic radiation decreases slightly when it passes through matter, such as when light passes through water.

The frequency and wavelength of a wave are related to each other by the speed at which the wave travels. For any electromagnetic wave, this relationship is written as

$$c = \lambda \nu$$

where c is the speed of light in m/s, λ is wavelength in m, and ν is the frequency in 1/s. Because c is the same for all electromagnetic radiation, the product $\lambda\nu$ is constant. Therefore, the wavelength of an electromagnetic wave is inversely proportional to its frequency.

Electromagnetic radiation goes by different names depending on its wavelength. Only waves with a wavelength of about 400 nm to 700 nm are visible to the human eye.

 READING CHECK

3. Define the term *electromagnetic wave* in your own words.

_____

_____

_____

_____

_____

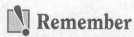 **Remember**

If two quantities are inversely proportional, when one quantity increases, the other quantity must decrease by the same factor.

> **When certain frequencies of light strike a metal, electrons are emitted.**

In the early 1900s, scientists conducted two experiments on light that could not be explained by a wave theory of light. One experiment involved the photoelectric effect.

In the **photoelectric effect,** a metal gives off electrons when light shines on it. The bulb at the right shows that light shining on the cathode causes the cathode to emit electrons. The electrons then travel to the anode and an electric current flows from the cathode and the anode. The photoelectric effect only happens if the frequency of the light is above a certain value.

In 1900 scientists knew that light is a form of energy. So the ability of light to cause a metal to give off electrons made sense. However, a new theory was needed to explain why light of lower frequencies did not cause the photoelectric effect.

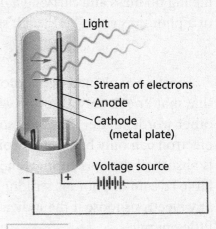

In the photoelectric effect, light strikes the surface of the metal, causing electrons to be ejected and an electric current to flow.

The Particle Description of Light

German physicist Max Planck provided part of the explanation for the photoelectric effect. Planck suggested that a hot object does not emit energy continuously, in the form of waves. He suggested that the object emits energy in small packets called quanta.

A **quantum** of energy is the minimum quantity of energy that can be lost or gained by an atom. The relationship between the frequency, ν, of radiation in 1/s and a quantum of energy, E, in joules is

$$E = h\nu$$

where h, also known as Planck's constant, is 6.626×10^{-34} J·s.

In 1905, Albert Einstein expanded on Planck's theory by hypothesizing that electromagnetic radiation can behave like a wave *and* like a particle. While light can exhibit wavelike properties, it can also be thought of as a stream of particles. Each particle carries a quantum of energy. Einstein called these particles photons.

 **CONNECT**

Many quantities in math and science are represented by Greek letters. For example, the symbol for wavelength, λ, is the Greek letter lambda. The symbol for frequency, ν, is the Greek letter nu.

✓ READING CHECK

4. Compare and contrast the way waves transmit energy and the way particles transmit energy.

Photons A **photon** is a particle of electromagnetic radiation having no mass and carrying a quantum of energy. The energy of a photon is given by Planck's formula for quanta of energy.

$$E_{photon} = h\nu$$

Einstein explained the photoelectric effect by proposing that matter can only absorb a whole number of photons. In other words, matter cannot absorb part of a photon. An electron can only be ejected from an object if one photon is absorbed that has enough energy to knock it loose. Even a large stream of photons striking an object will fail to knock any electrons loose if the individual photons contain too little energy.

The formula above relates the minimum energy to a frequency. Because electrons are bound with different force to different metals, the minimum frequency changes for each metal.

✓ **READING CHECK**

5. Use the quantites *mass* and *energy* to complete this sentence.

The _____ of a photon is zero, while the

_____ of a photon is greater than zero.

Electrons exist only in very specific energy states for atoms of each element.

In addition to the photoelectric effect experiments, a second set of experiments forced scientists to revise their ideas about light. These experiments focused on light emitted by gases. When electric current passes through a gas at low pressure, the gas gives off colored light. For example, when electric current passes through neon gas, a neon sign lights up.

A firefly, or lightning bug, uses a chemical reaction to produce light. The spectrum of light emitted by the chemical luciferin gives the bugs their yellow-green glow.

When scientists passed current through a tube containing hydrogen gas at low pressure, they observed a pinkish light. The wave theory of light predicted that hydrogen atoms would give off light in a continuous spectrum. A **continuous spectrum** is a continuous range of frequencies of electromagnetic radiation. A continuous spectrum of light appears white.

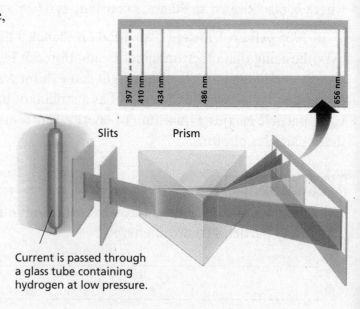

397 nm 410 nm 434 nm 486 nm 656 nm

Slits   Prism

Excited hydrogen atoms emit a pinkish light. This light is composed of four specific visible wavelengths of light. The line at 397 nm is not visible to the human eye.

Current is passed through a glass tube containing hydrogen at low pressure.

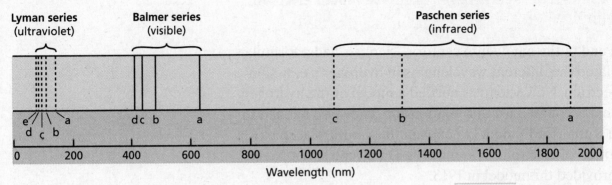

Lyman series
(ultraviolet)

Balmer series
(visible)

Paschen series
(infrared)

Wavelength (nm)

When passing the pinkish light emitted by hydrogen through a prism, scientists found that the light was composed of only four wavelengths, not a continuous spectrum. These four wavelengths are shown in the diagram at the bottom of the previous page. These four visible wavelengths of light are known collectively as the Balmer series, after their discoverer.

This diagram shows the emission-line spectrum for hydrogen. The letters below the lines label the various energy-level transitions.

The Balmer series is part of hydrogen's **emission-line spectrum,** shown at the top of this page. Additional sets of emission lines in the ultraviolet and infrared ranges of the electromagnetic spectrum are called the Lyman and Paschen series, after the scientists who discovered them.

Attempts to explain the emission-line spectrum of hydrogen led to the development of the *quantum theory* of atoms. The theory states that an atom's energy can only be at specific values, called states. The lowest energy state of an atom is its **ground state.** Any state that has a higher potential energy than the ground state is an **excited state.**

When an excited atom falls to its ground state or a lower-energy excited state, it gives off a photon. The energy of the photon ($E_{photon} = h\nu$) is equal to the difference in energy between the two states, as shown at the right. The fact that hydrogen atoms emit only specific frequencies of light suggests that the energy states of a hydrogen atom are fixed. Light can only be emitted with an amount of energy that is the difference between two of hydrogen's energy levels.

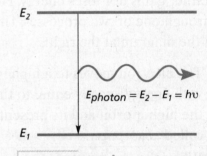

When an excited atom with energy E_2 falls back to energy E_1, it releases a photon with energy $E_2 - E_1$.

READING CHECK

6. How does the quantum theory of atoms explain the nature of the emission-line spectrum of hydrogen?

_____

_____

Bohr's model of the hydrogen atom explained electron transition states.

By the end of the nineteenth century, scientists had a formula that related the different wavelengths in hydrogen's emission-line spectrum. Now scientists needed a model of the hydrogen atom that accounted for this relationship. They also needed to update Rutherford's model to explain the nature, placement, and motion of electrons in atoms. The Danish physicist Niels Bohr provided this model in 1913.

According to Bohr's model, the electron in a hydrogen atom can only circle the nucleus in certain paths, or *orbits*. The orbit the electron is in determines the energy of the atom. The hydrogen atom is in its ground state when the electron is in the orbit closest to the nucleus. The electron cannot go closer to the nucleus than this orbit. If the electron enters an orbit that is farther from the nucleus, the atom has more energy. Each successive orbit represents a higher energy state.

The electron orbits, or atomic energy levels, can be compared to the rungs of a ladder. When you stand on the first rung, you have less potential energy than you would if you were standing on any other, higher, rung of the ladder. Because you cannot stand between the rungs, you can only have amounts of potential energy corresponding to each rung.

When the electron in a hydrogen atom is in one orbit, it neither gains nor loses energy. However, it can change orbits through one of two processes. These processes are summarized in the diagram at the right.

- The electron moves to a higher orbit if it absorbs a photon with energy exactly equal to the amount of energy between the higher orbit and its present orbit. This process is called *absorption*.
- When the electron falls to a lower orbit, it emits a photon with the difference in energy between the higher and lower orbits. This process is called *emission*.

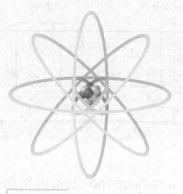

According to Bohr's model of the atom, electrons travel around the nucleus in specific energy levels.

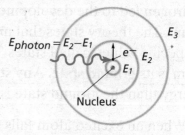

$E_{photon} = E_2 - E_1$

(a) Absorption

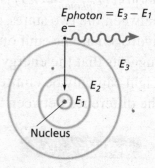

$E_{photon} = E_3 - E_1$

(b) Emission

(a) Absorption and (b) emission of a photon by a hydrogen atom according to Bohr's model.

✓ READING CHECK

7. When a hydrogen atom _____ a photon, it moves into a lower energy state.

8. When a hydrogen atom _____ a photon, it moves into a higher energy state.

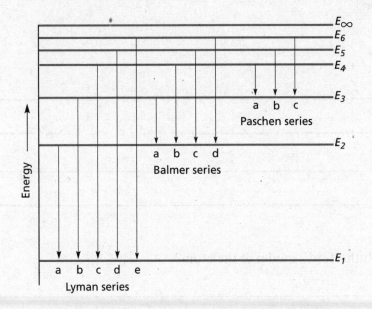

This energy-state diagram for a hydrogen atom shows some of the energy transitions for the Lyman, Balmer, and Paschen spectral series.

Photons emitted by a hydrogen atom can only have energies that represent the differences between its energy levels. The diagram above shows the possible energy states of the hydrogen atom according to Bohr's model. Bohr showed that the Lyman series of emission lines resulted from electrons dropping from orbits above the ground state (energies E_2, E_3, and so on) into the ground state (energy E_1).

Bohr also calculated the differences between energy level E_2 and higher energy levels. These differences corresponded to the energies of photons in the Balmer series. He also found that the Paschen series resulted from electrons falling to the energy level E_3.

This pattern provided convincing evidence that Bohr's model of the hydrogen atom was correct. This model consisted of an atom with a densely packed nucleus surrounded by electrons in various orbits far from the nucleus. However, Bohr's model was unable to explain the emission-line spectra of atoms other than hydrogen. Bohr's model also failed to explain the chemical behavior of atoms.

Critical Thinking

9. **Summarize** Explain how Bohr's model built on the ideas of Einstein and Planck.

_____

_____

VOCABULARY

1. Define the following.

a. electromagnetic radiation _____

_____

b. quantum _____

_____

REVIEW

2. What was the major shortcoming of Rutherford's model of the atom?

_____

_____

3. Write and label the equation that relates the speed, wavelength, and frequency of electromagnetic radiation.

$$\boxed{} = \boxed{}\ \boxed{}$$

4. What is meant by the dual wave-particle nature of light?

_____

_____

5. Describe the Bohr model of the hydrogen atom.

_____

_____

_____

Critical Thinking

6. INTERPRETING GRAPHICS Use the diagram on the previous page to answer (a) and (b):

a. Characterize each as absorption or emission:

- An electron moves from E_2 to E_1. _____

- An electron moves from E_1 to E_3. _____

- An electron moves from E_6 to E_3. _____

b. Which energy-level change above emits or absorbs the

- highest energy? _____

- lowest energy? _____

The Quantum Model of the Atom

The Bohr model of the atom seemed at first to contradict common sense. Bohr's model explained the experimental evidence of the hydrogen emission-line spectrum, but Bohr provided no reason for the atom's orbital structure.

Electrons have wave-like properties.

To explain Bohr's model, scientists had to change the way they viewed the nature of the electron. Scientists had thought that light behaved only as a wave. Now they were beginning to understand that it had a dual wave-particle nature. Electrons had always been thought of as particles. In 1924, French scientist Louis de Broglie asked if electrons could have a dual nature as well.

De Broglie pointed out the ways in which electrons in Bohr's model behaved like waves. For example, he knew that any wave confined within a certain space can have only certain frequencies. Electrons are confined to certain frequencies within an atom.

De Broglie suggested that electrons be thought of as waves confined to the space around an atomic nucleus. These electron waves can only exist at certain frequencies, and by the relationship $E = h\nu$, certain energies.

Scientists were soon able to confirm that electrons have other wave-like properties. For example, electrons can be diffracted. Diffraction is the bending of a wave through a small opening. Interference occurs when waves that diffract through a small opening overlap. In some areas of a target screen, the overlapping waves increase the energy and appear bright. In some areas the overlapping waves decrease the energy and appear dark. The result is a pattern of light and dark areas. A stream of particles would not be affected in this way, and would appear as a solid circle where the beam hits the screen.

READING CHECK

1. Name two properties of electrons that indicate a wave-like nature.

_____

_____

_____

_____

_____

The speed and position of an electron cannot be measured simultaneously.

The idea of electrons having a dual wave-particle nature troubled scientists. They wanted to be able to determine the specific locations of electrons within an atom. In 1927, German physicist Werner Heisenberg developed another principle that changed how scientists viewed the subatomic world.

Heisenberg hypothesized that the act of observing a particle would itself change the behavior of the particle. For example, to detect an electron, you use particles of light, or photons. You locate the electron by its absorption, emission, or other interaction with a photon. However, this interaction will change the course of the electron's movement. As a result, there is always uncertainty in trying to locate an electron, or any other particle.

The **Heisenberg uncertainty principle** states that it is impossible to determine the exact position and the exact velocity of a particle at the same time. This principle is now a foundation of current theories of the nature of light and matter.

Orbitals indicate probable electron locations.

In 1926, Austrian physicist Erwin Schrödinger successfully combined Bohr's model of the atom and the dual wave-particle nature of electrons. Bohr's model was a hypothesis based on the assumption that energy levels in an atom were fixed. Schrödinger used an equation to show that these fixed energy levels resulted from the wave nature of electrons.

Together with the Heisenberg uncertainty principle, Schrödinger's equation formed the foundation of a new atomic theory. **Quantum theory** describes mathematically the wave properties of electrons and other small particles.

One result of quantum theory is that the position of an electron in an atom cannot be determined precisely. Only the probability of finding it in a certain region can be determined. Electrons do not travel in specific orbits as in Bohr's model of the atom. Instead, they travel within **orbitals,** which are three-dimensional regions around the nucleus of the atom that indicate the probable location of an electron.

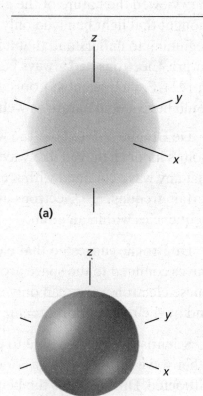

Here are two ways of visualizing an atomic orbital. (a) The electron is likely to be found in the dense regions of this cloud. (b) The electron is located within this surface 90% of the time.

The Four Quantum Numbers

Quantum Number	Symbol	Description
principal quantum number	n	main energy level of the electron
angular momentum quantum number	l	shape of the orbital
magnetic quantum number	m	orientation of the orbital around the nucleus
spin quantum number	$+\frac{1}{2}$ or $-\frac{1}{2}$	spin state of the electron

Quantum numbers describe atomic orbitals.

In Bohr's model of the atom, electrons of increasing energy occupy orbits farther and farther from the nucleus. According to the Schrödinger equation, electrons in orbitals also have quantized energies. Scientists can assign each orbital within an atom a specific value of energy.

Scientists need more numbers to completely describe the properties of an electron. **Quantum numbers** specify the properties of atomic orbitals and the properties of electrons in these orbitals. The four quantum numbers are summarized in the table above.

TIP The words *quantum,* and *quantized,* are related. A *quantum* is a specific value. A quantity is *quantized* if it is limited to certain values.

Principal Quantum Number

The **principal quantum number,** symbolized by n, indicates the main energy level occupied by the electron. The first six energy levels in an atom are shown at the right. If $n = 1$, an electron occupies the first energy level and is located closest to the nucleus. As n increases to 2, 3, 4, and so on, the electron increases in energy and average distance from the nucleus.

More than one electron can occupy the same energy level in an atom. These electrons are sometimes said to be in the same electron *shell*.

✓ READING CHECK

3. An electron at the $n = 3$ level of an atom has

_____ energy and is located _____

the nucleus than an electron at the $n = 2$ level.

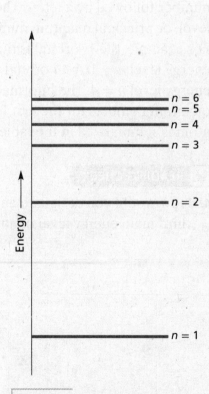

The principal quantum number, n, gives the main energy level occupied by an electron.

Angular Momentum Quantum Number

Not all orbitals are the same shape. At the $n = 1$ level, there is just one orbital and it has a spherical shape. For higher main energy levels, the orbitals can take on multiple shapes. The **angular momentum quantum number**, symbolized by l, indicates the shape of the orbital.

For a specific main energy level n, there are n possible shapes for the orbitals. Each shape is called a *sublevel*. For example, for the $n = 2$ level, there are two sublevels for the orbitals: spherical ($l = 0$) and dumbbell-shaped ($l = 1$). The $n = 3$ level includes three sublevels that include spherical ($l = 0$), dumbbell-shaped ($l = 1$), and more complex ($l = 2$) orbitals.

Each sublevel is also given a letter designation. The letter designations are given in the table at the right. Every main energy level includes an s orbital. Every energy level for $n = 2$ and higher also includes p orbitals. Every energy level for $n = 3$ and higher includes d orbitals. So $n = 3$ includes s orbitals, p orbitals, and d orbitals.

Every atomic orbital has a designation that includes a number followed by a letter. The number is the main energy level, or principal quantum number. The letter is the sublevel. For example, the $1s$ orbital is the only orbital on the main energy level $n = 1$. A $4d$ orbital is any one of the d orbitals on energy level $n = 4$. The information given by these first two quantum numbers for the first four main energy levels of an atom is summarized in the table on the next page.

Orbital Letter Designations According to Values of l	
l	Letter
0	s
1	p
2	d
3	f

✓ **READING CHECK**

4. How would you designate an orbital in the p sublevel of the third main energy level of an atom?

_____

s orbital   p orbital   d orbital

The orbitals s, p, and d have different shapes.

Orbital Types for the First Four Main Energy Levels

Principal quantum number, n (main energy level)	Number of orbital shapes possible	Possible values of angular momentum quantum number, l	Possible orbital types	Orbital designations
$n = 1$	1	$l = 0$	s	$1s$
$n = 2$	2	$l = 0, 1$	s, p	$2s, 2p$
$n = 3$	3	$l = 0, 1, 2$	s, p, d	$3s, 3p, 3d$
$n = 4$	4	$l = 0, 1, 2, 3$	s, p, d, f	$4s, 4p, 4d, 4f$

Magnetic Quantum Number

The total number of orbitals that exist in a given main energy level is equal to n^2. Therefore, the first energy level ($n = 1$) of an atom has one orbital. Every energy level higher than $n = 1$ has multiple orbitals. For example, the second energy level ($n = 2$) has two sublevels that include four orbitals. The third energy level ($n = 3$) has nine orbitals in three sublevels.

The orbitals of each main energy level are oriented so that they do not overlap. At the $n = 1$ level, there is only one orbital, so no overlap is possible. At the $n = 2$ level, there are four orbitals. The $2s$ orbital is spherically shaped. Three dumbbell-shaped $2p$ orbitals are oriented around the $2s$ orbital.

The **magnetic quantum number,** symbolized by m, indicates the orientation of an orbital around the nucleus. Values of m are whole numbers that range from $-l$ to $+l$. All s orbitals are spherical, so they can only have one orientation. Since the s orbital has an angular momentum quantum number of $l = 0$, all s orbitals have the magnetic quantum number $m = 0$.

The p orbitals have three possible orientations, depending on the axis with which the dumbbell is aligned. These p orbitals are designated as p_x, p_y, and p_z. Because $l = 1$ for p orbitals, they can be assigned the magnetic quantum numbers $m = -1, m = 0$, or $m = +1$.

✓ READING CHECK

5. Describe the main energy level, shape, and orientation of the $2p_x$ orbital.

_____

_____

_____

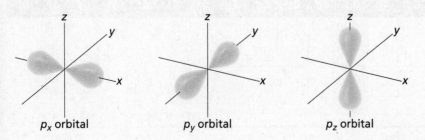

p_x orbital p_y orbital p_z orbital

The three p orbitals in any main energy level are oriented as shown. The letters x, y, and z on each orbital name describe the axis on which the dumbbell is oriented. The nucleus is at the intersection of the three axes.

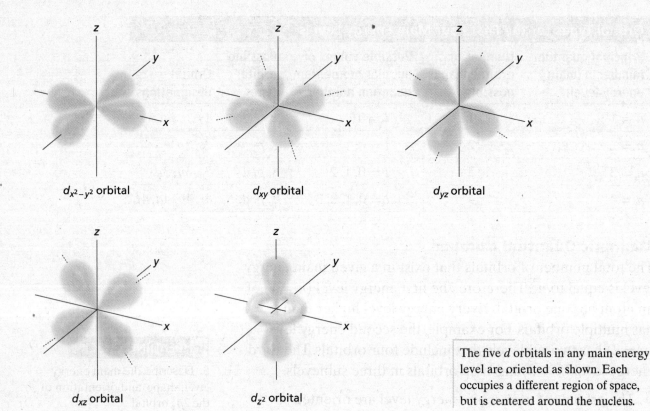

$d_{x^2-y^2}$ orbital d_{xy} orbital d_{yz} orbital

d_{xz} orbital d_{z^2} orbital

The five d orbitals in any main energy level are oriented as shown. Each occupies a different region of space, but is centered around the nucleus.

The d sublevel in every main energy level has five different orientations. The value of l for d orbitals is $l = 2$. This means that the five different orientations correspond to values of $|m = -2, m = -1, m = 0, m = +1,$ and $m = +2$.

With each move from simple to more complex orbitals, two more orientations in space become available. For example, the $n = 4$ level, has one s orbital, three p orbitals, five d orbitals, and seven f orbitals. The number of orbitals, $1 + 3 + 5 + 7 = 16$, is equal to the number of sublevels as defined by $n^2 = (4)^2 = 16$.

PRACTICE

A. Complete this chart defining the 16 sublevels in the $n = 4$ energy level of an atom.

Designation	4s	4p	4p	4p	4d	4d	4d	4d	4d	4f	4f	4f	4f	4f	4f	4f
angular momentum quantum number, l																
magnetic quantum number, m																

Spin Quantum Number

An electron in an orbital behaves in some ways like Earth spinning on its axis. Earth's spinning generates a magnetic field. An electron exists in one of two possible spin states. Each spin state creates a different magnetic field. To account for the magnetic properties of the electron, scientists assign electrons a spin quantum number.

The **spin quantum number** has only two possible values, +1/2 and −1/2, which indicate the two possible spin states of an electron in an orbital. Each orbital of an atom can contain up to two electrons. However, the electrons in the orbital must have opposite spin states.

For example, examine the $n = 2$ main energy level. It has two sublevels. The s sublevel includes one s orbital. The p sublevel includes three p orbitals. Each one of these four orbitals can contain two electrons if the electrons have opposite spin states. Therefore, the $n = 2$ level of an atom can hold up to 8 electrons. The structure of the atom given by these quantum numbers is summarized in the table below.

LOOKING CLOSER

6. Which quantum numbers define the properties of electrons in an orbital?

_____

_____

_____

7. Which quantum numbers define the properties of the orbitals?

_____

_____

_____

✓ READING CHECK

8. What is the difference between an orbital and a sublevel?

_____

_____

Quantum Number Relationships in Atomic Structure

Principal quantum number: main energy level (n)	Sublevels in main energy level (n sublevels)	Number of orbitals per sublevel	Number of orbitals per main energy level (n^2)	Number of electrons per sublevel	Number of electrons per main energy level ($2n^2$)
1	s	1	1	2	2
2	s	1	4	2	8
	p	3		6	
3	s	1	9	2	18
	p	3		6	
	d	5		10	
4	s	1	16	2	32
	p	3		6	
	d	5		10	
	f	7		14	

VOCABULARY

1. Define each of the following.

 a. main energy level _____

_____

 b. quantum number _____

_____

REVIEW

2. Identify the four quantum numbers by name and symbol.

_____

_____

_____

_____

3. What general information about atomic orbitals is provided by the quantum numbers?

_____

_____

4. Describe briefly what specific information is given by each of the four quantum numbers.

_____

_____

_____

Critical Thinking

5. INFERRING RELATIONSHIPS

 a. What are the possible values of the magnetic quantum number m for f orbitals?

_____

 b. What is the maximum number of electrons that can exist in the orbitals in the $4f$ sublevel?

_____

SECTION 4.3

Electron Configurations

Bohr's model of the atom described the possible energy states of the electron in a hydrogen atom. The energy states were deduced from observations of hydrogen's emission-line spectra, but no reason was given for the specific values.

The quantum model of the atom improves on Bohr's model in several ways. One improvement is that the energy states can be derived from Schrödinger's equation, and verified by observation. Another improvement is that the quantum model describes the arrangement of electrons in atoms other than hydrogen.

The arrangement of electrons in an atom is known as the atom's **electron configuration.** Atoms of different elements have different numbers of electrons. Therefore, each element has a unique electron configuration. The electrons in an atom tend to be arranged such that their total energy is as small as possible. The arrangement that has the least energy for each element is called the *ground-state electron configuration.*

✓ READING CHECK

1. Name two ways the quantum model of the atom is an improvement over Bohr's model of the atom.

_____

_____

Electrons fill in the lowest-energy orbitals first.

To determine the ground-state configuration of any atom, first determine the energy levels of the orbitals. The relationship between the energy levels of the orbitals is given in the diagram above. Next, place the electrons in orbitals, one by one, according to three basic rules.

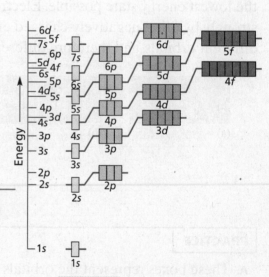

The energy of each atomic sublevel is shown on the vertical axis. Each individual box represents one orbital.

Aufbau Principle According to the **Aufbau principle,** an electron occupies the lowest-energy orbital that can receive it. The 1s orbital has the lowest energy. A hydrogen atom in the ground state has an electron in this orbital.

The next four sublevels are 2s, 2p, 3s, and 3p. However, the 4s sublevel has a lower energy than the 3d sublevel, so the 4s orbital is filled with electrons before any of the five 3d orbitals are filled.

Pauli Exclusion Principle According to the **Pauli exclusion principle,** no two electrons in the same atom can have the same set of four quantum numbers. The principal, angular momentum, and magnetic quantum numbers specify the energy, shape, and orientation of an electron's orbital. The fourth quantum number specifies the spin of the electron.

Because there are only two possible values for the spin of an electron, only two electrons can exist in the same orbital. As first stated in Section 2 of this chapter, two electrons in the same orbital must have opposite spin states.

Hund's Rule According to **Hund's rule,** orbitals of equal energy are each occupied by one electron before any are occupied by a second electron. In addition, all electrons in orbitals with just one electron must have the same spin state.

Hund's rule reflects the fact that electrons are arranged in the lowest energy state possible. Electrons are not repelled as strongly by other negatively-charged electrons if they are in different orbitals, and therefore different regions, of the atom.

1s orbital

The box shows the electron configuration of a helium atom. According to the Pauli exclusion principle, this orbital can only contain two electrons and they must have opposite spin states.

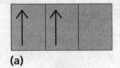
(a)

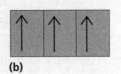
(b)

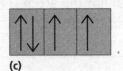
(c)

The figure shows how (a) two, (b) three, and (c) four electrons fill the p sublevel of any main energy level according to Hund's rule.

PRACTICE

A. These boxes represent the orbitals of a sulfur atom, with 16 electrons. Draw arrows to fill these orbitals with electrons.

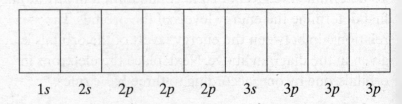

1s   2s   2p   2p   2p   3s   3p   3p   3p

There are three ways to indicate electron configuration.

Three types of notation are used to describe electron configurations. This page discusses two types of notation, and another part of this section will deal with noble-gas notation. The three notations are summarized as follows:

- *Orbital notation* represents an orbital by showing its number and letter below a horizontal line. Arrows above each line represent electrons.

- *Electron-configuration notation* eliminates the lines and arrows and represents the electrons by numbers listed to the top right of an orbital's name.

- *Noble-gas notation* uses the symbol for a noble gas in place of part of the electron-configuration notation.

Electron Configurations of First Period Elements

Name	Symbol	Orbital notation	Electron-configuration notation
Hydrogen	H	$\uparrow$ $1s$	$1s^1$
Helium	He	$\uparrow\downarrow$ $1s$	$1s^2$

Orbital Notation

Orbital notation is a horizontal line with the orbital's name below and the number of electrons above. The space above the line is left blank for an unoccupied orbital. An orbital containing one electron is represented as $\underline{\;\uparrow\;}$, and an orbital containing two electrons is represented as $\underline{\;\uparrow\downarrow\;}$. The table above shows the orbital notation for the elements in the first period of the periodic table: hydrogen and helium.

Electron-Configuration Notation

Electron-configuration notation eliminates the lines and arrows of orbital notation. Instead, this notation shows the number of electrons in a sublevel by placing a number to the top right of the sublevel's designation. For example, the electron configuration for sulfur is $1s^2 2s^2 2p^6 3s^2 3p^4$. The s sublevels of the sulfur atom all contain 2 electrons. The 2p sublevel contains 6 electrons, and the 3p sublevel contains 4 electrons. The table above also shows the electron configuration notations for hydrogen and helium.

Critical Thinking

2. Reasoning Why do you think orbital notation is rarely used for atoms with more than ten electrons?

_____

_____

_____

_____

The electron configuration of boron is $1s^2 2s^2 2p^1$. How many electrons are present in an atom of boron? What is the atomic number for boron? Write the orbital notation for boron.

SOLUTION

1 ANALYZE

Determine what information is given and unknown.

Given: The electron configuration of boron is $1s^2 2s^2 2p^1$.

Unknown: number of electrons, atomic number

2 PLAN

Determine the information necessary to answer the questions.

The number of electrons, which is equal to the atomic number, can be determined by adding the values in the electron configuration. The orbital notation for boron is simply another representation of the given information.

3 SOLVE

Answer the questions.

The number of electrons in a boron atom is $2 + 2 + 1 = 5$. This is also equal to the atomic number of boron. To write the orbital notation, first draw lines to represent the orbitals.

$$\underline{\quad} \quad \underline{\quad} \quad \underbrace{\underline{\quad}\ \underline{\quad}\ \underline{\quad}}$$
$$1s \qquad 2s \qquad\quad 2p$$

Next, fill in the electrons one at a time. Complete one sublevel before beginning the next sublevel.

$$\underline{\uparrow\downarrow} \quad \underline{\uparrow\downarrow} \quad \underbrace{\underline{\uparrow}\ \underline{\quad}\ \underline{\quad}}$$
$$1s \qquad 2s \qquad\quad 2p$$

4 CHECK YOUR WORK

Determine if the answers make sense.

The number of arrows in each orbital match the numbers to the top right of the orbital in the electron configuration.

PRACTICE

B. The electron configuration of nitrogen is $1s^2 2s^2 2p^3$.

What is the atomic number of nitrogen? _____
Write the orbital notation for nitrogen.

> No electron can occupy a higher energy sublevel until the energy sublevel below it is filled.

The elements in the second period of the periodic table can have up to five orbitals. The 1s orbital will be filled first, followed by the 2s orbital, and then the 2p orbitals. Thus, the first element of the second period, lithium, has a configuration of $1s^2 2s^1$.

The electron occupying the 2s sublevel of a lithium atom is in the atom's *highest-occupied energy level*. For the first period elements, the highest-occupied energy level is $n = 1$. For the second period elements, the highest-occupied energy level is $n = 2$. In these elements, the elements in the $n = 1$ level are *inner-shell electrons*. These electrons are at an energy level below the highest-occupied energy level.

The table at the bottom of the page illustrates the patterns that electron configurations follow as you move across the second period of the periodic table. Each element has the same electron configuration as the element just before it, but with the addition of one electron.

The last element in the second period is neon. In this element, all of the orbitals in the 2s and 2p sublevels have been filled with two electrons. Any atom that has its s and p sublevels filled in its highest-occupied energy level is said to have an *octet* of electrons. An octet is a group of eight.

Remember

The electrons within the same main energy level of an atom are said to be in the same electron *shell*.

READING CHECK

3. Use the information in the other rows of the table to complete the table.

Electron Configurations of Atoms of Second-Period Elements Showing Two Notations

| Name | Symbol | Orbital notation | | | | | Electron-configuration notation |
		1s	2s	2p			
Lithium	Li	↑↓	↑	___	___	___	$1s^2 2s^1$
Beryllium	Be	↑↓	↑↓	___	___	___	$1s^2 2s^2$
Boron	B	↑↓	↑↓	↑	___	___	$1s^2 2s^2 2p^1$
Carbon	C	↑↓	↑↓	↑	↑	___	$1s^2 2s^2 2p^2$
Nitrogen	N	___	___	___	___	___	$1s^2 2s^2 2p^3$
Oxygen	O	↑↓	↑↓	↑↓	↑	↑	
Fluorine	F	___	___	___	___	___	$1s^2 2s^2 2p^5$
Neon	Ne	___	___	___	___	___	

Elements of the Third Period

After the outer octet is filled in neon, the next electron enters the s sublevel in the $n = 3$ main energy level. Thus, an atom of sodium, the first element in the third period, has the electron configuration $1s^2 2s^2 2p^6 3s^1$. The third period elements have two sets of inner-shell electrons, the electrons in the $n = 1$ and $n = 2$ levels, and the additional electrons are placed in the $n = 3$ energy level.

Noble-Gas Notation

The Group 18 elements in the periodic table are called the **noble gases.** Neon is an example of a noble gas. The first ten electrons in a sodium atom have the same configuration as a neon atom. The same is true for all the third period elements. Scientists used this fact to develop a shortened version of electron-configuration notation called noble-gas notation. The symbol for neon is enclosed in brackets and substituted for that portion of the configuration. So, $[Ne] = 1s^2 2s^2 2p^6$, and the noble-gas notation for sodium is $[Ne]3s^1$.

The last element in the third period is a noble gas called argon. Argon, like neon, has an octet in its highest-occupied energy level. In fact, all noble gases other than helium have such an octet. A **noble-gas configuration** refers to an outer main energy level occupied, in most cases, by eight electrons.

READING CHECK

4. Use the information in the other rows of the table to complete the table.

Electron Configurations of Atoms of Third-Period Elements

Name	Symbol	Atomic number	Number of electrons in sublevels					Noble-gas notation
			1s	2s	2p	3s	3p	
Sodium	Na	11	2	2	6	1		*[Ne]$3s^1$
Magnesium	Mg	12	2	2	6	2		[Ne]$3s^2$
Aluminum	Al	13	2	2	6	2	1	[Ne]$3s^2 3p^1$
Silicon	Si	14	2	2	6	2	2	[Ne]$3s^2 3p^2$
Phosphorus	P	15						[Ne]$3s^2 3p^3$
Sulfur	S	16	2	2	6	2	4	
Chlorine	Cl	17						
Argon	Ar	18						[Ne]$3s^2 3p^6$

*[Ne] $= 1s^2 2s^2 2p^6$

Elements of the Fourth Period

The fourth period of the periodic table contains elements in which the highest-occupied energy level is the $n = 4$ level. Potassium, K, is the first element in the fourth period. It has an atomic number of 19. Its first 18 electrons are placed in the same way as the 18 electrons of the argon atom. These electrons fill the $1s$, $2s$, $2p$, $3s$, and $3p$ sublevels. However, according to the diagram on the first page of this section, the $4s$ sublevel has a lower energy than the $3d$ sublevel. Therefore, the 19th electron fills the $4s$ sublevel, not the $3d$ sublevel. Potassium atoms have the electron configuration $[Ar]4s^1$.

The next element is calcium, Ca, which has the electron configuration $[Ar]4s^2$ and an atomic number of 20. The next element after that is scandium, Sc, with an atomic number of 21. Its first 20 electrons are placed in the same way as the calcium atom. The 21st electron is placed at the next lowest energy sublevel, which is the $3d$ sublevel.

Scandium atoms have the electron configuration $[Ar]3d^14s^2$. Note that the $3d$ sublevel is written first, even though it has a higher energy than the $4s$ sublevel. Electron-configuration notation and noble-gas notation always show the sublevels in order from lowest to highest main energy level.

The next nine elements fill the other remaining positions within the $3d$ sublevel. The $4p$ sublevel is then filled starting with gallium, Ga, element number 31. Therefore, the electron configuration of a gallium atom is $[Ar]3d^{10}4s^24p^1$.

The diagram at the top right provides another way to remember the order in which atomic orbits are filled. Note that according to the diagram, the d sublevel for a given main energy level is never filled until the s sublevel of the next-highest main energy level is filled.

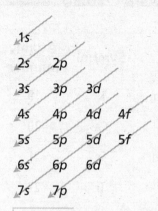

Follow the diagonal arrows from the top to get the order in which atomic orbitals are filled according to the Aufbau principle.

✓ READING CHECK

5. Why is the symbol [Ar] used in the electron configuration of potassium, and what does it represent?

_____

_____

Electron Configuration of Atoms of Elements in the Fourth Period

Name	Symbol	Atomic number	Number of electrons in sublevels above 2p					Noble-gas notation
			3s	3p	3d	4s	4p	
Potassium	K	19	2	6		1		*[Ar]$4s^1$
Calcium	Ca	20	2	6		2		[Ar]$4s^2$
Scandium	Sc	21	2	6	1	2		[Ar]$3d^14s^2$
Titanium	Ti	22	2	6	2	2		[Ar]$3d^24s^2$
Vanadium	V	23	2	6	3	2		[Ar]$3d^34s^2$
Chromium	Cr	24	2	6	5	1		[Ar]$3d^54s^1$
Manganese	Mn	25	2	6	5	2		[Ar]$3d^54s^2$
Iron	Fe	26	2	6	6	2		
Cobalt	Co	27						[Ar]$3d^74s^2$
Nickel	Ni	28	2	6	8	2		[Ar]$3d^84s^2$
Copper	Cu	29	2	6	10	1		[Ar]$3d^{10}4s^1$
Zinc	Zn	30	2	6	10	2		[Ar]$3d^{10}4s^2$
Gallium	Ga	31	2	6	10	2	1	
Germanium	Ge	32						[Ar]$3d^{10}4s^24p^2$
Arsenic	As	33	2	6	10	2	3	
Selenium	Se	34						[Ar]$3d^{10}4s^24p^4$
Bromine	Br	35						
Krypton	Kr	36	2	6	10	2	6	[Ar]$3d^{10}4s^24p^6$

*[Ar] = $1s^22s^22p^63s^23p^6$

The table above shows all 18 elements in the fourth period of the periodic table. There are two exceptions to the normal rules for placing electrons in orbitals that are reflected in the table. In each case, the configuration listed has the lowest possible energy. The first exception is chromium, in which one of the electrons in the 4s orbital switches to the 3d orbital. The second exception is copper, in which the same switch occurs. There is no simple explanation for this departure from the pattern.

READING CHECK

6. Use the information in the other rows of the table to complete the table.

Elements of the Fifth Period

The patterns seen in the first four periods of the periodic table continue with the fifth period. There are 18 elements in the fifth period. The sublevels are filled in the order $5s$, $4d$, and finally $5p$. All of the elements in the fifth period of the periodic table have a highest-occupied energy level of $n = 5$. The table at the bottom of the page shows the elements in the fifth period. This table also includes configurations that differ from those predicted by the rules given earlier in this chapter.

◯ Critical Thinking

7. Explain Describe why ruthenium, Ru, does not have a noble-gas configuration.

_____

_____

_____

Electron Configurations of Atoms of Elements in the Fifth Period

Name	Symbol	Atomic number	Number of electrons in sublevels above 3d					Noble-gas notation
			4s	4p	4d	5s	5p	
Rubidium	Rb	37	2	6		1		*$[Kr]5s^1$
Strontium	Sr	38	2	6		2		$[Kr]5s^2$
Yttrium	Y	39	2	6	1	2		$[Kr]4d^1 5s^2$
Zirconium	Zr	40	2	6	2	2		$[Kr]4d^2 5s^2$
Niobium	Nb	41	2	6	4	1		$[Kr]4d^4 5s^1$
Molybdenum	Mo	42	2	6	5	1		$[Kr]4d^5 5s^1$
Technetium	Tc	43	2	6	6	1		$[Kr]4d^6 5s^1$
Ruthenium	Ru	44	2	6	7	1		$[Kr]4d^7 5s^1$
Rhodium	Rh	45	2	6	8	1		$[Kr]4d^8 5s^1$
Palladium	Pd	46	2	6	10			$[Kr]4d^{10}$
Silver	Ag	47	2	6	10	1		$[Kr]4d^{10} 5s^1$
Cadmium	Cd	48	2	6	10	2		$[Kr]4d^{10} 5s^2$
Indium	In	49	2	6	10	2	1	$[Kr]4d^{10} 5s^2 5p^1$
Tin	Sn	50	2	6	10	2	2	$[Kr]4d^{10} 5s^2 5p^2$
Antimony	Sb	51	2	6	10	2	3	$[Kr]4d^{10} 5s^2 5p^3$
Tellurium	Te	52	2	6	10	2	4	$[Kr]4d^{10} 5s^2 5p^4$
Iodine	I	53	2	6	10	2	5	$[Kr]4d^{10} 5s^2 5p^5$
Xenon	Xe	54	2	6	10	2	6	$[Kr]4d^{10} 5s^2 5p^6$

*$[Kr] = 1s^2 2s^2 2p^6 3s^2 3p^6 3d^{10} 4s^2 4p^6$

Write the complete electron-configuration notation and the noble-gas notation for iron, Fe. How many electron-containing orbitals are in an atom of iron? How many of these orbitals are completely filled? How many unpaired electrons are there in an atom of iron? In what sublevel are the unpaired electrons located?

SOLUTION

1 ANALYZE   *Determine what information is given and unknown.*

No information is given. The information must be deduced from the periodic table and the rules for electron configurations.

2 PLAN   *Determine how to answer the questions.*

All of the questions can be answered by referring to the electron configuration of iron or to the periodic table.

3 SOLVE   *Write the configurations and answer the questions.*

Iron is not an exception to the rules, so its configuration can be determined using the normal procedure. Iron's electron configuration can be written as

$$1s^2 2s^2 2p^6 3s^2 3p^6 3d^6 4s^2 \quad \text{or} \quad [\text{Ar}]3d^6 4s^2$$

All of the s and p sublevels in the configuration are completely filled. The $3d$ sublevel is not filled. The notation $3d^6$ represents

$$3d \quad \uparrow\downarrow \quad \uparrow \quad \uparrow \quad \uparrow \quad \uparrow \ .$$

Each s sublevel has one orbital with electrons, each p sublevel has three orbitals with electrons, and the $3d$ sublevel has five orbitals with electrons. The total number of orbitals with electrons is given by $1 + 1 + 3 + 1 + 3 + 5 + 1 = 15$.

All of the p and s orbitals are filled, and one of the $3d$ orbitals is filled. So, 11 orbitals are filled. The other four $3d$ orbitals contain unpaired electrons.

4 CHECK YOUR WORK   *Check to see that the answer makes sense.*

The atomic number of iron is 26. The complete electron configuration of iron contains 26 electrons because $2 + 2 + 6 + 2 + 6 + 6 + 2 = 26$.

C. Write both the complete electron-configuration notation and the noble-gas notation for iodine, I.

_____

How many inner-shell electrons are in the configuration?

_____

How many orbitals contain electrons?

_____

How many orbitals are completely filled?

_____

How many unpaired electrons are in the configuration?

_____

D. Write the noble-gas notation for tin, Sn.

_____

How many unpaired electrons are in the configuration?

_____

How many *d* orbitals contain electrons?

_____

What fourth-period element has atoms with the same number of electrons in its highest-occupied energy level?

_____

E. Write the complete electron configuration for the element with atomic number 18.

_____

How many orbitals are completely filled?

_____

What is the name of this element?

_____

Elements of the Sixth Period

The sixth period of the periodic table contains 32 elements. It is much longer than the periods that precede it in the periodic table, because an f sublevel fills with electrons in this period. All of the elements in this period have a highest-occupied energy level of $n = 6$. The first element of the sixth period is cesium, Cs. It has the same electron configuration as the noble gas xenon, plus one electron in the $6s$ orbital. The next element, barium, Ba, has a $6s$ orbital that is completely filled.

Lanthanum, La, has one electron in the $5d$ orbital. In the next 13 elements, listed in the lanthanide series on the periodic table, electrons are added to the $4f$ orbital. Because the $4f$ and $5d$ orbitals are very close in energy, there are many deviations from the rules covered early in this section. The last six elements in the period fill the $6p$ orbital. Radon, a noble gas, has an octet of electrons in the $n = 6$ energy level.

The seventh period of the periodic table would contain 32 elements, except that not all of the elements have been discovered. Most of the elements in this period do not exist in nature. They are created artificially in a laboratory. These artificial elements break down rapidly into other elements, which is one reason they are not found in nature.

✓ READING CHECK

9. Why do the sixth and seventh period of the periodic table have many more elements than the previous periods?

_____

_____

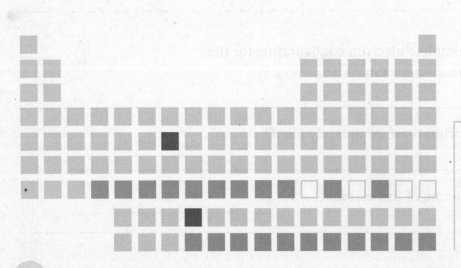

The two artificially-created dark blue elements fill gaps in the periodic table. The other highlighted elements are artificially-created and extend the periodic table beyond uranium, element 92. Empty squares represent elements that have been reported but have yet to be confirmed.

VOCABULARY

1. a. What is an atom's electron configuration?

_____

_____

b. What three principles guide the electron configuration of an atom?

_____

REVIEW

2. What three methods are used to represent the arrangement of electrons in atoms?

_____

3. What is an octet of electrons? Which elements contain an octet of electrons?

_____

_____

4. Identify the elements having the following electron configurations:

a. $1s^2 2s^2 2p^6 3s^2 3p^3$ _____

b. $[Ar]4s^1$ _____

c. contains four electrons in its third and outer main energy level _____

Critical Thinking

5. RELATING IDEAS Write the electron configuration for the following third-period elements.

a. aluminum, Al _____

b. silicon, Si _____

c. phosphorus, P _____

d. sulfur, S _____

e. chlorine, Cl _____

f. What is the relationship between the group number of each element and the number of electrons in the outermost energy level?

_____

_____

Math Tutor WEIGHTED AVERAGES AND ATOMIC MASS

The atomic masses listed on the periodic table are not whole numbers. Instead they are decimals that represent average atomic masses. The atomic masses are averages because most elements occur in nature as a specific mixture of isotopes. For example, 75.76% of chlorine atoms have a mass of 34.969 u, and 24.24% have a mass of 36.966 u. If the isotopes were in a 1:1 ratio, you could simply add the masses of the two isotopes together and divide by 2. However, to account for the differing abundance of the isotopes, you must calculate a weighted average. For chlorine, the weighted average is 35.45 u. The following two examples demonstrate how weighted averages are calculated.

Problem-Solving TIPS

- To find an average atomic mass, convert the abundance of each isotope from a percentage to a decimal equivalent.
- Multiply each decimal equivalent with the atomic mass of each isotope. The result is the contribution of the isotope to the weighted average.
- Add the contributions of each isotope. The sum is the average atomic mass.

SAMPLE

Naturally occurring silver consists of two isotopes: 51.839% Ag-107 (106.905 093 u) and 48.161% Ag-109 (108.904 756 u). What is the average atomic mass of silver?

Convert the percentages to decimals, multiply by the atomic masses, and add the results.

$$0.518\ 39 \times 106.905\ 093\ u \rightarrow \quad 55.419\ u$$
$$0.481\ 61 \times 108.904\ 756\ u \rightarrow \underline{+ 52.450\ u}$$
$$107.869\ u$$

Naturally occurring magnesium consists of 78.99% Mg-24 (23.985 042 u), 10.00% Mg-25 (25.985 837 u), and 11.01% Mg-26 (25.982 593 u). What is the average atomic mass of magnesium?

Convert the percentages to decimals, multiply by the masses, and add the results.

$$0.7899 \times 23.985\ 042\ u \rightarrow \quad 18.95\ u$$
$$0.1000 \times 24.985\ 837\ u \rightarrow \quad 2.499\ u$$
$$0.1101 \times 25.982\ 593\ u \rightarrow \underline{+ 2.861\ u}$$
$$24.31\ u$$

Practice Problems: Chapter Review practice problem 14

1. a. List five examples of electromagnetic radiation.

_____

_____

b. What is the speed of all forms of electromagnetic radiation in a vacuum? _____

2. In the early twentieth century, what two experiments involving light and matter could not be explained by the wave theory of light?

_____

3. a. How are wavelength and frequency of electromagnetic radiation related?

_____

b. How are the energy and frequency of electromagnetic radiation related?

_____

4. Distinguish between the ground state and an excited state of an atom.

_____

_____

5. According to Bohr's model of the hydrogen atom, how is hydrogen's emission spectrum produced?

_____

_____

6. Describe two major shortcomings of Bohr's model of the atom.

_____

_____

7. a. What is the principal quantum number and how is it symbolized? _____

b. What are shells? _____

_____

c. How does the principal quantum number relate to the number of electrons allowed per main energy level?

_____

8. For each of the following values of n, indicate the numbers and types of sublevels possible for that main energy level.

a. $n = 1$ _____   c. $n = 3$ _____

b. $n = 2$ _____   d. $n = 4$ _____

9. In your own words, explain the following rules of electron configuration.

a. the Aufbau principle _____

_____

b. Hund's rule _____

_____

c. Pauli exclusion principle _____

_____

10. a. What is meant by the term *highest-occupied energy level*?

_____

_____

b. What are inner shell electrons?

_____

_____

11. The electron configuration for oxygen is $1s^2 2s^2 2p^4$.

a. What is the atomic number of oxygen? _____

b. How many unpaired electrons does oxygen have? _____

c. What is the highest occupied energy level? _____

12. How does noble-gas notation simplify writing electron configurations?

_____

_____

13. Write both the complete electron-configuration notation and the noble-gas notation for each of the elements below.

a. sodium, Na _____

b. strontium, Sr _____

14. The element silicon occurs as a mixture of three isotopes: 92.22% Si-28, 4.69% Si-29, and 3.09% Si-30. The atomic masses of these three isotopes are Si-28 = 27.976 926 u, Si-29 = 28.976 495 u, and Si-30 = 29.973 770 u. Find the average atomic mass of silicon.

15. Determine the energy in joules of a photon whose frequency is 3.55×10^{17} Hz.

16. How long would it take a radio wave whose frequency is 7.25×10^5 Hz to travel from Mars to Earth if the distance between the two planets is approximately 8.00×10^7 km?

17. How does a $2s$ orbital differ from a $1s$ orbital? How does a $2p_x$ orbital differ from a $2p_y$ orbital?

_____

_____

_____

18. List the order in which the orbitals generally fill, from $1s$ to $7p$.

_____

19. How do the electron configurations of chromium and copper contradict the Aufbau principle?

_____

_____

The Periodic Law

Review Previous Concepts

1. What information is recorded on the periodic table of the elements?

_____

_____

_____

_____

2. Explain what is meant by the *electron configuration* of an atom.

_____

_____

_____

_____

History of the Periodic Table

By 1860, more than 60 elements had been discovered. Chemists had to learn the properties of these elements as well as those of the many compounds that the elements formed. The elements were not organized into any patterns and the factors that determined the properties of the elements were unknown.

In addition, there was no method for determining an element's atomic mass or the number of atoms of an element in a compound. Different chemists used different atomic masses for the same elements, resulting in different compositions being listed for the same compounds. This made communication of results between chemists difficult.

In 1860, Italian chemist Stanislao Cannizzaro presented a method for accurately measuring the relative masses of atoms. This allowed chemists to agree on standard values of atomic mass. It also allowed them to search for relationships between atomic mass and other properties of the elements.

Mendeleev's periodic table grouped elements by their properties.

A Russian chemist, Dmitri Mendeleev, decided to write a chemistry textbook and include the standard values of atomic masses. For the book, Mendeleev hoped to organize the elements according to their properties.

Mendeleev went about organizing elements much as you might organize information to study for a test or write a research paper. He placed the name of each known element on a card, together with its atomic mass and a list of its observed physical and chemical properties. He then arranged the cards according to various properties and looked for trends or patterns.

KEY TERMS

periodic law   lanthanides
periodic table   actinides

💡 Critical Thinking

1. Infer How could organizing the elements according to trends or patterns help chemists study the properties of the elements?

_____

_____

_____

_____

_____

Element B
average atomic
mass = 29.6 amu
d Element A
average atomic
mass = 201.9 amu
density = 27 g/cm³
m.P. = 660°C
b.P. = 2467°C

Element C
average atomic
mass = 123 amu
g/cm³

Element D

Element E

These note cards could be used to determine patterns in the properties of the elements.

Mendeleev's First Periodic Table

			Ti = 50	Zr = 90	? = 180
			V = 51	Nb = 94	Ta = 182
			Cr = 52	Mo = 96	W = 186
			Mn = 55	Rh = 104.4	Pt = 197.4
			Fe = 56	Ru = 104.4	Ir = 198
			Ni = Co = 59	Pl = 106.6	Os = 199
H = 1			Cu = 63.4	Ag = 108	Hg = 200
	Be = 9.4	Mg = 24	Zn = 65.2	Cd = 112	
	B = 11	Al = 27.4	? = 68	Ur = 116	Au = 197?
	C = 12	Si = 28	? = 70	Su = 118	
	N = 14	P = 31	As = 75	Sb = 112	Bi = 210
	O = 16	S = 32	Se = 79.4	Te = 128?	
	F = 19	Cl = 35.5	Br = 80	I = 127	
Li = 7	Na = 23	K = 39	Rb = 85.4	Cs = 133	Tl = 204
		Ca = 40	Sr = 87.6	Ba = 137	Pb = 207
		? = 45	Ce = 92		
		?Er = 56	La = 94		
		?Yt = 60	Di = 95		
		?In = 75.6	Th = 118?		

Mendeleev noticed that when the elements were arranged in order of increasing atomic mass, certain similarities in their properties appeared at regular intervals. For example, there are seven elements between F and Cl atoms, which have similar properties. There are also seven elements between two other atoms that have similar properties: Na and K.

This repeating pattern is referred to as *periodic*. Something is periodic if it repeats again and again. For example, the second hand on a clock is periodic because it passes over the same spot every 60 seconds.

Mendeleev's arrangement of the elements is shown in the table above. He switched two elements, iodine, I, and tellurium, Te, to maintain the patterns. He also hypothesized undiscovered elements to fill in the gaps in his pattern. By 1886, three of these elements had been discovered.

✓ READING CHECK

2. Name three things in everyday life that are periodic.

_____

_____

_____

Moseley arranged elements by their atomic numbers.

The **periodic law** states that the physical and chemical properties of the elements are periodic functions of their atomic numbers. In other words, when the elements are arranged in order of increasing atomic number, elements with similar properties appear at regular intervals.

Mendeleev's periodic table ordered the elements by atomic mass, not atomic number. In 1911, English scientist Henry Moseley found that the elements fit into patterns better when they were ordered by nuclear charge, or the amount of positive charge in the nucleus. Moseley's work led to the modern definition of the atomic number and also to the reorganization of the elements by atomic number instead of atomic mass.

Modern periodic tables arrange the elements by both atomic number and properties.

The periodic table has undergone extensive changes since Mendeleev's time. Chemists have discovered more than 40 new elements and, in more recent years, manufactured new ones in the laboratory. Each of these elements, however, can still be placed in a group of other elements using the same type of pattern originally described by Mendeleev. The modern **periodic table** is an arrangement of the elements in order of their atomic numbers so that elements with similar properties fall in the same column, or group.

The Noble Gases

An important addition to the periodic table was made near the end of the nineteenth century. In 1894, English physicist Lord Rayleigh and Scottish chemist William Ramsay discovered an unreactive gas called argon, with atomic mass 40. However, no spot was available for argon on the periodic table. In 1895, Ramsay isolated another such gas, helium, which previously had been observed in the Sun, using the Sun's emission spectrum. William Ramsay won the Nobel Prize for his discoveries in 1904.

Over the next several years, four more unreactive gases were discovered: neon, krypton, xenon, and radon. Scientists realized that a new column was needed to account for these elements, which they called noble gases.

READING CHECK

3. In what way is the periodic table *periodic*?

_____

_____

_____

_____

_____

			2 He
7 N	8 O	9 F	10 Ne
15 P	16 S	17 Cl	18 Ar
33 As	34 Se	35 Br	36 Kr
51 Sb	52 Te	53 I	54 Xe
83 Bi	84 Po	85 At	86 Rn

The noble gases, or Group 18 elements, are all unreactive.

The Lanthanides

The next step in the development of the periodic table was completed in the early 1900s. The **lanthanides** are the 14 elements with atomic numbers from 58 (cerium, Ce) to 71 (lutetium, Lu). These elements have very similar properties. The process of separating and identifying these elements required a large effort by many chemists. However, finally it was understood that the elements were best located in the sixth period, between Group 3 and Group 4.

The Actinides

Another major step in the development of the periodic table was the discovery of the actinides. The **actinides** are the 14 elements with atomic numbers from 90 (thorium, Th) to 103 (lawrencium, Lr). The actinides belong between Group 3 and Group 4 directly below the lanthanides. They are located in the seventh period of the table. To save space, the lanthanides and the actinides are often broken off and displayed below the rest of the periodic table. The periodic table in Section 2 is one example of this form of display.

Periodicity

The periodicity of the atomic numbers is one of the most important features of the periodic table. Consider the noble gases in Group 18. The first noble gas is helium, He. It has an atomic number of 2. The next element that has similar properties to helium is neon, Ne, with atomic number 10. The rest of the noble gases are argon (Ar, atomic number 18), krypton (Kr, atomic number 36), xenon (Xe, atomic number 54), and radon (Rn, atomic number 86). The progression of the differences between the atomic numbers of these elements is shown at the right.

The elements in Group 1 follow the same pattern. As the figure at the right shows, the atomic number of each successive element in the group is 8, 8, 18, 18, and 32 higher than the previous element.

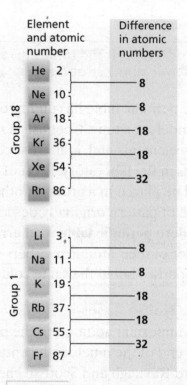

In Groups 1 and 18, the differences between the atomic numbers of successive elements are 8, 8, 18, 18, and 32, respectively.

🔍 Critical Thinking

4. **Calculate** What is the pattern of differences between the atomic numbers of Groups 2 and 13–17 of the periodic table?

VOCABULARY

1. State the periodic law.

_____

_____

REVIEW

2. a. Who is credited with developing a method that led to the
determination of standard atomic masses?

_____

b. Who discovered the periodic law?

_____

c. Who established atomic numbers as the basis for organizing the
periodic table?

_____

3. Name three sets of elements that have been added to the periodic table
after Mendeleev's time.

_____

4. How do the atomic numbers of the elements within each of Groups 1, 2, and
13–18 of the periodic table vary?

_____

_____

Critical Thinking

5. RELATING IDEAS Why are the atomic masses of the elements not strictly in
increasing order in the periodic table, even though the properties of the
elements are similar? For example, by atomic mass, tellurium, Te, should be
in Group 17 and iodine, I, should be in Group 16, but grouping by properties
has Te in Group 16 and I in Group 17.

_____

_____

_____

_____

SECTION 5.2

Electron Configuration and the Periodic Table

Mendeleev and the scientists who built upon his work arranged the elements in a periodic table that reflected the similarity of their properties. For example, all of the Group 18 elements, the noble gases, are stable, undergoing few chemical reactions. The reason for this stability has to do with the number of electrons in the highest-occupied energy level. Each noble gas, except for helium, has an octet of electrons in the highest-occupied energy level. This configuration is stable, making removal of electrons difficult.

The period of an element is determined by its electron configuration.

In the chapter "Arrangement of Electrons in Atoms," you learned that you can determine the period of an element directly from its configuration. The highest-occupied energy level for an atom of any element determines the element's period. For example, arsenic's electron configuration is $[Ar]3d^{10}4s^24p^3$. Therefore, the highest-occupied energy level for arsenic is the $n = 4$ level.

The table below restates the order at which sublevels fill with electrons. The table shows that the number of sublevels filled determines the length of the period.

KEY TERMS

alkali metal
alkaline-earth metal
transition element
main-group element
halogen

 **READING CHECK**

1. How many electrons does a noble gas, other than helium, have in its highest-occupied energy level?

Relationship Between Period Length and Sublevels Being Filled		
Period number	Number of elements in period	Sublevels in order of filling
1	2	1s
2	8	2s 2p
3	8	3s 3p
4	18	4s 3d 4p
5	18	5s 4d 5p
6	32	6s 4f 5d 6p
7	32	7s 5f 6d 7p

Periodic Table

Legend:
- s-block elements
- p-block elements
- d-block elements
- f-block elements

Group 1	Group 2	Group 3	Group 4	Group 5	Group 6	Group 7	Group 8	Group 9	Group 10	Group 11	Group 12	Group 13	Group 14	Group 15	Group 16	Group 17	Group 18
1 H																	2 He
3 Li	4 Be											5 B	6 C	7 N	8 O	9 F	10 Ne
11 Na	12 Mg											13 Al	14 Si	15 P	16 S	17 Cl	18 Ar
19 K	20 Ca	21 Sc	22 Ti	23 V	24 Cr	25 Mn	26 Fe	27 Co	28 Ni	29 Cu	30 Zn	31 Ga	32 Ge	33 As	34 Se	35 Br	36 Kr
37 Rb	38 Sr	39 Y	40 Zr	41 Nb	42 Mo	43 Tc	44 Ru	45 Rh	46 Pd	47 Ag	48 Cd	49 In	50 Sn	51 Sb	52 Te	53 I	54 Xe
55 Cs	56 Ba	57 La	72 Hf	73 Ta	74 W	75 Re	76 Os	77 Ir	78 Pt	79 Au	80 Hg	81 Tl	82 Pb	83 Bi	84 Po	85 At	86 Rn
87 Fr	88 Ra	89 Ac	104 Rf	105 Db	106 Sg	107 Bh	108 Hs	109 Mt	110 Ds	111 Rg	112 Cn		114 Fl		116 Lv		

58 Ce	59 Pr	60 Nd	61 Pm	62 Sm	63 Eu	64 Gd	65 Tb	66 Dy	67 Ho	68 Er	69 Tm	70 Yb	71 Lu
90 Th	91 Pa	92 U	93 Np	94 Pu	95 Am	96 Cm	97 Bk	98 Cf	99 Es	100 Fm	101 Md	102 No	103 Lr

In the first period, the $1s$ orbital is filled with two electrons. In the second and third periods, the s sublevel is filled with two electrons and the p sublevel is filled with six electrons, for a total of eight electrons. In the fourth and fifth periods, the d sublevel is filled with 10 electrons, for a total of 18 electrons. Finally, in the sixth and seventh periods, the f sublevel is filled with an additional 14 electrons, for a total of 32 electrons.

By examining the electron configurations of the elements, you can see that the horizontal location of an element in the periodic table is also related to its configuration. For example, in Group 2, the last electron fills the s sublevel. Therefore, the periodic table can be divided into four blocks depending on which sublevel the last electron fills. The periodic table above shows the result of this division. The four blocks are the s block, the p block, the d block, and the f block.

> The periodic table can be divided into four blocks based on the electron configurations of the elements.

✓ READING CHECK

2. The last electron in arsenic occupies a $4p$ level. What block of the periodic table is arsenic in?

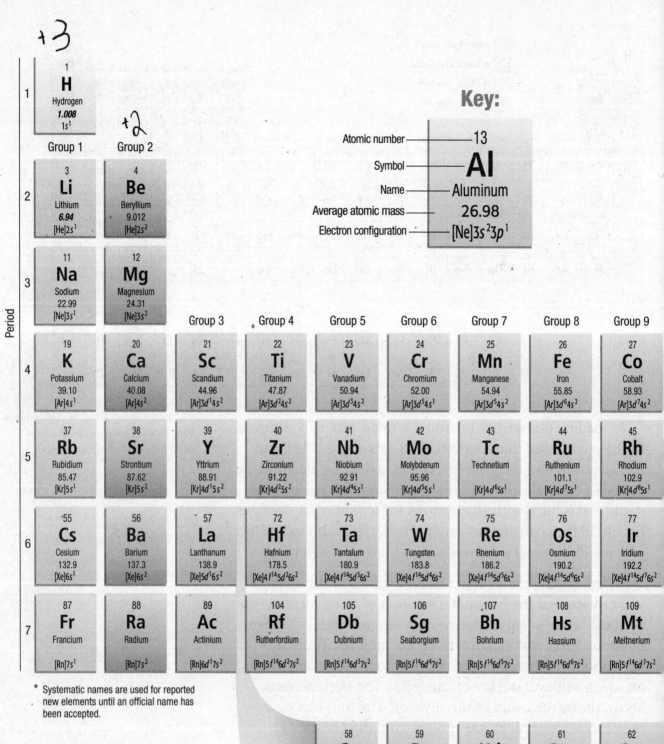

+3

1	Group 1
H	
Hydrogen	
1.008	
$1s^1$	

+2 Group 2

Key:

Atomic number — 13
Symbol — **Al**
Name — Aluminum
Average atomic mass — 26.98
Electron configuration — $[Ne]3s^23p^1$

Period

Period	Group 1	Group 2	Group 3	Group 4	Group 5	Group 6	Group 7	Group 8	Group 9
2	3 **Li** Lithium *6.94* $[He]2s^1$	4 **Be** Beryllium 9.012 $[He]2s^2$							
3	11 **Na** Sodium 22.99 $[Ne]3s^1$	12 **Mg** Magnesium 24.31 $[Ne]3s^2$							
4	19 **K** Potassium 39.10 $[Ar]4s^1$	20 **Ca** Calcium 40.08 $[Ar]4s^2$	21 **Sc** Scandium 44.96 $[Ar]3d^14s^2$	22 **Ti** Titanium 47.87 $[Ar]3d^24s^2$	23 **V** Vanadium 50.94 $[Ar]3d^34s^2$	24 **Cr** Chromium 52.00 $[Ar]3d^54s^1$	25 **Mn** Manganese 54.94 $[Ar]3d^54s^2$	26 **Fe** Iron 55.85 $[Ar]3d^64s^2$	27 **Co** Cobalt 58.93 $[Ar]3d^74s^2$
5	37 **Rb** Rubidium 85.47 $[Kr]5s^1$	38 **Sr** Strontium 87.62 $[Kr]5s^2$	39 **Y** Yttrium 88.91 $[Kr]4d^15s^2$	40 **Zr** Zirconium 91.22 $[Kr]4d^25s^2$	41 **Nb** Niobium 92.91 $[Kr]4d^45s^1$	42 **Mo** Molybdenum 95.96 $[Kr]4d^55s^1$	43 **Tc** Technetium $[Kr]4d^65s^1$	44 **Ru** Ruthenium 101.1 $[Kr]4d^75s^1$	45 **Rh** Rhodium 102.9 $[Kr]4d^85s^1$
6	55 **Cs** Cesium 132.9 $[Xe]6s^1$	56 **Ba** Barium 137.3 $[Xe]6s^2$	57 **La** Lanthanum 138.9 $[Xe]5d^16s^2$	72 **Hf** Hafnium 178.5 $[Xe]4f^{14}5d^26s^2$	73 **Ta** Tantalum 180.9 $[Xe]4f^{14}5d^36s^2$	74 **W** Tungsten 183.8 $[Xe]4f^{14}5d^46s^2$	75 **Re** Rhenium 186.2 $[Xe]4f^{14}5d^56s^2$	76 **Os** Osmium 190.2 $[Xe]4f^{14}5d^66s^2$	77 **Ir** Iridium 192.2 $[Xe]4f^{14}5d^76s^2$
7	87 **Fr** Francium $[Rn]7s^1$	88 **Ra** Radium $[Rn]7s^2$	89 **Ac** Actinium $[Rn]6d^17s^2$	104 **Rf** Rutherfordium $[Rn]5f^{14}6d^27s^2$	105 **Db** Dubnium $[Rn]5f^{14}6d^37s^2$	106 **Sg** Seaborgium $[Rn]5f^{14}6d^47s^2$	107 **Bh** Bohrium $[Rn]5f^{14}6d^57s^2$	108 **Hs** Hassium $[Rn]5f^{14}6d^67s^2$	109 **Mt** Meitnerium $[Rn]5f^{14}6d^77s^2$

* Systematic names are used for reported new elements until an official name has been accepted.

58 **Ce** Cerium 140.1 $[Xe]4f^15d^16s^2$	59 **Pr** Praseodymium 140.9 $[Xe]4f^36s^2$	60 **Nd** Neodymium 144.2 $[Xe]4f^46s^2$	61 **Pm** Promethium $[Xe]4f^56s^2$	62 **Sm** Samarium 150.4 $[Xe]4f^66s^2$
90 **Th** Thorium 232.0 $[Rn]6d^27s^2$	91 **Pa** Protactinium 231.0 $[Rn]5f^26d^17s^2$	92 **U** Uranium 238.0 $[Rn]5f^36d^17s^2$	93 **Np** Neptunium $[Rn]5f^46d^17s^2$	94 **Pu** Plutonium $[Rn]5f^67s^2$

Atomic masses are averages based upon the naturally occurring composition of isotopes on Earth. For elements that have slightly different isotopic composition depending on the source, IUPAC now reports a range of values for atomic masses. These atomic masses are shown here in bold italics. The atomic masses in this table have been rounded to values sufficiently accurate for everyday calculations. Per IUPAC convention, no values are listed for elements whose isotopes lack a characteristic abundance in natural samples.

Hydrogen
Semiconductors
(also known as metalloids)

Metals
- Alkali metals
- Alkaline-earth metals
- Transition metals
- Other metals

Nonmetals
- Halogens
- Noble gases
- Other nonmetals

O

+1   -3   -2   -1

Group 13	Group 14	Group 15	Group 16	Group 17	Group 18
					2 **He** Helium 4.003 $1s^2$
5 **B** Boron *10.81* $[He]2s^2 2p^1$	6 **C** Carbon *12.01* $[He]2s^2 2p^2$	7 **N** Nitrogen *14.007* $[He]2s^2 2p^3$	8 **O** Oxygen *15.999* $[He]2s^2 2p^4$	9 **F** Fluorine 19.00 $[He]2s^2 2p^5$	10 **Ne** Neon 20.18 $[He]2s^2 2p^6$
13 **Al** Aluminum 26.98 $[Ne]3s^2 3p^1$	14 **Si** Silicon *28.085* $[Ne]3s^2 3p^2$	15 **P** Phosphorus 30.97 $[Ne]3s^2 3p^3$	16 **S** Sulfur *32.06* $[Ne]3s^2 3p^4$	17 **Cl** Chlorine *35.45* $[Ne]3s^2 3p^5$	18 **Ar** Argon 39.95 $[Ne]3s^2 3p^6$

Group 10	Group 11	Group 12						
28 **Ni** Nickel 58.69 $[Ar]3d^8 4s^2$	29 **Cu** Copper 63.55 $[Ar]3d^{10}4s^1$	30 **Zn** Zinc 65.38 $[Ar]3d^{10}4s^2$	31 **Ga** Gallium 69.72 $[Ar]3d^{10}4s^2 4p^1$	32 **Ge** Germanium 72.63 $[Ar]3d^{10}4s^2 4p^2$	33 **As** Arsenic 74.92 $[Ar]3d^{10}4s^2 4p^3$	34 **Se** Selenium 78.96 $[Ar]3d^{10}4s^2 4p^4$	35 **Br** Bromine 79.90 $[Ar]3d^{10}4s^2 4p^5$	36 **Kr** Krypton 83.80 $[Ar]3d^{10}4s^2 4p^6$
46 **Pd** Palladium 106.4 $[Kr]4d^{10}$	47 **Ag** Silver 107.9 $[Kr]4d^{10}5s^1$	48 **Cd** Cadmium 112.4 $[Kr]4d^{10}5s^2$	49 **In** Indium 114.8 $[Kr]4d^{10}5s^2 5p^1$	50 **Sn** Tin 118.7 $[Kr]4d^{10}5s^2 5p^2$	51 **Sb** Antimony 121.8 $[Kr]4d^{10}5s^2 5p^3$	52 **Te** Tellurium 127.6 $[Kr]4d^{10}5s^2 5p^4$	53 **I** Iodine 126.9 $[Kr]4d^{10}5s^2 5p^5$	54 **Xe** Xenon 131.3 $[Kr]4d^{10}5s^2 5p^6$
78 **Pt** Platinum 195.1 $[Xe]4f^{14}5d^9 6s^1$	79 **Au** Gold 197.0 $[Xe]4f^{14}5d^{10}6s^1$	80 **Hg** Mercury 200.6 $[Xe]4f^{14}5d^{10}6s^2$	81 **Tl** Thallium *204.38* $[Xe]4f^{14}5d^{10}6s^2 6p^1$	82 **Pb** Lead 207.2 $[Xe]4f^{14}5d^{10}6s^2 6p^2$	83 **Bi** Bismuth 209.0 $[Xe]4f^{14}5d^{10}6s^2 6p^3$	84 **Po** Polonium $[Xe]4f^{14}5d^{10}6s^2 6p^4$	85 **At** Astatine $[Xe]4f^{14}5d^{10}6s^2 6p^5$	86 **Rn** Radon $[Xe]4f^{14}5d^{10}6s^2 6p^6$
110 **Ds** Darmstadtium $[Rn]5f^{14}6d^9 7s^1$	111 **Rg** Roentgenium $[Rn]5f^{14}6d^{10}7s^1$	112 **Cn** Copernicium $[Rn]5f^{14}6d^{10}7s^2$	113 **Uut*** Ununtrium $[Rn]5f^{14}6d^{10}7s^2 7p^1$	114 **Fl** Flerovium $[Rn]5f^{14}6d^{10}7s^2 7p^2$	115 **Uup*** Ununpentium $[Rn]5f^{14}6d^{10}7s^2 7p^3$	116 **Lv** Livermorium $[Rn]5f^{14}6d^{10}7s^2 7p^4$	117 **Uus*** Ununseptium $[Rn]5f^{14}6d^{10}7s^2 7p^5$	118 **Uuo*** Ununoctium $[Rn]5f^{14}6d^{10}7s^2 7p^6$

The discoveries of elements with atomic numbers 113, 115, and 117 -118 have been reported but not fully confirmed.

63 **Eu** Europium 152.0 $[Xe]4f^7 6s^2$	64 **Gd** Gadolinium 157.3 $[Xe]4f^7 5d^1 6s^2$	65 **Tb** Terbium 158.9 $[Xe]4f^9 6s^2$	66 **Dy** Dysprosium 162.5 $[Xe]4f^{10}6s^2$	67 **Ho** Holmium 164.9 $[Xe]4f^{11}6s^2$	68 **Er** Erbium 167.3 $[Xe]4f^{12}6s^2$	69 **Tm** Thulium 168.9 $[Xe]4f^{13}6s^2$	70 **Yb** Ytterbium 173.1 $[Xe]4f^{14}6s^2$	71 **Lu** Lutetium 175.0 $[Xe]4f^{14}5d^1 6s^2$
95 **Am** Americium $[Rn]5f^7 7s^2$	96 **Cm** Curium $[Rn]5f^7 6d^1 7s^2$	97 **Bk** Berkelium $[Rn]5f^9 7s^2$	98 **Cf** Californium $[Rn]5f^{10}7s^2$	99 **Es** Einsteinium $[Rn]5f^{11}7s^2$	100 **Fm** Fermium $[Rn]5f^{12}7s^2$	101 **Md** Mendelevium $[Rn]5f^{13}7s^2$	102 **No** Nobelium $[Rn]5f^{14}7s^2$	103 **Lr** Lawrencium $[Rn]5f^{14}6d^1 7s^2$

The *s*-Block Elements: Groups 1 and 2

The elements in the *s*-block are chemically reactive metals. The Group 1 metals are more reactive than the Group 2 metals. As you will learn in Section 3, Group 1 metals are reactive because the single electron in their highest-occupied energy level is easily lost.

The elements in Group 1 (lithium, sodium, potassium, rubidium, cesium, and francium) are known as the **alkali metals.** In their pure state, all of the alkali metals have a silvery appearance and are soft enough to cut with a knife. As you move down the column in the periodic table, the pure forms of these elements melt at lower and lower temperatures.

TIP Some groups in the periodic table are also represented by their own configuration. This notation reflects the fact that each element in the group has the same configuration in its highest-occupied energy level. For example, Group 1 has a group configuration of ns^1, and Group 2 has a group configuration of ns^2.

✓ **READING CHECK**

3. Which is more reactive, potassium or calcium?

(a) (b)

(a) Potassium reacts so strongly with water that (b) it must be stored in kerosene to prevent it from contacting moisture in the air.

However, because the alkali metals are so reactive, they are not found in nature as free elements. Each element reacts with water to form hydrogen gas and a solution known as an alkali. They also react with most nonmetals. To prevent pure forms of these elements from reacting, they are stored in jars and completely covered with kerosene.

The elements in Group 2 (beryllium, magnesium, calcium, strontium, barium, and radium) are called the **alkaline-earth metals.** Atoms of alkaline-earth metals have a pair of electrons in their outermost *s* sublevel. The Group 2 metals are harder and denser than the alkali metals. They also have higher melting points. Although they are less reactive than the alkali metals, the alkaline-earth metals are also too reactive to be found in nature as free elements.

Beryllium is found in the mineral compound beryl. Beryl crystals include the blue-green aquamarine and the dark green emerald.

a. **Without looking at the periodic table, identify the group, period, and block in which the element that has the electron configuration $[Xe]6s^2$ is located.**

b. **Without looking at the periodic table, write the electron configuration for the Group 1 element in the third period.**

	SOLUTION	
1	ANALYZE	*Determine what information is given and unknown.*

Given: a. $[Xe]6s^2$
   b. Group 1, third period

Unknown: a. group, period, block
   b. electron configuration

2	PLAN	*Determine the information necessary to answer the questions.*

The location of an element in the periodic table is directly related to its electron configuration.

3	SOLVE	*Determine the unknowns from the given information.*

a. The element is in the sixth period because its highest-occupied energy level is $n = 6$. Because its configuration is of the form ns^2, it is in Group 2, which is in the s block.

b. The group configuration of Group 1 elements is ns^2. Since the element is in the third period, $n = 3$, the electron configuration is $1s^2 2s^2 2p^6 3s^1$, or $[Ne]3s^1$.

4	CHECK YOUR WORK	*Determine if the answers make sense.*

The configuration of each element matches the group and period describing the element's location in the periodic table.

PRACTICE	*Answer without looking at the periodic table.*

A. Identify the following for the element with the electron configuration $[Kr]5s^1$.

Group number _____   Period number _____

Block designation _____

B. Write the noble-gas configuration for the Group 2 element in the fourth period. _____

Hydrogen and Helium

Hydrogen has the electron configuration $1s^1$, but does not share the same properties as the Group 1 elements. It is a unique element, whose properties do not closely resemble those of any group. It is usually placed above the Group 1 elements with a gap between it and lithium.

Helium has the same ns^2 configuration as the Group 2 elements. However, it has the stability of a noble gas because its outermost energy level is filled. It is placed in Group 18, instead of with the reactive, unstable Group 2 elements.

The *d*-Block Elements: Groups 3–12

The *d*-block elements are metals with typical metallic properties and are often referred to as **transition elements** or transition metals. They are good conductors of electricity and have a high luster. They are usually less reactive than the alkali metals and alkaline-earth metals. Some transition elements, such as gold, palladium, and platinum, are so unreactive that they exist in nature mostly as free elements.

The last electron placed in an atom of a *d*-block element is in a *d* orbital. The *d* block spans ten groups on the periodic table. The group configuration of Group 3 elements is $(n-1)d^1ns^2$. For example, scandium has the configuration $[Ar]3d^14s^2$, as shown below. The group configuration of Group 12 elements is $(n-1)d^{10}ns^2$. One example is mercury, with the configuration $[Xe]4f^{14}5d^{10}6s^2$. Groups 4–11 do not have regular configurations, but the sum of the electrons in the highest *s* and *d* sublevels is always equal to the group number.

The transition element copper is found in nature as part of copper ore and can be obtained from surface mines.

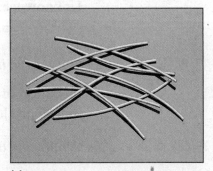

(a)

(b)

The pure forms of (a) tungsten and (b) vanadium are shown.

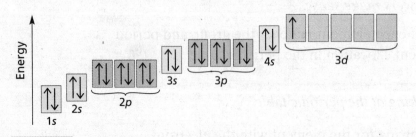

The electron configuration of the fourth-period, Group 3 element Scandium, Sc.

READING CHECK

4. Name at least three properties of a transition element.

An element has the electron configuration $[Kr]4d^55s^1$. Without looking at the periodic table, identify the period, block, and group in which this element is located. Then, consult the periodic table to identify this element.

SOLUTION

1 ANALYZE   *Determine what information is given and unknown.*

> **Given:** the electron configuration $[Kr]4d^55s^1$
> **Unknown:** period, block, group, other elements in group

2 PLAN   *Determine the information needed to answer the questions.*

The location of an element in the periodic table is directly related to its electron configuration.

3 SOLVE   *Determine the unknowns from the given information.*

The element is in the fifth period because its highest-occupied energy level is $n = 5$.

There are five electrons in the d sublevel, which means that the sublevel is not completely filled. It also means that the element is in the d block. The sum of the electrons in the highest s and d levels is six, so the element is in Group 6. The fifth-period element in Group 6 of the periodic table is molybdenum.

4 CHECK YOUR WORK   *Determine if the answers make sense.*

The configuration of molybdenum matches the group and period describing its location in the periodic table.

PRACTICE   *Answer without looking at the periodic table.*

> **C.** Identify the following for the element with the electron configuration $[Ar]3d^84s^2$.
>
> Period number _____ Block designation _____
>
> Group number _____
>
> **D.** Write the outer electron configuration for the Group 12 element in the fifth period.
>
> _____

Relationships Among Group Numbers, Blocks, and Electron Configurations

Group number	Group configuration	Block	Comments
1, 2	$ns^{1,2}$	s	One or two electrons in ns sublevel
3–12	$(n-1)d^{1-10}ns^{0-2}$	d	Sum of electrons in ns and $(n-1)d$ levels equals group number
13–18	ns^2n^{1-6}	p	Number of electrons in np sublevel group number minus 12

The *p*-Block Elements: Groups 13–18

The *p*-block elements consist of all the elements in Groups 13–18 except helium. In the atoms of these elements, the final electron fills the *p* sublevel. Because electrons are added to the *p* sublevel only after the *s* sublevel is filled, each element in the *p* block also has two electrons in every *s* sublevel. The *p*-block elements, along with the *s*-group elements are called the **main-group elements.**

The group configurations for the *p* block, as well as the *s* and *d* blocks, are summarized in the table at the top of the page. You can conclude from the table, for example, that the group configuration for Group 15 is ns^2np^3.

For atoms of *p*-block elements, the total number of electrons in the highest-occupied energy level is equal to the group number minus 10. For example, bromine is in Group 17. It has $17 - 10 = 7$ electrons in its highest energy level.

The properties of the elements in the *p* block vary greatly. The right side of the *p* block contains all of the *nonmetals* except hydrogen and helium. All six of the *metalloids* (boron, silicon, germanium, arsenic, antimony, and tellurium) are also in the *p* block. The bottom left of the *p* block contains eight metals.

Metals
Metalloids
Nonmetals

Groups 13–18 of the periodic table, which includes the *p* block and helium.

Remember

A *nonmetal* is a poor conductor of electricity and heat. A *metalloid*, or semiconductor, has some properties of metals and some properties of nonmetals.

READING CHECK

5. What is the group configuration of the elements in Group 17?

The halogens in Group 17 include (a) fluorine, (b) chlorine, (c) bromine, and (d) iodine.

The elements in Group 17 (fluorine, chlorine, bromine, iodine, and astatine) are called the **halogens.** The halogens are the most reactive nonmetals. They react vigorously with most metals to form salts. At room temperature, fluorine and chlorine are gases, bromine is a reddish liquid, and iodine is a purplish solid. Astatine is an artificial element.

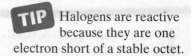

Halogens are reactive because they are one electron short of a stable octet.

The metalloids of the *p* block are mostly brittle solids. They have an electrical conductivity that is in between that of metals, which are good conductors, and nonmetals, which are poor conductors.

The metals of the *p* block are usually harder and denser than the alkali metals and alkaline-earth metals of the *s* block, but softer and less dense than the metals of the *d* block. With the exception of bismuth, these metals are reactive enough to be found in nature only in compounds. However, once a pure metal is obtained, the element is stable in the presence of air.

The *f*-Block Elements: Lanthanides and Actinides
The *f*-block elements are wedged between Group 3 and Group 4 of the periodic table. There are seven orbitals to be filled with two electrons each on the *f* sublevel. Therefore, the *f* block is $2 \times 7 = 14$ elements wide.

The lanthanides are the 14 elements in the sixth period. They are shiny metals similar in reactivity to the alkaline-earth metals. The actinides are the 14 elements in the seventh period. All of the actinides are radioactive. Only the first four actinides—thorium, protactinium, uranium, and neptunium—have been found on Earth. The others were made in the laboratory.

6. Which blocks of the periodic table contain elements that are considered metals?

_____

_____

Without looking at the periodic table, write the outer electron configuration for the Group 14 element in the second period. Then, name the element and identify it as a metal, nonmetal, or metalloid.

SOLUTION

1 ANALYZE *Determine what information is given and unknown.*

> **Given:** a second period element in Group 14
> **Unknown:** outer electron configuration, type of element

2 PLAN *Determine the information necessary to answer the questions.*

The electron configuration of an element in the periodic table is directly related to its location.

3 SOLVE *Determine the unknowns from the given information.*

Elements in Group 14 are in the p block. The total number of electrons in the highest occupied s and p sublevels for a Group 14 element is $14 - 10 = 4$. Two electrons fill the s sublevel first, so the other two electrons must be in the p sublevel. The outer configuration for a Group 14 element in the second period, $n = 2$, is $2s^2 2p^2$.

The second period element in Group 14 is carbon, C. Carbon is a nonmetal.

4 CHECK YOUR WORK *Determine if the answers make sense.*

The configuration of carbon matches the group and period describing its location in the periodic table.

PRACTICE *Answer without looking at the periodic table.*

E. Write the outer electron configuration for the Group 17 element in the third period.

_____

F. Identify the following for the element with the electron configuration $[Ar]3d^{10}4s^2 4p^3$.

Period number _____ Block designation _____

Group number _____

Use the given electron configuration to determine the period, group, and block for these four elements. Then use the periodic table to name each element, identify it as a metal, nonmetal, or metalloid, and describe its relative reactivity.

SOLVE

Electron configuration	Complete before looking at the periodic table			Complete while looking at the periodic table		
	Period	Block	Group	Name	Type	Reactivity
a. $[Xe]4f^{14}5d^{9}6s^{1}$	6	d	10	platinum	metal	low
b. $[Ne]3s^{2}3p^{5}$	3	p	17	chlorine	nonmetal	high
c. $[Ne]3s^{2}3p^{6}$	3	p	18	argon	nonmetal	low
d. $[Xe]4f^{6}6s^{2}$	6	f	N/A	samarium	metal	high

a. The $5d$ sublevel is not filled, so the element is in the d block. The group number is $9 + 1 = 10$. The element is platinum, which is a transition metal and has low reactivity.

b. The $3p$ sublevel is not filled, so the element is in the p block. The group number is $10 + 5 + 2 = 17$. The element is chlorine, a reactive nonmetal.

c. This element has a noble-gas configuration, so it is in Group 18. The element is argon, a nonreactive nonmetal.

d. The $4f$ sublevel is not filled, so the element is in the f block. This is a sixth-period element, so it a lanthanide, a reactive metal. The name of the element is samarium.

PRACTICE Complete the table below. Fill in the first three columns without consulting the periodic table.

Electron configuration	Complete before looking at the periodic table			Complete while looking at the periodic table		
	Period	Block	Group	Name	Type	Reactivity
G. $[He]2s^{2}2p^{5}$						
H. $[Ar]3d^{10}4s^{1}$						

VOCABULARY

1. What name is given to each of the following groups of elements in the periodic table?

   a. Group 1 _____

   b. Group 2 _____

   c. Group 3–12 _____

   d. Group 17 _____

   e. Group 18 _____

REVIEW

2. Into what four blocks can the periodic table be divided to illustrate the relationship between the elements' electron configurations and their placement in the periodic table?

   _____

3. What are the relationships between group configuration and group number for elements in the $s, p,$ and d blocks?

   _____

   _____

   _____

4. Without looking at the periodic table, write the outer electron configuration

   for the Group 15 element in the fourth period. _____

5. Without looking at the periodic table, identify the period, block, and group of the element that has the electron configuration $[Ar]3d^7 4s^2$.

   Period number _____ Block designation _____ Group number _____

Critical Thinking

6. **APPLYING MODELS** Period 7 contains elements in the $s, p, d,$ and f blocks. Suppose there were a Period 8 and it contained elements in the "g" block, where "g" had the angular momentum quantum number of 4. If a hypothetical element in Period 8 had an atomic number of 120, into what group in the periodic table would the element fit, and what properties might it have (assuming it does not radioactively decay)?

   _____

   _____

   _____

SECTION 5.3

Electron Configuration and Periodic Properties

So far, you have learned that elements are arranged in the periodic table according to their atomic number. There is also a rough correlation between the arrangement of the elements and their electron configurations.

In this section, the relationship between the periodic law and electron configurations will be further explored. This relationship allows several properties of an element to be predicted simply from its position relative to other elements on the periodic table.

Atomic radii are related to electron configuration.

Ideally, the size of an atom is defined by the edge of its outermost orbital. However, the location of this boundary is difficult to determine, and can vary under different conditions. Therefore, to estimate the size of an atom, the conditions to which it is subjected must be described.

One way to define the **atomic radius** is as one-half the distance between the nuclei of identical atoms that are bonded together. For example, a molecule of chlorine gas contains two atoms of chlorine bonded together. The distance between the two chlorine nuclei is 198 pm. Therefore, the atomic radius of a chlorine atom is 99 pm.

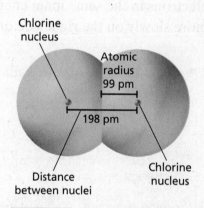

One method of determining atomic radius is to measure the distance between the nuclei of two identical atoms that are bonded together in an element or compound, then divide this distance by 2.

🔍 Critical Thinking

1. **Apply** In a gold block, individual atoms of gold are bonded together through metallic bonding. How would you use the gold block to determine the atomic radius of an atom of gold?

_____

_____

Period Trends

The table below lists the atomic radii of all of the elements in the periodic table in picometers. The graph on the next page plots the atomic radii of the elements versus their atomic number. By examining the table and the graph, several trends in the atomic radius can be observed.

Note that there is a gradual decrease in atomic radius as you move from left to right across the second period of the periodic table. The atomic radius of lithium in Group 1 is 152 pm, and the values decrease through neon in Group 18, which has an atomic radius of 71 pm.

The trend to smaller atoms across a period is caused by the increasing positive charge of the nucleus. As electrons are added to the *s* and *p* levels in the same main energy level, they are gradually pulled closer to the positively charged nucleus that contains more and more protons. This increased pull results in a decrease in atomic radius. Because the increased pull is offset somewhat by the repulsion of more and more electrons in the same main energy level, atomic radii decrease more slowly on the right side of the periodic table.

✓ READING CHECK

2. If two elements are from the same period, which element is most likely to have the largest atomic radius, the element from Group 13 or the element from Group 17?

Periodic Table of Atomic Radii (pm)

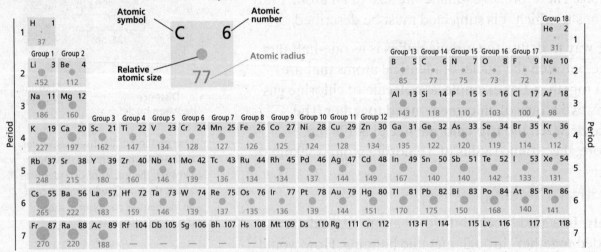

In general, atomic radii decrease from left to right across a period and increase from top to bottom down a group.

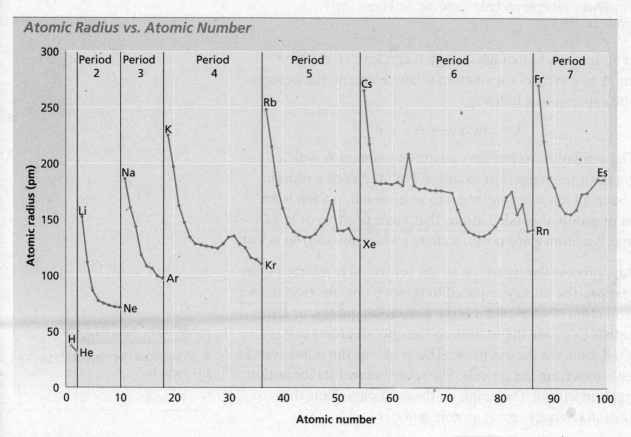

Atomic Radius vs. Atomic Number

Group Trends

Note that there is a gradual increase in atomic radius as you move down a group in the periodic table. The trend to larger atoms down a group results from the increase in the number of electron shells surrounding the nucleus.

There are some exceptions, such as gallium, which has a smaller atomic radius than aluminum. Gallium is an exception to the general rule because the pull of the extra 18 positively charged protons in its nucleus outweighs the presence of another electron shell.

The plot of atomic radius versus atomic number shows both period trends and group trends.

TIP The graph above shows trends within a period by the shape of the graph between the vertical lines that separate the periods. The graph shows trends within a group by the way the period plots increase from period to period.

PRACTICE

A. Of the elements Li, O, C, and F, which:

has the largest atomic radius? _____

has the smallest atomic radius? _____

B. Which of Ca, Be, Ba, and Sr has the largest atomic radius?
Explain your answer in terms of trends in the periodic table.

_____

_____

Removing electrons from atoms to form ions requires energy.

If an atom absorbs enough energy, it can lose an electron. Using A as a symbol for an atom of any element, the process can be expressed as follows.

$$A + energy \rightarrow A^+ + e^-$$

The symbol A^+ represents an ion of element A with a single positive charge. For example, Na^+ refers to a sodium ion. Such an ion is also referred to as a 1+ ion. An **ion** is an atom or group of bonded atoms that has a positive or negative charge. An atom gains positive charge when an electron is lost.

Any process during which an ion is formed is referred to as **ionization.** The energy required to remove one electron from a neutral atom of an element is the **ionization energy,** or **IE.** Scientists calculate the ionization energies of atoms using isolated atoms in the gas phase. This removes the influence of other atoms from the process. The table below lists ionization energies in kJ/mol. The graph on the next page plots the ionization energies versus atomic number.

✓ **READING CHECK**

3. What does the chemical symbol Li^+ refer to?

Periodic Table of Ionization Energies (kJ/mol)

Atomic number — 6
Symbol — C
First ionization energy — 1086

Period	Group 1	Group 2	Group 3	Group 4	Group 5	Group 6	Group 7	Group 8	Group 9	Group 10	Group 11	Group 12	Group 13	Group 14	Group 15	Group 16	Group 17	Group 18
1	1 H 1312																	2 He 2372
2	3 Li 520	4 Be 900											5 B 801	6 C 1086	7 N 1402	8 O 1314	9 F 1681	10 Ne 2081
3	11 Na 496	12 Mg 738											13 Al 578	14 Si 787	15 P 1012	16 S 1000	17 Cl 1251	18 Ar 1521
4	19 K 419	20 Ca 590	21 Sc 633	22 Ti 659	23 V 651	24 Cr 653	25 Mn 717	26 Fe 762	27 Co 760	28 Ni 737	29 Cu 746	30 Zn 906	31 Ga 579	32 Ge 762	33 As 947	34 Se 941	35 Br 1140	36 Kr 1351
5	37 Rb 403	38 Sr 550	39 Y 600	40 Zr 640	41 Nb 652	42 Mo 684	43 Tc 702	44 Ru 710	45 Rh 720	46 Pd 804	47 Ag 731	48 Cd 868	49 In 558	50 Sn 709	51 Sb 834	52 Te 869	53 I 1008	54 Xe 1170
6	55 Cs 376	56 Ba 503	57 La 538	72 Hf 659	73 Ta 761	74 W 770	75 Re 760	76 Os 839	77 Ir 878	78 Pt 868	79 Au 890	80 Hg 1007	81 Tl 589	82 Pb 716	83 Bi 703	84 Po 812	85 At —	86 Rn 1038
7	87 Fr —	88 Ra 509	89 Ac 490	104 Rf —	105 Db —	106 Sg —	107 Bh —	108 Hs —	109 Mt —	110 Ds —	111 Rg —	112 Cn —	113	114 Fl —	115	116 Lv —	117	118

Lanthanide series

58 Ce 534	59 Pr 527	60 Nd 533	61 Pm 536	62 Sm 545	63 Eu 547	64 Gd 592	65 Tb 566	66 Dy 573	67 Ho 581	68 Er 589	69 Tm 597	70 Yb 603	71 Lu 523

Actinide series

90 Th 587	91 Pa 570	92 U 598	93 Np 600	94 Pu 585	95 Am 578	96 Cm 581	97 Bk 601	98 Cf 608	99 Es 619	100 Fm 627	101 Md 635	102 No 642	103 Lr —

In general, first ionization energies increase from left to right across a period and decrease from top to bottom down a group.

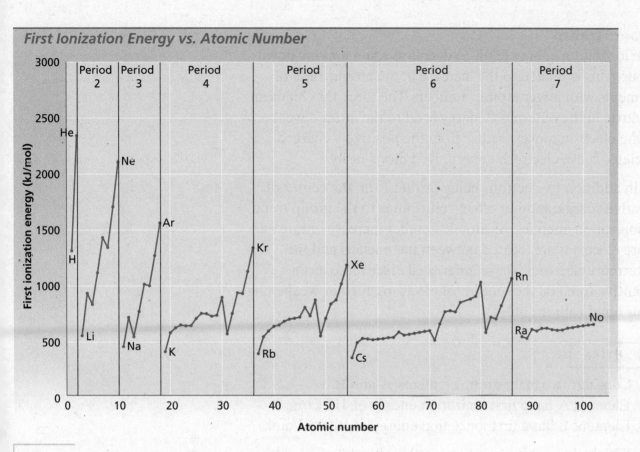

First Ionization Energy vs. Atomic Number

The plot of first ionization energy versus atomic number shows both period trends and group trends.

Period Trends

By examining the table on the previous page and the graph above, several trends in the ionization energy can be observed. Note that there is a gradual increase in ionization energy as you move from left to right across a period in the periodic table. Another trend is that nonmetals usually have higher ionization energies than metals.

The Group 1 metals have the lowest ionization energies in their respective periods. The ease with which these metals lose electrons is a major reason for their high reactivity. On the opposite side of the periodic table, the Group 18 elements have the highest ionization energies. This is a major reason why noble gases are so unreactive.

The general increase in ionization energies moving across a period is caused by the increasing charge in the nucleus. A higher positive charge in the nucleus attracts the negatively charged electrons more strongly.

TIP In the graph above, note that the period trends and group trends are less pronounced as the atomic number increases.

 **READING CHECK**

4. Suppose you have an alkaline-earth metal and a halogen. Which is more likely to have a higher ionization energy?

Group Trends

The ionization energy tends to decrease when moving down a group. This is related to the increase in the atomic radii of elements with larger atomic numbers. The force that binds an electron in the outermost energy level to the atom is weaker as the electron moves farther from the positively charged nucleus. These electrons are removed more easily.

In addition to electrons being farther from the center of positive charge, another effect contributes to the group trend in ionization energies. As atomic number increases, more and more electrons are located between the nucleus and the outermost electrons. These inner shell electrons exert a repulsive force on the outermost electrons, further weakening their bond with the atom.

PRACTICE

C. Consider two main-group elements, A and B.
Element A has a first ionization energy of 419 kJ/mol.
Element B has a first ionization energy of 1000 kJ/mol.

a. Which element is likely to be in the *s* block? _____

b. Which element is likely to be in the *p* block? _____

c. Which element is more likely to form a positive ion? _____

Removing Electrons from Positive Ions

If enough energy is provided, an electron can be removed from a neutral atom. If even more energy is provided, additional electrons can be removed from the positive ion. The different ionization energies are classified in the following way.

- The removal of an electron from a neutral atom is referred to as the ionization energy, *IE*, or the *first ionization energy, IE_1*.
- The removal of a second electron from an atom, or an electron from a 1+ ion, is called the *second ionization energy, IE_2*.
- The removal of a third electron from an atom, or an electron from a 2+ ion, is called the *third ionization energy, IE_3*.
- The removal of the *n*th electron from an atom, or an electron from an $(n-1)+$ ion, is called the *n*th ionization energy, IE_n.

READING CHECK

5. What name is given to the energy required to remove an electron from a 4+ ion?

_____

_____

Ionization Energies (in kJ/mol) for Elements of Periods 1–3									
	Period 1		**Period 2**							
	H	He	Li	Be	B	C	N	O	F	Ne
IE_1	1312	2372	520	900	801	1086	1402	1314	1681	2081
IE_2		5250	7298	1757	2427	2353	2856	3388	3374	3952
IE_3			11 815	14 849	3660	4621	4578	5300	6050	6122
IE_4				21 007	25 026	6223	7475	7469	8408	9370
IE_5					32 827	37 830	9445	10 990	11 023	12 178
	Period 3									
			Na	Mg	Al	Si	P	S	Cl	Ar
IE_1			496	738	578	787	1012	1000	1251	1521
IE_2			4562	1451	1817	1577	1903	2251	2297	2666
IE_3			6912	7733	2745	3232	2912	3361	3822	3931
IE_4			9544	10 540	11 578	4356	4957	4564	5158	5771
IE_5			13 353	13 628	14 831	16 091	6274	7013	6540	7238

The table above shows the first five ionization energies for the elements in the first three periods of the periodic table. For each element, IE_2 is always higher than IE_1, IE_3 is always higher than IE_2, and so on. This is because each successive electron removed from an ion feels a stronger and stronger effective nuclear charge from the nucleus. In other words, as each electron is removed, fewer electrons remain within the atom to shield the attractive force of the nucleus.

Removing the first electron from a noble gas is more difficult than removing the first electron from any other element. This is due to the stability of the octet in the highest-occupied energy level of the noble-gas atom. This concept also applies to ions that have a noble-gas configuration.

For example, when sodium, Na, loses a single electron, it has a noble-gas configuration. You can see why when you look at sodium's electron configuration, $[Ne]3s^1$. So, there is a large increase in sodium's IE_2 compared to its IE_1. In the same way, magnesium has a large jump in IE_3 from IE_2. Magnesium's electron configuration, $[Ne]3s^2$, shows that it has a noble-gas configuration after it loses two electrons. The table uses highlighting to emphasize the large jumps in ionization energies caused by the noble-gas configurations of some ions.

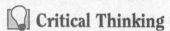 **Critical Thinking**

6. Infer. Suppose that the table above was extended to list the sixth ionization energies for the elements. Which element in the second period, and which element in the third period, would have the highest value for IE_6?

_____

_____

Adding electrons to atoms to form ions also requires energy.

Not only can neutral atoms lose electrons; they can gain electrons. The energy change that occurs when a neutral atom gains an electron is called the atom's **electron affinity.** Most atoms release energy when they gain an electron.

$$A + e^- \rightarrow A^- + \text{energy}$$

On the other hand, some atoms must absorb energy before they will gain an electron. An ion produced in this way is unstable and will usually lose the added electron quickly.

$$A + e^- + \text{energy} \rightarrow A^-$$

TIP In a chemical equation, energy is released if it is shown on the right side of the equation. Energy is absorbed if it is shown on the left side of a chemical equation.

Period Trends

The table below shows the electron affinities for most elements. The graph on the next page shows a plot of these data. The values are negative to show that the atom loses energy when it gains an electron. The electron affinities for atoms that gain energy when gaining an electron are difficult to determine, so they are given as zeros in parentheses.

The Group 17 elements, the halogens, have the electron affinities that are most negative. Their ability to attract electrons helps to explain why halogens are so reactive. The electron affinities generally become more negative when moving left to right across the *p* block.

READING CHECK

7. Why are most of the electron affinities in the table below negative?

Periodic Table of Electron Affinities (kJ/mol)

Key: 6 (Atomic number) C (Symbol) −126.3 (Electron affinity)

Period	Group 1	Group 2	Group 3	Group 4	Group 5	Group 6	Group 7	Group 8	Group 9	Group 10	Group 11	Group 12	Group 13	Group 14	Group 15	Group 16	Group 17	Group 18
1	1 H −75.4																	2 He (0)
2	3 Li −61.8	4 Be (0)											5 B −27.7	6 C −126.3	7 N (0)	8 O −146.1	9 F −339.9	10 Ne (0)
3	11 Na −54.8	12 Mg (0)											13 Al −44.1	14 Si −138.5	15 P −74.6	16 S −207.7	17 Cl −361.7	18 Ar (0)
4	19 K −50.1	20 Ca (0)	21 Sc −18.8	22 Ti −7.9	23 V −52.5	24 Cr −66.6	25 Mn (0)	26 Fe −16.3	27 Co −66.1	28 Ni −115.6	29 Cu −122.8	30 Zn (0)	31 Ga −30	32 Ge −135	33 As −81	34 Se −202.1	35 Br −336.5	36 Kr (0)
5	37 Rb −48.6	38 Sr (0)	39 Y −30.7	40 Zr −42.6	41 Nb −89.3	42 Mo −74.6	43 Tc −55	44 Ru −105	45 Rh −113.7	46 Pd −55.7	47 Ag −130.2	48 Cd (0)	49 In −30	50 Sn −120	51 Sb −107	52 Te −197.1	53 I −305.9	54 Xe (0)
6	55 Cs −47.2	56 Ba (0)	57 La −50	72 Hf (0)	73 Ta −32.2	74 W −81.5	75 Re −15	76 Os −110	77 Ir −156.5	78 Pt −212.8	79 Au −230.9	80 Hg (0)	81 Tl −20	82 Pb −36	83 Bi −94.6	84 Po −190	85 At −280	86 Rn (0)
7	87 Fr −47.0	88 Ra (0)	89 Ac —	104 Rf —	105 Db —	106 Sg —	107 Bh —	108 Hs —	109 Mt —	110 Ds —	111 Rg —	112 Cn —	113	114 Fl —	115	116 Lv —	117	118

This table shows the electron affinities for the *s*-, *p*-, and *d*-block elements. Values in parentheses are approximate. All of the lanthanides have an estimated electron affinity of −50 kJ/mol. All of the actinides have an estimated electron affinity of 0 kJ/mol.

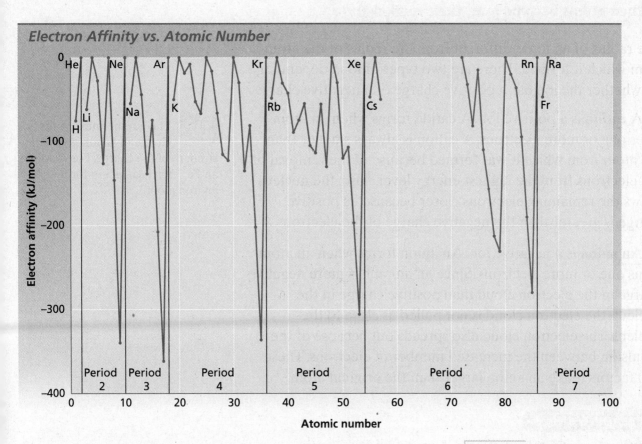

Electron Affinity vs. Atomic Number

Electron affinity (kJ/mol) (y-axis: 0, −100, −200, −300, −400)

Atomic number (x-axis: 0, 10, 20, 30, 40, 50, 60, 70, 80, 90, 100)

Labels: He, Ne, Ar, Kr, Xe, Rn, Ra, Li, H, Na, K, Rb, Cs, Fr

Period 2, Period 3, Period 4, Period 5, Period 6, Period 7

One exception to the trend is that it is easier to add an electron into the empty third *p* orbital of Group 14 elements than it is to add an electron into one of the partially filled *p* orbitals in the Group 15 elements. This makes the Group 14 electron affinities more negative than those in Group 15.

The plot of electron affinity versus atomic number shows that most atoms release energy when they acquire an electron because the electron affinity is negative.

Group Trends

Electron affinities become slightly less negative as you move down a group. Because atomic radii increase moving down a group, electrons are less likely to be attracted to the nucleus. The strength of the positively charged nucleus relative to the electrons around the nucleus also decreases.

Adding Electrons to Negative Ions

For an isolated ion in the gas phase, it is always more difficult to add a second electron to an already negatively charged ion. Therefore, second electron affinities are always positive.

The halogens form a noble-gas configuration when they gain an electron. Adding a second electron to a 1– halogen ion is so difficult that 2– halogen ions do not form. Group 16 elements form a noble gas configuration when they gain two electrons to form 2– ions.

 READING CHECK

8. Is an element with an electron affinity that is greater (less negative) than another element more or less likely to gain an electron?

When atoms become ions, their radii change.

The radius of an ion is different from the radius of the atom from which it formed. There are two types of ions, depending on whether the ion has a positive charge or a negative charge.

A **cation** is a positive ion. A cation forms when an atom loses one or more electrons. A cation is always smaller than the atom from which it was formed because of the removal of the electrons from the highest energy level. Also, the nucleus draws the remaining electrons closer because its positive charge is greater than the negative charge of the electrons.

An **anion** is a negative ion. An anion forms when an atom gains one or more electrons. Since an anion has more negative charge in the electron cloud than positive charge in the nucleus, the electron cloud is not pulled as close to the nucleus. The electron cloud also spreads out because of the repulsion between the increased number of electrons. These two factors make an anion larger than the original atom.

TIP The number next to the charge in an ion gives the strength of the charge. For example, an Fe^{2+} ion is a 2+ ion formed from an iron atom.

✓ READING CHECK

9. Classify each of the following ions as a cation or an anion.

a. Rb^+ _____   **d.** P^{3-} _____

b. F^- _____   **e.** Te^{2-} _____

c. Fe^{2+} _____   **f.** C^{4-} _____

Periodic Table of Ionic Radii (pm)

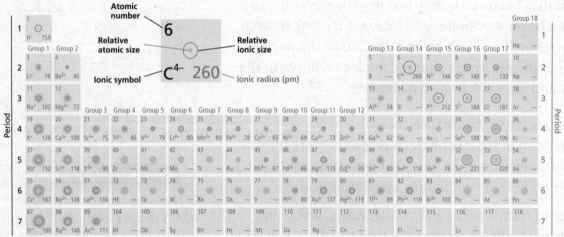

This table shows the ionic radii for the most common ions of the s-, p-, and d- block elements. Cations are smaller and anions are larger than the original atoms.

Period Trends

The metals at the left of the periodic table tend to form cations. This is because it is easier for one of these atoms to lose the few electrons in its highest-occupied energy level than it is for one of them to gain electrons to form an octet. On the other hand, the nonmetals at the upper right of the periodic table tend to form anions. It is easier for one of these atoms to form a stable octet by gaining a few electrons than to lose all of the electrons in the outermost energy level.

The ionic radii of cations decrease as the charge on the cation becomes stronger. For example, the lithium ion, Li^+ is much larger than the beryllium ion, Be^{2+}. The more the charges are unbalanced, the stronger the force with which the nucleus can pull on the electron cloud.

The ionic radii of anions increase as the charge on the anion becomes stronger. The more negative the charge on the ion, the less force with which the nucleus can pull on the electrons. Since the charge becomes less negative, moving from Group 15 to Group 17, the ionic radii of anions tend to decrease moving across a period from left to right.

The ionic radii of cations also tend to decrease moving across a period from left to right. Either the charge on the cation increases, or the positive charge of the nucleus increases without an increase in the highest-occupied energy level.

Group Trends

There is a gradual increase in ionic radii moving down a group for the same reason as there is a gradual increase in atomic radii moving down a group. The highest-occupied energy level increases when moving down a group, so the electron cloud extends farther from the nucleus of the ion.

 Critical Thinking

11. Infer Why are there no common ions or ionic radii listed for the noble-gas elements in Group 18 of the periodic table on the previous page?

_____

_____

_____

 READING CHECK

10. Describe whether the following pairs of particles repel each other or attract each other.

a. anion and anion

_____

b. cation and anion

_____

c. cation and cation

_____

D. Consider four hypothetical main-group elements, Q, R, T, and X, that have the outer electron configurations indicated below.

Q: $3s^23p^5$ R: $3s^1$ T: $4d^{10}5s^25p^5$ X: $4d^{10}5s^25p^1$

a. Identify the block location of each hypothetical element.

     Q: _____ block   T: _____ block

     R: _____ block   X: _____ block

b. Which of these elements are in the same period?

_____

c. Which of these elements are in the same group?

_____

d. Which would you expect to have the highest IE_1? Which would have the lowest IE_1?

_____

e. Which would you expect to have the highest IE_2?

_____

f. Which of these elements is most likely to form a 1+ ion?

_____

g. Which has an electron affinity that is the most negative?

_____

h. Which of these elements is most likely to form a 1– ion?

_____

i. Which would you expect to have the largest ionic radius?

_____

j. Which would you expect to have the smallest ionic radius?

_____

k. Using the letters Q, R, T, and X, write the symbol that represents the most common ion that each hypothetical element would form.

_____

Only the outer electrons are involved in forming compounds.

Chemical compounds form when atoms of two or more elements bond together. These bonds form when electrons are lost, gained, or shared between atoms. The electrons involved in the process of forming chemical bonds are the electrons in the outer energy levels. These electrons are the most likely to be influenced by other atoms or ions.

The electrons available to be lost, gained, or shared in the formation of chemical compounds are called **valence electrons.** Valence electrons are usually located in main energy levels that are incompletely filled. For example, a sodium atom has an electron configuration of $[Ne]3s^1$. The $n = 3$ level of the sodium atom only has a single electron. That one valence electron is lost when the Na^+ ion forms.

For main group elements, the valence electrons are the electrons in the outermost s and p sublevels. The other main energy levels are completely filled. The attraction between the nucleus and the inner-shell electrons is too strong for these electrons to become involved in forming chemical bonds.

The number of valence electrons in the atoms of a main-group element is determined by the group configuration. This configuration shows the number of electrons in the outermost s and p sublevels. For example, a Group 13 element has two electrons in its outermost s sublevel and one electron in its outermost p sublevel. Therefore, a Group 13 element has three valence electrons.

TIP If you look back to the table of ionic radii earlier in this section, you will see the most common ions listed for each main group element. For Groups 1, 2, and 13, the most common ion is a cation with a charge equal to the number of valence electrons in the atom. For Groups 15, 16, and 17, the most common ion is an anion with a charge equal to the number of valence electrons needed to form an octet of eight electrons.

READING CHECK

12. Use the information in the other rows of the table to complete the table.

Valence Electrons in Main-Group Elements

Group number	Group configuration	Number of valence electrons
1	ns^1	1
2	ns^2	
13	ns^2p^1	3
14		4
15	ns^2p^3	
16		6
17	ns^2p^5	
18		

Atoms have different abilities to capture electrons.

Valence electrons form the bonds that hold compounds together. In many compounds, the negative charge of the valence electrons is concentrated closer to one atom than to another. This uneven charge distribution helps to determine the chemical properties of a compound.

Electronegativity is a measure of the ability of an atom in a chemical compound to attract electrons from another atom of the compound. An American chemist named Linus Pauling devised a scale to measure this quantity. Fluorine, the most electronegative element, is assigned a value of 4.0. The values for the other elements are then given in relation to this value.

Critical Thinking

13. Apply Potassium has a relatively low electronegativity of 0.8. If potassium forms a compound with a Group 17 element, where is the electron most likely to be located within that compound?

____

____

Period Trends

The table below and the graph on the next page show the electronegativities of the elements. The graph shows that the electronegativities increase when moving across a period.

The alkali metals and alkaline-earth metals are the least electronegative elements. These elements tend to lose electrons when forming ions. Nitrogen, oxygen, and the halogens are the most electronegative elements. These atoms attract electrons strongly when in compounds.

This table shows the electronegativities for all of the elements. The highest values are in the upper right of the *p* block. The lowest values are in the lower part of the *s* block.

Periodic Table of Electronegativities

Key: 6 (Atomic number), C (Symbol), 2.5 (Electronegativity)

Period	Group 1	Group 2	Group 3	Group 4	Group 5	Group 6	Group 7	Group 8	Group 9	Group 10	Group 11	Group 12	Group 13	Group 14	Group 15	Group 16	Group 17	Group 18
1	1 H 2.1																	2 He —
2	3 Li 1.0	4 Be 1.5											5 B 2.0	6 C 2.5	7 N 3.0	8 O 3.5	9 F 4.0	10 Ne —
3	11 Na 0.9	12 Mg 1.2											13 Al 1.5	14 Si 1.8	15 P 2.1	16 S 2.5	17 Cl 3.0	18 Ar —
4	19 K 0.8	20 Ca 1.0	21 Sc 1.3	22 Ti 1.5	23 V 1.6	24 Cr 1.6	25 Mn 1.5	26 Fe 1.8	27 Co 1.8	28 Ni 1.8	29 Cu 1.9	30 Zn 1.6	31 Ga 1.6	32 Ge 1.8	33 As 2.0	34 Se 2.4	35 Br 2.8	36 Kr 3.0
5	37 Rb 0.8	38 Sr 1.0	39 Y 1.2	40 Zr 1.4	41 Nb 1.6	42 Mo 1.8	43 Tc 1.9	44 Ru 2.2	45 Rh 2.2	46 Pd 2.2	47 Ag 1.9	48 Cd 1.7	49 In 1.7	50 Sn 1.8	51 Sb 1.9	52 Te 2.1	53 I 2.5	54 Xe 2.6
6	55 Cs 0.7	56 Ba 0.9	57 La 1.1	72 Hf 1.3	73 Ta 1.5	74 W 1.7	75 Re 1.9	76 Os 2.2	77 Ir 2.2	78 Pt 2.2	79 Au 2.4	80 Hg 1.9	81 Tl 1.8	82 Pb 1.8	83 Bi 1.9	84 Po 2.0	85 At 2.2	86 Rn 2.4
7	87 Fr 0.7	88 Ra 0.9	89 Ac 1.1	104 Rf —	105 Db —	106 Sg —	107 Bh —	108 Hs —	109 Mt —	110 Ds —	111 Rg —	112 Cn —	113	114 Fl —	115	116 Lv —	117	118

Lanthanide series

58 Ce 1.1	59 Pr 1.1	60 Nd 1.1	61 Pm 1.1	62 Sm 1.2	63 Eu 1.1	64 Gd 1.2	65 Tb 1.1	66 Dy 1.2	67 Ho 1.2	68 Er 1.2	69 Tm 1.3	70 Yb 1.1	71 Lu 1.3

Actinide series

90 Th 1.3	91 Pa 1.5	92 U 1.4	93 Np 1.4	94 Pu 1.3	95 Am 1.3	96 Cm 1.3	97 Bk 1.3	98 Cf 1.3	99 Es 1.3	100 Fm 1.3	101 Md 1.3	102 No 1.3	103 Lr —

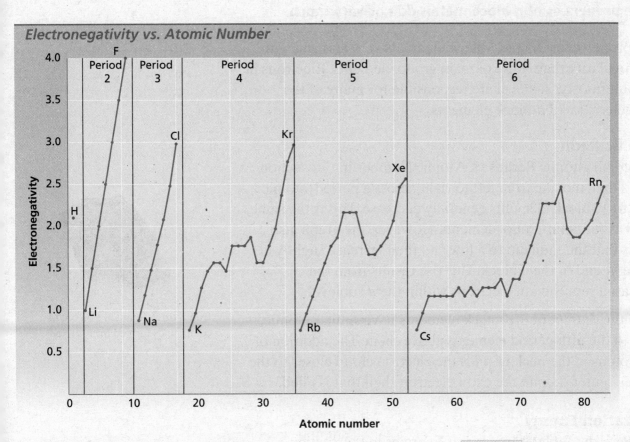

Electronegativity vs. Atomic Number

Electronegativities tend to decrease or remain the same when moving from top to bottom in a group. An exception to this trend is Group 18, the noble gases. Because helium, neon, and argon do not form compounds, they cannot be assigned electronegativities. The other noble gases rarely form compounds, but when they do they attract electrons strongly.

> The plot of electronegativity versus atomic number shows that electronegativity usually increases across a period.

PRACTICE

E. Of the elements Ga, Br, and Ca, which has the highest electronegativity? Explain in terms of periodic trends.

_____

_____

F. Consider five hypothetical main-group elements, with the outer electron configurations indicated below.

E: $2s^2 2p^5$ G: $4d^{10} 5s^2 5p^5$ J: $2s^2 2p^2$

L: $5d^{10} 6s^2 6p^5$ M: $2s^2 2p^4$

a. Which element(s) contain seven valence electrons? _____

b. Which element has the highest electronegativity? _____

The properties of *d*-block metals do not vary much.

The properties of *d*- and *f*-block elements vary less and with less regularity than those of main group elements. Electrons in the outermost *d* sublevel are responsible for many of the characteristics of *d*-block elements.

Atomic Radii

The graph Atomic Radius vs. Atomic Number in this section shows that, moving from left to right across a period, atomic radii for *d*-block elements generally decrease. This is the same trend as for main-group elements. However, the graph also shows that the radii dip to a low and then increase slightly at the right end of the *d* block. This rise results from the increased repulsion of electrons within the *d* sublevel.

In the sixth period, *d*-block elements have similar atomic radii to the fifth period elements above them. The addition of 32 protons in the nucleus pulls the electron cloud closer to the atom's center despite the extra electron shell that is filled.

Iron is often found in iron ore in compounds formed from 2+ ions.

Ionization Energy

The Periodic Table of Ionization Energies in this section shows that in the main-group elements, IE_1 increases moving across a period and decreases moving down a group. In the *d*-block, IE_1 increases when moving down a group. Because the *d* sublevels are incomplete in these elements, the outermost electrons are shielded less from the positively charged nucleus.

Ion Formation and Ionic Radii

In atoms of the *d*- and *f*-block elements, electrons in the outermost energy level are removed first. The *s* sublevel electrons are removed even though this sublevel is filled before the outermost *f* and *d* sublevels. As a result, most *d*-block elements commonly form 2+ ions. One exception is Group 3 elements, which also lose their *d*-sublevel electron and form 3+ ions. Since the ions in the *d* block typically have the same 2+ charge, their ionic radii decrease across a period.

Electronegativity

The *d*- and *f*-block elements all have relatively low electronegativities. The only elements with lower electronegativities are the reactive metals in Groups 1 and 2. The electronegativity increases as atomic radii decrease.

READING CHECK

14. In general, which element will have a higher value for each quantity, a Group 3 element or a Group 12 element?

Atomic radius _____

Ionization energy _____

Ionic radius _____

Electronegativity _____

VOCABULARY

1. What is electron affinity? What signs are associated with electron affinities and what is the significance of each sign?

_____

_____

_____

REVIEW

2. State the general period and group trends among main-group elements with respect to each of the following properties:

   a. atomic radii _____

   _____

   b. first ionization energy _____

   _____

   c. electronegativity _____

   _____

3. For each main-group element, what is the relationship between its group number and the number of valence electrons that the group members have?

   _____

   _____

   _____

Critical Thinking

4. **RELATING IDEAS** Graph the general trends (left to right and top to bottom) in the second ionization energy (IE_2) of an element as a function of its atomic number (Z), over the range $Z = 1 - 20$. Label the minima and maxima on the graph with the appropriate element symbol.

Math Tutor   WRITING ELECTRON CONFIGURATIONS

The arrangement of elements in the periodic table reflects the arrangement of electrons in an atom. Each period begins with an atom that has an electron in a new energy level. Each period ends with an atom that has a filled set of *p* orbitals (with the exception of the first period).

To write the electron configuration of an element, you must fill the sublevels in order of increasing energy. If you follow the arrows in either of the two types of mnemonic devices shown, you will get the correct configurations for most elements. You also need to know how many electrons can exist in each sublevel, as shown in the following table.

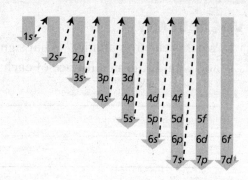

Sublevel	*s*	*p*	*d*	*f*
No. of orbitals	1	3	5	7
No. of electrons	2	6	10	14

Problem-Solving TIPS

- To write an electron configuration for an element, first find the atomic number of the element.
- Then, write the designation for a sublevel and the number of electrons that fill that sublevel to the top right of the designation.
- Continue adding filled sublevels to this list until the sum of top right numbers in the list exceeds or equals the atomic number. Adjust, if necessary, the last electron number so that the sum of the values exactly equals the atomic number.
- To write the noble-gas notation for an element, substitute the symbol of the noble gas in brackets for the first part of the electron configuration.

SAMPLE

Write the full electron configuration for phosphorus.

The atomic number for phosphorus is 15. The first four sublevels filled are $1s$, $2s$, $2p$, and $3s$. Filling these suborbitals results in an electron configuration of $1s^2 2s^2 2p^6 3s^2$, for a total of $2 + 2 + 6 + 2 = 12$ electrons.

Filling the next sublevel, $3p$, requires 6 more electrons. However, the atomic number of phosphorus is 15, so only $15 - 12 = 3$ electrons are necessary. Therefore, the electron configuration of phosphorus is $1s^2 2s^2 2p^6 3s^2 3p^3$.

Practice Problems: Chapter Review practice problems 8 and 11

1. Describe the contributions made by the following scientists to the development of the periodic table.

   a. Stanislao Cannizzaro _____

   _____

   b. Dmitri Mendeleev _____

   _____

   c. Henry Moseley _____

   _____

2. State the periodic law.

   _____

   _____

3. How do electron configurations within a group of elements compare?

   _____

   _____

4. Why are the noble gases relatively unreactive?

   _____

   _____

5. How do the properties of alkaline-earth metals compare with alkali metals?

   _____

   _____

6. What are valence electrons and where are they located?

   _____

   _____

7. For each group, indicate whether electrons are likely to be lost or gained to form compounds and give the typical number of electrons involved.

   a. Group 1 _____   **c.** Group 13 _____   **e.** Group 17 _____

   b. Group 2 _____   **d.** Group 16 _____   **f.** Group 18 _____

8. Write the noble-gas notation for the electron configuration of each of the following elements, and indicate the period in which each belongs.

a. lithium, Li   Configuration: _____   Period: _____

b. oxygen, O   Configuration: _____   Period: _____

c. copper, Cu   Configuration: _____   Period: _____

d. bromine, Br   Configuration: _____   Period: _____

9. Without looking at the periodic table, identify the period, block, and group in which the elements with the following electron configurations are located.

a. $[Ne]3s^2 3p^1$ Period: _____   Block: _____   Group: _____

b. $[Kr]4d^{10}5s^2 5p^2$ Period: _____   Block: _____   Group: _____

c. $[Xe]4f^{14}5d^{10}6s^2 6p^5$ Period: _____   Block: _____   Group: _____

10. Based on the information given below, give the group, period, block, and identity of each element described.

a. $[He]2s^2$ Group: _____   Period: _____   Block: _____   Identity: _____

b. $[Ne]3s^1$ Group: _____   Period: _____   Block: _____   Identity: _____

c. $[Kr]5s^2$ Group: _____   Period: _____   Block: _____   Identity: _____

d. $[Ar]3d^5 4s^1$ Group: _____   Period: _____   Block: _____   Identity: _____

11. Without looking at the periodic table, write the expected outer electron configuration for each of the following elements.

a. Group 7, fourth period _____

b. Group 3, fifth period _____

c. Group 12, sixth period _____

12. Complete the table below using the electron configurations.

Electron configuration	Complete before looking at the periodic table			Complete while looking at the periodic table		
	Period	Block	Group	Name	Type	Reactivity
a. $[Ne]3s^2 3p^1$						
b. $[Ar]3d^{10}4s^2 4p^6$						
c. $[Kr]4d^{10}5s^1$						
d. $[Xe]4f^1 5d^1 6s^2$						

13. Of cesium, Cs, hafnium, Hf, and gold, Au, which element has the smallest atomic radius? Explain your answer in terms of trends in the periodic table.

_____

_____

14. a. What is the difference between the first, second, and third ionization energies of an atom?

_____

_____

b. How do the values of successive ionization energies compare? Why?

_____

_____

15. Without looking at the electron affinity table, arrange the following elements in order of decreasing electron affinities: C, O, Li, Na, Rb, and F.

_____

16. a. Without looking at the ionization energy table, arrange these elements in order of decreasing first ionization energies: Li, O, C, K, Ne, and F.

_____

b. Which of the elements listed in (a) would you expect to have the

highest second ionization energy? Why? _____

_____

17. a. Which cation is least likely to form: Sr^{2+}, Al^{3+}, K^{2+}? _____

b. Which anion is least likely to form: I^-, Cl^-, O^{2-}? _____

18. Which element is the most electronegative among C, N, O, Br, and S? To which group does this element belong?

_____

19. The two ions K^+ and Ca^{2+} each have 18 electrons surrounding the nucleus. Which would you expect to have the smaller radius? Why?

_____

_____

Chemical Bonding

Review Previous Concepts

1. What are valance electrons?

_____

_____

_____

2. What quantity does the electronegativity of an atom represent?

_____

_____

_____

Introduction to Chemical Bonding

Nature favors arrangements in which potential energy is minimized. For example, a boulder is less likely to balance at the top of a hill than it is to roll to the bottom of a valley. The boulder at the top of the hill is not stable. Atoms are usually not stable when isolated. They usually combine to form more stable arrangements of matter.

KEY TERMS

chemical bond
ionic bonding
covalent bonding
nonpolar-covalent bond
polar
polar-covalent bond

Atoms become compounds by gaining, losing, or sharing electrons.

A **chemical bond** is a mutual electrical attraction between the nuclei and valence electrons of different atoms that binds the atoms together. When atoms form a chemical bond, their valence electrons are redistributed to make the atoms more stable. The way the electrons are redistributed determines the type of bond.

Chemical bonding that results from the electrical attraction between positive ions and negative ions is called **ionic bonding.** In a purely ionic bond, the metal atom gives up its electron or electrons to the nonmetal atom. In **covalent bonding,** a bond forms from the sharing of electron pairs between two atoms. In a purely covalent bond, the shared electrons are "owned" equally by the bonded atoms.

✓ READING CHECK

1. Why do atoms form chemical bonds?

_____

_____

_____

_____

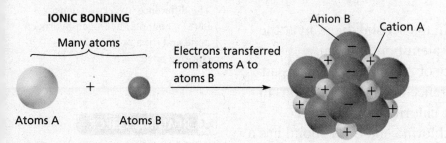

IONIC BONDING

Many atoms

Atoms A   +   Atoms B

Electrons transferred from atoms A to atoms B →

Anion B   Cation A

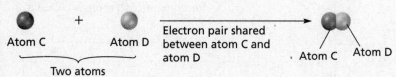

COVALENT BONDING

Atom C   +   Atom D

Electron pair shared between atom C and atom D →

Atom C   Atom D

Two atoms

In ionic bonding, many atoms transfer electrons. The atoms are then held together by the attraction of opposite charges. In covalent bonding, atoms share electrons and form independent molecules.

Ionic or Covalent?

Bonding between atoms of different elements is usually not purely ionic or purely covalent. It usually falls somewhere between the two extremes. The difference between the electronegativities of the two atoms determines the type of bond they form.

The first diagram at the right summarizes how the difference in electronegativity affects the percentage of the bond that is ionic in nature. If the difference in electronegativity of two atoms is 1.7 or greater, the bond is at least 50% ionic in nature, and the bond is considered an ionic bond.

The second diagram at the right shows that there are two types of covalent bonds. Bonding between two atoms of the same element is completely covalent, because the two atoms have the same electronegativity. For example, hydrogen is usually found in pairs of atoms that are bonded together covalently. The hydrogen-hydrogen bond is an example of a **nonpolar-covalent bond.** Any bond formed between atoms that have an electronegativity difference of 0.3 or less is considered nonpolar-covalent.

A nonpolar bond has an even distribution of charge. A bond that is **polar** has an uneven distribution of charge. The electrons are more strongly attracted to the more electronegative atom in a polar bond. A covalent bond in which the atoms have an uneven attraction for the electrons is called a **polar-covalent bond.** Bonds between atoms with a difference in electronegativities from 0.3 to 1.7 are considered polar-covalent bonds.

The hydrogen-chlorine bond in the second diagram at the right is an example of a polar-covalent bond. Because hydrogen has an electronegativity of 2.1 and chlorine has an electronegativity of 3.0, the difference is 0.9. The electrons in this bond tend to be closer to the chlorine atom than the hydrogen atom. As a result, the chlorine end of the bond has a partial negative charge, indicated by the symbol δ−. The hydrogen end of the bond has a partial positive charge, indicated by the symbol δ+.

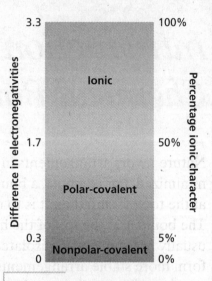

The electronegativity difference between two atoms determines the type of bond that forms.

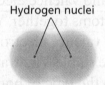

(a) Nonpolar-covalent bond

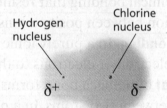

(b) Polar-covalent bond

The difference in electron density in (a) a nonpolar hydrogen-hydrogen bond and (b) a polar hydrogen-chlorine bond.

READING CHECK

2. A bond between two atoms in which the shared electron or electrons are equally likely to be found near each atom is called a

_____

SAMPLE PROBLEM

Use the electronegativity differences given in the chapter "The Periodic Law" and the first diagram on the previous page to classify bonding between sulfur, S, and the following elements: hydrogen, H; cesium, Cs; and chlorine, Cl. In each pair, which atom will be more negative?

SOLUTION

1 ANALYZE *Determine what information is given and unknown.*

> **Given:** electronegativity values for S, H, Cs, and Cl
> **Unknown:** bond types for S with H, Cs, and Cl

2 PLAN *Determine the information necessary to answer the questions.*

Look up the electronegativity values for each element. Find the difference between the electronegativities. Use the diagram on the previous page to determine the type of bond.

3 SOLVE *Determine the types of bonds from the given information.*

The electronegativities are 2.5 for S, 2.1 for H, 0.7 for Cs, and 3.0 for Cl. In each pair, the atom with the greater electronegativity will be the more negative atom.

Bonded atoms	Electronegativity difference	Bond type	More-negative atom
S and H	2.5 − 2.1 = 0.4	polar-covalent	S
S and Cs	2.5 − 0.7 = 1.8	ionic	S
S and Cl	3.0 − 2.5 = 0.5	polar-covalent	Cl

4 CHECK YOUR WORK *Determine if the answers make sense.*

Cs is a metal, so it is likely to form ionic compounds with a nonmetal. H and Cl are more likely to form covalent bonds.

PRACTICE *Complete the following table.*

Bonded atoms	Electronegativity difference	Bond type	More-negative atom
A. Cl and Ca			
B. Cl and O			
C. Cl and Br			

VOCABULARY

1. What is the main distinction between ionic and covalent bonding?

_____

_____

_____

REVIEW

2. How is electronegativity used in determining the ionic or covalent character of the bonding between two elements?

_____

_____

_____

_____

3. What type of bonding would be expected between the following pairs of atoms?

a. Li and F _____

b. Cu and S _____

c. I and Br _____

4. List the three pairs of atoms from Question 3 in order of increasing ionic character of the bonding between them.

_____

Critical Thinking

5. **INTERPRETING CONCEPTS** Compare the following two pairs of atoms: Cu and Cl; I and Cl.

a. Which pair would have a bond with a greater ionic character? _____

b. In which pair would Cl have the greater negative charge? _____

6. **INFERRING RELATIONSHIPS** The isolated K atom is larger than the isolated Br atom.

a. What type of bond is expected between K and Br? _____

b. Which ion in the compound KBr is larger? _____

SECTION 6.2

Covalent Bonding and Molecular Compounds

Most of the chemicals inside living things and produced by living things are molecules. A **molecule** is a neutral group of atoms that are held together by covalent bonds. A molecule formed by polar-covalent bonds is still considered neutral because the sum of the partial charges on either end of the bond is zero.

A **molecular compound** is any chemical compound whose simplest units are molecules. In other words, a single molecule of any molecular compound is an individual unit that is capable of existing on its own. A molecule may contain two or more atoms of the same element, as in oxygen. Or, a molecule may consist of two or more atoms of different elements, as in water and sugar.

The composition of a compound is given by its chemical formula. A **chemical formula** indicates the relative number of each type of atom necessary to form a single unit of a compound. For compounds that form molecules, the **molecular formula** shows the types and number of atoms necessary to form a single molecule.

The molecular formula for water, H_2O, shows that two hydrogen atoms and one oxygen atom are necessary to form a molecule of water. A molecule of oxygen, O_2, contains two atoms of oxygen and is an example of a diatomic molecule. A *diatomic molecule* contains only two atoms.

KEY TERMS

molecule
molecular compound
chemical formula
molecular formula
bond energy
electron-dot notation
Lewis structure
structural formula
single bond
multiple bond
resonance

✓ READING CHECK

1. The formula for sucrose, $C_{12}H_{22}O_{11}$, shows that a sucrose molecule contains

_____ carbon atoms,

_____ hydrogen atoms, and

_____ oxygen atoms.

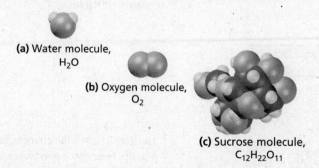

(a) Water molecule, H_2O

(b) Oxygen molecule, O_2

(c) Sucrose molecule, $C_{12}H_{22}O_{11}$

Three examples of molecular compounds are shown: (a) water, (b) oxygen, and (c) sucrose.

Covalent bonds form from shared electrons.

In Section 1, you learned that nature favors chemical bonding because atoms have lower potential energy when they are bonded than they have alone. Examining the formation of a hydrogen-hydrogen bond can illustrate the point.

The potential energy of two hydrogen atoms changes as the strengths of the attractive and repulsive forces between the atoms change. The electrons in each hydrogen atom repel each other, as do the protons. This repulsion corresponds to an increase in potential energy, similar to two boulders being pushed up opposite sides of a valley. On the other hand, the proton in one atom is attracted to the electron in the other atom, and vice versa. This corresponds to a decrease in potential energy, similar to two boulders falling down the sides of a valley toward each other.

The graph below shows the total potential energy of the two hydrogen atoms versus the distance between the atoms. Consider four stages shown on the graph.

(a) The two atoms do not influence each other. At this point, the potential energy is defined as zero.

(b) As the atoms approach each other, the electron-proton attractions are stronger than the electron-electron and proton-proton repulsions. The net potential energy decreases.

(c) When the atoms are 75 pm apart, the strengths of the attractions and repulsions are balanced. This is the point at which potential energy is at a minimum and a stable hydrogen molecule forms.

(d) If the atoms got any closer together, the repulsive forces would be stronger than the attractive forces, and would force them apart again.

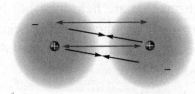

Both nuclei repel each other, as do both electron clouds.

→←The nucleus of one atom attracts the electron cloud of the other atom, and vice versa.

READING CHECK

2. Two atoms form a stable chemical bond when their potential energies are _____ than their potential energies as separate particles.

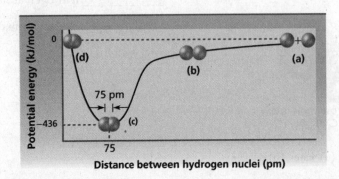

Distance between hydrogen nuclei (pm)

The graph shows the changes in potential energy of two atoms of hydrogen versus the distance between the two atoms.

Bond lengths and energy vary from molecule to molecule.

A stable covalent bond forms when the attractive forces between two atoms balance the repulsive forces between two atoms. In a hydrogen-hydrogen bond, the electrons of each hydrogen atom are shared between the two nuclei. The molecule's electrons can be pictured as occupying overlapping orbitals, moving freely in either orbital.

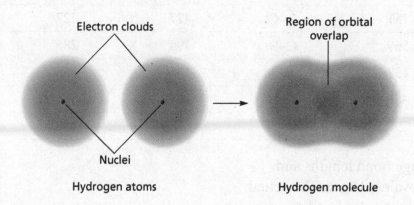

Electron clouds

Nuclei

Hydrogen atoms

Region of orbital overlap

Hydrogen molecule

The orbitals of two hydrogen atoms overlap when the atoms bond. Both electrons feel the attraction from both nuclei. As a result, the electron density between the nuclei increases.

The bonded atoms can vibrate, but they remain bonded as long as their potential energy remains close to the minimum value. *Bond length* is the average distance between two bonded atoms. The bond length for a hydrogen-hydrogen bond is 75 pm.

Energy in a closed system is always conserved. Therefore, when two atoms form a bond and their potential energy decreases by a certain amount, an equal amount of energy must be released by the atoms. The graph on the previous page shows that the hydrogen atoms must release 436 kJ/mol of energy when forming a bond. In other words, 436 kJ of energy are released when a mole of hydrogen molecules forms.

The same amount of energy that is released when a bond forms is required to force the atoms apart. **Bond energy** is the energy required to break a chemical bond and form neutral isolated atoms. The bond energy for a hydrogen-hydrogen bond is 436 kJ/mol. In other words, it takes 436 kJ of energy to break the bonds in a mole of hydrogen molecules.

READING CHECK

3. Define the following terms in your own words.

bond: _____

_____

_____

energy: _____

_____

_____

4. Consider a system consisting of one diatomic molecule. When the chemical bond is broken, is energy put into the system or is energy taken out of the system?

_____

Bond Lengths and Bond Energies for Selected Covalent Bonds

Bond	Average bond length (pm)	Average bond energy (kJ/mol)	Bond	Average bond length (pm)	Average bond energy (kJ/mol)
H–H	75	436	C–C	154	346
F–F	142	159	C–N	147	305
Cl–Cl	199	243	C–O	143	358
Br–Br	229	193	C–H	109	418
I–I	266	151	C–Cl	177	327
H–F	92	569	C–Br	194	285
H–Cl	127	432	N–N	145	163
H–Br	141	366	N–H	101	386
H–I	161	299	O–H	96	459

The table above shows the average bond lengths and bond energies for some common covalent bonds. The actual bond length and bond energy for a particular bond can vary depending on the influence of the other atoms in a molecule.

Atoms tend to form bonds to follow the octet rule.

As the diagram at the right shows, the overlapping orbital in a hydrogen molecule contains two electrons. This is the same electron configuration as in a helium atom, which is a stable noble gas. Each hydrogen atom in the molecule is said to have a noble-gas configuration, since its outermost electron shell (the $n = 1$ shell) is completely filled by the shared electrons.

Usually, the outermost electron shell of an atom in a noble-gas configuration contains 8 electrons, with 2 in the outermost s sublevel and 6 in the outermost p sublevel. Atoms tend to form bonds such that they obtain noble-gas configurations. Thus, the octet rule states that chemical compounds form so that each atom, by gaining, losing, or sharing electrons, has an octet of electrons in its highest-occupied energy level.

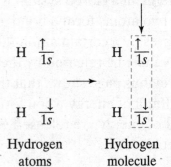

Bonding electron pair in overlapping orbitals

By sharing electrons in overlapping orbitals, each hydrogen atom in a hydrogen molecule experiences the stable effect of a stable $1s^2$ configuration.

Critical Thinking

5. **Compare** What feature do atoms in a noble gas and atoms in a molecule have in common?

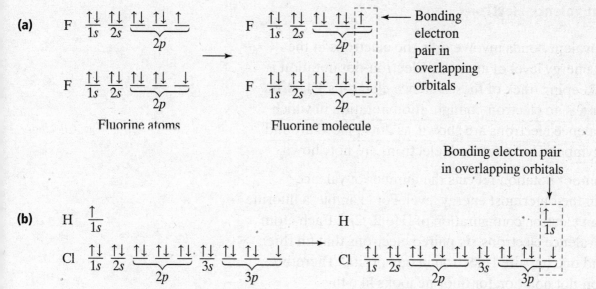

(a)

F $\uparrow\downarrow$ $\uparrow\downarrow$ $\uparrow\downarrow$ $\uparrow\downarrow$ $\uparrow$
   $1s$ $2s$ $\underbrace{\qquad\qquad}_{2p}$

F $\uparrow\downarrow$ $\uparrow\downarrow$ $\uparrow\downarrow$ $\uparrow\downarrow$ $\downarrow$
   $1s$ $2s$ $\underbrace{\qquad\qquad}_{2p}$

Fluorine atoms

$\longrightarrow$

F $\uparrow\downarrow$ $\uparrow\downarrow$ $\uparrow\downarrow$ $\uparrow\downarrow$ $\boxed{\uparrow}$
   $1s$ $2s$ $\underbrace{\qquad\qquad}_{2p}$

F $\uparrow\downarrow$ $\uparrow\downarrow$ $\uparrow\downarrow$ $\uparrow\downarrow$ $\boxed{\downarrow}$
   $1s$ $2s$ $\underbrace{\qquad\qquad}_{2p}$

Fluorine molecule

← Bonding electron pair in overlapping orbitals

Bonding electron pair in overlapping orbitals

(b)

H $\uparrow$
   $1s$

Cl $\uparrow\downarrow$ $\uparrow\downarrow$ $\uparrow\downarrow$ $\uparrow\downarrow$ $\uparrow\downarrow$ $\uparrow\downarrow$ $\uparrow\downarrow$ $\uparrow\downarrow$ $\downarrow$
    $1s$ $2s$ $\underbrace{\qquad}_{2p}$ $3s$ $\underbrace{\qquad}_{3p}$

Hydrogen and chlorine atoms

$\longrightarrow$

H $\boxed{\uparrow}$
   $1s$

Cl $\uparrow\downarrow$ $\uparrow\downarrow$ $\uparrow\downarrow$ $\uparrow\downarrow$ $\uparrow\downarrow$ $\uparrow\downarrow$ $\uparrow\downarrow$ $\uparrow\downarrow$ $\boxed{\downarrow}$
    $1s$ $2s$ $\underbrace{\qquad}_{2p}$ $3s$ $\underbrace{\qquad}_{3p}$

Hydrogen chloride molecule

One example of a stable molecule that follows the octet rule is the fluorine molecule shown above. A fluorine atom has seven electrons in its outermost energy level, including six paired electrons and one unpaired electron in a $2p$ orbital. When two fluorine atoms bond, they share the unpaired electrons. The result is that each atom essentially has an octet of electrons at the $n = 2$ level.

Another example is an HCl molecule. The chlorine atom achieves an octet by sharing an electron with a hydrogen atom. The chlorine essentially gets an eighth electron to give it an octet at the $n = 3$ level. The hydrogen atom receives a second electron to achieve helium's stable noble-gas configuration.

> (a) Both atoms in a fluorine molecule experience neon's stable $1s^2 2s^2 2p^6$ configuration. (b) Both atoms in an HCl molecule experience stable configurations.

Exceptions to the Octet Rule

Most main-group elements tend to form covalent bonds according to the octet rule. Hydrogen is one exception, as its atoms only form bonds with two electrons. Boron is another exception. Boron has three valence electrons, $[He]2s^2 2p^1$. It forms bonds by sharing all three of its electrons to form three electron pairs, such as in the molecule BF_3.

Other atoms have more than eight electrons in their outermost energy level when they combine with highly electronegative elements such as fluorine, oxygen, and chlorine. In these cases of expanded valence, bonding involves electrons in the d orbitals as well as the s and p orbitals. PF_5 and SF_6 are two examples of compounds with expanded valence.

🔎 **Critical Thinking**

6. Apply A chlorine atom has the electron configuration $[Ne]3s^2 3p^5$. Explain how atoms in a molecule of chlorine (Cl_2) follow the octet rule.

_____

_____

_____

_____

_____

Dots placed around an element's symbol can represent valence electrons.

Usually, covalent bonds involve only the electrons in the outermost energy level of an atom. Electron-dot notation is useful for keeping track of these valence electrons. **Electron-dot notation** is an electron-configuration notation in which only the valence electrons are shown, as dots placed around a chemical symbol. The inner-shell electrons are not shown.

Electron-dot notation reflects the number of valence electrons in the outermost energy level. For example, a fluorine atom has an electron configuration of $[He]2s^2 2p^5$. Each atom has seven valence electrons, six paired electrons that fill three orbitals and one unpaired electron in one orbital. Therefore, the electron-dot notation for fluorine looks like this.

$$:\ddot{F}:$$

The table below shows the electron-dot notation used in this book for the eight possible numbers of valence electrons in an atom.

Number of valence electrons	Electron-dot notation	Example
1	X·	Na·
2	·X·	·Mg·
3	·X·	·B·
4	·X·	·C·
5	·X:	·N:
6	:X·	:O·
7	:X:	:F:
8	:X:	:Ne:

Examples of electron-dot notation for atoms of elements with 1 to 8 valence electrons.

PRACTICE

Write the electron-dot notation for the following elements.

A. hydrogen _____

B. nitrogen _____

C. silicon _____

D. selenium _____

Electron-dot notations can represent compounds.

Electron-dot notation can also be used to represent molecules. A **Lewis structure,** named after American chemist G. N. Lewis, is any formula in which

- atomic symbols represent nuclei and inner-shell electrons
- dot-pairs or dashes between two atomic symbols represent electron pairs in covalent bonds
- dots adjacent to only one atomic symbol represent unshared electrons

For example, a hydrogen molecule, H_2, is represented by combining the notations of two individual hydrogen atoms. The pair of dots between the hydrogen symbols represents the shared electron pair in a hydrogen-hydrogen bond.

$$H \colon H$$

For a molecule of fluorine, F_2, the Lewis structure also includes the three *unshared pairs* of electrons in each fluorine atom. These pairs that are not shared in bonds are also called *lone pairs*.

$$\colon \ddot{F} \colon \ddot{F} \colon$$

Another way to write the Lewis structures of hydrogen molecules and fluorine molecules is to represent the shared pair of electrons by a long dash, as shown below.

$$H\!-\!H \quad \colon \ddot{F}\!-\!\ddot{F} \colon$$

Yet another way to write Lewis structures is only to use dashes to show the shared electrons. A **structural formula** indicates the kind, number, arrangement, and bonds, but not the unshared electrons of the atoms in a molecule. For example, F–F and H–Cl are structural formulas.

The sample problem on the next page shows the basic steps that can be used to draw the structural formula of many molecules. The single dash between two atomic symbols represents a **single bond.** A single bond is a covalent bond in which one pair of electrons is shared between two atoms.

> ✓ READING CHECK
>
> **7.** How is electron-dot notation related to Lewis structures?
>
> _____
>
> _____
>
> _____
>
> _____
>
> _____

Draw the Lewis structure of iodomethane, CH_3I.

SOLVE	
STEP 1	Determine the type and number of atoms in the molecule.
	Iodomethane has one C atom, three H atoms, and one I atom.
STEP 2	Write the electron-dot notation for each type of atom.
	C, I, and H atoms have 4, 7, and 1 valence electron, respectively.

$$\cdot \overset{\displaystyle\cdot}{C}\cdot \qquad :\overset{\displaystyle\cdot\cdot}{\underset{\displaystyle\cdot\cdot}{I}}: \qquad H\cdot$$

STEP 3	Determine the number of electrons available for bonding.

$$\text{4 electrons in each C atom} \rightarrow 1 \times 4e^- = 4e^-$$
$$\text{1 electron in each H atom} \rightarrow 3 \times 1e^- = 3e^-$$
$$\text{7 electrons in each I atom} \rightarrow 1 \times 7e^- = \underline{7e^-}$$
$$14e^-$$

STEP 4	Arrange the atoms to form a skeleton structure for the molecule. If carbon is present, make it the central atom. Otherwise, the most electronegative element besides hydrogen is central. Then connect the atoms with electron-pair bonds.

$$\begin{array}{c} H \\ H:\overset{\displaystyle H}{\underset{\displaystyle H}{C}}:I \\ H \end{array}$$

STEP 5	Add unshared pairs of electrons to each nonmetal atom (besides hydrogen) so that each is surrounded by an octet.

$$\begin{array}{c} H \\ H:\overset{\displaystyle H}{\underset{\displaystyle H}{C}}:\overset{\displaystyle\cdot\cdot}{\underset{\displaystyle\cdot\cdot}{I}}: \end{array} \quad \text{or} \quad \begin{array}{c} H \\ | \\ H-C-\overset{\displaystyle\cdot\cdot}{\underset{\displaystyle\cdot\cdot}{I}}: \\ | \\ H \end{array}$$

STEP 6	Count the electrons in the structure to be sure it shows the same number of available valence electrons as calculated in Step 3.
	The four covalent bonds add up to eight electrons, and the six unpaired electrons make a total of 14 electrons. This matches the number of available valence electrons.

E. Draw the Lewis structure of ammonia, NH_3.

One molecule has ☐ N atom(s) and ☐ H atom(s).

Each N atom has ☐ valence electrons.

Each H atom has ☐ valence electrons.

There are ☐ valence electrons available for bonding.

Use the space at the right to arrange the N and H atoms, using dots to represent electron pairs and lone pairs. Make sure the final result contains the same number of dots as there are valence electrons available for bonding.

F. Draw the Lewis structure of phosphorus trifluoride, PF_3.

One molecule has ☐ P atom(s) and ☐ F atom(s).

Each P atom has ☐ valence electrons.

Each F atom has ☐ valence electrons.

There are ☐ valence electrons available for bonding.

Use the space at the right to arrange the P and F atoms, using dots to represent electron pairs and lone pairs. Make sure the final result contains the same number of dots as there are valence electrons available for bonding.

G. Draw the Lewis structure for hydrogen sulfide, H_2S.

H. Draw the Lewis structure for silane, SiH_4.

Some atoms can share multiple pairs of electrons.

Atoms of some elements, especially carbon, nitrogen, and oxygen, can share more than one electron pair. A double covalent bond, or simply a *double bond*, is a covalent bond in which two pairs of electrons are shared between two atoms. A double bond is either shown by two side-by-side pairs of dots or by two parallel dashes. For example, in ethane, C_2H_4, two electron pairs are shared at the same time by two carbon atoms.

$$
\begin{array}{ccc}
\text{H} \quad\quad \text{H} & & \text{H} \quad\quad \text{H} \\
\;\;\diagdown\text{C::C}\diagup & \text{or} & \;\;\diagdown\text{C=C}\diagup \\
\text{H} \quad\quad \text{H} & & \text{H} \quad\quad \text{H}
\end{array}
$$

A triple covalent bond, or *triple bond*, is a covalent bond in which three pairs of electrons are shared between two atoms. A triple bond is either shown by three side-by-side pairs of dots or by three parallel dashes. For example, nitrogen normally exists as a diatomic molecule. The nitrogen atom has three unpaired electrons in its $2p$ orbitals. These unpaired electrons form an octet when two nitrogen atoms bond.

$$:\text{N}:::\text{N}: \quad\text{ or }\quad \text{N}\equiv\text{N}$$

Carbon can also form compounds with triple bonds. For example, ethyne, C_2H_2, contains a carbon-carbon triple bond.

$$\text{H}:\text{C}:::\text{C}:\text{H} \quad\text{ or }\quad \text{H}-\text{C}\equiv\text{C}-\text{H}$$

Double bonds and triple bonds are also referred to as multiple covalent bonds, or **multiple bonds.** In general, double bonds are shorter and have greater bond energies than single bonds. Triple bonds are even stronger and shorter. The table on the top of the next page compares single, double, and triple bonds.

It is important to remember that multiple bonds are possible when writing Lewis structures for molecules that contain carbon, nitrogen, or oxygen. A hydrogen atom, on the other hand, can only form single bonds.

🔍 Critical Thinking

8. Infer Why can an oxygen atom not form a triple bond?

Nitrogen molecule

In a molecule of nitrogen, N_2, each nitrogen atom is surrounded by an octet that includes one unshared pair and six shared electrons.

TIP If you are making a Lewis structure of a molecule, and it does not seem that there are enough electrons available to form complete octets, this often indicates that a double or triple bond is present.

Bond Lengths and Bond Energies for Single and Multiple Covalent Bonds

Bond	Average bond length (pm)	Average bond energy (kJ/mol)	Bond	Average bond length (pm)	Average bond energy (kJ/mol)
C–C	154	346	C–O	143	358
C=C	134	612	C=O	120	732
C≡C	120	835	C≡O	113	1072
C–N	147	305	N–N	145	163
C=N	132	615	N=N	125	418
C≡N	116	887	N≡N	110	945

Resonance structures show hybrid bonds.

Some molecules cannot be represented by a single Lewis structure. For example, ozone, O_3, can be represented by the two structures below. Each structure indicates that an ozone molecule includes one single bond and one double bond.

$$\ddot{O}=\ddot{O}-\ddot{O}\colon \quad \text{or} \quad \colon\ddot{O}-\ddot{O}=\ddot{O}$$

At one time, scientists hypothesized that ozone constantly switched between each structure. However, experiments have shown that the two oxygen-oxygen bonds are identical, not distinct as shown in the diagrams. Therefore, scientists now say that ozone has a single structure that is the average of the two structures above. The structures are referred to as *resonance structures*, or *resonance hybrids*.

In general, **resonance** refers to bonding in molecules or ions that cannot be represented by a single Lewis structure. To indicate resonance, a double arrow is placed between a molecule's resonance structures.

$$\ddot{O}=\ddot{O}-\ddot{O}\colon \quad \longleftrightarrow \quad \colon\ddot{O}-\ddot{O}=\ddot{O}$$

Some compounds are networks of bonded atoms.

All of the covalent molecules discussed so far have been molecular. However, there are other covalently bonded compounds that do not contain individual molecules, but are three-dimensional networks of bonded atoms. These covalently bonded networks will be discussed in the chapter "States of Matter."

✓ READING CHECK

9. Why can ozone not be represented by the structure O=O–O alone?

_____

_____

_____

_____

_____

Draw the Lewis structure for methanol, CH_2O.

SOLVE

STEP 1   *Determine the type and number of atoms in the molecule.*

Methanol has one C atom, two Ḣ atoms, and one O atom.

STEP 2   *Write the electron-dot notation for each type of atom.*

C, O, and H atoms have 4, 6, and
1 valence electron respectively.   ·Ċ·   :Ö: H·

STEP 3   *Determine the number of electrons available for bonding.*

$$1 \times 4e^- + 2 \times 1e^- + 1 \times 6e^- = 12e^-$$

STEP 4   *Arrange the atoms to form a skeleton structure for the molecule.*
Then connect the atoms with electron-pair bonds.

H
H:Ċ:O

STEP 5   *Add unshared pairs of electrons to each nonmetal atom*
(besides hydrogen) so that each is surrounded by an octet.

H
H:Ċ:Ö:

STEP 6   *Count the electrons in the structure to make sure the structure*
shows the sum of the available valence electrons calculated. If
it does not, subtract the extra electrons and change lone pairs
to shared pairs until each atom is surrounded by an octet.

Delete a lone pair from the O atom to get
12 electrons. Move the C lone pair so that
it is shared with the O atom.

    H   H
H:Ċ::Ö   or   H—C=Ö:

PRACTICE   *Draw the Lewis structure for each molecule.*

I. carbon dioxide, CO_2

J. hydrogen cyanide, HCN

VOCABULARY

1. Define the following.

a. bond length _____

_____

b. bond energy _____

_____

REVIEW

2. State the octet rule.

_____

_____

3. How many pairs of electrons are shared in the following types of covalent bonds?

a. a single bond _____

b. a double bond _____

c. a triple bond _____

4. Draw the Lewis structures for the following molecules.

a. CH_3Br

c. $SiCl_4$

b. C_2HCl

d. OF_2

Critical Thinking

5. APPLYING MODELS Compare the molecules H_2NNH_2 and HNNH. Which molecule has the stronger N–N bond?

SECTION 6.3

Ionic Bonding and Ionic Compounds

In Section 2, you learned about compounds that form covalent bonds. Most of the rocks and minerals on Earth are held together by another type of bond called an ionic bond. Compounds that are held together in this way are called ionic compounds.

An **ionic compound** is composed of positive and negative ions that are combined so that the amount of positive and negative charge is equal. One example of an ionic compound is table salt, which is also called sodium chloride. A sodium ion, Na^+, has a charge of 1+. A chloride ion, Cl^-, has a charge of 1−. Equal numbers of Na^+ and Cl^- ions attract each other to form a compound with a net charge of zero.

Most ionic compounds exist as crystalline solids, such as the cubes of sodium chloride shown at the right. A crystal of any ionic compound is a three-dimensional network of positive and negative ions that are all attracted to each other. Therefore, unlike a molecular compound, an ionic compound is not composed of independent units of a small number of atoms.

A **formula unit** is the simplest collection of atoms from which an ionic compound's formula can be established. It is the smallest number of atoms necessary to form a compound with zero charge. For sodium chloride, a formula unit is one sodium cation and one chloride anion. Therefore, the chemical formula of sodium chloride is NaCl.

Another example of an ionic compound is calcium fluoride. A calcium ion, Ca^{2+}, has a charge of 2+. A fluoride ion, F^-, has a charge of 1−. Two fluoride anions are required to balance the charge of one calcium cation. Therefore, the chemical formula for calcium fluoride is CaF_2.

KEY TERMS

ionic compound
formula unit

lattice energy
polyatomic ion

Sodium chloride, NaCl, is a crystalline solid.

TIP The name of an anion formed from a single ion ends with *-ide*. For example, a chloride ion forms from chlorine and an oxide ion forms from oxygen.

☑ READING CHECK

1. What is the difference between a formula unit for an ionic compound and a molecular formula for a molecule?

_____

_____

Ionic bonds form from attractions between positive and negative ions.

Electron-dot notation can be used to demonstrate the process of ionic bond formation. For example, consider a sodium atom and a chlorine atom. The sodium atom has one valence electron and the chlorine atom has seven valence electrons.

Alkali metals, such as sodium, readily lose their one valence electron to form a cation. Halogens, such as chlorine, readily gain a valence electron to form an anion. The two oppositely charged particles attract each other to form one formula unit of sodium chloride. The cations and anions all have noble-gas configurations.

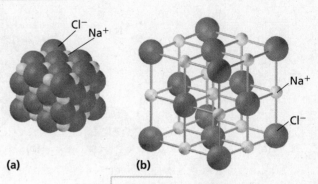

(a)   (b)

Two models of NaCl are shown:
(a) one that shows the actual arrangement and (b) one that has expanded to clarify the structure.

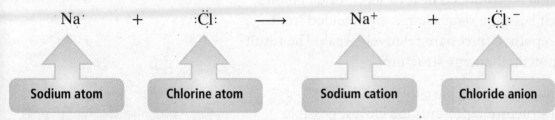

| Sodium atom | Chlorine atom | Sodium cation | Chloride anion |

Critical Thinking

2. **Identify** The equation below represents the formation of the formula unit CaF_2. Label the equation with the name of each particle.

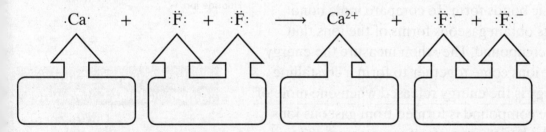

Characteristics of Ionic Bonding

Recall that nature favors arrangements with a minimum of potential energy. In an ionic crystal, ions minimize potential energy by forming an orderly arrangement called a *crystal lattice*. The distances between ions and the shape of the arrangement represent a balance between many forces. The forces include cation-anion and electron-proton attractive forces. They also include cation-cation, anion-anion, electron-electron, and proton-proton repulsive forces. A crystal's orderly structure balances all of these forces.

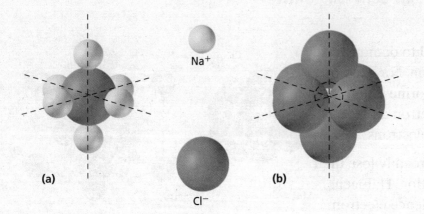

(a)

Na+

Cl−

(b)

Each anion or cation is surrounded by six particles to which it is attracted.

Within the crystal lattice of sodium chloride, the six particles closest to each chloride anion are the six sodium cations to which the anion is attracted. At the same time, each sodium cation is positioned next to six chloride anions. Because ions that have the same charge are shielded from each other, the repulsive forces are relatively weak. The result is a stable, low-potential-energy structure.

Different ionic compounds have different ionic structures. Each structure represents the closest possible packing in which positive and negative charges of the particles are balanced. In a calcium fluoride, CaF_2, crystal, each calcium cation is surrounded by eight fluoride anions. Each fluoride anion is surrounded by four calcium cations.

Just as in the formation of covalent bonds, energy is released when ionic bonds form. To compare ionic bond strengths, scientists obtain gaseous forms of the ions that make up an ionic compound. They then measure the energy released when the ions come together to form a crystalline solid. **Lattice energy** is the energy released when one mole of an ionic crystalline compound is formed from gaseous ions. The table shows the lattice energies of some common ionic compounds. The lattice energies are negative because energy is released when the compounds form.

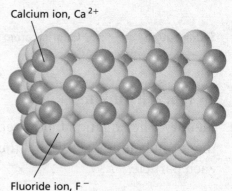

Calcium ion, Ca²⁺

Fluoride ion, F⁻

Lattice Energies of Some Common Ionic Compounds	
Compound	Lattice energy (KJ/mol)
NaCl	−787.5
NaBr	−751.4
CaF_2	−2634.7
LiCl	−861.3
LiF	−1032
MgO	−3760
KCl	−715

✓ READING CHECK

3. Energy is _____ when an ionic compound forms because the potential energy of the particles _____.

Differences in attraction strength give ionic and molecular compounds different properties.

The ionic bonds between ions in ionic compounds are strong attractions between particles of positive and negative charge. The covalent bonds that hold the atoms together in a molecule are also strong. However, intermolecular forces, the attraction between different molecules in a compound, are much weaker than the attraction between formula units in ionic compounds. Because of this difference, ionic compounds and molecular compounds have different properties.

Melting Point The attraction between ions in an ionic solid is strong. However, because the attraction between molecules in a solid is relatively weak, solid molecular compounds melt at lower temperatures than ionic compounds.

Boiling Point Boiling points for molecular compounds are also at lower temperatures than for ionic compounds. Many molecular compounds are gases at room temperature.

Hardness Because of their strong ionic attractions, ionic compounds are hard when in solid form. Repulsive forces between ions of the same charge help to hold the shape of the lattice.

Deformation Ionic compounds are brittle, which means they tend to shatter instead of bend. This is because it is easier to break off a smaller lattice of ions, such as the crystal plane in the diagram, than it is to change the shape of a lattice. In contrast, solid molecular compounds can often be deformed without breaking, similar to the way a stick of butter can be deformed.

Electrical Conductivity Molecular compounds do not normally conduct electricity because the attraction between molecules is weak. When solid, ionic compounds also do not conduct electricity because the electrons in the crystal lattice are difficult to dislodge. However, when an ionic compound dissolves in water, the ions separate from each other and are surrounded by water molecules. These ions are then free to move around and conduct electric charge. So, dissolved ionic compounds are good conductors.

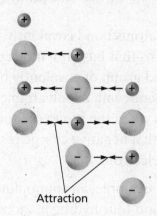

(a)

(b)

(a) The attraction between ions in a crystal causes layers of ions to resist motion. (b) Striking the crystal with enough force can shift a layer so that like-charged ions get too close to one another, causing the crystal to shatter.

✓ READING CHECK

4. The attractive force between formula units in an ionic compound is _____ than the attractive force between molecules in a molecular compound.

Multiple atoms can bond covalently to form a single ion.

Some atoms bond covalently with each other to form a group of atoms that has both molecular and ionic characteristics. A charged group of covalently bonded atoms is known as a **polyatomic ion.** A polyatomic ion with a positive charge results when the group of atoms loses electrons. A polyatomic ion with a negative charge results when the group of atoms gains electrons.

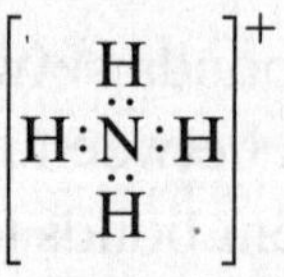

For example, an ammonium ion contains one nitrogen atom and four hydrogen atoms that are covalently bonded. The formula for an ammonium ion is NH_4^+. The electron in each hydrogen atom forms a shared pair with one of the electrons in the nitrogen atom's outermost energy level. However, a nitrogen atom has five valence electrons. The addition of four electrons from four hydrogen atoms would violate the octet rule. Therefore, the group of atoms loses an electron so that the nitrogen atom has a stable octet of electrons in its outermost energy level. The loss of an electron gives the ammonium ion a charge of 1+.

A few examples of polyatomic ions are shown at the right. The charge on each is determined by the number of valence electrons that were lost and gained in order for all of the atoms in the ion to satisfy the octet rule.

Polyatomic ions can combine with other ions to form ionic compounds. For example, an ammonium ion, NH_4^+, can combine with a chloride anion, Cl^-, to form the ionic compound ammonium chloride, NH_4Cl. Two sodium cations, Na^+, can combine with a sulfate ion to form sodium sulfate, Na_2SO_4. Two polyatomic ions can also combine to form ionic compounds, such as ammonium nitrate NH_4NO_3.

ammonium ion

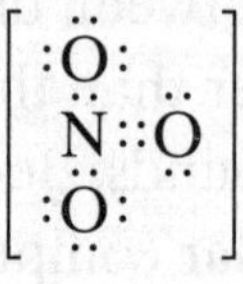

nitrate ion

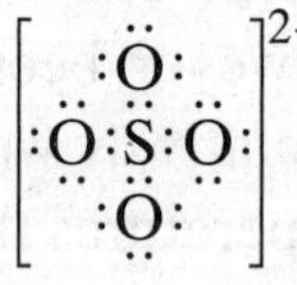

sulfate ion

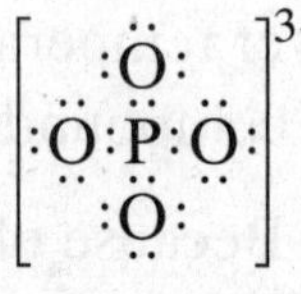

phosphate ion

The Lewis structures of four common polyatomic ions are shown.

PRACTICE

A. What is the Lewis structure of a carbonate ion, CO_3? What is the charge on a carbonate ion?

VOCABULARY

1. Distinguish between ionic and molecular compounds in terms of the basic units that each is composed of.

_____

_____

REVIEW

2. Give two examples of an ionic compound.

_____

3. Use electron-dot notation to demonstrate the formation of ionic compounds involving the following:

   a. Li and Cl

   ┌───┐
   │   │
   │   │
   │   │
   └───┘

   b. Ca and I

   ┌───┐
   │   │
   │   │
   │   │
   └───┘

4. Compound B has lower melting and boiling points than compound A. At the same temperature, compound B vaporizes faster than compound A. One of these compounds is ionic and the other is molecular.

   a. Which compound would you expect to be molecular? _____

   b. Which compound would you expect to be ionic? _____

   c. Explain the reasoning behind your answers to (a) and (b).

   _____

   _____

Critical Thinking

5. **ANALYZING DATA** The melting points for the compounds Li_2S, Rb_2S, and K_2S are 900°C, 530°C, and 840°C, respectively. List the three compounds in order of increasing lattice energy.

   _____

SECTION 6.4

Metallic Bonding

The previous sections discussed chemical bonds in ionic compounds and covalent compounds. Metals are held together by a different type of bond, resulting in some of the unique properties of metals.

Solid ionic compounds cannot conduct electricity. The electrons in an ionic crystal lattice are tightly bound to the atoms that make up the lattice. If the ionic compound melts, destroying the crystal structure, or if it is dissolved in water, then the ions can conduct electricity. The valence electrons in a molecular covalent bond are also locked inside bonds, making molecular compounds poor conductors.

One property shared by all metals is their ability to conduct electricity. A metal contains valence electrons that are mobile and able to move throughout the metal. They are much better conductors than molten ionic compounds.

Metal electrons move freely in empty, overlapping orbitals.

The outermost energy level of most metal atoms contains very few electrons. The s-block metals contain only one or two valence electrons. The highest p sublevel, which can hold up to six electrons, is empty. The d-block metals contain an empty p sublevel in their outermost energy level, and often empty d orbitals in the next lowest energy level.

Within a metal, the empty orbitals in the outer energy levels overlap. This overlapping of orbitals allows the outer electrons of metal atoms to move freely throughout the entire metal. The electrons do not belong to any specific atom, so they are called *delocalized* electrons.

Delocalized electrons in a metal form a *sea of electrons* around the metal's atoms. The atoms are packed together in a crystal lattice, similar to an ionic crystal lattice. The attraction between the metal atoms and the surrounding sea of electrons is called **metallic bonding.**

KEY TERMS

metallic bonding   ductility
malleability

Critical Thinking

1. Evaluate Which is most likely the better conductor of electricity: a block of solid sodium or a sodium chloride crystal? Explain.

_____

_____

_____

_____

_____

Solid sodium is arranged in a crystal lattice such that each atom is surrounded by eight other sodium atoms.

Metallic Properties

The sea of electrons in a metal allows electric current to flow freely. This makes metals good electrical conductors. Metallic bonding also causes metals to have other characteristic properties.

Thermal Conductivity The sea of electrons can transfer heat as well as carry electric current. Therefore, metals are good thermal conductors as well as electrical conductors.

Luster Metals are strong reflectors and absorbers of light. Metals contain many orbitals separated by extremely small energy differences, so they are able to absorb many frequencies of light. This excites the electrons, which rise to higher energy levels, then immediately fall back to lower energy levels and release light at similar frequencies. This re-radiated, or reflected, light gives metals their luster.

These stainless steel pans have a high luster. Stainless steel is a mixture of the metals iron and chromium.

Malleability Metals can be formed into many desired shapes. **Malleability** is the ability of a substance to be hammered into thin sheets. Metal is malleable because the layers in a metallic lattice can slide past each other without breaking bonds.

Ductility A property of metals related to malleability is ductility. **Ductility** is the ability of a substance to be pulled or drawn through a small opening to produce a wire.

Metallic Bond Strength

The strength of metallic bonds varies with the nuclear charge of the metal atoms and the number of electrons in a metal's sea of electrons. Both of these properties affect how much energy is required to vaporize a metal. A metal is vaporized when all of the metallic bonds are broken and the atoms form a gas. The energy required to vaporize a metal is called the metal's *enthalpy of vaporization*. Some enthalpies of vaporization are given in the table at the right.

✓ READING CHECK

2. Which property makes it possible to use a metal to make long, thin wires?

Enthalpies of Vaporization of Some Metals (kJ/mol)		
Period	Element	
Second	Li 147	Be 297	
Third	Na 97	Mg 128	Al 294
Fourth	K 77	Ca 155	Sc 333
Fifth	Rb 76	Sr 137	Y 365
Sixth	Cs 64	Ba 140	La 402

SECTION 6.4 REVIEW

VOCABULARY

1. a. What is metallic bonding?

b. How can the strength of metallic bonding be measured?

REVIEW

2. Describe the electron-sea model of metallic bonding.

3. What is the relationship between metallic bond strength and enthalpy of vaporization?

4. Explain why most metals are malleable and ductile but ionic crystals are not.

Critical Thinking

5. ORGANIZING IDEAS Explain why metals are good electrical conductors.

SECTION 6.5

Molecular Geometry

So far in this chapter you have learned about properties related to chemical bonding. The shape of a molecule also helps determine the properties of a molecular compound.

A covalent bond is either polar or nonpolar depending on the distribution of charge along the bond. The polarity of each bond contributes to the distribution of charge in a molecule. This *molecular polarity* influences the forces that act between molecules in liquids and solids.

Scientists have done many experiments to understand how the properties of a molecule are related to its shape. Scientists have developed two theories to explain these properties: VSEPR theory and hybridization models.

KEY TERMS

VSEPR theory
hybridization
hybrid orbitals
dipole
hydrogen bonding
London dispersion forces

Negative particles repel and move away from each other.

The abbreviation VSEPR stands for "Valence-Shell, Electron-Pair Repulsion." **VSEPR theory** states that the repulsion between sets of valence electrons surrounding an atom pushes these sets as far apart as possible.

Linear Molecules If a molecule contains two atoms, its shape must be linear. However, molecules that have more than two atoms can also be linear. Consider the molecule BeF_2. The Be atom has two valence electrons, each of which is shared with the only unpaired electron in an F atom. Beryllium does not follow the octet rule in this compound.

$$:\ddot{F}:Be:\ddot{F}:$$

According to VSEPR theory, the shared pairs will be as far apart as possible. The beryllium fluoride molecule has two shared pairs. For maximum distance between these shared pairs, the pairs are located on opposite sides of the beryllium atom. All three atoms lie along a straight line, and the molecule is linear, as shown in diagram (a) on the next page.

(a) Hydrogen, H_2

(b) Hydrogen chloride, HCl

All diatomic molecules are linear.

✓ READING CHECK

1. A molecule with two atoms will have a _____ shape.

Trigonal-Planar Molecules Some molecules contain three atoms bonded to a central atom, with no unshared pairs of electrons. Boron trifluoride is an example of such a molecule. The Lewis structure of boron trifluoride is given below.

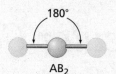

(a) Beryllium fluoride, BeF_2

:F̈:

:F̈:B:F̈:

VSEPR theory states that the three covalent bonds should be located as far apart as possible. The bonds must all be located in the same plane, because any three points lie in the same plane. The arrangement that spreads the bonds out as far as possible is the shape of an equilateral triangle, or a trigonal-planar shape. In this arrangement the bonds are each separated by the greatest angle possible, 120°.

(b) Boron trifluoride, BF_3

Tetrahedral Molecules Another possible shape occurs when a central atom is singly bonded to four other atoms. In a methane molecule, carbon is bonded to four hydrogen atoms.

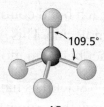

(c) Methane, CH_4

Three general molecular shapes: (a) AB_2 (linear), (b) AB_3 (trigonal-planar), and (c) AB_4 (tetrahedral).

H
|
H–C–H
|
H

In three-dimensions, the bonds point to the four corners of a tetrahedron. This allows each bond to be 109.5° distant from each of the other three covalent bonds. (If the bonds pointed at the four corners of a square, they would only be 90° apart.)

TIP A tetrahedron is a three-dimensional figure whose four sides are all triangles.

READING CHECK

2. What does VSEPR theory state about the orientation of the covalent bonds of a molecule?

_____

_____

VSEPR Theory and Unshared Electron Pairs
The first three molecular shapes discussed above involved molecules without any unshared electron pairs surrounding the central atom. VSEPR theory can also be applied to molecules whose central atoms have unshared pairs of electrons, or lone pairs.

Trigonal-Pyramidal Molecules Molecules of more than two atoms that only contain single bonds have central atoms surrounded by four pairs of electrons. In tetrahedral molecules, all four of these electron pairs are shared in covalent bonds. In other molecules, such as ammonia, NH_3, one pair of electrons is a lone pair.

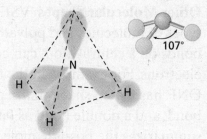

(a) Ammonia, NH_3

$$\text{H} \overset{..}{\text{N}} \text{H}$$
$$\text{H}$$

In a trigonal-pyramidal molecule, the four atoms occupy the four corners of a triangular pyramid. The sets of electrons surrounding the central atom point to the four corners of a tetrahedron.

VSEPR theory states that the four pairs of electrons, whether they are in bonds or not, should be separated as far as possible. The geometry that allows for the maximum separation is a tetrahedron. However, the shape of the molecule, as defined by the *position of the atoms only*, is not tetrahedral. As shown at the right, the shape of the molecule resembles a triangular pyramid.

Angular Molecules Water is similar to ammonia in that it has four pairs of electrons that surround a central atom. However, in water two of oxygen's electron pairs are shared with hydrogen atoms. The other two electron pairs are lone pairs.

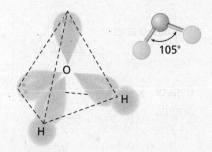

(b) Water, H_2O

$$\overset{..}{\overset{..}{\text{O}}}$$
$$\text{H} \qquad \text{H}$$

In an angular, or bent, molecule, the three atoms do not form a straight line. The sets of electrons surrounding the central atom point to the four corners of a tetrahedron.

Just as in tetrahedral molecules and trigonal-pyramidal molecules, the four pairs of electrons are oriented toward the four corners of a tetrahedron. However, there are only three atoms that make up the shape of the molecule as shown at the right. The molecule has an angular, or bent, shape. This shape is different from that of beryllium fluoride on the previous page, where the three atoms form a molecule with a linear shape.

In trigonal-pyramidal and angular molecules, the lone pairs repel the other sets of electrons more strongly. Therefore, the angle between the bonds is slightly less than the 109.5° angle between bonds in a tetrahedral molecule.

3. What defines the shape of a molecule: the shape of the electron pairs around the central atom or the shape of the atoms?

Other Molecular Shapes VSEPR theory also applies to other types of molecules and polyatomic ions. Double and triple bonds on a central atom can be treated like any other set of electrons. For example, in the table below, nitrosyl fluoride, ONF, has a bent shape that separates a lone pair, a single bond, and a double bond as far as possible. The table below summarizes the possible molecular shapes. Each shape is given a name and a type defined by the letters A, B, and E. A represents the central atom, B represents atoms bonded to the central atom, and E represents lone pairs.

READING CHECK

4. Use what you have learned in this section to complete the third and fourth columns on the table.

VSEPR Theory and Molecular Geometry

	Molecular shape	Atoms bonded to central atom	Lone pairs of electrons	Type of molecule	Formula example	Lewis structure
Linear		2	0	AB_2	BeF_2	$:\ddot{F}-Be-\ddot{F}:$
Trigonal-planar		3	0	AB_3	BF_3	$:\ddot{F}\diagdown \underset{:\ddot{F}:}{B} \diagup \ddot{F}:$
Bent or Angular		2	1	AB_2E	ONF	$\ddot{O} \diagdown \overset{\ddot{N}}{} \diagup \ddot{F}:$
Tetrahedral		4	0	AB_4	CH_4	$H-\underset{\underset{H}{\mid}}{\overset{\overset{H}{\mid}}{C}}-H$
Trigonal-pyramidal		3	1	AB_3E	NH_3	$\underset{H\ H\ H}{\overset{\ddot{N}}{\mid}}$
Bent or Angular		2	2	AB_2E_2	H_2O	$\underset{H\ \ \ \ H}{\overset{\ddot{O}}{\diagup\diagdown}}$
Trigonal-bipyramidal	90° 120°	5	0	AB_5	PCl_5	$:\ddot{Cl}-\underset{:\ddot{Cl}:}{\overset{}{P}}\diagdown\underset{\ddot{Cl}:}{\overset{\ddot{Cl}:}{}}$
Octahedral	90° 90° 90°	6	0	AB_6	SF_6	$:\ddot{F}\diagdown\underset{:\ddot{F}\ \ddot{F}:}{\overset{\overset{:\ddot{F}:}{\mid}}{S}}\diagup\ddot{F}:$

Use VSEPR theory to predict the shape of (a) a molecule of carbon dioxide, CO$_2$, and (b) a chlorate ion, ClO$_3^-$.

SOLUTION		
1	ANALYZE	*Determine what information is given and unknown.*
		Given: the molecular formula of each substance
		Unknown: the shape of each substance
2	PLAN	*Work out how the unknown information can be determined.*
		First, draw the Lewis structure for each substance. Then, use the electron pairs of the central atom to determine its shape.
3	SOLVE	*Determine the shape of each substance.*
		The Lewis structures of carbon dioxide and chlorate are:

$$\ddot{O}=C-\ddot{O} \qquad \left[\begin{array}{c} \ddot{Cl} \\ :\ddot{O} \quad \ddot{O}: \\ :\ddot{O}: \end{array} \right]^-$$

Carbon dioxide is an AB$_2$ molecule because the carbon atom has two sets of electron pairs. This means its shape is linear. Chlorate is an AB$_3$E molecule because the chlorine atom is surrounded by three single bonds and a lone pair. Its shape is trigonal-pyramidal.

4	CHECK YOUR WORK	*Check the answers to see if they make sense.*
		Because CO$_2$ has three atoms, it must be linear or bent. Chlorate ions resemble the ammonia molecule seen earlier in this section.

PRACTICE	*Determine the shape of these molecules.*
	A. sulfur difluoride _____
	$:\ddot{F}-\ddot{S}-\ddot{F}:$
	B. phosphorus trichloride _____
	$:\ddot{Cl}-\ddot{P}-\ddot{Cl}:$
	$\quad\quad :\ddot{Cl}:$

Multiple orbitals can combine to form hybrid orbitals.

VSEPR theory is useful for explaining the shape of molecules. However, it does not explain how the orbitals of a particular atom are affected by the formation of chemical bonds. **Hybridization** is a model that explains the mixing of two or more atomic orbitals of similar energies on the same atom to produce new hybrid atomic orbitals of equal energies.

For example, consider a molecule of methane, CH_4. The orbital notation shows that a carbon atom has four valence electrons, two in the $2s$ orbital and two in separate $2p$ orbitals.

$$C \quad \underset{1s}{\uparrow\downarrow} \quad \underset{2s}{\uparrow\downarrow} \quad \underset{2p}{\underbrace{\uparrow \quad \uparrow \quad \_\_}}$$

This orbital configuration shows that even though carbon atoms have four valence electrons, there are only two unpaired electrons available for forming covalent bonds. In addition, recall that the $2s$ and $2p$ orbitals have different shapes. Therefore, some reorganization must occur inside a carbon atom when it forms four bonds.

To achieve four equivalent single bonds, carbon's one $2s$ orbital and three $2p$ orbitals hybridize to form four identical orbitals called sp^3 orbitals. The numeral "3" above the p shows that three p orbitals are involved in the hybridization. The absence of a number over the s shows that one s orbital is involved.

The diagram below shows how the energy level of the orbitals changes during hybridization. The new sp^3 orbitals all have the same energy, which is in between the energy of the old $2s$ orbital and $2p$ orbitals.

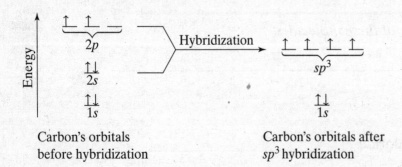

Carbon's orbitals before hybridization

Carbon's orbitals after sp^3 hybridization

 **CONNECT**

Computational chemistry is the study of molecules, their properties, and the interaction between molecules using mathematical equations. Computational chemists require expertise in mathematics, computers, and chemistry. Computational chemists help in the discovery of new medicines and new catalysts.

✓ READING CHECK

5. When hybridization of the outer orbitals of an atom occurs, the resulting hybrid orbitals have energy that is _____ the energy of the levels that were combined.

The sp^3 hybridization of carbon's outer orbitals combines one s orbital and three p orbitals.

Hybrid Orbitals Orbitals of equal energy produced by the combination of two or more orbitals on the same atom are called **hybrid orbitals.** The number of hybrid orbitals that form is always equal to the number of orbitals that have combined.

The diagram at the right shows how hybridization occurs within three elements: carbon, nitrogen, and oxygen. In each case, the 2s and 2p orbitals combine to form hybrid orbitals of equal energy. In carbon, all four orbitals are involved in bonds. In nitrogen, only three sets of electrons are involved in bonds because nitrogen only requires three additional electrons to form an octet. The other two electrons form a lone pair in a hybrid orbital. Oxygen forms two bonds to acquire two additional electrons to form an octet, and two sets of electrons form lone pairs.

The table below shows other types of hybridization possible for the outer electrons. Beryllium fluoride, as shown earlier in this section, has two *sp* hybrid orbitals formed from one 2s orbital and one 2p orbital. Boron trifluoride, also shown earlier, has three *sp*^{2} hybrid orbitals formed from one 2s orbital and two 2p orbitals.

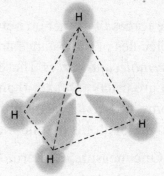

(a) Methane, CH_4

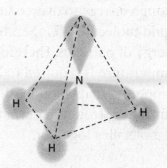

(b) Ammonia, NH_3

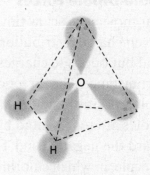

(c) Water, H_2O

Bonds formed by the overlap of the 1s orbitals of hydrogen and the *sp*^{3} orbitals of (a) carbon, (b) nitrogen, and (c) oxygen. Only the hybrid orbitals of the central atom are shown.

Geometry of Hybrid Orbitals

Atomic orbitals	Type of hybridization	Number of hybrid orbitals	Geometry
s, p	sp	2	180° Linear
s, p, p	sp^2	3	120° Trigonal-planar
s, p, p, p	sp^3	4	109.5° Tetrahedral

✓ READING CHECK

6. Explain hybridization.

_____

_____

_____

_____

Weak forces exist between molecules.

The forces of attraction between the different molecules of a substance are known as *intermolecular forces*. These forces vary in strength but are usually weaker than the forces that join atoms into molecules, ions into ionic compounds, and metal atoms in solid metals.

One measure of intermolecular forces is the boiling point of a liquid. For the liquid to become a gas, the molecules of the liquid must absorb enough energy to overcome the influence of other liquid molecules. Temperature is a measure of the energy of particles. Therefore, if a higher temperature is required to boil one molecular compound than another, then the first substance must have stronger intermolecular forces holding its molecules together.

Molecular Polarity and Dipole-Dipole Forces

Polar molecules act as tiny dipoles because of their uneven charge distribution. A **dipole** is created by equal but opposite charges that are separated by a short distance. The direction of a dipole is from the dipole's positive end toward its negative end. Dipoles are represented by arrows that point toward the negative end. For example, an HCl molecule, in which chlorine is the more electronegative atom, is shown as follows.

$$\overset{\xrightarrow{\hspace{1cm}}}{H-Cl}$$

The negative region in one polar molecule attracts the positive region in another molecule. The forces of attraction between polar molecules are known as *dipole-dipole forces*. An example of dipole-dipole forces in molecules of ICl is shown at the top of the following page.

All molecules involving two atoms are polar if the covalent bond between the two atoms is polar. However, the molecular polarity of larger molecules is determined by the shape of the molecule as well as the polarity of the bonds.

Boiling Points and Bonding Types

Bonding type	Substance	bp (1 atm,°C)
Nonpolar-covalent (molecular)	H_2	−253
	O_2	−183
	Cl_2	−34
	Br_2	59
	CH_4	−164
	CCl_4	77
	C_6H_6	80
Polar-covalent (molecular)	PH_3	−88
	NH_3	−33
	H_2S	−61
	H_2O	100
	HF	20
	HCl	−85
	ICl	97
Ionic	NaCl	1413
	MgF_2	2239
Metallic	Cu	2567
	Fe	2750
	W	5660

💡 Critical Thinking

7. Why are the boiling points of ionic and metallic substances higher than the boiling points of molecular substances?

_____

_____

_____

_____

_____

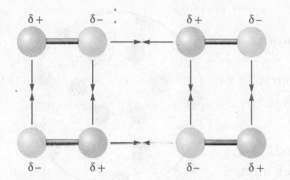

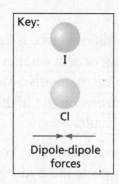

Key:

I

Cl

⟶⟵ Dipole-dipole forces

In each molecule of iodine chloride, ICl, the highly electronegative chlorine atom has a partial negative charge and the iodine atom has a partial positive charge. The neighboring positive and negative ends of ICl molecules attract each other.

In some molecules, such as water and ammonia, the dipoles point toward one end of the molecule, causing one end of the molecule to be negative. These molecules are highly polar. In other molecules, such as carbon tetrachloride and carbon dioxide, the inside of the molecule has a different charge than the outside of the molecule. However, because every end of the molecule has the same charge, there is no net attraction between the ends of different molecules. These molecules contain polar bonds, but their molecular polarity is zero.

A polar molecule can also *induce* a dipole in a nonpolar molecule by temporarily attracting its electrons. This short-range force is weaker than the dipole-dipole force. One example of an induced dipole is the interaction of oxygen gas and water. Water induces a dipole in oxygen, which attracts the oxygen molecules to the water molecules and allows oxygen gas to dissolve in water.

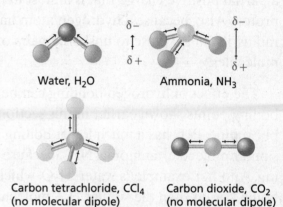

Water, H_2O

Ammonia, NH_3

Carbon tetrachloride, CCl_4 (no molecular dipole)

Carbon dioxide, CO_2 (no molecular dipole)

Water and ammonia are polar molecules. Carbon tetrachloride and carbon dioxide are nonpolar molecules.

✓ READING CHECK

8. Dipole-dipole forces are one example of what type of force that acts on molecules?

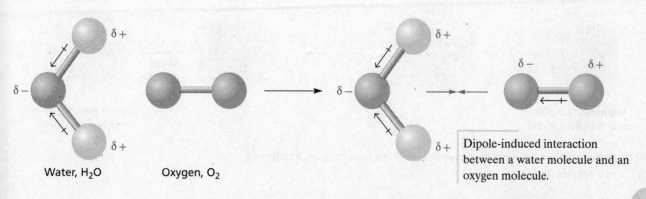

Water, H_2O

Oxygen, O_2

Dipole-induced interaction between a water molecule and an oxygen molecule.

Hydrogen Bonding

One especially strong type of dipole-dipole force is known as hydrogen bonding. **Hydrogen bonding** occurs when a hydrogen atom bonded to a highly electronegative atom is attracted to an unshared pair of electrons on the highly electronegative atom of another molecule.

Hydrogen bonding occurs because the covalent bonds H–F, H–O, and H–N are highly polar. This gives the hydrogen atom a partial positive charge that is almost half the charge of a proton. Also, because a hydrogen atom has a small atomic radius, it can get close to unshared pairs of electrons on other molecules.

The effect of hydrogen bonding can be seen in the table of boiling points shown earlier in this section. For example, phosphine, PH_3 has a much lower boiling point than the similar molecule, ammonia, NH_3, because of hydrogen bonding. Another example is water, H_2O, which has a much higher boiling point than the similar H_2S molecule.

London-Dispersion Forces

Electrons are always in motion, moving around an atom or in shared regions between atoms. Therefore, at any moment, the electron distribution in a molecule may be uneven. This temporary dipole can induce a dipole in another molecule, causing a brief attraction between the two molecules.

The intermolecular attractions resulting from the motion of electrons and temporary dipoles are called **London dispersion forces.** This is the only type of intermolecular force between nonpolar molecules and noble gas atoms. The strength of these forces increases as atomic mass increases, as reflected in the increasing boiling points of H_2, O_2, Cl_2, and Br_2 shown earlier in this section.

The dotted lines indicate the attraction between the negative oxygen ends of the water molecules and the positive hydrogen ends.

✓ READING CHECK

9. What is the only force that acts between the particles of helium gas?

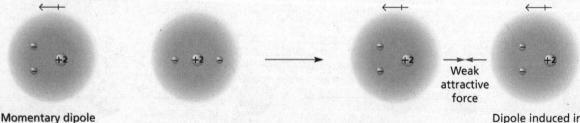

Momentary dipole in one helium atom

Weak attractive force

Dipole induced in neighboring atom

When an instantaneous, temporary dipole develops in a helium atom, it induces a dipole in a neighboring atom.

VOCABULARY

1. What two theories can be used to predict molecular geometry?

_____

_____

REVIEW

2. Draw the Lewis structures and predict the molecular geometry of the
following molecules:

a. SO_2

b. BCl_3

3. What factors affect the geometry of a molecule?

_____

_____

4. Explain what is meant by sp^3 hybridization.

_____

_____

5. What type of intermolecular force contributes to the high boiling point of
water? Explain.

_____

_____

_____

Critical Thinking

6. INFERRING RELATIONSHIPS What experimental property directly correlates
with the strength of the intermolecular forces? Briefly explain your answer.

_____

_____

_____

_____

Math Tutor DRAWING LEWIS STRUCTURES

Drawing Lewis structures can help you understand how valence electrons participate in bonding. Dots are placed around the symbol of an element to represent the element's valence electrons. For example, carbon has four valence electrons, and its Lewis structure is usually written as $\cdot\ddot{C}\cdot$. An atom of fluorine has seven valence electrons. Fluorine's Lewis dot structure can be written as $:\ddot{F}:$. When Lewis structures for covalently bonded atoms are written, the dots may be placed as needed to show the electrons shared in each bond. Most atoms bond in a way that gives them a stable octet of *s* and *p* electrons in the highest-occupied energy level. So, whenever possible, dots should be arranged in a way that represents a stable octet around each atom.

Problem-Solving TIPS

- Hydrogen is an exception to the octet rule because hydrogen has only one electron and becomes stable with two electrons.
- Some elements, such as boron, can form covalent bonds without achieving an octet because they have three or fewer electrons to share.

SAMPLE

Draw the Lewis structure for a molecule of sulfur dichloride, SCl_2.

First, write the electron-dot notation for each of the three atoms.

$$:\ddot{Cl}: \qquad :\ddot{Cl}: \qquad :\ddot{S}\cdot$$

Next, determine the total number of valence electrons in the atoms.

$$
\begin{array}{lll}
S & \longrightarrow & 1 \times 6e^- = 6e^- \\
2Cl & \longrightarrow & 2 \times 7e^- = 14e^- \\
\hline
\text{Total } e^- & \longrightarrow & 20e^-
\end{array}
$$

You can predict the arrangement of atoms by figuring out how many covalent bonds each atom must form in order to achieve a stable octet. Each chlorine atom, which has 7 valence electrons, must form a single covalent bond. Sulfur, which has 6 valence electrons, must form two covalent bonds. The only possible structure is Cl–S–Cl.

Finally, place two dots to represent each single covalent bond and dots for unshared electrons to give each atom a stable octet. Check the number of dots to make sure they match the sum calculated above. The arrangement shown below contains 20 electrons.

$$:\ddot{Cl}:\ddot{S}:\ddot{Cl}:$$

Practice Problems: Chapter Review practice problems 13 and 18

1. Identify and define the three major types of chemical bonding.

   _____

   _____

   _____

2. Describe the general location of the electrons in a covalent bond.

   _____

   _____

3. In writing Lewis structures, how is the need for multiple bonds generally determined?

   _____

   _____

4. In general, how do ionic and molecular compounds compare in terms of melting points, boiling points, and ease of vaporization?

   _____

   _____

5. List three general physical properties of ionic compounds.

   _____

6. How do the properties of metals differ from those of both ionic and molecular compounds?

   _____

   _____

   _____

7. How is VSEPR theory used to classify molecules?

   _____

   _____

8. What are intermolecular forces?

   _____

   _____

9. Complete the table with respect to bonds formed between the pairs of atoms.

Bonded atoms	Electronegativity difference	Bond type	More-negative atom
H and I			
S and O			
K and Br			
Si and Cl			
K and Cl			
Se and S			
C and H			

10. List the bonding pairs from Question 9 in order of increasing covalent character.

_____

11. The lattice energy of sodium chloride, NaCl, is −787.5 kJ/mol. The lattice energy of potassium chloride, KCl, is −715 kJ/mol. In which compound is the bonding between ions stronger? Why?

_____

_____

12. Use electron-dot notation to illustrate the number of valence electrons present in one atom of each of the following elements.

a. chlorine, Cl _____   **c.** carbon, C _____

b. calcium, Ca _____   **d.** phosphorus, P _____

13. Draw Lewis structures for each of the following molecules.

a. CF_4

c. $CClH_3$

b. H_2Se

d. N_2

14. According to the VSEPR theory, what molecular geometries are associated with the following types of molecules?

a. AB_3E _____ **b.** AB_2E_2 _____ **c.** AB_2E _____

15. For each of the following polar molecules, in which direction is the dipole oriented? (Which end would the dipole arrow point toward?)

a. H–F _____ **b.** H–Cl _____ **c.** H–I _____

16. Determine whether each of the following bonds would be polar or nonpolar.

a. H–H _____ **c.** H–F _____ **e.** H–Cl _____

b. H–O _____ **d.** Br–Br _____ **f.** H–N _____

17. On the basis of individual bond polarity and orientation, determine whether each of the following molecules would be polar or nonpolar.

a. H_2O _____ **c.** CF_4 _____ **e.** CO_2 _____

b. I_2 _____ **d.** NH_3 _____

18. Draw Lewis structures for each of the following molecules or ions, and then use VSEPR theory to determine the geometry of each.

a. SCl_2

e. $SiCl_3Br$

b. PI_3

f. ONCl

c. Cl_2O

g. NO_3^-

d. NH_2Cl

h. SO_4^{2-}

CHAPTER 7

Chemical Formulas and Chemical Compounds

Key Concepts

Review Previous Concepts

1. Why are most atoms more likely to be found in nature as part of compounds than as individual atoms?

_____

_____

_____

2. How can you determine the number of covalent bonds an atom can form in a molecule?

_____

_____

_____

SECTION 7.1

Chemical Names and Formulas

There are millions of chemical compounds that scientists have found in nature or made in the laboratory. Some compounds, such as table salt and water, have common names. These compounds also have chemical names that give information about their composition.

Formulas tell the number and kinds of atoms in a compound.

A compound's chemical name is often directly related to its chemical formula. The chemical formula for a molecular compound gives the number of each type of atom that goes into a single molecule. The chemical formula for octane is given below as an example.

READING CHECK

1. What information about a compound is given in a chemical formula?

_____

_____

_____

_____

_____

$$C_8H_{18}$$

| This molecule has 8 carbon atoms. | This molecule has 18 hydrogen atoms. |

In an ionic compound, a lattice of positive and negative ions is bonded together. The chemical formula for an ionic compound gives the simplest ratio of positive and negative ions that has no charge. The formula for aluminum sulfate is given below. Note that the polyatomic ion sulfate, SO_4^{2-}, is enclosed in parentheses. This means that the number 3 outside the parentheses applies to the whole polyatomic ion. So, a unit of aluminum sulfate includes 2 aluminum atoms, 3 sulfur atoms, and 12 oxygen atoms.

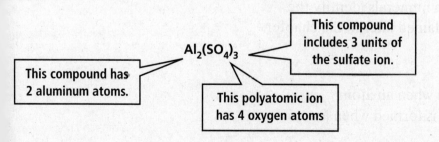

$$Al_2(SO_4)_3$$

This compound has 2 aluminum atoms.

This compound includes 3 units of the sulfate ion.

This polyatomic ion has 4 oxygen atoms

TIP If the symbol for an element in a chemical formula has no subscript number beside it, then the symbol represents one atom of the element. For example, the chemical formula for table salt, NaCl, represents one Na atom and one Cl atom.

Monatomic ions are made of only one type of atom.

In the ionic compound on the previous page, two aluminum cations bond with three polyatomic ions of sulfate. The aluminum cation, Al^{3+}, is known as a monatomic ion. Any ion that is formed from a single atom is a **monatomic ion.** In table salt, two monatomic ions, Na^+ and Cl^-, bond to form the formula unit NaCl.

The metals in Group 1 and Group 2 of the periodic table only need to lose one or two electrons to form a stable octet in their outermost energy levels. These elements readily form positive monatomic cations. Group 1 elements form 1+ ions, such as Na^+. Group 2 elements form 2+ ions.

The nonmetals in Group 15, Group 16, and Group 17 can form stable octets by gaining electrons. These elements readily form monatomic anions. Group 17 elements form 1– ions, such as Cl^-. Group 16 elements form 2– ions, and Group 15 elements form 3– ions.

Not all main-group elements readily form ions. Carbon and silicon usually form covalent bonds in which they share electrons with other atoms, rather than gain or lose electrons completely. The two metals in Group 14, tin and lead, tend to lose their two outermost p electrons but keep their two outermost s electrons. Tin and lead normally form 2+ ions, but they can also form 4+ ions in some compounds.

Elements in the d block usually form 2+ or 3+ ions. However, some form 1+ and 4+ ions as well. Many d-block elements can form multiple ions. For example, iron can form a 2+ ion and a 3+ ion. Vanadium can form 2+ ions, 3+ ions, and 4+ ions.

The table on the next page identifies some common monatomic ions. Some metals' cations have Roman numerals added to their names. The Roman numerals identify the charge of the ion, and will be explained later in the chapter.

✓ READING CHECK

3. A monatomic cation is formed when an atom _____ electrons. A monatomic anion is formed when an atom _____ electrons.

🔍 LOOKING CLOSER

2. List several other words that are formed using the prefix *mon-* or *mono-*. What do these words have in common?

_____

_____

_____

_____

_____

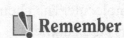 **Remember**

Usually, the charge of a cation formed from a main-group atom is the same as the group number. The charge of a main-group anion is usually 18 minus the group number.

Naming Monatomic Ions

The name of a monatomic ion is based on the name of the atom from which it formed.

- Monatomic cations are simply identified by the name of the element. For example, K is a potassium atom and K^+ is a potassium ion.

- Monatomic anions are identified by dropping the end of the element's name and adding the suffix *-ide*. For example, Cl is a chlorine atom and Cl^- is a chloride ion.

Some Common Monatomic Ions

Main-group elements

1+		2+		3+	
lithium	Li^+	beryllium	Be^{2+}	aluminum	Al^{3+}
sodium	Na^+	magnesium	Mg^{2+}		
potassium	K^+	calcium	Ca^{2+}		
rubidium	Rb^+	strontium	Sr^{2+}		
cesium	Cs^+	barium	Ba^{2+}		

1–		2–		3–	
fluoride	F^-	oxide	O^{2-}	nitride	N^{3-}
chloride	Cl^-	sulfide	S^{2-}	phosphide	P^{3-}
bromide	Br^-				
iodide	I^-				

***d*-Block elements and others with multiple ions**

1+		2+		3+		4+	
copper(I)	Cu^+	vanadium(II)	V^{2+}	vanadium(III)	V^{3+}	vanadium(IV)	V^{4+}
silver	Ag^+	chromium(II)	Cr^{2+}	chromium(III)	Cr^{3+}	tin(IV)	Sn^{4+}
		iron(II)	Fe^{2+}	iron(III)	Fe^{3+}	lead(IV)	Pb^{4+}
		cobalt(II)	Co^{2+}	cobalt(III)	Co^{3+}		
		copper(II)	Cu^{2+}				
		zinc	Zn^{2+}				
		cadmium	Cd^{2+}				
		tin(II)	Sn^{2+}				
		lead(II)	Pb^{2+}				

Binary compounds contain atoms of two elements.

Monatomic ions combine to form binary ionic compounds. A **binary compound** is any compound that is composed of exactly two elements. In a binary ionic compound, the total positive charge must balance the total negative charge. Therefore, the formula unit for a binary ionic compound can be established using the charges of the cation and the anion.

For example, the Group 2 metal magnesium forms 2+ magnesium cations, or Mg^{2+}. The Group 17 nonmetal bromine forms bromide anions, or Br^-. It takes two bromide anions to balance the charge of a single magnesium cation. Therefore, the formula unit for the ionic compound magnesium bromide is $MgBr_2$.

Note that the number 2 in the formula $MgBr_2$ refers to the number of bromide anions, not the charge of the bromide anion. The charges of the ions that make up an ionic compound are usually not referred to in the chemical formula for the compound.

One way to determine the chemical formula for an ionic compound is to "cross over" the charges. For example, here is how the method of crossing over can be used to determine the chemical formula for aluminum oxide.

1. Write the symbol for the cation followed by the symbol for the anion.

$$Al^{3+} \quad O^{2-}$$

2. Cross over the charges by taking the charge, without the positive or negative sign, from one atomic symbol and writing it below the other symbol.

$$Al_2^{3+} \quad O_3^{2-}$$

3. If necessary, divide each bottom number by the greatest common factor of the two numbers to reduce the ratio to lowest terms. Then delete the charges.

$$Al_2O_3$$

To check the answer, make sure the net charge on the formula unit is zero. The total positive charge on the two aluminum cations is 6+. The total negative charge on the two oxygen anions is 6−. The net charge on the formula unit is 0.

5. Define the terms binary and compound separately in your own words.

binary: _____

_____

_____

compound: _____

_____

_____

Remember

A formula unit for an ionic compound is the *smallest* ratio of positive cations and negative anions that sum to zero charge. That is why division by the greatest common factor is necessary.

Naming Binary Ionic Compounds

Nomenclature is the process of choosing names to identify things. Scientists have developed a nomenclature for naming chemical compounds. The process of naming a binary ionic compound involves combining the name of the positive cation and the name of the negative anion. For example, the name of the compound formed from aluminum cations, Al^{3+}, and oxide anions, O^{2-}, is aluminum oxide.

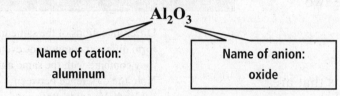

Name of cation:	Name of anion:
aluminum	oxide

Name of compound: **aluminum oxide**

Note that the nomenclature for binary ionic compounds does not include the number of atoms of each type. Because each ion has a specific charge associated with it, the ratio of the elements can be determined simply from the charges associated with each ion, as shown on the preceding page.

PRACTICE

A. Write formulas for the binary ionic compounds formed between the following elements:

a. potassium and iodine _____

b. magnesium and chlorine _____

c. sodium and sulfur _____

d. aluminum and sulfur _____

e. aluminum and nitrogen _____

B. Name the binary ionic compounds indicated by the following formulas:

a. AgCl _____

b. ZnO _____

c. $CaBr_2$ _____

d. SrF_2 _____

e. BaO _____

The Stock System of Nomenclature

Some elements form two or more cations with different charges. To distinguish these ions, scientists use the *Stock system* of nomenclature. A Roman numeral after the name of the cation indicates the amount of positive charge on the cation. Roman numerals are only associated with cations because there are no elements that form more than one monatomic anion. For example, there are two common ions formed from iron atoms.

iron(II): Fe^{2+} **iron(III):** Fe^{3+}

Most elements in the *d* block have ions that are named with Roman numerals. A few elements, such as silver and zinc, usually only form one ion. If a metal commonly forms only one monatomic ion, then there is no Roman numeral. So, for example, a silver ion is understood to have a charge of 1+.

The name of a binary ionic compound using the Stock system is also a combination of the name of the cation and the name of the anion. The metal cation name includes its charge when the element commonly forms two or more ions.

Different cations of the same metal form different compounds even when they combine with the same anion. Note the difference between (a) lead(IV) oxide, PbO_2, and (b) lead(II) oxide, PbO.

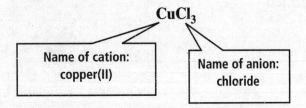

Name of compound: **copper(II) chloride**

PRACTICE

C. Write the formula and give the name for the compounds formed between the following ions:

   a. Pb^{2+} and Cl^- _____

   b. Hg^{2+} and S^{2-} _____

   c. Fe^{3+} and O^{2-} _____

D. Give the names of the following compounds.

   a. CuO _____   **c.** CoF_3 _____

   b. SnI_4 _____   **d.** FeS _____

Some Polyatomic Ions

1+		2+	
ammonium	NH_4^+	dimercury*	Hg_2^{2+}

1−		2−		3−	
acetate	CH_3COO^-	carbonate	CO_3^{2-}	arsenate	AsO_4^{3-}
bromate	BrO_3^-	chromate	CrO_4^{2-}	phosphate	PO_4^{3-}
chlorate	ClO_3^-	dichromate	$Cr_2O_7^{2-}$		
chlorite	ClO_2^-	hydrogen phosphate	HPO_4^{2-}		
cyanide	CN^-	oxalate	$C_2O_4^{2-}$		
dihydrogen phosphate	$H_2PO_4^-$	peroxide	O_2^{2-}		
hydrogen carbonate (bicarbonate)	HCO_3^-	sulfate	SO_4^{2-}		
hydrogen sulfate	HSO_4^-	sulfite	SO_3^{2-}		
hydroxide	OH^-				
hypochlorite	ClO^-				
nitrate	NO_3^-				
nitrite	$4NO_2^-$				
perchlorate	ClO_4^-				
permanganate	MnO_4^-				

*The mercury(I) cation exists as two Hg^+ ions joined together by a covalent bond and is written as Hg_2^{2+}.

Compounds Containing Polyatomic Ions

The table at the top of the page gives the names of some common polyatomic ions. Most of these ions are negatively charged. Most are also **oxyanions,** which are polyatomic anions that contain oxygen.

Elements That Form Two Oxyanions Note that some elements can combine with oxygen to form more than one polyatomic ion. For example, nitrogen can combine with oxygen to form NO_2^- and NO_3^-. The names of these ions are distinguished by the suffixes *-ate* and *-ite*. The ion that has the smaller number of oxygen atoms ends in *-ite*. The ion that has the greater number of oxygen atoms ends in *-ate*. For example, the two nitrogen-oxygen ions are

nitrite: NO_2^- nitrate: NO_3^-

LOOKING CLOSER

6. How do the roots that form the term oxyanion give a clue to the definition of the term?

_____

_____

_____

_____

_____

Elements That Form More Than Two Oxyanions Some elements can combine with oxygen to form more than two polyatomic ions. An ion that has fewer oxygen atoms than the -ite ion is given the prefix *hypo*-. An ion that has more oxygen atoms than the -ate ion is given the prefix *per*-. The four oxyanions that are formed by chlorine are shown on the right.

> **The four oxyanions of chlorine**
> Hypochlorite: ClO^-
> Chlorite: ClO_2^-
> Chlorate: ClO_3^-
> Perchlorate: ClO_4^-

Compounds containing polyatomic ions are named in the same way as binary ionic compounds. The name of the cation is given first, followed by the name of the anion. For example, silver cations and nitrogen oxyanions can form two compounds. Note that parentheses, such as those used on the formula for aluminum sulfate shown earlier in this section, are not necessary when a formula uses only one unit of a polyatomic ion.

silver nitrite: $AgNO_2$ **silver nitrate:** $AgNO_3$

PRACTICE

E. Write formulas for the following ionic compounds:

a. lithium nitrate _____

d. calcium nitrite _____

b. copper(II) sulfate _____

e. potassium perchlorate _____

c. sodium carbonate _____

F. Give the names for the following compounds:

a. $Ca(OH)_2$ _____

b. $KClO_3$ _____

c. NH_4OH _____

d. $Fe_2(CrO_4)_3$ _____

e. $KClO$ _____

Naming Binary Molecular Compounds

The names of ionic compounds do not include information on the ratio of atoms of each type included in the compound. The charges on each ion determine this ratio. However, molecules are not formed from charged particles. Therefore, the names of molecular compounds must refer to the number of atoms of each type that make up a compound.

Prefix System One system of naming binary molecular compounds is based on prefixes. The names of the elements are assigned prefixes based on the number of atoms that are in the molecule. The prefixes used are given in the table at the right. The rules for this naming system are as follows.

1. The element with the smallest group number is usually given first. If both elements are in the same group, the element with the greatest period number is given first. This element is given a prefix if the compound contains two or more atoms of this type.

2. The second element is named by combining (a) a prefix from the table above, (b) the root of the element's name, and (c) the suffix -*ide*.

3. The *o* or *a* at the end of a prefix is usually dropped when the element's name following the prefix starts with a vowel. For example, you would write *monoxide* and *pentoxide* instead of *mono-oxide* and *penta-oxide*.

Numerical Prefixes	
Number	**Prefix**
1	mono-
2	di-
3	tri-
4	tetra-
5	penta-
6	hexa-
7	hepta-
8	octa-
9	nona-
10	deca-

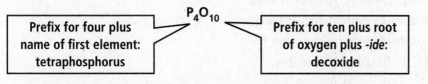

Prefix for four plus name of first element: **tetraphosphorus** → P_4O_{10} ← Prefix for ten plus root of oxygen plus -*ide*: **decoxide**

Name of compound: **tetraphosphorus decoxide**

TIP By convention, the order of the elements is usually given as C, P, N, H, S, I, Br, Cl, O, and F.

PRACTICE

G. Name the following binary molecular compounds:

a. SO_3 _____

b. ICl_3 _____

c. PBr_5 _____

H. Give the formulas for the following compounds:

a. carbon tetraiodide _____

b. phosphorus trichloride _____

c. dinitrogen trioxide _____

Covalent-Network Compounds

As you read in the chapter "Chemical Bonding," some covalent compounds do not consist of individual molecules. Instead, each atom is joined to all of its neighbors in a three-dimensional network. All of the bonds in this network are covalent bonds.

TIP Many of the compounds in this section have ended with -*ide*. With a few exceptions, the ending -*ide* is a clue that a compound only contains two elements.

These compounds, like ionic compounds, lack molecules with a set composition. Instead, a formula unit consists of the smallest whole-number ratio of the atoms in the compound. Here are some examples of the chemical formulas and chemical names of covalent-network compounds.

silicon carbide: SiC **silicon dioxide:** SiO_2

trisilicon tetranitride: Si_3N_4

Acids and Salts

Another type of covalent compound is an acid. An acid is a specific type of molecular compound that has special properties when dissolved in water. Usually, the term *acid* refers to a solution of the compound in water rather to the compound itself. For example, hydrochloric acid refers to compound hydrogen chloride, HCl, dissolved in water.

Most acids can be classified as one of two types. *Binary acids* consist of two elements, usually hydrogen and one of the halogens. *Oxyacids* contain hydrogen, oxygen, and a third element (usually a nonmetal). The table below lists some common binary acids and oxyacids.

⚗ Critical Thinking

7. **Compare** What do binary ionic compounds, binary molecular compounds, and binary acids have in common?

Common Binary Acids and Oxyacids					
HF	hydrofluoric acid	HNO_2	nitrous acid	HClO	hypochlorous acid
HCl	hydrochloric acid	HNO_3	nitric acid	$HClO_2$	chlorous acid
HBr	hydrobromic acid	H_2SO_3	sulfurous acid	$HClO_3$	chloric acid
HI	hydriodic acid	H_2SO_4	sulfuric acid	$HClO_4$	perchloric acid
H_3PO_4	phosphoric acid	CH_3COOH	acetic acid	H_2CO_3	carbonic acid

Bottles of nitric acid, hydrochloric acid, and sulfuric acid for the laboratory. Acids should be handled with care because drops of acid can burn the skin or burn holes in clothing.

Many polyatomic ions are produced by the loss of hydrogen atoms from an oxyacid. Two examples of an oxyacid and its oxyanion are given below.

sulfuric acid: H_2SO_4 $\longrightarrow$ sulfate: SO_4^{2-}

phosphoric acid: H_3PO_4 $\longrightarrow$ phosphate: PO_4^{3-}

A **salt** is an ionic compound formed from a cation and the anion from an acid. Table salt, NaCl, contains a sodium cation, Na^+, and the chloride anion, Cl^-, from hydrochloric acid, HCl. Calcium sulfate, $CaSO_4$, is an example of a salt formed from the sulfate ion of sulfuric acid.

Some salts contain anions in which one of more hydrogen atoms from the acid are retained. Such ions have names that start with the word *hydrogen* or the prefix *bi-*. For example, HCO_3^- is the anion that forms from carbonic acid, H_2CO_3. It is referred to as a hydrogen carbonate ion, or a bicarbonate ion.

✓ READING CHECK

8. What happens to an acid that causes the formation of a polyatomic ion?

_____

_____

VOCABULARY

1. What is a salt? Give two examples of salts.

_____

_____

REVIEW

2. What is the significance of a chemical formula?

_____

_____

3. Write formulas for the compounds formed between the following pairs.

a. aluminum and bromine _____

e. Sn^{2+} and I^- _____

b. sodium and oxygen _____

f. Fe^{3+} and S^{2-} _____

c. magnesium and iodine _____

g. Cu^{2+} and NO_3^- _____

d. Pb^{2+} and O^{2-} _____

h. NH_4^+ and SO_4^{2-} _____

4. Name the following compounds by using the Stock system.

a. NaI _____

d. K_2S _____

b. MgS _____

e. CuBr _____

c. CaO _____

f. $FeCl_2$ _____

5. Write formulas for the following compounds.

a. sodium hydroxide _____

e. carbon diselenide _____

b. lead(II) nitrate _____

f. acetic acid _____

c. iron(II) sulfate _____

g. chloric acid _____

d. diphosphorus trioxide _____

h. sulfurous acid _____

Critical Thinking

6. RELATING IDEAS Draw the Lewis structure, give the name, and predict the molecular geometry of SCl_2.

Name: _____   Shape: _____

Oxidation Numbers

The charges on the ions in an ionic compound reflect the electron distribution of the compound. Scientists also need to describe how the electrons are distributed between the covalently bonded atoms of a molecule. Oxidation numbers serve this purpose.

Oxidation numbers, or **oxidation states,** indicate the general distribution of electrons among the bonded atoms in a molecular compound or a polyatomic ion. Each atom is assigned its own oxidation number. Oxidation numbers do not have physical meanings, but they are useful for naming compounds, writing formulas, and balancing equations.

Specific rules are used to assign oxidation numbers.

Oxidation numbers assigned to the atoms in a polyatomic ion or molecule represent the charge of the unit as a whole. Here are three rules for assigning oxidation numbers:

1. The shared electrons in a covalent bond are usually assigned to the atom that is more electronegative.

2. For a molecule, the sum of the oxidation numbers of all of its atoms is zero.

3. For a polyatomic ion, the sum of the oxidation numbers of all of its atoms is equal to the charge on the ion.

Consider hydrogen fluoride, HF. The shared electrons are assigned to fluorine since it is more electronegative. Then, fluorine has an extra electron and its oxidation state is –1. Because the sum of the oxidation states in any molecule is equal to zero, hydrogen has an oxidation number of +1.

In water, H_2O, oxygen is the more electronegative atom. It is assigned the electrons from water's two covalent bonds. This gives oxygen two extra electrons and an oxidation state of –2. The sum of the oxidation states will be zero if each hydrogen atom is assigned the oxidation state +1.

READING CHECK

1. What is the sum of the oxidation states on the atoms in the following three substances?

   a. H_2SO_4 _____

   b. SO_4^{2-} _____

   c. He _____

Pure Elements The oxidation number for pure elements is always zero. For example, the atoms in sodium, Na, oxygen, O_2, phosphorus, P_4, and sulfur, S_8, all have oxidation states of zero.

Fluorine The oxidation number for fluorine is always –1. Fluorine, the most electronegative element, will always have a greater attraction for its shared electrons than will other elements in the same compounds.

Oxygen The oxidation number for oxygen is usually –2. One exception is OF_2, in which oxygen has the oxidation state +2 because fluorine is so electronegative. Another exception is in peroxide compounds such as H_2O_2, where oxygen has an oxidation state of –1.

Hydrogen The oxidation number for hydrogen is +1 in compounds containing more electronegative atoms. In compounds containing metals, hydrogen has an oxidation state of –1.

Ionic Compounds Oxidation numbers can also be applied to atoms in ionic compounds. Monatomic ions have oxidation numbers equal to their charge. So, Na^+, Ca^{2+}, and Cl^- have oxidation numbers of +1, +2, and –1, respectively.

✓ READING CHECK

2. Explain why the sum of the oxidation states on the atoms in a molecule of H_2O_2 is zero.

_____

_____

_____

_____

_____

SAMPLE PROBLEM

Assign oxidation numbers to each atom in UF_6.

SOLVE		
STEP 1	*Write the known oxidation numbers above the elements.*	$\overset{-1}{UF_6}$
	Fluorine always has an oxidation number of –1.	
STEP 2	*Write the total of the oxidation states below these elements.*	$\overset{-1}{\underset{-6}{UF_6}}$
	The six F atoms have a total oxidation state of $-1 \times 6 = -6$.	
STEP 3	*Find the oxidation state of the unknown element.*	$\overset{+6\ -1}{\underset{+6\ -6}{UF_6}}$
	In order to sum to zero, the uranium atom must have an oxidation state of +6.	

Assign oxidation numbers to each atom in the following compounds or ions:

a. H_2SO_4

b. ClO_3^-

SOLVE

STEP 1

Write the known oxidation numbers above the elements.

Oxygen is in both of these substances, but neither contains fluorine or is a peroxide. So, the oxidation state of oxygen is –2. Hydrogen has an oxidation state of +1 with nonmetals.

$$\overset{+1\ -2}{\text{a. } H_2SO_4} \qquad \overset{-2}{\text{b. } ClO_3^-}$$

STEP 2

Write the total of the oxidation states below these elements.

Multiplying the oxidation number by the number of atoms yields the total oxidation state for each element.

$$\overset{+1\ \ -2}{\underset{+2\ \ -8}{\text{a. } H_2SO_4}} \qquad \overset{-2}{\underset{-6}{\text{b. } ClO_3^-}}$$

STEP 3

Find the oxidation state of the unknown element.

a. $+2 + -8 +$ oxidation state of sulfur $= 0$, so oxidation state of sulfur $= 0 - 2 + 8 = +6$.

b. $-6 +$ oxidation state of chlorine $= -1$, so oxidation state of chlorine $= -1 + 6 = +5$.

$$\overset{+1\ +6\ -2}{\underset{+2\ +6\ -8}{\text{a. } H_2SO_4}} \qquad \overset{+5\ -2}{\underset{+5\ -6}{\text{b. } ClO_3^-}}$$

PRACTICE | *Assign oxidation numbers to each atom in these compounds.*

A. CF_4

What is the oxidation state of one fluorine atom? _____

What is the total oxidation state of the fluorine atoms? _____

What is the oxidation state of the chlorine atom? _____

B. HCl   **E.** HNO_3 **H.** $HClO_3$

C. PCl_3 **F.** KH   **I.** N_2O_5

D. SO_2 **G.** P_4C_{10} **J.** $GeCl_2$

Common Oxidation Numbers of Some Nonmetals That Have Variable Oxidation States*

Group 14	carbon	−4, +2, +4
Group 15	nitrogen	−3, +1, +2, +3, +4, +5
	phosphorus	−3, +3, +5
Group 16	sulfur	−2, +4, +6
Group 17	chlorine	−1, +1, +3, +5, +7
	bromine	−1, +1, +3, +5, +7
	iodine	−1, +1, +3, +5, +7

*In addition to the values shown, atoms of each element in its pure state are assigned an oxidation number of zero.

Many nonmetals have multiple oxidation numbers.

Many nonmetals can have more than one oxidation number. Some of these nonmetals and their multiple oxidation states are shown in the table above. These numbers can sometimes be used the same way as ionic charges to determine formulas.

For example, suppose you want to know the formula of a compound formed from sulfur and oxygen. Since oxygen usually has the oxidation number −2, and sulfur can have the oxidation number of +4 or +6, you would expect that sulfur and oxygen would form the compounds SO_2 and SO_3.

In Section 1 you learned how to use Roman numerals to name ionic compounds through the Stock system. This system is actually based on oxidation numbers. In the Stock system, the prefixes are dropped and the oxidation state of the less electronegative element is given by the Roman numeral.

✓ READING CHECK

3. How does the prefix system of naming binary molecular compounds differ from the Stock system of naming compounds?

_____

_____

_____

_____

_____

Names of compounds

Formula	Prefix system	Stock system
SO_2	sulfur dioxide	sulfur(IV) oxide
SO_3	sulfur trioxide	sulfur(VI) oxide
PCl_3	phosphorus trichloride	phosphorus(III) chloride
PCl_5	phosphorus pentachloride	phosphorus(V) chloride
N_2O	dinitrogen monoxide	nitrogen(I) oxide
NO	nitrogen monoxide	nitrogen(II) oxide

SECTION 7.2 REVIEW

VOCABULARY

1. a. What are oxidation numbers?

b. What useful functions do oxidation numbers serve?

REVIEW

2. Assign oxidation numbers to each atom in the following compounds or ions.

a. HF
b. CI_4
c. H_2O
d. PI_3
e. CS_2
f. Na_2O_2
g. H_2CO_3
h. NO_2^-
i. SO_4^{2-}

3. Name each of the following binary molecular compounds according to the Stock system.

a. CI_4
b. SO_3
c. As_2S_3
d. NCl_3

Critical Thinking

4. **DRAWING CONCLUSIONS** Determine the oxidation numbers for iron oxide, Fe_3O_4. (Recall that oxidation numbers must be integers.)

SECTION 7.3

Using Chemical Formulas

Many quantities that describe the compound can be calculated using the information in a chemical formula. Three of these quantities are the *formula mass*, *molar mass*, and *percentage composition* (by mass) of a compound.

Formula mass is the sum of the average atomic masses of a compound's elements.

The **formula mass** of any molecule, formula unit, or ion is the sum of the average atomic masses of the atoms represented in its formula. If the particle is a molecule, then the formula mass is also called the *molecular mass*.

Hydrogen atoms have an average atomic mass of 1.01 u and oxygen atoms have an average atomic mass of 16.00 u. These values can be used to calculate the formula mass, or molecular mass, of a molecule of water.

The chemical formula for water is H_2O. Therefore, the molecular mass of water is twice the average atomic mass of hydrogen plus the average atomic mass of water. Another way to consider the calculation is to use the average atomic mass as a conversion factor.

$$2 \text{ H atoms} = 2 \text{ H atoms} \times \frac{1.01 \text{ u}}{\text{H atom}} = 2.02 \text{ u}$$

$$1 \text{ O atom} = 1 \text{ O atom} \times \frac{16.00 \text{ u}}{\text{O atom}} = 16.00 \text{ u}$$

$$\text{average mass of } H_2O \text{ molecule} = 18.02 \text{ u}$$

The molar mass of a compound is numerically equal to its formula mass.

In the chapter "Atoms: The Building Blocks of Matter," you learned that the molar mass of a substance is equal to the mass in grams of one mole of the substance, or the mass in grams of 6.022×10^{23} particles of the substance. This means that a compound's molar mass is the mass in grams of one mole of the compound.

Critical Thinking

1. Infer Why is the formula mass of an ionic compound not referred to as the molecular mass of the compound?

_____

_____

_____

TIP When atomic masses are used in calculations in this book, they are rounded to two decimal places.

Calculating Molar Mass Calculating the molar mass of a compound is similar to calculating its formula mass. First, recall that the molar mass of an element in grams per mole is equal to the average atomic mass of its atoms in amu. Second, each particle, or unit, of a compound contains the number of atoms given in the compound's chemical formula. As a result, the molar mass of a compound is the sum of the molar mass contribution of each element to the compound.

$$2 \text{ mol H} = 2 \text{ mol H} \times \frac{1.01 \text{ g H}}{\text{mol H}} = 2.02 \text{ g H}$$

$$1 \text{ mol O} = 1 \text{ mol O} \times \frac{16.00 \text{ g H}}{\text{mol O}} = 16.00 \text{ g O}$$

$$\text{mass of 1 mol H}_2\text{O} = 18.02 \text{ g}$$

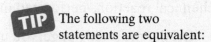 **TIP** The following two statements are equivalent:

1. The mass of one mole of water is 18.02 g.

2. The molar mass of water is 18.02 g/mol.

The same values are used in the calculation of molar mass as in the calculation of formula mass. So, the molar mass of a compound in grams is equal to the formula mass of a unit of the compound.

PRACTICE

A. Find the formula mass of $Ca(NO_3)_2$.

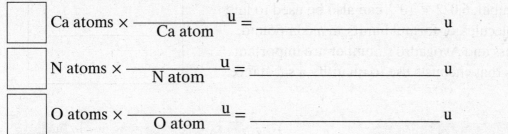

$$\boxed{} \text{Ca atoms} \times \frac{\text{u}}{\text{Ca atom}} = \underline{\hspace{3cm}} \text{ u}$$

$$\boxed{} \text{N atoms} \times \frac{\text{u}}{\text{N atom}} = \underline{\hspace{3cm}} \text{ u}$$

$$\boxed{} \text{O atoms} \times \frac{\text{u}}{\text{O atom}} = \underline{\hspace{3cm}} \text{ u}$$

average mass of $Ca(NO_3)_2$ molecule = \underline{\hspace{5cm}}

B. How many moles of atoms are there in each compound?

a. Al_2S_3 \underline{\hspace{2.5cm}}   **b.** $NaNO_3$ \underline{\hspace{2.5cm}}   **c.** $Ba(OH)_2$ \underline{\hspace{2.5cm}}

C. Find the molar mass of Al_2S_3

$$\boxed{} \text{mol Al} \times \frac{\text{g Al}}{\text{mol Al}} = \underline{\hspace{4cm}} \text{ g Al}$$

$$\boxed{} \text{mol S} \times \frac{\text{g S}}{\text{mol S}} = \underline{\hspace{4cm}} \text{ g S}$$

mass of 1 mol Al_2S_3 = \underline{\hspace{6cm}}

Molar mass is used to convert from moles to grams.

The molar mass of a compound is an important characteristic to a chemist. A chemist normally measures the amount of a substance involved in a reaction by measuring the mass of the substance in grams with a scale. However, the proportions of substances that are consumed or produced in a chemical reaction are normally given in moles. Molar mass is an important conversion factor for analyzing the results of chemical reactions performed in the laboratory.

On the preceding page, you used molar mass as a conversion factor to express the amount of a substance given in moles as an amount in grams. That is one of the two ways that molar mass can be used as a conversion factor.

- To convert from mass to moles, use the following equation.

  amount in moles × molar mass (g/mol) = mass in grams

- To convert from moles to mass, use the following equation.

  mass in grams × $\dfrac{1}{\text{molar mass (g/mol)}}$ = amount in moles

Avogadro's number, 6.022×10^{23}, can also be used to find the number of molecules, or formula units, in a compound. So, both molar mass and Avogadro's number are important conversion factors that chemists use to quantify a substance.

🔎 Critical Thinking

2. Apply Write two conversion factors using the information that the molar mass of chlorine is 35.45 g/mol. Then circle the conversion factor that would be necessary to find the number of moles of chlorine in 100 g of NaC.

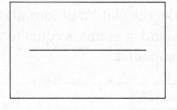

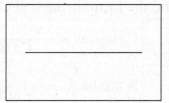

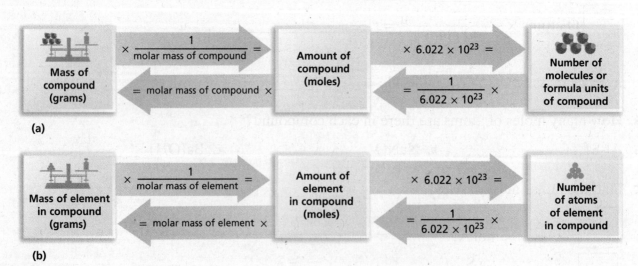

The diagram shows the relationships between the mass in grams, amount in moles, and number of units for a compound or for one element of the compound. Notice the similarity between this diagram and the one in Section 3 of the chapter "Atoms: The Building Blocks of Matter."

What is the mass in grams of 2.50 mol of oxygen gas?

SOLUTION		
1 ANALYZE	*Determine the information that is given and unknown.*	

    Given: 2.50 mol O_2
    Unknown: mass of O_2 in grams

2 PLAN   *Write the equation that can be used to find the unknown.*

To convert from moles to mass, use this equation.

    amount in moles × molar mass (g/mol) = mass in grams

3 SOLVE   *Substitute known values to find the value of the unknown.*

The molar mass of an atom of oxygen is 16.00 g/mol. There are two moles of oxygen atoms in one mole of oxygen gas. Therefore,

$$\text{molar mass of } O_2 = 2 \text{ mol O} \times \frac{16.00 \text{ g O}}{\text{mol O}} = 32.00 \text{ g O}$$

Now, this value can be used to convert moles of O_2 into grams.

$$2.50 \text{ mol } O_2 = 2.50 \text{ mol } O_2 \times \frac{32.00 \text{ g } O_2}{\text{mol } O_2} = 80.0 \text{ g } O_2$$

4 CHECK YOUR WORK   *Check the answer to see if it is reasonable.*

The answer is correctly expressed to three significant figures. The answer is reasonable because 2.5 moles of oxygen gas contain 5 moles of oxygen atoms and 5 × 16 = 80.

PRACTICE

    D. How many moles are in 4.5 kg of $Ca(OH)_2$?

    What is the mass of Ca in one mole of $Ca(OH)_2$? _____

    What is the mass of O in one mole of $Ca(OH)_2$? _____

    What is the mass of H in one mole of $Ca(OH)_2$? _____

    What is the molar mass of $Ca(OH)_2$? _____

$$25.0 \text{ g Ca(OH)}_2 \times \frac{\_\_\_\_ \text{ g}}{1 \text{ kg}} \times \frac{1 \text{ mol Ca(OH)}_2}{\_\_\_\_ \text{ g Ca(OH)}_2} = _____$$

Ibuprofen, $C_{13}H_{18}O_2$, is the active ingredient in many nonprescription pain relievers. Its molar mass is 206.31 g/mol.

a. If a bottle of tablets contains 33 g of ibuprofen, how many moles of ibuprofen are in the bottle?

b. How many molecules of ibuprofen are in the bottle?

c. What is the total mass in grams of carbon in the bottle?

SOLUTION		
1 ANALYZE	*Determine the information that is given and unknown.*	

        Given: 33 g of $C_{13}H_{18}O_2$, molar mass = 206.31 g/mol

        Unknown: a. moles $C_{13}H_{18}O_2$ **c.** total mass of C

                    b. molecules $C_{13}H_{18}O_2$

2 PLAN   *Write the conversion factors used to find the unknowns.*

$$\textbf{a.}\ \frac{1\ \text{mol}\ C_{13}H_{18}O_2}{206.31\ \text{g}\ C_{13}H_{18}O_2} \qquad\qquad \textbf{c.}\ \frac{13\ \text{mol}\ C}{\text{mol}\ C_{13}H_{18}O_2},\ \frac{12.01\ \text{g}\ C}{\text{mol}\ C}$$

$$\textbf{b.}\ \frac{6.022\times10^{23}\ \text{molecules}}{\text{mol}}$$

3 SOLVE   *Substitute known values to find the value of the unknown.*

$$\textbf{a.}\ 33\ \text{g}\ C_{13}H_{18}O_2 \times \frac{1\ \text{mol}\ C_{13}H_{18}O_2}{206.31\ \text{g}\ C_{13}H_{18}O_2} = 0.16\ \text{mol}\ C_{13}H_{18}O_2$$

$$\textbf{b.}\ 0.16\ \text{mol} \times \frac{6.022\times10^{23}\ \text{molecules}}{\text{mol}} = 9.6\times10^{22}\ \text{molecules}$$

$$\textbf{c.}\ 0.16\ \text{mol}\ C_{13}H_{18}O_2 \times \frac{13\ \text{mol}\ C}{\text{mol}\ C_{13}H_{18}O_2} \times \frac{12.01\ \text{g}\ C}{\text{mol}\ C} = 25\ \text{g}\ C$$

To summarize, the bottle contains 0.16 mol of ibuprofen, or 9.6×10^{22} molecules of ibuprofen. Out of 33 g of ibuprofen, 25 g are carbon atoms.

4 CHECK YOUR WORK   *Check the answer to see if it is reasonable.*

Each answer is given to two significant figures and the units canceled correctly. The answer to part (c) is less than the total mass of the bottle. Also, judging from the chemical formula, most of ibuprofen is carbon (since hydrogen atoms have little mass), so 25 g out of 33 g is reasonable.

E. How many molecules are in 25.0 g of H_2SO_4?

What is the mass of H in one mole of H_2SO_4? _____

What is the mass of S in one mole of H_2SO_4? _____

What is the mass of O in one mole of H_2SO_4? _____

What is the molar mass of H_2SO_4? _____

25.0 g H_2SO_4

$$= 25.0 \text{ g } H_2SO_4 \times \frac{1 \text{ mol } H_2SO_4}{\text{g } H_2SO_4} \times \frac{6.022 \times 10^{23} \text{ molecules}}{\text{mol}}$$

= _____

F. How many molecules are in 125 g of sugar, $C_{12}H_{22}O_{11}$?

What is the molar mass of $C_{12}H_{22}O_{11}$?

Convert 125 g of $C_{12}H_{22}O_{11}$ to molecules of $C_{12}H_{22}O_{11}$.

G. What is the mass in grams of 6.25 mol of copper(II) nitrate?

What is the chemical formula for copper(II) nitrate? _____

What is the molar mass of copper (II) nitrate?

Convert 6.25 mol of copper(II) nitrate to grams of copper(II) nitrate.

Percent composition is the number of grams in one mole of a compound.

Another quantity that scientists often want to know is what proportion of a compound's mass is taken up by each element. **Percentage composition** is the percentage by mass of each element in the compound.

For example, suppose a chemist is using the compound potassium chlorate, $KClO_3$, to fill a container with oxygen gas. It would be helpful to know what percentage of the compound's mass is made up of oxygen atoms. The percentage composition of the compound is the ratio of each element's contribution to the compound's mass and the total mass of the compound. This ratio is expressed as a percentage, using the following formula.

$$\frac{\text{mass of element in sample}}{\text{mass of sample}} \times 100\% = \% \text{ element in compound}$$

The percentage composition of a compound is the same regardless of the size of the sample. This is because a compound has a fixed composition. Therefore, the compound's chemical formula can be used to determine the percentage of each element in one unit of the compound. The following formula is used to determine the percentage composition of a compound using the chemical formula.

$$\frac{\text{mass of element in 1 mol}}{\text{molar mass}} \times 100\% = \% \text{ element in compound}$$

LOOKING CLOSER

3. Define each of the following two terms separately in your own words.

percentage: _____

_____

_____

composition: _____

_____

_____

SAMPLE PROBLEM

Find the percentage composition of copper(I) sulfide, Cu_2S.

	SOLUTION	
1	**ANALYZE**	*Determine the information that is given and unknown.*
		Given: chemical formula, Cu_2S
		Unknown: percentage composition of Cu_2S
2	**PLAN**	*Determine the procedure used to find the unknown.*
		First, determine the molar mass of the compound. Then, find the ratio of each element's contribution to the molar mass.

Perform the calculations to find the unknown.

$$2 \text{ mol Cu} = 2 \text{ mol Cu} \times \frac{63.55 \text{ g Cu}}{\text{mol Cu}} = 127.1 \text{ g Cu}$$

$$1 \text{ mol S} = 1 \text{ mol S} \times \frac{32.07 \text{ g S}}{\text{mol S}} = 32.07 \text{ g S}$$

$$\text{mass of 1 mol Cu}_2\text{S} = 159.2 \text{ g}$$

$$\text{contribution of Cu} = \frac{127.1 \text{ g Cu}}{159.2 \text{ g Cu}_2\text{S}} \times 100\% = 79.85\% \text{ Cu}$$

$$\text{contribution of S} = \frac{32.07 \text{ g S}}{159.2 \text{ g Cu}_2\text{S}} \times 100\% = 20.15\% \text{ Cu}$$

Check the answer to see if it is reasonable.

A good way to check percentage composition problems is to make sure that the percentages add up to 100%.

PRACTICE

H. Find the percentage composition of $PbCl_2$.

What is the molar mass of $PbCl_2$?

contribution of Pb = 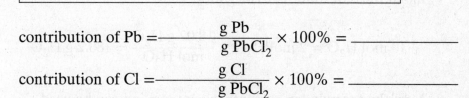 $\dfrac{\text{g Pb}}{\text{g PbCl}_2} \times 100\% = $ _____

contribution of Cl = $\dfrac{\text{g Cl}}{\text{g PbCl}_2} \times 100\% = $ _____

I. Find the percentage composition of $Ba(NO_3)_2$.

What is the molar mass of $Ba(NO_3)_2$?

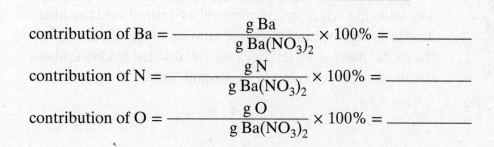

contribution of Ba = $\dfrac{\text{g Ba}}{\text{g Ba(NO}_3)_2} \times 100\% = $ _____

contribution of N = $\dfrac{\text{g N}}{\text{g Ba(NO}_3)_2} \times 100\% = $ _____

contribution of O = $\dfrac{\text{g O}}{\text{g Ba(NO}_3)_2} \times 100\% = $ _____

As some salts crystallize from a water solution, they bind water molecules in their crystal structure. Sodium carbonate forms such a hydrate, in which 10 water molecules are present for every formula unit of sodium carbonate. Find the mass percentage of water in $Na_2CO_3 \cdot 10H_2O$ with a molar mass of 286.19 g/mol.

SOLUTION

1 ANALYZE *Determine the information that is given and unknown.*

> **Given:** chemical formula and molar mass of $Na_2CO_3 \cdot 10H_2O$
>
> **Unknown:** mass percentage of H_2O

2 PLAN *Write the conversion factors to be used to find the unknowns.*

First, find the mass of water per mole of sodium carbonate. Then, compute the ratio of this mass to the molar mass of the hydrate.

3 SOLVE *Substitute known values to find the value of the unknown.*

Earlier in this section, the molar mass of water was calculated from the average atomic masses of hydrogen and oxygen. The molar mass of water is 18.02 g/mol.

$$10 \text{ mol } H_2O = 2 \text{ mol } H_2O \times \frac{18.02 \text{ g } H_2O}{\text{mol } H_2O} = 180.2 \text{ g } H_2O$$

Now, the formula for percentage composition can be used.

$$\text{contribution of } H_2O = \frac{180.2 \text{ g } H_2O}{286.19 \text{ g } Na_2CO_3 \cdot 10H_2O} \times 100\%$$

$$= 62.97\% \ H_2O$$

4 CHECK YOUR WORK *Check the answer to see if it is reasonable.*

The units in each calculation cancel as desired, and the final answer is expressed in the same number of significant figures as the molar mass of water. Because 180 divided by 300 is about 0.6, the final answer should be around 60%.

J. Find the mass percentage of water in $ZnSO_4 \cdot 7H_2O$.

What is the molar mass of $ZnSO_4 \cdot 7H_2O$?

What proportion of the molar mass of $ZnSO_4 \cdot 7H_2O$ consists of water?

$$\text{contribution of } H_2O = \frac{\text{g } H_2O}{\text{g } ZnSO_4 \cdot 7H_2O} \times 100\%$$

= _____

K. Magnesium hydroxide is 54.87% oxygen by mass. How many grams of oxygen are in 175 g of the compound? How many moles of oxygen is this?

What is the chemical formula of magnesium hydroxide? _____

What is the molar mass of magnesium hydroxide?

What portion, in grams, of the molar mass is oxygen?

$54.87\% \times$ _____ g magnesium hydroxide = _____ g O

How many moles of oxygen are in 1 mol magnesium hydroxide?

_____

VOCABULARY

1. Define *formula mass*. In what unit is formula mass expressed?

_____

_____

REVIEW

2. Determine both the formula mass and molar mass of ammonium carbonate, $(NH_4)_2CO_3$.

3. Calculate the percentage composition of $(NH_4)_2CO_3$.

Critical Thinking

4. RELATING IDEAS A sample of hydrated copper(II) sulfate $(CuSO_4 \cdot nH_2O)$ is heated to 150°C and produces 103.74 g of $CuSO_4$ and 58.55 g of H_2O. How many moles of H_2O molecules are present in one mole of hydrated copper(II) sulfate?

How many moles of $CuSO_4$ are in 103.74 g of $CuSO_4$? _____

How many moles of H_2O are in every mole of $CuSO_4 \cdot nH_2O$? _____

Use the answer to these two questions to determine the number of moles of water in the sample.

SECTION 7.4

Determining Chemical Formulas

When scientists discover or produce a new compound, they analyze it to learn its composition. Often what they measure is the percentage composition of the substance. Using the molar masses of the elements in the compound, they can convert the percentages into mole ratios. These molar ratios give the empirical formula for a compound.

An **empirical formula** consists of the symbols for the elements combined in a compound, with subscripts showing the smallest whole-number mole ratio of the different elements. An empirical formula is often the same as the compound's chemical formula. However, some molecular compounds, such as diborane, B_2H_6, consist of molecules that do not have the lowest whole-number ratio of atoms possible. The empirical formula for diborane is BH_3.

> ### KEY TERMS
>
> empirical formula

> **TIP** For ionic compounds, the empirical formula is almost always the same as the formula unit. However, the empirical formula would not reflect the presence of a polyatomic ion. For example, the empirical formula of $Ba(NO_3)_2$ is BaN_2O_6.

Empirical formulas show the whole number ratio of elements in a compound.

Empirical formulas are calculated from the percentage composition of a sample. The following steps will convert a percentage composition into an empirical formula.

1. Assume that you have 100 g of the sample. The mass of each element in this sample is numerically equivalent to the percentage composition for that element.

2. Convert each mass into a number of moles by using each element's molar mass as a conversion factor. Express the result as a molar ratio of the elements in the sample.

3. Divide the ratio from Step 2 by the number of moles of the element with the least amount of moles. If the result is a ratio of numbers very close to whole numbers, then this ratio gives the empirical formula of the sample.

4. If Step 3 does not yield a ratio of whole numbers, multiply the ratio by the smallest number that will give a whole-number ratio.

> ### 💡 Critical Thinking
>
> **1. Apply** An analysis of a sample of a compound determines that the compound contains 1 mol of phosphorus atoms for every 2.497 mol of oxygen atoms. What is the empirical formula of the compound?

Quantitative analysis shows that a compound contains
32.38% sodium, 22.65% sulfur, and 44.99% oxygen. Find the
empirical formula of the compound.

	SOLUTION	
1	**ANALYZE**	*Determine the information that is given and unknown.*

> **Given:** Sample is 32.38% Na, 22.65% S, 44.99% O by mass.
>
> **Unknown:** empirical formula

2	**PLAN**	*Describe the steps that will be used to find the unknown.*

The procedure on the previous page will convert a percentage
composition into an empirical formula.

3	**SOLVE**	*Calculate the unknown using the given information.*

A 100.0 g sample of the compound contains 32.38 g Na,
22.65 g S, and 44.99 g O.

$$32.38 \text{ g Na} = 32.38 \text{ g Na} \times \frac{1 \text{ mol Na}}{22.99 \text{ g Na}} = 1.408 \text{ mol Na}$$

$$22.65 \text{ g S} = 22.65 \text{ g S} \times \frac{1 \text{ mol S}}{32.07 \text{ g S}} = 0.7063 \text{ mol S}$$

$$44.99 \text{ g O} = 44.99 \text{ g O} \times \frac{1 \text{ mol O}}{16.00 \text{ g O}} = 2.812 \text{ mol O}$$

Then, divide the mole ratio of the three elements by 0.7063,
which is the least of the three amounts above.

$$\frac{1.408 \text{ mol Na}}{0.7063} : \frac{0.7063 \text{ mol S}}{0.7063} : \frac{2.812 \text{ mol O}}{0.7063}$$

$$= 1.993 \text{ mol Na} : 1.000 \text{ mol S} : 3.981 \text{ mol O}$$

This ratio is close to the ratio of whole numbers 2:1:4.
Therefore, the empirical formula of the compound is Na_2SO_4.

4	**CHECK YOUR WORK**	*Check the answer to see if it is reasonable.*

The result is an ionic compound formed from Na^+ cations
and SO_4^{2-} anions, which is a plausible combination.

A. A compound is found to contain 63.52% iron and 36.48% sulfur. Find its empirical formula.

What mass of Fe is present in a 100 g sample of this compound? _____

What mass of S is present in a 100 g sample of this compound? _____

Convert each mass above into moles.

_____ g Fe = _____ g Fe $\times$ $\dfrac{1 \text{ mol Fe}}{\text{g Fe}}$ = _____

_____ g S = _____ g S $\times$ $\dfrac{1 \text{ mol S}}{\text{g S}}$ = _____

Write the results above as a ratio and divide by the smallest amount.

_____ mol Fe: _____ mol S, divided by _____

= _____ **mol Fe:** _____ **mol S**

What is the empirical formula of the compound? _____

B. Find the empirical formula of a compound containing 26.56% potassium, 35.41% chromium, and the remainder oxygen.

What mass of K is present in a 100 g sample of this compound? _____

What mass of Cr is present in a 100 g sample of this compound? _____

What mass of O is present in a 100 g sample of this compound? _____

Convert each mass above into moles.

_____ g K = _____ g K $\times$ $\dfrac{1 \text{ mol K}}{\text{g K}}$ = _____

_____ g Cr = _____ g Cr $\times$ $\dfrac{1 \text{ mol Cr}}{\text{g Cr}}$ = _____

_____ g O = _____ g O $\times$ $\dfrac{1 \text{ mol O}}{\text{g O}}$ = _____

Write the results above as a ratio and divide by the smallest amount.

_____ mol K: _____ mol Cr: _____ mol O,

divided by _____

= _____ mol K: _____ mol Cr: _____ mol O

What is the empirical formula of the compound? _____

The empirical formula may or may not be equivalent to the molecular formula of a compound. Some compounds that have different molecular formulas have the same empirical formula. For example, examine the formulas for the two compounds, ethene and cyclopropane.

Ethene: molecular formula: C_2H_4
empirical formula: CH_2

Cyclopropane: molecular formula: C_3H_6
empirical formula: CH_2

The empirical formula is always the smallest whole-number mole ratio of the elements in a compound. A molecular formula does not have to be the smallest ratio, but it must be a whole-number multiple of the smallest ratio. In other words,

x(empirical formula) = molecular formula

where x is some whole number greater than or equal to 1. The numbers of atoms of each element in the empirical formula are each multiplied by x to obtain the molecular formula.

In order to determine the value of x, a chemist must have an additional piece of information. The chemist must be able to calculate the formula mass of the compound. The relationship between the empirical formula mass and the molecular formula mass is given by

x(empirical formula mass) = molecular formula mass

where x is the same whole number greater than or equal to 1 as defined in the first equation.

For example, from percentage composition measurements, a chemist might determine that the empirical formula of a compound is BH_3, with an empirical formula mass of 13.84 u. If separate measurements determine that the formula mass of the compound is 27.67 u, then the value of x is

$$x = \frac{\text{molecular formula mass}}{\text{empirical formula mass}} = \frac{27.67 \text{ u}}{13.84 \text{ u}} = 2.000$$

Therefore, the chemical formula of the compound is B_2H_6, and the compound is diborane.

Remember

The formula mass of a compound in u is equal to its molar mass in g/mol.

READING CHECK

2. Calculate The empirical formula for ethene, C_2H_4, and cyclopropane, C_3H_6, is CH_2. Use the relationship given above to calculate the value of x for each compound.

ethene: _____

cyclopropane: _____

The empirical formula of a compound of phosphorus and
oxygen is P_2O_5. Experimentation shows that the molar mass
of this compound is 283.89 g/mol. What is the compound's
molecular formula?

SOLUTION	
1 ANALYZE	*Determine the information that is given and unknown.*
	Given: empirical formula
	Unknown: molecular formula
2 PLAN	*Give the equations that will be used to find the unknown.*
	First, the value of x can be determined by this relationship.
	$$x = \frac{\text{molecular formula mass}}{\text{empirical formula mass}}$$
	Then, x can be used to calculate the molecular formula.
	$$x(\text{empirical formula}) = \text{molecular formula}$$
3 SOLVE	*Calculate the unknown using the given information.*
	The molar mass of the compound is 283.89 g/mol, so the molecular formula mass is 283.89 u.
	$$\text{Mass of P in } P_2O_5 = 2 \text{ P atoms} \times \frac{30.97 \text{ u}}{\text{P atom}} = 61.94 \text{ u}$$
	$$\text{Mass of O in } P_2O_5 = 5 \text{ O atoms} \times \frac{16.00 \text{ u}}{\text{O atom}} = 80.00 \text{ u}$$
	$$\text{empirical formula mass} = 141.94 \text{ u}$$
	$$x = \frac{\text{molecular formula mass}}{\text{empirical formula mass}} = \frac{238.89 \text{ u}}{141.94 \text{ u}} = 2.001$$
	Therefore, the molecular formula is $2(P_2O_5) = P_4O_{10}$.
4 CHECK YOUR WORK	*Check the answer to see if it is reasonable.*
	The empirical formula mass is about equal to $2 \times 30 + 5 \times 16 = 140$, which is half of the given molar mass.

c. Determine the molecular formula of the compound with an empirical formula of CH and a formula mass of 78.110 u.

The empirical formula mass of CH is

_____ u + _____ u = _____ u

$$x = \frac{\text{molecular formula mass}}{\text{empirical formula mass}} = \frac{_____ \, u}{_____ \, u} = _____$$

The molecular formula is _____ × (CH) = _____ .

D. A sample of a compound with a formula mass of 34.00 u is found to consist of 0.44 g H and 6.92 g O. Find its molecular formula.

_____ g H = _____ g H × $\dfrac{1 \text{ mol H}}{\text{g H}}$ = _____

_____ g O = _____ g O × $\dfrac{1 \text{ mol O}}{\text{g O}}$ = _____

Write the results above as a ratio and divide by the smallest amount.

_____ mol H: _____ mol O, divided by _____

= _____ mol H: _____ mol O

What is the empirical formula of the sample? _____

The empirical formula mass of the sample is

_____ u + _____ u = _____ u

$$x = \frac{\text{molecular formula mass}}{\text{empirical formula mass}} = \frac{_____ \, u}{_____ \, u} = _____$$

The molecular formula is _____ × _____ = _____ .

VOCABULARY

1. What is the relationship between the empirical formula and the molecular formula of a compound?

_____

_____

_____

REVIEW

2. A compound contains 36.48% Na, 25.41% S, and 38.11% O. Find its empirical formula.

3. If 4.04 g of N combine with 11.46 g O to produce a compound with a formula mass of 108.0 u, what is the molecular formula of the compound?

Critical Thinking

4. **RELATING IDEAS** A compound containing sodium, chlorine, and oxygen is 25.42% sodium by mass. A 3.25 g sample gives 4.33×10^{22} atoms of oxygen. What is its empirical formula?

Math Tutor CALCULATING PERCENTAGE COMPOSITION

Chemists can analyze an unknown substance by determining its percentage composition by mass. Percentage composition is determined by finding the mass of each element in a sample as a percentage of the whole sample. The results of this analysis can then be compared with the percentage composition of known compounds to determine the probable identity of the unknown substance. Once you know a compound's formula, you can determine its exact percentage composition by mass.

Problem-Solving TIPS

- To determine the percentage composition for a compound using its chemical formula, first determine the contribution of each element to the molar mass of the compound.
- Use this information to determine the molar mass of the compound.
- Then calculate the ratio of the mass contribution of each element to the total molar mass and express the ratio as a percentage.

SAMPLE

Determine the percentage composition of potassium chlorate, $KClO_3$.

First, calculate the molar mass of $KClO_3$.

Mass of 1 mol K = 39.10 g K

Mass of 1 mol Cl = 35.45 g Cl

Mass of 3 mol O = 3(16.00 g O) = 48.00 g O

The molar mass of $KClO_3$ is 39.10 g + 35.45 g + 48.00 g = 122.55 g.

The percentage composition of $KClO_3$ is determined by using the following formula to calculate the percentage of each element.

$$\frac{\text{mass of element in 1 mol}}{\text{molar mass}} \times 100\% = \% \text{ element in compound}$$

$$\text{Percent K by mass in } KClO_3 = \frac{39.10 \text{ g K}}{122.55 \text{ g } KClO_3} \times 100\% = 31.91\%$$

$$\text{Percent Cl by mass in } KClO_3 = \frac{35.45 \text{ g Cl}}{122.55 \text{ g } KClO_3} \times 100\% = 28.93\%$$

$$\text{Percent O by mass in } KClO_3 = \frac{48.00 \text{ g O}}{122.55 \text{ g } KClO_3} \times 100\% = 39.17\%$$

Practice Problems: Chapter Review practice problems 17 and 18

1. What are monatomic ions? Give three examples.

_____

_____

2. Using only the periodic table, write the symbol of the ion most typically formed by each of the following elements.

a. K _____ b. S _____ c. Ca _____

3. Write the formula for and indicate the charge on each of the following ions.

a. sodium ion _____ c. chloride ion _____ e. iron(II) ion _____

b. aluminum ion _____ d. nitride ion _____ f. iron(III) ion _____

4. Write formulas for the binary ionic compounds formed between the following elements.

a. sodium and iodine _____ c. barium and fluorine _____

b. calcium and sulfur _____ d. lithium and oxygen _____

5. Give the name of each of the following binary ionic compounds.

a. KCl _____ c. Li_2O _____

b. $CaBr_2$ _____ d. $MgCl_2$ _____

6. Write formulas for each of the following binary molecular compounds.

a. carbon tetrabromide _____ c. tetraphosphorus decoxide _____

b. silicon dioxide _____ d. diarsenic trisulfide _____

7. Name each of the following acids.

a. HF _____ c. HNO_3 _____

b. HBr _____ d. H_3PO_4 _____

8. Name each of the following ions according to the Stock system.

a. Fe^{2+} _____ c. Pb^{2+} _____ e. Sn^{2+} _____

b. Fe^{3+} _____ d. Pb^{4+} _____ f. Sn^{4+} _____

9. What three types of information are used to find an empirical formula from percentage composition?

_____

10. Write formulas for each of the following compounds.

a. sodium fluoride _____

b. calcium oxide _____

c. potassium sulfide _____

d. iron(II) oxide _____

e. aluminum bromide _____

f. lithium nitride _____

11. Name each of the following ionic compounds by using the Stock system.

a. NaCl _____

b. KF _____

c. CaS _____

d. $FePO_4$ _____

e. Hg_2SO_4 _____

f. $Hg_3(PO_4)_2$ _____

12. Assign oxidation numbers to each atom in the following.

a. HI

b. PBr_3

c. H_3PO_4

d. As_2O_5

e. NO_3^-

f. ClO_4^-

g. $Cr_2O_7^{2-}$

h. CO_3^{2-}

13. Determine the formula mass of each of the following compounds or ions.

a. glucose, $C_6H_{12}O_6$

b. ammonium ion, NH_4^+

14. Determine the number of moles of each ion in one mole of the following compounds. For each polyatomic ion, also determine the number of moles of each atom present in one mole of the ion.

a. $Ca_3(PO_4)_2$ _____

b. $Al_2(CrO_4)_3$ _____

15. Determine the molar mass of $Al_2(CrO_4)_3$.

16. Determine the number of moles in 4.50 g of H_2O.

17. Determine the percentage composition of $Mg(OH)_2$.

18. Determine the percentage by mass of water in $CuSO_4 \bullet 5H_2O$.

19. Determine the empirical formula of a compound containing 52.11% carbon, 13.14% hydrogen, and 34.75% oxygen.

20. What is the molecular formula of the molecule that has an empirical formula of CH_2O and a molar mass of 120.12 g/mol?

21. A compound with a formula mass of 42.08 u is 85.64% carbon and 14.36% hydrogen by mass. Find its molecular formula.

CHAPTER 8

Chemical Equations and Reactions

Key Concepts

Section 1 *Describing Chemical Reactions*
What signs tell you a chemical reaction has occurred?
What is a chemical equation, and what can it tell you?
How do you write and balance a chemical equation?

Section 2 *Types of Chemical Reactions*
What types of chemical reactions are there?
How can you predict the products of simple reactions?

Section 3 *Activity Series of the Elements*
What is an activity series, and why is it significant?
How do you know if a particular reaction will occur?

Review Previous Concepts

1. Explain how the charge of each ion in an ionic compound may be used to determine the simplest chemical formula for the compound.

2. Explain why oxidation numbers are useful in naming compounds and writing formulas.

SECTION 8.1

Describing Chemical Reactions

When iron rusts, oxygen combines with iron to make iron oxide. Iron and oxygen undergo a process called a chemical reaction. A chemical reaction is when one or more substances interact and produce one or more new substances. The original substances in a chemical reaction are called *reactants*. The new substances that are formed are called the *products*. In a chemical reaction, the total mass of the original reactants always equals the mass of the products. This is known as the law of conservation of mass.

Chemical reactions are described by chemical equations. A **chemical equation** is a way of showing the results of a chemical reaction using symbols and formulas. A chemical equation also shows the relative amounts of the reactants and products. For example, the chemical equation below shows that ammonium dichromate breaks down into nitrogen gas, chromium(III) oxide, and water.

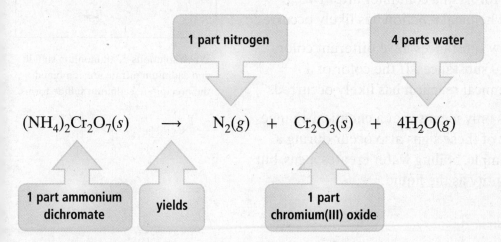

1 part nitrogen   4 parts water

$$(NH_4)_2Cr_2O_7(s) \longrightarrow N_2(g) + Cr_2O_3(s) + 4H_2O(g)$$

1 part ammonium dichromate   yields   1 part chromium(III) oxide

✓ READING CHECK

1. In the chemical equation above, name the reactant(s) and product(s).

_____

_____

Chemical reactions have physical indicators.

The only way to really know that a chemical reaction has occurred is to analyze all the substances before and after the reaction. If the chemical identities of the reactants are different from those of the products, then you know a chemical reaction took place. There are, however, other changes that are easier to observe that often indicate a chemical reaction is taking place. Here are some of the common signs of a chemical reaction:

Energy Release When ammonium dichromate decomposes, it releases energy very quickly. This energy can be observed in the form of heat and light. Many chemical reactions release energy in the form of heat or light or both. However, the release of energy can also occur during a physical change, so other factors must also be considered to determine if a reaction did take place.

Gas Formation When vinegar is mixed with baking soda, bubbles of carbon dioxide gas form. The formation of a gas when two substances are mixed is a good indicator that the original substances are reacting.

Precipitate A **precipitate** is a solid that forms during a chemical reaction in a solution and separates from the solution. If a precipitate forms in a container after two substances are mixed, a chemical reaction has likely occurred.

Color Change Often new substances have different colors from those of the original substances. If the color of a substance changes, a chemical reaction has likely occurred.

Observing these signs only means that a chemical change possibly occurred. Many of these signs also occur during a physical change. For example, boiling water creates a gas, but the gas has the same identity as the liquid.

This ammonium dichromate reaction releases energy very quickly.

When solutions of ammonium sulfide and cadmium nitrate are combined, the precipitate cadmium sulfide forms.

✓ READING CHECK

2. You mix two clear liquids and a colored solid forms at the bottom of the beaker. Do you think this is a chemical change? How can you know for certain?

_____

_____

_____

Chemical equations must satisfy the law of conservation of mass.

A good chemical equation will tell you everything you need to know about a specific reaction. Here are the requirements for a good chemical equation:

1. **The equation must represent known facts.** It accurately shows all the reactants and products. These can be identified by experiments and chemical analysis, or by using reliable sources for information.

2. **The equation must contain the correct formulas for the reactants and products.** Remember what you have already learned about writing symbols and formulas. Know the oxidation states of the elements, as this will help you write correct formulas. Remember that some elements, such as oxygen and hydrogen, are usually diatomic molecules. Some of these elements are shown in the table below. If an element is not usually found in molecular form, just use the atomic symbol.

3. **The law of conservation of mass must be satisfied.** Atoms are not created or destroyed in a chemical reaction. Check to make sure you have the same numbers and types of atoms on both sides of your chemical equation.

In order to balance equations, add coefficients before each substance in an equation. A **coefficient** is a small whole number that goes in front of a formula in a chemical equation. It indicates the relative number of moles of a substance. For example, $3H_2O$ represents three moles of water molecules in a chemical equation.

READING CHECK

3. Why should the numbers and types of atoms be the same on both sides of your chemical equation?

_____

_____

_____

Critical Thinking

4. Apply Write a chemical formula that indicates two moles of chlorine molecules.

_____

Element	Symbol	Molecular formula	Physical state at room temperature
Hydrogen	H	H_2	gas
Nitrogen	N	N_2	gas
Oxygen	O	O_2	gas
Fluorine	F	F_2	gas
Chlorine	Cl	Cl_2	gas
Bromine	Br	Br_2	liquid
Iodine	I	I_2	solid

Elements That Normally Exist as Diatomic Molecules

Word and Formula Equations

TIP Word equations are descriptions of a reaction. They do not tell you anything about the quantities of the substances.

1. The first step in writing a chemical equation is to identify the facts about a reaction that are known. It is often useful to represent these facts using a word equation. **A word equation** is an equation in which the reactants and products are written down in words.

   For example, when methane burns in air, it combines with oxygen to produce carbon dioxide and water vapor. To turn this information into a word equation, first identify the reactants and the products.

   REACTANTS: methane, oxygen
   PRODUCTS: carbon dioxide, water

   List the reactants on the left side of the equation and the products on the right side of the equation. Then draw an arrow pointing from the reactants to the products.

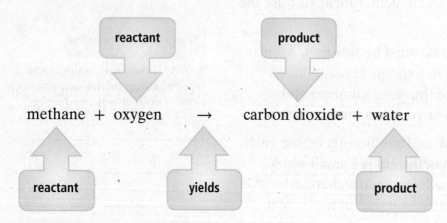

   The result is a word equation. This equation reads "methane and oxygen react to yield carbon dioxide and water."

PRACTICE

Write a word equation for each chemical reaction.

A. Solid calcium reacts with solid sulfur to produce solid calcium sulfide.

B. Hydrogen gas reacts with fluorine gas to produce hydrogen fluoride gas.

---

2. The next step in writing a chemical equation is to replace the words with the appropriate chemical formulas. A **formula equation** is an equation that uses chemical formulas and symbols to represent the reactants and products.

Consider the word equation from the previous page. Methane is a molecule that has one carbon atom and four hydrogen atoms. Its chemical formula is CH_4. Oxygen exists as a diatomic molecule, so its chemical formula is O_2. Carbon dioxide is CO_2 and water is H_2O. Therefore, the unbalanced formula equation is shown below:

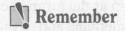 **Remember**

In a chemical formula, the state of the substance is shown in parentheses.

(*g*) is a gas

(*l*) is a liquid

(*s*) is a solid

(*aq*) is an aqueous solution, or a solution in water

$$CH_4(g) \ + \ O_2(g) \ \longrightarrow \ CO_2(g) \ + \ H_2O(g)$$

The formula equation also includes information about the state of each substance in the reaction. For example, all four of the chemical formulas above indicate that the substances are in gaseous form during the reaction. A substance can be designated as a solid, as a liquid, as a gas, or as part of an aqueous solution.

The formula equation states the substances that are involved in the reaction. However, it still does not give any information about the relative quantities of the reactants and the products.

PRACTICE

Write a formula equation for each of the following chemical reactions. Refer to the word equations you wrote on the previous page.

C. Solid calcium reacts with solid sulfur to produce solid calcium sulfide.

_____

D. Hydrogen gas reacts with fluorine gas to produce hydrogen fluoride gas.

_____

3. Look again at the formula equation for the reaction between methane and oxygen, shown below. In order to satisfy the conservation of mass, there should be an equal number of each type of atom on both sides of the equation.

$$CH_4(g) \ + \ O_2(g) \ \longrightarrow \ CO_2(g) \ + \ H_2O(g)$$

PRACTICE

E. Fill in the chart, showing the number of atoms on each side of the equation. The number of a given atom in each formula is equal to the product of the coefficient in front of the formula and the subscript on the atom.

UNBALANCED EQUATION		
Number of atoms of	Reactants	Products
carbon		
hydrogen		
oxygen		

Notice that the number of carbon atoms is the same on both sides. However, the numbers of hydrogen and oxygen atoms do not balance. We need to add coefficients to some of the formulas to make the equation balance. If we had two moles of oxygen on the reactant side, and two moles of water on the product side, the equation would be as follows.

$$CH_4(g) \ + \ 2O_2(g) \ \longrightarrow \ CO_2(g) \ + \ 2H_2O(g)$$

This balanced equation is a chemical equation. It contains an accurate description of the reaction and tells you about the relative quantities of the reactants and the products. One mole of methane gas will react with two moles of molecular oxygen to form one mole of carbon dioxide gas and two moles of water vapor.

Critical Thinking

5. **Evaluate** Show that there are the same number of each type of atom on both sides of the balanced equation.

_____

_____

_____

Additional Symbols Used in Chemical Equations

The table below shows some other symbols used in chemical equations. Some symbols may already be familiar to you.

Symbols Used in Chemical Equations	
Symbol	**Explanation**
$\longrightarrow$	"Yields"; indicates result of reaction
$\rightleftharpoons$	Used in place of a single arrow to indicate a reversible reaction
(s)	A reactant or product in the solid state; also used to indicate a precipitate
$\downarrow$	Alternative to (s), but used only to indicate a precipitate
(l)	A reactant or product in the liquid state
(aq)	A reactant or product in an aqueous solution (dissolved in water)
(g)	A reactant or product in the gaseous state
$\uparrow$	Alternative to (g), but used only to indicate a gaseous product
$\xrightarrow{\Delta}$ or $\xrightarrow{\text{heat}}$	Reactants are heated
$\xrightarrow{\text{2 atm}}$	Pressure at which reaction is carried out, in this case 2 atm
$\xrightarrow{\text{pressure}}$	Pressure at which reaction is carried out exceeds normal atmospheric pressure
$\xrightarrow{\text{0°C}}$	Temperature at which reaction is carried out, in this case 0°C
$\xrightarrow{\text{MnO}_2}$	Formula of catalyst, in this case manganese dioxide, used to alter the rate of the reaction

> A **reversible reaction** is a chemical reaction in which the products re-form the original reactants. Not all reactions are reversible.

> Some reactants must be heated for the reaction to take place.

> For some reactions, it is important to show the temperature or pressure at which the reaction took place.

> Some reactions can happen faster or at a lower temperature if a catalyst is present. A *catalyst* is a substance that has a temporary role in a chemical reaction, but is recovered unchanged when the reaction is complete.

Critical Thinking

6. **Analyze** Write the following chemical equation as a descriptive sentence. Include all the information available in the equation.

$$2\text{HgO}(s) \xrightarrow{\Delta} 2\text{Hg}(l) + \text{O}_2(g)$$

Write word and formula equations for the chemical reaction that occurs when solid sodium oxide is added to water at room temperature and forms sodium hydroxide dissolved in water. Include symbols for physical states in the formula equation. Then balance the formula equation to give a balanced chemical equation.

SOLVE	
STEP 1	*Write the word equation from the given information.*
	sodium oxide + water → sodium hydroxide
STEP 2	*Replace each compound's name with its chemical formula.*
	Sodium has an oxidation state of +1. Oxygen usually has an oxidation state of −2. Therefore, two sodium atoms will combine with one oxygen atom according to the chemical formula Na_2O. The hydroxide ion has an oxidation state equal to its charge of −1. Therefore, one sodium atom will combine with one hydroxide ion according to the chemical formula NaOH.
	$Na_2O + H_2O \rightarrow$ NaOH (not balanced)
STEP 3	*Indicate the state each compound is in.*
	$Na_2O(s) + H_2O(l) \rightarrow$ NaOH(aq) (not balanced)
STEP 4	*Balance the equation by adding coefficients.*
	There are two of each type of atom on the left side of the equation. To balance the equation, add a coefficient of two to the product.
	Solution: $Na_2O(s) + H_2O(l) \rightarrow 2NaOH(aq)$

Critical Thinking

7. Analyze Why would it be incorrect to balance the equation by changing NaOH to Na_2OH_2 instead of 2NaOH?

_____

_____

F. Write word and balanced chemical equations for the following reaction. Include symbols for the physical states of the substances when indicated.

Solid aluminum metal reacts with aqueous zinc chloride to produce solid zinc metal and aqueous aluminum chloride.

Word equation:

_____

Formula equation:

_____

Formula equation with states:

_____

Balanced chemical equation:

TIP Sometimes drawing the compounds can help you balance the equation.

Translate the following chemical equations into sentences.

G. $CS_2(l) + 3O_2(g) \rightarrow CO_2(g) + 2SO_2(g)$

_____

_____

_____

H. $NaCl(aq) + AgNO_3(aq) \rightarrow NaNO_3(aq) + AgCl(s)$

_____

_____

_____

When a chemical equation is balanced, it gives you a lot of information about the chemical reaction.

 Remember

The arrow in a balanced chemical equation is like an equals sign in a mathematical equation. The coefficients tell you the relative amount of each substance.

1. **The coefficients in a chemical equation tell you the relative, not absolute, amounts of the reactants and products.** The smallest units of matter that can undergo a chemical reaction are atoms, molecules, and ions. The law of conservation of mass determines how many of these small units are needed for a chemical reaction to take place.

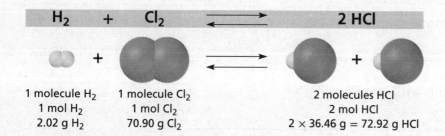

1 molecule H_2	1 molecule Cl_2	2 molecules HCl
1 mol H_2	1 mol Cl_2	2 mol HCl
2.02 g H_2	70.90 g Cl_2	2×36.46 g $= 72.92$ g HCl

For example, one molecule of hydrogen will react with one molecule of chlorine to form two molecules of hydrogen chloride. Similarly, one mole of hydrogen molecules will react with one mole of chlorine molecules to produce two moles of hydrogen chloride.

2. **The relative masses of the reactants and products of a chemical reaction can be determined from the reaction's coefficients.** When you have the relative amounts of the reactants and products, you can use these amounts to calculate the relative masses involved.

$$1 \text{ mol } H_2 \cdot \frac{2.02 \text{ g } H_2}{1 \text{ mol } H_2} = 2.02 \text{ g } H_2$$

$$1 \text{ mol } Cl_2 \cdot \frac{70.90 \text{ g } Cl_2}{1 \text{ mol } Cl_2} = 70.90 \text{ g } Cl_2$$

$$2 \text{ mol } HCl \cdot \frac{36.46 \text{ g } HCl}{1 \text{ mol } HCl} = 72.92 \text{ g } HCl$$

3. **The reverse reaction for a chemical equation has the same relative amounts of substances as the forward reaction.** Because a chemical equation is like an algebraic equation, the equality can be read in either direction. Two moles of hydrogen chloride will break down into one mole of molecular hydrogen gas and one mole of chlorine gas.

 **Critical Thinking**

8. Apply Use the molar masses to show that mass was conserved in the reaction.

_____

_____

Chemical equations can be balanced with step-by-step inspection.

Sometimes it is easy to balance a chemical equation just by looking at it. Other times, you may need to use trial and error until you find the solution. There is a step-by-step process to help you balance equations.

Consider the reaction that occurs when electric current is passed through water, as shown in the photograph at the right. An electric current is passed through water that has been made slightly conductive. The water molecules break down to yield hydrogen in the right tube and oxygen in the left tube.

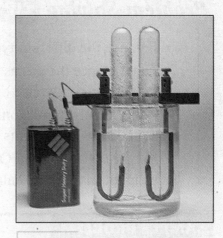

When an electric current is passed through impure water, oxygen gas bubbles into the left tube and hydrogen gas bubbles into the right tube.

1. **Identify the names of the reactants and the products, and write a word equation.**

   water $\rightarrow$ hydrogen + oxygen

2. **Write a formula equation by substituting correct formulas for the names of the reactants and the products.**

   $H_2O(l) \rightarrow H_2(g) + O_2(g)$ (not balanced)

   TIP Remember to check for diatomic molecules when writing chemical formulas for elements.

3. **Balance the formula equation according to the law of conservation of mass.** In this equation, hydrogen appears to be balanced but oxygen is not. Determine the coefficient for the reactant that will bring the oxygen atoms into balance. Then determine if the hydrogen atoms can be balanced by adding a coefficient to the hydrogen gas product.

   $2H_2O(l) \rightarrow H_2(g) + O_2(g)$ (partially balanced)

   Balance the oxygen atoms first. You need 2 more on the left.

   $2H_2O(l) \rightarrow 2H_2(g) + O_2(g)$ (balanced)

   TIP Make sure that equal numbers of atoms of each element appear on both sides of the arrow in a balanced equation.

   Next, balance the hydrogen atoms. You now need a total of 4 H on the right.

4. **Count atoms to be sure that the equation is balanced.**

   $2H_2O(l) \rightarrow 2H_2(g) + O_2(g)$

   $4H + 2O = 4H + 2O$ ✓

Problem-Solving TIPS

- Balance the different types of atoms one at a time.
- First balance the atoms of elements that are combined and that appear only once on each side of the equation.
- Balance polyatomic ions that appear on both sides of the equation as single units.
- Balance H atoms and O atoms after atoms of all other elements have been balanced.

SAMPLE PROBLEM

The reaction of zinc with aqueous hydrochloric acid produces a solution of zinc chloride and hydrogen gas. Write a balanced chemical equation for the reaction.

SOLUTION

1 ANALYZE

Write the word equation from the given information.

zinc + hydrochloric acid → zinc chloride + hydrogen

2 PLAN

Write the formula equation that needs to be balanced.

$Zn(s) + HCl(aq) \rightarrow ZnCl_2(aq) + H_2(g)$ (not balanced)

3 SOLVE

Adjust the coefficients to balance the equation.

Zinc is balanced. Next, look at chlorine. To balance chlorine, add a coefficient of 2 to HCl. Check hydrogen. Hydrogen is now also balanced. No more adjustments are needed.

$Zn(s) + 2HCl(aq) \rightarrow ZnCl_2(aq) + H_2(g)$

4 CHECK YOUR WORK

Count atoms to check the balance.

$Zn(s) + 2HCl(aq) \rightarrow ZnCl_2(aq) + H_2(g)$

Zinc reacts with hydrochloric acid.

BALANCED EQUATION		
Number of atoms of	Reactants	Products
zinc	1	1
chlorine	2	2
hydrogen	2	2

I. Balance the following equation:

$$Al_4C_3(s) + H_2O(l) \rightarrow CH_4(g) + Al(OH)_3(s)$$

Start by balancing the aluminum atoms on each side.

How many are on the left? _____ on the right? _____

Now add the coefficient to $Al(OH)_3$ that balances the aluminum atoms:

$$Al_4C_3(s) + H_2O(l) \rightarrow CH_4(g) + \boxed{}\,Al(OH)_3(s)$$

Next, balance the carbon atoms.

How many are on the left? _____ on the right? _____

$$Al_4C_3(s) + H_2O(l) \rightarrow \boxed{}\,CH_4(g) + \boxed{}\,Al(OH)_3(s)$$

Now look at the oxygen atoms. The compound $Al(OH)_3$ has three oxygen atoms. Multiply this by the coefficient to determine the total number of oxygen atoms on the reactant side. Then balance these atoms by putting a coefficient by H_2O.

$$Al_4C_3(s) + \boxed{}\,H_2O(l) \rightarrow \boxed{}\,CH_4(g) + \boxed{}\,Al(OH)_3(s)$$

Finally, look at the hydrogen atoms.

How many are on the left? _____ on the right? _____

Write the balanced equation and check that it is balanced.

_____

BALANCED EQUATION		
Number of atoms of	Reactants	Products

VOCABULARY

1. Describe the differences between word equations, formula equations, and chemical equations.

_____

_____

_____

REVIEW

2. List three signs that indicate a chemical reaction has probably taken place.

_____

_____

3. Translate the following chemical equation into a sentence:

$$2K(s) + 2H_2O(l) \rightarrow 2KOH(aq) + H_2(g)$$

_____

_____

4. Write the word, formula, and chemical equations for the reaction between hydrogen sulfide gas and oxygen gas that produces sulfur dioxide gas and water vapor.

_____

_____

_____

Critical Thinking

5. **INTEGRATING CONCEPTS** The reaction of vanadium(II) oxide with iron(III) oxide results in the formation of vanadium(V) oxide and iron(II) oxide. Write the balanced chemical equation for the reaction.

Word Equation:

_____

Formula Equation:

_____

Balanced Chemical Equation:

_____

SECTION 8.2

Types of Chemical Reactions

Chemical reactions occur in living systems, in industrial processes, and in chemical laboratories. Chemists often need to be able to predict what products will form during a chemical reaction. One strategy they use is to classify chemical reactions by their similarities. These classifications can be used to predict what products will result when certain substances react.

There are many different classification schemes for chemical reactions. One common way to classify reactions is to group them into five basic types:

- synthesis reactions
- decomposition reactions
- single-displacement reactions
- double-displacement reactions
- combustion reactions

KEY TERMS

synthesis reaction
decomposition reaction
electrolysis
single-displacement reaction
double-displacement reaction
combustion reaction

Substances are combined in synthesis reactions.

In a **synthesis reaction,** two or more substances combine to form a new compound. Synthesis reactions are also called composition reactions. A synthesis reaction is represented by the following general equation:

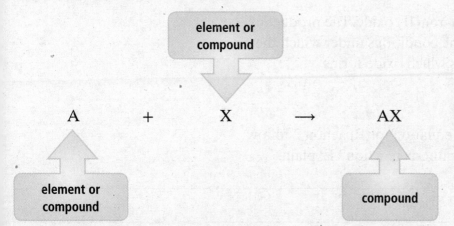

$$A \quad + \quad X \quad \longrightarrow \quad AX$$

A and X can be elements or compounds. AX is a compound.

READING CHECK

1. What is a synthesis reaction?

_____

_____

_____

_____

 TIP In a specific synthesis reaction, A, X, and AX will generally have subscripts and coefficients in the balanced equation.

Reactions of Elements with Oxygen and Sulfur

There are many examples of synthesis reactions that can occur in nature. For example, the Group 16 elements oxygen and sulfur readily combine with other elements to form compounds. A compound that is a combination of oxygen and another element is an *oxide*. A compound that is a combination of sulfur and another element is a *sulfide*.

Metal Oxides One simple synthesis reaction is the reaction between a metal and oxygen. This reaction produces an oxide of the metal. Most metals react with oxygen to form oxides. For example, magnesium reacts with oxygen to form magnesium oxide. The general formula for these oxides is MO, where M is the metal.

When this strip of magnesium is placed in an open flame, it will react with oxygen in the air.

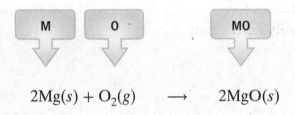

$$2Mg(s) + O_2(g) \longrightarrow 2MgO(s)$$

The Group 2 elements react with oxygen in a similar way to form oxides. However, the general formula for oxides formed from Group 1 metals is M_2O. Lithium, for example, reacts with oxygen to form lithium oxide, Li_2O.

Some metals can react with oxygen in different ways to form different types of oxides. For example, consider iron. There are two reactions that can each form an oxide.

Reaction 1 $2Fe(s) + O_2(g) \longrightarrow 2FeO(s)$

Reaction 2 $4Fe(s) + 3O_2(g) \longrightarrow 2Fe_2O_3(s)$

The reaction between magnesium and oxygen produces magnesium oxide, MgO, a fine white powder.

The product of Reaction 1 is iron(II) oxide. The product of Reaction 2 is iron(III) oxide. The conditions under which the reaction takes place determines which oxide forms.

Critical Thinking

2. **Analyze** Does the chemical equation for Reaction 2 follow the general equation for a synthesis reaction? Explain.

_____

_____

Metal Sulfides Group 1 and Group 2 elements also react with sulfur to form sulfides. For example, the Group 1 element rubidium reacts with sulfur to form rubidium sulfide. The general formula for a sulfide of a Group 1 metal is M_2S, where M is the Group 1 metal.

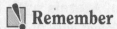
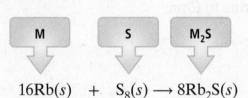

$$16Rb(s) + S_8(s) \longrightarrow 8Rb_2S(s)$$

Group 2 metals form sulfides with a different general chemical formula. The Group 2 element barium reacts with sulfur to form barium sulfide. The general formula for a sulfide of a Group 2 metal is MS.

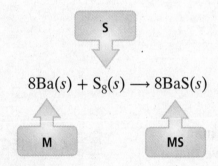

$$8Ba(s) + S_8(s) \longrightarrow 8BaS(s)$$

✓ READING CHECK

3. What is the general chemical equation for a Group 2 synthesis reaction that forms a sulfide?

_____

Nonmetal Oxides Nonmetals can also undergo a synthesis reaction to form oxides. Sulfur, for example, reacts with oxygen to form sulfur dioxide.

$$S_8(s) + 8O_2(g) \longrightarrow 8SO_2(g)$$

When carbon is burned in air, carbon dioxide is produced.

$$C(s) + O_2(g) \longrightarrow CO_2(g)$$

If the supply of oxygen is limited, carbon monoxide is formed.

$$2C(s) + O_2(g) \longrightarrow 2CO(g)$$

TIP Remember that *mono-* means one and *di-* means two. Knowing these prefixes can help you write the chemical formulas.

CONNECT

One very familiar nonmetal oxide is dihydrogen monoxide, or H_2O, better known as water.

Reactions of Metals with Halogens

Most metals react with the Group 17 elements, the halogens, to form either ionic or covalent compounds. For example, Group 1 metals react with halogens to form ionic compounds with the formula MX, where M is the metal and X is the halogen. For example, sodium reacts with chlorine to form sodium chloride.

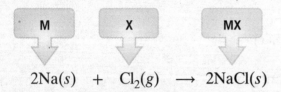

$$2Na(s) + Cl_2(g) \longrightarrow 2NaCl(s)$$

Group 2 metals react with the halogens to form ionic compounds with the formula MX_2. Magnesium reacts with fluorine to form magnesium fluoride.

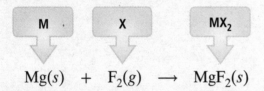

$$Mg(s) + F_2(g) \longrightarrow MgF_2(s)$$

The halogens undergo synthesis reactions with many different metals. Fluorine in particular is so reactive that it combines with almost all metals. For example, fluorine reacts with sodium to produce sodium fluoride. Similarly, it reacts with cobalt to form cobalt(III) fluoride and with uranium to form uranium(VI) fluoride.

$$2Na(s) + F_2(g) \longrightarrow 2NaF(s)$$

$$2Co(s) + 3F_2(g) \longrightarrow 2CoF_3(s)$$

$$U(s) + 3F_2(g) \longrightarrow UF_6(g)$$

 **CONNECT**

Sodium fluoride, NaF, is added to municipal water supplies in trace amounts to provide fluoride ions, which help to prevent tooth decay in the people who drink the water.

Natural uranium is converted to uranium(VI) fluoride, UF_6, as the first step in processing uranium for use in nuclear power plants.

PRACTICE

Complete the following chemical equations that show synthesis reactions involving metals and halogens.

A. $2K(s) + I_2(g) \longrightarrow$ _____ (s)

B. $Sr(s) + Br_2(l) \longrightarrow$ _____ (s)

C. $2V(s) + 3Cl_2(g) \longrightarrow$ _____ (s)

Synthesis Reactions with Oxides

Active metals are highly reactive metals. Oxides of active metals react with water to produce metal hydroxides. For example, calcium oxide reacts with water to form calcium hydroxide, an ingredient in some stomach antacids.

$$CaO(s) \quad + \quad H_2O(l) \quad \longrightarrow \quad Ca(OH)_2(s)$$

Calcium oxide, CaO, also known as lime or quicklime, is manufactured in large quantities.	The addition of water to lime to produce $Ca(OH)_2$, which is also known as slaked lime, is a crucial step in the setting of cement.	Calcium hydroxide, a base, can be used to neutralize hydrochloric acid in your stomach.

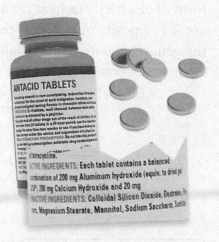

These antacid tablets contain two metal hydroxides in equal amounts: aluminum hydroxide, $Al(OH)_3$, and calcium hydroxide, $Ca(OH)_2$.

Many oxides of nonmetals in the upper right portion of the periodic table react with water to produce oxyacids. Remember that an oxyacid is an acid that contains oxygen. For example, sulfur dioxide, SO_2, reacts with water to produce sulfurous acid.

$$SO_2(g) + H_2O(l) \rightarrow H_2SO_3(aq)$$

In air polluted with sulfuric acid, sulfurous acid further reacts with oxygen. Sulfuric acid forms as a result. Sulfuric acid is one of the main ingredients in acid rain, and its acidity is responsible for damage to structures and the environment.

$$2H_2SO_3(aq) + O_2(g) \rightarrow 2H_2SO_4(aq)$$

Certain metal oxides and nonmetal oxides react with each other in synthesis reactions to form salts. For example, calcium sulfite, $CaSO_3$, is formed by the reaction of calcium oxide and sulfur dioxide.

PRACTICE

D. *Write the balanced chemical equation for the synthesis reaction showing how calcium oxide and sulfur dioxide form calcium sulfite.*

_____

_____

Substances are broken down in decomposition reactions.

In a **decomposition reaction,** a single compound undergoes a reaction that produces two or more simpler substances. Most decomposition reactions take place only when energy in the form of electricity or heat is added. Decomposition reactions are the opposite of synthesis reactions and are represented by the general equation given below. Substances A and X can be elements or compounds.

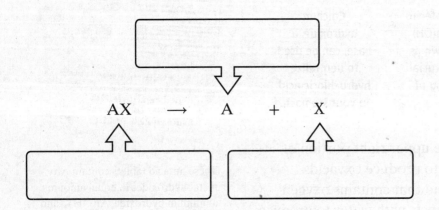

LOOKING CLOSER

4. Fill in the boxes to indicate whether each chemical formula can be an element, a compound, or both.

Decomposition of Binary Compounds

The simplest kind of decomposition reaction is the decomposition of a binary compound into its elements. Recall that passing an electric current through water will break the water molecules down into hydrogen and oxygen. The decomposition of a substance by an electric current is called **electrolysis.**

$$2H_2O(l) \xrightarrow{\text{electricity}} 2H_2(g) + O_2(g)$$

Oxides of the less-active metals, which are located in the lower center of the periodic table, decompose into their elements when heated. For example, mercury(II) oxide decomposes into mercury and oxygen when heated.

$$2HgO(s) \xrightarrow{\Delta} 2Hg(l) + O_2(g)$$

CONNECT

Joseph Priestley discovered oxygen in 1774, when he heated mercury(II) oxide to produce mercury and oxygen.

✓ READING CHECK

5. What is a decomposition reaction?

_____

_____

Decomposition of Metal Carbonates

When a metal carbonate is heated, it breaks down to produce a metal oxide and carbon dioxide gas. For example, calcium carbonate decomposes to produce calcium oxide and carbon dioxide, as shown below.

$$CaCO_3(s) \xrightarrow{\Delta} CaO(s) + CO_2(g)$$

Decomposition of Metal Hydroxides

All metal hydroxides except those containing Group 1 metals decompose when heated to yield metal oxides and water. For example, calcium hydroxide decomposes to produce calcium oxide and water through the following reaction.

$$Ca(OH)_2(s) \xrightarrow{\Delta} CaO(s) + H_2O(g)$$

Decomposition of Metal Chlorates

When a metal chlorate is heated, it decomposes to produce a metal chloride and oxygen. For example, potassium chlorate, $KClO_3$, decomposes to produce potassium chloride and oxygen when the catalyst $MnO_2(s)$ is present, as shown below.

$$2KClO_3(s) \xrightarrow[MnO_2(s)]{\Delta} 2KCl(s) + 3O_2(g)$$

Decomposition of Acids

Certain acids decompose into nonmetal oxides and water. Carbonic acid, for example, is unstable and decomposes readily at room temperature to produce carbon dioxide and water through the following reaction.

$$H_2CO_3(aq) \longrightarrow CO_2(g) + H_2O(l)$$

When heated, sulfuric acid decomposes into sulfur trioxide and water. Sulfurous acid, H_2SO_3, decomposes in a similar way.

$$H_2SO_4(aq) \xrightarrow{\Delta} SO_3(g) + H_2O(l)$$

 Remember

The "delta" symbol represents a reaction in which heat must be added in order for the reaction to occur. The decomposition of potassium chlorate below also requires the presence of a catalyst.

Critical Thinking

6. **Compare and Contrast** Compare the equation for the decomposition of sulfuric acid to the general formula for a decomposition reaction.

_____

_____

_____

One element replaces another in single-displacement reactions.

A **single-displacement reaction** is a reaction in which one element replaces a similar element in a compound. Single-displacement reactions are also called replacement reactions. Many single displacement reactions take place in aqueous solution. Single-displacement reactions can be represented by the following general equations.

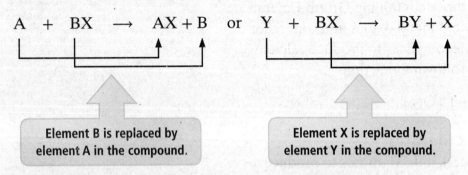

$$A \ + \ BX \ \longrightarrow \ AX + B \ \text{ or } \ Y \ + \ BX \ \longrightarrow \ BY + X$$

Element B is replaced by element A in the compound.

Element X is replaced by element Y in the compound.

A, B, X, and Y are elements. AX, BX, and BY are compounds. The amount of energy involved in a single-displacement reaction is usually smaller than the amount of energy involved in synthesis or decomposition reactions.

Displacement of a Metal in a Compound by Another Metal

If one metal is more reactive than another metal, the more reactive metal will often replace the less active metal in an aqueous solution. For example, when solid aluminum is placed in a solution of lead(II) nitrate, $Pb(NO_3)_2(aq)$, the aluminum replaces the lead. The lead precipitates out of solution, and the aluminum replaces the lead in the solution. Solid lead and aqueous aluminum nitrate are formed as a result.

$$2Al(s) + 3Pb(NO_3)_2(aq) \longrightarrow 3Pb(s) + 2Al(NO_3)_3(aq)$$

READING CHECK

7. Describe in your own words what happens when solid aluminum is put in a solution of lead(II) nitrate.

_____

_____

Displacement of Hydrogen in Water by a Metal

The most-active metals, such as those in Group 1, react vigorously with water to produce metal hydroxides and hydrogen. For example, sodium reacts with water to form sodium hydroxide and hydrogen gas.

$$2Na(s) + 2H_2O(l) \longrightarrow 2NaOH(aq) + H_2(g)$$

Less-active metals react with steam to form a metal oxide and hydrogen gas. Iron is one such metal.

$$3Fe(s) + 4H_2O(g) \longrightarrow Fe_3O_4(s) + 4H_2(g)$$

Displacement of Hydrogen in an Acid by a Metal

The more-active metals react with certain acidic solutions, such as hydrochloric acid and dilute sulfuric acid, replacing the hydrogen in the acid. The reaction products are a metal compound (a salt) and hydrogen gas. For example, solid magnesium reacts with hydrochloric acid to produce hydrogen gas and aqueous magnesium chloride.

$$Mg(s) + 2HCl(aq) \longrightarrow H_2(g) + MgCl_2(aq)$$

Displacement of Halogens

In another type of single-displacement reaction, one halogen replaces another halogen in a compound. Each halogen is less active than the one above it in the periodic table. Therefore, each element in Group 17 can replace any element below it, but not any element above it. For example, chlorine can replace bromine in potassium bromide to produce potassium chloride, as shown below.

$$Cl_2(g) + 2KBr(aq) \longrightarrow 2KCl(aq) + Br_2(l)$$

However, chlorine cannot replace fluorine in an aqueous solution of potassium fluoride. When a reaction does not typically occur, it is shown as follows.

$$Cl_2(l) + KF(aq) \longrightarrow \text{no reaction}$$

LOOKING CLOSER

8. As you study the equations on these two pages, draw arrows like those on the previous page to show the single displacements that occur.

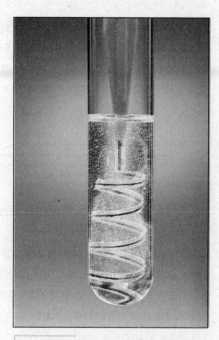

In *this single displacement reaction, the hydrogen in hydrochloric acid, HCl, is replaced by magnesium, Mg.*

READING CHECK

9. Explain why the following chemical equation is true.

$$Br_2(l) + KCl(aq) \longrightarrow \text{no reaction}$$

_____

_____

_____

_____

Single Replacement by Fluorine The element at the top of Group 17 is fluorine. This element is the most active halogen element. It can replace any other Group 17 element in a single-replacement reaction. For example, the combination of fluorine and sodium chloride produces sodium fluoride and solid chlorine.

$$F_2(g) + 2NaCl(aq) \longrightarrow 2NaF(aq) + Cl_2(g)$$

In double-displacement reactions, two compounds exchange ions.

In **double-displacement reactions,** the ions of two compounds exchange places in an aqueous solution to form two new compounds. A double-displacement reaction is represented by the following general equation.

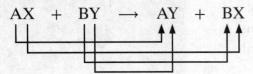

A, X, B, and Y in the reactants represent ions. AY and BX represent ionic or molecular compounds. One of the compounds formed is usually a precipitate, an insoluble gas that bubbles out of the solution, or a molecular compound, usually water. The other compound is often soluble and remains dissolved in solution.

When solutions of ammonium sulfide and cadmium nitrate are combined, the precipitate cadmium sulfide forms.

✓ READING CHECK

10. List three forms that the products of a double-displacement reaction usually take.

_____

_____

_____

11. What is the difference between a single-replacement reaction and a double-replacement reaction?

_____

_____

_____

Formation of a Precipitate

When the cations of one reactant combine with the anions of another reactant to form an insoluble or slightly soluble compound, a precipitate forms. For example, when a solution of potassium iodide is added to a solution of lead(II) nitrate, the yellow precipitate lead(II) iodide forms.

$$2KI(aq) + Pb(NO_3)_2(aq) \longrightarrow PbI_2(s) + 2KNO_3(aq)$$

The precipitate forms because there are very strong attractive forces between the Pb^{2+} cations and the I^- anions. The potassium and nitrate remain in solution as aqueous ions.

Formation of a Gas

In some double-displacement reactions, one of the products is an insoluble gas that bubbles out of the mixture. For example, iron(II) sulfide reacts with hydrochloric acid to form hydrogen sulfide gas and iron(II) chloride.

$$FeS(s) + 2HCl(aq) \longrightarrow H_2S(g) + FeCl_2(aq)$$

Formation of Water

In some double-displacement reactions, a very stable molecular compound, such as water, is one of the products. For example, hydrochloric acid reacts with an aqueous solution of sodium hydroxide, producing aqueous sodium chloride and water.

$$HCl(aq) + NaOH(aq) \longrightarrow NaCl(aq) + H_2O(l)$$

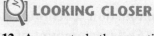 **LOOKING CLOSER**

12. As you study the equations on this page, draw arrows like those on the preceding page to show the double displacements that occur.

Critical Thinking

13. Analyze Write the reaction between hydrochloric acid and sodium hydroxide using the general form for the double-displacement reaction. How does this equation compare to the one above?

_____

_____

_____

Combustion reactions involve oxygen.

In a **combustion reaction,** a substance combines with oxygen, releasing a large amount of energy in the form of light and heat. The products of the combustion depend on the composition of the substance that is combusted. The most common products of a combustion reaction are carbon dioxide and water.

For example, the combustion of hydrogen gas produces water vapor. No other products form because all of the elements in the reactants are accounted for in the elements in water vapor.

$$2H_2(g) + O_2(g) \longrightarrow 2H_2O(g)$$

Other combustion reactions involve substances that contain carbon as well as hydrogen. These combustion reactions release heat and result in the formation of carbon dioxide and water vapor. For example, natural gas, propane, gasoline, and wood all consist of carbon and hydrogen atoms, and sometimes oxygen atoms. The equation for the combustion of propane, C_3H_8, is shown below.

$$C_3H_8(g) + 5O_2(g) \longrightarrow 3CO_2(g) + 4H_2O(g)$$

A candle supplies heat to a balloon filled with hydrogen gas.

The heat triggers an explosive combustion reaction.

🔲 Critical Thinking

15. **Analyze** What products would you predict from the combustion of methane? Explain your reasoning.

   $CH_4 + O_2 \rightarrow$ _____

_____

_____

VOCABULARY

1. Describe the following types of chemical reactions.

synthesis:_____

decomposition:_____

single displacement:_____

double displacement:_____

combustion:_____

REVIEW

2. Classify each of the following reactions as a synthesis, decomposition, single-displacement, double-displacement, or combustion reaction:

a. $N_2(g) + 3H_2(g) \longrightarrow 2NH_3(g)$ _____

b. $2Li(s) + 2H_2O(l) \longrightarrow 2LiOH(aq) + H_2(g)$ _____

c. $2NaNO_3(s) \longrightarrow 2NaNO_2(s) + O_2(g)$ _____

3. For each of the following reactions, identify the missing reactant(s) or products(s) and then balance the resulting equation. Note that each empty slot may require one or more substances.

a. decomposition:

_____ $Mg(ClO_3)_2 \longrightarrow$ _____

b. double displacement:

_____ $HNO_3 +$ _____ $Ca(OH)_2 \longrightarrow$ _____

c. combustion:

_____ $C_5H_{12} +$ _____ $O_2 \longrightarrow$ _____

Critical Thinking

4. INFERRING RELATIONSHIPS In an experiment, an iron sample is oxidized to form iron(III) oxide. The oxygen necessary for this oxidation reaction is generated from the thermal decomposition of potassium chlorate. Write these two chemical reactions in the correct sequence.

_____

_____

Activity Series of the Elements

The ability of an element to react is referred to as the element's *activity*. The more readily an element reacts with other substances, the greater its activity is. For metals, greater activity means it is easier to lose electrons to form positive ions. For nonmetals, greater activity means it is easier to gain electrons to form negative ions.

KEY TERMS

activity series

> **An activity series helps determine what substances will displace others in chemical reactions.**

An **activity series** is a list of elements organized according to the ease with which they undergo certain chemical reactions. Some chemical equations that can be written may not actually take place. Activity series are used to help predict whether certain chemical reactions will occur.

The order in which the elements are listed is usually determined by single-displacement reactions. The most-active element is listed at the top of the series. This element can replace any of the elements below it in a single-displacement reaction. An element farther down can replace any element that is below it but not any above it.

The table on the next page shows an activity series for the elements. The information in the table can be used as a general guide for predicting reaction outcomes.

Critical Thinking

1. Apply In the diagram, copper replaces the silver in a silver nitrate solution. Given that this reaction occurs, is copper above or below silver on the activity series?

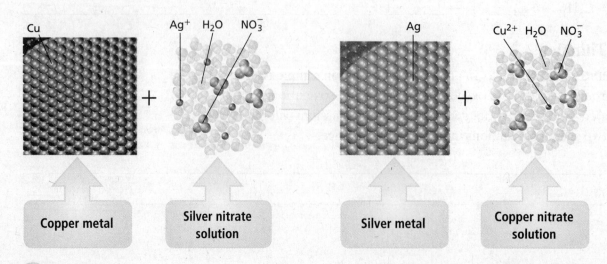

| Copper metal | Silver nitrate solution | Silver metal | Copper nitrate solution |

Activity Series of the Elements

Activity of metals		Activity of halogen nonmetals
Li Rb K Ba Sr Ca Na	React with cold H_2O and acids, replacing hydrogen. React with oxygen, forming oxides.	F_2 Cl_2 Br_2 I_2
Mg Al Mn Zn Cr Fe Cd	React with steam (but not cold water) and acids, replacing hydrogen. React with oxygen, forming oxides.	
Co Ni Sn Pb	Do not react with water. React with acids, replacing hydrogen. React with oxygen, forming oxides.	
H_2 Sb Bi Cu Hg	React with oxygen, forming oxides.	
Ag Pt Au	Fairly unreactive, forming oxides only indirectly.	

The halogens are listed in the same order as they are in the periodic table.

These elements are all alkali metals and alkaline-earth metals.

These elements are transition metals with *d* sublevels that are filled or nearly filled.

The activity series can be used to determine if a metal will react with acids or with water. Some metals (potassium, K, for example) react vigorously with water and acids, replacing hydrogen to form new compounds. Other metals, such as zinc, Zn, replace hydrogen in acids but react with water only when it is hot enough to become steam. Nickel, Ni, will replace hydrogen in acids but will not react with steam. And gold, Au, will not react with acids or water, either as a liquid or as steam.

✓ READING CHECK

2. Name three elements that are less reactive than mercury.

_____

_____

_____

Using the Activity Series In the activity series for metals, aluminum replaces zinc, because aluminum is listed higher on the activity series then zinc. Therefore, we would predict that the following reaction between aluminum metal and a solution of zinc chloride does occur.

$$2Al(s) + 3ZnCl_2(aq) \longrightarrow 3Zn(s) + 2AlCl_3(aq)$$

Cobalt, however, is listed below sodium on the activity series. Therefore, cobalt cannot replace sodium in a single-replacement reaction. Therefore, we would write the following.

$$Co(s) + 2NaCl(aq) \longrightarrow \text{no reaction}$$

SAMPLE PROBLEM

Using the activity series shown in the table on the previous page, explain whether each of the possible reactions listed below will occur. For those reactions that will occur, predict what the products will be.

SOLVE

a. $Zn(s) + H_2O(l) \xrightarrow{50°C} ?$

This is a reaction between a metal and water at 50°C. Zinc does not react with water when it is in liquid form. Therefore, no reaction will occur.

Answer: $Zn(s) + H_2O(l) \xrightarrow{50°C} \text{no reaction}$

b. $Cd(s) + Pb(NO_3)_2(aq) \rightarrow ?$

Cadmium, Cd, is above lead, Pb, in the activity series, therefore a reaction will occur to produce lead metal and cadmium nitrate, $Cd(NO_3)_2$.

Answer: $Cd(s) + Pb(NO_3)_2(aq) \rightarrow Pb(s) + Cd(NO_3)_2(aq)$

PRACTICE

Using the activity series, predict whether each of the possible reactions listed below will occur. For the reactions that will occur, write the products and balance the equation.

A. _____ $Cr(s) +$ _____ $H_2O(l) \rightarrow$ _____

B. _____ $Cd(s) +$ _____ $HBr(aq) \rightarrow$ _____

C. _____ $Mg(s) +$ _____ $H_2O(g) \rightarrow$ _____

VOCABULARY

1. What is the activity series, and how is the activity series useful in predicting chemical behavior?

_____

_____

_____

_____

REVIEW

2. Based on the activity series, predict whether each of the following possible reactions will occur. For the reactions that will occur, write the products and balance the equation.

   a. $Ni(s) + H_2O(l) \rightarrow$ _____

   _____

   b. $Br_2(l) + KI(aq) \rightarrow$ _____

   _____

   c. $Au(s) + HCl(aq) \rightarrow$ _____

   _____

   d. $Cd(s) + HCl(aq) \rightarrow$ _____

   _____

   e. $Mg(s) + Co(NO_3)_2(aq) \rightarrow$ _____

   _____

Critical Thinking

3. **PREDICTING OUTCOMES** A mixture contains cobalt metal, copper metal, and tin metal. This mixture is mixed with nickel nitrate. Which metals, if any, will react and why? Write the chemical equation for any reaction.

_____

_____

_____

_____

Math Tutor   BALANCING CHEMICAL EQUATIONS

A chemical equation represents exactly what happens in a specific chemical reaction. A balanced chemical equation shows that all of the atoms present in reactants are still present in products.

Problem-Solving TIPS

- First, identify reactants and products. (Write a word equation first.)
- Using correct formulas and symbols, write an unbalanced equation for the reaction.
- Balance atoms one element at a time by inserting coefficients.
- Identify elements that appear in only one reactant and one product, and balance the atoms of those elements first.
- If a polyatomic ion appears on both sides of the equation, treat it as a single unit.
- Double-check to be sure that the number of atoms of each element is the same on both sides of the equation.

SAMPLE

An aqueous solution of ammonium sulfate, $(NH_4)_2SO_4(aq)$, is combined with an aqueous solution of silver nitrate, $AgNO_3(aq)$. A precipitate of solid silver sulfate, $Ag_2SO_4(s)$, forms, leaving ammonium nitrate, $NH_4NO_3(aq)$, in solution. Balance the equation for this reaction.

First write an equation with the correct chemical formulas for all reactants and products.

$$(NH_4)_2SO_4(aq) + AgNO_3(aq) \rightarrow NH_4NO_3(aq) + Ag_2SO_4(s)$$

Look at the number of silver atoms on each side—one on the left and two on the right. The equation is not balanced.

In many reactions, polyatomic ions, such as sulfate, nitrate, and ammonium, do not change. NO_3 is present on both sides, as are SO_4 and NH_4. Balance the equation by treating the groups as if they were single atoms.

To balance the NH_4 groups, place a 2 in front of NH_4NO_3. This gives you two ammonium groups on the left and two on the right.

Because you have two nitrate groups on the right, place a 2 in front of $AgNO_3$ to give two nitrate groups on the left. Finally, check silver atoms and sulfate groups, and you find that they balance.

$$(NH_4)_2SO_4(aq) + 2AgNO_3(aq) \rightarrow 2NH_4NO_3(aq) + Ag_2SO_4(s)$$

Practice Problems: Chapter Review practice problems 11, 13–18

1. List the three requirements for a correctly written chemical equation.

_____

_____

_____

2. Give one example of a word equation, one example of a formula equation, and one example of a chemical equation.

_____

_____

_____

3. Write formulas for each of the following compounds.

   a. potassium hydroxide _____

   b. calcium nitrate _____

4. How many atoms of each type are represented in each of the following chemical formulas?

   a. $3N_2$ _____

   b. $4HNO_3$ _____

   c. $2Ca(OH)_2$ _____

5. How are most decomposition reactions initiated?

_____

_____

6. A substance is decomposed by an electric current. What is the name of this type of reaction?

_____

7. In what environment do single-displacement reactions commonly occur?

_____

8. What is the basis for the ordering of the elements in the activity series?

_____

9. Write the chemical equation for the following word equations. Include symbols for physical states in the equation.

a. solid zinc sulfide + oxygen gas → solid zinc oxide + sulfur dioxide gas

_____

b. aqueous hydrochloric acid + aqueous barium hydroxide → aqueous barium chloride + water

_____

10. Translate each of the following chemical equations into a sentence.

a. $2ZnS(s) + 3O_2(g) \rightarrow 2ZnO(s) + 2SO_2(g)$

_____

_____

b. $CaH_2(s) + 2H_2O(l) \rightarrow Ca(OH)_2(aq) + 2H_2(g)$

_____

_____

11. Balance each of the following equations.

a. $H_2 + Cl_2 \rightarrow HCl$

_____

b. $Al + Fe_2O_3 \rightarrow Al_2O_3 + Fe$

_____

12. Complete each of the following word equations for synthesis reactions.

a. sodium + oxygen → _____

b. magnesium + fluorine → _____

13. Complete and balance the equations for the decomposition reactions.

a. $HgO \xrightarrow{\Delta}$ _____

_____

b. $H_2O(l) \xrightarrow{\text{electricity}}$ _____

_____

14. Complete and balance the equations for the single-displacement reactions.

   a. $Zn + Pb(NO_3)_2 \rightarrow$ _____

_____

   b. $Al + NiSO_4 \rightarrow$ _____

_____

15. Complete and balance the equations for the double-displacement reactions.

   a. $AgNO_3(aq) + NaCl(aq) \rightarrow$ _____

_____

   b. $Mg(NO_3)_2(aq) + KOH(aq) \rightarrow$ _____

_____

16. Complete and balance the equations for the combustion reactions.

   a. _____ $CH_4 +$ _____ $O_2 \rightarrow$ _____

_____

   b. _____ $C_3H_6 +$ _____ $O_2 \rightarrow$ _____

_____

   c. _____ $C_5H_{12} +$ _____ $O_2 \rightarrow$ _____

_____

17. Circle the element within each pair of elements that is more likely to replace the other in a compound. Base your answer on the activity series of metals and halogens.

   a. K   and   Na   **c.** Au   and   Ag

   b. Al   and   Ni   **d.** Cl   and   I

18. Use the activity series to predict whether the following synthesis reaction will occur. Write the chemical equations for the reaction if it is predicted to occur.

   _____ $Ca(s) +$ _____ $O_2(g) \rightarrow$ _____

_____

CHAPTER 9

Stoichiometry

Key Concepts

Section 1 *Introduction to Stoichiometry*

What is stoichiometry?

What is the significance of mole ratios in stoichiometry?

How do you write mole ratios for substances in an equation?

Section 2 *Ideal Stoichiometric Calculations*

How do you find the molar amount of a reactant or product?

How do you find the mass amount of a reactant or product?

Section 3 *Limiting Reactants and Percentage Yield*

How can you determine which reactant is a limiting reactant?

How do limiting reactants affect stoichiometric calculations?

What is the difference between theoretical and actual yields?

What is percentage yield and how do you calculate it?

Review Previous Concepts

1. Describe how a balanced chemical equation gives you information about the relative amounts of reactants and products.

_____

_____

_____

_____

2. What is the general equation for a synthesis reaction? What is the general equation for a decomposition reaction?

_____

_____

SECTION 9.1

Introduction to Stoichiometry

Earlier you learned about **composition stoichiometry,** which describes the mass relationships of elements in a compound. **Reaction stoichiometry** describes the mass relationships between the reactants and products in a chemical reaction. Reaction stoichiometry is based on the law of conservation of mass. Mass is conserved in balanced chemical equations, so reaction stoichiometry problems always start with balanced chemical equations.

✓ READING CHECK

1. Write the definition of reaction stoichiometry in your own words.

_____

_____

Ratios of substances in chemical reactions can be used as conversion factors.

Reaction stoichiometry problems can be approached by looking at what information is given and what is unknown. There are four basic types of problems. Each type of problem requires taking the amount or mass of one substance and converting it to the amount or mass of another substance. These conversions are done using two quantities that will be discussed later in this section: the *mole ratio* and the *molar mass*.

1. **Both the given and unknown quantities are amounts in moles.** In this type of problem, you are given the amount of a substance in moles and asked to calculate the amount in moles of another substance in a reaction. The general plan to solve this type of problem is shown below. Only one conversion is necessary to solve this type of problem.

convert | amount of *given* substance (mol) | into → | amount of *unknown* substance (mol)

2. **The given quantity is an amount in moles and the unknown quantity is a mass in grams.** In this type of problem, you are given the amount in moles of one substance and asked to calculate the mass of another substance in the chemical reaction.

TIP If you are asked to find a mass, look at the units. Most of the time the masses will be in grams, but sometimes they will be in larger units, such as kilograms.

The general plan to solve this type of problem is shown below. Two conversions are necessary to solve this type of problem.

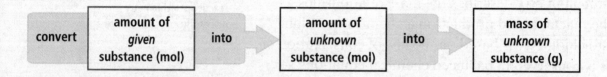

convert | amount of *given* substance (mol) | into | amount of *unknown* substance (mol) | into | mass of *unknown* substance (g)

3. **The given quantity is a mass in grams and the unknown quantity is an amount in moles.** In this type of problem, you are given the mass of one substance and asked to calculate the amount in moles of another substance in the chemical reaction.

The general plan to solve this type of problem is shown below. Two conversions are also necessary to solve this type of problem.

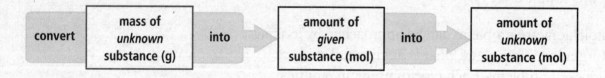

convert | mass of *unknown* substance (g) | into | amount of *given* substance (mol) | into | amount of *unknown* substance (mol)

4. **Both the given and unknown quantities are masses in grams.** In this type of problem, you are given the mass of one substance and asked to calculate the mass of another substance in the chemical reaction.

The general plan to solve this type of problem is shown below. Three conversions are necessary to solve this type of problem.

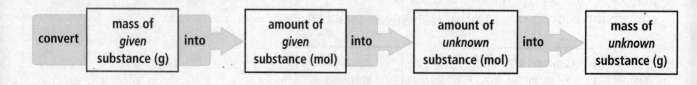

convert | mass of *given* substance (g) | into | amount of *given* substance (mol) | into | amount of *unknown* substance (mol) | into | mass of *unknown* substance (g)

Mole Ratio

A **mole ratio** is a conversion factor that compares the amounts of any two substances involved in a chemical reaction. The mole ratio of the substances is determined by the coefficients in the balanced chemical equation.

Consider, for example, the chemical equation for the electrolysis of melted aluminum oxide to produce aluminum and oxygen. The equation states that 3 mol of aluminum oxide yield 4 mol of aluminum and 3 mol of oxygen gas.

$$2Al_2O_3(l) \longrightarrow 4Al(s) + 3O_2(g)$$

If you are given the amount in moles for one substance, multiply by the appropriate mole ratio to find the moles of the other substance. The appropriate mole ratio is one that causes the units to cancel correctly. For example, to find the amount of aluminum that can be produced from 13.0 mol of aluminum oxide, the mole ratio needed is that of Al to Al_2O_3.

$$13.0 \text{ mol } Al_2O_3 \times \frac{4 \text{ mol Al}}{2 \text{ mol } Al_2O_3} = 26.0 \text{ mol Al}$$

Mole Ratios		
$\dfrac{2 \text{ mol } Al_2O_3}{4 \text{ mol Al}}$	**or**	$\dfrac{4 \text{ mol Al}}{2 \text{ mol } Al_2O_3}$
$\dfrac{2 \text{ mol } Al_2O_3}{3 \text{ mol } O_2}$	**or**	$\dfrac{3 \text{ mol } O_2}{2 \text{ mol } Al_2O_3}$
$\dfrac{4 \text{ mol Al}}{3 \text{ mol } O_2}$	**or**	$\dfrac{3 \text{ mol } O_2}{4 \text{ mol Al}}$

PRACTICE

A. How many moles of O_2 would 13.0 mol of Al_2O_3 produce?

Molar Mass

Remember that the *molar mass* of a substance is the mass, in grams, of one mole of that substance. The molar mass can be determined using the periodic table. It is the same value as the atomic mass of the substance, but given in grams. For the decomposition of aluminum oxide shown above, the molar mass of Al is 26.98 g/mol, the molar mass of O_2 is 32.00 g/mol, and the molar mass of Al_2O_3 is 101.96 g/mol.

Suppose you needed to find the mass of aluminum in grams that is equivalent to 26.0 mol of aluminum. You would convert moles to grams using the molar mass as shown below. In Section 2, several examples of how to use mole ratios and molar masses in stoichiometric calculations will be presented.

TIP To find the molar mass of a compound, add together the molar masses of each atom in the compound. Remember to multiply by any subscripts.

The molar mass of Al_2O_3 is two times the molar mass of Al plus three times the molar mass of O.

$$26.0 \text{ mol Al} = 26.0 \text{ mol Al} \times \frac{26.98 \text{ g Al}}{1 \text{ mol Al}} = 701 \text{ g Al}$$

VOCABULARY

1. What is stoichiometry?

_____

_____

2. What is a mole ratio, and how is it used in stoichiometry?

_____

_____

REVIEW

3. For each equation, write all possible mole ratios.

   a. $2HgO(s) \rightarrow 2Hg(l) + O_2(g)$

   [ ]

   b. $4NH_3(g) + 6NO(g) \rightarrow 5N_2(g) + 6H_2O(l)$

   [ ]

Critical Thinking

4. **RELATING IDEAS** What step must be performed before any stoichiometry problem is solved? Explain.

_____

_____

_____

SECTION 9.2

Ideal Stoichiometric Calculations

Balanced chemical equations are important for stoichiometric calculations. This is because the mole ratio can be directly found from balanced chemical equations. With a chemical equation, you can predict the relative amounts of the reactants and products that are needed for or produced in the reaction.

The chemical equation predicts what will happen for a reaction that takes place under *ideal conditions*. Under ideal conditions, all the reactants are completely converted into the products. Many real reactions proceed in a such a way that not all reactants are converted to products. However, stoichiometric calculations will tell you the maximum amount of the products that can form for a given amount of reactants.

Balanced equations give amounts of reactants and products under ideal conditions.

You are given the quantity in moles of one of the substances in a reaction. You must find the quantity in moles of another substance in the reaction. The general plan is shown below.

| convert | amount of *given* substance (mol) | into | amount of *unknown* substance (mol) |

This plan requires only one conversion factor—the mole ratio of the unknown substance to the given substance. To solve this problem, multiply the known amount by the conversion factor to get the unknown amount.

TIP Use the coefficients in the chemical equation to figure out the appropriate mole ratio conversion factors.

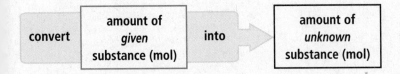

Amount of *given* substance (mol)

GIVEN IN THE PROBLEM

$\times \dfrac{\text{mol } unknown}{\text{mol } given} =$

Mole ratio (Balanced equation)

CONVERSION FACTOR

Amount of *unknown* substance (mol)

CALCULATED

In a spacecraft, the carbon dioxide exhaled by astronauts can be removed by its reaction with lithium hydroxide, LiOH, according to the following chemical equation.

$$CO_2(g) + 2LiOH(s) \rightarrow Li_2CO_3(s) + H_2O(l)$$

How many moles of lithium hydroxide are required to react with 20 mol CO_2, the average amount exhaled by a person each day?

1 ANALYZE

Determine the information that is given and unknown.

Given: amount of CO_2 = 20 mol

Unknown: amount of LiOH in moles

2 PLAN

Write an equation that can be used to find the unknown.

The mole ratio is obtained from the balanced chemical equation. Because you are given moles of CO_2, select a mole ratio that will cancel mol CO_2 and give you mol LiOH in your final answer. The correct ratio has the following units.

$$\frac{\text{mol LiOH}}{\text{mol CO}_2}$$

This ratio cancels mol CO_2 and gives the units mol LiOH in the answer.

$$\text{mol CO}_2 \times \frac{\text{mol LiOH}}{\text{mol CO}_2} = \text{mol LiOH}$$

mole ratio

3 SOLVE

Substitute the values in the equation and compute the answer.

$$20 \text{ mol CO}_2 = 20 \text{ mol CO}_2 \times \frac{2 \text{ mol LiOH}}{1 \text{ mol CO}_2} = 40 \text{ mol LiOH}$$

4 CHECK YOUR WORK

Check the answer to determine if it makes sense.

The answer is written correctly with one significant figure to match the number of significant figures in the given value of 20 mol CO_2. The units correctly cancel to leave mol LiOH, which is the unknown. The equation shows that twice the amount of LiOH reacts with CO_2. Therefore, the answer should be $2 \times 20 = 40$.

A. The decomposition of potassium chlorate, $KClO_3$, is used as a source of oxygen in the laboratory. How many moles of potassium chlorate are needed to produce 15 mol of oxygen gas?

Write the balanced equation for the decomposition reaction. Refer to Section 2 of the chapter "Chemical Equations and Reactions" for more information about decomposition reactions.

_____

What is the given quantity? _____

What is the unknown quantity? _____

Use the chemical equation to find the appropriate mole ratio and write the conversion equation.

```
+--------------------------------------------------+
|                                                  |
|                                                  |
|                                                  |
|                                                  |
+--------------------------------------------------+
```

Substitute numbers into the equation and calculate your answer.

```
+--------------------------------------------------+
|                                                  |
|                                                  |
|                                                  |
+--------------------------------------------------+
```

B. Ammonia, NH_3, is widely used as a fertilizer and in many household cleaners. How many moles of ammonia are produced when 6 mol of hydrogen gas react with an excess of nitrogen gas?

Write the balanced equation for the synthesis reaction.

_____

Use the chemical equation to find the appropriate mole ratio and write the conversion equation. Then substitute numbers into the equation and calculate your answer.

```
+--------------------------------------------------+
|                                                  |
|                                                  |
|                                                  |
|                                                  |
+--------------------------------------------------+
```

Mole-to-gram calculations require two conversion factors.

You are asked to calculate the mass (usually in grams) of a substance that will react with or be produced from a given amount in moles of a second substance. The plan for these mole-to-gram conversions is given below.

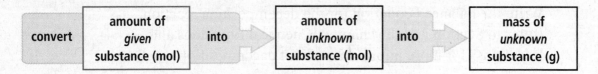

Two conversion factors are needed. The mole ratio of the *unknown* substance to the *given* substance is needed, as is the molar mass of the *unknown* substance.

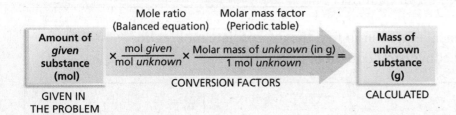

SAMPLE PROBLEM

In photosynthesis, plants use energy from the sun to produce glucose, $C_6H_{12}O_6$, and oxygen from the reaction of carbon dioxide and water. What mass, in grams, of glucose is produced when 3.00 mol of water react with carbon dioxide?

SOLUTION

1 ANALYZE   *Determine the information that is given and unknown.*

Given: amount of H_2O = 3.00 mol

Unknown: mass of $C_6H_{12}O_6$ produced in grams

2 PLAN   *Write an equation that can be used to find the unknown.*

Two conversion factors are needed—the mass ratio of glucose to water and the molar mass of glucose.

$$\text{mol } H_2O \times \frac{\text{mol } C_6H_{12}O_6}{\text{mol } H_2O} \times \frac{\text{g } C_6H_{12}O_6}{\text{mol } C_6H_{12}O_6} = \text{g } C_6H_{12}O_6$$

mole ratio molar mass factor

3 SOLVE

Substitute the values in the equation and compute the answer.

First, write the balanced equation for the reaction.

$$6CO_2(g) + 6H_2O(l) \rightarrow C_6H_{12}O_6(s) + 6O_2(g)$$

Then, compute the molar mass of $C_6H_{12}O_6$.

$$\text{g/mol } C_6H_{12}O_6$$
$$= 6(12.01 \text{ g/mol C}) + 12(1.01 \text{ g/mol H}) + 6(16.00 \text{ g/mol O})$$
$$= 180.18 \text{ g/mol}$$

Finally, use both conversion factors to find the answer.

$$3.00 \text{ mol } H_2O \times \frac{1 \text{ mol } C_6H_{12}O_6}{6 \text{ mol } H_2O} \times \frac{180.19 \text{ g } C_6H_{12}O_6}{1 \text{ mol } C_6H_{12}O_6} = 90.1 \text{ g } C_6H_{12}O_6$$

4 CHECK YOUR WORK

Check the answer to determine if it makes sense.

The answer is correctly rounded to three significant figures, to match those in 3.00 mol H_2O. The units cancel correctly, leaving g $C_6H_{12}O_6$ as the units for the answer. The answer is reasonable because it is about three-sixths, or one-half, of 180.

PRACTICE

c. When magnesium burns in air, it combines with oxygen to form magnesium oxide according to the following equation. What mass in grams of magnesium oxide is produced from 2.00 mol of magnesium?

$$2Mg(s) + O_2(g) \rightarrow 2MgO(s)$$

What is the given quantity? _____

What is the unknown quantity? _____

Write the two conversion factors needed to solve the problem.

Calculate the molar mass of the unknown using the given quantity and the two conversion factors.

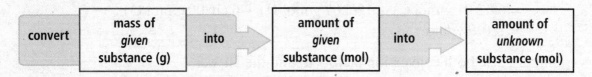

Gram-to-mole conversions require the molar mass of the given substance and the mole ratio.

You are asked to calculate the amount in moles of one substance that will react with or be produced from a given mass of another substance. In this type of problem, you are starting with a mass (probably in grams) of some substance. The plan for this conversion is given below.

| convert | mass of *given* substance (g) | into | amount of *given* substance (mol) | into | amount of *unknown* substance (mol) |

This procedure is similar to the previous procedure. You need two additional pieces of data—the molar mass of the *given* substance and the mole ratio of the two substances. You can use the units of the molar mass conversion factor to guide you in your calculations. Because the known quantity is a mass, the conversion factor will need to be 1 mol divided by the molar mass. This will cancel grams and leave moles.

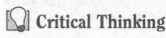 **Critical Thinking**

2. Compare and Contrast How does this procedure compare to the previous procedure?

_____

_____

_____

_____

_____

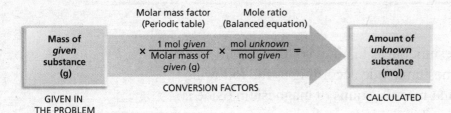

PRACTICE

D. The following reaction produced 10.0 g of O_2.

$$6CO_2(g) + 6H_2O(l) \rightarrow C_6H_{12}O_6(aq) + 6O_2(g)$$

What two conversion factors would you need in order to determine the number of moles of H_2O used to run the reaction?

SAMPLE PROBLEM

The first step in the industrial manufacture of nitric acid is the catalytic oxidation of ammonia.

$$NH_3(g) + O_2(g) \rightarrow NO(g) + H_2O(g) \text{ (unbalanced)}$$

The reaction is run using 824 g NH_3 and excess oxygen. How many moles of NO are formed?

	SOLUTION	
1	ANALYZE	*Determine the information that is given and unknown.*
		Given: mass of NH_3 = 824 g
		Unknown: amount of NO produced in moles
2	PLAN	*Write an equation that can be used to find the unknown.*

Two conversion factors are needed—the molar mass factor for NH_3 and the mole ratio of NO to NH_3.

$$\text{g } NH_3 \quad \times \quad \frac{\text{mol } NH_3}{\text{g } NH_3} \quad \times \quad \frac{\text{mol NO}}{\text{mol } NH_3} \quad = \quad \text{mol NO}$$

molar mass factor   mole ratio

3	SOLVE	*Substitute the values in the equation and compute the answer.*

First, balance the equation for the reaction.

$$\text{molar mass} = 14.01 \text{ g/mol N} + 3(1.01 \text{ g/mol H}) = 17.04 \text{ g/mol } NH_3$$

Then use the periodic table to compute the molar mass of NH_3 and use the chemical equation to find the mole ratio. Then substitute the numbers into the conversion equation to find the answer.

$$4NH_3(g) + 5O_2(g) \rightarrow 4NO(g) + 6H_2O(g)$$

Finally, compute the molar mass of NH_3 and apply the conversion factors to find the answer.

$$824 \text{ g } NH_3 \times \frac{1 \text{ mol } NH_3}{17.04 \text{ g } NH_3} \times \frac{4 \text{ mol NO}}{4 \text{ mol } NH_3} = 48.4 \text{ mol NO}$$

4	CHECK YOUR WORK	*Check the answer to determine if it makes sense.*

The answer is correctly given to three significant figures. The units cancel out to leave the unknown.

Mass-to-mass calculations use the mole ratio and the molar masses of the given and unknown substances.

Mass-mass calculations are usually more useful than the other calculations. You cannot measure moles directly, but you can measure the masses of the products and reactants involved. The plan for solving mass-mass problems is given below.

TIP Mass-mass problems can be viewed as the combination of the other types of problems.

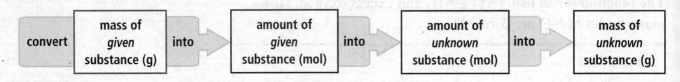

To solve mass-mass problems, you need three conversion factors. They are the molar mass of the given substance, the mole ratio, and the molar mass of the unknown substance.

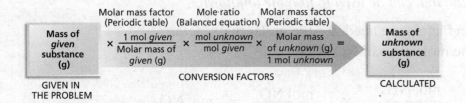

SAMPLE PROBLEM

How many grams of SnF_2 are produced from the reaction of 30.00 g HF with Sn? The reaction is given by this equation.

$$Sn(s) + 2HF(g) \rightarrow SnF_2(s) + H_2(g)$$

	SOLUTION	
1	ANALYZE	**Given:** amount of HF = 30.00 g
		Unknown: mass of SnF_2 produced in grams
2	PLAN	Three conversion factors are needed.
		$$g\ HF \times \frac{mol\ HF}{g\ HF} \times \frac{mol\ SnF_2}{mol\ HF} \times \frac{g\ SnF_2}{mol\ SnF_2} = g\ SnF_2$$
3	SOLVE	The molar masses are 20.01 g/mol HF and 156.71 g/mol SnF_2.
		$$30.00\ g\ HF \times \frac{mol\ HF}{20.01\ g\ HF} \times \frac{1\ mol\ SnF_2}{2\ mol\ HF} \times \frac{156.71\ g\ SnF_2}{mol\ SnF_2} = 117.5\ g\ SnF_2$$

E. What mass of aluminum is produced by the decomposition of 5.0 kg Al_2O_3? How many moles of oxygen are produced?

What is the given quantity? _____

What is the unknown quantity? _____

Write the balanced decomposition reaction.

_____

What conversion factors are needed to find the mass of aluminum produced? The moles of oxygen produced?

mass Al

mol O

Find the molar mass ratios needed for both problems.

_____

_____

Substitute numbers into the conversion factors and calculate your answers.

mass Al

mol O

Check your answers.

_____

REVIEW

1. Balance the following equation. Then, given the moles of reactant or product below, determine the corresponding amount in moles of each of the other reactants and products.

$$NH_3 + O_2 \rightarrow N_2 + H_2O$$

_____

a. 4 mol NH_3

b. 4.5 mol O_2

2. One reaction that produces hydrogen gas can be represented by the following unbalanced chemical equation:

$$Mg(s) + HCl(aq) \rightarrow MgCl_2(aq) + H_2(g)$$

What mass of HCl is consumed by the reaction of 2.50 mol of magnesium?

Critical Thinking

3. **RELATING IDEAS** Carbon and oxygen react to form carbon monoxide as in the equation $2C + O_2 \rightarrow 2CO$. What masses of carbon and oxygen are needed to make 56.0 g CO?

Which law does this illustrate?

_____

SECTION 9.3

Limiting Reactants and Percentage Yield

In the laboratory, a reaction is rarely carried out with exactly the required amount of each of the reactants. Usually, one or more of the reactants is present in excess: there is more than the exact amount required to react.

Once one of the reactants is used up, the reaction stops. No more product can be formed. The substance that is completely used up first in a reaction is called the limiting reactant. The **limiting reactant** is the reactant that limits the amount of the other reactant that can combine and the amount of product that can form in a chemical reaction. A limiting reactant may also be referred to as a *limiting reagent*. The substance that is not used up completely in a reaction is called the **excess reactant.**

Consider the reaction between carbon and oxygen to form carbon dioxide. According to the equation, one mole of carbon reacts with one mole of oxygen to form one mole of carbon dioxide.

$$C(s) + O_2(g) \rightarrow CO_2(g)$$

Suppose you could mix 5 mol C with 10 mol O_2. The following diagram summarizes what would take place.

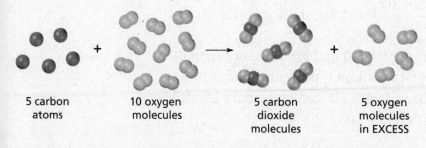

| 5 carbon atoms | 10 oxygen molecules | 5 carbon dioxide molecules | 5 oxygen molecules in EXCESS |

There is more oxygen than is needed to react with the carbon. Carbon is the limiting reactant in this situation, and it limits the amount of CO_2 that is formed. Oxygen is the excess reactant, and 5 mol O_2 will be left over at the end of the reaction.

KEY TERMS

limiting reactant   actual yield
excess reactant   percentage yield
theoretical yield

 READING CHECK

1. If 15 mol C is mixed with 10 mol O_2 to form CO_2, which reactant is the limiting reactant?

_____

Which reactant would be the excess reactant?

_____

Silicon dioxide (quartz) is usually quite unreactive but reacts readily with hydrogen fluoride according to the following equation.

$$SiO_2(s) + 4HF(g) \rightarrow SiF_4(g) + 2H_2O(l)$$

If 6.0 mol HF is added to 4.5 mol SiO_2, which is the limiting reactant?

	SOLUTION	
1	**ANALYZE**	*Determine the information that is given and unknown.*

Given: amount of HF = 6.0 mol, amount of SiO_2 = 4.5 mol

Unknown: limiting reactant |
| **2** | **PLAN** | *Determine how the unknown value can be calculated.*

First, calculate the amount of a product that can be formed with each of the given reactant amounts.

$$\text{mol HF} \times \frac{\text{mol SiF}_4}{\text{mol HF}} \text{ mol} = \text{mol SiF}_4 \text{ produced}$$

$$\text{mol SiO}_2 \times \frac{\text{mol SiF}_4}{\text{mol SiO}_2} = \text{mol SiF}_4 \text{ produced}$$

One amount will be less than the other. The lesser amount represents the maximum amount of that product that can possibly be formed. The limiting reactant is the reactant that gives this lesser amount of product. |
| **3** | **SOLVE** | *Substitute the given values to determine the limiting reactant.*

$$6.0 \text{ mol HF} \times \frac{1 \text{ mol SiF}_4}{4 \text{ mol HF}} = 1.5 \text{ mol SiF}_4 \text{ produced}$$

$$4.5 \text{ mol SiO}_2 \times \frac{1 \text{ mol SiF}_4}{1 \text{ mol SiO}_2} = 4.5 \text{ mol SiF}_4 \text{ produced}$$

Under ideal conditions, the 6.0 mol HF present can make 1.5 mol SiF_4, and the 4.5 mol SiO_2 present can make 4.5 mol SiF_4. Because 6.0 mol HF can make only 1.5 mol SiF_4, HF is the limiting reactant. |
| **4** | **CHECK YOUR WORK** | *Check the answer to see if it makes sense.*

The reaction requires four times the number of moles of HF as it does moles of SiO_2. Because the amount of HF available is less than four times the amount of SiO_2 available, HF is the limiting reactant. |

A. Some rocket engines use a mixture of hydrazine, N_2H_4, and hydrogen peroxide, H_2O_2, as the propellant. The reaction is given by the following equation.

$$N_2H_4(l) + 2H_2O_2(l) \rightarrow N_2(g) + 4H_2O(g)$$

a. Which is the limiting reactant in this reaction when 0.750 mol N_2H_4 is mixed with 0.500 mol H_2O_2?

b. How much of the excess reactant, in moles, remains unchanged?

a. What is given? _____

What is unknown? _____

What quantity of N_2 is produced by 0.750 mol N_2H_4?

What quantity of N_2 is produced by 0.500 mol H_2O_2?

Which reactant is the limiting reactant? _____

b. Using the amount of the limiting reactant calculated above, find the amount of the excess reactant that is used in the reaction.

Subtract the amount of the excess reactant used in the reaction from the total amount of excess reactant. How much of the excess reactant, in moles, remains unchanged?

_____

Check your answers. _____

Iron oxide, Fe_3O_4, can be made in the laboratory by the reaction between red-hot iron and steam according to the following equation.

$$3Fe(s) + 4H_2O(g) \rightarrow Fe_3O_4(s) + 4H_2(g)$$

a. When 36.0 g H_2O is mixed with 67.0 g Fe, which reactant is the limiting reactant?

b. What mass in grams of black iron oxide is produced?

c. What mass in grams of excess reactant remains when the reaction is completed?

SOLUTION

1 ANALYZE *Determine the information that is given and unknown.*

Given: mass of H_2O = 36.0 g, mass of Fe = 67.0 g

Unknown: a. limiting reactant
b. mass of Fe_3O_4 produced
c. mass of excess reactant left over

2 PLAN *Determine how the unknown values can be calculated.*

a. The reactant yielding the smaller number of moles of product is the limiting reactant.

molar mass factor	mole ratio

$$g\ Fe \quad \times \quad \frac{mol\ Fe}{g\ Fe} \quad \times \quad \frac{mol\ Fe_3O_4}{mol\ Fe} \quad = \quad mol\ Fe_3O_4$$

molar mass factor	mole ratio

$$g\ H_2O \quad \times \quad \frac{mol\ H_2O}{g\ H_2O} \quad \times \quad \frac{mol\ Fe_3O_4}{mol\ H_2O} \quad = \quad mol\ Fe_3O_4$$

b. To find the maximum mass of Fe_3O_4 that can be produced, use the amount of Fe_3O_4 in moles from the limiting reactant.

molar mass factor

$$mol\ Fe_3O_4\ \text{from limiting reactant} \times \frac{g\ Fe_3O_4}{mol\ Fe_3O_4} = g\ Fe_3O_4$$

c. Use the moles of product found using the limiting reactant to determine the amount of the excess reactant that is consumed. Then subtract the amount consumed from the original amount.

$$\text{mol product} \times \frac{\text{mol excess reactant}}{\text{mol product}} \times \frac{\text{g excess reactant}}{\text{mol excess reactant}}$$

= grams of excess reactant consumed

original mass − mass consumed = mass of reactant remaining

3 SOLVE

Substitute the given values to determine the unknown values.

a. The molar masses are 18.02 g/mol H_2O, 55.85 g/mol Fe, and 231.55 g/mol Fe_3O_4.

$$67.0 \text{ g Fe} \times \frac{1 \text{ mol Fe}}{55.85 \text{ g Fe}} \times \frac{1 \text{ mol Fe}_2O_4}{3 \text{ mol Fe}} = 0.400 \text{ mol Fe}_3O_4$$

$$36.0 \text{ g H}_2O \frac{1 \text{ mol H}_2O}{18.02 \text{ g H}_2O} \times \frac{1 \text{ mol Fe}_3O_4}{4 \text{ mol H}_2O} = 0.499 \text{ mol Fe}_3O_4$$

Fe is the limiting reactant because the given amount of Fe can make only 0.400 mol Fe_3O_4, which is less than the 0.499 mol Fe_3O_4 that the given amount of H_2O would produce.

b. $0.400 \text{ mol Fe}_3O_4 \times \frac{231.55 \text{ g Fe}_3O_4}{1 \text{ mol Fe}_3O_4} = 92.6 \text{ g Fe}_3O_4$

c. $0.400 \text{ mol Fe}_3O_4 \times \frac{4 \text{ mol H}_2O}{1 \text{ mol Fe}_3O_4} \times \frac{18.02 \text{ g H}_2O}{1 \text{ mol H}_2O}$

$= 28.8 \text{ g H}_2O \text{ consumed}$

$36.0 \text{ g H}_2O - 28.8 \text{ g H}_2O \text{ consumed} = 7.2 \text{ g H}_2O \text{ remaining}$

4 CHECK YOUR WORK

Check the answer to see if it makes sense.

The mass of original reactants is 67.0 g + 36.0 g = 103.0 g. The mass of Fe_3O_4 + unreacted water is 92.6 g + 7.2 g = 99.8 g. The difference of 3.2 g is the mass of hydrogen that is produced with the Fe_3O_4. Therefore, the answers make sense in the context of the conservation of mass.

Critical Thinking

2. Evaluate How could you check the statement in Step 4 that the 3.2 g difference is the mass of hydrogen that is produced?

_____

_____

Comparing the actual and theoretical yields help chemists determine the reaction's efficiency.

The product amounts that you calculate in ideal stoichiometry problems give you the theoretical yields for a reaction. The **theoretical yield** is the maximum amount of the product that can be produced from a given amount of reactant. In most chemical reactions, the amount of product obtained is less than the theoretical yield.

There are many reasons that the actual yield is usually less than the theoretical yield. Reactants may contain impurities or may form byproducts in competing side reactions. Also, many reactions do not go to completion. As a result, less product is produced than ideal stoichiometric calculations predict. The **actual yield** of a product is the measured amount of that product obtained from a reaction.

Chemists are usually interested in the efficiency of a reaction. The efficiency is expressed by comparing the actual and theoretical yields. The **percentage yield** is the ratio of the actual yield to the theoretical yield, multiplied by 100.

$$\text{percentage yield} = \frac{\text{actual yield}}{\text{theoretical yield}} \times 100$$

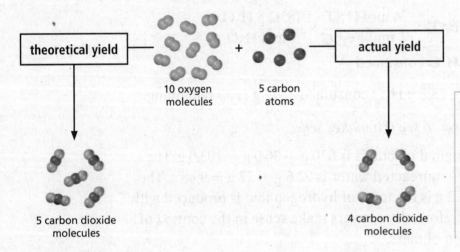

theoretical yield

10 oxygen molecules

5 carbon atoms

actual yield

5 carbon dioxide molecules

4 carbon dioxide molecules

Consider the synthesis of carbon dioxide from carbon and oxygen as discussed earlier in this section. In theory, 10 oxygen molecules and 5 carbon atoms can combine to form 5 carbon dioxide molecules. In practice, a reaction with an 80% percentage yield will only produce 4 carbon dioxide molecules.

✓ READING CHECK

3. Give two reasons that the actual yield of a reaction might be less than the theoretical yield of a reaction.

One industrial method of preparing chlorobenzene, C_6H_5Cl, is to react benzene, C_6H_6, with chlorine, as represented by the following equation.

$$C_6H_6(l) + Cl_2(g) \rightarrow C_6H_5Cl(l) + HCl(g)$$

When 36.8 g C_6H_6 react with an excess of Cl_2, the actual yield of C_6H_5Cl is 38.8 g. What is the percentage yield of C_6H_5Cl?

	SOLUTION	
1	ANALYZE	*Determine the information that is given and unknown.*

Given: mass of C_6H_6 = 36.8 g, mass of Cl_2 = excess
actual yield of C_6H_5Cl = 38.8 g

Unknown: percentage yield of C_6H_5Cl

2 PLAN

Determine how the unknown value can be calculated.

First do a mass-mass calculation to find the theoretical yield of C_6H_5Cl. Then the percentage yield can be found.

molar mass factor   molar mass factor

$$g\ C_6H_6 \times \frac{mol\ C_6H_6}{g\ C_6H_6} \times \frac{mol\ C_6H_5Cl}{mol\ C_6H_6} \times \frac{g\ C_6H_5Cl}{mol\ C_6H_5Cl} = g\ C_6H_5Cl$$

mole ratio

$$\text{percentage yield } C_6H_5Cl = \frac{\text{actual yield}}{\text{theoretical yield}} \times 100$$

3 SOLVE

Substitute the given values to determine the unknown values.

The molar masses are 78.12 g/mol C_6H_6 and 112.56 g/mol C_6H_5Cl.

$$36.8\ g\ C_6H_6 \times \frac{mol\ C_6H_6}{78.12\ g\ C_6H_6} \times \frac{1\ mol\ C_6H_5Cl}{1\ mol\ C_6H_6} \times \frac{112.56\ g\ C_6H_5Cl}{mol\ C_6H_5Cl}$$

$$= 53.0\ g\ C_6H_5Cl \text{ (theoretical yield)}$$

$$\text{percentage yield} = \frac{38.8\ g}{53.0\ g} \times 100 = 73.2\%$$

B. Methanol can be produced through the reaction of CO and H_2 in the presence of a catalyst.

$$CO(g) + 2H_2(g) \rightarrow CH_3OH(l)$$

If 75.0 g of CO react to produce 68.4 g CH_3OH, what is the percentage yield of CH_3OH?

What is known? _____

What is unknown? _____

Write the mass-mass calculation needed to find the theoretical yield of CH_3OH.

Use the periodic table to find the molar mass of CO and the molar mass of CH_3OH.

_____

_____

Compute the theoretical yield.

Use the actual yield and the theoretical yield to compute the percentage yield.

Check your answer.

_____

_____

_____

VOCABULARY

1. Describe the difference between actual yield and theoretical yield.

_____

_____

REVIEW

2. Carbon disulfide burns in oxygen to yield carbon dioxide and sulfur dioxide according to the following chemical equation.

$$CS_2(l) + 3O_2(g) \rightarrow CO_2(g) + 2SO_2(g)$$

If 1.00 mol CS_2 is combined with 1.00 mol O_2, identify the limiting reactant.

3. Quicklime, CaO, can be prepared by roasting limestone, $CaCO_3$, according to the following reaction.

$$CaCO_3(s) \rightarrow CaO(s) + CO_2(g)$$

When 2.00×10^3 g $CaCO_3$ are heated, the actual yield of CaO is 1.05×10^3 g. What is the percentage yield?

Critical Thinking

4. ANALYZING DATA A chemical engineer calculated that 15.0 mol H_2 were needed to react with excess N_2 to prepare 10.0 mol NH_3. But the actual yield is 60.0%. Write a balanced chemical equation for the reaction. Is the amount of H_2 needed to make 10.0 mol NH_3 more, the same, or less than 15 mol? How many moles of H_2 are needed?

_____

_____

_____

Math Tutor USING MOLE RATIOS

The coefficients in a balanced equation represent the relative amounts in moles of reactants and products. You can use the coefficients of two of the substances in the equation to set up a mole ratio. A mole ratio is a conversion factor that relates the amounts in moles of any two substances involved in a chemical reaction.

Problem-Solving TIPS

- When solving stoichiometric problems, always start with a balanced chemical equation.
- Identify the amount known from the problem (in moles or mass).
- If you are given the mass of a substance, use the molar mass factor as a conversion factor to find the amount in moles. If you are given the amount in moles of a substance, use the molar mass factor as a conversion factor to find the mass.

SAMPLE

If 3.61 g of aluminum react completely with excess $CuCl_2$, what mass of copper metal is produced? Use the balanced equation below.

$$2Al(s) + 3CuCl_2(aq) \rightarrow 2AlCl_3(aq) + 3Cu(s)$$

First, convert the amount of aluminum from a mass in grams to a number of moles by using the molar mass of aluminum.

$$3.61 \text{ g Al} = 3.61 \text{ g Al} \times \frac{1 \text{ mol Al}}{26.98 \text{ g Al}} = 0.134 \text{ mol Al}$$

Next, apply the mole ratio of aluminum to copper to find the moles of copper produced.

$$\text{mol Al} \times \frac{3 \text{ mol Cu}}{2 \text{ mol Al}} = \text{mol Cu}$$

$$0.134 \text{ mol Al} = 0.134 \text{ mol Al} \times \frac{3 \text{ mol Cu}}{2 \text{ mol Al}} = 0.201 \text{ mol Cu}$$

Then, convert moles of copper to mass of copper in grams by using the molar mass of copper.

$$0.201 \text{ mol Cu} = 0.201 \text{ mol Cu} \times \frac{63.55 \text{ g Cu}}{1 \text{ mol Cu}} = 12.8 \text{ g Cu}$$

Practice Problems: Chapter Review practice problems 8 and 9

1. Explain the concept of mole ratio as used in reaction stoichiometry problems. What is the source of mole ratios used in these problems?

_____

_____

_____

2. For each of the following balanced chemical equations, write all possible mole ratios.

   a. $2Ca + O_2 \rightarrow 2CaO$

   b. $Mg + 2HF \rightarrow MgF_2 + H_2$

3. What is the role of molar mass in reaction stoichiometry?

_____

_____

4. What is the difference between the limiting reactant and the excess reactant in a chemical reaction?

_____

_____

5. How does the value of the theoretical yield generally compare with the value of the actual yield?

_____

6. Why are actual yields usually less than calculated theoretical yields?

_____

_____

_____

7. Given the following chemical equation, determine to two decimal places the molar masses of all substances involved.

$$Na_2CO_3(aq) + Ca(OH)_2(aq) \rightarrow 2NaOH(aq) + CaCO_3(s)$$

_____

_____

_____

_____

8. Hydrogen and oxygen react under a specific set of conditions to produce water according to the following equation.

$$2H_2(g) + O_2(g) \rightarrow 2H_2O(g)$$

a. How many moles of hydrogen would be required to produce 5.0 mol of water?

b. How many moles of oxygen would be required?

9. In a blast furnace, iron(lll) oxide is used to produce iron by the following (unbalanced) reaction. First, balance the equation.

_____ $Fe_2O_3(s)$ + _____ $CO(g)$ → _____ $Fe(s)$ + _____ $CO_2(g)$

If 4.00 kg Fe_2O_3 are available to react, how many moles of CO are needed?

10. Calculate the indicated quantity associated with the two given values.

a. theoretical yield = 20.0 g, actual yield = 15.0 g, percentage yield = _____

b. theoretical yield = 1.0 g, percentage yield = 90.0%, actual yield = _____

11. Methanol, CH_3OH, is an important industrial compound that is produced from the following (unbalanced) reaction. First, balance the equation.

_____ $CO(g)$ + _____ $H_2(g) \rightarrow$ _____ $CH_3OH(g)$

Determine the mass of each reactant that would be needed to produce 100.0 kg of methanol.

12. In the reaction below, 2.0 mol HCl react with 2.5 mol NaOH. What is the limiting reactant?

$HCl + NaOH \rightarrow NaCl + H_2O$

13. In the reaction below, 2.5 mol Zn react with 6.0 mol HCl. What is the limiting reactant?

$Zn + HCl \rightarrow ZnCl_2 + H_2$

14. Sulfuric acid reacts with aluminum hydroxide by double replacement. If 30.0 g of sulfuric acid react with 25.0 g of aluminum hydroxide, identify the limiting reactant. Then determine the mass of excess reactant remaining.

Limiting reactant: _____

States of Matter

Review Previous Concepts

1. What is the difference between a physical and chemical change?

_____

_____

_____

2. What forces act between molecules in a molecular compound and formula units in an ionic compound?

_____

_____

_____

SECTION 10.1

The Kinetic-Molecular Theory of Matter

In the late nineteenth century, scientists developed a theory to account for the particles that make up matter. This theory explains the differences between the three states of matter: solid, liquid, and gas.

The **kinetic-molecular theory** is based on the idea that particles of matter are always in motion. The properties of solids, liquids, and gases are a result of the energy of their particles and forces acting between the particles.

> **The kinetic-molecular theory explains the constant motion of gas particles.**

The kinetic-molecular theory provides a model of what is called an ideal gas. An **ideal gas** is a theoretical gas that perfectly fits these five assumptions of the kinetic-molecular theory.

1. **Gases consist of large numbers of tiny particles that are far apart relative to their size.** Most of the volume occupied by a gas is empty space.

2. **Collisions between particles or a particle and a container are elastic.** In an **elastic collision** no kinetic energy is lost, but energy may be transferred between particles. A gas exerts pressure on its container through the collisions of its particles with the container.

3. **Gas particles are always in motion, so they always have kinetic energy.** They can move freely in all directions.

4. **There are no forces of attraction between particles.** They behave like billiard balls. When they collide they immediately bounce apart, instead of sticking together.

5. **The temperature of a gas depends on the average kinetic energy of its particles.** If the temperature of a gas increases, the average speed of its particles increases. If it decreases, the average speed of its particles decreases.

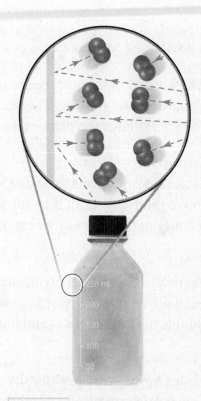

Gas particles travel in straight lines until they collide with each other or a container wall.

✓ READING CHECK

1. What is always true about the kinetic energy of a single particle in a gas?

Kinetic Energy and Temperature The kinetic energy of any moving object is given by the following equation.

$$KE = \frac{1}{2}mv^2$$

The quantity m is the mass of the particle and v is the speed of the particle. In a specific gas, the mass of each particle is the same, so the kinetic energy of the gas, and thus its temperature, depends only on the speed of the particles.

In a mixture of gases, the particles of each gas have the same temperature and the average kinetic energy. Consider such a mixture of hydrogen gas and oxygen gas. The hydrogen particles are moving much faster on average than the oxygen particles because they have less mass.

> **The kinetic-molecular theory explains the constant motion of gas particles.**

The kinetic-molecular theory states that particles in an ideal gas are always moving. This section will describe how the theory explains the physical properties of an ideal gas.

Expansion

Gases do not have a definite shape or volume. The particles move randomly until they fill any container. A gas that enters a container twice as large expands to fill the new container.

Fluidity

Particles in a gas feel no attractive forces, so they slide past each other. In other words, gases flow in the same way that liquids flow. Both gases and liquids are referred to as *fluids*.

Low Density

Gases have a very low density compared to liquids and solids. Gas particles typically occupy a volume 1000 times greater than an equal number of particles in a liquid or solid.

Compressibility

A compression is a reduction in volume. Because particles in a gas are so far apart, the volume of a gas can be dramatically decreased. Gases are often kept compressed in high-pressure steel cylinders for industrial purposes. These cylinders can hold over 100 times more gas than unpressurized cylinders.

2. If the temperature of a gas increases, then its particles move

_____.

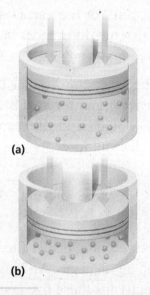

(a) Gas particles expand to fill the cylinder when the piston is raised.
(b) Lowering the piston exerts pressure on the gas, compressing it into a smaller volume.

Gas cylinders used in scuba diving hold compressed air so that the diver can carry more air at one time.

Diffusion and Effusion

Diffusion is the mixing of the particles of two substances caused by their random motions. Because gas particles are so spread out, two gases that are released into a container can easily occupy the same space. The gases will mix together just through the natural motion of their particles; they do not require additional stirring.

Gas particles passing through a tiny opening is called **effusion.** The rate of effusion depends on the velocities of the particles. A low-mass gas such as hydrogen effuses through an opening more rapidly than other gases in a mixture, because its particles travel at higher speeds at a given temperature.

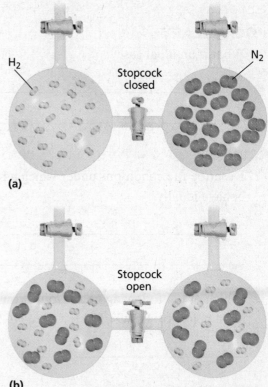
(a)

(b)

Gases diffuse readily into one another. When the stopcock is open, both gases act as if they are occupying an identical, larger container and spread out to fill the entire volume together.

Real gases do not behave according to the kinetic-molecular theory.

The kinetic-molecular theory only applies to ideal gases. However, ideal gases do not actually exist. Kinetic-molecular theory is still useful because, as long as the pressure is not too high or the temperature too low, many gases behave like ideal gases.

A **real gas** is a gas that does not behave completely according to the assumptions of kinetic-molecular theory. Real gas particles feel some attractive forces from other particles. These effects are minor, unless the temperature is low or the pressure is high. Then the particles are either too close together or do not have enough energy to escape the influence of attractive forces.

Noble gases such as helium and neon behave more like ideal gases because their particles have little attraction for each other. These gases consist of monatomic particles, which are neutrally charged and stable.

For the same reason, nonpolar gases such as hydrogen and nitrogen also behave like ideal gases. Gases with polar molecules, such as water vapor and ammonia, deviate the most from ideal gas behavior because of attractive forces between the molecules.

✓ READING CHECK

3. What is the difference between an ideal gas and a real gas?

_____

_____

_____

_____

_____

VOCABULARY

1. What is an ideal gas?

_____

_____

REVIEW

2. Describe the conditions under which a real gas is most likely to behave ideally.

_____

_____

3. Which of the following gases would you expect to deviate significantly from ideal behavior: He, O_2, H_2, H_2O, N_2, HCl, or NH_3?

_____

4. How does kinetic-molecular theory explain the pressure exerted by gases?

_____

_____

5. What happens to gas particles when a gas is compressed?

_____

_____

6. What happens to gas particles when a gas is heated?

_____

_____

Critical Thinking

7. **DRAWING CONCLUSIONS** Molecules of hydrogen escape from Earth, but molecules of oxygen and nitrogen are held to the surface and remain in the atmosphere. Explain.

_____

_____

_____

SECTION 10.2

Liquids

The liquid state is the least common state of matter in the universe. This is because a substance exists as a liquid in a relatively narrow range of temperatures. What happens as a liquid changes to a solid or a gas, as well as the properties of liquids themselves, can be explained by the kinetic-molecular theory of matter.

The intermolecular forces of liquids determine their properties.

A liquid has a definite volume but takes the shape of its container. This is in contrast to a gas, which has neither a definite shape nor a definite volume. As in a gas, the particles in a liquid are constantly moving. However, they are packed much closer together than gas particles. Intermolecular forces such as dipole-dipole forces, London dispersion forces, and hydrogen bonding have more impact on liquid particles.

Liquid particles are not bound to fixed positions, as particles within a solid are. Liquid particles can move freely within the liquid. This is similar to the behavior of gases, except that intermolecular forces prevent liquid particles from separating from the rest of the liquid.

A **fluid** is a substance that can flow and take the shape of its container. Both gases and liquids are considered fluids. However, a gas expands to take the shape of its container. A liquid has a definite volume, and is compelled by the force of gravity to flow downhill to fill the bottom of its container.

Relatively High Density

Most substances are hundreds of times denser than gases at normal atmospheric pressures. Solids and liquids have similar densities, although most substances are slightly less dense as liquids than as solids.

KEY TERMS

fluid	vaporization
surface tension	evaporation
capillary action	freezing

✓ READING CHECK

1. Name three ways that a liquid is different from a gas.

_____

_____

_____

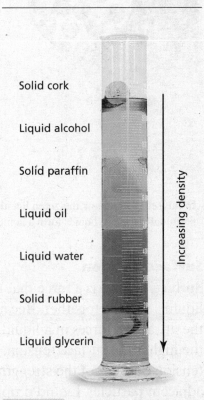

Solid cork

Liquid alcohol

Solid paraffin

Liquid oil

Liquid water

Solid rubber

Liquid glycerin

Increasing density

Solids and liquids of different densities are shown. The densest materials are at the bottom, and the least dense are at the top. Dyes added to the liquid layers make them more visible.

Relative Incompressibility

When the pressure on a gas increases by a factor of 1000, its volume decreases by a factor of 1000. On the other hand, liquid particles, already packed close together, do not compress nearly as much. When the pressure on liquid water at room temperature increases by a factor of 1000, its volume only decreases 4%. But liquids do resemble gases in that they exert pressure on a container equally in all directions.

Ability to Diffuse

Liquids diffuse and mix with other liquids the same way that gases diffuse and mix with other gases. However, diffusion occurs more slowly in liquids, because the more closely packed particles and intermolecular forces slow the process down. Diffusion occurs more quickly if the temperature rises.

2. Use the words *definite* and *indefinite* to complete the statement.

Even though a liquid has a(n)

_____ shape, it is relatively

incompressible because it has a(n)

_____ volume.

Water molecule

Dye molecule

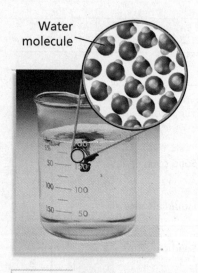

In this series of photos, the green liquid dye diffuses into the beaker of water. Eventually, the two liquids form a homogeneous mixture.

Surface Tension

Surface tension is a force that tends to pull adjacent parts of a liquid's surface together. Because surface tension is a result of the attractive forces in a liquid, the higher the attractive forces the higher the surface tension. Water has a high surface tension because of the strength of hydrogen bonds between adjacent particles. Liquid droplets with high surface tension tend to take on a spherical shape. For a given volume, a sphere has the smallest surface area. The particles around the outside surface of the spherical drop are all pulled toward the center, helping the drop to maintain its shape.

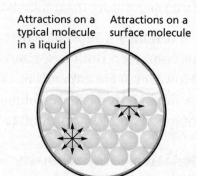

Attractions on a typical molecule in a liquid | Attractions on a surface molecule

Molecules on the surface of a liquid are pulled inward because the net intermolecular force is downward.

(a)

(b)

In paper chromatography, water rises up a piece of paper through capillary action. (a) Because each component of the ink in the line is attracted to the water molecules and cellulose molecules in different strengths, (b) the ink separates as it is drawn up with the water.

Capillary action is the attraction of the surface of a liquid to the surface of a solid. It is closely related to surface tension, except that it relates to intermolecular forces between a liquid substance and a solid substance. The meniscus on a graduated cylinder is a result of capillary action, caused by the attraction of the liquid to the sides of the cylinder. Plants make use of capillary action to transport water from roots up through leaves.

Evaporation and Boiling

A liquid can change state to a solid or gas if the conditions change. **Vaporization** occurs when a liquid becomes a gas. Two processes through which vaporization occurs are evaporation and boiling. Boiling, the change of a liquid into large bubbles of gas, will be discussed further in Section 4.

Evaporation is the process by which particles escape from the surface of a nonboiling liquid to become a gas. Evaporation occurs because particles in a liquid do not all have the same kinetic energy. Though temperature describes the average kinetic energy of the particles, some are moving more rapidly and some are moving more slowly. A particle with enough kinetic energy can overcome the intermolecular forces at the surface of a liquid and escape to become a gas.

Formation of Solids

Freezing is the physical change of a liquid into a solid by the removal of heat. When the average kinetic energy of the particles decreases enough, attractive forces can pull the particles into the more orderly arrangement of a solid. Now the particles can no longer move freely, as they did in the liquid. This process is also called solidification.

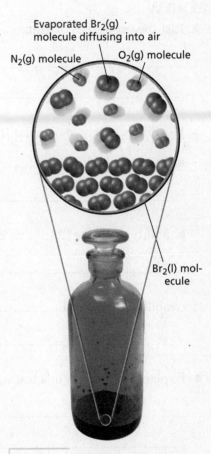

Evaporated $Br_2(g)$ molecule diffusing into air

$N_2(g)$ molecule

$O_2(g)$ molecule

$Br_2(l)$ molecule

Liquid bromine, Br_2, evaporates near room temperature. The resulting brownish-red gas diffuses into the air.

✓ READING CHECK

3. Of the three states of water (ice, liquid water, and water vapor), in which state are the intermolecular forces the strongest? _____

In which state are they the weakest? _____

VOCABULARY

1. Compare vaporization and evaporation.

_____

_____

_____

REVIEW

2. List the properties of liquids.

_____

_____

3. How does kinetic-molecular theory explain these properties of liquids?

   a. relatively high density _____

   _____

   b. ability to diffuse _____

   _____

   c. ability to evaporate _____

   _____

4. Explain why liquids in a test tube form a meniscus.

   _____

   _____

   _____

Critical Thinking

5. **INTERPRETING CONCEPTS** The evaporation of liquid water from the surface of Earth is an important step in the water cycle. How do water molecules obtain enough kinetic energy to escape into the gas state?

   _____

   _____

   _____

SECTION 10.3

Solids

A gas has neither a definite volume nor a definite shape. A liquid has a definite volume, but not a definite shape. A solid, the third state, has a definite volume *and* a definite shape.

The particles in a solid hold relatively fixed positions.

The particles in a solid are more closely packed than the particles of a liquid or a gas. Therefore, intermolecular forces have much more influence over the motion of the particles. These forces tend to hold the particles of a solid in relatively fixed positions.

The particles in a solid still have kinetic energy, according to kinetic-molecular theory. However, the motion of the particles is mostly restricted to vibrating about their fixed positions. Particles in a solid have less average kinetic energy than the same particles in the liquid state.

The two types of solids are crystalline solids and amorphous solids. A **crystal** is a substance in which the particles are arranged in an orderly, repeating pattern. **Crystalline solids** consist of crystals. On the other hand, the particles of **amorphous solids** are arranged randomly. Glass and plastic are two examples of amorphous solids.

💡 Critical Thinking

1. Infer If the particles in a crystalline solid substance gain enough energy to escape their fixed positions and move about the substance, what happens to the substance as a whole?

_____

_____

_____

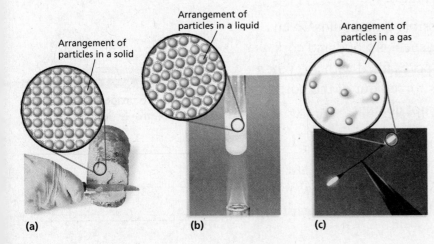

Arrangement of particles in a solid

Arrangement of particles in a liquid

Arrangement of particles in a gas

(a)   (b)   (c)

Sodium is shown as (a) a solid block, (b) a liquid in a test tube, and (c) as a gas in a sodium-vapor lamp.

Definite Shape and Volume

Unlike a liquid or a gas, a solid can maintain a definite shape without a container. A crystalline solid maintains a geometric shape that reflects its internal structure, even when it is broken into pieces. An amorphous solid maintains a shape, but this shape can vary. Some amorphous solids, such as glass and plastic, can be molded into whatever shape is desired.

The volume of a solid changes only slightly with increases in pressure or temperature. This is because there is very little space in which the particles can be compressed.

The plastic polyethylene can be molded into different shapes for different purposes.

Definite Melting Point

Melting is the physical change of a solid to a liquid by the addition of energy as heat. Melting is the reverse of the process of freezing. The temperature at which a solid becomes a liquid is its **melting point.** At this temperature, the particles have enough kinetic energy to overcome the attractive forces. They break out of their fixed positions and flow.

Crystalline solids have definite melting points. Amorphous solids, like glass and plastics, have no definite melting point. They have the ability to flow over a range of temperatures.

High Density and Incompressibility

In general, substances have their highest density in the solid state. The high density is a result of the particles being packed more closely together than in other states.

Solids are generally less compressible than liquids. Even solids that seem to be compressible, such as wood and cork, are not compressible. They contain pores filled with air. When pressure on cork increases, the air is forced out of the pores, but the material of the cork itself is not compressed.

Low Rate of Diffusion

Scientists have found that a zinc plate and a copper plate clamped together will experience the diffusion of a few atoms. However, the rate of diffusion is millions of times slower than in liquids.

✓ READING CHECK
2. Name three properties of a solid that are not properties of a liquid.

_____

_____

_____

Crystal particles are arranged in a 3-dimensional lattice.

Crystalline solids exist either as single crystals or as groups of crystals stuck together. The total three-dimensional arrangement of particles in a crystal is called a **crystal structure.** This arrangement can be represented by a coordinate system called a *lattice*. The smallest portion of a crystal lattice that shows the three-dimensional pattern of the entire lattice is called a **unit cell.** Each lattice contains many unit cells packed together.

A crystal and its unit cells can have any one of seven types of symmetry. This allows scientists to classify crystals by their shape. The seven types of crystal are summarized below.

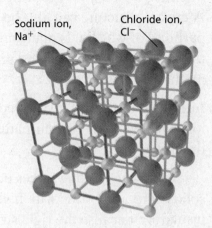
Sodium ion, Na⁺   Chloride ion, Cl⁻

A unit cell of a sodium chloride crystal is outlined in black.

Sodium chloride crystals have a cubic shape.

The Seven Types of Crystalline Solids

A **cubic** unit cell is the shape of a cube

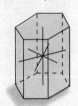
A **hexagonal** unit cell is a hexagonal prism.

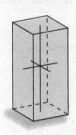
A **tetragonal** unit cell is a rectangular prism with a square base.

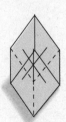
A **trigonal** unit cell is either a hexagonal prism or a slanted cube with faces that are rhombuses or squares.

An **orthorhombic** unit cell is a rectangular prism without any square bases.

A **monoclinic** unit cell is a slanted rectangular prism with faces that are rectangles or parallelograms.

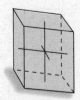
A **triclinic** unit cell has three sides of different lengths and no right angles on its faces.

Critical Thinking

3. Infer Why are amorphous solids not classified by their shape the way crystalline solids are?

_____

_____

_____

_____

_____

Binding Forces in Crystals

A crystal structure can also be described by the type of particles of which it is made and the type of binding that holds the particles together. There are four types of solids in this method of classification.

Ionic Crystals Ionic crystals consist of positive and negative ions arranged in a regular pattern. The ions can be monatomic or polyatomic.

The strong binding forces between the ions make these solids hard and brittle with high melting points. They are good insulators, because the rigid structure conducts heat poorly.

Covalent Network Crystals In covalent network crystals, each atom is covalently bonded to its nearest neighboring atoms. The bonding extends throughout a network that includes a very large number of atoms. Examples of these solids include diamond, C_x, quartz, $(SiO_2)_x$, silicon carbide, $(SiC)_x$, and many oxides of transition metals. These solids are essentially giant molecules. The x in each chemical formula indicates that the unit within the parentheses extends indefinitely.

Covalent network solids are very hard and brittle. They have high melting points and usually are nonconductors or semiconductors of electricity.

Metallic Crystals Metallic crystals consist of metal cations surrounded by a sea of unbound electrons. The electrons originate with the metal atoms, but belong to the crystal as a whole.

The freedom of these electrons gives metallic solids a high electric conductivity. The electrons are free to flow throughout the metal and transfer charge from place to place.

Covalent Molecular Crystals Molecules that are held together by intermolecular forces make up a covalent molecular crystal. Nonpolar molecules are held together only by weak London dispersion forces. Polar molecules can be held together by dispersion forces, dipole-dipole forces, or hydrogen bonding.

Overall, these forces are weaker than in other crystals, so covalent molecular solids have low melting points. They are also good insulators, soft, and vaporize easily.

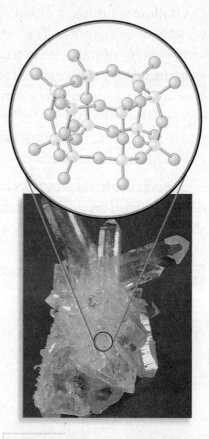

Quartz, $(SiO_2)_x$, is shown here with its three-dimensional atomic structure.

READING CHECK

4. What is the main difference between a covalent network crystal and a covalent molecular crystal?

_____

_____

_____

Melting and Boiling Points of Representative Crystalline Solids

Type of substance	Formula	Melting point (°C)	Boiling point at 1 atm (°C)
Ionic	NaCl	801	1413
	MgF_2	1266	2239
Covalent network	$(SiO_2)_x$	1610	2230
	C_x (diamond)	3500	3930
Metallic	Hg	−39	357
	Cu	1083	2567
	Fe	1535	2750
	W	3410	5660
Covalent molecular (nonpolar)	H_2	−259	−253
	O_2	−218	−183
	CH_4	−182	−164
	CCl_4	−23	77
	C_6H_6	6	80
Covalent molecular (polar)	NH_3	−78	−33
	H_2O	0	100

The particles in amorphous solids are not arranged in a regular pattern.

The word *amorphous* comes from the Greek word for "without shape." The particles of amorphous solids are arranged in a random pattern, and therefore have no regular or lattice structure. Amorphous solids such as glass and plastic can flow at a large range of temperatures. This property is one reason that amorphous solids are sometimes classified as supercooled liquids. **Supercooled liquids** are substances that retain some properties of a liquid even at temperatures at which they appear to be solid.

Glass is made by cooling certain molten materials in a way that prevents crystallization. Glass is suitable for many uses, including as windows, light bulbs, and optical fibers. Plastics can be molded at high temperatures and pressures and then cooled to form strong structures. Other amorphous solids that have semiconducting properties are used in electronic devices such as solar cells, laser printers, and flat-panel televisions and computer monitors.

Glass is strong enough to be shaped and then etched with acid to make artwork.

READING CHECK

5. A substance that looks solid but also has some liquid properties is a

_____

VOCABULARY

1. What is the difference between an amorphous solid and a crystalline solid?

_____

_____

_____

REVIEW

2. Account for each of the following properties of solids.

a. definite volume _____

_____

b. relatively high density _____

_____

c. extremely low rate of diffusion _____

_____

3. Compare and contrast the four types of crystals.

_____

_____

_____

_____

4. Why do crystalline solids shatter into regularly shaped fragments when they
are broken?

_____

_____

Critical Thinking

5. RELATING IDEAS Explain why ionic crystals melt at much higher
temperatures than typical covalent molecular crystals.

_____

_____

_____

SECTION 10.4

Changes of State

Matter can exist in any one of three main states—gas, liquid, or solid. There are six possible ways to change between these three states, as shown in the table below.

Possible Changes of State

Change of state	Process	Example
solid → liquid	melting	ice → water
solid → gas	sublimation	dry ice → CO_2 gas
liquid → solid	freezing	water → ice
liquid → gas	vaporization	liquid Br_2 → Br_2 vapor
gas → liquid	condensation	water vapor → water
gas → solid	deposition	water vapor → ice

Substances in equilibrium change back and forth between states at equal speeds.

A **phase** is any part of a system that has uniform composition and properties. Consider a liquid in a sealed container, such as a bottle of perfume. The perfume is present in two phases: a liquid phase and a gas phase.

Some molecules at the surface of the liquid gain enough kinetic energy to escape the attraction of neighboring particles. These molecules are said to *evaporate*. The molecules leave the liquid phase and enter the gas phase. If the perfume bottle is opened, the molecules in the gas phase escape and mix with air. Some of these molecules enter your nose, and you detect the perfume's smell.

Inside the perfume bottle, some gas molecules strike the surface of the liquid and lose kinetic energy. These molecules can no longer overcome the attractive forces of the liquid and reenter the liquid phase. **Condensation** is the process by which a gas changes into a liquid. A gas in contact with its liquid or solid phase is often called a vapor.

A perfume bottle contains molecules in the liquid phase and the gas phase.

READING CHECK

1. What process is the reverse of condensation?

Liquid-Vapor Equilibrium The rate of evaporation in the perfume bottle depends on temperature. On the other hand, the rate of condensation depends on the number of molecules in the vapor phase. Condensation occurs very slowly when there are few molecules of vapor striking the surface of a liquid.

When perfume is poured into a bottle and capped, at first all the molecules are in the liquid phase. The perfume then starts to evaporate. As more molecules enter the gas phase, the rate of condensation starts to rise. At some point in time, the rate of evaporation will equal the rate of condensation. **Equilibrium** is a condition in which two opposing changes occur at equal rates in a closed system. At equilibrium, the amount of perfume in the liquid phase and the amount in the gas phase are constant.

(a)

(b)

(c)

Equilibrium is reached between a liquid and a vapor in a closed system. (a) Some molecules of liquid begin to evaporate. (b) Evaporation continues at a constant rate, but a little condensation occurs. (c) Evaporation and condensation occur at the same rate.

Equilibrium Vapor Pressure of a Liquid

The collisions of the molecules in a vapor on the surface of a liquid exert pressure on the liquid. The **equilibrium vapor pressure** of a liquid is the pressure exerted by its corresponding vapor at equilibrium. The equilibrium vapor pressure increases with temperature because the rate of evaporation increases with temperature. More vapor must be present for condensation to balance evaporation.

The equilibrium vapor pressure of a liquid is determined by the strength of the attractive forces in the liquid. If the attractive forces are strong, the rate of evaporation is low, and less vapor is required for condensation to balance evaporation. These liquids are called nonvolatile liquids. **Volatile liquids** evaporate readily. These liquids, such as ether, have weak forces of attraction between molecules and a high equilibrium vapor pressure.

🔍 Critical Thinking

2. **Infer** Which type of liquid is more likely to be volatile, a liquid with polar molecules or a liquid with nonpolar molecules? Explain.

_____

_____

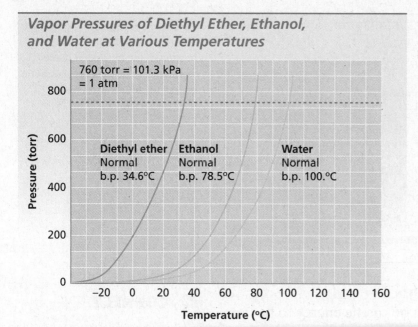

Vapor Pressures of Diethyl Ether, Ethanol, and Water at Various Temperatures

760 torr = 101.3 kPa = 1 atm

Diethyl ether
Normal
b.p. 34.6°C

Ethanol
Normal
b.p. 78.5°C

Water
Normal
b.p. 100.°C

The vapor pressure of any liquid increases as its temperature increases. A liquid boils when its vapor pressure equals the pressure of the atmosphere.

A liquid boils when it has absorbed enough energy to evaporate.

Boiling is the conversion of a liquid into a vapor within the liquid as well as at its surface. The boiling point of a liquid is the temperature at which the equilibrium vapor pressure of the liquid equals the atmospheric pressure.

Below the boiling point, only particles at the surface of a liquid enter the gas phase. Evaporation and condensation are in equilibrium. As the temperature of the liquid rises, the equilibrium vapor pressure also rises. When equilibrium vapor pressure equals atmospheric pressure, evaporation and condensation can no longer maintain equilibrium. More energy added to the liquid makes the liquid molecules move fast enough to enter the gas phase. The liquid is now boiling.

Energy and Boiling

At the boiling point, the temperature of the liquid does not rise. Instead, the energy is used to overcome the attractive forces of the other molecules in the liquid. The energy required to turn a liquid into a gas is stored in the resulting vapor as potential energy.

Energy must be added continuously to keep a liquid boiling. A pot of water stops boiling almost immediately upon being removed from the stove. Without the input of energy, molecules in the interior of the liquid cannot enter the gas phase.

 CONNECT

A pressure cooker works on the principle that the boiling point can change if the pressure on the liquid changes. A pressure cooker increases the pressure, allowing the equilibrium vapor pressure to rise to higher values and the temperature of the liquid to continue to increase. Food submerged in water inside the pressure cooker can then be cooked at a higher temperature.

A vacuum evaporator works on the opposite principle. By decreasing the pressure, the evaporator causes boiling to occur at a lower temperature. This allows water to be removed from sugar or milk solutions without burning the sugar or milk.

✓ READING CHECK

3. Why does the temperature of a liquid that is at its boiling point remain constant when more energy is added to the liquid?

_____

_____

_____

_____

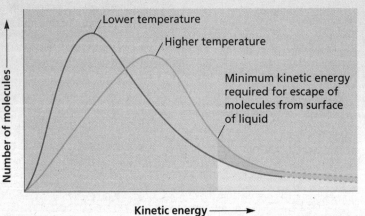

Energy Distribution of Molecules in a Liquid at Different Temperatures

Number of molecules (vertical axis)

Lower temperature

Higher temperature

Minimum kinetic energy required for escape of molecules from surface of liquid

Kinetic energy →

The two lines show two liquids at two different temperatures. A larger portion of the molecules in the warmer liquid have enough kinetic energy to enter the gas phase.

Molar Enthalpy of Vaporization

A molecule needs a certain amount of kinetic energy to be able to escape from the surface of a liquid and become a vapor. A higher percentage of particles in a warmer liquid have this required energy than particles in the same liquid if it were at a lower temperature, as shown in the graph above.

The amount of energy as heat that is needed to vaporize one mole of liquid at its boiling point at constant pressure is called the **molar enthalpy of vaporization,** ΔH_v. This quantity is a measure of the attractive forces between the particles in a liquid. The stronger the attractive forces, the more energy is required to vaporize the liquid.

> **Freezing is when a substance loses enough heat energy to solidify.**

Freezing The boiling point of a substance can vary greatly depending on the atmospheric pressure. In contrast, a crystalline solid has a fairly constant melting point and freezing point. The **freezing point** is the temperature at which the solid and liquid are in equilibrium at a pressure of 1 atm. Freezing involves a loss of energy, as shown in this equation.

$$\text{liquid} \rightarrow \text{solid} + \text{energy}$$

At the freezing point, the particles in the liquid and the solid have the same average kinetic energy. Therefore, the energy that is released during freezing must have been energy stored in the liquid. Because a liquid is much less ordered than its solid form at the same temperature, this stored energy represents a less orderly arrangement of particles.

 **CONNECT**

Water has a high molar enthalpy of vaporization, which makes it an effective cooling agent. When sweat evaporates from your skin, it must absorb energy to change from a liquid to a gas. The removal of energy in the form of heat from your skin makes your skin feel cooler.

Critical Thinking

4. Explain How does the equation at the left show that energy is released during the process of freezing.

_____

_____

_____

_____

Melting The reverse process of freezing is melting. As a solid melts, it continuously absorbs energy as heat, as shown in this equation.

$$\text{solid} + \text{energy} \rightarrow \text{liquid}$$

For a crystalline solid, the melting point is the same as the freezing point. At that temperature, without any additional input of energy, the processes of melting and freezing occur at the same rates.

$$\text{solid} + \text{energy} \rightleftharpoons \text{liquid}$$

If heat is added to a system that is in equilibrium, the balance will shift so that more liquid forms than solid. The temperature will continue to remain the same. Only after all of the solid is turned into liquid will the temperature rise.

Molar Enthalpy of Fusion

The amount of energy required to melt one mole of solid at the solid's melting point is its **molar enthalpy of fusion.** Just like the molar enthalpy of vaporization, this quantity is a measure of the attractive forces between particles. As a solid particle absorbs energy at the melting point, its kinetic energy stays the same. But, the potential energy increases until the attractive forces are overcome and the particles have a less ordered arrangement.

Sublimation and Deposition

If the pressure and temperature are low enough, a liquid cannot exist. In these conditions, a gas achieves a state of equilibrium with a solid, as represented by this equation.

$$\text{solid} + \text{energy} \rightleftharpoons \text{gas}$$

The change of state from a solid directly to a gas is known as **sublimation.** The reverse process of a gas changing directly into a solid is known as **deposition.** Dry ice (solid carbon dioxide) and iodine sublime at ordinary temperatures.

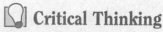

Critical Thinking

5. Illustrate Write an equation that represents the equilibrium condition in a closed system between a substance in the liquid phase and the same substance in the gas phase.

_____

_____

CONNECT

Frost is an example of deposition. Water changes from water vapor to solid ice on a surface below its freezing point (0°C). On the other hand, snow can disappear from the ground even when the temperature is below freezing because of the slow sublimation of solid water into water vapor.

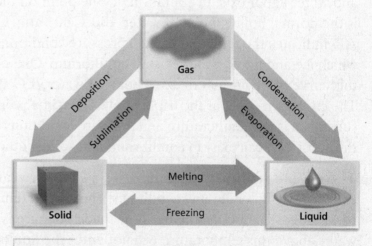

The diagram shows a summary of the possible changes of state that can occur for a substance. The processes on the outside of the triangle release energy. The processes on the inside of the triangle absorb energy.

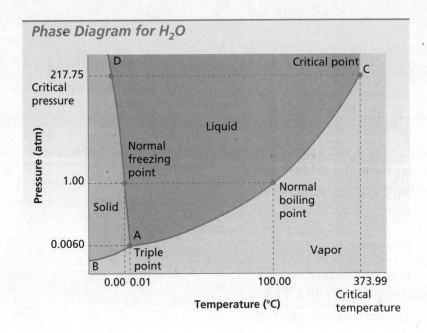

Phase Diagram for H₂O

Pressure (atm) vs *Temperature (°C)*

D — Critical point C
217.75 Critical pressure
Liquid
Normal freezing point
1.00
Normal boiling point
Solid
A
0.0060
Triple point
B
Vapor

0.00 0.01   100.00   373.99 Critical temperature

The phase diagram for water shows the relationship between the phases of water and its temperature and pressure. The pressure and temperature scales on this graph are logarithmic.

Under certain conditions, water can exist in all three phases at the same time.

A **phase diagram** is a graph of pressure versus temperature that shows the conditions under which a substance's phases exist. The graph above is the phase diagram for water.

Note that the graph includes three curves. Curve AB indicates the temperature and pressure conditions in which ice and water vapor exist in equilibrium. Curve AC indicates the temperature and pressure conditions in which liquid water and water vapor exist in equilibrium. One point on the curve is the normal boiling point of water, 100°C at 1 atm. Curve AD indicates the temperature and pressure conditions in which ice and liquid water exist in equilibrium. One point on this curve is the normal freezing point of water, 0°C at 1 atm. The curves intersect at the triple point. The **triple point** of a substance is the temperature and pressure conditions at which the substance can exist in equilibrium as a solid, liquid, or gas.

Above the **critical temperature** (t_c), a substance cannot exist as a liquid under any conditions. The critical temperature of water is 373.99°C. No matter how much pressure is applied, water above this temperature will not enter the liquid state. The **critical pressure** (P_c), is the lowest pressure at which the substance can exist as a liquid at its critical temperature. The critical pressure for water is 217.75 atm. The point on the phase diagram indicated by the critical temperature and the critical pressure is called the **critical point.**

 CONNECT

The slope of line AC in the diagram above shows that the temperature of sublimation decreases with decreasing pressure. This fact is used in freeze-dried foods. The food is frozen, then the pressure is decreased. The ice in the food sublimes rather than melts, leaving the food free of water.

✓ **READING CHECK**

6. What forms can water take at the conditions described by its triple point?

_____

_____

_____

VOCABULARY

1. What is equilibrium?

_____

_____

REVIEW

2. What happens when a liquid-vapor system at equilibrium experiences an increase in temperature?

_____

_____

_____

3. What is the equilibrium vapor pressure of a liquid and how is it measured?

_____

_____

_____

Critical Thinking

4. **INTERPRETING GRAPHICS** Refer to the phase diagram of water on the preceding page to answer these questions.

a. Describe all the changes a sample of solid water would undergo when heated from –10°C to its critical temperature at a pressure of 1.00 atm.

_____

_____

b. Describe all the changes a sample of water vapor would undergo when cooled from 110°C to 5°C at 1.00 atm pressure.

_____

_____

c. At what pressures will water be a vapor at 0°C?

_____

d. Within what range of pressures will water be a liquid at temperatures above its normal boiling point?

_____

SECTION 10.5

Water

Water commonly exists in all three physical states on Earth, where it is by far the most abundant liquid. It covers nearly three-quarters of Earth's surface. Water is an essential component of life; from 70% to 90% of the mass of living things is water. Chemical reactions that are necessary for life take place in water, and often involve water as a reactant or a product. The structure of a water molecule gives water the unique properties that make it such an important molecule.

The properties of water in all phases are determined by its structure.

Water molecules consist of two atoms of hydrogen linked to one atom of oxygen by polar-covalent bonds. A molecule of water is bent, with its two bonds forming an angle of about 105°.

$$H\overset{\ddot{O}}{\underset{105°}{\frown}}H$$

Different molecules of water are linked by hydrogen bonding. The number of linked molecules decreases with increasing temperature because hydrogen bonds have difficulty forming between molecules with greater kinetic energies. Usually, four to eight molecules of water are linked in a group, as shown at the right.

This ability of water molecules to form groups prevents molecules from escaping to become gas particles. Water would be a gas at room temperature without this ability.

The diagram on the next page shows water molecules in the solid state. These molecules form an orderly, hexagonal arrangement in ice crystals. The large empty spaces between molecules in this pattern explain why solid water has the unusual property of being less dense than its liquid form.

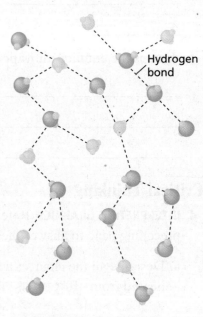

Hydrogen bond

Liquid water

In a group of liquid water molecules, hydrogen and oxygen are bonded within each molecule, and different molecules are held together by hydrogen bonds.

 READING CHECK

1. Order the three forms of water from least dense to densest.

The diagrams of water molecules to the right and on the preceding page represent water in the liquid state and the solid state at 0°C. Liquid water has fewer and more disorderly hydrogen bonds than ice. When energy is added to ice, and the crystal structure breaks down, the water molecules can actually crowd closer together in the liquid state. This is why water is more dense than ice.

As liquid water is warmed from 0°C, its particles pack closer together until the temperature of 3.98°C is reached. At temperatures above 3.98°C, the kinetic energy of the water molecules moving around in the liquid keeps the molecules from being packed so closely together.

This unusual property of water helps protect organisms that live in water. Most liquids freeze from the bottom up. Water freezes from the top down, because the surface water is cooler than the deeper water. In addition, the ice stays on the surface of a lake or pond because it is less dense than water and acts as an insulator. This effect makes it difficult for a large body of water to freeze solid.

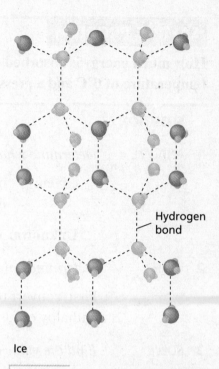

Hydrogen bond

Ice

Ice contains the same types of bonding as liquid water. However, the structure of the hydrogen bonding is more rigid than in liquid water.

The molar enthalpy of water determines many of its physical characteristics.

At room temperature, liquid water is transparent, odorless, tasteless, and nearly colorless. Any observed odor or taste is a result of dissolved substances in the water. The density of water is 0.999 84 g/cm^3, while the density of ice is 0.917 g/cm^3.

Water has a relatively high boiling point. A large amount of kinetic energy is necessary for the water molecules to completely overcome the hydrogen bonding.

At atmospheric pressure, ice's molar enthalpy of fusion is 6.009 kJ/mol. That value is relatively large compared to other solids. Water also has a relatively high molar enthalpy of vaporization, 40.79 kJ/mol. These high values both result from the strong attractive forces in hydrogen bonds. The high molar enthalpy of vaporization makes steam (vaporized water) ideal for household heating systems. Steam can store a great deal of energy as heat. When the steam condenses in a radiator, it releases this energy.

✓ READING CHECK

2. Why is a relatively large amount of energy required to turn liquid water into water vapor?

_____

_____

_____

_____

_____

How much energy is absorbed when 47.0 g of ice melt at a temperature of 0°C and a pressure of 1 atm?

SOLUTION		
1 ANALYZE		*Determine what information is given and unknown.*

Given: mass of $H_2O(s) = 47.0$ g
molar enthalpy of fusion = 6.009 kJ/mol

Unknown: energy absorbed when ice melts

2 PLAN   *Determine how to find the value of the unknown.*

First, convert the mass of water to moles. Then use the molar enthalpy of fusion as a conversion factor.

3 SOLVE   *Find the value of the unknown using the given information.*

$$47.0 \text{ g } H_2O = 47.0 \text{ g } H_2O \times \frac{1 \text{ mol } H_2O}{18.02 \text{ g } H_2O}$$

$$= 2.61 \text{ mol } H_2O$$

$$\text{Energy absorbed} = 2.61 \text{ mol } H_2O \times \frac{6.009 \text{ kJ } H_2O}{1 \text{ mol } H_2O}$$

$$= 15.7 \text{ kJ}$$

4 CHECK YOUR WORK   *Check to see if the answers make sense.*

A mass of 47 g of water is about 3 mol and $3 \times 6 = 18$. The answer has the right units and is close to the estimate.

PRACTICE

A. What mass of steam is required to release 4.97×10^5 kJ of energy on condensation?

$$\text{Moles of steam required} = 4.97 \times 10^5 \text{ kJ} \times \frac{1 \text{ mol } H_2O}{40.79 \text{ kJ } H_2O}$$

$$= \underline{\hspace{2cm}}$$

$$\text{Mass of steam required} = \underline{\hspace{2cm}} \text{ mol } H_2O \times \frac{18.02 \text{ g } H_2O}{1 \text{ mol } H_2O}$$

$$= \underline{\hspace{2cm}}$$

Water plays a unique role in biological systems.

Life as we know it would be impossible without water. Water's physical and chemical properties are necessary to support life on Earth. Water is one of the few naturally occurring liquids on this planet.

Physical Properties

Water is the only substance on Earth's surface that occurs naturally in all three common physical states (solid, liquid, gas). This fact makes the water cycle possible —the natural process of evaporation and condensation that carries water from the oceans to the clouds and then to the land.

Another property of water is that it has the ability to remain a liquid under a wide range of temperatures. Even though Earth's surface experiences wide fluctuations in temperature, the oceans don't freeze completely or boil.

Water can also absorb a large amount of heat energy, making the oceans a climate moderator. When the sun shines, the oceans absorb this energy. They then radiate it back when the sun is not shining. This helps to maintain a more constant average temperature on Earth's surface.

An additional property of water is its ability to increase its volume as it freezes. This means that ice floats on liquid water, allowing many aquatic organisms to survive in the water.

Earth appears blue from outer space because two-thirds of its surface is covered in liquid water.

 READING CHECK

3. Describe three of water's physical properties.

_____

_____

_____

_____

_____

_____

_____

_____

Solubility and Metabolism

Animals Animals could not survive long without water. Water gives the body of a living thing a way to transport the nutrients it needs to the places where it needs them. Water's ability to remain a liquid across a wide range of temperatures makes this possible.

Water also can dissolve just about anything, making it the ideal carrier for all the soluble nutrients a body needs. Here are some examples.

- Some compounds, known as electrolytes, dissolve in water and regulate such things as proper muscle function. Many sports drinks advertise that they replenish electrolytes.
- Water is involved in all aspects of a body's metabolism (processing of chemicals). It helps pull together larger molecules the body needs for energy storage and then disassemble the molecules when the body needs them for fuel. Water helps flush fat cells and sugar out of the body.
- Water enables enzymes to take part in chemical reactions. Enzyme molecules are catalysts. Catalysts are chemicals that speed up reactions. Without water, chemical reactions inside the body's cells would happen at a much slower rate.

Plants Of course, plants need water as well as animals. During photosynthesis, plants use energy from the sun to break off the hydrogen atoms from water and put them on to a molecule of carbon dioxide. The eventual result is a molecule of glucose, which is used for energy.

TIP **Solubility** is the ability of one substance to dissolve in another at a given temperature and pressure.

A **solution** is a homogeneous mixture of two or more substances uniformly dispersed throughout a single phase.

TIP **Metabolism** is the sum of all chemical processes that occur in an organism.

Critical Thinking

4. **Apply Concepts** What would happen to solubility and metabolism of a body if water was NOT able to remain a liquid across a wide range of temperatures?

_____

_____

_____

_____

_____

_____

REVIEW

1. Why is the water molecule polar?

_____

_____

2. How is the structure of water responsible for its unique characteristics?

_____

_____

3. Describe the arrangement of molecules in liquid water and ice.

_____

_____

4. Why does ice float? Why is this phenomenon important?

_____

_____

5. Why is ice less dense than liquid water?

_____

_____

6. Is more energy required to melt one gram of ice at 0°C or to boil one gram
of water at 100°C? How do you know?

_____

_____

Critical Thinking

7. RELATING IDEAS Why is exposure to steam dangerous?

_____

_____

_____

Math Tutor CALCULATING USING ENTHALPIES OF FUSION

When one mole of a liquid freezes to a solid, a certain amount of energy is released. The attractive forces between particles pull the disorderly particles of the liquid into a more orderly crystalline solid. When the solid melts to a liquid, the solid must absorb the same amount of energy in order to separate the particles of the crystal and overcome the attractive forces opposing separation. The energy used to melt or freeze one mole of a substance at its melting point is called its molar enthalpy of fusion, ΔH_f.

Problem-Solving TIPS

- The enthalpy of fusion of a substance can be given as either joules per gram or kilojoules per mole.
- *Molar* enthalpy of fusion (kilojoules per mole) is the value that is most commonly used in calculations.
- The enthalpy of fusion is the energy absorbed or given off as heat when a substance melts or freezes at its melting point.
- No net change in temperature occurs as the change in state occurs.

SAMPLE

Determine the quantity of energy that will be needed to melt 2.50×10^5 kg of iron at its melting point, 1536°C. The ΔH_f of iron is 13.807 kJ/mol.

The number of moles of a substance that is equal to a given mass of a substance can be determined from the following equation.

moles of a substance = mass of substance/molar mass of substance

The energy as heat absorbed by a substance as it is going through a phase change from a solid to a liquid is

energy absorbed = $\Delta H_f \times$ moles of a substance

The first equation can be substituted into the second equation to give the energy absorbed in terms of the given information. The given information can then be used to solve the problem.

$$\text{energy absorbed} = \Delta H_f \times \frac{\text{mass of substance}}{\text{molar mass of substance}}$$

$$\text{energy absorbed} = \frac{13.807 \text{ kJ}}{1 \text{ mol}} \times \frac{2.50 \times 10^8 \text{ g Fe}}{55.847 \text{ g Fe/mol}}$$

$$= 6.18 \times 10^7 \text{ kJ}$$

Practice Problems: Chapter Review practice problems 16–18

1. What idea is the kinetic-molecular theory based on?

_____

_____

2. State the five basic assumptions of kinetic-molecular theory.

(1)_____

(2)_____

(3)_____

(4)_____

(5)_____

3. How do gases compare with liquids and solids in terms of the distance between their molecules?

_____

_____

_____

4. What is the relationship among the temperature, speed, and kinetic energy of gas molecules?

_____

_____

_____

5. What factors affect the rate of diffusion of one gas through another?

_____

_____

_____

6. What is surface tension?

_____

_____

_____

7. List at least three properties of solids and explain each in terms of the kinetic-molecular theory of solids.

_____

_____

_____

_____

8. List and describe the four types of crystals in terms of the nature of the component particles and the type of bonding between them.

_____

_____

_____

_____

_____

_____

9. Using the graph "Energy Distribution of Molecules in a Liquid at Different Temperatures," estimate the equilibrium vapor pressure of each of the following at the specified temperature.

a. water at 80°C _____   **b.** ethanol at 60°C _____

10. Explain how the attractive forces between the particles of a liquid are related to the equilibrium vapor pressure of that liquid.

_____

_____

_____

11. Explain the relationship between the atmospheric pressure and the actual boiling point of water.

_____

_____

12. Explain the relationship between the molar enthalpy of fusion of a solid and the strength of attraction between that solid's particles.

_____

_____

_____

13. List at least eight physical properties of water.

_____

_____

_____

14. Express the molar enthalpy of vaporization for water (40.79 kJ/mol) and the molar enthalpy of fusion for water (6.009 kJ/mol) in joules per gram.

15. Calculate the molar enthalpy of vaporization of a substance given that 0.433 mol of the substance absorbs 36.5 kJ of energy when it is vaporized.

16. Given that a substance has a molar mass of 259.0 g/mol and a 71.8 g sample of the substance absorbs 4.307 kJ when it melts, calculate the molar enthalpy of fusion.

17. Calculate the number of moles in a liquid sample of a substance that has a molar enthalpy of fusion of 3.811 kJ/mol, given that the sample releases 83.2 kJ when it freezes.

18. What volume and mass of steam at 100°C and 1.00 atm would release the same amount of energy during condensation as 100 cm^3 of liquid water would release during freezing?

CHAPTER 11

Gases

Key Concepts

Section 1 *Gases and Pressure*

What is pressure and how is it measured?

How are partial pressures calculated?

Section 2 *The Gas Laws*

What are Boyle's law, Charles's law, and Gay-Lussac's law?

How are volume, temperature, and pressure related for a gas?

Section 3 *Gas Volumes and the Ideal Gas Law*

What is the law of combining volumes of gases?

What is Avogadro's law and what is its significance?

What is the ideal gas law and how is it used?

Section 4 *Diffusion and Effusion*

How are molecular velocities and molar masses related?

Review Previous Concepts

1. What is a mole? What information does the molar mass of a substance relate about the substance?

_____

_____

_____

_____

2. What is the kinetic-molecular theory of matter?

_____

_____

_____

_____

SECTION 11.1

Gases and Pressure

In the chapter "States of Matter," you read about the kinetic-molecular theory of matter. You were also introduced to how this theory explains some of the properties of ideal gases. In this chapter, you will study the predictions of kinetic-molecular theory for gases in more detail. This includes the relationship among the temperature, pressure, volume, and amount of gas in a sample.

Collisions of air molecules generate pressure.

You may be familiar with the concept of tire pressure. When you pump more air into a tire, the number of molecules of air inside the tire increases. This causes an increase in the number of collisions between air molecules and the sides of the tire. An increase in pressure is the result of the increase in collisions.

Pressure depends on force and area.

Pressure is the force per unit area on a surface. The SI unit for force is the newton, N. The pressure exerted by a particular force is given by this equation.

$$\text{pressure} = \frac{\text{force}}{\text{area}}$$

READING CHECK

1. Compute the pressure exerted by the dancer for photos (b) and (c) below.

Force = 500 N

a. Area of contact = 325 cm^2

$\text{Pressure} = \frac{\text{force}}{\text{area}}$

$= \frac{500 \text{ N}}{325 \text{ cm}^2}$

$= 1.5 \text{ N/cm}^2$

Force = 500 N

b. Area of contact = 13 cm^2

$\text{Pressure} = \frac{\text{force}}{\text{area}}$

$=$

$=$

Force = 500 N

c. Area of contact = 6.5 cm^2

$\text{Pressure} = \frac{\text{force}}{\text{area}}$

$=$

$=$

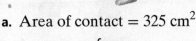

The pressure a dancer exerts against the floor depends on the area of contact. The smaller the area, the greater the pressure.

Pressure One way to think of force is to consider it the result of a mass times an acceleration. A **newton** is the force that will increase the speed of a one-kilogram mass by one meter per second each second that the force is applied.

Consider the ballet dancer on the previous page. Earth exerts a gravitational force on all objects on its surface that accelerates them toward Earth at 9.8 m/s². The ballet dancer has a mass of 51 kg. Therefore, the force that Earth exerts on her is given by the following equation.

$$51 \text{ kg} \times 9.8 \text{ m/s}^2 = 500 \text{ N}$$

As a result of gravity, the dancer is pulled against the floor with a force of 500 N. The pressure that the dancer exerts on the floor depends on the surface area of the dancer touching the floor. If the dancer is standing on one toe, she exerts more pressure on that part of the floor than if she is standing on two flat feet. The same force applied to a smaller area results in greater pressure.

Atmospheric Pressure The atmosphere, which is the air that surrounds Earth, exerts pressure on Earth's surface. This pressure is equivalent to a 1.03 kg mass sitting on every square centimeter of Earth. The resulting pressure is 10.1 N/cm². This quantity is also called 1 atmosphere, or 1 atm.

Atmospheric pressure is the result of all of the different gases in the air striking Earth's surface. The atmosphere contains 78% nitrogen gas, 21% oxygen gas, and 1% other gases by volume.

Atmospheric pressure decreases higher up in the atmosphere. This is because there are fewer air particles farther away from Earth's surface. When you fly in an airplane, the decrease in pressure outside your ears relative to the pressure inside your ears makes your ears "pop."

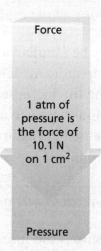

Force

1 atm of pressure is the force of 10.1 N on 1 cm²

Pressure

☑ READING CHECK

2. What element is responsible for most of the pressure exerted by the atmosphere on the surface of Earth?

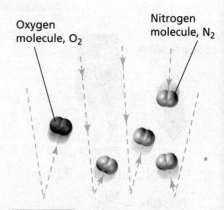

Oxygen molecule, O₂

Nitrogen molecule, N₂

Air molecules, mostly nitrogen and oxygen, collide with Earth's surface, exerting a pressure of 10.1 N/cm².

Measuring Pressure

A **barometer** is a device used to measure atmospheric pressure. The first type of barometer was introduced by Evangelista Torricelli in the early 1600s. Torricelli wondered why water pumps could only raise water to a height of 34 ft. He hypothesized that the height of the water depends on the weight of the water compared with the weight of air. He predicted that mercury, which is 14 times as dense as water, would only rise 1/14 as high as water.

To find out if he was right, Torricelli held a tube upside down over a dish of liquid mercury. The top of the tube was a vacuum, so only the weight of the liquid mercury pressed down on the mercury in the dish. This column of fluid was prevented from falling because air pushed down on the liquid in the dish, preventing it from rising due to fluid leaving the tube. Torricelli found that the pressure of the air was equivalent to the pressure of about a 760 mm column of mercury. And 760 mm was about 1/14 the height of 34 feet (10.4 m).

The atmospheric pressure at any place on Earth depends on elevation and weather conditions. If the pressure rises, then the column of mercury in Torricelli's barometer becomes taller. If the pressure drops, then the column becomes shorter. So, air pressure can be measured by the height of a column of mercury in a barometer.

A manometer uses a similar method to measure the pressure of a specific gas sample. The gas is enclosed but is able to exert pressure on a column of mercury in a U-shaped tube. The difference in height of the mercury columns in the two arms of the "U" is a measure of the pressure exerted by the gas.

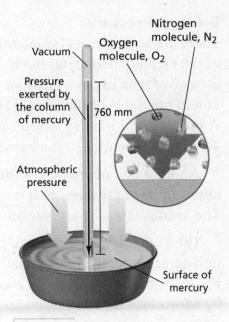

This barometer measures the pressure exerted by the gas in the atmosphere in millimeters of mercury. Atmospheric pressure can support the weight of a column of mercury that is about 760 mm high.

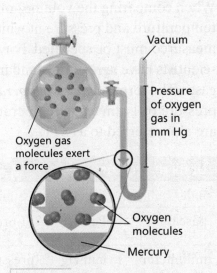

This manometer is measuring the pressure in a sample of oxygen gas. The pressure is indicated by the difference in height of the mercury in the two arms of the U-shaped tube.

Critical Thinking

3. **Apply** Suppose the air is completely removed from inside an empty plastic water bottle. What happens to the water bottle? Explain your answer.

_____

_____

_____

Units of Pressure

There are several units for measuring pressure. The usefulness of the mercury barometer has led to the use of the height of a column of mercury as a measure of pressure. The common unit of pressure is **millimeters of mercury,** or mm Hg. A pressure of 1 mm Hg is also called 1 torr in honor of Torricelli's invention of the barometer.

Another unit of pressure is the atmosphere. One **atmosphere of pressure,** atm, is the equivalent of 760 mm Hg. The average atmospheric pressure at sea level at 0°C is 1 atm.

The SI unit of pressure is the pascal. A pascal is a derived unit named after the French mathematician and philosopher Blaise Pascal. One **pascal,** Pa, is equal to the pressure exerted by a force of 1 N acting on an area of 1 m². In many situations, it is more convenient to use the unit kilopascal, kPa. For example, one atmosphere of pressure, 1 atm, is equal to 101.325 kPa. The units of pressure used in this book are summarized in the table.

Standard Temperature and Pressure

When comparing the volumes of two different gases, the temperature and pressure at which the volumes were measured must be specified. For purposes of comparison, scientists have agreed on standard conditions for comparing gases. The term *standard temperature and pressure* refers to a pressure of 1 atm and a temperature of 0°C. These conditions are also referred to as STP.

> **Remember**
>
> A derived unit is a unit that is a combination of two or more base units in the SI system. The pascal is a derived unit equal to one kilogram per meter per second squared.

 READING CHECK

4. What does each letter in the acronym STP stand for?

S_____

T_____

P_____

Units of Pressure		
Unit	Symbol	Definition/relationship
pascal	Pa	SI pressure unit, $1\ Pa = \dfrac{1\ N}{m^2}$
millimeter of mercury	mm Hg	pressure that supports a 1 mm mercury column in a barometer
torr	torr	1 torr = 1 mm Hg
atmosphere	atm	average atmospheric pressure at sea level and 0°C 1 atm = 760 mm Hg = 760 torr = $1.013\ 25 \times 10^5$ Pa = 101.325 kPa
pounds per square inch	psi	1 psi = $6.892\ 86 \times 10^3$ Pa 1 atm = 14.700 psi

The total pressure of a gas mixture is the sum of the pressures of the gases in it.

The pressure exerted by each gas in a mixture is called the **partial pressure** of that gas. John Dalton, the English chemist who proposed the atomic theory, also studied gas mixtures. He proposed that the pressure exerted by each gas in an unreactive mixture is independent of the pressures exerted by the other gases in the mixture. In other words, if a sample of oxygen gas exerts a pressure of 0.28 atm when it is isolated, then the molecules of that sample will exert a partial pressure of 0.28 atm when mixed with one or more gases.

Dalton's law of partial pressures states that the total pressure exerted by a gas mixture is the sum of the partial pressures of the component gases. Dalton's law may be expressed as an equation

$$P_T = P_1 + P_2 + P_3 + \ldots$$

where P_T is the total pressure of the mixture, P_1 is the partial pressure of the first gas, P_2 is the partial pressure of the second gas, and so on.

The kinetic-molecular theory of matter can explain Dalton's law. Each particle in a mixture of gases has an equal chance of colliding with the walls of a container. Therefore, each collection of gas molecules exerts a pressure independent of that exerted by the other gases. The total pressure is the result of the total number of collisions on a unit of wall area in a given time.

LOOKING CLOSER

5. Define each of these terms separately in your own words.

partial: _____

_____

_____

pressure: _____

_____

_____

PRACTICE

A. Convert a pressure of 1.75 atm to kPa and mm Hg.

B. What is the partial pressure of O_2 in a mixture of CO_2, N_2, and O_2 at 1 atm if $P_{CO_2} = 0.285$ torr and $P_{N_2} = 593.525$ torr?

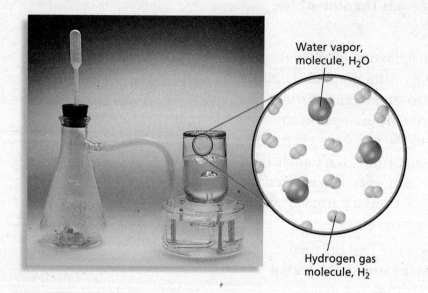

Water vapor, molecule, H$_2$O

Hydrogen gas molecule, H$_2$

Gases Collected by Water Displacement

Often it is difficult to determine the amount of gas given off by a chemical reaction. The low density of the gas makes it hard to measure the mass that a gas adds to a container. Scientists have developed a method of collecting gases by water displacement to address this problem.

In this method, a collection bottle is partially filled with water and placed upside down over a reservoir of water. The gas released by a reaction passes into the collection bottle through a tube. When the gas enters the bottle, it displaces water from the bottle. The pressure of the gas forces the water down toward the reservoir.

After the gas is collected, the collection bottle does not contain a pure sample of the gas from the chemical reaction. The gas in the bottle is a mixture of the gas from the reaction and water vapor that is in a state of equilibrium with the water in the bottle. During the collection, the water level adjusts so that the total pressure on the water surface inside the water bottle equals the atmospheric pressure, P_{atm}. Therefore, the partial pressures of the two gases, the gas from the reaction and water vapor, must satisfy this equation:

$$P_{atm} = P_{gas} + P_{H_2O}$$

The value of P_{atm} can be read from a barometer in the laboratory. The value of P_{H_2O} can be found in the table on the next page, using the recorded temperature of the experiment. The value of P_{gas} can be determined using these two values.

READING CHECK

6. What law states that the sum of the partial pressures of two gases in a mixture is the total pressure of the mixture?

_____

_____

Water-Vapor Pressure

Temperature (°C)	Pressure (mm Hg)	Pressure (kPa)	Temperature (°C)	Pressure (mm Hg)	Pressure (kPa)
0.0	4.6	0.61	23.0	21.1	2.81
10.0	9.2	1.23	23.5	21.7	2.90
15.0	12.8	1.71	24.0	22.4	2.98
16.0	13.6	1.82	25.0	23.8	3.17
16.5	14.1	1.88	26.0	25.2	3.36
17.0	14.5	1.94	27.0	26.7	3.57
17.5	15.0	2.00	28.0	28.3	3.78
18.0	15.5	2.06	29.0	30.0	4.01
18.5	16.0	2.13	30.0	31.8	4.25
19.0	16.5	2.19	35.0	42.2	5.63
19.5	17.0	2.27	40.0	55.3	7.38
20.0	17.5	2.34	50.0	92.5	12.34
20.5	18.1	2.41	60.0	149.4	19.93
21.0	18.6	2.49	70.0	233.7	31.18
21.5	19.2	2.57	80.0	355.1	47.37
22.0	19.8	2.64	90.0	525.8	70.12
22.5	20.4	2.72	100.0	760.0	101.32

For example, suppose oxygen gas is collected by water displacement from a decomposition reaction of potassium chlorate, $KClO_3$. If the temperature during the experiment is 20.0°C, then the partial pressure of water vapor atmospheric pressure is 17.5 torr. If the atmospheric pressure during the experiment is 731.0 torr, then the partial pressure of the oxygen gas can be determined as follows.

$$P_{O_2} = P_{atm} - P_{H_2O} = 731.0 \text{ torr} - 17.5 \text{ torr} = 713.5 \text{ torr}$$

PRACTICE

C. Some hydrogen gas is collected over water at 20.0°C. The levels of water inside and outside the gas-collection bottle are the same. The partial pressure of the hydrogen is 742.5 torr. What is the barometric pressure at the time the gas is collected?

$P_{atm} =$ _____ $+ P_{H_2O} =$ _____ torr + _____ torr = _____ torr

VOCABULARY

1. Define *pressure*.

_____

_____

REVIEW

2. Name at least four different units that are used to express measurements of pressure.

_____

_____

3. Convert the following pressures to pressures in standard atmospheres.

   a. 151.98 kPa

   [   ]

   b. 456 torr

   [   ]

4. A sample of nitrogen gas is collected over water at a temperature of 23.0°C. What is the pressure of the nitrogen gas if atmospheric pressure is 785 mm Hg?

   [   ]

Critical Thinking

5. **EVALUATING METHODS** Clean rooms used for sterile biological research are sealed and operate at slightly above atmospheric pressure. Explain why.

_____

_____

_____

6. **INFERRING RELATIONSHIPS** Explain why helium-filled balloons deflate over time faster than air-filled balloons do.

_____

_____

_____

SECTION 11.2

The Gas Laws

The *gas laws* are simple mathematical relationships among the volume, temperature, pressure, and amount of a gas. They are the result of hundreds of years of study on the physical properties of gases. The scientists who discovered them made careful observations of the relationship between two or more variables in samples of various gases. The gas laws can all be explained using the kinetic-molecular theory of matter.

<table>
<tr><td colspan="2">KEY TERMS</td></tr>
<tr><td>absolute zero</td><td>Gay-Lussac's law</td></tr>
<tr><td>Boyle's law</td><td>combined gas law</td></tr>
<tr><td>Charles's law</td><td></td></tr>
</table>

In this section, four gas laws will be covered. These gas laws are listed in the table at the right. These four laws are true for any choice of units for pressure and volume. The units of the constant k depend on the units of pressure and volume. In any comparison between a sample of a gas at two different times, the same units of pressure and volume should be used.

Gas law	Equation	Variables held constant
Boyle's law	$PV = k$	temperature, amount of gas
Charles's law	$\frac{V}{k} = k$	pressure, amount of gas
Gay-Lussac's law	$\frac{P}{T} = k$	volume, amount of gas
combined gas law	$\frac{PV}{T} = k$	amount of gas

The gas laws are only true if temperature is measured in kelvins. The Kelvin temperature scale starts at absolute zero and expresses temperatures in kelvins, K. **Absolute zero** is the temperature –273.15°C. The relationship between the Celsius scale and the Kelvin scale is given by

$$K = 273.15 + °C$$

So, the temperature –273.15°C is equivalent to 0 K.

TIP For calculations in this book, the value of absolute zero is rounded off to –273°C. The temperature 0°C is then considered equivalent to 273 K.

PRACTICE

Convert the following temperatures to either the Celsius temperature scale or the Kelvin temperature scale.

A. 20°C _____

C. –10°C _____

E. 273°C _____

B. 300 K _____

D. 100 K _____

F. 297 K _____

Gas volume and pressure are indirectly proportional.

The first relationship that was discovered between quantities in a sample of gas was between the pressure and the volume. In 1662, Robert Boyle discovered that doubling the pressure on a gas at constant temperature reduced its volume by one-half. Reducing the pressure on a gas by one-half allowed the volume of the gas to double.

The kinetic-molecular theory explains why this pressure-volume relationship exists. Pressure is caused by gas particles hitting the walls of a container. If the volume of the container is decreased, the particles will strike the container walls more frequently. If the volume of the container is increased, the particles will spread out and fewer collisions will occur.

Boyle's law states that the volume of a fixed mass of gas varies inversely with the pressure at constant temperature. Mathematically, Boyle's law is expressed as

$$PV = k$$

where P is pressure, V is volume, and k is a constant.

Another way to express Boyle's law is to consider two sets of measurements at different times on the same sample of a gas. If P_1 and V_1 are the first set of measurements of pressure and volume, and P_2 and V_2 are the second set, then

$$P_1V_1 = P_2V_2$$

Volume vs. Pressure for a Gas at Constant Temperature

This graph shows the inverse relationship between volume and pressure for a gas sample at a constant temperature.

✓ READING CHECK

1. If a gas is pumped from a smaller container to a container that is twice the size, what happens to the pressure of the gas?

_____

_____

_____

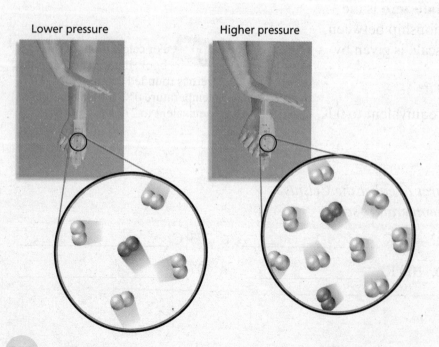

Lower pressure   Higher pressure

When the plunger is pressed in, the molecules collide with the walls of the plunger more frequently, raising the pressure.

A sample of oxygen gas has a volume of 150.0 mL when its pressure is 0.947 atm. What will the volume of the gas be at a pressure of 0.987 atm if the temperature remains constant?

SOLUTION		
1	ANALYZE	*Determine what information is given and unknown.*

Given: $V_1 = 150.0$ mL
$P_1 = 0.947$ atm
$P_2 = 0.987$ atm

Unknown: V_2

2	PLAN	*Write the equation that can be used to find the unknown.*

Because the given data are pressure and volume, and the unknown is volume, use Boyle's law.

$$P_1V_1 = P_2V_2$$

Rearranging the equation to isolate the unknown value:

$$V_2 = \frac{P_1V_1}{P_2}$$

3	SOLVE	*Substitute the given information and find the unknown value.*

$$V_2 = \frac{(0.947 \text{ atm})(150.0 \text{ mL O}_2)}{0.987 \text{ atm}} = 144 \text{ mL O}_2$$

4	CHECK YOUR WORK	*Check to see if the answer makes sense.*

The pressure increased slightly at constant temperature. Therefore the volume should decrease slightly.

PRACTICE

G. A balloon filled with helium gas has a volume of 500 mL at a pressure of 1 atm. The balloon is released and reaches an altitude of 6.5 km, where the pressure is 0.5 atm. If the temperature has remained the same, what volume does the gas occupy at 6.5 km?

$$V_2 = \frac{P_1V_1}{P_2} = \underline{\hspace{4cm}}$$

$$= \underline{\hspace{4cm}}$$

Gas volume and temperature are directly related.

A balloonist makes use of the expansion of a gas when it is heated at a constant pressure. When the temperature of a gas increases, the average kinetic energy of its particles increases. Because the particles are moving faster, they collide with the walls of a container more frequently. For the number of collisions, and therefore the pressure, to remain constant, the volume of the container must increase.

French scientist Jacques Charles discovered the relationship between volume and temperature in 1787. He found that each time a gas was heated from 0°C to 1°C, its volume increased by a factor of 1/273. If the temperature was increased from 0°C to 273°C, then the volume doubled.

Charles's law states that the volume of a fixed mass of gas at constant pressure varies directly with the Kelvin temperature. Mathematically, Charles's law is expressed as

$$V = kT \qquad \text{or} \qquad \frac{V}{T} = k$$

where V is volume, T is temperature in kelvins, and k is a constant. Just as for Boyle's law, Charles's law can be used to consider two sets of measurements at different times on the same sample of a gas. In the equation below, V_1 and T_1 are the first set of measurements, and V_2 and T_2 are the second set.

$$\frac{V_1}{T_1} = \frac{V_2}{T_2}$$

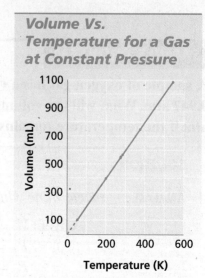

Volume Vs. Temperature for a Gas at Constant Pressure

This graph shows the linear relationship between the volume and the temperature in kelvins for a gas sample at constant pressure.

✓ READING CHECK

2. If a gas is pumped from a smaller container to a container that is twice the size, and its pressure is kept the same, then what happens to the temperature of the gas?

_____

_____

_____

As balloons filled with air are placed in a beaker of liquid nitrogen, the extremely cold temperature inside the beaker causes them to shrink. When the balloons are removed from the beaker, they expand to their original volume.

A sample of neon gas occupies a volume of 752 mL at 25°C. What volume will the gas occupy at 50°C if the pressure remains constant?

SOLUTION		
1	**ANALYZE**	*Determine what information is given and unknown.*
		Given: $V_1 = 752$ mL
		$T_1 = 25°C$
		$T_2 = 50°C$
		Unknown: V_2
2	**PLAN**	*Write the equation that can be used to find the unknown.*
		Because the given data are volume and temperature, use Charles's law and solve for the value of V_2.
		$$V_2 = \frac{T_2 V_1}{T_1}$$
3	**SOLVE**	*Substitute the given information and find the unknown value.*
		First, convert the given temperatures from degrees Celsius to Kelvin: $T_1 = 25°C + 273 = 298$ K; $T_2 = 50°C + 273 = 323$ K.
		$$V_2 = \frac{(323\ K)(752\ \text{mL Ne})}{298\ K} = 815\ \text{mL Ne}$$
4	**CHECK YOUR WORK**	*Check to see if the answer makes sense.*
		The temperature doubled in the Celsius scale, but not in kelvins. The temperature increased slightly at constant pressure, therefore the volume should increase slightly.

PRACTICE

H. A sample of nitrogen gas is contained in a piston with a freely moving cylinder. At 0.0°C, the volume of the gas is 375 mL. To what temperature must the gas be heated to occupy a volume of 500.0 mL?

$$T_2 = \frac{(\quad)(\quad)}{(\quad)} = \underline{\hspace{4cm}}$$

$$= \underline{\hspace{4cm}}$$

Gas pressure and temperature are directly related.

When the temperature of a gas is increased, Charles's law explains that the gas must expand for the pressure to remain constant. However, suppose that the volume were held constant when the temperature was increased. When the temperature of a gas in a rigid container increases, the average kinetic energy of its particles increases. Since the volume of the container is fixed, the increased speed of the particles leads to more collisions with the walls of the container. As a result, the gas exerts a greater pressure on the walls of the container.

French scientist Joseph Gay-Lussac is given credit for discovering the relationship between the pressure and temperature of a gas in 1802. His results were similar to the results of Charles's experiments. Each time a gas was heated from 0°C to 1°C, the pressure of the gas increased by a factor of 1/273. And an increase from 0°C to 273°C led to a doubling of the pressure.

Gay-Lussac's law states that the pressure of a fixed mass of gas at constant volume varies directly with the Kelvin temperature. Gay-Lussac's law can be expressed as

$$P = kT \quad \text{or} \quad \frac{P}{T} = k$$

where P is pressure, T is temperature in kelvins, and k is a constant. If P_1 and T_1 are a set of measurements on a sample of gas, and P_2 and T_2 are a second set taken at a later time, then the following equation is true.

$$\frac{P_1}{T_1} = \frac{P_2}{T_2}$$

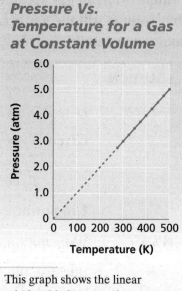

Pressure Vs. Temperature for a Gas at Constant Volume

This graph shows the linear relationship between the pressure and the temperature in kelvins for a gas sample at constant volume.

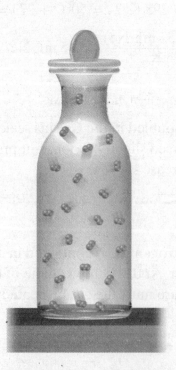

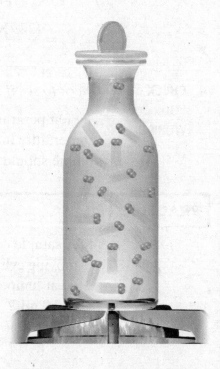

As the temperature of a gas inside a sealed container increases, the pressure of the gas increases.

The gas in a container is at a pressure of 3.00 atm at 25°C. Directions on the container warn the user not to keep it in a place where the temperature exceeds 52°C. What would the gas pressure in the container be at 52°C?

SOLUTION

1 ANALYZE

Determine what information is given and unknown.

Given: $P_1 = 3.00$ atm
$T_1 = 25°C$
$T_2 = 52°C$

Unknown: P_2

2 PLAN

Write the equation that can be used to find the unknown.

Because the given data are pressure and temperature, use Gay-Lussac's law and solve for the value of P_2.

$$P_2 = \frac{T_2 P_1}{T_1}$$

3 SOLVE

Substitute the given information and find the unknown value.

First, convert the given temperatures from degrees Celsius to Kelvin.

$$T_1 = 25°C + 273 = 298 \text{ K}$$

$$T_2 = 52°C + 273 = 325 \text{ K}$$

$$P_2 = \frac{(325 \text{ K})(3.00 \text{ atm})}{298 \text{ K}} = 3.27 \text{ atm}$$

4 CHECK YOUR WORK

Check to see if the answer makes sense.

The temperature increased slightly at constant volume. Therefore the pressure should increase slightly.

PRACTICE

1. A sample of helium gas has a pressure of 1.20 atm at 22°C. At what Celsius temperature will the helium reach a pressure of 2.00 atm, assuming constant volume?

$$T_2 = \frac{(\quad)(\quad)}{(\quad)} = \underline{\hspace{3cm}}$$

$$= \underline{\hspace{3cm}}$$

Gas pressure, temperature, and volume are interrelated.

The preceding pages of this section discussed the relationships between two quantities that describe a gas sample. However, in many cases, the pressure, volume, and temperature of a gas can all change between different sets of measurements.

The **combined gas law** expresses the relationship among pressure, volume, and temperature of a fixed amount of gas. The combined gas law can be expressed as follows.

$$\frac{PV}{T} = k$$

In this equation, the constant k depends on the amount of gas in the sample. The combined gas law can also be written as the following equation for two sets of measurements on the same sample of gas.

$$\frac{P_1 V_1}{T_1} = \frac{P_2 V_2}{T_2}$$

In this equation, P_1, V_1, and T_1 are the pressure, volume and temperature of a gas at one time, and P_2, V_2, and T_2 are the pressure, volume, and temperature of the gas at a later time.

The combined gas law is a combination of Boyle's law, Charles's law, and Gay-Lussac's law. If one of the quantities (pressure, volume, or temperature) is constant, then the combined gas law simplifies to one of the original three laws.

For example, if $T_1 = T_2$, then both sides of the equation above can be multiplied by T_1 to cancel the temperature variables.

$$\cancel{T_1} \times \frac{P_1 V_1}{\cancel{T_1}} = \cancel{T_1} \times \frac{P_2 V_2}{\cancel{T_2}}$$

$$P_1 V_1 = P_2 V_2$$

The result is Boyle's law. Because Boyle's law describes the relationship when temperature is a constant, the derivation makes sense.

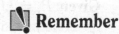

Remember

Two quantities are *inversely proportional* if their product is a constant. Two quantities are *directly proportional* if their ratio is a constant.

Critical Thinking

3. **Identify** Which of the three gas laws discussed so far describes a relationship that is directly proportional?

A helium-filled balloon has a volume of 50.0 L at 25°C and 1.08 atm. What volume will it have at 0.855 atm and 10.0°C?

	SOLUTION	
1	**ANALYZE**	*Determine what information is given and unknown.*

Given: $P_1 = 1.08$ atm, $T_1 = 25°C$, $V_1 = 50.0$ L

$\qquad P_2 = 0.855$ atm, $T_2 = 10°C$

Unknown: V_2

2 PLAN

Write the equation that can be used to find the unknown.

Use the combined gas law because the pressure, volume, and temperature are all changing. Rearrange to solve for V_2.

$$V_2 = \frac{P_1 V_1 T_2}{P_2 T_1}$$

3 SOLVE

Substitute the given information and find the unknown value.

$T_1 = 25°C + 273 = 298$ K

$T_2 = 10°C + 273 = 283$ K

$$V_2 = \frac{(1.08 \text{ atm})(50.0 \text{ L He})(283 \text{ K})}{(0.855 \text{ atm})(298 \text{ K})} = 60.0 \text{ L He}$$

4 CHECK YOUR WORK

Check to see if the answer makes sense.

The temperature decreased slightly, which should have decreased the volume slightly. The pressure decreased by a larger factor, which should have increased the volume by a larger factor. The answer reflects the net effect of a slight increase in volume.

PRACTICE

J. A 700.00 mL gas sample at STP is compressed to a volume of 200 mL, and the temperature is increased to 30.0°C. What is the new pressure of the gas in Pa?

$$P_2 = \frac{(\quad)(\quad)(\quad)}{(\quad)} = \underline{\hspace{4cm}}$$

$$= \underline{\hspace{4cm}}$$

VOCABULARY

1. Explain Charles's law in terms of the kinetic-molecular theory.

_____

_____

_____

REVIEW

2. Relate the effect of temperature and pressure on a gas to the model of a gas given by the kinetic-molecular theory.

_____

_____

_____

3. A sample of helium gas has a volume of 200.0 mL at 0.960 atm. What pressure, in atmospheres, is needed to reduce the volume at constant temperature to 50.0 mL?

4. A gas occupies 2.0 m³ at 100.0 K and exerts a pressure of 100.0 kPa. What volume will the gas occupy if the temperature is increased to 400.0 K and the pressure is increased to 200.0 kPa?

Critical Thinking

5. ANALYZING RESULTS A student has the following data: $V_1 = 822$ mL, $T_1 = 75°C$, and $T_2 = -25°C$. He calculates V_2 and gets –274 mL. Is this value correct? Explain why or why not.

_____

_____

_____

SECTION 11.3

Gas Volumes and the Ideal Gas Law

Section 2 presented laws that describe the relationship between the pressure, temperature, and volume of a gas. The volume of a gas is also related to the number of moles in gas. Using this relationship and the combined gas law, a single equation can be derived to describe all of the characteristics of a gas, called the *ideal gas law*.

KEY TERMS

Gay-Lussac's law of combining volumes of gases
Avogadro's law
standard molar volume of a gas
ideal gas law
ideal gas constant

Gases react in whole number ratios.

In the early nineteenth century, Joseph Gay-Lussac noticed a relationship between the volume of the reacted gases in a chemical reaction and the volume of the produced gases. For example, consider the synthesis of water vapor.

hydrogen gas   +   oxygen gas   ⟶   water vapor

| 2 L (2 volumes) | 1 L (1 volume) | 2 L (2 volumes) |

The 2:1:2 relationship for this reaction also applied to other proportions of volume, such as 600 L, 300 L, and 600 L. Gay-Lussac noticed that simple relationships existed for many other reactions, such as the following:

hydrogen gas + chlorine gas   ⟶   hydrogen chloride gas

| 1 L (1 volume) | 1 L (1 volume) | 2 L (2 volumes) |

Gay Lussac's law of combining volumes of gases states that the volumes of gaseous reactants and products can be expressed as ratios of small whole numbers.

Critical Thinking

1. Explain Which equation on this page is evidence that volume is not conserved in a chemical reaction? Why?

_____

_____

_____

_____

_____

READING CHECK

2. In a lab, 400 mL of hydrogen gas reacts with 400 mL of chlorine gas. What product would form and how much of the product would form?

_____

_____

Equal volumes of gases under the same conditions contain equal numbers of molecules.

Gay-Lussac's results contradicted Dalton's theory of the atom, which was still the leading theory at the time. Dalton believed that atoms are indivisible. He also believed that gaseous elements were isolated single atoms.

The first reaction on the previous page shows that it is possible for two gases with a combined volume of 3 L to produce a gas with less volume. Therefore, either 1 L of oxygen gas has the same number of particles as 2 L of hydrogen gas, or one of the gases contained particles with multiple atoms.

In 1811, Amedeo Avogadro developed a theory to explain Gay-Lussac's simple law. He rejected Dalton's idea that elements in a chemical reaction are always in the form of single atoms. He reasoned that the elements could consist of molecules that contain multiple atoms.

Avogadro also introduced an idea known today as Avogadro's law. **Avogadro's law** states that equal volumes of gases at the same temperature and pressure contain equal numbers of molecules. In other words, the volume of a gas varies directly with the number of molecules in the gas. This relationship can be expressed using the equation

$$V = kn$$

where n is the amount of gas in moles and k is a constant.

✓ READING CHECK

3. For a gas at constant pressure and temperature, the number of moles of the gas and the volume of the gas are

_____ proportional.

◐ CONNECT

The inflation of automobile air bags results from a rapid series of chemical reactions producing a volume of nitrogen gas. An igniter starts a series of reactions in which two nitrogen-containing solids produce molecules of nitrogen. In as few as 40 milliseconds (0.04 s) the air bag fills to prevent impacts with the dashboard or steering wheel.

At the same temperature and pressure, balloons of equal volume have equal numbers of molecules, regardless of which gas they contain.

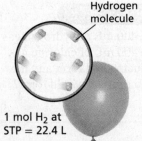

Hydrogen molecule

1 mol H₂ at
STP = 22.4 L

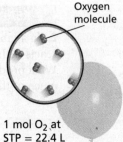

Oxygen molecule

1 mol O₂ at
STP = 22.4 L

Carbon dioxide molecule

1 mol CO₂ at
STP = 22.4 L

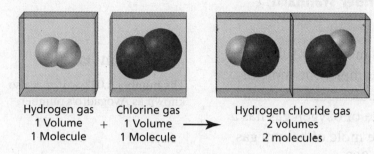

Hydrogen gas
1 Volume
1 Molecule

+

Chlorine gas
1 Volume
1 Molecule

→

Hydrogen chloride gas
2 volumes
2 molecules

Hydrogen molecules combine with
chlorine molecules in a 1:1 volume
ratio to produce 2 volumes of
hydrogen chloride.

Recall that 1 L of hydrogen gas combines with 1 L of chlorine gas to form 2 L of hydrogen chloride gas. According to Avogadro's law, there are twice as many particles in hydrogen chloride as there are in the other two gases. Since the compound must have at least two atoms, the reactants must contribute at least two atoms each to the reaction. The simplest equation that also satisfies Avogadro's law is shown.

$$H_2(g) \quad + \quad Cl_2(g) \quad \longrightarrow \quad 2HCl(g)$$

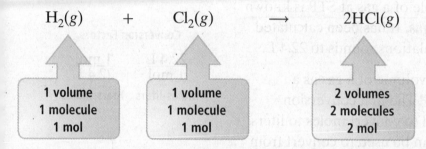

1 volume
1 molecule
1 mol

1 volume
1 molecule
1 mol

2 volumes
2 molecules
2 mol

Experiments eventually showed that all elements that are gases near room temperature, except for the noble gases, are diatomic molecules in their most common form. Therefore, the equation above, using Gay-Lussac's results and Avogadro's reasoning, is correct.

The reaction for water is also consistent with Avogadro's law and the idea that gaseous elements are diatomic. Gay-Lussac's results imply that the simplest combination of reactants is two diatomic molecules of hydrogen and one diatomic molecule of oxygen. If the product is to satisfy a 2:1:2 ratio, then it must be a molecule with two hydrogen atoms and one oxygen atom in each molecule.

$$2H_2(g) \quad + \quad O_2(g) \quad \longrightarrow \quad 2H_2O(g)$$

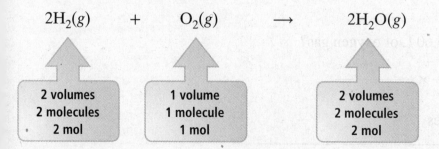

2 volumes
2 molecules
2 mol

1 volume
1 molecule
1 mol

2 volumes
2 molecules
2 mol

🎧 Critical Thinking

4. Compare Order the following samples of gas from the gas with the smallest volume to the largest volume: (a) 1.8 mol of H_2 gas, (b) 2.3 mol of AsH_3 gas, (c) 4 mol of Ar gas, (d) 1.7 mol of H_2O gas.

All gases have a volume of 22.4 L under standard conditions.

Earlier, you learned that one mole of a molecular substance contains 6.022×10^{23} molecules. For example, one mole of oxygen gas contains 6.022×10^{23} molecules, each of which consists of two oxygen atoms. One mole of oxygen gas has a mass of 32.00 g. On the other hand, one mole of helium gas has 6.022×10^{23} atoms and a mass of 4.003 g.

According to Avogadro's law, one mole of any gas will occupy the same volume as one mole of any other gas at the same temperature and pressure. Even though oxygen gas consists of diatomic molecules that are 8 times the mass of the monatomic helium atoms, one mole of each gas at STP will occupy the same volume.

The volume occupied by one mole of a gas at STP is known as the **standard molar volume of a gas.** It has been calculated as 22.414 10 L, which for most calculations rounds to 22.4 L.

You can use the standard molar volume of a gas as a conversion factor for any gas at STP. The first conversion factor listed at the right can be used to convert moles to liters, and the second conversion factor can be used to convert from liters to moles.

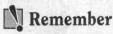 **Remember**

The number 6.022×10^{23} is also known as Avogadro's number.

Conversion Factors	
$\dfrac{22.4 \text{ L}}{1 \text{ mol}}$	$\dfrac{1 \text{ mol}}{22.4 \text{ L}}$
moles-liters	liters-moles

PRACTICE

A. At STP, what is the volume of 7.08 mol of nitrogen gas?

$7.08 \text{ mol} = 7.08 \text{ mol} \times \underline{\qquad\qquad}$

$= \underline{\qquad} \text{ L}$

B. A sample of hydrogen gas occupies 14.1 L at STP. How many moles of the gas are present?

$14.1 \text{ L} = 14.1 \text{ L} \times \underline{\qquad\qquad}$

$= \underline{\qquad} \text{ mol}$

C. How many molecules are in 5.60 L of oxygen gas?

$5.60 \text{ L} = 5.60 \text{ L} \times \underline{\qquad\qquad} \times \underline{\qquad\qquad}$

$= \underline{\qquad} \text{ molecules}$

> **In a chemical equation, the coefficients can indicate moles, molecules, or volume.**

Reaction stoichiometry is the study of the relationships between the substances that participate in a chemical reaction. In the chapter "Stoichiometry," the simple molar ratios given by a chemical equation were used to calculate the mass relationships between the various products and reactants. For reactions involving gases, Avogadro's law can also be used to calculate the relative volumes of two or more gases, assuming the pressure and temperature conditions remain the same.

Avogadro's law implies that the molar ratios established in a chemical equation also apply to the volume ratios of the gases in the equation. For example, consider the reaction of carbon monoxide gas with oxygen gas to form carbon dioxide gas.

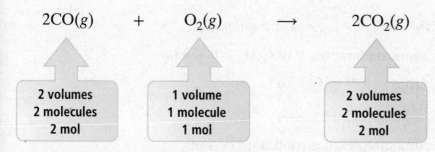

$$2CO(g) \quad + \quad O_2(g) \quad \longrightarrow \quad 2CO_2(g)$$

2 volumes	1 volume	2 volumes
2 molecules	1 molecule	2 molecules
2 mol	1 mol	2 mol

This equation states that the number of moles of the gases that participate in the reaction are in a 2:1:2 ratio. The volumes of the gases are also in this same 2:1:2 ratio. That means that the relationships between any two of the gases can be expressed in the following ways.

Ratio of CO to O₂: $\dfrac{1 \text{ volume } O_2}{2 \text{ volumes } CO}$ or $\dfrac{2 \text{ volumes } CO}{1 \text{ volume } O_2}$

Ratio of CO to CO₂: $\dfrac{2 \text{ volumes } CO}{2 \text{ volumes } CO_2}$ or $\dfrac{2 \text{ volumes } CO_2}{2 \text{ volumes } CO}$

Ratio of O₂ to CO₂: $\dfrac{1 \text{ volume } O_2}{2 \text{ volumes } CO_2}$ or $\dfrac{2 \text{ volumes } CO_2}{1 \text{ volume } O_2}$

| PRACTICE |

D. What is the ratio of the volume of oxygen gas to the volume of water vapor in the following reaction? _____

$$C_3H_8(g) + 5O_2(g) \quad \longrightarrow \quad 3CO_2(g) + 4H_2O(g)$$

SAMPLE PROBLEM

Propane, C_3H_8, is a gas that is sometimes used as a fuel for cooking and heating. The complete combustion reaction of propane occurs according to the following balanced equation.

$$C_3H_8(g) + 5O_2(g) \longrightarrow 3CO_2(g) + 4H_2O(g)$$

Assuming that all volumes are measured at the same temperature and pressure:

a. What will be the volume, in liters, of oxygen required for the complete combustion of 0.350 L of propane?

b. What will be the volume of carbon dioxide produced in the reaction?

SOLUTION

1 ANALYZE

Determine the information that is given and unknown.

Given: balanced chemical equation, V of C_3H_8 = 0.350 L

Unknown: a. V of O_2 in L, **b.** V of CO_2 in L

2 PLAN

Describe how to find the unknown values.

Since the temperature and pressure conditions do not change, the volume ratios are equal to the mole ratios of the substances. These ratios can be used as conversion factors to get from the volume of C_3H_8 to the volumes of O_2 and CO_2.

3 SOLVE

Calculate the unknowns from the given information.

a. The volume ratio of C_3H_8 gas to O_2 gas is 1:5.

$$0.350 \text{ L } C_3H_8 = 0.350 \text{ L } C_3H_8 \times \frac{5 \text{ L } O_2}{1 \text{ L } C_3H_8} = 1.75 \text{ L } O_2$$

b. The volume ratio of C_3H_8 gas to CO_2 gas is 1:3.

$$0.350 \text{ L } C_3H_8 = 0.350 \text{ L } C_3H_8 \times \frac{3 \text{ L } CO_2}{1 \text{ L } C_3H_8} = 1.05 \text{ L } CO_2$$

4 CHECK YOUR WORK

Check the answer to see if it is reasonable.

The answers are correctly expressed to three significant figures. The answers are reasonable because the chemical equation indicates that there should be a larger volume of oxygen than carbon dioxide, and a larger volume of carbon dioxide than propane.

E. Assuming all volume measurements are made at the same temperature and pressure, what volume of H_2 is needed to react completely with 4.55 L of O_2 to produce water vapor?

Balanced equation for the reaction:

_____$H_2(g)$ + _____$O_2(g)$ $\longrightarrow$ _____$H_2O(g)$

4.55 L O_2 = 4.55 L O_2 × ———————— =

F. What volume of oxygen gas is needed to react completely with 0.626 L of CO to form CO_2? Assume that all volume measurements are made at the same temperature and pressure.

Balanced equation for the reaction:

_____$CO(g)$ + _____$O_2(g)$ $\longrightarrow$ _____$CO_2(g)$

0.626 L CO = 0.626 L CO × ———————— =

G. Nitric acid can be produced by the reaction of NO_2 with water, according to the following balanced equation.

$3NO_2(g) + H_2O(l) \longrightarrow 2HNO_3(l) + NO(g)$

If 708 L of NO_2 gas react with water, what volume of NO gas will be produced? Assume the gases are measured under the same conditions before and after the reaction.

708 L NO_2 = 708 L NO_2 × ———————— =

H. If 29.0 L of methane, CH_4, undergoes complete combustion at 0.961 atm and 140°C, how many liters of each product would be present at the same temperature and pressure?

Balanced equation for the reaction:

_____$CH_4(g)$ + _____$O_2(g)$ $\longrightarrow$ _____$CO_2(g)$ + _____$H_2O(g)$

29.0 L CH_4 = 29.0 L CH_4 × ———————— =

29.0 L CH_4 = 29.0 L CH_4 × ———————— =

Pressure, volume, and temperature are related to the number of moles of a gas.

Avogadro's law states that the number of molecules in a gas is proportional to its volume. The law can be stated as the equation $n = Vk$, where k is a constant. Just like Boyle's law, Charles's law, and Gay-Lussac's law, Avogadro's law is the relationship between two quantities of a gas and a constant.

The other three gas laws were used to form the combined gas law, relating three different variables: pressure, temperature, and volume. When Avogadro's law is also included, the relationship can be expanded to include the number of molecules in a gas. The **ideal gas law** is the mathematical relationship among pressure, volume, temperature, and the number of moles in a gas, and is given by this equation, where the quantity R is a constant.

$$PV = nRT$$

Other gas laws can be derived from this equation by holding some variables constant. For example, if the number of moles of the gas is held constant, then the combined-gas law results. If the pressure and temperature are held constant, then Avogadro's law results.

The ideal gas law shows that at least one quantity will change when the number of molecules in a gas changes. If more gas is added to a container at a fixed temperature, the pressure will increase. If more molecules are added to a flexible container at constant temperature and pressure, then the volume will increase.

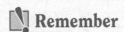

Remember

Boyle's law: $PV = k$

Charles's law: $\dfrac{V}{T} = k$

Gay-Lussac's law: $\dfrac{P}{T} = k$

Avogadro's law: $\dfrac{n}{V} = k$

Critical Thinking

5. Which gas law is derived from the ideal gas law if the number of moles and the temperature are held constant?

_____

(a) When volume and temperature are constant, pressure increases as the number of molecules increases.
(b) When pressure and temperature are constant, volume increases as the number of molecules increases.

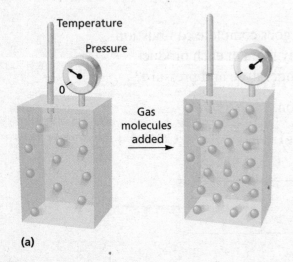

(a)

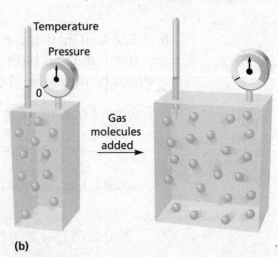

(b)

The ideal gas law relates pressure to volume to temperature.

One major difference between the ideal gas law and the combined gas law is the nature of the constant. The value of k in the combined gas law stays the same when the conditions of a particular sample of gas change. However, its value changes for different samples. The combined gas law can only be used to compare two sets of measurements for the same sample.

The constant R in the ideal gas law is known as the **ideal gas constant.** Its value is the same for every sample of gas. Therefore, the ideal gas law can be used to determine an unknown value from just one set of measurements.

The value of R can be calculated by solving for R in the ideal gas equation, and then substituting values for one mole of an ideal gas at STP. The result is the following equation.

TIP For the calculations in this book, use the rounded value 0.0821 L·atm/(mol·K)

$$R = \frac{PV}{nT} = \frac{(1\ \text{atm})(22.414\ 10\ \text{L})}{(1\ \text{mol})(273.15\ \text{K})} = 0.082\ 058\ \frac{\text{L·atm}}{\text{mol·K}}$$

Other values of R for different units are shown in the table.

Numerical Values of Gas Constant, R					
Unit of R	Numerical value of R	Unit of P	Unit of V	Unit of T	Unit of n
$\dfrac{\text{L·mmHg}}{\text{mol·K}}$	62.4	mm Hg	L	K	mol
$\dfrac{\text{L·atm}}{\text{mol·K}}$	0.0821	atm	L	K	mol
$\dfrac{\text{J}}{\text{mol·K}}$	8.314	Pa	m^3	K	mol
$\dfrac{\text{L·kPa}}{\text{mol·K}}$	8.314	kPa	L	K	mol
Note: 1 L·atm = 101.325 J; 1 J = 1 Pa·m³					

Finding *P*, *V*, *T*, or *n* from the Ideal Gas Law

The ideal gas law can be applied to determine the current conditions of a gas sample if three of the four variables are known. It can also be used to calculate the molar mass or density of a gas sample. Be sure to match the units in all of the given values to the correct value for R before applying the ideal gas law.

 READING CHECK

6. To use the ideal gas law to determine the number of moles in a gas sample, what three quantities must be measured?

_____

_____

What is the pressure in atmospheres exerted by a 0.500 mol sample of nitrogen gas in a 10.0 L container at 298 K?

	SOLUTION	
1	**ANALYZE**	*Determine the information that is given and unknown.*
		Given: $V = 10.0$ L, $n = 0.500$ mol, $T = 298$ K
		Unknown: P in atm
2	**PLAN**	*Write the equation that can be used to determine the unknown.*
		The ideal gas law can be used because three quantities are given. Rearranging to solve for P gives this equation.

$$P = \frac{nRT}{V}$$

3	**SOLVE**	*Substitute known values to find the value of the unknown.*
		Because the given values are in moles, liters, and kelvins, use $R = 0.0821$ L·atm/(mol·K). No conversions are necessary.

$$P = \frac{nRT}{V} = \frac{(0.500 \text{ mol})\left(\dfrac{0.0821 \text{ L} \cdot \text{atm}}{\text{mol} \cdot \text{K}}\right)(298 \text{ K})}{10.0 \text{ L}} = 1.22 \text{ atm}$$

4	**CHECK YOUR WORK**	*Check the answer to see if it is reasonable.*
		The units cancel as desired, and the final answer is expressed in the correct number of significant figures. The answer is also close to an estimated value of

$$\frac{(0.5 \times 0.1 \times 300)}{10} = 1.5$$

PRACTICE

I. What pressure, in atmospheres, is exerted by 0.325 mol of hydrogen gas in a 4.08 L container at 35°C?

$$P = \frac{nRT}{V} = \underline{\hspace{5cm}}$$

$$= \underline{\hspace{4cm}}$$

VOCABULARY

1. State Avogadro's law and explain its significance.

_____

_____

_____

REVIEW

2. What volume (in mL) at STP will be occupied by 0.0035 mol of CH_4?

3. What would be the units for R if P is in pascals, T is in kelvins, V is in

liters, and n is in moles? _____

4. A 4.44 L container holds 15.4 g of oxygen at 22.55°C. What is the pressure?

Critical Thinking

5. ANALYZING DATA Nitrous oxide is sometimes used as a source of oxygen gas:

$$2N_2O(g) \longrightarrow 2N_2(g) + O_2(g)$$

a. What volume of each product will be formed from 2.22 L N_2O?

b. At STP, what is the density of the product gases when they are mixed?

Diffusion and Effusion

The kinetic-molecular theory of matter, as applied to gases, states that a gas is a large group of fast moving particles that are far apart and travel in all directions. Two processes that can be explained by examining a gas at the particle level are *diffusion* and *effusion*.

In diffusion, the particles from two different gases mix together. In the diagram below, perfume molecules diffuse into the air when a bottle of perfume is opened. At the same time, the nitrogen gas and oxygen gas in the air diffuse into the perfume bottle.

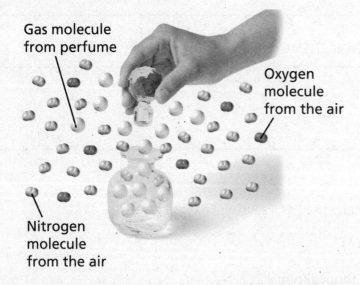

Gas molecule from perfume

Oxygen molecule from the air

Nitrogen molecule from the air

Air molecules diffuse into a bottle of perfume when it is opened. At the same time, perfume molecules diffuse into the air outside the bottle.

The rate of diffusion depends on the speed of the molecules. If the particles in a gas are moving faster than the particles in another gas, then the first gas will diffuse more quickly. Since the two gases are usually at the same temperature, then the average kinetic energy of the particles in two mixed gases is the same. Therefore, the gas whose particles have a smaller mass will have a greater speed. For the perfume example, the perfume molecules have a greater mass than the particles in the air, so they diffuse into the air more slowly than the air particles diffuse into the bottle.

Critical Thinking

1. Apply A container filled with oxygen gas is connected to a container filled with nitrogen gas. Which gas will diffuse more quickly to fill both containers?

The rates of effusion and diffusion for gases depend on the velocities of their molecules.

In the mid-1800s, the Scottish chemist Thomas Graham studied the effusion and diffusion of gases. Recall that effusion occurs when the random motions of a gas result in some of the molecules passing through a small opening. One of Graham's discoveries was a relationship between the rate of effusion of gases and their molar mass.

The mass and velocity of a gas molecule determines its kinetic energy, through the expression $mv^2/2$. If two different gases are at the same temperature, then the following relationship is true.

$$\frac{1}{2} M_A v_A^{\,2} = \frac{1}{2} M_B v_B^{\,2}$$

where v_A and v_B are the average velocities of the particles in the two gases and M_A and M_B are the molar masses of the two gases.

The rate of effusion of a gas is proportional to the average velocity of its particles. Therefore, the equation above can be used to show that the following relationship is true.

$$\frac{\text{rate of effusion of A}}{\text{rate of effusion of B}} = \frac{\sqrt{M_B}}{\sqrt{M_A}}$$

This equation, **Graham's law of effusion,** states that the rates of effusion of gases at the same temperature and pressure are inversely proportional to the square roots of their molar masses. So, a gas that effuses twice as fast as a second gas has one-fourth of the mass of the second gas.

✓ READING CHECK

2. A gas that has a greater mass than another gas will have a

_____ rate of

diffusion and a _____

rate of effusion than the other gas.

3. Which gas, nitrogen or oxygen, will effuse out of the tire in the photograph faster?

_____

Molecules of oxygen and nitrogen from inside the bicycle tire effuse out through a small nail hole.

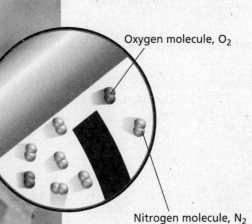

Oxygen molecule, O_2

Nitrogen molecule, N_2

SAMPLE PROBLEM

Compare the rates of effusion of hydrogen and oxygen at the same temperature and pressure.

SOLUTION	
1 ANALYZE	*Determine the information that is given and unknown.*
	Given: identities of two gases, H_2 and O_2
	Unknown: relative rates of effusion
2 PLAN	*Write the equation that can be used to find the unknown.*
	The molar masses of the two gases can be determined from the periodic table. Graham's law can then be used to write the relative rates of effusion.
	$$\frac{\text{rate of effusion of A}}{\text{rate of effusion of B}} = \frac{\sqrt{M_B}}{\sqrt{M_A}}$$
3 SOLVE	*Calculate the unknown using the given information.*
	$$\frac{\text{rate of effusion of } H_2}{\text{rate of effusion of } O_2} = \frac{\sqrt{M_{O_2}}}{\sqrt{M_{H_2}}} = \frac{\sqrt{32.00 \text{ g/mol}}}{\sqrt{2.02 \text{ g/mol}}} = 3.98$$
	Hydrogen effuses 3.98 times faster than oxygen.
4 CHECK YOUR WORK	*Check the answer to see if it is reasonable.*
	Oxygen is about 16 times more massive than hydrogen. The square root of 16 is 4, and 3.98 is very close to 4.

PRACTICE

A. A sample of hydrogen effuses through a porous container about 9 times faster than an unknown gas. Estimate the molar mass of the unknown gas.

What value is given for $\dfrac{\text{rate of effusion of } H_2}{\text{rate of effusion of unknown gas}}$? _____

Write an equation for M_B and then substitute the known values.

380 *CHAPTER 11*

VOCABULARY

1. Compare diffusion with effusion.

_____

_____

_____

REVIEW

2. State Graham's law of effusion.

_____

_____

_____

3. Estimate the molar mass of a gas that effuses at 1.6 times the effusion rate of carbon dioxide.

4. Determine the molecular mass ratio of two gases whose rates of effusion have a ratio of 16:1.

_____

5. List the following gases in order of increasing average molecular velocity at 25°C: H_2O, He, HCl, BrF, and NO_2.

_____

Critical Thinking

6. ANALYZING INFORMATION An unknown gas effuses at one-half the speed of oxygen. What is the molar mass of the unknown? The gas is known to be either HBr or HI. Which gas is it?

Math Tutor ALGEBRAIC REARRANGEMENTS OF GAS LAWS

When using the gas laws, you do not need to memorize all of the equations, because they can be derived from the combined gas law. In each of Boyle's, Charles's, and Gay-Lussac's laws, one of the quantities—T, P, or V—does not change. By eliminating that factor from the equation, you obtain the equation for one particular gas law. The conditions stated in the problem should make clear which factors change and which are held constant. This information will tell you which law's equation you need to use.

Gas law	Held constant	Cancellation	Result
Combined gas law	none	$\dfrac{P_1V_1}{T_1} = \dfrac{P_2V_2}{T_2}$	$\dfrac{P_1V_1}{T_1} = \dfrac{P_2V_2}{T_2}$
Boyle's law	temperature	$\dfrac{P_1V_1}{\cancel{T_1}} = \dfrac{P_2V_2}{\cancel{T_2}}$	$P_1V_1 = P_2V_2$
Charles's law	pressure	$\dfrac{\cancel{P_1}V_1}{T_1} = \dfrac{\cancel{P_2}V_2}{T_2}$	$\dfrac{V_1}{T_1} = \dfrac{V_2}{T_2}$
Gay-Lussac's law	volume	$\dfrac{P_1\cancel{V_1}}{T_1} = \dfrac{P_2\cancel{V_2}}{T_2}$	$\dfrac{P_1}{T_1} = \dfrac{P_2}{T_2}$

Problem-Solving TIPS

- When you solve problems in chemistry, it is usually a bad idea to just start entering numbers into a calculator.
- Try to manipulate an equation in variable form to solve for the unknown variable before you start computation. This way, you can substitute all of the values at the very end and save having to keep track of intermediate results.

SAMPLE

A cylinder of nitrogen gas has a volume of 35.00 L at a pressure of 11.50 atm. What pressure will the nitrogen have if the contents of the cylinder are allowed to flow into a sealed reaction chamber whose volume is 140.0 L, and if the temperature remains constant?

Start with the combined gas law, and cancel the temperature.

$$\frac{P_1V_1}{T_1} = \frac{P_2V_2}{T_2} \rightarrow P_1V_1 = P_2V_2$$

The unknown value is P_2, so solve the above equation for P_2.

$$P_2 = \frac{P_1V_1}{V_2}$$

Substitute the given values into the equation to find the answer.

$$P_2 = \frac{(11.50 \text{ atm})(35.00 \text{ L})}{140.0 \text{ L}} = 2.875 \text{ atm}$$

Practice Problems: Chapter Review practice problems 11 and 12

1. State the assumptions that the kinetic-molecular theory makes about the characteristics of gas particles.

_____

_____

_____

2. Why does a gas in a closed container exert pressure?

_____

_____

3. Explain what is meant by the partial pressure of a gas within a mixture of gases. How do these partial pressures affect the other gases in the mixture?

_____

_____

4. Explain why pressure increases as a gas is compressed into a smaller volume.

_____

_____

5. Explain Gay-Lussac's law in terms of the kinetic-molecular theory.

_____

_____

6. When using the ideal gas law, why do you have to pay particular attention to the units used in the calculations?

_____

_____

7. Describe in your own words the process of diffusion.

_____

_____

8. Ammonia, NH_3, and alcohol, C_2H_6O, are released together across a room.

Which will you smell first? _____

9. The atmosphere can support a column of mercury 760 mm high at sea level. What height of a liquid whose density was 1.40 times the density of mercury could the atmosphere support at sea level?

10. In a sample of air at exactly 1 atm containing a mixture of N_2, O_2, and CO_2, $P_{CO_2} = 0.323$ torr and $P_{N_2} = 593.525$ torr. What is the partial pressure of O_2?

11. The pressure on a gas at $-73°C$ is doubled, but its volume is held constant. What will the final temperature be in degrees Celsius?

12. A flask containing 155 cm^3 of hydrogen was collected at 22.5 kPa pressure. What pressure would have been needed to collect the same gas at the same temperature using a flask with a volume of 90 cm^3?

13. A meteorological balloon contains 250.0 L He at 22°C and 740.0 mm Hg. The volume of the balloon can vary according to external conditions, but it will burst if its volume reaches 400.0 L. At what temperature, in degrees Celsius, will the balloon burst if its pressure at that bursting point is 0.475 atm?

14. Suppose a 5.00 L sample of O_2 at a given temperature and pressure contains 1.08×10^{23} molecules. How many molecules would be contained in each gas at the same temperature and pressure?

a. 5.0 L CO_2 _____

b. 10.0 L NH_3 _____

15. Find the volume, in liters, of 8.00 g O_2 at STP.

16. Acetylene gas, C_2H_2, undergoes combustion to produce carbon dioxide and water vapor, and 75.0 L CO_2 is produced.

a. Balance the equation: _____ C_2H_2 + _____ $O_2 \rightarrow$ _____ CO_2 + _____ H_2O

b. Find the volume of each reactant and the volume of water produced.

17. Calculate the pressure exerted by 2.50 L HF containing 1.35 mol at 320.0 K.

18. Determine the number of moles in 1.25 L of gas at 250.0 K and 1.06 atm.

19. Compare the rates of effusion for fluorine and chlorine.

Solutions

Review Previous Concepts

1. What is the difference between a mixture and a compound, and what are some different types of mixtures?

_____

_____

_____

_____

2. What does the term *equilibrium* mean?

_____

_____

_____

_____

SECTION 12.1

Types of Mixtures

The chapter "Matter and Change" discussed the various types of matter. One type of matter is a mixture. Some materials are easy to identify as mixtures, because the different components are visible. For example, soil is a mixture of rock debris, clay, and decomposed animal and plant matter.

Other mixtures are less obvious. Milk is a mixture of water, fats, proteins, and sugar. Both milk and soil are *heterogeneous* mixtures, because their composition is not uniform. Salt water is a mixture of salt and water, but it has a uniform composition. Salt water is an example of a *homogeneous* mixture.

This section will discuss three types of mixtures. A **solution** is a homogeneous mixture of two or more substances in a single phase. The other two types of mixtures are heterogeneous: suspension and colloids. A **suspension** is a mixture in which the particles are so large that they settle out unless the mixture is constantly stirred or agitated. **Colloids** form when the particle size is in between those of solutions and suspensions.

KEY TERMS

solution   solvent
suspension   solute
colloid   electrolyte
soluble   nonelectrolyte

Both milk and salt water look like homogeneous mixtures, but milk is a heterogeneous mixture called a colloid.

Properties of Solutions, Colloids, and Suspensions

Solutions	Colloids	Suspensions
Homogeneous	Heterogeneous	Heterogeneous
Particle size: 0.01–1 nm; can be atoms, ions, molecules	Particle size: 1–1000 nm, dispersed; can be aggregates or large molecules	Particle size: over 1000 nm, suspended; can be large particles or aggregates
Do not separate on standing	Do not separate on standing	Particles settle out
Cannot be separated by filtration	Cannot be separated by filtration	Can be separated by filtration
Do not scatter light	Scatter light (Tyndall effect)	May scatter light, but are not transparent

✓ READING CHECK

1. Order the three types of mixtures from those with the smallest to largest in particle size.

_____

_____

_____

_____

Solutions are homogeneous mixtures.

When a sugar cube is dropped in water, it dissolves. The cube gradually disappears as sugar molecules leave the surface of the cube and mix with water molecules. Eventually, all of the sugar molecules become spread out evenly among the water molecules. None of the original sugar cube will be visible. If you taste the sugar water after it is completely dissolved, then every sip will have the same proportion of sugar and water. The sugar is **soluble,** which means that it can dissolve.

Components of Solutions

In a solution, all of the molecules, atoms, or ions are thoroughly mixed. The solution has the same composition and properties throughout. The medium that dissolved the other substance is called the **solvent.** In the sugar-water example, water is the solvent. The substance that was dissolved is called the **solute.** The sugar is the solute in a sugar water solution. In general, the component with the smaller amount in the solution is called the solute.

In a solution, the dissolved particles are so small they cannot be seen. They also remain mixed with the solvent indefinitely, as long as the conditions do not change. If a solution is poured through filter paper, it will remain a solution. This is because the particles in a solution are less than a nanometer in diameter.

 **TIP** When a solution is close to a 50%-50% mixture of two substances, it is difficult and unnecessary to designate one substance the solute and the other substance the solvent.

✓ **READING CHECK**

2. What will happen to the solute in a jar of a sugar-water solution if you leave it in a dark place for several days without disturbing it?

_____

_____

_____

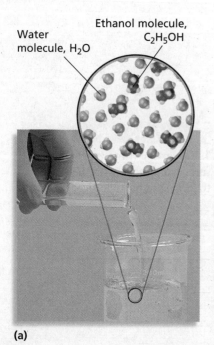

Water molecule, H₂O — Ethanol molecule, C₂H₅OH

(a)

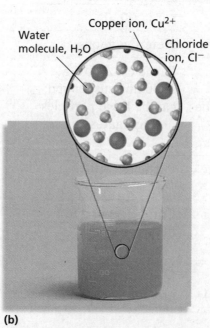

Water molecule, H₂O — Copper ion, Cu²⁺ — Chloride ion, Cl⁻

(b)

(a) An ethanol-water solution has a liquid solvent and a liquid solute.
(b) A copper(II) chloride–water solution has a liquid solvent and a solid solute. Both solutions have a uniform composition.

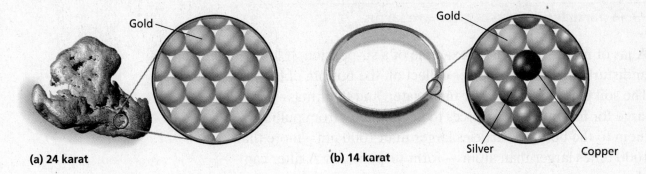

(a) 24 karat

(b) 14 karat

Gold

Gold

Silver

Copper

(a) 24-karat gold is pure gold.
(b) 14-karat gold is an alloy of gold with silver and copper. Gold makes up 14/24 of the alloy.

Types of Solutions

Most of the examples of solutions that have been discussed so far have been made up of a solid in a liquid or a liquid in a liquid. However, there are many other types of solutions. A liquid can, in fact, dissolve substances in any of the three main states of matter: solid, liquid, or gas. For example, oxygen gas dissolves in water. This dissolved oxygen is what oceanic animals, such as fish, breathe when they pass water through their gills.

Liquids are not the only substances that can be solutes. A gas can dissolve another gas. For example, air is a homogeneous solution of nitrogen, oxygen, and other gases. In air, nitrogen is the solvent and the other gases are the solutes.

A solid can also be a solvent. An *alloy* is a solution of two of more elements that are metallically bonded. The metal that makes up the greatest percentage of the alloy is the solvent. The atoms in an alloy are distributed evenly, as shown in the diagram above.

The mixing of metals in alloys yields desirable properties. Pure gold (also called 24-karat gold) is too soft to use in jewelry. Therefore, silver and copper are mixed with the gold to give it greater strength and hardness while maintaining its color and resistance to corrosion. Other common alloys include brass (zinc and copper), sterling silver (silver and copper), and steel (iron and usually carbon).

✓ READING CHECK

3. Give at least three examples of solutions in which the solvent is either a gas or a solid.

_____

_____

_____

The particles in a suspension are large.

A jar of muddy water is an example of a suspension. If left undisturbed, the soil particles collect on the bottom of the jar. The soil particles are denser than water, and their mass is too large for intermolecular forces to keep gravity from pulling them to the bottom. Particles larger than 1000 nm—more than 1000 times larger than atoms—form suspensions. A filter can also remove particles from a suspension.

Colloids have particles of intermediate size.

Particles that are between 1 nm and 1000 nm in diameter may form colloids. After large soil particles settle out of muddy water, the water is often still cloudy because colloidal particles remain in the water. In this colloid, the water is the *dispersing medium*. The colloidal particles are called the *dispersed phase*.

The motion of the surrounding particles prevents colloidal particles from settling out, even after long periods of time. Under a microscope, these particles can appear as rapidly moving tiny specks of light. The random motion and collisions of these particles is called *Brownian motion*.

The particles in a colloid will scatter a beam of light, while the particles in a solution will not. The left-hand jar holds salt water, a true solution. The right-hand jar holds a colloid of gelatin and water.

Tyndall Effect

Many colloids, such as milk, appear homogeneous because the individual particles cannot be seen. However, the particles are large enough to scatter light. The *Tyndall effect* is the scattering of light by colloidal particles in a transparent medium. This effect is responsible for a headlight beam being visible from the side on a foggy night. The Tyndall effect can be used to distinguish a colloid from a solution.

> ✓ **READING CHECK**
>
> **4.** In the gelatin-water colloid above, _____ is the dispersing medium and
>
> _____ is the dispersed phase.

Classes of Colloids		
Class of colloid	**Phases**	**Example**
Sol	solid dispersed in liquid	paints, mud
Gel	solid network throughout liquid	gelatin
Liquid emulsion	liquid dispersed in a liquid	milk, mayonnaise
Foam	gas dispersed in liquid	shaving cream, whipped cream
Solid aerosol	solid dispersed in gas	smoke, auto exhaust
Liquid aerosol	liquid dispersed in gas	fog, mist, clouds, aerosol spray
Solid emulsion	liquid dispersed in solid	cheese, butter

Electrolytes are ionic solutions that conduct electricity.

Substances that dissolve in water are classified by the nature of the particles in solution. If the substance dissolves in water to form a solution that can conduct electric current, then the substance is called an **electrolyte.**

Any soluble ionic compound will separate into its positive and negative ions when it dissolves in water. For example, sodium chloride is an electrolyte that separates into an Na^+ cation and a Cl^- anion in water. Another example of an electrolyte is a highly polar molecular compound. Hydrogen chloride, HCl, forms the ions H_3O^+ and Cl^- when dissolved in water.

If the substance dissolves in water to form a solution that cannot conduct electric current, then the substance is called a **nonelectrolyte.** These substances form neutral solute particles, usually molecules. Sugar is an example of a nonelectrolyte.

One way to test the electrical conductivity of a solution is shown below. Two electrodes are connected to a power supply and a light bulb and lowered into water without touching. For an electric current to flow, the solution must be able to conduct charge from one electrode to the other. If the light bulb does not light up, the solution contains nonelectrolytes.

 CONNECT

For electric current to flow, a complete circuit must be formed. A complete circuit includes a power source, usually a battery. The current must be able to flow uninterrupted from the positive terminal of the battery to the negative terminal of the battery.

 READING CHECK

5. A substance that dissolves in water and forms molecules in solution is called a(n) _____. A substance that dissolves in water and forms ions in solution is called a(n) _____.

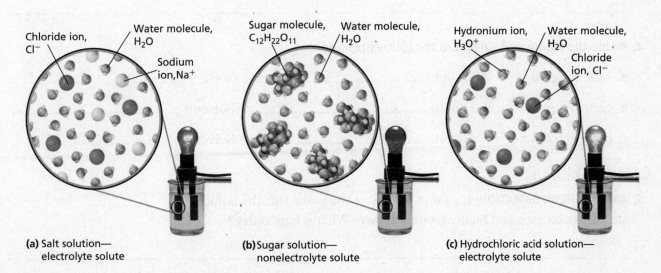

(a) Salt solution— electrolyte solute

(b) Sugar solution— nonelectrolyte solute

(c) Hydrochloric acid solution— electrolyte solute

Of the three dissolved substances above, (a) sodium chloride is an electrolyte, (b) sucrose is a nonelectrolyte, and (c) hydrogen chloride is an electrolyte.

VOCABULARY

1. Classify the following as either a heterogeneous or homogeneous mixture, and explain your answers.

a. orange juice _____

_____

b. tap water _____

_____

REVIEW

2. a. Make a drawing of the particles in an NaCl solution to show why this solution conducts electricity.

b. Make a drawing of the particles in an NaCl crystal to show why pure salt does not conduct electricity.

3. Describe one way to prove that a mixture of sugar and water is a solution and that a mixture of sand and water is not a solution.

_____

_____

4. Name the solute and solvent in the following solutions.

a. 14-karat gold   Solute: _____   Solvent: _____

b. corn syrup   Solute: _____   Solvent: _____

c. carbonated water   Solute: _____   Solvent: _____

Critical Thinking

5. ANALYZING INFORMATION If a jar of sea water sits in the sun, the liquid level steadily decreases, and finally crystals appear. What is happening?

_____

_____

_____

SECTION 12.2

The Solution Process

In Section 1 you learned about the nature of solutions. Now you will learn about the process of *dissolution*—the dissolving of a solute in a solvent to make a solution.

Several factors affect dissolving.

A crystalline solid dissolves as its particles leave the surface of the crystal and mix with solvent molecules. The molecules or ions of the solid are attracted to the solvent. The rate at which a substance dissolves depends on many factors.

Increasing the Surface Area of the Solute

One way to speed up dissolution is to increase the surface area of the solute. Crushing larger crystals into smaller ones increases the amount of crystal surfaces in contact with the liquid. Dividing something into smaller parts will increase its exposed surface area, and make it dissolve faster.

Agitating a Solution

As a solid is dissolving, there are more dissolved particles close to the undissolved crystal than there are away from the crystal. Stirring or shaking a solution will help spread dissolved particles throughout the solvent. This makes it easier for new particles to dissolve into the solvent.

Heating a Solvent

You may have found it more difficult to mix sugar into iced tea than hot tea. The more energy a solvent's particles have, the more they will collide with the dissolving solid, and the more energy they can transfer to the solid. So, a solid will dissolve more quickly in a warm liquid than a cool liquid.

✓ READING CHECK

1. Name three ways to make sugar dissolve in water faster.

_____

_____

large surface area exposed to solvent—faster rate

$CuSO_4 \cdot 5H_2O$ powdered
Increased surface area

Small surface area exposed to solvent—slow rate

Solvent particle

Solute

$CuSO_4 \cdot 5H_2O$ large crystals

The surface area of a powdered solute is larger. Therefore, the powder will dissolve faster.

Solubility is a measure of how well one substance dissolves another.

When solid sugar is added to water, sugar molecules leave the solid surface and mix with the water molecules. These molecules move about the water and sugar molecules at random, as do all particles in a liquid. However, some of these dissolved molecules collide with the crystal and transfer energy to the crystal. They no longer have enough energy to pull away from the crystal again. As a result, these molecules recrystallize, rejoining the crystal lattice.

When the sugar is first added, there is no solute in the water. Therefore, there is also no recrystallization of solute. Over time, the concentration of solute in the water increases, and the rate of recrystallization increases. Eventually, if there is enough sugar, the rate of dissolution and the rate of recrystallization are equal. At this point, the solution is in equilibrium. **Solution equilibrium** is the physical state in which the opposing processes of dissolution and crystallization of a solute occur at equal rates.

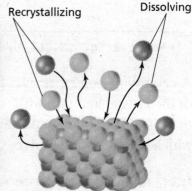
Recrystallizing Dissolving

There are three types of solutions.

- A **saturated solution** contains the maximum amount of dissolved solute that is possible under the current conditions. The dissolution of any new solute immediately results in crystallization to keep the total amount of solute constant.

- An **unsaturated solution** contains less than the maximum amount of dissolved solute possible.

- A **supersaturated solution** contains more than the maximum amount of dissolved solute that is normally possible. This solution is in a state of equilibrium that is unstable.

Critical Thinking

2. **Synthesize** How does the equilibrium between a solute and a solvent compare with the equilibrium between a liquid and its vapor?

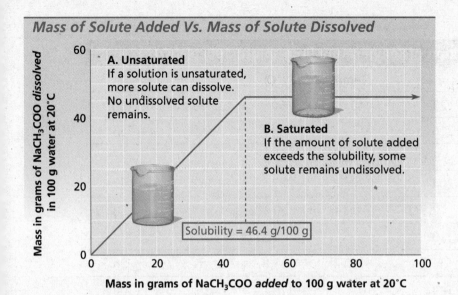

Mass of Solute Added Vs. Mass of Solute Dissolved

A. Unsaturated
If a solution is unsaturated, more solute can dissolve. No undissolved solute remains.

B. Saturated
If the amount of solute added exceeds the solubility, some solute remains undissolved.

Solubility = 46.4 g/100 g

Mass in grams of NaCH₃COO dissolved in 100 g water at 20°C (y-axis)

Mass in grams of NaCH₃COO added to 100 g water at 20°C (x-axis)

The graph shows the maximum mass of sodium acetate, NaCH$_3$COO, that can be dissolved in water.

Saturated Versus Unsaturated Solutions

One way to tell the difference between a saturated solution and an unsaturated solution is to add more of the dissolved substance. If the substance collects at the bottom of the solution and does not dissolve, the solution is saturated. In an unsaturated solution, all of the available solute is dissolved.

The maximum amount that can be dissolved is a ratio of the solute amount to solvent amount. If more solvent is added to a saturated solution, the solution becomes unsaturated.

Supersaturated Solutions

When a saturated solution is cooled, usually some of the solute will come out of the solution. This is because the amount that a solvent can dissolve depends on its temperature. But sometimes, if the solution is cooled without being disturbed, it can become a supersaturated solution.

Once a supersaturated solution is disturbed, and crystals start to form, the recrystalization process will continue until the solution is saturated without being supersaturated. Another way to start recrystallization is by introducing a "seed" crystal. This seed will rapidly grow as molecules of solute begin to come out of solution.

✓ READING CHECK

3. For a given substance, order an unsaturated, saturated, and supersaturated solution from smallest amount of solute to largest.

🔗 CONNECT

One example of a supersaturated solution in nature is honey. If honey is unprocessed or left undisturbed for a long period of time, the sugar in the honey will crystallize.

Solubility of Solutes as a Function of Temperature (in g solute/100. g H₂O)						
	Temperature (°C)					
Substance	0	20	40	60	80	100
AgNO₃	122	216	311	440	585	733
Ba(OH)₂	1.67	3.89	8.22	20.94	101.4	—
C₁₂H₂₂O₁₁	179	204	.238	287	362	487
Ca(OH)₂	0.189	0.173	0.141	0.121	—	0.07
Ce₂(SO₄)₃	20.8	10.1	—	3.87	—	—
KCl	28.0	34.2	40.1	45.8	51.3	56.3
KI	128	144	162	176	192	206
KNO₃	13.9	31.6	61.3	106	167	245
LiCl	69.2	83.5	89.8	98.4	112	128
Li₂CO₃	1.54	1.33	1.17	1.01	0.85	0.72
NaCl	35.7	35.9	36.4	37.1	38.0	39.2
NaNO₃	73	87.6	102	122	148	180
CO₂ (gas at SP)	0.335	0.169	0.0973	0.058	—	—
O₂ (gas at SP)	0.00694	0.00537	0.00308	0.00227	0.00138	0.00

Solubility Values

The **solubility** of a substance is the amount of that substance required to form a saturated solution with a certain amount of solvent at a given temperature. For example, at 20°C the solubility of sodium acetate is 46.4 g per 100 g of water. Solubility is usually given in grams of solute per 100 grams of solvent or grams of solute per 100 milliliters of solvent.

Like Dissolves Like

Whether a substance is soluble in another substance is often hard to predict. Lithium chloride is highly soluble in water, but gasoline is not. Gasoline is highly soluble in benzene, C_6H_6, but lithium chloride is not.

A rough way of determining whether a substance will dissolve into another substance is the phrase "like dissolves like." For example, polar substances tend to dissolve in polar solvents, but not in nonpolar solvents.

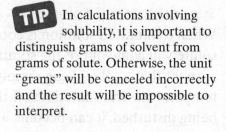

TIP In calculations involving solubility, it is important to distinguish grams of solvent from grams of solute. Otherwise, the unit "grams" will be canceled incorrectly and the result will be impossible to interpret.

READING CHECK

4. As temperature increases, the solubility of a substance

_____.

Dissolving Ionic Compounds in Aqueous Solution

The polarity of water molecules plays an important role in the formation of solutions of ionic compounds in water. The positive and negative ends of a water molecule are attracted to different parts of a crystal. These attractions are strong enough to pull the molecules or ions out of the crystal and into solution. **Hydration** occurs when the attraction of the charged ends of water molecules dissolve an ionic compound or a substance whose molecules are polar.

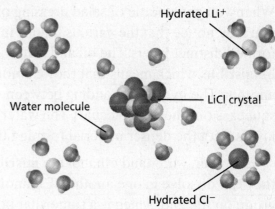

When LiCl dissolves, the ions are hydrated. The attraction between ions and water molecules is strong enough that each ion in solution is surrounded by water molecules.

The diagram at the right shows how the process of hydration works for a lithium chloride crystal. The positive end of the water molecule, where the hydrogen atoms are, is attracted to a chloride anion. The negative end, the end away from the hydrogen atoms, is attracted to a lithium cation. When the attraction is strong enough to pull the ion out of the crystal, the ion eventually becomes surrounded by water molecules. The lithium cations and chloride ions that are in solution are said to be *hydrated*.

When some ionic compounds recrystallize out of solution, the new crystals include water molecules. These compounds are called *hydrates*. The formula unit for the crystal structure contains a specific number of water molecules in a regular structure. For example, the copper(II) sulfate crystal shown at the right has the formula $CuSO_4 \cdot 5H_2O$. The water can be removed from the crystal using heat, leaving the anhydrous, or water-free, salt. When a hydrate dissolves in water, it breaks up into ions, and the water molecules become part of the solvent.

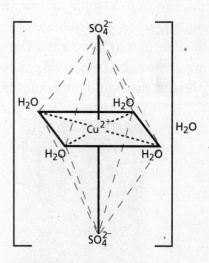

Hydrated copper(II) sulfate has the formula $CuSO_4 \cdot 5H_2O$. Heating releases the water and the anhydrous crystal $CuSO_4$ forms.

Nonpolar Solvents

Ionic compounds are not generally soluble in nonpolar solvents, such as carbon tetrachloride, CCl_4, or toluene, $C_6H_5CH_3$. The nonpolar solvent molecules do not attract the ions of the crystal strongly enough to overcome the forces holding the crystals together.

✓ READING CHECK

5. What force of attraction is responsible for the dissolution of an ionic crystal in water?

Liquid Solutes and Solvents

When you get a bottle of salad dressing out of the refrigerator, you may notice that the various liquids in the bottle have formed distinct layers. The oil and water in the bottle are **immiscible,** which means that they cannot dissolve in one another. The hydrogen bonding between water molecules squeezes out the oil molecules. The water and oil form two layers, with the denser material forming the bottom layer.

However, water and ethanol are **miscible,** which means they can dissolve in one another. Ethanol contains an —OH group on the end, which is a somewhat polar bond.

$$
\begin{array}{c}
\quad\ \ H\ \ H \\
\quad\ \ |\ \ \ | \\
H\!-\!C\!-\!C\!-\!OH \\
\quad\ \ |\ \ \ | \\
\quad\ \ H\ \ H
\end{array}
$$

This —OH group can form hydrogen bonds with water molecules. The molecular forces in the mixture of water and ethanol are so similar to those of a pure liquid that the liquids mix freely with one another.

Another example of miscible liquids is a mixture of fat, oil, or grease with toluene or gasoline. All of these substances have nonpolar molecules. The only intermolecular forces are the weak London dispersion forces. These forces do not prevent the liquid molecules from moving freely in solution.

READING CHECK

6. A liquid with polar molecules and a liquid with _____ molecules are generally miscible. A liquid with polar molecules and a liquid with _____ molecules are generally immiscible.

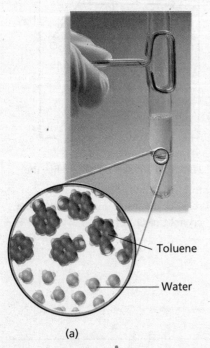

- Toluene
- Water

(a)

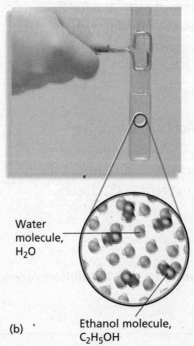

Water molecule, H_2O

Ethanol molecule, C_2H_5OH

(b)

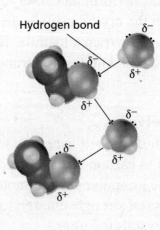

Hydrogen bond

δ^- δ^- δ^+ δ^+ δ^- δ^- δ^+ δ^+

(a) Toluene and water are immiscible.
(b) Ethanol and water are miscible. Hydrogen bonding between water and ethanol molecules enhances the ability of the ethanol to dissolve in water.

Effects of Pressure on Solubility

Pressure does not generally affect the solubility of liquids or solids in liquid solvents. However, an increase in the pressure of a gas can increase the solubility of a gas in a liquid.

A gas and a solvent are normally in a state of equilibrium in which gas molecules enter or leave the liquid phase at the same rate.

$$gas \ + \ solvent \ \leftrightarrows \ solution$$

If the pressure on the gas is increased, more gas molecules will collide with the liquid solvent and the rate of dissolution increases. Eventually, a new equilibrium is reached with a higher solubility. SO, an increase in pressure will increase solubility and result in more of the gas entering the liquid phase.

Henry's Law

Henry's law states that the solubility of a gas in a liquid is directly proportional to the partial pressure of that gas on the surface of the liquid. The law is named after English chemist William Henry, and applies to liquid gas solutions at constant temperature.

In the chapter "Gases," you learned that the same amount of gas exerts the same amount of pressure whether it is in a mixture or occupies a space alone. For this reason, the amount of the gas that will dissolve in a liquid also does not depend on the other gases in a mixture.

A manufacturer of carbonated beverages forces CO_2 into a bottle with flavored water. As stated in Henry's law, the carbon dioxide will dissolve in the water. When the bottle is opened, the gas rapidly escapes from the liquid. This causes the liquid to bubble and fizz, and is called **effervescence**.

READING CHECK

7. When happens when the partial pressure of a gas on a liquid decreases?

 CONNECT

A scuba diver must be aware of Henry's law. Deep under water, as pressure increases, the amount of air that can dissolve in blood increases. The extra nitrogen can affect the nervous system of the diver and lead to disorientation. Therefore, scuba divers often use a mixture of air with less nitrogen than normal.

In addition, when a scuba diver returns to the surface, the amount of nitrogen that can dissolve in the blood decreases. If the diver ascends too quickly, the nitrogen gas will form bubbles in tissues and blood vessels.

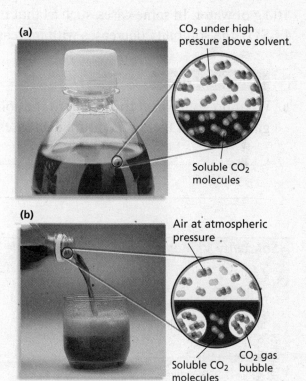

(a)

CO$_2$ under high pressure above solvent.

Soluble CO_2 molecules

(b)

Air at atmospheric pressure

Soluble CO_2 molecules

CO_2 gas bubble

(a) The unopened bottle has no gas bubbles because of the pressure of the CO_2 inside the bottle. (b) When the bottle is opened, the pressure is reduced and some of the dissolved CO_2 enters the gas phase through effervescence.

Effects of Temperature on Solubility

As shown in the graph below on the left, an increase in temperature usually decreases the solubility of a gas in a liquid. At higher temperatures, the average kinetic energy of the solvent and the solute particles increases. The attractive forces between the solvent and solute decrease, and more molecules are able to escape from the surface of the liquid.

Usually an increase in temperature increases the solubility of a solid. However, the effect can be more pronounced for some substances than for other substances.

For example, look at the graphs of potassium nitrate, KNO_3, and sodium chloride, NaCl. The solubility of potassium nitrate increases from 14 g per 100 g of water at 0°C to 167 g per 100 g of water at 80°C. However, the solubility of sodium chloride barely changes under the same temperature increase. Its solubility increases from 36 g per 100 g of water to 38 g per 100 g of water. In some cases, such as that of lithium sulfate, Li_2SO_4, the solubility decreases with increasing temperature.

☑ READING CHECK

8. What do you expect to happen to the solubility of nitrogen gas in water if the temperature decreases?

_____

_____

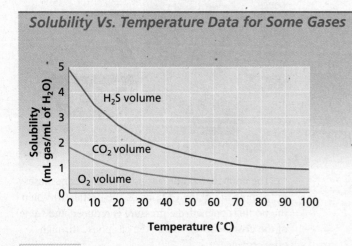

Solubility Vs. Temperature Data for Some Gases

The solubility of gases in water decreases with increasing temperature. The solubility of a solid in water generally increases with temperature, although the effect is more pronounced in some compounds than in others.

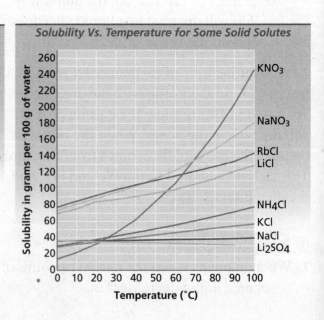

Solubility Vs. Temperature for Some Solid Solutes

A change in energy accompanies solution formation.

The formation of a solution is accompanied by an energy change. If you dissolve some potassium iodide, KI, in water, you will find that the outside of the container feels cold to the touch. However, if you dissolve some sodium hydroxide, NaOH, the outside of the container feels hot. The formation of a solid-liquid solution can absorb energy as heat or release energy as heat.

The net amount of energy that is absorbed as heat by the solution when a specific amount of solute enters solution is called the **enthalpy of solution.** The formation of a solution can be pictured as a result of three steps, which are summarized in the graph below. Each step involves the absorption or release of energy.

1. Solute particles are separated from the solid. Energy is required to break the bonds between the particles and the rest of the solid.

2. The solute particles push apart the solvent particles. This requires energy to act against the attractive forces between the solvent particles.

3. The solvent particles are attracted to and surround the solute particles. Instead of breaking apart or pushing against attractive forces, this involves the forming of new intermolecular bonds. Energy is released and stored as potential energy in the bonds.

🔍 Critical Thinking

9. Analyze Does the graph below show a reaction with a positive enthalpy of solution or a negative enthalpy of solution? Explain.

_____

_____

_____

_____

_____

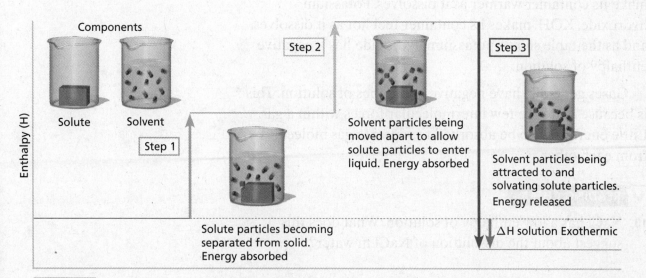

The graph shows the changes in enthalpy that occur during the formation of a solution.

Enthalpies of Solution (kJ/mol solute at 25°C)

Substance	Enthalpy of solution	Substance	Enthalpy of solution
$AgNO_3(s)$	+22.59	$KOH(s)$	−57.61
$CH_3COOH(l)$	−1.51	$MgSO_4(s)$	+15.9
$HCl(g)$	−74.84	$NaCl(s)$	+3.88
$HI(g)$	−81.67	$NaNO_3(s)$	+20.50
$KCl(s)$	+17.22	$NaOH(s)$	−44.51
$KClO_3(s)$	+41.38	$NH_3(g)$	−30.50
$KI(s)$	+20.33	$NH_4Cl(s)$	+14.78
$KNO_3(s)$	+34.89	$NH_4NO_3(s)$	+25.69

The end result of the dissolving process is the surrounding of solute particles by solvent particles. A solute particle that is surrounded by solvent particles is said to be **solvated.**

Two of the steps of dissolving a substance involve the absorption of energy. One step involves the release of energy. If more energy is absorbed than released, the reaction has a positive enthalpy of solution. As a result, a container in which the process has occurred will feel colder than it did before. As the table shows, potassium chloride is an example of a substance with a positive enthalpy of solution.

The graph on the previous page represents a process in which more energy is released than absorbed. This substance has a negative enthalpy of solution. Such a substance will make its container warmer as it dissolves. Potassium hydroxide, KOH, makes its container feel hot as it dissolves, and as the table shows, potassium hydroxide has a negative enthalpy of solution.

Gases generally have negative enthalpies of solution. This is because there are few intermolecular forces within a gas. Little energy has to be absorbed to separate gas molecules from each other.

✓ READING CHECK

10. NaCl has a low enthalpy of solution. What does this suggest about the dissolution of NaCl in water?

_____

_____

VOCABULARY

1. What is the difference between a saturated and an unsaturated solution?

_____

_____

REVIEW

2. Why would you expect sugar to dissolve faster in hot tea than in iced tea?

_____

_____

3. Explain how you prepare a saturated solution of sugar in water. Then explain how you would turn this solution into a supersaturated solution.

_____

_____

_____

4. Explain why ethanol will dissolve in water and carbon tetrachloride will not.

_____

_____

_____

Critical Thinking

5. PREDICTING OUTCOMES You get a small amount of lubricating oil on your clothing. Which would work better to remove the oil, water or toluene? Explain your answer.

_____

_____

6. INTERPRETING CONCEPTS A commercial "fizz saver" pumps helium under pressure into a soda bottle to keep gas from escaping. Will this keep CO_2 in the drink? Explain.

_____

_____

_____

SECTION 12.3

Concentration of Solutions

The **concentration** of a solution is a measure of the amount of solute in a given amount of solvent or solution. A *dilute* solution is a solution that has a relatively small amount of solute, or a low concentration. A *concentrated* solution is a solution that has a relatively high amount of solute. These terms are not necessarily related to the solubility of a substance. However, a substance with a very low solubility can only form dilute solutions, even if they are saturated.

This section covers two ways of expressing the concentration of a solution. **Molarity** is the number of moles of solute in a liter of solution. **Molality** is the number of moles of solute in a kilogram of solvent. In other words, molarity is a measure of moles per volume, and molality is a measure of moles per mass.

Molarity is moles of solute per liter of solution.

Molarity is one way to express the concentration of a solution. The symbol for molarity is M. For example, a 1 M NaOH solution contains one mole of NaOH in every liter of solution. The series of photographs at the right details how to create a 0.5 M solution of $CuSO_4 \cdot 5H_2O$.

✓ READING CHECK

1. What is the difference between concentration and solubility?

_____

_____

_____

_____

Start by calculating the mass of $CuSO_4 \cdot 5H_2O$ needed. Making a liter of this solution requires 0.5000 mol of solute. Convert the moles to mass by multiplying by the molar mass of $CuSO_4 \cdot 5H_2O$. This mass is calculated to be 124.8 g.

Add some solvent to the solute to dissolve it, and then pour it into a 1.0 L volumetric flask.

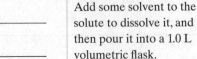

Rinse the weighing beaker with more solvent to remove all the solute, and pour the rinse into the flask. Add water until the volume of the solution nears the neck of the flask.

Calculating Molarity One mole of NaOH has a mass of 40.0 g. If this quantity is dissolved in enough water to make exactly 1.00 L of solution, a 1 M solution results. Dissolving 20.0 g of NaOH, or 0.500 mol, in enough water to make 1.00 L of solution produces a 0.500 M NaOH solution. Likewise, if 80.0 g of NaOH is added to water to make 1.00 L of solution, then a 2 M NaOH solution results.

TIP The word *molar* is often used to describe the molarity of a solution. For example, a one molar solution of NaOH is the same as a 1 M NaOH solution.

Note that the solute is not added to 1.00 L of water to make these solutions. The total volume of the solution should be 1.00 L, so adding solute to a 1.00 L solution will yield a solution that is more than 1.00 L. The proper amount of solute must be dissolved in a smaller quantity of water, and then water added to bring the solution to a 1.00 L volume.

The following equation can be used to compute the molarity of any solution. Note that the amount of solute must be converted from grams to moles if necessary.

$$\text{molarity (M)} = \frac{\text{amount of solute (mol)}}{\text{volume of solution (L)}}$$

☑ READING CHECK

2. Why does 40.0 g NaOH added to 1.00 L of water not make a 1 M NaOH solution?

_____

_____

Put the stopper in the flask, and swirl the solution thoroughly.

Carefully fill the flask to the 1.0 L mark with water.

Restopper the flask, and invert it at least 10 times to ensure complete mixing.

The resulting solution has 0.5000 mol of solute dissolved in 1.000 L of solution, which is a 0.5000 M concentration.

You have 3.50 L of solution that contains 90.0 g of sodium chloride. What is the molarity of the solution?

	SOLUTION
1 ANALYZE	*Determine the information that is given and unknown.*
	Given: solute mass = 90.0 g NaCl
	solution volume = 3.50 L
	Unknown: molarity of NaCl solution
2 PLAN	*Describe how to use the given information to find the unknown.*

Molarity is the number of moles of solute per liter of solution. First, convert the given solute mass into moles of solute.

$$\text{g NaCl} \times \frac{1\ \text{mol NaCl}}{\text{g NaCl}} = \text{mol NaCl}$$

Then use the formula for molarity to calculate the molarity of the solution.

$$\text{molarity of solution (M)} = \frac{\text{amount of solute (mol)}}{\text{volume of solution (L)}}$$

3 SOLVE   *Calculate the unknown from the given information.*

First, the molar mass of NaCl must be calculated.

$$\text{molar mass of NaCl} = \text{molar mass of Na} + \text{molar mass of Cl}$$

$$= 22.99\ \text{g/mol} + 35.45\ \text{g/mol}$$

$$= 58.44\ \text{g/mol}$$

$$90.0\ \text{g NaCl} = 90.0\ \text{g NaCl} \times \frac{1\ \text{mol NaCl}}{58.44\ \text{g NaCl}} = 1.54\ \text{mol NaCl}$$

$$\text{molarity of solution} = \frac{1.54\ \text{mol NaCl}}{3.50\ \text{L NaCl}} = 0.440\ \text{M NaCl}$$

4 CHECK YOUR WORK   *Check the answer to see if it is reasonable.*

The answer is correctly limited to three significant digits. Because the molar mass of NaCl is about 60 g/mol, 210 g of NaCl would form a 1 M solution in 3.5 L of solvent. The actual solute mass of 90 g is a little less than half that amount, which matches the answer of 0.440 M.

A. What is the molarity of a solution composed of 5.85 g of potassium iodide, KI, dissolved in enough water to make 1.25 L of solution?

What is the molar mass of KI? _____

$$5.85 \text{ g KI} = 5.85 \text{ g KI} \times \frac{1 \text{ mol NaCl}}{\text{g KI}} = \underline{\hspace{3cm}}$$

$$\text{molarity of solution} = \frac{\text{mol KI}}{1.25 \text{ L KI}} = \underline{\hspace{3cm}}$$

B. You have 0.8 L of a 0.5 M HCl solution. How many moles of HCl does the solution contain?

Rearrange the equation for molarity to solve for the number of moles of solute in the solution.

$$\text{amount of solute (mol)} = \underline{\hspace{5cm}}$$

Substitute the given information into your equation to find the number of moles of HCl.

C. How many moles of H_2SO_4 are present in 0.500 L of a 0.150 L H_2SO_4 solution?

To produce 40.0 g of silver chromate, Ag_2CrO_4 you will need at least 23.4 g of potassium chromate, K_2CrO_4, in solution as a reactant. All you have on hand is 5 L of a 6.0 M K_2CrO_4 solution. What volume of the solution is needed to give you the 23.4 g K_2CrO_4 needed for the reaction?

SOLUTION

1 ANALYZE

Determine the information that is given and unknown.

Given: available solution volume = 5 L
concentration of solution = 6.0 M K_2CrO_4 solution
mass of solute = 23.4 g K_2CrO_4
mass of product = 40.0 g Ag_2CrO_4

Unknown: volume of K_2CrO_4 needed in L

·2 PLAN

Describe how to use the given information to find the unknown.

To calculate the volume of solution needed, use the following equation.

$$\text{volume of solution (L)} = \frac{\text{amount of solute (mol)}}{\text{molarity of solution (M)}}$$

The molarity is given. The amount of solute can be calculated by converting the given mass of K_2CrO_4 into moles. The mass of product is not needed for this calculation. The 5 L of solution available sets an upper limit on the answer.

3 SOLVE

Calculate the unknown from the given information.

molar mass of K_2CrO_4
$$= 2(39.10 \text{ g/mol}) + 52.00 \text{ g/mol} + 4(16.00 \text{ g/mol})$$

$$= 194.20 \text{ g/mol}$$

$$23.4 \text{ g } K_2CrO_4 = 23.4 \text{ g } K_2CrO_4 \times \frac{1 \text{ mol } K_2CrO_4}{194.20 \text{ g } K_2CrO_4} = 0.120 \text{ mol } K_2CrO_4$$

$$\text{volume of solution} = \frac{0.120 \text{ mol } K_2CrO_4}{6.0 \text{ M } K_2CrO_4} = 0.020 \text{ L}$$

4 CHECK YOUR WORK

Check the answer to see if it is reasonable.

The answer is below the 5 L amount available. The units cancel correctly, and dividing moles by molarity yields liters.

D. What volume of 3.00 M NaCl is needed for a reaction that requires 146.3 g of NaCl?

What is the molar mass of NaCl? _____

How many moles of NaCl are in 146.3 g of NaCl?

What volume of 3.00 M NaCl solution contains that number of moles?

E. What volume of 1.0 M AgNO$_3$ is needed to provide 169.9 g of pure AgNO$_3$?

What is the molar mass of AgNO$_3$? _____

How many moles of AgNO$_3$ are in 169.9 g of AgNO$_3$?

What volume of 1.0 M AgNO$_3$ solution contains that number of moles?

While molarity is a measure of solute mass per unit volume of solution, molality is a measure of solute mass per unit mass of solvent. The symbol of molality is *m*. A 1 *m* NaOH solution contains one mole of NaOH dissolved in 1 kg of water.

In general, the molality of a solution can be calculated using the following equation.

$$\text{molality } (m) = \frac{\text{amount of solute (mol)}}{\text{mass of solvent(kg)}}$$

Note the similarity between this representation of concentration and molarity. Also note that the mass of the solvent must be expressed in kilograms.

The series of photographs that starts below details how to create a 0.5 *m* solution of $CuSO_4 \cdot 5H_2O$. Note that the process is simpler because the necessary amount of solvent is defined, whereas with molarity the total volume is defined, not the volume of the solvent.

Molality is commonly used when discussing the properties of solutions related to vapor pressure and temperature changes. This is because the molality of a solution will not change with temperature.

TIP The word *molal* is often used to describe the molality of a solution. For example, a one molal solution of NaOH is the same as a 1 *m* NaOH solution.

✓ READING CHECK

3. Why is a one molal solution easier to prepare than a one molar solution?

_____

_____

_____

_____

_____

Calculate the mass of $CuSO_4 \cdot 5H_2O$ needed. Making this solution will require 0.5000 mol of $CuSO_4 \cdot 5H_2O$ per kilogram of solvent(1000 g). This mass is calculated to be 124.8 g.

Add 1.000 kg of solvent to the solute in the beaker. Because the solvent is water, 1.000 kg will equal 1000 mL.

Mix thoroughly.

The resulting solution has 0.5000 mol of solute dissolved in 1.000 kg of solvent.

A solution was prepared by dissolving 17.1 g of sucrose (table sugar, $C_{12}H_{22}O_{11}$) in 125 g of water. Find the molal concentration of this solution.

	SOLUTION	
1	**ANALYZE**	*Determine the information that is given and unknown.*

Given: solute mass = 17.1 g $C_{12}H_{22}O_{11}$, solvent mass = 125 g H_2O

Unknown: molality of $C_{12}H_{22}O_{11}$ solution

2 PLAN

Describe how to use the given information to find the unknown.

Molality is the number of moles of solute per kilogram of solvent. First, convert the given solute mass into moles of solute. Then use the formula for molality to calculate the molality of the solution.

$$\text{molality } (m) = \frac{\text{amount of solute (mol)}}{\text{mass of solvent (kg)}}$$

3 SOLVE

Calculate the unknown from the given information.

First, the molar mass of $C_{12}H_{22}O_{11}$ must be calculated.

$$\begin{aligned}\text{molar mass of } C_{12}H_{22}O_{11}\\ = 12(12.01 \text{ g/mol}) + 22(1.01 \text{ g/mol}) + 11(16.00 \text{ g/mol})\\ = 342.34 \text{ g/mol}\end{aligned}$$

$$17.1 \text{ g } C_{12}H_{22}O_{11} \times \frac{1 \text{ mol } C_{12}H_{22}O_{11}}{342.34 \text{ g } C_{12}H_{22}O_{11}} = 0.0500 \text{ mol } C_{12}H_{22}O_{11}$$

Convert the mass of the water to kilograms before using it in the equation for molality.

$$\text{molality} = \frac{0.0500 \text{ mol } C_{12}H_{22}O_{11}}{0.125 \text{ kg } C_{12}H_{22}O_{11}} = 0.400 \text{ } m \text{ } C_{12}H_{22}O_{11}$$

4 CHECK YOUR WORK

Check the answer to see if it is reasonable.

The answer is correctly limited to three significant digits. A mass of 125 g is one-eighth of 1 kg. Because the molar mass of $C_{12}H_{22}O_{11}$ is about 340 g/mol, a 1 molal solution of $C_{12}H_{22}O_{11}$ would contain about 340 ÷ 8, or about 40 g. The actual solute mass is 17 g, which is a little less than half of 40 g.

F. What is the molality of acetone, $(CH_3)_2CO$, in a solution composed of 255 g of acetone dissolved in 200. g of water?

What is the molar mass of acetone? _____

_____

255 g acetone $= 255$ g acetone $\times \dfrac{1 \text{ mol acetone}}{\text{g acetone}} =$ _____

$\text{molality} = \dfrac{\text{mol acetone}}{1.25 \text{ kg acetone}} =$ _____

G. What quantity, in grams, of methanol, CH_3OH, is required to prepare a 0.244 *m* solution in 400. g of water?

Rearrange the equation for molarity to solve for the number of moles of solute in the solution.

$$\text{amount of solute (mol)} = \underline{\qquad\qquad\qquad}$$

Substitute the given information into your equation to find the number of moles of HCl.

_____

What is the molar mass of methanol?

_____

What is the mass, in g, of that number of moles of methanol?

_____

VOCABULARY

1. What quantity represents the ratio of the number of moles of solute for a given volume of solution?

_____

REVIEW

2. You dissolve 5.00 g of sugar, $C_{12}H_{22}O_{11}$, in water to make 1.000 L of solution. What is the concentration of this solution expressed as molarity?

_____

3. A solution is prepared by dissolving 17.1 g of sucrose, $C_{12}H_{22}O_{11}$, in 275 g of H_2O. What is the molality of the solution?

Critical Thinking

4. ANALYZING DATA You evaporate all of the water from 100. mL of NaCl solution and obtain 11.3 g of NaCl. What was the molarity of the NaCl solution?

5. RELATING IDEAS Suppose you know the molarity of a solution. What additional information would you need to calculate the molality of the solution?

_____

_____

Math Tutor CALCULATING SOLUTION CONCENTRATION

You can use the relationship below to calculate the concentration in molarity of any solution.

$$\text{molarity (M)} = \frac{\text{amount of solute (mol)}}{\text{volume of solution (L)}}$$

Suppose you dissolve 20.00 g of NaOH in some water and dilute the solution to a volume of 250.0 mL (0.2500 L). You do not know the molarity of this solution until you know how many moles of NaOH have been dissolved. You know that the number of moles of a substance can be found by dividing the mass of the substance by the mass of 1 mol of the substance. The molar mass of NaOH is 40.00 g/mol, so the number of moles of NaOH dissolved is

$$40.00 \text{ g NaOH} = 20.00 \text{ g NaOH} \times \frac{1 \text{ mol NaOH}}{40.00 \text{ g NaOH}} = 0.5000 \text{ mol NaOH}$$

Now you know that the solution has 0.5000 mol NaOH dissolved in 0.2500 L of solution, so you can calculate molarity.

$$\text{molarity of solution} = \frac{\text{moles of NaOH}}{\text{liters of solution}} = \frac{0.5000 \text{ mol NaOH}}{0.2500 \text{ L NaOH}} = 2.000 \text{ M NaOH}$$

Problem-Solving TIPS

- Remember that balances measure mass, not moles, so you often have to convert between mass and moles of solute when making or using solutions.

SAMPLE

A 0.5000 L volume of a solution contains 36.49 g of magnesium chloride, $MgCl_2$. What is the molarity of the solution?

The molar mass of $MgCl_2$ is 24.30 g/mol + 2(35.45 g/mol) = 95.20 g/mol.

The number of moles of $MgCl_2$ can be determined by using the molar mass to convert grams to moles.

$$36.49 \text{ g MgCl}_2 = 36.49 \text{ g MgCl}_2 \times \frac{1 \text{ mol MgCl}_2}{95.20 \text{ g MgCl}_2} = 0.3833 \text{ mol MgCl}_2$$

Molarity can be computed using the equation above.

$$\text{molarity of solution} = \frac{\text{moles of MgCl}_2}{\text{liters of solution}} = \frac{0.3833 \text{ mol MgCl}_2}{0.5000 \text{ L MgCl}_2}$$

$$= 0.7666 \text{ M MgCl}_2$$

Practice Problems: Chapter Review practice problems 13–16

1. Given an unknown mixture consisting of two or more substances, explain how to determine whether the mixture is a solution, colloid, or suspension.

_____

_____

2. Explain why a suspension is considered a heterogeneous mixture.

_____

_____

3. Does a solution have to involve a liquid? Explain your answer.

_____

_____

4. What is the difference between an electrolyte and a nonelectrolyte?

_____

_____

5. What is solution equilibrium? What factors determine the point at which a given solute-solvent combination reaches equilibrium?

_____

_____

_____

6. Two bottles of soda are opened. One is a cold bottle and the other is at room temperature. Which bottle would show more effervescence and why?

_____

_____

7. What rule of thumb is useful for predicting whether one substance will dissolve in another? Describe what the rule means in terms of various combinations of polar and nonpolar solutes and solvents.

_____

_____

_____

8. What visible evidence indicates that a solution is saturated?

_____

_____

9. If the pressure of a gas above a liquid is increased, what happens to the amount of the gas that will dissolve in the liquid, if all other conditions remain constant?

_____

_____

10. Use the Solubility vs. Temperature graph in Section 2 to determine the solubility of each of the following in grams of solute per 100. g H_2O.

a. $NaNO_3$ at 10°C _____ **b.** KNO_3 at 60°C _____ **c.** NaCl at 50°C _____

11. The enthalpy of solution for $AgNO_3$ is +22.8 kJ/mol.

a. Does the dissolution process absorb energy or release energy? _____

b. As $AgNO_3$ dissolves, how does the temperature of the solution change? _____

c. How do the rates of dissolution and crystallization compare at equilibrium?

_____

d. If the solution is then heated, how will the rates of dissolution and crystallization be affected? Why?

_____

_____

e. How does the solubility of $AgNO_3$ change after heating?

_____

12. On which property of solutions does the concept of concentration rely?

_____

_____

13. If you dissolve 2.00 mol KI in 1.00 L of water, will you get a 2.00 M solution? Explain.

_____

_____

14. Suppose you dissolve 106 g of Na_2CO_3 in enough H_2O to make 6.00 L of solution. What is the molarity of the solution?

15. Suppose you wanted to produce 1.00 L of a 3.50 M aqueous solution of H_2SO_4. How many grams of solute are needed?

16. a. Balance the equation:

_____ H_3PO_4 + _____ $Ca(OH)_2$ → _____ $Ca_3(PO_4)_2$ + _____ H_2O

b. What mass of each product results if 750 mL of 6.00 M H_3PO_4 react according to this equation?

17. How many kilograms of H_2O must be added to 75.5 g of $Ca(NO_3)_2$ to form a 0.500 m solution?

CHAPTER 13

Ions in Aqueous Solutions and Colligative Properties

Key Concepts

Section 1 *Compounds in Aqueous Solutions*

How can a chemical equation represent dissolution?

When will a precipitate form during a chemical reaction?

How does dissociation compare with ionization?

What is a hydronium ion and what is its significance?

What distinguishes strong and weak electrolytes?

Section 2 *Colligative Properties of Solutions*

What is a colligative property?

Why does a solute change the properties of a liquid?

Why do observed properties differ from theoretical ones?

Review Previous Concepts

1. What is a chemical equation and what does it represent?

_____

_____

_____

2. Explain the process of dissolution at a molecular level.

_____

_____

_____

3. What are two ways to express the concentration of a solution and how is each value determined?

_____

_____

_____

SECTION 13.1

Compounds in Aqueous Solutions

Ionic compounds and molecular compounds have different properties. Ionic compounds form a crystal lattice that consists of a regular pattern of charged particles held together by ionic attractions. Although molecules are held together by strong covalent bonds, molecules within a molecular compound are held together by relatively weak intermolecular forces. This difference in nature causes the two types of compound to behave differently when they dissolve in water.

Ions separate from each other when ionic compounds are dissolved in water.

Dissociation is the separation of ions that occurs when an ionic compound dissolves. For example, the dissociation of sodium chloride in water can be represented by this equation. Note that a formula unit for sodium chloride produces two ions in solution.

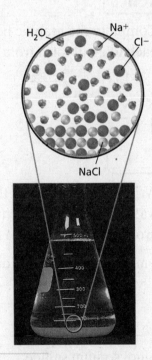

a formula unit of solid sodium chloride

one dissolved sodium ion

$$NaCl(s) \xrightarrow{\ H_2O\ } Na^+(aq) + Cl^-(aq)$$

yields when added to water

one dissolved chloride ion

When NaCl dissolves in water, the ions separate as they leave the crystal.

 **READING CHECK**

1. What is the difference between dissociation and dissolution?

_____

_____

_____

Moles of Dissolved Ions Chemical equations representing dissolution reflect the number of moles of each substance that are reacted and produced. So, for the dissolution of sodium chloride in water, 1 mol of sodium chloride dissociates into 2 mol of ions (1 mol of Na^+ ions and 1 mol of Cl^- ions).

TIP It is important not to confuse the terms *dissociation* and *dissolution*. Dissociation is the process of splitting apart or separating. Dissolution is the process of dissolving.

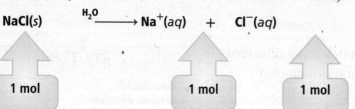

$$NaCl(s) \xrightarrow{\text{H}_2\text{O}} Na^+(aq) + Cl^-(aq)$$

| 1 mol | 1 mol | 1 mol |

This relationship only holds if the compound undergoes 100% dissociation. In other words, one mole of sodium chloride will only form one mole of each type of ion if every formula unit in the mole of sodium chloride dissociates.

PRACTICE

A. Complete the graphic below to show how many moles of each ion will form from the 100% dissociation of $CaCl_2$.

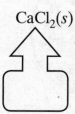 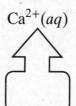 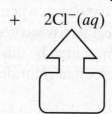

$$CaCl_2(s) \xrightarrow{\text{H}_2\text{O}} Ca^{2+}(aq) + 2Cl^-(aq)$$

B. Write the equation for the dissolution of each sample in water. Then determine the number of moles of each ion produced as well as the total moles of ions produced.

a. 1 mol aluminum chloride

_____

_____

b. 1 mol sodium sulfide

_____

_____

c. 0.5 mol barium nitrate

_____

_____

Precipitation Reactions

Every ionic compound is soluble to some degree. Some compounds, such as sodium chloride, form clear solutions in water. Others form solutions with a characteristic color. The solutions are still homogeneous even though the solute particles change the appearance of the water.

However, there are some ionic compounds that have a very low solubility. Those compounds are considered insoluble for practical purposes. The photograph shows some ionic compounds that are soluble and some that are insoluble.

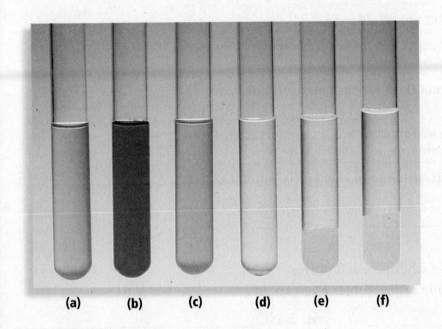

(a) $NiCl_2$ forms a green solution in water. (b) $KMnO_4$ forms a purple solution in water. (c) $CuSO_4$ forms a blue solution in water. (d) $Pb(NO_3)_2$ forms a clear solution in water. (e) AgCl and (f) CdS are insoluble in water.

(a)   (b)   (c)   (d)   (e)   (f)

PRACTICE

C. If possible, write dissociation equations for the six compounds shown in the photograph. Otherwise write "no dissociation."

a. $NiCl_2(aq) \xrightarrow{H_2O}$ _____

b. $KMnO_4(aq) \xrightarrow{H_2O}$ _____

c. $CuSO_4(aq) \xrightarrow{H_2O}$ _____

d. $Pb(NO_3)_2(aq) \xrightarrow{H_2O}$ _____

e. $AgCl(aq) \xrightarrow{H_2O}$ _____

f. $CdS(aq) \xrightarrow{H_2O}$ _____

Solubility Guidelines The table below gives some general guidelines about whether an ionic compound is soluble in water or not. According to the table, sodium carbonate, Na_2CO_3, is soluble. Most carbonate compounds are insoluble according to Rule 5. However, Rule 5 also states that the compounds listed in Rule 1 are an exception. As another example, calcium phosphate is insoluble. According to Rule 5, most phosphates are insoluble and calcium is not one of the exceptions.

General Solubility Guidelines
1. Sodium, potassium, and ammonium compounds are soluble in water.
2. Nitrates, acetates, and chlorates are soluble.
3. Most chlorides are soluble, except those of silver, mercury(I), and lead. Lead(II) chloride is soluble in hot water.
4. Most sulfates are soluble, except those of barium, strontium, lead, calcium, and mercury.
5. Most carbonates, phosphates, and silicates are insoluble, except those of sodium, potassium, and ammonium.
6. Most sulfides are insoluble, except those of calcium, strontium, sodium, potassium, and ammonium.

PRACTICE

D. Use the table above to predict whether each of the following compounds is soluble or insoluble.

a. KCl _____

b. $NaNO_3$ _____

c. AgCl _____

d. $BaSO_4$ _____

e. $Ca_3(PO_4)_2$ _____

f. $Pb(ClO_3)_2$ _____

Formation of Precipitates The solubility guidelines listed above are also important for determining what happens when two different soluble compounds are mixed. Two sets of cations and two sets of anions would be present in such a mixture. If the attraction between the two types of ions is greater than the attraction between the ions and the polar water molecules, then the ions will bond and precipitation will occur. This happens if a double-displacement reaction between the compounds results in an insoluble compound. If the attraction between the water molecules and the ions is greater, then both compounds will remain dissolved.

Critical Thinking

2. Infer Assuming no additional energy is supplied, what do you expect will happen if you mix two insoluble compounds in water, and why?

_____

_____

_____

_____

Before reaction

H_2O

NH_4^+

S^{2-}

$(NH_4)_2S(aq)$

NO_3^-

Cd^{2+}

$Cd(NO_3)_2(aq)$

CdS(s)

After reaction

$CdS(s) + NH_4NO_3(aq)$

For example, consider the mixture shown in the photograph above. The test tube contains a solution of ammonium sulfide and the beaker contains a solution of cadmium nitrate. The dissociation equations for the two substances are shown below.

$$(NH_4)_2S(s) \xrightarrow{H_2O} 2NH_4^+(aq) + S^{2-}(aq)$$

$$Cd(NO_3)_2(s) \xrightarrow{H_2O} Cd^{2+}(aq) + 2NO_3^-(aq)$$

The following equation represents a potential double-displacement reaction between the two compounds. The question marks indicate that states that are undetermined.

$$(NH_4)_2S(aq) + Cd(NO_3)_2(aq) \longrightarrow 2NH_4NO_3(?) + CdS(?)$$

According to Rules 1 and 2 in the table on the previous page, ammonium nitrate is soluble in water. However, according to Rule 6, cadmium sulfide is insoluble in water. Therefore, the cadmium sulfide will precipitate out of solution. The completed equation for the reaction in the photograph is

$$(NH_4)_2S(aq) + Cd(NO_3)_2(aq) \longrightarrow 2NH_4NO_3(aq) + CdS(s)$$

Ammonium sulfide and cadmium nitrate are mixed, resulting in the formation of the yellow precipitate cadmium sulfide.

Remember

A double-displacement reaction is a reaction in which two ionic compounds swap ions so that the cation from one compound bonds with the anion from the other compound.

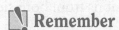

READING CHECK

3. If one product of a double-displacement reaction is a precipitate, what is the state of that product?

Net Ionic Equations

A reaction between ions in aqueous solutions is usually represented by the component ions instead of by the ionic compounds themselves. One reason is that the ions are the important units in the reaction, not the formula units of the compound's crystal lattice. An equation that represents aqueous solutions of ionic compounds as ions is called an *ionic equation*.

A **net ionic equation** is a chemical reaction that includes only those compounds and ions that undergo a chemical change in a reaction in an aqueous solution. Ions that do not participate in the reaction are not included. These **spectator ions** are found in solution before and after the reaction occurs.

The first step in writing a net ionic equation is to write a complete ionic equation. Consider the reaction that was discussed on the previous page. The double-displacement reaction can be written as follows, by writing all of the substances in an aqueous state as dissociated ions.

$$2NH_4^+(aq) + S^{2-}(aq) + Cd^{2+}(aq) + 2NO_3^-(aq) \longrightarrow$$
$$2NH_4^+(aq) + 2NO_3^-(aq) + CdS(s)$$

This ionic equation shows that aqueous ammonium ion, NH_4^+, appears on both sides of the equation. The aqueous nitrate ion, NO_3^+, also appears on both sides of the equation. These ions are spectator ions. To form the net ionic equation, cancel the spectator ions from both sides of the equation.

$$\cancel{2NH_4^+(aq)} + S^{2-}(aq) + Cd^{2+}(aq) + \cancel{2NO_3^-(aq)} \longrightarrow$$
$$\cancel{2NH_4^+(aq)} + \cancel{2NO_3^-(aq)} + CdS(s)$$

$$Cd^{2+}(aq) + S^{2-}(aq) \longrightarrow CdS(s)$$

This net ionic equation applies to other reactions besides the one between ammonium sulfide and cadmium nitrate. It applies to any reaction in which ions are combined in solution and cadmium sulfide forms. For example, the reaction of cadmium sulfate, $CdSO_4$, and hydrogen sulfide, H_2S, also has the same net ionic equation.

LOOKING CLOSER

4. Write separate definitions for these terms in your own words.

spectator: _____

_____

_____

ion: _____

_____

_____

Critical Thinking

5. Apply What are the two spectator ions in the reactions of cadmium sulfate and hydrogen sulfide?

_____

_____

A molecular compound ionizes in a polar solvent.

Ionic compounds form ions in solution through the process called dissociation. Molecular compounds can also form ions in solution. However, molecular compounds undergo a different process. Ions are formed from solute molecules by the action of the solvent in a process called **ionization.**

The extent to which a solute ionizes depends on the strength of the bonds within the molecule of the solute and the strength of the attraction between the solute and the solvent molecules. If the strength of the bonds in the solute molecule are weaker, then the covalent bond breaks and the molecule separates into ions. The ions form because the more electronegative atom holds on to the electrons that were shared in the covalent bond.

One example of ionization is in the dissolution of hydrogen chloride, HCl. The hydrogen-chlorine bond is highly polar. The attraction between the polar HCl molecule and the polar water molecules is strong enough to break the covalent bond. The chlorine atom keeps the shared electrons and forms a chloride ion, while the hydrogen atom forms a hydrogen ion.

$$HCl(g) \xrightarrow{\text{H}_2\text{O}} H^+(aq) + Cl^-(aq)$$

The Hydronium Ion

The hydrogen ion, H^+, is equivalent to a proton, a concentrated area of positive charge. This ion is attracted to negatively charged particles so strongly that it does not normally exist alone. In an aqueous solution, the hydrogen ion will be attracted to the negative end of a water molecule. The result is the formation of an H_3O^+ ion, known as a **hydronium ion.**

The ionization of hydrogen chloride is better represented by the transfer of a proton from a hydrogen chloride molecule to a water molecule. The chemical reaction is shown below.

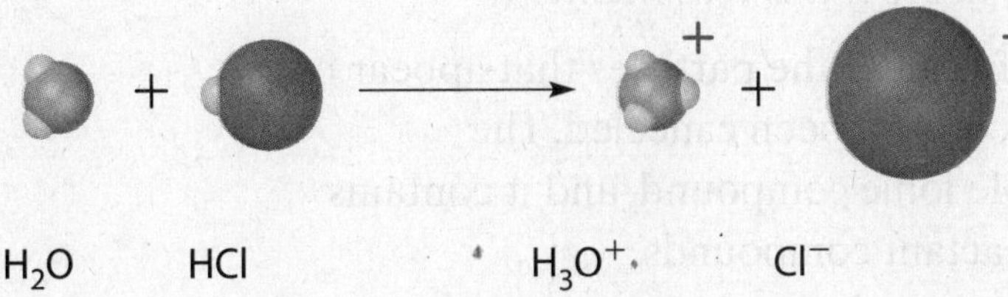

✔ READING CHECK

6. How is ionization different from dissociation?

_____

_____

_____

_____

_____

📝 **Remember**

A hydrogen-1 atom consists of a single electron that orbits a nucleus consisting of a single proton. If the electron is stripped away to form a hydrogen ion, only the proton remains.

| H_2O | HCl | | H_3O^+ | Cl^- |

SAMPLE PROBLEM

Write the net ionic equation for the reaction of aqueous solutions of zinc nitrate and ammonium sulfide.

SOLUTION		
1 ANALYZE	*Determine the information that is given and unknown.*	

Given: reactants are zinc nitrate and ammonium sulfide

Unknown: net ionic equation

2 PLAN — *Describe how to write the net ionic equation.*

First, determine the possible double-displacement reaction between the two reactants. Then determine if either of the products forms a precipitate. Then write the ionic equation for the reaction and cancel the particles that appear unchanged on both sides.

3 SOLVE — *Use the plan above to write the equation for the reaction.*

Zn^{2+} combines with NO_3^- to form $Zn(NO_3)_2$. NH_4^+ combines with S^{2-} to form $(NH_4)_2S$. The balanced double-displacement reaction is as follows.

$$Zn(NO_3)_2(aq) + (NH_4)_2S(aq) \longrightarrow ZnS(?) + 2NH_4NO_3(?)$$

According to the "Solubility Guidelines" table earlier in this chapter, zinc sulfide is insoluble, so it forms a precipitate in this reaction. The completed equation for the reaction is as follows.

$$Zn(NO_3)_2(aq) + (NH_4)_2S(aq) \longrightarrow ZnS(s) + 2NH_4NO_3(aq)$$

The aqueous compounds in this reaction are written as ions to produce the complete ionic equation. Canceling the spectator ions yields the net ionic equation for the reaction.

$$Zn^{2+}(aq) + 2NO_3^-(aq) + 2NH_4^+(aq) + S^{2-}(aq) \longrightarrow$$
$$+ 2NO_3^-(aq) + 2NH_4^+(aq) + ZnS(s)$$

$$Zn^{2+}(aq) + S^{2-}(aq) \longrightarrow ZnS(s)$$

4 CHECK YOUR WORK — *Check the final equation to see if it is reasonable.*

The chemical formulas for all of the particles that appear on both sides of the equation have been canceled. The precipitate is an insoluble ionic compound, and it contains ions from both of the reactant compounds.

E. Will a precipitate form if solutions of potassium sulfate and barium nitrate are combined? If so, write the net ionic equation for the reaction.

Chemical formulas: potassium sulfate: _____

barium nitrate: _____

Which of the products are soluble? _____

Complete double-displacement reaction:

_____

Complete ionic equation:

_____

Net ionic equation:

_____

F. Will a precipitate form if solutions of potassium nitrate and magnesium sulfate are combined? If so, write the net ionic equation for the reaction.

Chemical formulas: potassium nitrate: _____

magnesium sulfate: _____

Which of the products will be soluble? _____

Complete double-displacement reaction:

_____

Complete ionic equation:

_____

Net ionic equation:

_____

G. Will a precipitate form if solutions of barium chloride and sodium sulfate are combined? If so, write the net ionic equation for the reaction.

_____

_____

TIP If both ionic compounds are soluble, the complete ionic equation has the same four ions on both sides of the equation. In any of these practice problems in which this is the case, write "does not apply" for the net ionic equation.

An electrolyte's strength depends on how many dissolved ions it contains.

As discussed in the chapter "Solutions," substances that yield ions and conduct an electric current in solution are electrolytes. However, not all electrolytes have the same ability to conduct electricity. Electrolytes that conduct electricity well are called **strong electrolytes.** Electrolytes that conduct electricity poorly are called **weak electrolytes.**

The factor that determines whether a substance is a strong or a weak electrolyte is the proportion of the substance that is found as aqueous ions in solution. A strong electrolyte is composed of all, or nearly all, ions in solution. A weak electrolyte mostly consists of molecules in solution, with just a few molecules that are ionized.

Consider the group of substances known as hydrogen halides. Hydrogen halides are polar molecules that are gases at room temperature and soluble in water. Hydrogen chloride, hydrogen bromide, and hydrogen iodide are strong electrolytes. However, hydrogen fluoride is a weak electrolyte. If solutions of these four substances are made at the same concentration, the first three will conduct electricity strongly and hydrogen fluoride will conduct electricity poorly.

Recall that a nonelectrolyte is a substance that does not have the ability to conduct electricity at all when it is in solution. Because all of the substance remains in molecular form, no charge can be transmitted by the movement of charged particles in the solution. The diagram at the right shows a molecular view of a sucrose solution. Sucrose, $C_{12}H_{22}O_{11}$, is a nonelectrolyte. Compare this diagram to the diagrams of strong and weak electrolytes on the next page.

TIP Be careful not to confuse the classification of an electrolyte as strong or weak with the concentration of a solution. Strong and weak electrolytes differ in the percentage of dissolved solute ionization or dissociation. Concentration is a measure of the percentage of solute that is dissolved. A dilute solution can still be a strong electrolyte.

TIP A hydrogen halide forms from a hydrogen atom and an atom from Group 17, the halogens. The term *halide* is derived in the same way as that of a negative ion. The ending *-ide* is appended to the root of the term *halogen*.

Nonelectrolyte

$C_{12}H_{22}O_{11}$

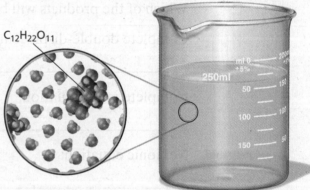

$C_{12}H_{22}O_{11}$(aq)

✓ READING CHECK

7. Order the following substances from lowest to highest percentage of ions in solution: a nonelectrolyte, a strong electrolyte, and a weak electrolyte.

Strong Electrolytes

The distinguishing feature of a strong electrolyte is that it exists in ionic form when dissolved in water. This feature is observable for dilute concentrations as well as high concentrations of the solute. Even if the compound has a low solubility, the amount that does dissolve is only present in ionic form. The diagram at the right shows the molecular view of sodium chloride, which is a strong electrolyte.

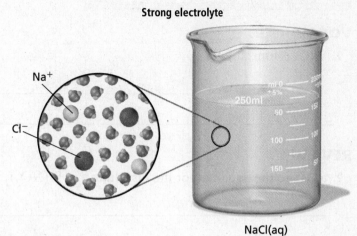

Strong electrolyte

Na$^+$

Cl$^-$

250ml

NaCl(aq)

All soluble ionic compounds are strong electrolytes. Strong electrolytes also include the halides hydrogen chloride, hydrogen bromide, and hydrogen iodide. Several other acids are strong electrolytes as well.

Weak Electrolytes

Some molecular compounds form aqueous solutions that contain not only dissolved ions, but also dissolved molecules that are not ionized. For example, hydrogen fluoride dissolves in water to form hydrofluoric acid. The diagram at the right shows that hydrofluoric acid consists of both ions and molecules. The hydrogen-fluorine bond, the strongest of the polar bonds in the hydrogen halides, is difficult for the polar water molecules to break.

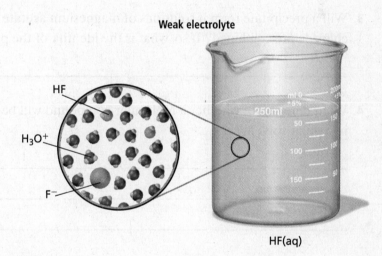

Weak electrolyte

HF

H$_3$O$^+$

F$^-$

250ml

HF(aq)

Weak electrolytes exist in a state of equilibrium in which molecules are being ionized and other molecules are re-forming at equal rates. For example, the equilibrium reaction for hydrofluoric acid is shown below.

$$HF(aq) + H_2O(l) \rightleftharpoons H_3O^+(aq) + F^-(aq)$$

✓ READING CHECK

8. Is sodium nitrate a strong electrolyte, a weak electrolyte, or a nonelectrolyte? Explain.

_____

_____

VOCABULARY

1. What is ionization?

_____

_____

REVIEW

2. a. Write the equation for the dissolution of $Sr(NO_3)_2$ in water.

_____

   b. How many moles of strontium ions and nitrate ions are produced by dissolving 0.5 mol of strontium nitrate?

_____

3. Will a precipitate form if solutions of magnesium acetate and strontium chloride are combined? If so, what is the identity of the precipitate?

_____

4. What determines whether a molecular compound will be ionized in a polar solvent?

_____

_____

_____

5. Explain why HCl is a strong electrolyte and HF is a weak electrolyte.

_____

_____

_____

Critical Thinking

6. PREDICTING OUTCOMES For each of the following pairs, tell which solution contains the larger total concentration of ions.

   a. 0.10 M HCl and 0.05 M HCl _____

   b. 0.10 M HCl and 0.10 M HF _____

   c. 0.10 M HCl and 0.10 M $CaCl_2$ _____

Colligative Properties of Solutions

The presence of solutes in a solution affects the properties of the solution. Some of these properties do not depend on the nature of the solutes. **Colligative properties** are properties that depend on the concentration of solute particles but not on their identity. Recall that molality is the amount of solute per kilogram of solvent. This section covers the colligative properties of solutions, and how they change with changes in molality.

Most of the solutes discussed in this section are nonvolatile substances. A **nonvolatile substance** has little tendency to become a gas under the existing conditions.

Critical Thinking

1. **Apply** In ocean water, which of the following is a nonvolatile substance: dissolved carbon dioxide, dissolved oxygen, or dissolved salt?

_____

Lowering vapor pressure depends on nonelectrolyte solute concentration.

When a nonvolatile substance is dissolved in a solvent, the boiling point of the solvent increases. The diagram at the right helps to explain why this occurs. A volume of an aqueous solution contains fewer water molecules than the same volume of pure water. Therefore, fewer molecules must exist in the gas phase for the processes of evaporation and condensation to balance. The equilibrium vapor pressure of the solution is less than the equilibrium vapor pressure of pure water.

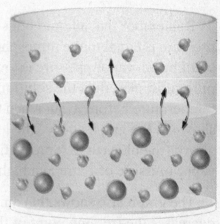

Aqueous solution of nonvolatile solute

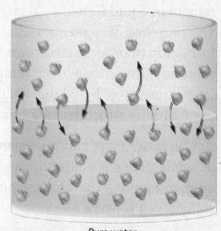

Pure water

At a given temperature, the vapor pressure of water over pure water is greater than the vapor pressure of water over an aqueous solution of sucrose.

⬤ Used to represent $C_{12}H_{22}O_{11}$, sucrose

⬤ Used to represent H_2O, water

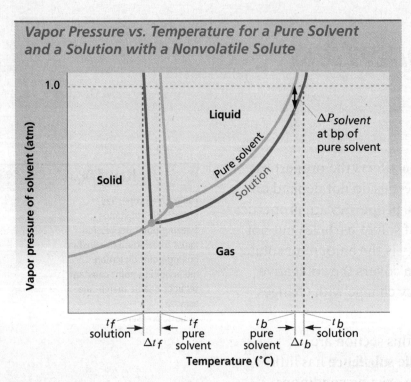

Vapor Pressure vs. Temperature for a Pure Solvent and a Solution with a Nonvolatile Solute

The graph shows that a solution has a higher boiling point and a lower freezing point than the pure solvent. This is because the vapor pressure of a solution is lower than the vapor pressure of the solvent alone. Note that Δt_f is the change in freezing point temperature, Δt_b is the change in boiling point temperature, and $\Delta P_{solvent}$ is the change in vapor pressure of the solvent at the boiling point.

Remember that a liquid boils when its equilibrium vapor pressure is equal to the atmospheric vapor pressure. If equilibrium vapor pressure is lowered for a solution versus a pure substance, then the solution must be raised to a higher temperature before it can reach the boiling point. This is shown in the graph above. The lower curve on the graph above (the blue curve representing the solution) reaches a vapor pressure of 1 atm at a higher temperature.

The graph also shows that a nonvolatile substance decreases the freezing point of the solution versus the pure solvent. The lower vapor pressure allows the solution to remain in liquid form over a larger range of temperatures. The presence of solute molecules interferes with the formation of ordered structures within the solvent. The solution must reach a lower temperature to get the average kinetic energy of liquid molecules low enough to form the more orderly structures of a solid.

The lowering of vapor pressure resulting from the presence of solute depends on the concentration of solute particles, not on their identity. Therefore, vapor-pressure lowering is a colligative property.

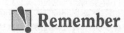 The vapor pressure of water is lowered by 5.5×10^{-4} atm by a 1 m solution of any nonelectrolyte solute.

Remember

The *freezing point* of a substance is the temperature at which the solid and liquid forms of the substance are at equilibrium at atmospheric pressure.

READING CHECK

2. Salt water has a _____ boiling point and a _____ freezing point than pure water.

The freezing point depression is directly proportional to the molal concentration of a solution.

Adding solute to a solution lowers its freezing point. One reason people sprinkle salt on sidewalks is to prevent ice from forming by lowering the freezing point of water. The salt also dissolves in ice as it melts, preventing the ice from refreezing.

Scientists have found that the freezing point of a 1 m solution of any nonelectrolyte in water is −1.86°C instead of 0.00°C. In other words, 1 mol of solute dissolved in water lowers the freezing point of water by 1.86°C. Through experiments, scientists have found that 2 mol of solute lowers the freezing point of water by 3.72°C. By studying the effect of different concentrations of solute on the freezing point, scientists have found that the concentration of solute and the change in freezing point are directly proportional.

The **freezing-point depression,** Δt_f, is the difference between the freezing point of the pure solvent and that of a solution of a nonelectrolyte in the solvent. Because this quantity and concentration are directly proportional, they can be related by a constant, as in the equation below.

$$\Delta t_f = K_f m$$

In the equation, m is molality, and Δt_f is expressed in °C. The constant, K_f, is called the molal freezing-point constant. The **molal freezing-point constant** is the freezing point of the solvent in a 1-molal solution of a nonvolatile, nonelectrolyte solute. As stated above, the molal freezing-point constant for water is −1.86°C. The table shows the molal freezing-point constants for other substances.

 CONNECT

Even though the concepts of freezing and melting are familiar, scientists have only just begun to understand these processes. Starting several degrees below the melting point of ice, a fluid surface layer forms that is a few molecules thick. This "quasiliquid layer" could help explain many features of ice, such as the unique shapes of snowflakes or the physics of ice skating.

 Critical Thinking

3. Calculate Assuming that ocean water has 1.04 mol of dissolved salt, what is ocean water's freezing point?

Molal Freezing-Point Constants		
Solvent	Normal freezing point (°C)	Molal freezing-point constant, K_f (°C/m)
Acetic acid	16.6	−3.90
Camphor	178.8	−39.7
Ether	−116.3	−1.79
Naphthalene	80.2	−6.94
Phenol	40.9	−7.40
Water	0.00	−1.86

SAMPLE PROBLEM

What is the actual freezing point of water in a solution of 17.1 g of sucrose, $C_{12}H_{22}O_{11}$, in 200. g of water?

	SOLUTION	
1	**ANALYZE**	*Determine the information that is given and unknown.*

Given: solute: 17.1 g $C_{12}H_{22}O_{11}$
solvent: 200. g H_2O

Unknown: freezing point of the solution

2	**PLAN**	*Describe how to use the given information to find the unknown.*

First, determine the amount of solute in moles. Then, determine the molality of the solution. Finally, use the equation for freezing-point depression to determine the amount that the freezing point decreases below 0°C.

3	**SOLVE**	*Use the plan above to calculate the unknown.*

molar mass of $C_{12}H_{22}O_{11}$

$$= 12(12.01 \text{ g/mol}) + 22(1.0 \text{ g/mol}) + 11(16.00 \text{ g/mol})$$

$$= 342.34 \text{ g/mol}$$

$$17.1 \text{ g } C_{12}H_{22}O_{11} \times \frac{1 \text{ mol } C_{12}H_{22}O_{11}}{342.34 \text{ g } C_{12}H_{22}O_{11}} = 0.0500 \text{ mol } C_{12}H_{22}O_{11}$$

The mass of the solvent is 200. g = 0.200 kg.

$$\text{molality} = \frac{\text{amount of solute (mol)}}{\text{mass of solvent (kg)}}$$

$$= \frac{0.0500 \text{ mol } C_{12}H_{22}O_{11}}{0.200 \text{ kg } H_2O}$$

$$= 0.250 \text{ } m$$

The freezing-point depression constant for water is −1.86°C/m.

$$\Delta t_f = K_f m = (-1.86°C/m)(0.250 \text{ } m) = -0.465°C$$

Therefore, the freezing point of the solution is −0.465°C.

4	**CHECK YOUR WORK**	*Check the final answer to see if it is reasonable.*

The correct units were used in each step and the final answer has the correct number of significant digits.

A. A solution consists of 10.3 g of the nonelectrolyte glucose, $C_6H_{12}O_6$, dissolved in 250. g of water. What is the freezing-point depression of the solution?

What is the molar mass of $C_6H_{12}O_6$?

$$\text{moles of solute} = 10.3 \text{ g } C_6H_{12}O_6 \times \frac{1 \text{ mol } C_6H_{12}O_6}{\text{g } C_6H_{12}O_6}$$

$$= \underline{\hspace{3cm}}$$

$$\text{molality of solution} = \frac{\text{amount of solute (mol)}}{\text{mass of solvent (kg)}} =$$

$$\Delta t_f = K_f m =$$

B. If 0.500 mol of a nonelectrolyte solute are dissolved in 500.0 g of ether, what is the freezing point of the solution?

What is the molality of the solution?

What is the freezing-point depression of the solution? _____

What is the normal freezing point of ether? _____

What is the freezing point of the solution?

A water solution containing an unknown quantity of a nonelectrolyte solute is found to have a freezing point of –0.23°C. What is the molal concentration of the solution?

SOLUTION

1 ANALYZE *Determine the information that is given and unknown.*

Given: freezing point of solution = –0.23°C

Unknown: molality of the solution

2 PLAN *Write an equation that can be used to find the unknown.*

The equation for the freezing-point depression of a solution is $\Delta t_f = K_f m$. Therefore, the molality of the solution can be written as follows.

$$m = \frac{\Delta t_f}{K_f}$$

The value of Δt_f can be derived from the given information and the freezing point of pure water.

3 SOLVE *Substitute the given information into the equation.*

The freezing-point depression of the solution is –0.23°C, because the freezing point of the solution is 0.23°C below 0.00°C. The molal freezing-point constant, K_f, for water is found in the table on page 425.

$$m = \frac{\Delta t_f}{K_f} = \frac{-0.23°C}{-1.86°C/m} = 0.12\ m$$

4 CHECK YOUR WORK *Check the final answer to see if it is reasonable.*

The correct units were used in each step and the final answer has the correct number of significant digits.

PRACTICE

C. In a laboratory experiment, the freezing point of an aqueous solution of glucose is found to be –0.325°C. What is the molal concentration of this solution?

A solution with a nonelectrolyte solvent will have a higher boiling point than pure solvent.

Adding solute to a solution raises its boiling point. The vapor pressure of the solution is lower than it would be for the pure solvent. More heat must be added to the solution before the vapor pressure equals the atmospheric pressure. A liquid will boil when these two quantities are equal.

Scientists have found that the boiling point of a 1 m solution of any nonelectrolyte in water is 100.51°C instead of 100.00°C. Just as with freezing-point depression, scientists have found that the concentration of solute and the change in freezing point are directly proportional.

The **boiling-point elevation,** Δt_b, is the difference between the boiling point of the pure solvent and that of a solution of a nonelectrolyte in the solvent. This quantity and the molality of a solution are related by the equation below.

$$\Delta t_b = K_b m$$

Once again, m is molality, and Δt_b is expressed in °C. The constant, K_b, the **molal boiling-point constant,** is the boiling point of the solvent in a 1-molal solution of a nonvolatile, nonelectrolyte solute. The molal boiling-point constant for water is 0.51°C. The molal boiling-point constants, and for comparison the molal-freezing point constants, for several substances are shown in the table.

✓ **READING CHECK**

4. The molal _____ constant is always a negative value because the _____ of a solution is always lower. Conversely, the molal _____ constant is always a positive value because the _____ of a solution is always higher.

Molal Freezing-Point and Boiling-Point Constants

Solvent	Normal freezing point (°C)	Molal freezing-point constant, K_f (°C/m)	Normal boiling point (°C)	Molal boiling-point constant, K_b (°C/m)
Acetic acid	16.6	−3.90	117.9	3.07
Camphor	178.8	−39.7	207.4	5.61
Ether	−116.3	−1.79	34.6	2.02
Naphthalene	80.2	−6.94	217.7	5.80
Phenol	40.9	−7.40	181.8	3.60
Water	0.00	−1.86	100.0	0.51

What is the boiling point of a solution made from 20.1 g of a nonelectrolyte solute and 400.0 g of water? The molar mass of the solute is 62.0 g/mol.

SOLUTION		
1 ANALYZE	*Determine the information that is given and unknown.*	

Given: solute mass = 17.1 g, molar mass of solute
= 62.0 g/mol
solvent: 400.0 g of water

Unknown: boiling-point elevation

2 PLAN *Describe how to find the unknown value.*

First, determine the amount of solute in moles. Then, determine the molality of the solution. Finally, use the equation for boiling-point elevation to determine the amount that the boiling point increases above 100°C.

3 SOLVE *Use the plan above to calculate the unknown value.*

$$20.1 \text{ g solute} \times \frac{1 \text{ mol solute}}{62.0 \text{ g solute}} = 0.324 \text{ mol solute}$$

The mass of the solvent is 400.0 g = 0.4000 kg.

$$\text{molality} = \frac{\text{amount of solute (mol)}}{\text{mass of solvent (kg)}} = \frac{0.324 \text{ mol solute}}{0.4000 \text{ kg H}_2\text{O}}$$
$$= 0.810 \, m$$

The boiling point elevation constant for water is 0.51°C/*m*.

$$\Delta t_b = K_b m = (0.51°C/m)(0.810 \, m) = 0.41°C$$

The boiling point of the solution is the normal boiling point of water plus the boiling point elevation.

boiling point of solution = b.p. of water + Δt_b

$$= 100.00°C + 0.41°C$$
$$= 100.41°C$$

4 CHECK YOUR WORK *Check the final answer to see if it is reasonable.*

The correct units were used in each step and the final answer has the correct number of significant digits.

D. A solution contains 450.0 g of sucrose, $C_{12}H_{22}O_{11}$, a nonelectrolyte, dissolved in 250.0 g of water. What is the boiling point of the solution?

What is the molar mass of $C_{12}H_{22}O_{11}$?

$$\text{moles of solute} = 450.0 \text{ g } C_{12}H_{22}O_{11} \times \frac{1 \text{ mol } C_{12}H_{22}O_{11}}{\text{g } C_{12}H_{22}O_{11}}$$

$$= \underline{\hspace{10cm}}$$

$$\text{molality of solution} = \frac{\text{amount of solute (mol)}}{\text{mass of solvent (kg)}} =$$

$$\Delta t_b = K_b m =$$

boiling point of solution = _____ + _____ = _____

E. If the boiling-point elevation of an aqueous solution containing a nonvolatile electrolyte is 1.02°C, what is the molality of the solution?

F. The boiling point of an aqueous solution containing a nonvolatile nonelectrolyte is 100.75°C?

a. What is the boiling point elevation of the solution? _____

b. What is the molality of the solution? _____

Osmotic pressure is determined by the concentration of dissolved solute particles.

Another colligative property is related to the pressure that fluids of different concentrations exert on each other. This property is important to the function of the cells in living things.

A cell is surrounded by a semipermeable membrane. A **semipermeable membrane** allows the passage of some particles while blocking the passage of others. For example, a cell membrane might allow the passage of water molecules but block the passage of large solute molecules.

Suppose the cell membrane separates two fluids that have different concentrations of solute. Particles from both fluids will strike the membrane at the same rate, but more of the particles from the dilute fluid will be small enough to pass through the membrane. The result is a net flow of water from one side to the other. The movement of solvent through a semipermeable membrane from the side of lower concentration to the side of higher concentration is called **osmosis.**

Pressure would have to be exerted on the membrane from the side with the more concentrated solution in order to prevent osmosis. **Osmotic pressure** is the external pressure that is necessary to stop osmosis. Because this pressure is dependent on the difference in concentrations, not on the identity of the solutes, it is a colligative property.

CONNECT

Regulation of osmosis is vital to the life of a cell. Cells lose water and shrink when placed in a solution of higher concentration than their interior fluid. Cells gain water and swell when placed in a solution of lower concentration. The cells of vertebrates are protected from swelling and shrinking by the blood and lymph that surround the cells. These fluids are kept at a concentration equal to the concentration inside cells.

LOOKING CLOSER

5. Draw an arrow on diagram (b) below to represent the osmotic pressure that is preventing osmosis through the semipermeable membrane.

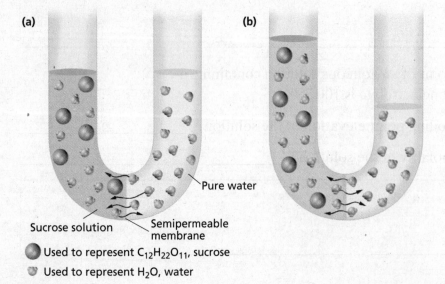

(a)   (b)

Pure water

Sucrose solution   Semipermeable membrane

🔴 Used to represent $C_{12}H_{22}O_{11}$, sucrose

⚪ Used to represent H_2O, water

(a) Pure water and an aqueous sucrose solution are separated by a semipermeable membrane. The net movement of water molecules through the membrane is from the pure water side into the sucrose solution. (b) The height of the solution rises until the pressures on both sides of the membrane balance. The difference in the heights of the fluids exerts pressure on the membrane toward the pure water side. The difference in concentrations exerts pressure on the membrane toward the solution side.

The total molality of all dissolved particles determines changes in colligative properties.

The examples and problems discussed in this section so far have involved nonelectrolytes. The same principles also apply to electrolytes, so long as the dissociation and ionization of the solutes are taken into account.

For example, consider two solutions, a 1 m solution of sucrose and a 1 m solution of sodium chloride. Sucrose is a nonelectrolyte. One mole of sucrose dissolves to form one mole of solute particles. However, sodium chloride is a strong electrolyte. Each mole of sodium chloride dissolves to form two moles of solute particles, one mole of sodium ions and one mole of chloride ions. Therefore, a sodium chloride solution will have twice as many solute particles as a sugar solution at the same molality. Since colligative properties are dependent on particle concentration only, not the type of particles, you would expect sodium chloride to have twice the effect as sugar on the properties of solutions.

Calculated Values for Electrolyte Solutions

The changes in colligative properties caused by electrolytes is proportional to the total molality of all dissolved particles, not to formula units. The sample problem on the next page shows how to apply a conversion factor that accounts for the number of moles of ions that form from a mole of electrolyte.

CONNECT

Reverse osmosis can purify water. Exerting more pressure on the semipermeable membrane than is coming from the osmotic pressure can reverse the direction of osmosis. So, if the membrane separates pure water and salt water, the water molecules will move from the salt water to the pure water. Over time, more and more pure water can accumulate. The largest desalination plant in Florida uses reverse osmosis to produce 12 million gallons of fresh water a day.

Critical Thinking

6. Apply Assume that all three solutions below have the same molality. If the sodium chloride solution has a boiling-point elevation of 1.0°C, what are the boiling-point elevations of the other two solutions?

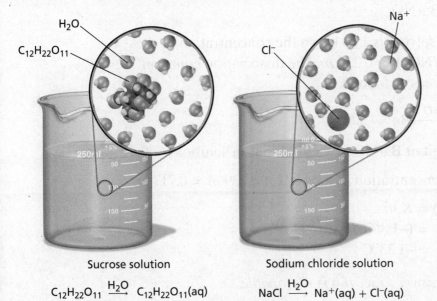

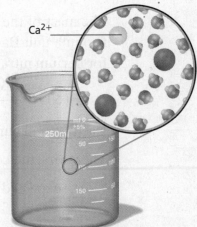

Sucrose solution
$$C_{12}H_{22}O_{11} \xrightarrow{H_2O} C_{12}H_{22}O_{11}(aq)$$

Sodium chloride solution
$$NaCl \xrightarrow{H_2O} Na^+(aq) + Cl^-(aq)$$

Calcium chloride solution
$$CaCl_2 \xrightarrow{H_2O} Ca^{2+}(aq) + 2Cl^-(aq)$$

From left to right, these three solutions include 1 mol, 2 mol, and 3 mol of solute particles per formula unit. A 1:2:3 ratio reflects the effect of equal concentrations of these solutions on colligative properties.

What is the expected change in the freezing point of water in a solution of 62.5 g of barium nitrate, Ba(NO₃)₂, in 1.00 kg of water?

SOLUTION		
1 ANALYZE	*Determine the information that is given and unknown.*	

Given: solute: 62.5 g Ba(NO₃)₂, solvent: 1.00 kg H₂O

Unknown: expected freezing-point depression

2 PLAN   *Describe how to find the unknown value.*

First, determine the amount of solute in moles and determine the molality of the solution. Then convert the concentration from molality of formula units to molality of ions. This adjusted molality can then be used to calculate the freezing-point depression of the solution.

3 SOLVE   *Use the plan above to calculate the unknown.*

molar mass of $Ba(NO_3)_2$

$= 137.33 \text{ g/mol} + 2(14.01 \text{ g/mol}) + 6(16.00 \text{ g/mol})$

$= 261.35 \text{ g/mol}$

$62.5 \text{ g Ba(NO}_3)_2 \times \dfrac{1 \text{ mol Ba(NO}_3)_2}{261.35 \text{ g Ba(NO}_3)_2}$

$= 0.239 \text{ mol Ba(NO}_3)_2$

The mass of the solvent is 1.00 kg, so the concentration of the formula unit $Ba(NO_3)_2$ is 0.239 m. The dissociation equation for barium nitrate is as follows.

$$Ba(NO_3)_2 \xrightarrow{\text{H}_2\text{O}} Ba^+ + 2NO_3^-$$

Each formula unit of $Ba(NO_3)_2$ yields 3 ions in solution.

Therefore, the concentration of ions is $3 \times 0.239 \ m = 0.717 \ m$.

$\Delta t_f \text{ (expected)} = K_f m$

                  $= (-1.86°C/m)(0.717 \ m)$

                  $= -1.33°C$

4 CHECK YOUR WORK   *Check the final answer to see if it is reasonable.*

The correct units were used in each step and the final answer has the correct number of significant digits.

G. What is the expected freezing-point depression for a solution that contains 2.0 mol of magnesium sulfate dissolved in 1.0 kg of water?

What is the molality of $MgSO_4$ formula units in the solution? _____

What is the dissociation equation for magnesium sulfate?

_____

What is the molality of ions in the solution? _____

$\Delta t_f = K_f m =$

H. What is the expected boiling-point elevation of water for a solution that contains 150 g of sodium chloride dissolved in 1.0 kg of water?

What is the molar mass of sodium chloride? _____

How many moles of sodium chloride are in the solution?

```
┌─────────────────────────────────────────────────┐
│                                                   │
│                                                   │
│                                                   │
└─────────────────────────────────────────────────┘
```

What is the molality of the NaCl formula units in the solution? _____

What is the dissociation equation for sodium chloride?

_____

What is the molality of ions in the solution? _____

$\Delta t_b = K_b m =$

I. The freezing point of an aqueous sodium chloride solution is $-0.20°C$. What is the molality of the solution?

$$m = \frac{(\quad)}{(\quad)} = \frac{(\qquad)}{(\qquad)} = \underline{\qquad} \; m \text{ ions in solution}$$

The molality of the solution is _____ m NaCl.

Actual Values for Electrolyte Solutions

The method shown on the previous two pages calculates the expected value of a colligative property for an electrolytic solution. The actual values for strong electrolytes are almost the same, but not exactly the same, as these expected values. The table below shows some actual values.

Molal Freezing-Point Depressions for Aqueous Solutions of Ionic Solutes				
Solute	Concentration (m)	Δt_f observed (°C)	Δt_f nonelectrolyte solution (°C)	$\dfrac{\Delta t_f \text{ observed}}{\Delta t_f \text{ nonelectrolyte solution}}$
KCl	0.1	−0.345	−0.186	1.85
	0.01	−0.0361	−0.0186	1.94
	0.001	−0.00366	−0.00186	1.97
MgSO$_4$	0.1	−0.225	−0.186	1.21
	0.01	−0.0285	−0.0186	1.53
	0.001	−0.00338	−0.00186	1.82
BaCl$_2$	0.1	−0.470	−0.186	2.53
	0.01	−0.0503	−0.0186	2.70
	0.001	−0.00530	−0.00186	2.84

The table shows that a dilute concentration of an electrolyte that forms two ions in solution, such as KCl or MgSO$_4$, has a freezing-point depression that is almost twice the nonelectrolytic value. An electrolyte that forms three ions, such as BaCl$_2$, has a value almost three times as large.

The table also shows that as concentration decreases, the actual value is closer to the expected value. This suggests a reason for the actual values not being the same as the expected values. Ions in solution feel some attraction to ions of opposite charge as they move through a fluid. This attraction partially hinders the movement of the charges and lowers the solute's effective concentration. In more dilute solutions a solute particle encounters oppositely charged ions less frequently, so the attraction has less effect.

Another trend the table shows is that ions of greater charge cause values that vary farther from expected values. Both KCl and MgSO$_4$ form two moles of ions in solution, but the charges on the Mg^{2+} and SO$_4^{2-}$ ions are twice that of K$^+$ and Cl$^-$ ions. The variance between expected values and actual values is larger because the attractive forces between ions in MgSO$_4$ solutions are greater.

✓ READING CHECK

7. What attractive force accounts for electrolytic solutions having lower values of colligative properties than expected?

_____

_____

_____

VOCABULARY

1. What colligative property is displayed by each of the following situations?

a. Antifreeze is added to a car's cooling system to prevent freezing when

the temperature is below 0°C. _____

b. Ice melts on sidewalks after salt has been spread on them. _____

REVIEW

2. Two moles of a nonelectrolytic solute are dissolved in 1 kg of an unknown solvent. The solution freezes at 7.8°C below its normal freezing point.

a. What is the molal freezing-point constant of the unknown solvent? _____

b. Suggest a possible identity of the solvent. _____

3. If two solutions of equal amounts in a U-tube are separated by a semipermeable membrane, will the level of the more-concentrated solution or the less-concentrated solution rise?

_____

_____

4. a. Calculate the expected freezing-point depression of a 0.200 *m* KNO$_3$ solution.

_____

b. Will the value you calculated match the actual freezing-point depression for this solution? Why or why not?

_____

_____

Critical Thinking

5. INFERRING RELATIONSHIPS The freezing-point depressions of aqueous solutions A, B, and C are –2.3°C, –1.2°C, and –4.1°C, respectively. Predict the order of the boiling-point elevations of these solutions, from lowest to highest. Explain your ranking.

_____

_____

_____

Math Tutor
BOILING AND FREEZING POINTS OF SOLUTIONS

The presence of a nonvolatile solute causes the freezing point of a solution to be lower and the boiling point to be higher than those of the pure solvent. The freezing-point depression, Δt_f, is the amount that the freezing point is lowered. It is calculated by using the formula $\Delta t_f = K_f m$. The boiling-point elevation, Δt_b, is the amount that the boiling point is elevated. It is found by using the equation $\Delta t_b = K_b m$. To determine Δt_f or Δt_b, you need to know the molal concentration of the solution, m (moles of solute per kilogram of solvent). You also need to know the molal freezing-point constant, K_f, or the molal boiling-point constant, K_b.

Problem-Solving TIPS

- Make sure that you find the molal concentration, not the molar concentration.
- For electrolytes, calculate the total number of moles of ions in solution.

SAMPLE

What is the theoretical boiling point of a solution of 247 g of potassium chloride, KCl, dissolved in 2.90 kg of water? Potassium chloride is a strong electrolyte.

First, determine the molality of the KCl that dissolved. The amount of KCl must be converted from grams to moles, using the molar mass of KCl (74.55 g/mol).

$$247 \text{ g KCl} = 247 \text{ g KCl} \times \frac{1 \text{ mol KCl}}{74.55 \text{ g KCl}} = 3.31 \text{ mol KCl}$$

$$\text{molality} = \frac{\text{solute particles (mol)}}{\text{mass of solvent (kg)}} = \frac{3.31 \text{ mol KCl}}{2.90 \text{ kg H}_2\text{O}} = 1.14 \text{ } m$$

Because KCl is an electrolyte, the total moles of ions in solution must be determined. The dissociation equation is as follows.

$$\text{KCl}(s) \xrightarrow{\text{H}_2\text{O}} \text{K}^+(aq) + \text{Cl}^-(aq)$$

So, 2 mol of ions form for every 1 mol of solute. Therefore, a 1.14 m solution will form a solution with an ion concentration of $2 \times 1.14 \text{ } m = 2.28 \text{ } m$.

Finally, calculate the boiling-point elevation for the solution. The molal boiling point constant for water is 0.51°C/m.

$$\Delta t_b = K_b m = (0.51°\text{C}/m)(2.28 \text{ } m) = 1.16°\text{C}$$

The boiling point is the sum of the solvent's boiling point and Δt_b.

$$\text{boiling point of solution} = 100.00°\text{C} + 1.16°\text{C} = 101.16°\text{C}$$

Practice Problems: Chapter Review practice problems 16–18

1. How many moles of ions are contained in 1 L of a 1 M solution of the
following compounds?

a. KCl _____   **b.** $Mg(NO_3)_2$ _____

2. Use the "Solubility Guidelines" table in this chapter to predict whether each
of the following compounds is considered soluble or insoluble.

a. $(NH_4)_2S$ _____   **c.** FeS _____

b. $PbCl_2$ (in cold water) _____   **d.** $Al_2(SO_4)_3$ _____

3. What is a net ionic equation?

_____

_____

4. What determines the strength of a solute as an electrolyte?

_____

_____

5. Distinguish between the use of the terms *strong* and *weak* and the use of the
terms *dilute* and *concentrated* when describing electrolyte solutions.

_____

_____

_____

6. How does the presence of a nonvolatile solute affect each of the following
properties of the solvent in which the solute is dissolved?

a. vapor pressure _____

b. freezing point _____

c. boiling point _____

d. osmotic pressure _____

7. What is the relationship between the freezing-point depression, Δt_f, for a
solution with x concentration of solute and one with $2x$ concentration?

_____

_____

_____

8. Why does the level of the more-concentrated solution rise when two solutions are separated by a semipermeable membrane?

_____

_____

9. Write the equation for the dissolution of each of the following ionic compounds in water.

a. $MgCl_2 \longrightarrow$ _____

b. $Na_2SO_4 \longrightarrow$ _____

10. Using the "Solubility Guidelines" table, write the balanced chemical equation and the net ionic equation for the reaction of aqueous mercury(II) chloride and aqueous potassium sulfide.

_____

_____

11. What precipitate, if any, forms when aqueous copper(II) chloride reacts with

aqueous ammonium phosphate? _____

12. Identify the spectator ions in the reaction between KCl and $AgNO_3$ in an

aqueous solution. _____

13. Copper(II) chloride and lead(II) nitrate react in aqueous solutions by double displacement.

a. Write the balanced chemical equation, the overall ionic equation, and the net ionic equation for this reaction.

_____

_____

_____

b. If 13.45 g of copper(II) chloride react, what is the maximum amount of precipitate that could be formed?

14. How many grams of antifreeze, $C_2H_4(OH)_2$, would be required per 500. g of water to prevent the water from freezing at a temperature of $-20.0°C$?

15. Pure benzene, C_6H_6, freezes at $5.45°C$. A solution containing 7.24 g $C_2Cl_4H_2$ in 115 g of benzene freezes at $3.55°C$. Based on these data, what is the molal freezing-point constant for benzene?

16. Determine the molality of a water solution that has the boiling point of $102.805°C$.

17. Determine the expected boiling point of a solution made by dissolving 25.0 g of barium chloride in 0.150 kg of water.

18. Experimental data for a 1.00 m MgI_2 aqueous solution indicate an actual change in the freezing point of water of $-4.78°C$.

a. Find the expected change in the freezing point of water.

b. Suggest a reason for the discrepancy between the experimental and the expected values.

CHAPTER 14

Acids and Bases

Key Concepts

Section 1 *Properties of Acids and Bases*

What are the general properties of acids and bases?

What are the names of some common acids?

What is Arrhenius's theory of ionization?

How do strong and weak acids and bases differ?

Section 2 *Acid-Base Theories*

What are Brønsted-Lowry acids and bases?

What are Lewis acids and bases?

Section 3 *Acid-Base Reactions*

What are conjugate acids and amphoteric compounds?

How does the process of neutralization work?

What is acid rain and how does it affect the environment?

Review Previous Concepts

1. What is the relationship between the chemical formula and the chemical name of a compound?

_____

_____

_____

_____

2. What happens when a molecular compound ionizes in an aqueous solution?

_____

_____

_____

_____

SECTION 14.1

Properties of Acids and Bases

Acids and bases are special chemical compounds. You may already be familiar with many acids. Most often when you detect a sour taste in food, it is an acid that you are tasting. Here are some examples of acids in foods.

- *Lactic acid* is found in milk.

- *Acetic acid* is found in vinegar and fermented foods.

- *Phosphoric acid* gives a tart flavor to many carbonated beverages.

- *Citric acid* is found in citrus fruits such as lemons, oranges, and grapefruits.

- *Malic acid* is found in apples.

- *Tartaric acid* is found in grape juice.

Bases, another type of chemical compound, have a bitter taste. Bases, such as those listed below, are found in many household products.

- *Ammonia* in solution with water is useful for all types of general cleaning.

- *Lye,* which is the common name of sodium hydroxide, NaOH, is found in some commercial cleaners.

- *Magnesium hydroxide,* $Mg(OH)_2$, is called milk of magnesia when in suspension with water. It is used as an antacid to relieve stomach pain.

- *Aluminum hydroxide,* $Al(OH)_3$, and *sodium hydrogen carbonate,* $NaHCO_3$, are also commonly found in antacids.

KEY TERMS

binary acid	Arrhenius base
oxyacid	strong acid
Arrhenius acid	weak acid

Benzoic acid, $HC_7H_5O_2$
Sorbic acid, $HC_6H_7O_2$
Phosphoric acid, H_3PO_4
Carbonic acid, H_2CO_3

Citric acid, $H_3C_6H_5O_7$
Ascorbic acid, $H_2C_6H_6O_6$

(a)

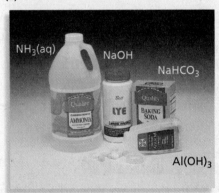

$NH_3(aq)$ NaOH $NaHCO_3$

$Al(OH)_3$

(b)

(a) Fruits, fruit juices, and carbonated beverages all contain acids.
(b) Household cleaners and antacids contain bases.

✓ READING CHECK

1. List three common objects or substances that contain an acid and three that contain a base.

_____

_____

Acids are identified by their properties.

Acids were first recognized as a distinct class of compounds because of the common properties of their aqueous solutions. Those properties are summarized below.

1. **Aqueous solutions of acids have a sour taste.** Although many fruits contain acids, acids are not always safe to eat. Acids are corrosive, which means they break down body tissue or clothing. Many acids are also poisonous.

2. **Acids change the color of acid-base indicators.** When pH paper is used as an indicator, the paper turns certain colors in acidic solutions, as shown in the photograph.

3. **Some acids react with active metals and release hydrogen gas.** Recall that metals can be ordered in terms of an activity series. Metals above hydrogen in the series undergo single-displacement reactions with certain acids. Hydrogen gas is formed as a product. One example of this type of reaction is shown when barium reacts with sulfuric acid.

$$Ba(s) + H_2SO_4(aq) \longrightarrow BaSO_4(s) + H_2(g)$$

4. **Acids react with bases to produce salts and water.** When equal amounts of acids and bases react, the acid is *neutralized*. This means that the properties listed above are no longer present. The products of this neutralization reaction are water and an ionic compound called a salt.

5. **Acids conduct electric current.** All acids are electrolytes because they separate into ions in water. Some acids are strong electrolytes because they completely ionize. Other acids are weak electrolytes.

TIP Taste should NEVER be used as a test to identify or analyze any chemical substance.

A strip of pH paper dipped into vinegar turns red, showing that vinegar is an acid.

☑ READING CHECK

2. Why do all acids conduct electric current?

_____

_____

Acid Nomenclature

A **binary acid** is an acid that contains only two different elements: hydrogen and a highly electronegative element. The hydrogen halides are all binary acids. The procedure for naming binary acids is demonstrated at the top of the next page for the acidic compound hydrobromic acid, HBr.

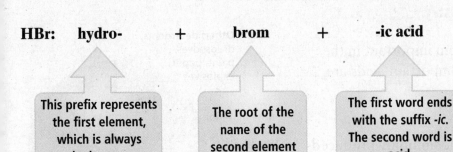

HBr: hydro-   +   brom   +   -ic acid

This prefix represents the first element, which is always hydrogen.

The root of the name of the second element

The first word ends with the suffix -ic. The second word is acid.

PRACTICE

Name the following binary acids.

A. HF _____

B. HCl _____

C. HI _____

D. H_2S _____

An **oxyacid** is an acid that is composed of hydrogen, oxygen, and a third element, usually a nonmetal. Oxyacids are one type of ternary acid. *Ternary* means composed of three parts, just as the term *binary* means composed of two parts. The table below shows some common oxyacids. The chemical formula usually includes one or more hydrogen atoms and a polyatomic anion. The name of the anion is related to the name of the acid.

(a) H_3PO_4

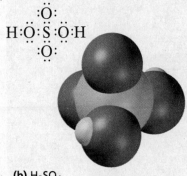

(b) H_2SO_4

The structure of (a) phosphoric acid and (b) sulfuric acid is shown. The hydrogen atoms are bonded to the oxygen atoms in oxyacids.

Names of Common Oxyacids and Oxyanions

Formula	Acid name	Anion
CH_3COOH	acetic acid	CH_3COO^-, acetate
H_2CO_3	carbonic acid	CO_3^{2-}, carbonate
$HClO$	hypochlorous acid	ClO^-, hypochlorite
$HClO_2$	chlorous acid	ClO_2^-, chlorite
$HClO_3$	chloric acid	ClO_3^-, chlorate
$HClO_4$	perchloric acid	ClO_4^-, perchlorate
HIO_3	iodic acid	IO_3^-, iodate
HNO_2	nitrous acid	NO_2^-, nitrite
HNO_3	nitric acid	NO_3^-, nitrate
H_3PO_3	phosphorous acid	PO_3^{3-}, phosphite
H_3PO_4	phosphoric acid	PO_4^{3-}, phosphate
H_2SO_3	sulfurous acid	SO_3^{2-}, sulfite
H_2SO_4	sulfuric acid	SO_4^{2-}, sulfate

Some acids are useful in industry.

The properties of acids make them important in the laboratory and in industry. Five important acids are discussed below.

Sulfuric Acid

Sulfuric acid, H_2SO_4, is the most commonly produced industrial chemical in the world. More than 37 million metric tons are made each year in the United States alone. Sulfuric acid is used in large quantities in oil refineries and in extracting metals from ores. It is involved in the production of paper, paint, detergents, fertilizers, and automobile batteries.

Because it attracts water, sulfuric acid is often used to dehydrate (remove water from) other compounds. It can dehydrate nonreactive gases, sugar, and some carbon compounds. Because sulfuric acid also attacks the carbon compounds in skin, it can cause serious burns.

Nitric Acid

Pure nitric acid, HNO_3, is a volatile, unstable liquid. Forming an aqueous solution of nitric acid makes it more stable. These solutions are widely used in industry. The producers of rubber, plastics, dyes, fertilizers, and medical drugs use these solutions.

Nitric acid solutions are initially colorless, but upon standing they turn yellow as a portion of the acid decomposes into NO_2 gas. Nitric acid can stain proteins yellow, as shown below. It has a suffocating odor and can stain and burn skin.

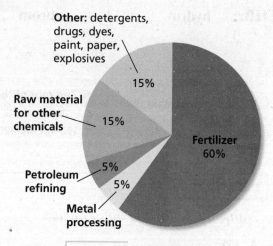

Other: detergents, drugs, dyes, paint, paper, explosives — 15%

Raw material for other chemicals — 15%

Fertilizer 60%

Petroleum refining — 5%

Metal processing — 5%

The pie chart shows the uses of sulfuric acid in the U.S.

✓ READING CHECK

3. Why are sulfuric acid and nitric acid dangerous?

_____

_____

_____

_____

_____

Concentrated nitric acid can stain a feather.

Phosphoric Acid

Phosphorus, along with nitrogen and potassium, is an essential element for plants and animals. The bulk of phosphoric acid, H_3PO_4, produced each year is used directly for making fertilizers and animal feed. Dilute phosphoric acid has a pleasant but sour taste and is not toxic. It is used as a flavoring agent in beverages and as a cleaning agent for dairy equipment. Phosphoric acid is also important in the manufacture of detergents and ceramics.

Hydrochloric Acid

The stomach produces hydrochloric acid, HCl, to aid in digestion. In industry, hydrochloric acid is important for "pickling" iron and steel. Pickling is the immersion of metals in acids to remove surface impurities. This acid is also used as a cleaning agent, in food processing, in getting magnesium from sea water, and in the production of other chemicals.

Concentrated solutions of hydrochloric acid, also known as *muriatic acid,* can be found in hardware stores. It is used to correct acidity in swimming pools and to clean masonry.

Acetic Acid

Pure acetic acid, CH_3COOH, is a clear, colorless, and pungent liquid known as *glacial acetic acid.* This name results from pure acetic acid having a freezing point of 17°C. It can form crystals in a cold room. Fermentation of certain plants produces vinegars containing acetic acid. White vinegar contains 4% to 8% acetic acid.

Acetic acid is important industrially in producing chemicals used in the manufacture of plastics. It is also a raw material in the production of food supplements. For example, it is used to make lysine, an essential amino acid. Acetic acid also helps prevent the growth of molds and other fungi.

Top Ten Chemicals Produced in the U.S.			
Rank	Chemical	Physical state	Formula
1	sulfuric acid	*l*	H_2SO_4
2	nitrogen	*g*	N_2
3	oxygen	*g*	O_2
4	ethylene	*g*	C_2H_4
5	calcium oxide (lime)	*s*	CaO
6	ammonia	*g*	NH_3
7	phosphoric acid	*l*	H_3PO_4
8	sodium hydroxide	*s*	NaOH
9	propylene	*g*	C_3H_6
10	chlorine	*g*	Cl_2

Zinc and hydrochloric acid react in a single-replacement reaction and hydrogen gas is released.

✓ READING CHECK

4. Which of these five acids are used in fertilizers?

The properties of bases differ from those of acids.

Like acids, bases in the form of an aqueous solution have several common properties. Those properties are summarized below.

1. **Aqueous solutions of bases taste bitter.** You may have noticed the bitterness of a base if you have ever gotten soap in your mouth. Many bases also break down tissues or cause burns.

2. **Bases change the color of acid-base indicators.** When pH paper is used as an indicator, the paper turns certain colors in basic solutions, as shown in the photograph. The color is always different from the color the indicator turns in an acid.

3. **Dilute aqueous solutions of bases feel slippery.** Soap is an example of this property of bases. A wet bar of soap is slippery, and it also slides along your skin easily.

4. **Bases react with acids to produce salts and water.** When equal amounts of acids and bases react, the base is also said to be *neutralized*. The properties listed above are no longer present in the base. The products of this neutralization reaction between an acid and a base are water and a salt.

5. **Bases conduct electric current.** Just like acids, all bases are electrolytes because they separate into ions in water. Some bases are strong electrolytes and others are weak electrolytes.

 **Remember**

Taste should NEVER be used as a test to identify or analyze any chemical substance.

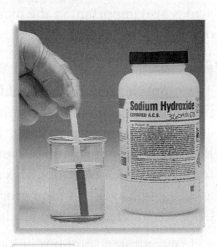

A strip of pH paper dipped into sodium hydroxide turns blue, showing that sodium hydroxide is a base.

Critical Thinking

5. **Compare and Contrast** Use the properties of bases listed above and the properties of acids listed earlier in this chapter to determine how acids and bases are alike and how they are different.

_____

_____

_____

_____

_____

Arrhenius acids and bases produce ions in solution.

Svante Arrhenius was a Swedish chemist who lived from 1859 to 1927. He understood that acids and bases conducted electric current. To explain this property, he theorized that acids and bases formed ions in solution. He defined two types of substances, depending on how they affected solutions in water.

- An **Arrhenius acid** is a chemical compound that increases the concentration of hydrogen ions, H^+, in aqueous solutions. This increase is caused by the ionization of the acid, leading to the formation of H^+ cations.

- An **Arrhenius base** is a chemical compound that increases the concentration of hydroxide ions, OH^-, in aqueous solutions. Some bases dissociate in solution to release hydroxide ions, causing this increase. Other bases react with water molecules to remove a hydrogen ion, resulting in more hydroxide ions in the solution.

Aqueous Solutions of Acids

Arrhenius acids are molecular compounds with ionizable hydrogen atoms. The solutions of these compounds in water are called *aqueous acids*.

Acid molecules are polar enough to be attracted to the water molecules. This attraction is strong enough to pull the hydrogen ion apart from the acid. Negatively charged anions are left behind. As explained in the chapter "Ions in Aqueous Solutions," the hydrogen ion does not remain in solution by itself. It forms a hydronium ion, H_3O^+, by combining with a water molecule. The ionization of nitric acid, HNO_3, is shown below.

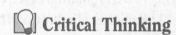 **Critical Thinking**

6. Apply What are the products of the ionization of hydrochloric acid, HCl, in water?

_____

_____

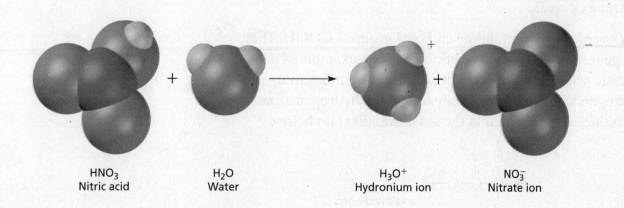

| HNO₃ | H₂O | H₃O⁺ | NO₃⁻ |
| Nitric acid | Water | Hydronium ion | Nitrate ion |

Strength of Acids

The strength of an acid depends on the polarity of the bond between hydrogen and the element to which it is bonded. It also depends on how easily that bond can be broken. Acid strength increases with increasing polarity and decreasing bond energy.

A **strong acid** is one that ionizes completely in aqueous solutions. A strong acid is also a strong electrolyte. Three examples of strong acids are perchloric acid, $HClO_4$, hydrochloric acid, HCl, and nitric acid, HNO_3. In all of these acids, 100% of the acid molecules are ionized.

A **weak acid** is an acid that releases few H^+ ions in aqueous solution. The aqueous solution of a weak acid contains hydronium ions, anions, and dissolved acid molecules. Weak acids exist in a state of equilibrium between the processes of ionization and its reverse reaction (de-ionization).

One example of a weak acid is hydrocyanic acid. For every 100 000 molecules in a 1 M HCN solution, 99 998 remain as HCN and 2 molecules ionize. The chemical equation that represents the equilibrium between ionization of HCN and the reverse process is as follows.

$$HCN(aq) + H_2O(l) \rightleftharpoons H_3O^+(aq) + CN^-(aq)$$

The table above shows some strong acids and weak acids. Note that the number of hydrogen atoms in the chemical formula of the acid does not determine whether or not an acid is strong or weak.

Organic acids contain the carboxyl group $-COOH$. They are generally weak acids. Acetic acid is one example of an organic acid. Each molecule of acetic acid contains four hydrogen atoms. However, only one of the hydrogen atoms is ionizable, as highlighted in the structural diagram below.

acidic hydrogen

Common Aqueous Acids
Strong acids
$HI + H_2O \rightarrow H_3O^+ + I^-$
$HClO_4 + H_2O \rightarrow H_3O^+ + ClO_4^-$
$HBr + H_2O \rightarrow H_3O^+ + Br^-$
$HCl + H_2O \rightarrow H_3O^+ + Cl^-$
$H_2SO_4 + H_2O \rightarrow H_3O^+ + HSO_4^-$
$HClO_3 + H_2O \rightarrow H_3O^+ + ClO_3^-$
Weak acids
$HSO_4^- + H_2O \rightleftharpoons H_3O^+ + SO_4^{2-}$
$H_3PO_4 + H_2O \rightleftharpoons H_3O^+ + H_2PO_4^-$
$HF + H_2O \rightleftharpoons H_3O^+ + F^-$
$CH_3COOH + H_2O \rightleftharpoons H_3O^+ + CH_3COO^-$
$H_2CO_3 + H_2O \rightleftharpoons H_3O^+ + HCO_3^-$
$H_2S + H_2O \rightleftharpoons H_3O^+ + HS^-$
$HCN + H_2O \rightleftharpoons H_3O^+ + CN^-$
$HCO_3^- + H_2O \rightleftharpoons H_3O^+ + CO_3^{2-}$

LOOKING CLOSER

7. Which would be a better conductor of electricity, a strong acid or a weak acid?

Aqueous Solutions of Bases

Most bases are ionic compounds containing metal cations and the hydroxide anion, OH^-. Because these bases are ionic, they dissociate when dissolved in water. When a base completely dissociates in water to yield aqueous OH^- ions, the solution is referred to as a strong base. Sodium hydroxide, NaOH, is a common strong base used in the laboratory. Its dissociation equation is shown below.

$$NaOH(s) \xrightarrow{H_2O} Na^+(aq) + OH^-(aq)$$

You have learned that Group 1 elements are called alkali metals. This group gets its name from the fact that lithium hydroxide, sodium hydroxide, potassium hydroxide, rubidium hydroxide, and cesium hydroxide are all basic solutions. Another word for basic is alkaline.

Not all bases are ionic compounds. Many household cleaners use ammonia, NH_3, which is molecular. Ammonia is a base because it produces hydroxide ions when reacting with water molecules, as shown in the equation below.

$$NH_3(aq) + H_2O(l) \rightleftharpoons NH_4^+(aq) + OH^-(aq)$$

✓ READING CHECK

8. Describe two ways that basic compounds in solutions with water result in an increase in hydroxide ions.

_____

_____

_____

Remember

Dissociation of ionic compounds is similar to the ionization of molecules but not the same thing. Dissociation involves the splitting of two ions that are bonded. Ionization is the formation of an ion or ions from a neutrally charged particle.

Common Aqueous Bases	
Strong bases	**Weak bases**
$Ca(OH)_2 \rightarrow Ca^{2+} + 2OH^-$	$NH_3 + H_2O \rightleftharpoons NH_4^+ + OH^-$
$Sr(OH)_2 \rightarrow Sr^{2+} + 2OH^-$	$C_6H_5NH_2 + H_2O \rightleftharpoons C_6H_5NH_3^+ + OH^-$
$Ba(OH)_2 \rightarrow Ba^{2+} + 2OH^-$	
$NaOH \rightarrow Na^+ + OH^-$	
$KOH \rightarrow K^+ + OH^-$	
$RbOH \rightarrow Rb^+ + OH^-$	
$CsOH \rightarrow Cs^+ + OH^-$	

Strength of Bases

As with acids, the strength of a base also depends on the extent to which the base dissociates or adds hydroxide ions to the solution. Potassium hydroxide, KOH, is an example of a strong base. Strong bases are strong electrolytes, just as strong acids are strong electrolytes. A strong base completely dissociates into its ions in dilute aqueous solutions.

$$NaOH(s) \xrightarrow{H_2O} Na^+(aq) + OH^-(aq)$$

Bases that are not very soluble do not produce a large number of hydroxide ions when added to water. One example is copper hydroxide, $Cu(OH)_2$, as shown in the diagram below. The number of hydroxide ions in an undissolved compound does not affect the strength of the base. Only those hydroxide ions that dissolve and dissociate contribute to the strength of the base.

Bases that are highly soluble can still be weak bases if they form few ions in solution. Ammonia is one example of a weak base that is highly soluble. Many organic compounds that contain nitrogen atoms are also weak bases. For example, the weak base codeine, $C_{18}H_{21}NO_3$, is a pain reliever and cough suppressant found in prescription cough medicine.

CONNECT

Many people are unaware of the level of acidity of the tap water in their homes. Acidic water can cause damage to pipes, increasing the amount of dissolved lead or copper in the water. Lead poisoning is especially dangerous for young children. Some noticeable effects of highly acidic water are blue rings in sinks, water heaters breaking unexpectedly, or tropical fish that die suddenly.

✓ READING CHECK

9. Why is solubility not necessarily related to the strength of a base?

_____

_____

_____

_____

Chloride ion, Cl^-

$Na^+(aq) + OH^-(aq)$

Chloride ion, Cl^-

Sodium ion, Na^+

Copper(II) ion, Cu^{2+}

Water molecule, H_2O

$Cu^{2+}(aq) + 2OH^-(aq) \longrightarrow Cu(OH)_2(s)$

$Cu(OH)_2(s)$

Sodium hydrozide, NaOH, is mixed with a solution of copper chloride, $CuCl_2$. The hydroxides of most d-block metals are nearly insoluble in water, as shown by the gelatinous precipitate, copper(II) hydroxide, $Cu(OH)_2$, in the beaker on the right.

SECTION 14.1 REVIEW

VOCABULARY

1. a. Why are strong acids also strong electrolytes?

b. Is every strong electrolyte also a strong acid?

REVIEW

2. Name the following acids.

a. HBrO ____________ **b.** $HBrO_3$ ____________

3. What are five general properties of aqueous acids?

4. Name some common acids and common bases.

Critical Thinking

5. RELATING IDEAS A classmate states, "All compounds containing H atoms are acids, and all compounds containing OH groups are bases." Do you agree? Give evidence to support your answer.

SECTION 14.2

Acid-Base Theories

Scientists have found that substances can behave like acids or bases even if they are not in a water solution. Because the Arrhenius definitions rely on water being the solvent, other theories are needed to explain these substances.

KEY TERMS

Brønsted-Lowry acid
Brønsted-Lowry base
Brønsted-Lowry acid-base reaction
monoprotic acid
polyprotic acid
diprotic acid
triprotic acid
Lewis acid
Lewis base
Lewis acid-base reaction

Brønsted-Lowry acids and bases donate or accept protons.

In 1923, two chemists expanded the Arrhenius definition of acids and bases. One was Danish chemist J. N. Brønsted and the other was English chemist T. M. Lowry.

Brønsted-Lowry Acids A **Brønsted-Lowry acid** is a molecule or ion that is a proton donor. All Arrhenius acids are also Brønsted-Lowry acids, because H^+ ions are protons. However, other substances can donate protons to another substance besides water.

For example, hydrochloric acid behaves like an acid when it is in solution with ammonia. Recall that hydrochloric acid donates a hydrogen ion to water to form the hydronium ion. In a similar way, hydrochloric acid donates a proton to ammonia to form the ammonium ion.

$$HCl(g) + NH_3(l) \longrightarrow NH_4^+(l) + Cl^-(l)$$

$$H\!:\!\ddot{C}l\!: + H\!:\!\ddot{N}\!:\!H \rightarrow \left[H\!:\!\overset{H}{\underset{H}{\ddot{N}}}\!:\!H \right]^+ + :\!\ddot{C}l\!:^-$$

Water can also act as a Brønsted-Lowry acid. When water reacts with ammonia it donates a hydrogen ion to form an ammonium ion and a hydroxide ion.

$$H_2O(l) + NH_3(aq) \rightleftharpoons NH_4^+(aq) + OH^-(aq)$$

$$H\!:\!\ddot{O}\!: + H\!:\!\ddot{N}\!:\!H \rightleftharpoons \left[H\!:\!\overset{H}{\underset{H}{\ddot{N}}}\!:\!H \right]^+ + \left[:\!\overset{..}{\underset{H}{\ddot{O}}}\!: \right]^-$$

READING CHECK

1. What is the difference between a Brønsted-Lowry acid and an Arrhenius acid?

Brønsted-Lowry Bases A **Brønsted-Lowry base** is a molecule or ion that accepts a donated proton. Ammonia is a Brønsted-Lowry base in both of the reactions shown above. However, many Arrhenius bases are not, strictly speaking, Brønsted-Lowry bases. Sodium hydroxide, NaOH, does not accept a proton. Its hydroxide ion, OH^-, is the particle that accepts a proton in solution and becomes a water molecule.

In a **Brønsted-Lowry acid-base reaction** protons are transferred from one reactant (the acid) to another (the base). The two reactions discussed on the previous page are examples of Brønsted-Lowry acid-base reactions. The photograph at the right shows another acid-base reaction.

Vapors of hydrogen chloride, HCl, and ammonia, NH_3, react in air. The resulting cloud is solid ammonium chloride that is dispersed in the air.

 **READING CHECK**

2. What is the difference between a Brønsted-Lowry base and an Arrhenius base?

_____

_____

Monoprotic and Polyprotic Acids

Brønsted-Lowry acids are classified by how many protons they can donate per molecule. These acids are either classified as monoprotic acids or polyprotic acids.

- A **monoprotic acid** can only donate one proton (hydrogen ion) per molecule.

- A **polyprotic acid** can donate more than one proton per molecule. Polyprotic acids are further classified by the exact number of protons they can donate. A **diprotic acid** can donate two protons per molecule. A **triprotic acid** can donate three protons per molecule.

TIP The prefixes on these vocabulary terms are the same as those used to name binary compounds, . The prefix *poly-* means "many."

Perchloric acid, $HClO_4$, hydrochloric acid, HCl, and nitric acid, HNO_3, are all monoprotic acids. The following equation shows how a molecule of the monoprotic acid HCl donates a proton to a water molecule. The HCl ionizes to form H_3O^+ ions and Cl^- ions.

$$HCl(g) + H_2O(l) \longrightarrow H_3O^+(aq) + Cl^-(aq)$$

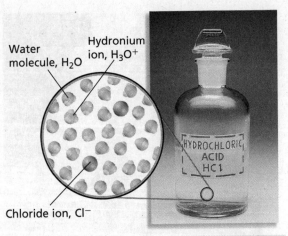

Water molecule, H₂O

Hydronium ion, H₃O⁺

Chloride ion, Cl⁻

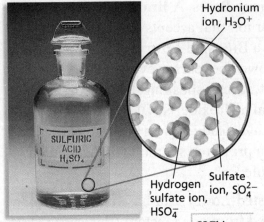

Hydronium ion, H₃O⁺

Sulfate ion, SO₄²⁻

Hydrogen sulfate ion, HSO₄⁻

$$HCl + H_2O \longrightarrow H_3O^+ + Cl^-$$

$$H_2SO_4 + H_2O \longrightarrow H_3O^+ + HSO_4^-$$
$$HSO_4^- + H_2O \rightleftharpoons H_3O^+ + SO_4^{2-}$$

HCl is a strong monoprotic acid. A dilute HCl solution contains hydronium and chloride ions. H_2SO_4 is a strong diprotic acid. A dilute H_2SO_4 solution contains hydrogen sulfate ions from the first ionization, sulfate ions from the second ionization, and hydronium ions from both.

Sulfuric acid, H_2SO_4, and phosphoric acid, H_3PO_4, are examples of polyprotic acids. The ionization of a polyprotic acid occurs in stages. It loses its hydrogen ions one at a time. In polyprotic acids, concentration of ions formed in the first ionization is the greatest. There are lesser concentrations of ions formed in each succeeding step.

Sulfuric acid is a diprotic acid. Its ionization occurs in two stages. In the first stage, the strong acid donates a proton to a water molecule to form a hydronium ion and hydrogen sulfate ions, HSO_4^-. The hydrogen sulfate ion itself is a weak Brønsted-Lowry acid, so it establishes an equilibrium in solution between ionization and the reverse reaction. The stages of sulfuric acid ionization are summarized below.

$$H_2SO_4(aq) + H_2O(l) \longrightarrow H_3O^+(aq) + HSO_4^-(aq)$$

$$HSO_4^-(aq) + H_2O(l) \rightleftharpoons H_3O^+(aq) + SO_4^{2-}(aq)$$

The anion from the first stage becomes the acid in the second stage.

Both stages occur in the same solution. Therefore, there are three types of ions present in the solution at equilibrium: H_3O^+, $HSO_4^-(aq)$ and $SO_4^{2-}(aq)$.

Phosphoric acid is a triprotic acid. It is a weak acid in all three stages of ionization, as shown below.

$$H_3PO_4(aq) + H_2O(l) \rightleftharpoons H_3O^+(aq) + H_2PO_4^-(aq)$$

$$H_2PO_4^-(aq) + H_2O(l) \rightleftharpoons H_3O^+(aq) + HPO_4^{2-}(aq)$$

$$HPO_4^{2-}(aq) + H_2O(l) \rightleftharpoons H_3O^+(aq) + PO_4^{3-}(aq)$$

The anion from the first stage becomes the acid in the second stage.

The anion from the second stage becomes the acid in the third stage.

🔍 **LOOKING CLOSER**

3. Look at the ionization equations for phosphoric acid below. What ions are present in a solution of phosphoric acid at equilibrium?

_____

A Lewis acid or base accepts or donates a pair of electrons.

The Arrhenius and Brønsted-Lowry definitions describe most acids and bases. However, both definitions assume that the acid contains or produces hydrogen ions. A third acid classification includes acids that do not contain hydrogen at all.

A **Lewis acid** is an atom, ion, or molecule that accepts an electron pair to form a covalent bond. In 1923 G. N. Lewis, the American chemist whose name was given to electron-dot structures, introduced this definition of acids. His definition emphasizes the role of electron pairs in acid-base reactions.

The Lewis definition is the broadest of the three acid definitions you have read about so far. It can apply to particles in any phase. Here are some examples of Lewis acids.

1. A bare proton (a hydrogen ion) is a Lewis acid in reactions in which it forms a covalent bond. This includes the HCl reactions discussed earlier in this section where a proton was donated to a water molecules to form a hydronium ion or to an ammonia molecule to form an ammonium ion. However, only the H^+ ion is considered an acid, not the HCl molecule. The equation below shows the H^+ ion forming a covalent bond in an ammonium ion.

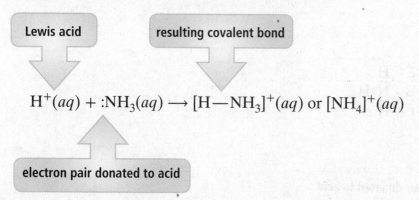

$$H^+(aq) + :NH_3(aq) \longrightarrow [H\text{---}NH_3]^+(aq) \text{ or } [NH_4]^+(aq)$$

2. Any ion that accepts electron pairs from another compound to form a covalent bond is an acid. For example, in this silver reaction, the silver ion accepts two electron pairs and forms covalent bonds with two ammonia molecules.

$$Ag^+(aq) + 2:NH_3(aq) \longrightarrow [H_3N\text{---}Ag\text{---}NH_3]^+(aq) \text{ or}$$

$$[Ag(NH_3)_2]^+(aq)$$

Remember

An electron-dot structure is a representation of a particle that shows the valence electrons of each atom in the particle.

TIP

Note that the total charge on either side of the equation is conserved. For example, the hydrogen ion has a charge of 1+, and the ammonia molecule has no charge. The product, an ammonium ion, has a charge of 1+.

Critical Thinking

4. Infer Explain why the Na^+ ion is not a Lewis acid when it bonds with Cl^- to form NaCl.

_____

_____

_____

_____

_____

_____

3. A compound in which the central atom has three single bonds can react as a Lewis acid. These compounds accept a pair of electrons to form a fourth covalent bond and obtain a stable octet of electrons. Boron trifluoride is a good example of this type of Lewis acid.

$$BF_3(aq) + F^-(aq) \longrightarrow BF_4^-(aq)$$

Acid-Base Definitions		
Type	Acid	Base
Arrhenius	H^+ or H_3O^+ producer	OH^- producer
Brønsted-Lowry	proton (H^+) donor	proton (H^+) acceptor
Lewis	electron-pair acceptor	electron-pair donor

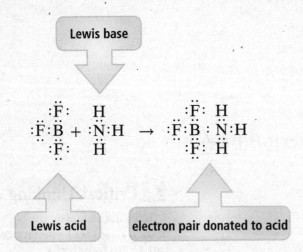

A **Lewis base** is an atom, ion, or molecule that donates an electron pair to form a covalent bond. In the two examples on the preceding page, ammonia molecules were the Lewis bases. In the example above, a fluoride ion is a Lewis base.

The formation of one or more covalent bonds between an electron-pair donor and an electron-pair acceptor is a **Lewis acid-base reaction.** The reaction of boron trifluoride and ammonia is one example of a Lewis acid-base reaction.

Lewis base

Lewis acid   electron pair donated to acid

The three definitions of acids and bases are summarized in the table at the top of the page. Although the definitions are very different, many compounds may be categorized as acids or bases according to all three definitions. For example, ammonia is an Arrhenius base in aqueous solution because of the creation of OH^- ions. It is a Brønsted-Lowry base whenever it accepts a proton in a reaction. It is a Lewis base whenever it donates an electron pair to form a covalent bond.

✓ READING CHECK

5. A Lewis _____ donates an electron pair to a Lewis _____ to form a covalent bond in a Lewis acid-base reaction.

✓ READING CHECK

6. Which definition(s) of acids can apply to substances that are in a phase other than the liquid phase?

_____

_____

SECTION 14.2 REVIEW

VOCABULARY

1. Distinguish between a monoprotic acid, a diprotic acid, and a triprotic acid.

_____

_____

REVIEW

2. Label each reactant in the reaction below as a proton donor or a proton acceptor and as acidic or basic.

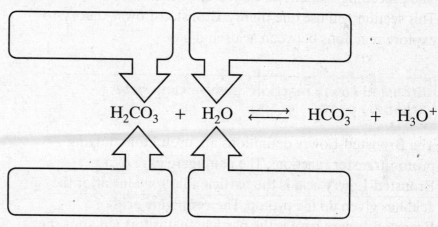

$$H_2CO_3 + H_2O \rightleftharpoons HCO_3^- + H_3O^+$$

3. For the reaction below, label each reactant as an electron pair acceptor or electron pair donor and as a Lewis acid or a Lewis base.

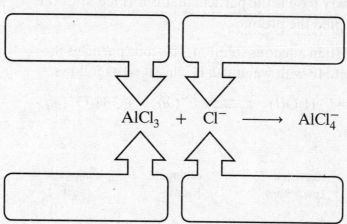

$$AlCl_3 + Cl^- \longrightarrow AlCl_4^-$$

Critical Thinking

4. ANALYZING INFORMATION For the following three reactions, identify the reactants that are Arrhenius bases, Brønsted-Lowry bases, and/or Lewis bases. State which type(s) of bases each reactant is. Explain your answers.

a. $NaOH(s) \longrightarrow Na^+(aq) + OH^-(aq)$ _____

_____

b. $HF(aq) + H_2O(l) \longrightarrow F^-(aq) + H_3O^+(aq)$ _____

_____

c. $H^+(aq) + NH_3(aq) \longrightarrow NH_4^+(aq)$ _____

_____

SECTION 14.3

Acid-Base Reactions

The preceding sections discussed three acid-base theories. This section will use one theory, Brønsted-Lowry theory, to explore reactions between acids and bases.

KEY TERMS

conjugate base   salt
conjugate acid   neutralization
amphoteric

Brønsted-Lowry reactions involve conjugate acid-base pairs.

The Brønsted-Lowry definitions are useful for studying proton-transfer reactions. The **conjugate base** of a Brønsted-Lowry acid is the particle that remains after the acid has given up the proton. The **conjugate acid** of a Brønsted-Lowry base is the particle that is formed after the base has accepted the proton.

Consider HF in aqueous solution. The four particles in the reaction of HF with water can be classified as follows.

$$HF(aq) \;+\; H_2O(l) \;\rightleftharpoons\; F^-(aq) \;+\; H_3O^+(aq)$$

| Brønsted-Lowry acid | Brønsted-Lowry base | conjugate base | conjugate acid |

Brønsted-Lowry reactions are usually equilibrium systems. Both the forward and backward reactions occur. The reaction involves two acid-base pairs, known as *conjugate acid-base pairs.*

LOOKING CLOSER

1. One meaning of the word *conjugate* is "to join together as a pair." Explain how this definition applies to the term *conjugate base*.

_____

_____

_____

_____

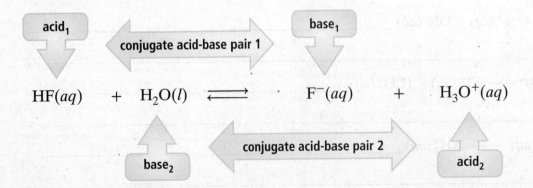

Strength of Conjugate Acids and Bases

One way Brønsted-Lowry theory sheds light on acid-base reactions is in predicting the extent of a reaction. Brønsted-Lowry theory can predict whether the particles on the left side or on the right side of the equation will be more numerous. Consider the reaction of perchloric acid, $HClO_4$, and water.

$$HClO_4(aq) + H_2O(l) \xrightleftharpoons{?} H_3O^+(aq) + ClO_4^-(aq)$$

| stronger acid | stronger base | weaker acid | weaker base |

In solution, perchloric acid is a much stronger acid than hydronium ions. Therefore, protons donated in acid-base reactions in this solution will usually come from perchloric acid molecules. Water is a much stronger base than the perchlorate ion, ClO_4^-. Therefore, water will usually accept the donated protons. The result is that proton donation will almost always favor the forward (left-to-right) reaction.

$$HClO_4(aq) + H_2O(l) \longrightarrow H_3O^+(aq) + ClO_4^-(aq)$$

Now consider a similar reaction of acetic acid and water.

$$CH_3COOH(aq) + H_2O(l) \xrightleftharpoons{?} H_3O^+(aq) + CH_3COO^-(aq)$$

| weaker acid | weaker base | stronger acid | stronger base |

In this reaction, acetic acid is a much weaker acid than hydronium ions. Water is a weaker base than the acetate ion, CH_3COO^-. The result is that the reverse reaction (the right-to-left reaction) is the favored reaction.

$$CH_3COOH(aq) + H_2O(l) \longleftarrow H_3O^+(aq) + CH_3COO^-(aq)$$

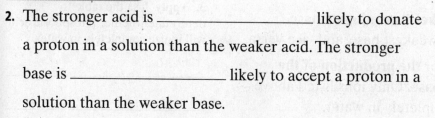

> ### CONNECT
>
> The saying "It's a bitter pill to swallow" may refer to the bitter taste of many medicines. This bitterness results from some of the basic ingredients. One such ingredient, caffeine, $C_8H_{10}O_2N_4$, is a stimulant for the nervous system and the respiratory system. The structure of caffeine includes a nitrogen atom that can accept a proton.

> **TIP** The question mark above the equation indicates that the direction of the reaction is undetermined.

✓ **READING CHECK**

2. The stronger acid is _____ likely to donate a proton in a solution than the weaker acid. The stronger base is _____ likely to accept a proton in a solution than the weaker base.

Relative Strengths of Acids and Bases

	Conjugate acid	Formula	Conjugate base	Formula	
↑	hydriodic acid*	HI	iodide ion	I^-	Increasing base strength
	perchloric acid*	$HClO_4$	perchlorate ion	ClO_4^-	
	hydrobromic acid*	HBr	bromide ion	Br^-	
	hydrochloric acid*	HCl	chloride ion	Cl^-	
	sulfuric acid*	H_2SO_4	hydrogen sulfate ion	HSO_4^-	
	chloric acid*	$HClO_3$	chlorate ion	ClO_3^-	
	nitric acid*	HNO_3	nitrate ion	NO_3^-	
	hydronium ion	H_3O^+	water	H_2O	
	chlorous acid	$HClO_2$	chlorite ion	ClO_2^-	
	hydrogen sulfate ion	HSO_4^-	sulfate ion	SO_4^{2-}	
	phosphoric acid	H_3PO_4	dihydrogen phosphate ion	$H_2PO_4^-$	
	hydrofluoric acid	HF	fluoride ion	F^-	
	acetic acid	CH_3COOH	acetate ion	CH_3COO^-	
	carbonic acid	H_2CO_3	hydrogen carbonate ion	HCO_3^-	
	hydrosulfuric acid	H_2S	hydrosulfide ion	HS^-	
	dihydrogen phosphate ion	$H_2PO_4^-$	hydrogen phosphate ion	HPO_4^{2-}	
	hypochlorous acid	HClO	hypochlorite ion	ClO^-	
	ammonium ion	NH_4^+	ammonia	NH_3	
	hydrogen carbonate ion	HCO_3^-	carbonate ion	CO_3^{2-}	
	hydrogen phosphate ion	HPO_4^{2-}	phosphate ion	PO_4^{3-}	
	water	H_2O	hydroxide ion	OH^-	
	ammonia	NH_3	amide ion†	NH_2^-	
	hydrogen	H_2	hydride ion†	H^-	↓

Increasing acid strength

* Strong acids † Strong bases

The table shows the relative strengths of acids and bases. Two important generalizations can be made about acid-base reactions from the table and from the examples on the previous page.

1. **The stronger an acid, the weaker its conjugate base.** The strongest acid forms the weakest base, and vice versa.

2. **Proton-transfer reactions favor the production of the weaker acid and the weaker base.** Only ions listed above the hydronium ion ionize completely in water.

Critical Thinking

3. Apply Use the table to determine whether phosphoric acid will ionize completely in water.

_____

_____

Some substances act as either acids or bases.

On the previous page, water is listed on both sides of the table. Water is in a special class of compounds that can be both an acid or a base. Any particle that can behave as an acid or a base is called **amphoteric.**

In any ionization reaction in which water accepts a proton to form a hydronium ion, water acts as a base. For example, recall the first stage of ionization for sulfuric acid. As a stronger acid than water, sulfuric acid acts as an acid and water acts as a base.

Water normally acts as a base. However, water acts as an acid in the presence of strong bases, such as hydride ions. In the photograph, calcium hydride crystals react vigorously when water is added to produce hydrogen gas in the reaction: $CaH_2(s) + 2H_2O(l) \rightarrow Ca(OH)_2(aq) + 2H_2(g)$.

$$H_2SO_4(aq) + H_2O(l) \longrightarrow H_3O^+(aq) + HSO_4^-(aq)$$

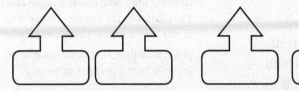

However, consider the reaction of water and ammonia. Water is a stronger acid than ammonia, so water will act as the acid and ammonia as the base.

$$NH_3(g) \ + \ H_2O(l) \ \rightleftharpoons \ NH_4^+(aq) \ + \ OH^-(aq)$$

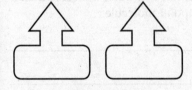

LOOKING CLOSER

4. Label the conjugate acid-base pairs for the two reactions shown to the left.

–OH in a Molecule

Molecular compounds containing –OH groups can be either acidic or amphoteric. The covalently bonded –OH group is called a *hydroxyl group*. A compound with a hydroxyl group is acidic only if a water molecule can attract a hydrogen atom from the –OH group.

The ability of water molecules to attract a proton from this group depends on the polarity of the bond. The polarity of the bond changes depending on the structure of the rest of the molecule. If the structure enhances the polarity of the bond, the compound is more acidic. Oxyacids are examples of these types of compounds.

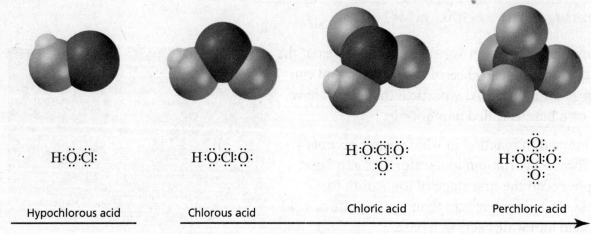

H:Ö:Cl:

Hypochlorous acid

H:Ö:Cl:Ö:

Chlorous acid

H:Ö:Cl:Ö:
      :Ö:

Chloric acid

      :Ö:
H:Ö:Cl:Ö:
      :Ö:

Perchloric acid

→ Acidity increases

The diagram above shows four oxyacids of chlorine. The hydrogen atom is bonded to an oxygen atom. All of the oxygen atoms are bonded to the chlorine atom. Each addition of an oxygen atom adds an atom that is much more electronegative than hydrogen. This pulls the electron density away from the –OH end of the molecule and causes the molecule to become more and more polar. As a result, the acidity of the chlorine oxyacids increases as the number of oxygen atoms increases.

While chlorine oxyacids change in acidity, other compounds can change from basic to acidic depending on the polarity of the –OH group. For example, chromium compounds with –OH groups change from basic to acidic as the number of oxygen atoms increases.

Basic: $Cr(OH)_2$, chromium(II) hydroxide

Amphoteric: $Cr(OH)_3$, chromium(III) hydroxide

Acidic: H_2CrO_4, chromic acid

Each oxyacid of chlorine contains one chlorine atom and one hydrogen atom. They differ in the number of oxygen atoms they contain. The increasing polarity of the O–H bond leads to an increase in the strength of an acid.

✓ READING CHECK

5. Explain why a more polar molecule is more likely to donate a proton to a water molecule than a nonpolar molecule.

_____

_____

_____

_____

        H   :Ö:
H:C:C:
        H   :Ö:H

(a) CH_3COOH
Acetic acid

        H H
H:C:C:Ö:H
        H H

(b) C_2H_5OH
Ethanol

Acetic acid and ethanol demonstrate how an additional oxygen atom increases the polarity of the –OH group and makes a compound more acidic. The second oxygen atom increases the polarity by drawing electrons towards it: Ethanol, on the other hand, is essentially neutral.

Neutralization reactions produce water and a salt.

The properties of strong acids and strong bases can be *neutralized* by mixing them together in the correct proportions. For example, consider the strong acid hydrochloric acid and the strong base sodium hydroxide. In aqueous solutions of each compound, only ions are found.

$$HCl(aq) + H_2O(l) \longrightarrow H_3O^+(aq) + Cl^-(aq)$$

$$NaOH(aq) \longrightarrow Na^+(aq) + OH^-(aq)$$

If the two solutions mix, the two sets of ions displayed on the right side of the equations above will mix. The hydronium ion will donate its extra proton to a hydroxide ion to form two water molecules. The Na^+ cation and Cl^- anion will form an aqueous solution of sodium chloride. This reaction is summarized in this equation.

$$HCl(aq) + NaOH(aq) \longrightarrow NaCl(aq) + H_2O(l)$$

A **salt** is an ionic compound composed of a cation from a base and an anion from an acid. The aqueous sodium chloride is a salt formed during an acid-base reaction.

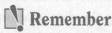

Remember

Sodium hydroxide, an ionic compound, dissociates into its component ions. Hydrochloric acid, a molecular compound, ionizes.

READING CHECK

6. What is a salt?

_____

_____

_____

_____

_____

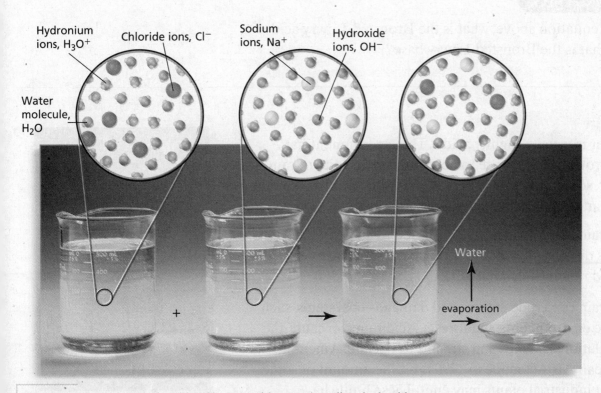

When aqueous hydrochloric acid, HCl, reacts with aqueous sodium hydroxide, NaOH, the reaction produces aqueous sodium chloride, NaCl.

Strong Acid–Strong Base Neutralization

The overall ionic equation for the reaction of hydrochloric acid and sodium hydroxide is given below. This equation is determined by the dissociation of sodium hydroxide and the ionization of hydrochloric acid.

$$H_3O^+(aq) + Cl^-(aq) + Na^+(aq) + OH^-(aq) \longrightarrow$$
$$Na^+(aq) + Cl^-(aq) + 2H_2O(l)$$

Note that the sodium ion and the chloride ion, which are present on both sides of the reaction, are spectator ions. The net ionic equation for the reaction is as follows.

$$H_3O^+(aq) + OH^-(aq) \longrightarrow 2H_2O(l)$$

When an equal number of moles of each solution are mixed, an equal number of hydronium and hydroxide ions will react. Therefore, in the mixture, all of these ions are converted into neutral water molecules. In aqueous solutions, **neutralization** is the reaction of hydronium ions and hydroxide ions to form water molecules. A completely neutralized mixture will not have any of the properties of an acid or a base.

✓ READING CHECK

7. In the equation above, what is the Brønsted-Lowry acid and what is the Brønsted-Lowry base?

Acid Rain

Rainwater is usually slightly acidic. The environment has natural protections in place to neutralize the acidity of rain. However, sometimes rain is very acidic. Rain that has a much higher than normal acidity is called acid rain.

Acid rain results when gases released by industrial processes dissolve in water to form acidic solutions. Gases that cause acid rain include NO, NO_2, CO_2, SO_2, and SO_3.

Acid rain can erode statues and damage ecosystems, such as aquatic environments and forests. Acid rain can cause the fish populations of lakes and streams to decline. Amendments to the Clean Air Act made in 1990 limit the amount of some gases that industrial plants may emit. These limits have decreased, but not eliminated, acid rain in the United States.

Acid rain causes extensive damage to the environment.

VOCABULARY

1. What is meant by the term *amphoteric*? Give an example of a substance that has amphoteric characteristics.

_____

_____

_____

REVIEW

2. Complete and balance the equations for the following acid-base reactions.

a. _____ H_2CO_3 + _____ $Sr(OH)_2 \longrightarrow$ _____

b. _____ $HClO_4$ + _____ $NaOH \longrightarrow$ _____

c. _____ HBr + _____ $Ba(OH)_2 \longrightarrow$ _____

d. _____ $NaHCO_3$ + _____ $H_2SO_4 \longrightarrow$ _____

3. Consider the equation for acetic acid plus water. Use the table "Relative Strengths of Acids and Bases," earlier in this chapter, to answer the questions below.

$$CH_3COOH + H_2O \rightleftharpoons CH_3COO^- + H_3O^+$$

a. Compare the strength of the two acids.

_____

b. Compare the strength of the two bases.

_____

c. Which direction, forward or reverse, is favored for this reaction?

_____

Critical Thinking

4. **INFERRING RELATIONSHIPS** Explain how the presence of several oxygen atoms in a compound containing an –OH group can make the compound acidic.

_____

_____

_____

_____

Math Tutor

Many chemical reactions that occur in water solutions are reactions involving ions. Soluble ionic compounds dissociate into ions when they dissolve, and some molecular compounds, including acids, ionize when they dissolve. An ionic equation represents what is actually present in a solution more accurately than an equation that uses full formulas.

Problem-Solving TIPS

- All dissolved substances in ionic reactions are dissociated into ions. Therefore, soluble ionic compounds are shown as separated ions in the full ionic equation. Strong acids and bases are also shown as separated ions in the full ionic equation because they are 100% ionized.

- Ions that do not take part in the reaction are called *spectator ions*. In other words, spectator ions stay in solution and will be labeled "(aq)" on both sides of the equation. Eliminating spectator ions reduces the "clutter" of the full ionic equation and produces a net ionic equation that shows only the particles that actually react.

SAMPLE

Write full and net ionic equations for the reaction that occurs when hydrochloric acid solution is combined with silver nitrate solution.

When hydrochloric acid, HCl, and silver nitrate, $AgNO_3$, are combined in solution, a double-displacement reaction will occur. The products are nitric acid, HNO_3, and silver chloride, AgCl. Although most chlorides are soluble, silver chloride is insoluble, so it forms a precipitate. The following equation summarizes this information.

$$HCl(aq) + AgNO_3(aq) \longrightarrow AgCl(s) + HNO_3(aq)$$

The full ionic equation shows the three aqueous compounds in ionic form. The H^+ ions are not found separate in solution. Instead, they bond with water molecules to form hydronium ions.

$$\cancel{H_3O^+(aq)} + Cl^-(aq) + Ag^+(aq) + \cancel{NO_3^-(aq)} \longrightarrow$$
$$AgCl(s) + \cancel{H_3O^+(aq)} + \cancel{NO_3^-(aq)}$$

Spectator ions are the ions found on both sides of the equation. These are the hydronium ion, H_3O^+, and the nitrate ion, NO_3^-. These ions are dropped to form the net ionic equation.

$$Cl^-(aq) + Ag^+(aq) \longrightarrow AgCl(s)$$

Practice Problems: Chapter Review practice problems 12 and 13

1. Although HCl(*aq*) exhibits properties of an Arrhenius acid, pure HCl gas and HCl dissolved in a nonpolar solvent exhibit none of the properties of an Arrhenius acid. Explain why.

_____

_____

_____

2. What distinguishes strong acids from weak acids?

_____

_____

3. What determines the strength of an Arrhenius base?

_____

_____

4. Which of the three acid definitions is the broadest? Explain.

_____

_____

_____

5. What is the trend in the favored direction of proton-transfer reactions?

_____

_____

6. Use the table "Relative Strengths of Acids and Bases" from Section 3 to determine which of HF, H_2S, HNO_3, and CH_3COOH is:

   a. the strongest acid _____

   b. the strongest base _____

7. Explain why the conjugate base of a strong acid is a weak base and the conjugate acid of a weak base is a strong acid.

_____

_____

_____

8. Name each of the following acids.

a. HCl _____

b. H_2S _____

c. HNO_3 _____

d. H_2SO_3 _____

e. $HClO_3$ _____

f. HNO_2 _____

9. Write formulas for the following acids.

a. hydrofluoric acid _____

b. hydroiodic acid _____

c. phosphoric acid _____

d. hypochlorous acid _____

10. Write the balanced equations that describe the two-stage ionization of sulfuric acid in a dilute aqueous solution. Then compare the degrees of ionization in the two stages.

First stage: _____

Second stage: _____

_____

11. Write the formula equation and net ionic equation for each reaction.

a. $H_3PO_4(aq) + NaOH(aq) \longrightarrow$ _____

_____

b. $Zn(s) + HCl(aq) \longrightarrow$ _____

_____

c. $Al(s) + H_2SO_4(aq) \longrightarrow$ _____

_____

12. Complete the following neutralization reactions. Balance each equation, and then write the overall ionic and net ionic equation for each.

a. _____ $HNO_3(aq) +$ _____ $KOH(aq) \longrightarrow$ _____

_____

_____

b. _____ $Ca(OH)_2(aq) +$ _____ $HNO_3(aq) \longrightarrow$ _____

_____

_____

13. Write the balanced chemical equation for each of the following reactions between water and the non-metallic oxide to form an acid.

a. _____ $CO_2(g)$ + _____ $H_2O(l)$ ⟶ _____

b. _____ $SO_3(g)$ + _____ $H_2O(l)$ ⟶ _____

c. _____ $N_2O_5(g)$ + _____ $H_2O(l)$ ⟶ _____

14. Write the formula equation, the overall ionic equation, and the net ionic equation for a neutralization reaction that would form the salt $RbClO_4$.

_____

_____

_____

15. A 211 g sample of barium carbonate, $BaCO_3$, reacts with a solution of nitric acid to give barium nitrate, carbon dioxide, and water. If the acid is present in excess, what mass and volume of carbon dioxide gas at STP will form?

16. Acid rain is the term used to describe rain or snow that is more acidic than it normally is. One cause of acid precipitation is the formation of sulfuric and nitric acids from various sulfur and nitrogen oxides produced in volcanic eruptions, forest fires, and thunderstorms. In a typical volcanic eruption, for example, 3.50×10^8 kg SO_2 may be produced. If this amount of SO_2 were converted to H_2SO_4 according to the two-step process given below, how many kilograms of H_2SO_4 would be produced from such an eruption?

$$SO_2 + \frac{1}{2} O_2 \longrightarrow SO_3$$

$$SO_3 + H_2O \longrightarrow H_2SO_4$$

CHAPTER 15

Acid-Base Titration and pH

Key Concepts

Section 1 *Aqueous Solutions and the Concept of pH*

How does water self-ionize?

What is the pH scale?

How do amounts of hydronium and hydroxide ions affect pH?

Section 2 *Determining pH and Titrations*

How does an acid-base indicator work?

How is an acid-base titration performed?

How are titration data used to calculate pH?

Review Previous Concepts

1. What is the molarity of a solution and how is it calculated?

2. What are an Arrhenius acid and an Arrhenius base?

3. What is the hydronium ion and what is its relationship to hydrogen ions in an aqueous solution?

SECTION 15.1

Aqueous Solutions and the Concept of pH

You have already seen that acids and bases form hydronium ions, H_3O^+, and hydroxide ions, OH^-, in aqueous solutions. However, ions formed by the solute are not the only ions present in an aqueous solution. Water molecules also form hydronium ions and hydroxide ions through their own interactions.

Self-ionization of water forms hydronium and hydroxide ions.

You might not expect a beaker of pure liquid water to conduct electricity. Without any dissolved solute contributing particles of positive and negative charge, there would be no means of transmitting electric current in the liquid. However, experiments have shown that pure water is a weak electrolyte rather than a nonelectrolyte. This implies that electric charge is being transmitted through the solution by a means other than ions of solute.

Self-Ionization of Water

The process that explains the fact that water is a weak electrolyte is called self-ionization. In the **self-ionization of water,** two water molecules produce a hydronium ion and a hydroxide ion by a transfer of a proton. The diagram below shows the equation for the equilibrium state of pure water.

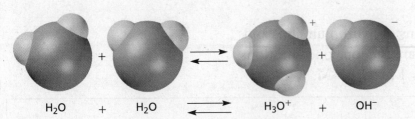

$$H_2O \quad + \quad H_2O \quad \rightleftharpoons \quad H_3O^+ \quad + \quad OH^-$$

Conductivity measurements show that only one out of every 560 million molecules of water self-ionizes. In pure water, at 25°C, the concentration of hydronium ions and hydroxide ions is 1.0×10^{-7} mol/L.

Critical Thinking

1. Apply How do the Brønsted-Lowry definitions of acids and bases apply to the self-ionization of water?

_____

_____

_____

_____

_____

Ion Concentration There is a standard notation to represent concentration in moles per liter. The formula of the particular ion is enclosed in brackets. For example, the symbol $[H_3O^+]$ means "hydronium ion concentration in moles per liter" or "molar hydronium ion concentration." In pure water at 25°C, $[H_3O^+] = 1.0 \times 10^{-7}$ M and $[OH^-] = 1.0 \times 10^{-7}$ M.

Two water molecules react to form one hydronium ion and one hydroxide ion. Therefore, when pure water self-ionizes, there should be an equal number of hydronium ions and hydroxide ions. This is reflected in the concentrations given above.

The degree to which water self-ionizes remains constant in water and dilute aqueous solutions at constant temperature. This is reflected in the following formula.

$$K_w = [H_3O^+][OH^-]$$

K_w is called the ionization constant of water. Different values of K_w for different temperatures are given in the table at the right. The value for water at 25°C can be verified by substituting the concentrations for water given above.

$$K_w = [H_3O^+][OH^-] = (1.0 \times 10^{-7} \text{ M})(1.0 \times 10^{-7} \text{ M})$$

$$= 1.0 \times 10^{-14} \text{ M}$$

The table shows that the ionization of water increases as temperature increases. This is because there is more kinetic energy available for chemical reactions at warmer temperatures. For the calculations in this book, the value of $K_w = 1.0 \times 10^{-14}$ M is assumed to be constant within the conditions of the problem unless otherwise indicated.

K_w at Selected Temperatures	
Temperature (°C)	K_w
0	1.2×10^{-15}
10	3.0×10^{-15}
25	1.0×10^{-14}
50	5.3×10^{-14}

PRACTICE

A. Assuming that the concentrations of hydronium ions and hydroxide ions are equal, what are the ion concentrations in pure water at 0°C? Use $K_w = 1.2 \times 10^{-15}$ M.

Neutral, Acidic, and Basic Solutions

The Arrhenius definitions of acids and bases in aqueous solutions can be used to classify an aqueous solution based on a comparson of its hydronium and hydroxide ion concentrations. A solution is either acidic, basic, or neutral.

- **Acidic solutions** An *acidic solution* is one in which $[H_3O^+]$ is greater than $[OH^-]$. In acidic solutions, the value of $[H_3O^+]$ is greater than 1.0×10^{-7} M and the value of $[OH^-]$ is less than 1.0×10^{-7} M.

- **Basic solutions** A *basic solution* is one in which $[H_3O^+]$ is less than $[OH^-]$. In basic solutions, the value of $[H_3O^+]$ is less than 1.0×10^{-7} M and the value of $[OH^-]$ is greater than 1.0×10^{-7} M.

- **Neutral solutions** A *neutral solution* is one in which $[H_3O^+]$ and $[OH^-]$ are equal. In a neutral solution, $[H_3O^+] = [OH^-] = 1.0 \times 10^{-7}$ M. Pure water is an example of a neutral liquid.

The diagram below shows how the concentration of ions varies from acidic solutions to basic solutions. This variation occurs because K_w remains constant. If the concentration of one type of ion goes up, then the concentration of the other ion must go down.

 Remember

An Arrhenius acid is a substance that increases the concentration of hydrogen ions, and therefore hydronium ions, in solution. An Arrhenius base is a substance that increases the concentration of hydroxide ions in solution.

PRACTICE

Label the solutions acidic or basic using the given data.

B. $[H_3O^+] = 1.0 \times 10^{-10}$ M _____

C. $[H_3O^+] = 1.0 \times 10^{-4}$ M _____

D. $[OH^-] = 1.0 \times 10^{-5}$ M _____

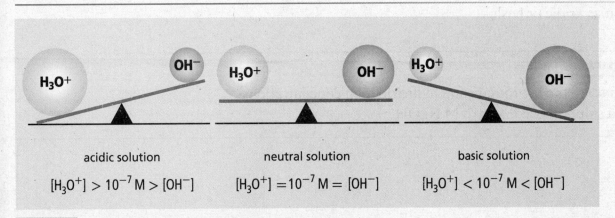

acidic solution
$[H_3O^+] > 10^{-7} M > [OH^-]$

neutral solution
$[H_3O^+] = 10^{-7} M = [OH^-]$

basic solution
$[H_3O^+] < 10^{-7} M < [OH^-]$

When the concentration of hydronium ions goes up, the concentration of hydroxide ions goes down, and vice versa.

Calculating $[H_3O^+]$ and $[OH^-]$

Strong Bases Recall that strong acids and bases are considered completely ionized or dissociated in weak aqueous solutions. A review of strong acids and bases is given in the table at the right. One example of a strong base is sodium hydroxide, NaOH. In a strong base, the solute completely dissociates or ionizes in solution. The dissociation equation for NaOH is shown below.

$$NaOH(s) \xrightarrow{H_2O} Na^+(aq) + OH^-(aq)$$

Therefore, 1 mol of NaOH dissociates into 1 mol of sodium ions and 1 mol of hydroxide ions. The mole ratio for NaOH and OH^- can be used to convert an amount of NaOH into an amount of OH^-. For a solution of 1.0×10^{-2} M NaOH, the following shows how to compute the concentration of OH^-.

$$1.0 \times 10^{-2} \text{ M NaOH} = \frac{1.0 \times 10^{-2} \text{ mol NaOH}}{1 \text{ L solution}} \times \frac{1 \text{ mol OH}^-}{1 \text{ mol NaOH}}$$

$$= \frac{1.0 \times 10^{-2} \text{ mol OH}^-}{1 \text{ L solution}} = 1.0 \times 10^{-2} \text{ M OH}^-$$

Because K_w is a constant, it can help determine the concentration of $[H_3O^+]$.

$$K_w = [H_3O^+][OH^-], \text{ therefore}$$

$$[H_3O^+] = \frac{K_w}{[OH^-]} = \frac{1.0 \times 10^{-14}}{1.0 \times 10^{-2}} = 1.0 \times 10^{-12} \text{ M}$$

Because $[OH^-]$ is greater than 1.0×10^{-7} M, and $[H_3O^+]$ is less than 1.0×10^{-7} M, the solution is basic. This is expected because NaOH is a strong base. Note that only one concentration value must be determined to classify a solution as acidic or basic.

Common Strong Acids and Bases

Strong Acids	Strong Bases
HCl	LiOH
HBr	NaOH
HI	KOH
$HClO_4$	RbOH
$HClO_3$	CsOH
HNO_3	$Ca(OH)_2$
H_2SO_4	$Sr(OH)_2$
	$Ba(OH)_2$

TIP You can check your answers by making sure that the product of the ion concentrations is equal to K_w.

PRACTICE

E. What are the hydronium and hydroxide ion concentrations in a solution of 3.0×10^{-2} M NaOH?

Strong Acids Now consider a 2.0×10^{-4} M HCl solution. In a strong base, the solute completely dissociates in solution. The ionization equation for HCl is

$$HCl(g) + H_2O(l) \longrightarrow H_3O^+ (aq) + Cl^-(aq)$$

Therefore, 1 mol of HCl ionizes to form into 1 mol of hydronium ions and 1 mol of chloride ions. The mole ratio for NaOH and OH$^-$ can be used to convert an amount of HCl into an amount of H_3O^+.

$$2.0 \times 10^{-4} \text{ M HCl} = \frac{2.0 \times 10^{-4} \text{ mol HCl}}{1 \text{ L solution}} \times \frac{1 \text{ mol } H_3O^+}{1 \text{ mol HCl}}$$

$$= \frac{2.0 \times 10^{-4} \text{ mol } H_3O^+}{1 \text{ L solution}}$$

$$= 2.0 \times 10^{-4} \text{ M } H_3O^+$$

This value can be used to calculate [OH$^-$].

$K_w = [H_3O^+][OH^-]$; therefore

$$[OH^-] = \frac{K_w}{[H_3O^+]} = \frac{1.0 \times 10^{-14}}{2.0 \times 10^{-4}} = 5.0 \times 10^{-10} \text{ M}$$

Because [H_3O^+] is greater than 1.0×10^{-7} M, and [OH$^-$] is less than 1.0×10^{-7} M, the solution is acidic. This is expected because HCl is a strong acid.

> **READING CHECK**
>
> **2.** Explain why calculating the [H_3O^+] of an aqueous solution is enough to determine whether the solution is acidic, basic, or neutral.
>
> _____
>
> _____
>
> _____
>
> _____
>
> _____

PRACTICE

F. What are the hydronium and hydroxide ion concentrations in a solution of 1.0×10^{-4} M HCl?

G. What are the hydronium and hydroxide ion concentrations in a solution of 1.0×10^{-4} M Ca(OH)$_2$.

The concentrations of hydronium and hydroxide ions determine pH and pOH.

Expressing the concentrations of hydronium ions and hydroxide ions can be cumbersome because the values tend to be very small. A more convenient quantity, called pH, also indicates the hydronium ion concentration of a solution. The **pH** of a solution is defined as the negative of the common logarithm of the hydronium ion concentration. The pH of a solution is expressed by the following equation.

$$pH = -\log [H_3O^+]$$

The common logarithm of a number is the power to which 10 must be raised to equal the number. For example, the logarithm of 100 is 2 and the logarithm of 1 000 000 is 6. The logarithms of numbers greater than 1 are positive and the logarithms of numbers less than 1 but greater than 0 are negative.

The logarithm of $[H_3O^+]$ is almost always a negative number. Therefore, The pH of a solution will almost always be a positive number. For example, consider a neutral solution. The solution has a value of $[H_3O^+] = 1.0 \times 10^{-7}$ M. The logarithm of 1.0×10^{-7} M is -7.0. Therefore, the pH of the solution is given by the following.

$$pH = -\log [H_3O^+] = -\log (1.0 \times 10^{-7} \text{ M}) = -(-7.0) = 7.0$$

The diagram below shows the relationship between pH values and the concentration of hydronium ions. At 25°C, the range of pH values of aqueous solution generally falls between 0 and 14.

CONNECT

The letters pH stand for the French words *pouvoir hydrogène,* meaning "hydrogen power."

READING CHECK

3. Compute the following.

a. log 1000 _____

b. log 10 _____

c. log 0.1 _____

d. log 0.000 01 _____

e. log 10^{-8} _____

TIP If $[H_3O^+]$ for a solution is of the form 1.0×10^{-n}, the pH of the solution is equal to n. In other words, the pH of the solution is the negative of the exponent of the hydronium ion concentration expressed in scientific notation.

PRACTICE

What is the pH of the following solutions?

H. $[H_3O^+] = 1 \times 10^{-13}$ M _____

I. $[H_3O^+] = 1 \times 10^{-6}$ M _____

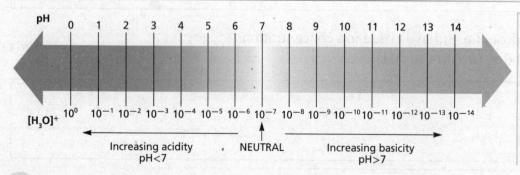

As the concentration of hydronium ions increases, the solution becomes more acidic and the pH decreases. As the concentration of hydronium ions decreases, the solution becomes more basic and the pH increases.

Approximate pH Range of Some Common Materials (at 25°C)

Material	pH	Material	pH	Material	pH
Gastric juice	1.0–3.0	Cherries	3.2–4.7	Saliva	6.5–7.5
Lemons	1.8–2.4	Tomatoes	4.0–4.4	Pure water	7.0
Vinegar	2.4–3.4	Bananas	4.5–5.7	Blood	7.3–7.5
Soft drinks	2.0–4.0	Bread	5.0–6.0	Eggs	7.6–8.0
Apples	2.9–3.3	Rainwater	5.5–5.8	Sea water	8.0–8.5
Grapefruit	2.9–3.4	Potatoes	5.6–6.0	Milk of magnesia	10.5
Oranges	3.0–4.0	Milk	6.3–6.6		

The **pOH** of a solution is defined as the negative of the common logarithm of the hydroxide ion concentration. The value of pOH is given by the equation $pH = -\log[OH^-]$. The pOH of a neutral solution is also 7.0.

For a neutral solution, the sum of the pH and the pOH is 14. This is directly related to the value of K_w being 1.0×10^{-14} M under normal conditions, and the fact that $K_w = [H_3O^+][OH^-]$. Similarly, this relationship holds under normal conditions: $\log K_w = \log[H_3O^+] + \log[OH^-] = pH + pOH$. Therefore, the following relationship holds true for all solutions.

$$pH + pOH = 14.0$$

For example, if you know that the pH of a solution is 4.2, the pOH of the solution is $14.0 - 4.2 = 9.8$. In fact, the pH of any acidic solution is always less than 7.0, and the pH of any basic solution is greater than 7.0. A summary of the relationships between $[H_3O^+]$, $[OH^-]$, pH, pOH is given in the table below.

CONNECT

The logarithm of the product of two numbers is equal to the sum of the logarithms of the two numbers. Before the invention of calculators, logarithms were used to multiply complicated numbers quickly. Using a device called a slide rule, it was faster to find the logarithms of the numbers and add them than it was to multiply the two numbers.

READING CHECK

4. Classify the following solutions as acidic, basic, or neutral.

a. pH = 3.1 _____

b. pH = 7.1 _____

c. pH = 13.2 _____

$[H_3O^+]$, $[OH^-]$, pH, and pOH of Solutions

Solution	General condition	At 25°C
Neutral	$[H_3O^+] = [OH^-]$ $pH = pOH$	$[H_3O^+] = [OH^-] = 1 \times 10^{-7}$ M $pH = pOH = 7.0$
Acidic	$[H_3O^+] > [OH^-]$ $pH < pOH$	$[H_3O^+] > 1 \times 10^{-7}$ M $[OH^-] < 1 \times 10^{-7}$ M $pH < 7.0$ $pOH > 7.0$
Basic	$[H_3O^+] < [OH^-]$ $pH > pOH$	$[H_3O^+] < 1 \times 10^{-7}$ M $[OH^-] > 1 \times 10^{-7}$ M $pH > 7.0$ $pOH < 7.0$

If either the $[H_3O^+]$ or the pH of a solution is known, then the other can be calculated using the relationship shown earlier. Significant figures involving pH must be handled differently. The significant figures of a logarithm are determined by the number of digits to the right of the decimal. Therefore, both $[H_3O^+] = 1 \times 10^{-7}$ M and pH = 7.0 have one significant digit.

Calculating pH from $[H_3O^+]$

You have already practiced the simplest type of pH problems. In these problems, $[H_3O^+]$ is an integral power of 10, such as 0.1 M or 0.01 M. These values of concentration are all of the form 1.0×10^{-n} M. The pH for a solution with this concentration of hydronium ions is equal to the value of the exponent with the sign changed, or n.

The diagrams below list the steps necessary to find the pH of a solution. The starting point in the diagram is determined by what information is given in the problem. For example, if you are given the concentration of the hydronium ions in the solution, you can solve the problem in one step. If you are given a basic solution, then you need three steps to solve the problem.

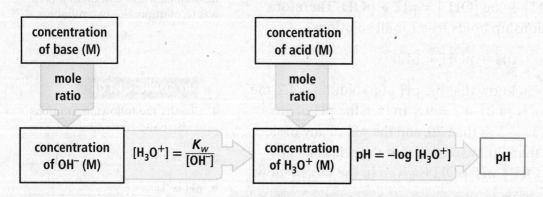

J. What is the pH of 1.0×10^{-5} M HNO_3 solution?

K. What is the pH of 1.0×10^{-2} M KOH solution?

Using a Calculator to Calculate pH from [H_3O^+]

Most problems involve hydronium ion concentrations that are not equal to powers of 10. These problems require a calculator. Most scientific calculators have a "log" key that can be used to find the logarithm of any number.

For example, consider a solution that has an [H_3O^+] of 3.4×10^{-5}. Only one step is necessary to determine the pH of the solution. This step uses the equation for pH in terms of the hydronium ion concentration. Substituting the given value into the equation yields the following.

$$pH = -\log [H_3O^+]$$
$$= -\log(3.4 \times 10^{-5})$$

On most calculators, the following set of keystrokes can be used to evaluate the expression above.

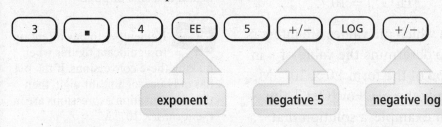

| 3 | . | 4 | EE | 5 | +/− | LOG | +/− |

exponent **negative 5** **negative log**

A calculator finds that the pH of the solution is 4.47. An estimate of pH can be used to check the answer. The value of [H_3O^+] is between the values of 1.0×10^{-5} and 1.0×10^{-4}. Therefore, the pH of the solution should be between 4 and 5.

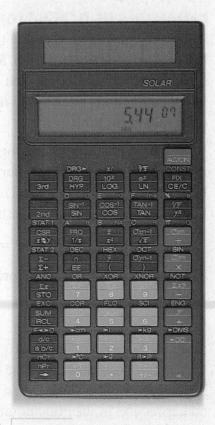

This calculator has a "log" key in the top row. It is being used to calculate the pH of a solution that has a hydronium ion concentration of 5.44×10^{-7} M.

PRACTICE

L. What is the pH of a solution if [H_3O^+] = 6.7×10^{-4} M? _____

M. What is the pH of a solution if [H_3O^+] = 2.5×10^{-2} M? _____

N. What is the pH of a 2.5×10^{-6} M HNO_3 solution? _____

O. What is the pH of a 2.0×10^{-2} M $Sr(OH)_2$ solution?

Calculating [H₃O⁺] and [OH⁻] from pH

You have learned to calculate the pH of a solution given its hydronium ion concentration. Suppose instead that you only have the pH of a solution. You can convert the relationship between pH and $[H_3O^+]$ into one in which $[H_3O^+]$ is determined from pH.

The base of the common logarithm is 10. The mathematical relationship between a number and its base-10 logarithm can be given in one of two ways. These equalities can be used to find the value of $[H_3O^+]$ in terms of the pH of the solution.

$$x = \log(10^x) \qquad \text{or} \qquad x = 10^{\log x}$$

$$\text{pH} = -\log [H_3O^+]; \text{ therefore } \log [H_3O^+] = -\text{pH}$$

$$10^{\log[H_3O^+]} = 10^{-\text{pH}}$$

$$[H_3O^+] = 10^{-\text{pH}}$$

The simplest cases are those in which pH values are integers. The value of pH is simply used to determine the value of n in an expression in scientific notation of the form 1.0×10^{-n} M. For $[H_3O^+]$, the value of n is simply the pH. For $[OH^-]$, the value of n is equal to 14 − pH. For example, a solution that has a pH of 2.00 has values $[H_3O^+] = 1.0 \times 10^{-2}$ M and $[OH^-] = 1.0 \times 10^{-12}$ M.

 CONNECT

One use for pH is in the monitoring of the environment. The pH of normal rainwater is about 5.5, but values as low as 4.3 have been recorded. Prolonged exposure to lower values of pH can cause damage to organisms in the environment.

Monitoring can detect low pH values in bodies of water. This allows measures to be taken to reduce the damage. Sometimes a basic substance such as calcium carbonate (limestone) can be continuously released into the water in an attempt to protect organisms dependent on the health of a lake or pond.

TIP Remember to pay attention to significant figures when making these conversions. If the pH has only one significant digit, then the concentration expressions are in the form 1×10^{-n} M.

PRACTICE

P. The pH of a solution is determined to be 5.0. What is the hydronium ion concentration of this solution?

Q. The pH of a solution is determined to be 12.0. What is the hydronium ion concentration of this solution?

R. The pH of a solution is determined to be 14.0. What is the hydronium ion concentration of this solution?

S. What are the hydroxide ion concentrations for the solutions given above?

---

pH Calculations and the Strength of Acids and Bases

So far, we have discussed only solutions that contain strong acids or strong bases. Weak acids and weak bases can also affect the pH of a solution of water.

The table at the bottom of the page lists five substances: two basic substances, two acidic substances, and one neutral substance. The pH of the strong base, 1.0×10^{-2} M KOH, can be determined using the methods discussed in this section. The pH of the strong acid, 1.0×10^{-3} M HCl, can also be determined using the methods in this section. The pH of pure water will always be 7.0, assuming normal conditions. For these three substances, the experimental values calculated in the laboratory will always match the theoretical values calculated in this section.

This is not true of solutions of weak acids, such as acetic acid, CH_3COOH. The ion concentrations cannot be calculated directly from the molar concentration because not all of the acetic acid molecules are ionized. The same problem also occurs for weak bases, such as ammonia, NH_3. The pH of these solutions must be determined experimentally. The ion concentrations can then be calculated from the measured pH values.

 Remember

The degree to which a substance ionizes or dissociates determines whether it is strong or weak. The concentration does not affect this determination. A 1.0×10^{-0} M HCl solution, a 1.0×10^{-2} M HCl solution, and a 1.0×10^{-6} M HCl solution are all strong acids even though the third acid is much more dilute than the other two.

✓ READING CHECK

5. Suppose you have a solution of 1.0×10^{-2} M CH_3COOH. Can you use the methods discussed in this section to calculate the values of $[H_3O^+]$, $[OH^-]$, and pH for the solution? Why or why not?

_____

_____

Relationship of $[H_3O^+]$ to $[OH^-]$ and pH (at 25°C)			
Solution	$[H_3O^+]$	$[OH^-]$	pH
1.0×10^{-2} M KOH	1.0×10^{-12}	1.0×10^{-2}	12.00
1.0×10^{-2} M NH_3	2.4×10^{-11}	4.2×10^{-4}	10.63
Pure H_2O	1.0×10^{-7}	1.0×10^{-7}	7.00
1.0×10^{-3} M HCl	1.0×10^{-3}	1.0×10^{-11}	3.00
1.0×10^{-1} M CH_3COOH	1.3×10^{-3}	7.5×10^{-12}	2.87

SAMPLE PROBLEM

The pH of a solution is measured and determined to be 7.52.

a. What is the hydronium ion concentration?

b. What is the hydroxide ion concentration?

c. Is the solution acidic or basic?

	SOLUTION	
1	**ANALYZE**	*Determine the information that is given and unknown.*

Given: pH = 7.52

Unknown: a. $[H_3O^+]$ **c.** type of solution: acidic or basic

b. $[OH^-]$ |

2 PLAN   *Describe how to find the unknown values.*

a. $[H_3O^+] = 10^{-pH}$ **b.** $[OH^-] = \dfrac{K_w}{[H_3O^+]}$

3 SOLVE   *Substitute the given values into the equations.*

a. $[H_3O^+] = 10^{-pH} = 10^{-7.52}$

On most calculators, this value is found by using one of the following two sets of keystrokes.

$$\boxed{7} \quad \boxed{.} \quad \boxed{5} \quad \boxed{2} \quad \boxed{+/-} \quad \boxed{\text{2nd}} \quad \boxed{10^x}$$

or

$$\boxed{7} \quad \boxed{.} \quad \boxed{5} \quad \boxed{2} \quad \boxed{+/-} \quad \boxed{\text{2nd}} \quad \boxed{\text{LOG}}$$

The calculator gives the result 3.0×10^{-8} M.

b. $[OH^-] = \dfrac{K_w}{[H_3O^+]} = \dfrac{1.0 \times 10^{-14}}{3.0 \times 10^{-8}} = 3.3 \times 10^{-7}$ M

c. Because the pH is greater than 7, the solution is basic.

4 CHECK YOUR WORK   *Check the answers to see if they are reasonable.*

A basic solution with a pH just over 7 should have a value of $[H_3O^+]$ a little less than 1.0×10^{-7} M and a value of $[OH^-]$ a little greater than 1.0×10^{-7} M.

T. The pH of an aqueous solution is measured as 1.50. Calculate the values of $[H_3O^+]$ and $[OH^-]$.

What equation can be used to find the value of $[H_3O^+]$?

Substitute values into that equation and determine $[H_3O^+]$.

What equation can be used to find the value of $[OH^-]$?

Substitute values into that equation and determine $[OH^-]$.

Describe two methods you could use to check to see if these answers make sense.

U. The pH of an aqueous solution is 3.67. What is the value of $[H_3O^+]$ for the solution?

What equation can be used to find the value of $[H_3O^+]$?

Substitute values into that equation and determine $[H_3O^+]$.

VOCABULARY

1. Describe what is meant by the pH of a solution. Then write a formula that can be used to determine pH.

_____

_____

_____

REVIEW

2. Why does the pH scale generally range from 0 to 14 in aqueous solutions?

_____

_____

3. Why does a pH of 7 represent a neutral solution at 25°C?

_____

_____

4. A solution contains 4.5×10^{-3} M HCl. Determine the values of $[H_3O^+]$, $[OH^-]$, and pH for the solution.

5. A $Ca(OH)_2$ solution has a pH of 8.0. Determine the values of $[H_3O^+]$, $[OH^-]$, and $[Ca(OH)_2]$ for the solution.

Critical Thinking

6. **PREDICTING OUTCOMES** Arrange the following solutions in order from lowest to highest pH: 0.10 M HCl, 0.10 M H_2SO_4, and 0.10 M HF.

_____

Determining pH and Titrations

The pH of weak acids and weak bases cannot be determined using the methods from the previous section. The pH of these substances is determined in the laboratory instead. One way to determine the pH of a solution experimentally is by using an acid-base indicator.

Indicators can determine pH, pOH, and strength.

An **acid-base indicator** is a compound whose color is sensitive to pH. In other words, the color of the substance changes as the pH of a solution changes.

Indicators themselves are either weak acids or weak bases. For example, a weak acid indicator will ionize in solution according to the following equilibrium equation.

$$HIn \rightleftarrows H^+ + In^-$$

The symbol In^- represents the anion of the indicator. Because the reaction is reversible, both HIn molecules and In^- anions are present. If they are different colors, then the color of the solution will change as the proportion of ionized indicator molecules changes. This proportion depends on the type of solution the indicator is in.

- **Acidic solutions** If the indicator is in an acidic solution, any In^- ions that are present accept protons from the acid. The indicator is present mostly in its molecular form, HIn, and takes on the color associated with this form.
- **Basic solutions** If the indicator is in a basic solution, HIn molecules will also ionize and donate protons. The indicator is present mostly in its ionic form, In^-, and takes on the color associated with this form.

Critical Thinking

1. Explain Why is the HIn molecule given in the equation on this page considered a weak acid?

_____

_____

_____

_____

In basic solution →
In acidic solution ←

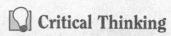

Acidic solutions cause more HIn molecules of the indicator litmus to form, turning the solution pink. Basic solutions cause more In^- ions to form, turning the solution purple.

Color Ranges of Various Indicators Used in Titrations

Titration type	Indicator	Transition interval	Acid color	Transition color	Base color
Strong acid/ strong base	methyl red	4.4–6.2	red	orange	yellow
	bromthymol blue	6.2–7.6	yellow	green	blue
Strong acid/ weak base	methyl orange	3.1–4.4	red	orange	yellow
	bromphenol blue	3.0–4.6	yellow	pink	purple
Weak acid/ strong base	phenolphthalein	8.0–10.0	colorless	pink	fuschia
	phenol red	6.4–8.0	yellow	orange	fuschia

The exact pH range over which an indicator changes colors varies with the indicator used. The pH range over which an indicator changes color is called its **transition interval.** Within the transition interval, both H*In* molecules and *In*⁻ anions are present. The table above gives the transition intervals for a number of common acid-base indicators.

Another way to measure pH is by using a universal indicator. Universal indicators are a mixture of several different indicators. The pH paper shown in the diagram below is dipped in such a mixture. It can be used to distinguish pH values that encompass the entire pH scale from 0 to 14.

An even more accurate way of measuring pH is by using a pH meter. A **pH meter** determines the pH of a solution by measuring the voltage between two electrodes placed in a solution. The voltage is dependent on the value of $[H_3O^+]$.

✓ READING CHECK

2. List three methods for determining the pH of a substance.

_____

_____

_____

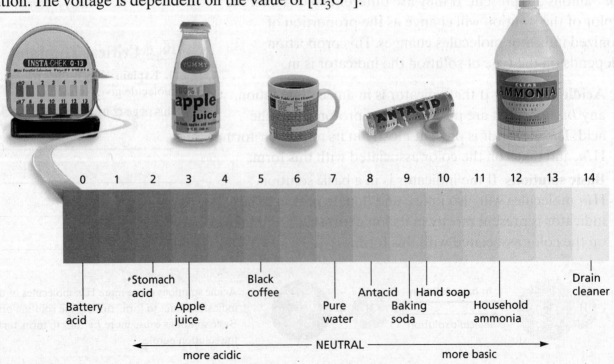

| 0 | 1 | 2 | 3 | 4 | 5 | 6 | 7 | 8 | 9 | 10 | 11 | 12 | 13 | 14 |

Stomach acid — Black coffee — Antacid — Hand soap — Drain cleaner

Battery acid — Apple juice — Pure water — Baking soda — Household ammonia

NEUTRAL

more acidic ← → more basic

Titration is used to determine exact concentrations.

As you learned in the chapter "Acids and Bases," reactions between acids and bases are called neutralization reactions. The hydronium ions formed by the acid and the hydroxide ions formed by the base will react. The hydronium ion will donate a proton to the hydroxide ion, resulting in two neutral water molecules.

$$H_3O^+(aq) + OH^-(aq) \rightarrow 2H_2O(l)$$

The equation shows that H_3O^+ ions and OH^- ions combine in a one-to-one mole ratio. Neutralization occurs when the two types of ions are provided in equal amounts by the reactants.

For example, consider a reaction of 1 L of 0.10 M HCl solution and 1 L of 0.10 M NaOH. The HCl solution contains 0.10 mol of hydronium ions. The NaOH contains 0.10 mol of hydroxide ions. When the two solutions are combined, the hydronium and hydroxide ions combine until the product $[H_3O^+][OH^-] = 1 \times 10^{-14}$. The sodium and chloride ions also combine to form NaCl. The resulting solution is neutral.

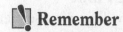

Remember

A proton is chemically equivalent to a hydrogen ion.

Strong acid turns pH paper red.

Strong base turns pH paper blue.

Neutral solution turns pH paper green.

The reaction of a strong acid with a certain number of hydronium ions and and a strong base with an equal number of hydroxide ions results in a neutral solution and a dissolved or precipitated salt.

Critical Thinking

3. Infer Can a base mixed with an acid ever increase the pH of an acid? Why or why not?

The progressive addition of an acid to a base (or a base to an acid) can be used to compare the concentrations of the acid and the base. **Titration** is the controlled addition and measurement of the amount of a solution of known concentration required to react completely with a measured amount of a solution of unknown concentration.

Equivalance Point

Titration provides a precise means of determining unknown concentrations of acids and bases. In a titration, the goal is to determine the equivalence point of a reaction. The **equivalance point** is the point at which two solutions used in a titration are present in chemically equivalent amounts. The pH changes rapidly as the equivalance point approaches.

If an indicator is used to measure pH, it must change color over a range that includes the equivalence point. The point at which an indicator changes color is called the **end point.** A suitable indicator for a particular titration will have an end point that corresponds to the equivalance point of the titration.

Some indicators, such as litmus, change color at about a pH of 7. However, the transition interval for litmus is very broad, stretched from pH values of 5.5 to 8. This broad range makes litmus impractical for determining a precise pH value. Of the indicators listed in the table earlier in this section, bromthymol blue has the narrowest range that also includes a pH of 7 in the range. This indicator is the most useful for titrations of strong acids and strong bases because neutralization of these substances produces a salt solution with a pH of 7.

A titration of a strong acid and a weak base has an equivalence point that is at a pH less than 7. The salt formed in such a neutralization reaction is a weak acid. A different indicator that changes color at a lower pH is needed for these titrations. Methyl orange and bromphenol blue are indicators that may be suitable for strong-acid/weak-base titrations.

Similarly, a titration of a weak acid and strong base has an equivalence point at a pH greater than 7. The salt formed in this neutralization reaction is a weak base. Phenolphthalein and phenol red are suitable for weak-acid/strong-base titrations.

✓ READING CHECK

4. Name three types of titrations and compare the values of the equivalence points for the three types.

_____

_____

_____

CONNECT

The primary job of an analytical chemist is to obtain information by making precise measurements. Analytical chemists use state-of-the-art instruments to analyze for barely detectable amounts of materials. Analytical chemists work in all areas of chemistry, including environmental chemistry. An analytical chemist analyzes water, soil, and air samples to determine the precise levels of pollutants or contaminants.

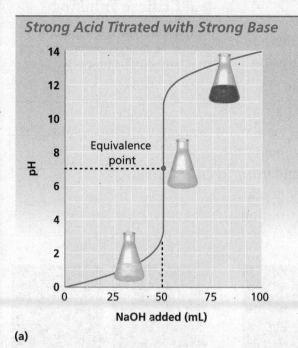

Strong Acid Titrated with Strong Base

pH vs NaOH added (mL)

Equivalence point

(a)

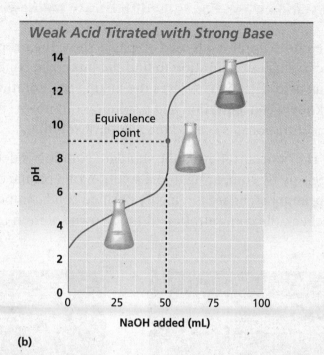

Weak Acid Titrated with Strong Base

pH vs NaOH added (mL)

Equivalence point

(b)

(a) When 50 mL of 1.0 M HCl is titrated with a 1.0 M NaCl solution, the equivalence point occurs at a pH of 7.00. (b) When 50 mL of 1.0 M CH_3COOH is titrated with a 1.0 M NaCl solution, the equivalence point occurs at a higher pH. In both cases, the equivalence point involves a rapid change in pH with a very slight increase in the amount of base added.

In a titration a carefully measured amount of aqueous base is slowly added to a measured volume of aqueous acid. As base is added, the pH changes from a lower numerical value to a higher one. The change in pH occurs slowly at first, then rapidly through the equivalence point, and then slowly again as the solution becomes more basic.

Near the equivalence point, one drop can cause a dramatic change in the pH of a solution. The pH can change by as much as 3 to 5 pH units. The graphs above compare a strong-acid/strong-base titration and a weak-acid/strong-base titration.

You may be wondering about the titration of a weak acid by a weak base, or vice versa. Since the pH value does not change dramatically at the equivalence point, a weak-acid/weak-base titration would not yield a very precise measurement of the original solution. If the concentration of a weak acid is unknown, titration should be performed with a strong base. If the concentration of a weak base is unknown, titration should be performed with a strong acid.

TIP The photographs on the next two pages lay out a procedure that allows chemists to precisely determine the amounts that are mixed in a titration.

READING CHECK

5. A titration of two solutions has an equivalence point at a pH of 8.3. What type of titration does this mixture represent?

_____

_____

A standard solution is used to titrate unknowns.

The photographs on these two pages show the proper method of carrying out a titration to find the unknown concentration of an acid. Titration involves the mixing of a solution of unknown concentration and a solution of known concentration, also called the **standard solution.**

The concentration of the standard solution is determined precisely by comparing it to a solution of a primary standard. A **primary standard** is a highly purified solid compound used to check the concentration of the known solution in a titration.

Critical Thinking

6. Explain Why is it important to determine the concentration of the standard solution precisely?

_____

_____

_____

_____

_____

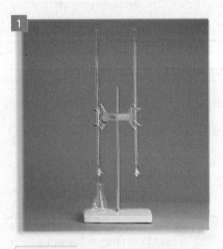

Set up two clean burets as shown. Rinse each buret three times with the solution that is to be used in that buret.

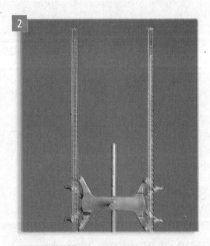

Fill the first buret to a point above the 0 mL calibration mark with the acid of unknown concentration.

Release some acid from the buret to remove any air bubbles from the tip and to lower the volume to the calibrated portion of the buret.

Record the volume of the acid in the buret to the nearest 0.01 mL as the initial volume. Remember to read the volume at the bottom of the meniscus.

Allow approximately the volume of acid that was determined by your teacher or lab procedure to flow into a clean Erlenmeyer flask.

Subtract the initial volume reading on the buret from the final reading. This is the exact volume of the acid released into the flask. Record it to the nearest 0.01 mL.

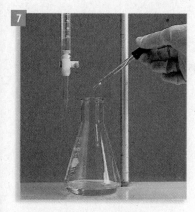

7 Add three drops of the appropriate indicator (in this case phenolphthalein) to the flask.

8 Fill the other buret with the standard base solution, whose concentration has already been determined, to a point above the calibration mark.

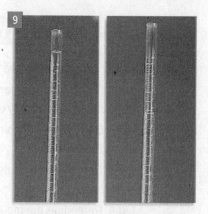

9 Release some base from the buret to remove any air bubbles and to lower the volume to the calibrated portion of the buret.

10 Record the volume of the base to the nearest 0.01 mL as your initial volume. Remember to read the volume at the bottom of the meniscus.

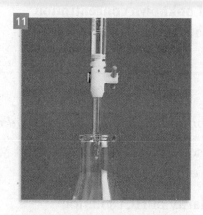

11 Place the Erlenmeyer flask under the base buret as shown. Notice that the tip of the buret extends into the mouth of the flask.

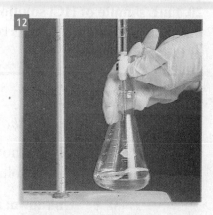

12 Slowly release base from the buret into the flask while constantly swirling the contents of the flask. The pink color of the indicator should fade with swirling.

13 The titration is nearing the end point when the pink color stays for longer periods of time. At this point, add base drop by drop.

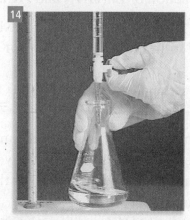

14 The equivalence point is reached when a very light pink color remains after 30 seconds of swirling.

15 Subtract the initial volume reading on the buret from the final reading. This is the exact volume of the base released into the flask. Record it to the nearest 0.01 mL.

Problem-Solving TIPS

To analyze the data collected from a titration experiment, follow these four steps:

- Step 1: Start with the balanced equation for the neutralization reaction and determine the chemically equivalent amounts of the acid and the base.
- Step 2: Determine the moles of acid (or base) from the known solution used during the titration.
- Step 3: Determine the moles of solute of the unknown solution used during the titration.
- Step 4: Determine the molarity of the unknown solution.

SAMPLE PROBLEM

In a titration, 27.4 mL of 0.0154 M $Ba(OH)_2$ is added to a 20.0 mL sample of HCl solution of unknown concentration until the equivalence point is reached. What is the molarity of the acid solution?

SOLUTION

1 ANALYZE

Determine the information that is given and unknown.

Given: known solution is 27.4 mL of 0.0154 M $Ba(OH)_2$, volume of HCl solution is 20.0 mL

Unknown: molarity of HCl solution

2 PLAN

Write the sequence of steps used to determine the unknown.

First, determine the mole ratio from the neutralization equation for the reaction of $Ba(OH)_2$ and HCl.

Second, determine the amount (in mol) of the known basic solution used from the volume of known solution used.

$$mL \cdot Ba(OH)_2 \times \frac{1\ L}{1000\ mL} \times \frac{mol\ Ba(OH)_2}{1\ L} = mol\ Ba(OH)_2$$

Third, determine the amount of moles of the unknown solution that reacted in the titration. Use the volume of known solution used and the mole ratio of the two substances.

$$mol\ Ba(OH)_2 \times \frac{mol\ HCl}{mol\ Ba(OH)_2} = mol\ HCl$$

Finally, determine the molarity of the unknown solution by dividing the amount in moles of the solution by the volume of the solution.

$$\frac{\text{amount of HCl (mol)}}{\text{volume of HCl (mL)}} \times \frac{1000\ \text{mL}}{1\ \text{L}} = \text{molarity of HCl solution}$$

3 SOLVE

Find the value of the unknown using the problem solving plan.

The neutralization equation for the reaction is:

$$Ba(OH)_2(aq) + 2HCl(aq) \rightarrow Ba(OH)_2(aq) + 2H_2O(l)$$

Therefore, the mole ratio of $Ba(OH)_2$ to HCl is 1:2.

The amount (in mol) of the known solution used is:

$$27.4\ \text{mL Ba(OH)}_2 \times \frac{1\ \text{L}}{1000\ \text{mL Ba(OH)}_2} \times \frac{0.0154\ \text{mol Ba(OH)}_2}{1\ \text{L}}$$

$$= 4.22 \times 10^{-4}\ \text{mol Ba(OH)}_2$$

The amount (in mol) of the unknown solution used is:

$$4.22 \times 10^{-4}\ \text{mol Ba(OH)}_2 \times \frac{2\ \text{mol HCl}}{1\ \text{mol Ba(OH)}_2}$$

$$= 8.44 \times 10^{-4}\ \text{mol HCl}$$

The molarity of the unknown solution is:

$$\frac{8.44 \times 10^{-4}\ \text{mol HCl}}{20\ \text{mL HCl}} \times \frac{1000\ \text{mL HCl}}{1\ \text{L}} = 4.22 \times 10^{-2}\ \text{M HCl}$$

4 CHECK YOUR WORK

Check the answer to see if it is reasonable.

The problem-solving plan outlined on the previous page was followed. At each step in the process, the units cancel as desired. There are the correct number of significant digits in the final answer.

💡 Critical Thinking

7. Analyze In the problem above, the volume of HCl that reacted was smaller than the volume of the basic solution that reacted. However, the concentration of the basic solution was smaller. Explain why these two facts do not contradict each other.

_____

_____

A. By titration, 17.6 mL of aqueous H_2SO_4 neutralized 27.4 mL of 0.0165 M LiOH solution. What was the molarity of the aqueous acid solution?

Summarize the steps necessary to determine the answer to the question from the given information.

_____

_____

_____

_____

What is the balanced neutralization equation for the reaction?

_____

What is the mole ratio of H_2SO_4 and LiOH?

_____

What was the volume of known solution used?

_____

What was the amount (in mol) of known solution used?

What was the amount (in mol) of unknown solution used?

What was the volume of unknown solution used?

_____

What was the molarity of the unknown solution?

VOCABULARY

1. What is meant by the transition interval of an indicator?

_____

_____

REVIEW

2. Name an appropriate indicator for titrating the following:

a. a strong acid and a weak base _____

b. a strong base and a weak acid _____

3. If 20.0 mL of 0.0100 M aqueous HCl is required to neutralize 30.0 mL of an aqueous solution of NaOH, determine the molarity of the NaOH solution.

4. Suppose that 20.0 mL of 0.010 M $Ca(OH)_2$ is required to neutralize 12.0 mL of aqueous HCl solution. What is the molarity of the HCl solution?

Critical Thinking

5. PREDICTING OUTCOMES
Sketch the titration curve for 50.0 mL of 0.10 M NH_3 that is titrated with 0.10 M HCl.

Math Tutor USING LOGARITHMS AND pH

When you work with acids and bases, you often need to state the hydronium ion concentration, $[H_3O^+]$, of a solution. One simple way is to use the negative logarithm of $[H_3O^+]$. This quantity is called *pH*. For example, pure water has an $[H_3O^+]$ of 1.00×10^{-7} M. So, the pH of pure water is $-\log(1.00 \times 10^{-7} \text{ M}) = 7.00$. A solution of 0.1 M HCl has a pH of 1.00 or pH $= -\log(1.00 \times 10^{-1} \text{ M}) = 1.00$.

The term *pOH* is also used for the negative logarithm of the hydroxide ion concentration, $[OH^-]$. The pOH of pure water is also 7.00.

Problem-Solving TIPS

- For pure water at 25°C, $[H_3O^+] = [OH^-] = 1.00 \times 10^{-7}$ M.
- The ionization constant of water, K_w, is the product of $[H_3O^+]$ and $[OH^-]$.
  $K_w = [H_3O^+][OH^-] = (1.00 \times 10^{-7} \text{ M})(1.00 \times 10^{-7} \text{ M}) = 1.00 \times 10^{-14}$ M at 25°C.
- If you know either $[H_3O^+]$ or $[OH^-]$, you can determine the other concentration.
- In terms of pH and pOH, pH + pOH = 14.00 for an aqueous solution at 25°C.
- Because pH calculations involve scientific notation and changes in signs, you should always check to see if answers make sense.

SAMPLE

What is the pH of a 0.0046 M solution of KOH?

KOH completely dissociates into equal numbers of $K^+(aq)$ ions and $OH^-(aq)$ ions. Therefore, the concentration of OH^- is the same as the concentration of dissolved KOH, 0.0046 M.

$$pOH = -\log[OH^-] = -\log(4.6 \times 10^{-3} \text{ M}) = 2.34$$

For an aqueous solution at 25°C, pH + pOH = 14.00

$$pH = 14.00 - pOH = 14.00 - 2.34 = 11.66$$

What is the hydronium ion concentration, $[H_3O^+]$, of a solution with a pH of 4.08? What is the pOH of the solution?

From the equation for pH, pH $= -\log[H_3O^+]$,

$$\log[H_3O^+] = -4.08$$

$$10^{\log[H_3O^+]} = 10^{-4.08}$$

$$[H_3O^+] = 10^{-4.08} = 0.000\,083 \text{ M} = 8.3 \times 10^{-5} \text{ M}$$

For an aqueous solution at 25°C, pH + pOH = 14.00

$$pOH = 14.00 - pH = 14.00 - 4.08 = 9.92$$

Practice Problems: Chapter Review practice problems 10–12

1. Why is pure water a very weak electric conductor?

_____

_____

2. What does it mean when a chemical formula is enclosed in brackets?

_____

_____

3. What is always true about the $[H_3O^+]$ value of acidic solutions?

_____

4. Identify each of the following solutions as acidic, basic, or neutral.

a. $[H_3O^+] = 1.0 \times 10^{-7}$ M _____

d. $[H_3O^+] = [OH^-]$ _____

b. $[H_3O^+] = 1.0 \times 10^{-10}$ M _____

e. pH = 13.0 _____

c. $[OH^-] = 1.0 \times 10^{-11}$ M _____

f. pH = 3.0 _____

5. Explain how changes in pH affect the color of an indicator.

_____

_____

6. On what basis is an indicator selected for a particular titration experiment?

_____

_____

7. For each titration, indicate the approximate pH at the end point. Also name
a suitable indicator for detecting that end point.

a. strong-acid/strong-base _____

b. strong-acid/weak-base _____

c. weak-acid/strong-base _____

d. weak-acid/weak-base _____

8. An unknown solution is colorless when tested with phenolphthalein but
causes the indicator phenol red to turn red. Use this information to find the
approximate pH of this solution.

_____

9. Calculate $[H_3O^+]$ and $[OH^-]$ for each of the following.

a. 0.030 M HCl $[H_3O^+] =$ _____ $[OH^-] =$ _____

b. 5.0×10^{-3} M HNO_3 $[H_3O^+] =$ _____ $[OH^-] =$ _____

c. 0.010 M $Ca(OH)_2$ $[H_3O^+] =$ _____ $[OH^-] =$ _____

10. Determine the pH of each of the following solutions.

a. 1.0×10^{-2} M HCl   pH = _____

b. 1.0×10^{-2} M NaOH   pH = _____

c. $[H_3O^+] = 3.8 \times 10^{-3}$ M   pH = _____

11. Calculate $[H_3O^+]$ and $[OH^-]$ for solutions with the following pH values.

a. 11.00 $[H_3O^+] =$ _____ $[OH^-] =$ _____

b. 4.23 $[H_3O^+] =$ _____ $[OH^-] =$ _____

c. 7.65 $[H_3O^+] =$ _____ $[OH^-] =$ _____

d. 9.48 $[H_3O^+] =$ _____ $[OH^-] =$ _____

12. A nitric acid solution is found to have a pH of 2.70.

a. What is the value of $[H_3O^+]$? _____

b. What is the value of $[OH^-]$? _____

c. What number of moles is required to prepare 5.50 L of this solution?

d. What mass of HNO_3 is required to make a 5.50 L solution?

e. What volume of concentrated acid, in milliliters, is needed to prepare
a 5.50 L solution? (Concentrated nitric acid is 69.5% HNO_3 by mass
and has a density of 1.42 g/mL.)

13. For each of the following acid-base titration combinations, determine the number of moles of the first substance that would be the chemically equivalent amount of the second substance.

a. HNO_3 with 0.75 mol KOH

b. $Ba(OH)_2$ with 0.20 mol HF

c. H_2SO_4 with 0.90 mol $Mg(OH)_2$

14. Suppose that 15.0 mL of 2.50×10^{-2} M aqueous H_2SO_4 is required to neutralize 10.0 mL of an aqueous solution of KOH. What is the molarity of the KOH solution?

15. In a titration experiment, a 12.5 mL sample of 1.75×10^{-2} M $Ba(OH)_2$ just neutralized 14.5 mL of HNO_3 solution. Calculate the molarity of the HNO_3 solution.

CHAPTER 16

Reaction Energy

Key Concepts

Section 1 *Thermochemistry*

What is temperature and what are the units of temperature?

What is the difference between heat and temperature?

What is the significance of the specific heat of a substance?

What is enthalpy and how is it calculated?

Section 2 *Driving Force of Reactions*

What determines whether a reaction is likely to occur?

What is free energy and how is it calculated?

Review Previous Concepts

1. Explain what the conservation of energy within a closed system means.

_____

_____

_____

2. What is the bond energy of a chemical compound?

_____

_____

_____

3. What is the kinetic theory of matter?

_____

_____

_____

SECTION 16.1

Thermochemistry

In the chapter "States of Matter" you learned that energy is absorbed or released during a physical change of matter, such as a change of state. Nearly all chemical changes also result in the release or absorption of energy. **Thermochemistry** is the study of transfers of energy as heat that accompany chemical reactions and physical changes.

Temperature and heat are related but not identical.

Temperature is a measure of the average kinetic energy of the particles in a sample of matter. The greater the kinetic energy of the particles, the higher the temperature.

To assign a numerical value to temperature, a temperature scale must be defined. Calculations in thermochemistry use the Celsius and Kelvin temperature scales. These two scales are related by this equation.

$$K = 273.15 + °C$$

In thermochemistry, scientists are interested in the transfer of energy as heat during a reaction, not the temperature. However, the transfer of energy as heat is not directly measurable. So, scientists measure temperature changes and then use the relationship between temperature and heat to convert the measurements into units of energy. The tool used in thermochemistry to perform this task is a calorimeter. A **calorimeter** measures the energy absorbed or released as heat in a chemical or physical change.

In one kind of calorimeter, known amounts of reactants are sealed in a chamber. The chamber is immersed in a known amount of water. The energy given off (or absorbed) during the reaction is equal to the energy absorbed (or lost) by the water. The calorimeter measures the temperature change of the water. The measurement can then be converted into a measure of energy transferred as heat.

KEY TERMS

thermochemistry
temperature
calorimeter
heat
joule
specific heat
enthalpy change
enthalpy of reaction
thermochemical equation
molar enthalpy of formation
enthalpy of combustion
Hess's law

✓ READING CHECK

1. A calorimeter measures changes in _____ because the energy lost or gained by a reaction cannot be directly measured.

This thermometer can be used to monitor temperature changes in a substance.

(a)
(b)

Heat can be thought of as energy transferred between samples of matter because of a difference in their temperatures. Energy transferred as heat always moves from matter at a higher temperature to matter at a lower temperature. In the photographs above, energy flows from the hotter cylinder to the cooler water. As the thermometer shows, the temperature of the water increases as this energy is absorbed by the water as heat. The temperature of the cylinder decreases as it loses this energy. This process continues until the water and the cylinder have the same temperature. At that point, there is no temperature difference, so no energy is transferred.

The amount of energy transferred as heat is usually measured in joules. A **joule,** J, is the SI unit of heat as well as all other forms of energy. A joule is derived from the units of force and length, as shown below.

$$J = N \times m = kg \times \frac{m^2}{s^2}$$

Several factors determine the transfer of heat.

Different materials have differing abilities to transfer heat. It takes a lot more energy to raise the temperature of 1 kg of water by 1°C than it does to raise the temperature of 1 kg of iron by 1°C.

(a) A brass cylinder is heated.
(b) Energy is transferred as heat from the brass cylinder to the water, making the temperature of the water rise. This energy transfer will continue until the cylinder and the water reach the same temperature.

READING CHECK

2. Explain the relationship between heat and temperature.

_____

_____

_____

_____

Specific Heats of Some Common Substances at 298.15 K	
Substance	Specific heat J/(g•K)
Water (*l*)	4.18
Water (*s*)	2.06
Water (*g*)	1.87
Ammonia (*g*)	2.09
Benzene (*l*)	1.74
Ethanol (*l*)	2.44
Ethanol (*g*)	1.42
Aluminum (*s*)	0.897
Calcium (*s*)	0.647
Carbon, graphite (*s*)	0.709
Copper (*s*)	0.385
Gold (*s*)	0.129
Iron (*s*)	0.449
Mercury (*l*)	0.140
Lead (*s*)	0.129

Water has one of the highest specific heats of common substances.

Metals commonly have low specific heats.

The amount of energy transferred as heat during a temperature change depends on three factors:

- the nature of the material that is changing temperature
- the mass of the material changing temperature
- the amount of the temperature change

These three factors are reflected in the equation below. It gives an expression for the quantity of energy, q, gained or lost by a sample with mass m that changes in temperature by ΔT.

$$q = c_p \times m \times \Delta T$$

The symbol c_p represents the specific heat of a material at constant pressure. **Specific heat** is the energy in joules required to raise the temperature of one gram of a substance by 1°C.

Specific heat is a measure of the ability of the material to absorb energy. One gram of iron that cools from 100°C to 50°C releases 22.5 J of energy. One gram of silver would only release 11.8 J of energy. So, iron has a higher specific heat than silver. The table at the top of the page shows some values of specific heat for some common substances.

Critical Thinking

3. Calculate Rewrite the equation for energy at the left so that the specific heat of a substance can be calculated from the other three quantities.

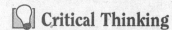

$c_p =$ _____

TIP The definition at the left requires specific heat to be reported in units of J/(g•°C). However, specific heat can also be given in other units, such as cal/(g•°C). Also, remember that changes in Celsius temperature are equivalent to changes in Kelvin temperature.

A 4.0 g sample of glass was heated from 274 K to 314 K, a temperature increase of 40 K, and was found to have absorbed 32 J of energy as heat. What is the specific heat of this type of glass? How much energy will the same glass sample gain when it is heated from 314 K to 344 K?

SOLUTION

1 ANALYZE   *Determine the information that is given and unknown.*

Given: $m = 4.0$ g
$T_{initial} = 274$ K
$T_{final} = 314$ K
$q = 32$ J

Unknown: c_p of glass, energy absorbed when heated from 314 K to 344 K

2 PLAN   *Write the equations needed to determine the unknowns.*

The specific heat, c_p, of glass can be found from the given information by using the equation

$$c_p = \frac{q}{m \times \Delta T}$$

The same equation can be used to find the energy absorbed during the second heating by solving for the quantity q.

$$q = c_p \times m \times \Delta T$$

3 SOLVE   *Substitute the given information to find the unknown values.*

ΔT for the first heating is 314 K − 274 K = 40 K.

$$c_p = \frac{32 \text{ J}}{(4.0 \text{ g})(40 \text{ K})} = 0.20 \text{ J/(g} \cdot \text{K)}$$

ΔT for the second heating is 344 K − 314 K = 30 K.

$$q = (0.20 \text{ J/(g} \cdot \text{K)})(4.0 \text{ g})(30 \text{ K}) = 24 \text{ J}$$

PRACTICE

A. Determine the specific heat of a material if a 35 g sample absorbed 96 J as it was heated from 293 K to 313 K.

$$c_p = \frac{q}{m \times \Delta T} = \underline{\hspace{3cm}} =$$

Heat energy is transferred during a reaction.

The energy absorbed as heat during a chemical reaction at constant pressure is represented by ΔH, where H represents a quantity called *enthalpy*. It is not practical to discuss the enthalpy, H, of a quantity, because it cannot be measured. However, changes in enthalpy, ΔH, can be measured. An **enthalpy change** is the amount of energy absorbed by a system as heat during a process at constant pressure.

The following equation expresses an enthalpy change for a reaction. The **enthalpy of reaction** is the energy transferred as heat during a chemical reaction. You can think of the enthalpy of reaction as the difference between the stored energy of the reactants and the stored energy of the products. This quantity is sometimes referred to as the *heat of reaction*.

$$\Delta H = H_{products} - H_{reactants}$$

A **thermochemical equation** is an equation that includes the quantity of energy released or absorbed as heat during the reaction. A general way to express a thermochemical equation is as follows.

$$\text{reactants} + \Delta H \longrightarrow \text{products}$$

Here are four things to keep in mind when using thermochemical equations.

1. The coefficients in a balanced thermochemical equation represent the numbers of moles of the reactants and products and never the number of molecules. This allows us to write the coefficients as fractions rather than whole numbers when necessary.

2. The physical state of the product or reactant involved in a reaction is an important factor and must be included in the thermochemical equation.

3. The change in enthalpy represented by a thermochemical equation is directly proportional to the number of moles of substances undergoing a change. For example, if 2 mol of H_2O are decomposed, twice as much enthalpy, 483.6 kJ, is needed than for the decomposition of 1 mol of H_2O, which requires 241.8 kJ of enthalpy.

4. The value of the enthalpy change, ΔH, is usually not influenced by changing temperature.

 Remember

The symbol "Δ" before a variable means "change in." So, ΔT is change in temperature, and ΔH is the change in enthalpy.

✓ READING CHECK

4. What is the difference between a regular chemical equation and a thermochemical equation?

_____

_____

_____

_____

_____

Exothermic Reactions If a mixture of hydrogen and oxygen is ignited, water will form and energy will be released explosively. The released energy comes from the reactants as they form products. More energy is stored in the bonds of the reactants than in the bonds of the products. The excess energy is released to the environment.

A reaction is *exothermic* if it releases energy to the environment. Experiments have shown that the exothermic reaction of hydrogen and water releases 483.6 kJ of energy for every 2 mol of water vapor that form. This information can be summarized in the following thermochemical equation.

$$2H_2(g) + O_2(g) \longrightarrow 2H_2O(g) + 483.6 \text{ kJ}$$

The amount of energy that is released is proportional to the number of moles that react. So, the formation of 4 mol of water and the formation of 1 mol of water can be expressed in the following thermochemical equations.

$$4H_2(g) + 2O_2(g) \longrightarrow 4H_2O(g) + 967.2 \text{ kJ}$$

$$H_2(g) + \tfrac{1}{2}O_2(g) \longrightarrow H_2O(g) + 241.8 \text{ kJ}$$

The graph below shows the evolution of an exothermic reaction. The enthalpy change, ΔH, is always negative because the energy of the products is less than the energy of the reactants.

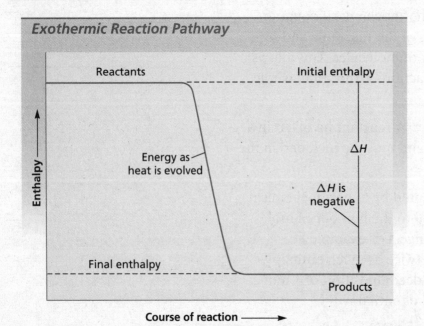

Exothermic Reaction Pathway

Reactants — Initial enthalpy

Energy as heat is evolved

ΔH

ΔH is negative

Final enthalpy

Products

Enthalpy

Course of reaction ⟶

TIP An enthalpy change is the amount of energy absorbed during a reaction. Note that enthalpy changes for combustion reactions are written on the right side of the equation, instead of on the left as in the general model on the preceding page. When an enthalpy change is negative, it is often written on the right side of the equation so it can be expressed as a positive value (amount of energy released).

TIP The ability to express chemical equations in fractional moles is useful when calculating molar enthalpy changes, as shown later in this section. Note that, because this equation expresses the formation of 1 mol of water, the energy required to form water from hydrogen and oxygen can be expressed as 241.8 kJ/mol.

READING CHECK

5. Write a thermochemical equation for the formation of 5 mol of water from hydrogen gas and oxygen gas.

_____

_____

In an exothermic chemical reaction, the enthalpy change is negative, meaning that energy is released from the system as heat.

Endothermic Reactions When water decomposes into hydrogen and oxygen, the opposite of an exothermic reaction occurs. A reaction is *endothermic* if it absorbs energy from the environment. The following thermochemical equation summarizes the decomposition of water.

$$2H_2O(g) + 483.6 \text{ kJ} \longrightarrow 2H_2(g) + O_2(g)$$

The energy absorbed by the decomposition of water is the same as the energy released by the formation of water. However, because the energy is absorbed, the enthalpy change, ΔH, has a positive value instead of a negative value. This positive value of enthalpy change is demonstrated in the graph below.

Thermochemical equations are usually written by giving the value of ΔH rather than writing the energy as a reactant or product. For example, the reactions for the formation and decomposition of water can be written as follows.

$$2H_2(g) + O_2(g) \longrightarrow 2H_2O(g); \Delta H = -483.6 \text{ kJ}$$

$$2H_2O(g) \longrightarrow 2H_2(g) + O_2(g); \Delta H = 483.6 \text{ kJ}$$

When the equations are written in this way, the sign of ΔH always reflects whether the reaction absorbs or releases energy. When ΔH is positive, the reaction is endothermic and the reaction absorbs energy. When ΔH is negative, the reaction is exothermic and the reaction releases energy.

 Remember

The physical states of the substances in a thermochemical equation are important. More energy would be required to decompose water if the water were in the liquid or solid phase.

 READING CHECK

6. If energy is released by a chemical reaction, the reaction is

_____ .

If energy is absorbed by a chemical reaction, the reaction is

_____ .

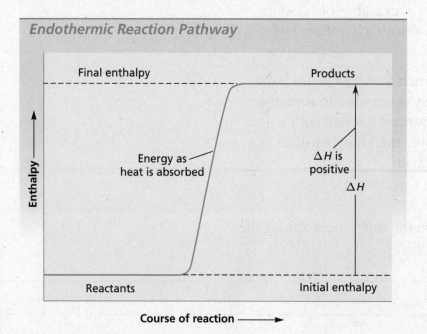

Endothermic Reaction Pathway

- Final enthalpy
- Products
- Enthalpy
- Energy as heat is absorbed
- ΔH is positive
- ΔH
- Reactants
- Initial enthalpy
- Course of reaction →

In an endothermic chemical reaction, the enthalpy change is positive, meaning that energy is absorbed into the system as heat.

Enthalpy of formation is the energy change when elements form one mole of a compound.

A *composition reaction* is the formation of a compound from its elements in their standard form. The formation of water from hydrogen and oxygen is a composition reaction.

The **molar enthalpy of formation**, ΔH_f, is the enthalpy change that occurs when one mole of a compound is formed from its elements in their standard state at 25°C and 1 atm. As shown earlier in this section, the molar enthalpy of formation of water vapor is −241.8 kJ/mol.

To make comparisons meaningful, enthalpies of formation are given for the standard states of reactants and products. The standard state of a substance is the state found at atmospheric pressure and room temperature. The molar enthalpy of formation of water vapor given above is not a standard enthalpy of formation because water is primarily in the liquid phase under normal conditions. The standard enthalpy of formation of water, ΔH_f^0, is −285.8 kJ/mol.

TIP The ^{0} sign that is added to an enthalpy symbol indicates that the standard enthalpy of a reaction is being given.

Compounds with large negative heats of formation tend to be stable.

If a large amount of energy is released as heat when a compound forms, the compound has a large negative enthalpy of formation. Such compounds are very stable, because the molecules of the compound must absorb a lot of energy before their bonds can be broken.

Stable Compounds Elements in their standard states have $\Delta H_f^0 = 0$ kJ/mol, because no energy is required to form the elements from themselves. For this reason water, with a $\Delta H_f^0 = -285.8$ kJ/mol, is more stable than the hydrogen and oxygen from which it was formed.

 Critical Thinking

7. **Compare and Contrast** Explain the differences among the following values: ΔH, ΔH_f, and ΔH_f^0.

Unstable Compounds Compounds with positive values of ΔH_f^0, or only slightly negative values, are typically unstable. For example, hydrogen iodide, HI, is a colorless gas that decomposes somewhat when stored at room temperature. It has a value of $\Delta H_f^0 = +26.5$ kJ/mol.

Compounds with a high positive enthalpy of formation are sometimes very unstable and react or decompose violently. For example, ethyne (acetylene), C_2H_2, reacts violently with oxygen and must be stored in cylinders as a solution in acetone. It has a value of $\Delta H_f^0 = +226.7$ kJ/mol.

Ethyne is the fuel used in oxyacetylene torches. The torches can reach temperatures over 3000°C as the ethyne combusts with oxygen.

Enthalpy changes in combustion.

Combustion reactions produce a large amount of energy in the form of light and heat. The enthalpy change that occurs during the complete combustion of one mole of a substance is called the **enthalpy of combustion,** ΔH_c, of the substance.

The enthalpy of formation is defined in terms of one mole of the product that is formed. The enthalpy of combustion, on the other hand, is defined in terms of one mole of the reactant that combusts. The value of ΔH_c for ethyne is -1301.1 kJ/mol. All enthalpies of combustion are negative because combustion reactions always release energy, and therefore are exothermic.

A combustion calorimeter is a common instrument used to determine ΔH_c. The diagram below shows a fixed-volume calorimeter.

✓ **READING CHECK**

8. What is the sign of the enthalpy of combustion for sucrose? Explain your answer.

_____

_____

_____

_____

_____

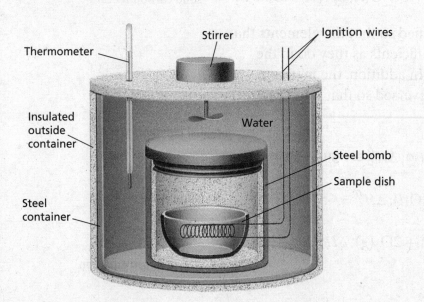

Thermometer — Stirrer — Ignition wires

Insulated outside container

Steel container

Water

Steel bomb

Sample dish

In this combustion calorimeter, a weighed sample is ignited by an electric spark and burned in the dish in an atmosphere of pure oxygen. The energy released by the reaction warms the steel bomb and the water surrounding it. The thermometer is used to measure the temperature change in the water, from which the energy transferred as heat can be calculated.

Change in enthalpy is calculated using Hess's Law.

Thermochemical reactions can be rearranged and added to give enthalpy changes for reactions in which the enthalpy change is unknown. According to **Hess's law**, the overall enthalpy change in a reaction is equal to the sum of the enthalpy changes for the individual steps in the process. As a consequence of this law, the energy difference between reactants and products is independent of the route taken to get from one to the other. The general principles for combining thermochemical equations are as follows.

1. If a reaction is reversed, the sign of ΔH is also reversed.

2. All coefficients in a chemical equation can be multiplied by a number as long as ΔH is also multiplied by that number.

3. Equations can be added and subtracted from each other.

Consider the formation of methane gas, CH_4, from its elements, solid carbon (graphite) and hydrogen gas.

$$C(s) + 2H_2(g) \longrightarrow CH_4(g); \Delta H_f^0 = ?$$

Suppose that the energy of formation for methane is unknown. However, suppose a combustion calorimeter is used to determine the enthalpies of combustion for each of the three substances in the equation above.

$$C(s) + O_2(g) \longrightarrow CO_2(g); \Delta H_c^0 = -393.5 \text{ kJ}$$

$$H_2(g) + \frac{1}{2}O_2(g) \longrightarrow H_2O(l); \Delta H_c^0 = -285.8 \text{ kJ}$$

$$CH_4(g) + 2O_2(g) \longrightarrow CO_2(g) + 2H_2O(l); \Delta H_c^0 = -890.8 \text{ kJ}$$

Each equation should be modified so that the elements that are combusted have the same coefficients as they do in the equation for methane formation. In addition, the methane combustion equation should be reversed so that it is a product instead of a reactant.

$$C(s) + O_2(g) \longrightarrow CO_2(g); \Delta H_c^0 = -393.5 \text{ kJ}$$

original equation

$$2H_2(g) + O_2(g) \longrightarrow 2H_2O(l); \Delta H_c^0 = -571.6 \text{ kJ}$$

equation multiplied by 2

$$CO_2(g) + 2H_2O(l) \longrightarrow CH_4(g) + 2O_2(g); \Delta H^0 = +890.8 \text{ kJ}$$

reversed equation

 READING CHECK

9. Explain What is the relationship between Hess's law and the conservation of energy?

_____

_____

_____

_____

_____

TIP Note that the composition equation for carbon dioxide from elemental carbon and oxygen is equivalent to the combustion equation for solid carbon.

Applying Hess's Law Hess's law allows the three equations at the bottom of the preceding page to be added together. This will result in the equation for the formation of methane. The sum of the enthalpies is the heat of formation of methane.

$$\Delta H^0_f = (-393.5 \text{ kJ}) + (-571.6 \text{ kJ}) + (+890.8 \text{ kJ}) = -74.3 \text{ kJ}$$

Note that there are two oxygen molecules on the reactant side and two on the product side of the equations, so oxygen can be cancelled from the sum of the equations. Similarly, there are two molecules of water on each side of the equations, and they can be canceled. The same is true for CO_2.

> **Hess's law can be used to determine reaction enthalpies not measurable directly.**

The process above can also be applied to finding the enthalpy of formation of carbon monoxide. This value cannot be measured directly because its formation always occurs in partnership with the formation of carbon dioxide.

$$C(s) + \tfrac{1}{2} O_2(g) \longrightarrow CO(g); \Delta H^0_f = ?$$

The unknown ΔH^0_f above can be calculated from the combustion equation for $C(s)$ and the reverse of the combustion equation for $CO_2(g)$.

$$C(s) + O_2(g) \longrightarrow CO_2(g); \qquad \Delta H^0_c = -393.5 \text{ kJ}$$

$$CO_2(g) \longrightarrow CO(g) + \tfrac{1}{2}O_2(g); \Delta H^0 = +283.0 \text{ kJ}$$

$$C(s) + \tfrac{1}{2}O_2(g) \longrightarrow CO(g); \qquad \Delta H^0_f = -110.5 \text{ kJ}$$

combustion equation for C(s)

reversed combustion equation of CO(g)

sum of the two equations

TIP  Substances cannot be cancelled from an equation unless they are in the same state. For this reason, it is important to track the states of the substances through each step in the process.

✓ **READING CHECK**

10. Is the formation of carbon monoxide an exothermic or endothermic reaction?

_____

_____

Enthalpies of Reaction

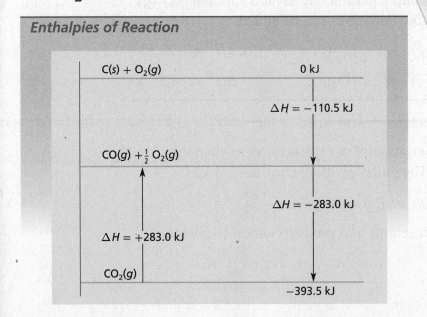

A graphical representation of the formation of $CO(g)$ and the formation of $CO_2(g)$ from elemental carbon and oxygen is shown.

Calculate the enthalpy of reaction for the combustion of nitrogen monoxide gas, NO, to form nitrogen dioxide gas, as given by the following thermochemical equation.

$$NO(g) + \frac{1}{2}O_2(g) \longrightarrow NO_2(g)$$

Use these formation equations for nitrogen monoxide and nitrogen dioxide.

$$\frac{1}{2}N_2(g) + \frac{1}{2}O_2(g) \longrightarrow NO(g); \Delta H_f^0 = +90.3 \text{ kJ}$$

$$\frac{1}{2}N_2(g) + O_2(g) \longrightarrow NO_2(g); \Delta H_f^0 = +33.2 \text{ kJ}$$

SOLUTION

1 ANALYZE   *Determine the information that is given and unknown.*

Given: ΔH_f^0 for $NO(g)$

ΔH_f^0 for $NO_2(g)$

Unknown: ΔH_c^0 for $NO(g)$

2 PLAN   *Write a plan that can be used to determine the unknown.*

Rewrite the two given equations to match the coefficients of $NO(g)$ and $NO_2(g)$ for the unknown enthalpy of reaction. Then add the two revised equations.

3 SOLVE   *Execute the plan to find the unknown values.*

The first equation needs to be reversed to get 1 mol of $NO(g)$ on the left. The second equation already has 1 mol of $NO_2(g)$ on the right. Then the equations can be added.

$$NO(g) \longrightarrow \frac{1}{2}\cancel{N_2(g)} + \frac{1}{2}\cancel{O_2(g)}; \Delta H^0 = -90.3 \text{ kJ}$$

$$\frac{1}{2}\cancel{N_2(g)} + O_2(g) \longrightarrow NO_2(g); \qquad \Delta H^0 = +33.2 \text{ kJ}$$

$$NO(g) + \frac{1}{2}O_2(g) \longrightarrow NO_2(g); \qquad \Delta H_f^0 = -57.1 \text{ kJ}$$

0.5 mol of $N_2(g)$ and 0.5 mol of $O_2(g)$ cancel to yield the correct equation. The enthalpy of reaction is –57.1 kJ.

4 CHECK YOUR WORK   *Check the answer to see if it makes sense.*

The unnecessary reactants and products cancel to give the correct equation.

B. Carbon occurs in two distinct forms. It can be the soft, black material found in pencils and lock lubricants, called graphite. Or, it can be the hard, brilliant gem we know as diamond. Calculate ΔH^0 for the conversion of graphite to diamond in the following reaction.

$$C_{graphite}(s) \longrightarrow C_{diamond}(s)$$

Use the following combustion equations to find the answer.

$$C_{graphite}(s) + O_2(g) \longrightarrow CO_2(g); \Delta H_c^0 = -394 \text{ kJ}$$

$$C_{diamond}(s) + O_2(g) \longrightarrow CO_2(g); \Delta H_c^0 = -396 \text{ kJ}$$

How many moles of $C_{graphite}(s)$ are in the reaction where ΔH^0 is unknown? _____

Is $C_{graphite}(s)$ on the reactant side or the product side of the equation where ΔH^0 is unknown? _____

How many moles of $C_{diamond}(s)$ are in the reaction where ΔH^0 is unknown? _____

Is $C_{diamond}(s)$ on the reactant side or the product side of the equation where ΔH^0 is unknown? _____

Write the first combustion equation, revising it if necessary so that the correct number of moles of $C_{graphite}(s)$ is on the correct side of the equation. Then, write the second combustion equation, revising it if necessary so that the correct number of moles of $C_{graphite}(s)$ is on the correct side of the equation. Finally, add the two equations, canceling terms if necessary.

_____ $\longrightarrow$ _____; $\Delta H^0 =$ _____

_____ $\longrightarrow$ _____; $\Delta H^0 =$ _____

_____ $\longrightarrow$ _____; $\Delta H^0 =$ _____

Check your answer. Does your sum above match the graphite-diamond reaction given in the problem?

_____

Calculate the enthalpy of formation of pentane, C_5H_{12}.

$$5C(s) + 6H_2(g) \longrightarrow C_5H_{12}(g)$$

Use the combustion equations for the three compounds.

$$C(s) + O_2(g) \longrightarrow CO_2(g); \Delta H_c^0 = -393.5 \text{ kJ}$$

$$H_2(g) + \frac{1}{2}O_2(g) \longrightarrow H_2O(l); \Delta H_c^0 = -285.8 \text{ kJ}$$

$$C_5H_{12}(g) + 8O_2(g) \longrightarrow 5CO_2(g) + 6H_2O(l); \Delta H_c^0 = -3535.6 \text{ kJ}$$

SOLUTION

1 ANALYZE   *Determine the information that is given and unknown.*

Given: ΔH_c^0 for $C(s)$, ΔH_c^0 for $H_2(g)$, ΔH_c^0 for $C_5H_{12}(g)$

Unknown: ΔH_f^0 for $C_5H_{12}(g)$

2 PLAN   *Write a plan that can be used to determine the unknown.*

Rewrite the three given equations to match the coefficient of $C(s)$, $H_2(g)$, and $C_5H_{12}(g)$ for the unknown enthalpy of formation. Then add the two revised equations.

3 SOLVE   *Execute the plan to find the unknown values.*

The first equation needs to be multiplied by 5 to get 5 mol of $C(s)$ on the left. The second equation needs to be multiplied by 6 to get 6 mol of $H_2(g)$ on the left. The third equation needs to be reversed to get 1 mol of $C_5H_{12}(g)$ on the right. Then the equations can be added.

$$5C(s) + 5O_2(g) \longrightarrow 5CO_2(g); \qquad \Delta H_c^0 = -1967.5 \text{ kJ}$$

$$6H_2(g) + 3O_2(g) \longrightarrow 6H_2O(l); \qquad \Delta H_c^0 = -1714.8 \text{ kJ}$$

$$5CO_2(g) + 6H_2O(l) \longrightarrow C_5H_{12}(g) + 8O_2(g); \Delta H^0 = +3535.6 \text{ kJ}$$

$$\overline{5C(s) + 6H_2(g) \longrightarrow C_5H_{12}(g) \qquad \Delta H_f^0 = -146.7 \text{ kJ}}$$

The 8 mol of $O_2(g)$, 5 mol of $CO_2(g)$, and 6 mol of $H_2O(l)$ cancel to yield the correct equation. The enthalpy of formation for pentane is −146.7 kJ.

4 CHECK YOUR WORK   *Check the answer to see if it makes sense.*

The unnecessary reactants and products cancel to give the correct equation.

c. Calculate the enthalpy of formation for sulfur dioxide, SO_2, from its elements, sulfur and oxygen. Use the balanced chemical equation and the following information.

$$S(s) + \frac{3}{2}O_2(g) \longrightarrow SO_3(g); \Delta H_c^0 = -395.2 \text{ kJ}$$

$$2SO_2(g) + O_2(g) \longrightarrow 2SO_3(g); \Delta H^0 = -198.2 \text{ kJ}$$

Write the balanced composition equation for $SO_2(g)$.

_____

How many moles of $S(s)$ are in the composition equation?

_____

Is $S(s)$ on the reactant side or the product side of the composition equation?

_____

How many moles of $SO_2(g)$ are in the composition equation?

_____

Is $SO_2(g)$ on the reactant side or the product side of the composition equation?

_____

Write the first combustion equation, revising it if necessary so that the correct number of moles of $S(s)$ is on the correct side of the equation. Then, write the second combustion equation, revising it if necessary so that the correct number of moles of $SO_2(g)$ is on the correct side of the equation. Finally, add the two equations, canceling terms if necessary.

_____ $\longrightarrow$ _____ ; $\Delta H^0 =$ _____

_____ $\longrightarrow$ _____ ; $\Delta H^0 =$ _____

_____ $\longrightarrow$ _____ ; $\Delta H_f^0 =$ _____

Check your answer. Does your sum above match the balanced composition equation for $SO_2(g)$?

_____

VOCABULARY

1. What is meant by enthalpy of reaction?

_____

_____

REVIEW

2. How much energy would be absorbed as heat by 75 g of iron when heated from 295 K to 301 K?

Critical Thinking

3. INTEGRATING CONCEPTS Isooctane, C_8H_{18}, is a major component of gasoline. Using the following thermodynamic data, calculate the change in enthalpy for the combustion of 1.0 gal of isooctane.

$$H_2(g) + \frac{1}{2}O_2(g) \longrightarrow H_2O(g); \Delta H_c^0 = -241.8 \text{ kJ}$$

$$C(s) + O_2(g) \longrightarrow CO_2(g); \Delta H_c^0 = 393.5 \text{ kJ}$$

$$8C(s) + 9H_2(g) \longrightarrow C_8H_{18}(l); \Delta H_f^0 = -224.1 \text{ kJ}$$

First, write the combustion equation for isooctane.

_____

Then, add the three given equations in such a way as to produce the combustion equation for isooctane.

_____

_____

_____

One gallon of isooctane has a mass of 2.6 kg. What is the change in enthalpy for the combustion of 1.0 gal of isooctane?

Driving Force of Reactions

The change in energy of a reaction system, or enthalpy change, is one of two factors that allow chemists to predict whether a reaction will occur spontaneously and to explain how it occurs. A second factor is related to the random motion of the particles in a system, according to the kinetic-molecular theory of matter.

Reactions generally move to a lower-energy state.

The change in enthalpy between reactants and products is one factor that explains why chemical reactions happen. Chemical reactions that occur in nature are exothermic. This means that the reactions release energy, and that the products have less potential energy than the reactants. The tendency in natural systems is for a reaction to proceed in a direction that leads to a lower energy state, or enthalpy, and a more stable structure. The products are more stable than the original reactants.

Endothermic reactions also occur in nature. These reactions produce products that have a higher potential energy than the reactants. This goes against the tendency of natural systems to move into lower energy states.

A continual input of energy in the form of heat can cause an endothermic reaction to occur. For example, melting is a naturally occurring endothermic process. Energy being transferred from room-temperature air to an ice cube will cause the ice to melt. Energy is conserved as it moves from warm air to cold ice.

The melting of ice goes against the tendency of natural systems to move into a state of lower enthalpy, because a liquid has more energy than a solid. Whenever a system moves from one state to another without a decrease in enthalpy, it does so with an increase in *entropy* instead.

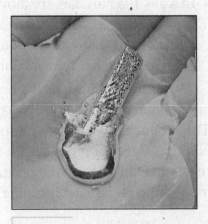

Gallium will melt spontaneously when in contact with a warm human hand. The enthalpy of the gallium increases as it absorbs energy. The melting point of gallium is 29.77°C.

READING CHECK

1. The tendency of systems in nature is for matter to move from a state of _____ enthalpy to a state of _____ enthalpy.

Entropy measures randomness in a system.

There is a tendency in natural systems to proceed in a direction that increases the randomness of the system. A random system is one that lacks a regular arrangement in its parts. **Entropy,** S, can be defined as a measure of the degree of randomness of the particles in a system. To understand the concept of entropy, consider solids, liquids, and gases.

- In a solid, the particles are fixed in position, vibrating back and forth. Their exact position can be pinned down to a small region of space. The degree of randomness is low, so the entropy in a solid is low.

- In a liquid, the particles are still very close together, but they can move about somewhat. The system is more random, and it is more difficult to describe the location of the particles. The entropy is higher in a liquid than a solid.

- In a gas, the particles are moving more rapidly and they are farther apart. Locating an individual particle is more difficult, and the system is more random. The entropy of a gas is even higher than a liquid.

For example, consider the decomposition reaction of ammonium nitrate below. Two gases and a liquid are formed. The products have a higher entropy than the reactant. In addition, 7 mol of products are formed for every 2 mol of reactant. Determining the position of seven particles is much more difficult than determining the position of two particles.

$$2NH_4NO_3(s) \longrightarrow 2N_2(g) + 4H_2O(l) + O_2(g)$$

TIP See the chapter "States of Matter" for more information on how the particles in the different states of matter behave according to the kinetic-molecular theory of matter.

✓ READING CHECK

2. Explain the term *entropy* in your own words.

_____

_____

_____

_____

_____

When ammonium nitrate, NH_4NO_3, decomposes, the entropy increases as (a) one solid reactant becomes (b) two gaseous products and one liquid product.

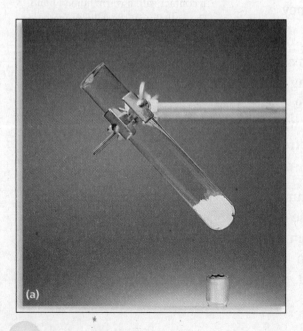

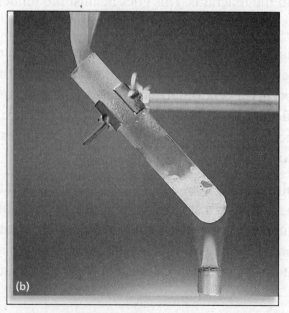

(a)

(b)

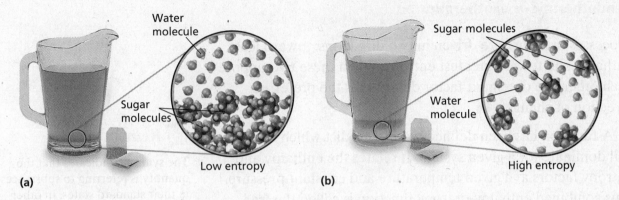

Water molecule

Sugar molecules

Low entropy

(a)

Sugar molecules

Water molecule

High entropy

(b)

The entropy of a pure crystalline solid is zero at absolute zero. In this theoretical state, the particles are not moving and their positions are defined precisely. As energy is added, the randomness of the molecular motion increases as the particles start to vibrate.

> When a solid dissolves in a liquid, the entropy of the system increases.

The standard molar entropy for a substance is reported in values with the units kJ/(mol•K). Entropy change, ΔS, is defined as the difference between the entropy of the products and the entropy of the reactants. An increase in entropy is represented by a positive value of ΔS, and a decrease in entropy is represented by a negative value of ΔS.

A natural process that almost always involves a positive value of ΔS is the formation of a solution. The diagram above demonstrates how this process increases entropy. When solid sugar is still at the bottom of the tea, most sugar molecules can be found within a small region of the pitcher. When the sugar has dissolved completely in the tea, the sugar molecules are thoroughly mixed and moving at random throughout the pitcher. The entropy is higher when the sugar is completely dissolved.

✓ READING CHECK

3. In natural systems, physical and chemical changes tend to

occur that have _____ values of ΔH and

_____ values of ΔS.

4. Explain the difference between enthalpy and entropy.

_____

_____

_____

Free energy changes determine if a reaction is endothermic or exothermic.

Processes in nature are driven in two directions: toward least enthalpy and toward greatest entropy. When these two oppose each other, the dominant factor determines the preferred direction of change.

A function has been defined to help predict which factor will dominate for a given system. It relates the enthalpy and entropy factors at a given temperature and constant pressure. This combined enthalpy-entropy function is called the **free energy,** G, of the system, or the Gibbs free energy of the system. Natural processes move in a direction that lowers the free energy of a system.

Only the change in the free energy can be measured. At a constant pressure and temperature, the **free-energy change,** ΔG, of a system is defined as the difference between the change in enthalpy, ΔH, and the product of the Kelvin temperature and the entropy change. Because the entropy change for a system is $T\Delta S$, where T is the temperature, the free-energy change can be summarized by the following equation.

$$\Delta G^0 = \Delta H^0 - T\Delta S^0$$

The quantities ΔG, ΔH, and $T\Delta S$, are typically measured in kilojoules. If ΔG is less than zero, then a reaction is spontaneous, because natural systems tend toward states with a lower free energy. Based on the values of ΔH and ΔS, there are four possible combinations of these terms. These combinations are summarized in the table below.

Critical Thinking

5. Analyze Can an endothermic process, $\Delta H > 0$, have a free-energy change that is less than zero? Explain your answer.

_____

_____

_____

_____

Relating Enthalpy, Entropy, and Free-Energy Changes to Reaction Occurrence		
ΔH	ΔS	ΔG
– value (exothermic)	+ value (more random)	always negative
– value (exothermic)	– value (less random)	negative at *lower* temperatures
+ value (endothermic)	+ value (more random)	negative at *higher* temperatures
+ value (endothermic)	– value (less random)	never negative

Negative ΔH, Positive ΔS If a reaction is exothermic and causes an increase in randomness, or entropy, then the free-energy change associated with the reaction will always be less than zero. This reaction will occur spontaneously in nature, and both factors contribute to its occurrence.

Positive ΔH, Negative ΔS If a reaction is endothermic and causes a decrease in entropy, then the free-energy change associated with the reaction will always be greater than zero. This reaction will not occur spontaneously in nature and must be assisted by an energy input or some other factor.

Values of ΔH and ΔS Have the Same Sign If one factor favors a spontaneous reaction and the other opposes it, then either factor could have more influence, depending on the reaction. For example, consider the reaction of ethene, C_2H_4, and hydrogen gas to form ethane, C_2H_6.

$$C_2H_4(g) + H_2(g) \longrightarrow C_2H_6(g)$$

There is a fairly large decrease in entropy in this reaction, $\Delta S^0 = -0.1207$ kJ/(mol•K), because two moles of gas combine into one. However, the reaction is strongly exothermic, with a $\Delta H^0 = -136.9$ kJ/mol. The value of ΔG is negative under standard conditions, so this reaction will occur spontaneously in nature, despite its decrease in entropy.

$$\Delta G^0 = \Delta H^0 - T\Delta S^0 = (-136.9 \text{ kJ/mol}) - (298 \text{ K})(-0.1207 \text{ kJ/mol•K})$$

$$= -100.9 \text{ kJ/mol}$$

On the other hand, consider the formation equation for syngas, given below. At standard conditions, this reaction is endothermic, with $\Delta H^0 = +206.1$ kJ/mol. However, the entropy change is also positive, $\Delta S^0 = +0.215$ kJ/(mol•K), because more moles of gas result. The resulting ΔG is positive at room temperature, and so the reaction does not occur even though the entropy change would normally favor the reaction.

$$CH_4(g) + H_2O(g) \longrightarrow CO(g) + 3H_2(g)$$

 **CONNECT**

The free-energy change for the conversion of diamond to graphite under standard conditions is slightly negative, –3 kJ/mol. However, this reaction occurs much too slowly to be noticeable. So, while diamonds are not "forever," they will last a very long time.

 **CONNECT**

Syngas is a commercial gas mixture of carbon monoxide and hydrogen. It is a starting point for the synthesis of a number of commercial chemicals, such as methanol, CH_3OH.

PRACTICE

A. Verify that ΔG for syngas formation is a positive value.

For the decomposition of ammonium chloride, at 298 K,
$\Delta H^0 = 176$ kJ/mol and $\Delta S^0 = 0.285$ kJ/(mol·K). Calculate ΔG^0,
and determine whether this reaction is spontaneous in the forward
direction at 298 K.

SOLUTION

1 ANALYZE *Determine the information that is given and unknown.*

Given: $\Delta H^0 = 176$ kJ/mol, $\Delta S^0 = 0.285$ kJ/(mol·K), $T = 298$ K

Unknown: ΔG^0

2 PLAN *Write the equation that can be used to determine the unknown.*

$\Delta G^0 = \Delta H^0 - T\Delta S^0$

3 SOLVE *Substitute the given information into the equation.*

$\Delta G^0 = 176$ kJ/mol $- 298$ K $[0.285$ kJ/(mol·K)$]$

$= 176$ kJ/mol $- 84.9$ kJ/mol

$= 91$ kJ/mol

The positive value of ΔG^0 indicates that this reaction does not
occur spontaneously under normal conditions.

4 CHECK YOUR WORK *Check the answer to see if it is reasonable.*

The units canceled properly and the correct number of
significant digits were used. An estimate of the calculation is
$200 - 300(0.3) = 110$, which is close to the actual answer.

PRACTICE

B. For the vaporization reaction of liquid bromine,
$\Delta H^0 = 31.0$ kJ/mol and $\Delta S^0 = 93.0$ J/(mol·K). At what
temperature will this process be spontaneous?

$\Delta G^0 = \Delta H^0 - T\Delta S^0$; therefore $T = \underline{\hspace{3cm}}$

VOCABULARY

1. What is entropy, and how does it relate to the spontaneity of reactions?

_____

_____

2. Define free energy, and explain how its change is calculated.

_____

_____

REVIEW

3. List several changes that result in an entropy increase.

_____

_____

4. Explain how free-energy change is related to the spontaneity of reactions.

_____

_____

5. In the reaction $CH_4(g) + H_2O(g) \longrightarrow CO(g) + 3H_2(g)$, why does the entropy increase?

_____

_____

Critical Thinking

6. **APPLYING MODELS** Most biological enzymes become denatured when they are heated and lose their ability to catalyze reactions. This process (original enzyme → denatured enzyme) is endothermic and spontaneous. Which structure, the original enzyme or the denatured enzyme, is more ordered? Explain your reasoning using thermodynamic concepts.

_____

_____

_____

_____

Math Tutor HESS'S LAW

You may have seen a popular comic strip in which a little boy takes a long, twisting path between the school-bus stop and home. No matter which path the boy takes, the result is always the same: He goes from the bus stop to the door of his house. Hess's law covers a similar situation in thermochemistry. No matter how many steps occur in changing one or more substances into one or more other substances, the overall change in enthalpy is always the same. Hess's law can be used to predict the enthalpy change, ΔH^0, of a reaction without actually carrying out the reaction.

Problem-Solving TIPS

- Always write the states of matter as part of the thermochemical equations. When canceling terms make sure that the states match.
- When multiplying all of the coefficients of an equation by a number, remember to multiply the heat of reaction by the same number.
- When reversing a reaction, remember to change the sign of the heat of reaction.

SAMPLE

Determine ΔH for the burning of carbon disulfide in oxygen.

$$CS_2(l) + 3O_2(g) \longrightarrow CO_2(g) + 2SO_2(g); \Delta H^0 = ?$$

Use the following information:

$$C(s) + O_2(g) \longrightarrow CO_2(g); \Delta H_f^0 = -393.5 \text{ kJ}$$

$$S(s) + O_2(g) \longrightarrow SO_2(g); \Delta H_f^0 = -296.8 \text{ kJ}$$

$$C(s) + 2S(s) \longrightarrow CS_2(l); \Delta H_f^0 = 87.9 \text{ kJ}$$

Rearrange the given formation equations so that the formed compounds are in the same position they hold in the equation in which the enthalpy of reaction, ΔH^0, is unknown.

The first equation is in the correct form. The second equation should be multiplied by 2 to form 2 mol of SO_2. The third equation should be reversed so that CS_2 is on the reactant side of the equation. Add the three equations, canceling like terms, and the combustion equation for CS_2 remains..

$\cancel{C(s)} + O_2(g) \longrightarrow CO_2(g);$	$\Delta H_f^0 = -393.5 \text{ kJ}$
$2\cancel{S(s)} + 2O_2(g) \longrightarrow 2SO_2(g);$	$\Delta H_f^0 = -593.6 \text{ kJ}$
$CS_2(l) \longrightarrow \cancel{C(s)} + 2\cancel{S(s)};$	$\Delta H_f^0 = -87.9 \text{ kJ}$

$$CS_2(l) + 3O_2(g) \longrightarrow CO_2(g) + 2SO_2(g); \Delta H^0 = -1075.0 \text{ kJ}$$

Practice Problems: Chapter Review practice problems 13 and 14

1. How does the enthalpy of the products of a reaction system compare with the enthalpy of the reactants when the system is

   a. exothermic? _____

   b. endothermic? _____

2. On what basis are the enthalpy of formation and the enthalpy of combustion defined?

   _____

   _____

3. What factors affect the value of ΔH in a reaction system?

   _____

   _____

4. Describe a combustion calorimeter. What information can it give?

   _____

   _____

   _____

5. Would entropy increase or decrease for changes in state in which the

   reactant is a gas or liquid and the product is a solid? _____

6. How does the increase in temperature affect the entropy of a system?

   _____

   _____

7. What combination of ΔH and ΔS values always produces a negative free-energy change?

   _____

8. Explain the relationship between temperature and the tendency for reactions to occur spontaneously.

   _____

   _____

   _____

9. How much energy is needed to raise the temperature of a 55 g sample of aluminum from 22.4°C to 94.6°C? The specific heat of aluminum is 0.897 J/(g•K).

10. If 3.5 kJ of energy are added to a 28.2 g sample of iron at 20°C, what is the final temperature of the iron in kelvins? The specific heat of iron is 0.449 J/(g•K).

11. For each equation listed below, determine the ΔH and type of reaction (endothermic or exothermic).

    a. $CH_4(g) + 2O_2(g) \longrightarrow CO_2(g) + 2H_2O(l) + 890.31$ kJ

    b. $CaCO_3(s) + 176$ kJ $\longrightarrow CaO(s) + CO_2(g)$

12. Rewrite each equation below with the ΔH value included with either the reactants or the products, and identify the reaction as endothermic or exothermic.

    a. $2Mg(s) + O_2(g) \longrightarrow 2MgO(s); \Delta H^0 = -1200$ kJ

    b. $I_2(s) \longrightarrow I_2(g); \Delta H^0 = +62.4$ kJ

13. The reaction below is involved in the smelting of iron. Calculate the enthalpy change during the formation of one mole of iron. Use the information that $\Delta H_f^0 = -824.2$ for $Fe_2O_3(s)$ and $\Delta H_f^0 = -393.5$ for $CO_2(g)$.

    $2Fe_2O_3(s) + 3C(s) \longrightarrow 4Fe(s) + 3CO_2(g)$

14. The enthalpy of formation of ethanol, C_2H_5OH, is -277.0 kJ/mol at 298 K. Calculate the enthalpy of combustion of one mole of ethanol, as given in the equation below. Use the information that $\Delta H_f^0 = -285.8$ for $H_2O(l)$ and $\Delta H_f^0 = -393.5$ for $CO_2(g)$.

_____ $C_2H_5OH(l) +$ _____ $O_2(g) \longrightarrow$ _____ $H_2O(l) +$ _____ $CO_2(g)$

15. A reaction has $\Delta H = -356$ kJ and $\Delta S = -36$ J/K. Calculate ΔG at 25°C to confirm that the reaction is spontaneous.

16. A reaction has $\Delta H = 98$ kJ and $\Delta S = 292$ J/K. Investigate the spontaneity of the reaction at room temperature. Would increasing the temperature have any effect on the spontaneity of the reaction?

17. The gas-phase reaction of H_2 with CO_2 to produce H_2O and CO has $\Delta H = 11$ kJ and $\Delta S = 41$ J/K. Is the reaction spontaneous at 298 K? What is ΔG?

18. The ΔS^0 for the reaction shown at 298 K is 0.003 00 kJ (mol•K). Calculate the ΔG^0 for this reaction, and determine whether it will occur spontaneously at 298 K.

$C(s) + O_2(g) \longrightarrow CO_2(g) + 393.51$ kJ

APPENDIX

Quick Topics

Contents

TEKS 11A

TOPIC 1

For more details, see the student edition chapters on reaction
kinetics and chemical equilibrium.

Reaction Rates
and Equilibrium

Chemical reactions, even spontaneous ones, do not occur at
the same rate. For example, iron rusts in air very slowly, but
the methane in natural gas burns quickly. The speed at which a
chemical reaction occurs depends on several factors.

KEY TERMS

reaction rate
catalyst
reversible reaction
chemical equilibrium
equilibrium constant

Molecular collisions need the right energy and orientation to react.

According to *collision theory*, particles must collide with
enough energy and in the correct orientation for a chemical
interaction to occur. Consider a hypothetical reaction between
two molecules of compound AB.

$$AB + AB \rightleftharpoons A_2 + 2B$$

The diagrams below show three ways the molecules could
collide. In diagram (a), the molecules are able to interact
chemically. In diagram (b), the molecules do not collide with
enough energy to overcome the forces binding the molecules
together, and they bounce away. In diagram (c), the molecules
collide in an orientation that is unfavorable for the formation
of A_2 molecules, so these molecules also bounce away.

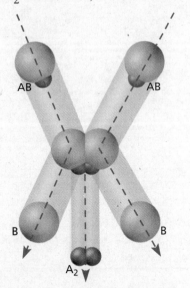

(a) Effective collision,
favorable orientation and energy

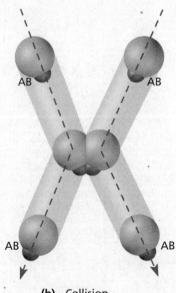

(b) Collision
too gentle

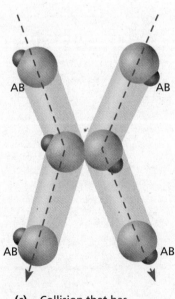

(c) Collision that has
poor orientation

Several factors can influence reaction rates.

The change in concentration of reactants per unit time as a reaction proceeds is called the **reaction rate.** The reaction rate depends on the number of collisions that result in chemical interactions. Any factor that influences the number of collisions, the energy of the collisions, or the efficiency of the collisions will affect the reaction rate.

Nature of Reactants Substances vary greatly in their tendencies to react. The rate of reaction depends on the reactants and the bonds involved. For example, sodium and oxygen combine much more rapidly than iron and oxygen under the same conditions.

Surface Area If two substances in different phases are reacting, the reaction only occurs where the two phases are in contact. The reaction rate depends on the surface area of this boundary. For example, a cube of zinc dropped into an acid reacts much more slowly than a zinc powder dropped into an acid, because the powder has a greater surface area exposed to the acid.

Temperature For a collision to cause an interaction, two particles must collide with enough energy. Temperature is a measure of the average kinetic energy of particles. Reaction rates increase with increasing temperature and decrease with decreasing temperature.

Concentration If more particles are present in a substance or mixture, then more collisions will occur. Reaction rates increase with increasing concentration and decrease with decreasing concentration.

Catalysts A **catalyst** is a substance that changes the rate of a chemical reaction without being consumed itself. Catalysts can lower the energy necessary for a reaction, or they can locally increase the concentration of reactants. For example, metal surfaces can catalyze a reaction by absorbing the reactants so that they have a higher concentration inside the metal.

(a)

(b)

Carbon burns faster (a) in pure oxygen than (b) in air because the concentration of the reactant in combustion, oxygen, is greater.

READING CHECK

1. What are two factors that determine whether two colliding particles will interact chemically?

_____

_____

2. Name three ways to decrease a reaction rate.

_____

_____

Some reactions favor products, and others reactants.

In theory, every chemical reaction can proceed in two opposing directions, forward and reverse. However, under normal conditions, only certain reactions act in both directions. For example, a strong base will only dissociate under normal conditions, while a weak base will dissociate and recombine. A chemical reaction in which the products can react to re-form the reactants is called a **reversible reaction.** Reversible reactions are shown with a double arrow, $\rightleftharpoons$.

If the reaction rates of the forward reaction and the reverse reaction are the same, then the reaction is said to be in **chemical equilibrium.** If a system is in a state of chemical equilibrium, then the concentrations of the reactants and the products do not change.

Chemical equilibrium is a dynamic state, not a static state. In other words, chemical equilibrium does not indicate that a reaction is not occurring. It means that the products are forming at the same rate that the reactants are re-forming.

 READING CHECK

3. Why is the forward reaction rate of a system in chemical equilibrium not equal to zero?

The graph below shows how an equilibrium is reached for a general reaction of the following form.

$$n\text{A} + m\text{B} \rightleftharpoons x\text{C} + y\text{D}$$

At first, only the reactants are present and no products are present. As the forward reaction occurs, the concentration of the products builds up over time, and the reverse reaction rate increases. At the same time, the concentration of the reactants decreases, so the forward reaction rate decreases. Eventually, the two reactions reach a point where both reactions occur at the same rate. The system enters a state of chemical equilibrium.

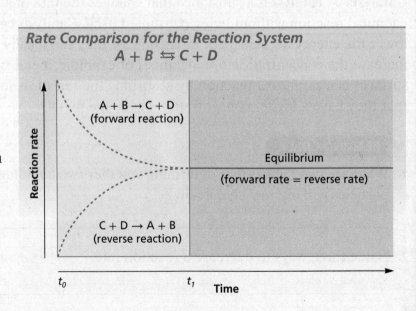

Rate Comparison for the Reaction System
$A + B \rightleftharpoons C + D$

A + B → C + D
(forward reaction)

Equilibrium
(forward rate = reverse rate)

C + D → A + B
(reverse reaction)

Reaction rate

t_0 t_1 Time

The Equilibrium Constant

At equilibrium, the concentrations of the products and reactants remain constant. The **equilibrium constant**, K, for a reaction is the ratio of the mathematical product of the concentrations of substances formed at equilibrium to the mathematical product of the concentrations of reacting substances. Each concentration is raised to a power equal to the coefficient of that substance in the chemical equation. The equilibrium constant for the equation on the previous page is

$$K = \frac{[C]^x[D]^y}{[A]^n[B]^m}$$

For a given reaction at a particular temperature, the value of K is constant. The constant K is independent of initial conditions. This means that a particular system will always arrive at the same equilibrium in the same conditions, as long as the environmental conditions are the same.

The equilibrium constant provides a measure of whether a system favors the formation of products or formation of the reactants. If K is small, then the amounts of the reactants in the system are much greater than the amounts of the products. If K is relatively large, then the amounts of the products are greater than the amounts of the reactants.

For example, consider this reversible reaction.

$$N_2(g) + O_2(g) \rightleftharpoons 2NO(g)$$

If $[N_2] = 6.4 \times 10^{-3}$ mol/L, $[O_2] = 1.7 \times 10^{-3}$ mol/L, and if $[NO] = 1.1 \times 10^{-5}$ mol/L, then K is calculated as follows.

$$K = \frac{[NO]^2}{[N_2][O_2]} = \frac{(1.1 \times 10^{-5}\text{mol/L})^2}{(6.4 \times 10^{-3}\text{mol/L}(1.7 \times 10^{-3}\text{mol/L})}$$

$$= 1.1 \times 10^{-5}$$

This value of K is very small, which suggests that equilibrium is shifted toward the reactants.

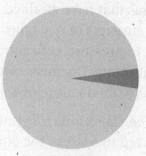

$K = 0.02$

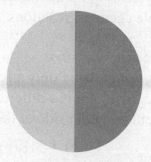

$K = 1$

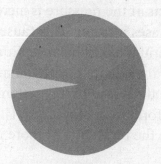

$K = 50$

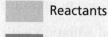
Reactants

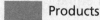
Products

These pie charts show the relative amounts of reactants and products for three different values of K for a reaction.

✓ READING CHECK

4. What is the expression for the equilibrium constant for the reaction $N_2(g) + 3H_2(g) \rightleftharpoons 2NH_3(g)$?

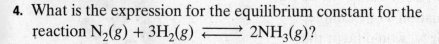

Equilibrium shifts to relieve stress on the system.

In systems that have attained chemical equilibrium, the relative amounts of reactants and products stay the same. But changes to pressure, concentration, or temperature can alter the equilibrium. Chemists often shift the equilibrium of a reaction to obtain more or less of a particular substance.

Le Châtelier's principle states that if a system at equilibrium is subjected to a stress, the equilibrium is shifted in the direction that tends to relieve the stress. This principle is true for all systems in a state of dynamic equilibrium, not just reversible chemical reactions.

Changes in Pressure

A change in pressure only affects systems in which gases are involved. In addition, a different amount of gas in moles must be present on either side of the equation, as in this system.

$$N_2(g) + 3H_2(g) \rightleftharpoons 2NH_3(g)$$

This system has 4 mol of reactants for every 2 mol of products. If the pressure is increased, the concentrations of all three gases increase. This causes stress by throwing the equilibrium out of balance. Equilibrium is restored as the side of the equation with the most moles of gas reacts to relieve the stress. In this system, an increase in pressure leads to the formation of more NH_3. A decrease in pressure would lead to the formation of more N_2 and H_2.

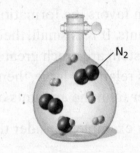

(a) at equilibrium

☑ READING CHECK

5. An increase in pressure increases the stress on the side of a chemical equation with a _____ amount of moles of gas.

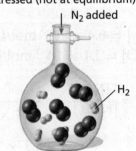

(b) stressed (not at equilibrium)
N₂ added

Changes in Concentration

A change in concentration of one substance can also put stress on a system. In the diagrams at the right, the equilibrium is disturbed by the addition of more N_2. To restore the system to equilibrium and relieve the stress, more NH_3 is formed. A decrease in the concentration of a substance would put stress on the other side of the equation. For example, a decrease in the concentration of N_2 would favor the formation of more N_2 so as to relieve the stress.

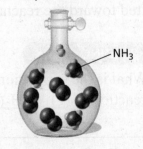

(c) at new equilibrium

Changes in Temperature

Changes in pressure and concentration do not change the equilibrium constant for a reaction. The change in pressure or concentration brings the system out of equilibrium. The reaction rates adjust until equilibrium is restored, with the same value of K.

However, the value of K for a system depends on temperature. A change in temperature changes the value of K. The concentrations of the substances in the system adjust until equilibrium is restored at the new value of K.

If the temperature of a system increases, the system relieves the stress by absorbing some of the energy. Therefore, the endothermic reaction is favored. If the temperature of a system decreases, the system relieves the stress by releasing energy as heat. The exothermic reaction is favored.

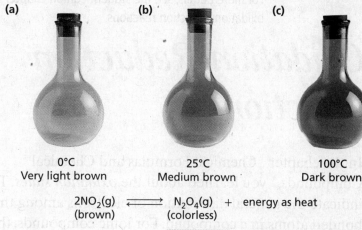

(a)	(b)	(c)
0°C	25°C	100°C
Very light brown	Medium brown	Dark brown

$$2NO_2(g) \rightleftharpoons N_2O_4(g) + \text{energy as heat}$$
$$\text{(brown)} \qquad \text{(colorless)}$$

A rise in temperature causes stress on the product in this system. The stress is relieved by the absorption of energy through the endothermic process. Therefore, the concentration of brown NO_2 gas increases with increasing temperature.

REVIEW

1. List five ways to increase the rate at which a reaction occurs.

_____

_____

2. How does the value of an equilibrium constant relate to the relative quantities of reactants and products at equilibrium?

_____

_____

3. Predict the effect on the equilibrium system in terms of the direction of equilibrium shift (forward, reverse, or neither).

$$H_2(g) + Cl_2(g) \rightleftharpoons 2HCl(g) + 184 \text{ kJ}$$

   a. addition of Cl_2 _____

   b. removal of HCl _____

   c. increased pressure _____

   d. decreased temperature _____

   e. addition of a catalyst _____

   f. decreased system volume _____

TOPIC 2 For more details, see the student edition chapter on oxidation-reduction reactions.

Oxidation-Reduction Reactions

In the chapter "Chemical Formulas and Chemical Compounds," you learned about the *oxidation states*. They indicate the general distribution of electrons among the bonded atoms in a compound. For ionic compounds, the oxidation state reflects the charge on each ion. For covalent compounds and ions, the oxidation state reflects the relative distribution of the shared electrons. The rules for assigning oxidation states to the elements in a molecule are summarized in the table below. In a chemical equation, the net charge of the products is always equal to the net charge of the reactants.

 **READING CHECK**

1. What does the oxidation state of an atom in a compound represent?

_____

Rules for Assigning Oxidation Numbers	
Rule	Example Oxidation Numbers
1. The oxidation number of any pure element is 0.	$Na(s)$: 0
2. The oxidation number of a monatomic ion equals the charge on the ion.	Cl^-: -1
3. The more electronegative element is assigned the number equal to the charge it would have if it were an ion.	O in NO: -2
4. The oxidation number of fluorine in a compound is always -1.	F in LiF: -1
5. Oxygen has an oxidation number of -2 unless it is combined with F ($+1$ or $+2$) or is in a peroxide (-1).	O in NO_2: -2
6. Hydrogen's oxidation state in most of its compounds is $+1$ unless it is combined with a metal, in which case it is -1.	H in LiH: -1
7. In compounds, Group 1 and 2 elements and aluminum have oxidation numbers of $+1$, $+2$, and $+3$, respectively.	Ca in $CaCO_3$: $+2$
8. The sum of the oxidation numbers of all atoms in a neutral compound is 0.	C in $CaCO_3$: $+4$
9. The sum of the oxidation numbers of all atoms in a polyatomic ion equals the charge of the ion.	P in $H_2PO_4^-$: $+5$

Oxidation occurs when valence electrons are lost.

Processes in which the atoms or ions of an element experience an increase in oxidation state are **oxidation** processes. For example, the combustion of metallic sodium in an atmosphere of chlorine gas produces sodium and chloride ions. The chemical equation for this reaction is written as follows.

$$2Na(s) + Cl_2(g) \longrightarrow 2NaCl(s)$$

The formation of sodium ions illustrates an oxidation process because each sodium atom loses an electron to become a sodium ion. The oxidation state of sodium has changed from 0, its elemental state, to the +1 state of the ion. A particle whose oxidation number increases is **oxidized.** The sodium atom is oxidized to form a sodium ion. Charge is conserved for sodium ion formation because the charge of the sodium ion plus the charge of the electron that is lost is zero.

$$\overset{0}{Na} \longrightarrow \overset{+1}{Na^+} + e^-$$

Sodium and chlorine react violently to form NaCl. The synthesis of NaCl from its elements illustrates the oxidation-reduction process.

Reduction occurs when valence electrons are gained.

Processes in which the oxidation state of an element decreases are **reduction** processes. The chlorine atom in the reaction above accepts an electron to become a chloride ion. The oxidation state decreases from 0 to –1. A particle that undergoes a decrease in oxidation state is **reduced.** The chlorine atom is reduced to form a chloride ion.

$$\overset{0}{Cl_2} + 2e^- \longrightarrow \overset{-1}{2Cl^-}$$

The two reactions above, for the oxidation of sodium and the reduction of chlorine, are called half-reactions. A **half-reaction** is a reaction that involves just oxidation or just reduction, but not both.

Zinc displaces copper ions from a copper(II) sulfate solution. The zinc atom is oxidized to form zinc cations. The copper ions are reduced to form copper atoms.

✓ READING CHECK

2. Label each of the following half-reactions as an oxidation half-reaction or a reduction half-reaction.

a. $\overset{0}{Br_2} + 2e^- \longrightarrow \overset{-1}{2Br^-}$ _____

b. $\overset{0}{Fe} \longrightarrow \overset{+2}{Fe^{2+}} + 2e^-$ _____

c. $\overset{+2}{Cu^{2+}} + 2e^- \longrightarrow \overset{0}{Cu}$ _____

d. $\overset{+3}{Fe^{3+}} + e^- \longrightarrow \overset{+2}{Fe^{2+}}$ _____

Oxidation and reduction reactions are balanced separately, then added together.

Electrons are released in oxidation and acquired in reduction. Therefore, for oxidation to occur during a chemical reaction, reduction must also occur. A transfer of electrons causes changes in the oxidation states of one or more elements. Any chemical process in which elements undergo changes in oxidation number is an **oxidation-reduction reaction.** This name is often shortened to **redox reaction.**

A redox reaction is the sum of two half-reactions. For example, consider the reaction between copper metal and nitric acid. The copper metal is oxidized and the nitrate ion is reduced. The electrons released by the copper are acquired by the nitrate ion, so they are canceled in the overall reaction.

Copper reacts with concentrated nitric acid in a redox reaction.

$$\overset{0}{Cu} \longrightarrow \overset{+2}{Cu^{2+}} + \cancel{2e^-} \qquad \text{(oxidation half-reaction)}$$

$$\overset{+5\,-2}{2NO_3^-} + \cancel{2e^-} + \overset{+1}{4H^+} \longrightarrow \overset{+4\,-2}{2NO_2} + \overset{+1\,-2}{2H_2O} \qquad \text{(reduction half-reaction)}$$

$$\overset{0}{Cu} + \overset{+5}{2NO_3^-} + 4H^+ \longrightarrow \overset{+2}{Cu^{2+}} + \overset{+4}{2NO_2} + 2H_2O \quad \text{(redox reaction)}$$

If none of the atoms in a reaction change oxidation state, the reaction is not a redox reaction. For example, sulfur dioxide gas, SO_2, dissolves in water to form an acidic solution containing a low concentration of sulfurous acid, H_2SO_3. All of the elemental oxidation states remain unchanged during the reaction. The reaction is not a redox reaction.

$$\overset{+4\,-2}{SO_2} + \overset{+1\,-2}{H_2O} + \longrightarrow \overset{+1\,+4\,-2}{H_2SO_3}$$

✓ READING CHECK

3. Sodium chloride is mixed with silver nitrate to form sodium nitrate and a silver chloride precipitate, as shown below. Is the reaction a redox reaction? Why or why not?

$$\overset{+1}{Na^+} + \overset{-1}{Cl^-} + \overset{+1}{Ag^+} + \overset{+5\,-2}{NO_3^-} \longrightarrow \overset{+1}{Na^+} + \overset{+5\,-2}{NO_3^-} + \overset{+1\,-1}{AgCl}$$

Redox Reactions and Covalent Bonds

The examples given so far have been reactions involving ionic compounds. Redox reactions can also involve covalent compounds. For example, when hydrogen burns in chlorine, a covalent bond forms from the sharing of two electrons.

$$\overset{0}{H_2} + \overset{0}{Cl_2} \longrightarrow \overset{+1\ -1}{2HCl}$$

The nitrate ion is a polyatomic ion held together by covalent bonds. In the reaction on page 540, the nitrate ion was reduced, to form nitrogen dioxide, which is also held together by covalent bonds.

Redox Reactions in Living Systems

Redox reactions play an important role in the cellular processes that are necessary for life. For example, cellular respiration and photosynthesis are both redox reactions involved in providing cells with energy. Nitrogen-fixing bacteria make use of redox reactions to convert nitrogen gas into forms that are useful to living things.

Nitrogen-fixing bacteria, *Rhizobium*, live in these small nodules that grow on the roots of soybeans.

REVIEW

1. How are oxidation numbers assigned?

_____

2. Which of the following reactions represent redox reactions?

   a. $2KNO_3(s) \longrightarrow 2KNO_2(s) + O_2(g)$ _____

   b. $H_2(g) + CuO(s) \longrightarrow Cu(s) + H_2O(l)$ _____

   c. $NaOH(aq) + HCl(aq) \longrightarrow NaCl(aq) + H_2O(l)$ _____

   d. $H_2(g) + Cl_2(g) \longrightarrow 2HCl(g)$ _____

   e. $SO_3(g) + H_2SO_4(aq)$ _____

3. For each reaction in Question 2, determine which element is oxidized and which is reduced, if any.

   a. _____   d. _____

   b. _____   e. _____

   c. _____

TOPIC 3   For more details, see the student edition chapters on organic chemistry and biochemistry.

Biochemistry

The carbon atom has special properties that make it suitable for forming large, complex molecules. These molecules form the basis of life on Earth. Most covalently bonded compounds that include carbon are **organic compounds,** because they are associated with organisms. The inorganic carbon compounds are oxides and carbonates, such as CO_2 and Na_2CO_3.

KEY TERMS	
organic compound	polymer
hydrocarbon	protein
alkane	carbohydrate
alkene	lipid
alkyne	nucleic acid

The uniqueness of carbon bonding results in many organic compounds.

Carbon-Carbon Bonding Carbon atoms are unique in their ability to form long chains and rings of covalently bonded atoms. In addition, carbon atoms in these structures can be linked by single, double, and triple covalent bonds.

Carbon Bonding to Other Elements Carbon atoms bond readily to elements with similar electronegativities. Organic compounds consist of carbon and these other elements. **Hydrocarbons** are the simplest organic compounds; they consist only of carbon atoms and hydrogen atoms. Organic compounds typically contain hydrocarbon backbones with O, N, S, and halogen atoms attached.

Arrangement of Atoms Some carbon compounds may contain the same atoms but have different properties because the atoms are arranged differently. For example, both butane and methylpropane have the molecular formula C_4H_{10}, but their structures and properties are very different.

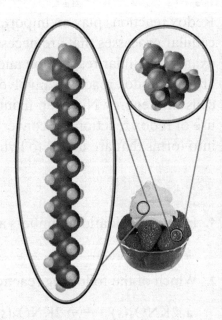

The fatty acids found in cream are long chains of carbon, while the fructose in strawberries forms rings of carbon.

```
         H  H  H  H                              H    H    H
         |  |  |  |                              |    |    |
butane: H-C--C--C--C-H    methylpropane:  H-C——————C————C-H
         |  |  |  |                          |    |        |
         H  H  H  H                          H  H-C-H H    H
```

✓ READING CHECK

1. What properties allow carbon to form complex molecules?

Hydrocarbons contain only hydrogen and carbon atoms.

Hydrocarbons are the simplest class of organic compounds. All other organic compounds can be thought of as hydrocarbons in which one or more hydrogen atoms have been replaced by other atoms or other groups of atoms.

Saturated Hydrocarbons

In saturated hydrocarbons each carbon atom in the molecule forms four single covalent bonds with other atoms. Another name for a saturated hydrocarbon is an alkane. An **alkane** is a hydrocarbon that contains only single bonds.

Unbranched-Chain Alkanes The simplest alkanes form straight, unbranched chains. The prefixes shown in the table at the right refer to the number of carbon atoms in the compound. Some examples of straight-chain alkanes are shown in the table below. Note that the structural formulas in the table are in shorthand—compare the structural formula of butane on the previous page with its representation in the table.

Carbon-Atom Chain Prefixes	
Number of carbon atoms	Prefix
1	meth-
2	eth-
3	prop-
4	but-
5	pent-
6	hex-
7	hept-
8	oct-
9	non-
10	dec-

Some Straight-Chain Alkyl Groups

Alkane	Name	Alkyl group	Name
CH_4	methane	$-CH_3$	methyl
CH_3-CH_3	ethane	$-CH_2-CH_3$	ethyl
$CH_3-CH_2-CH_3$	propane	$-CH_2-CH_2-CH_3$	propyl
$CH_3-CH_2-CH_2-CH_3$	butane	$-CH_2-CH_2-CH_2-CH_3$	butyl
$CH_3-CH_2-CH_2-CH_2-CH_3$	pentane	$-CH_2-CH_2-CH_2-CH_2-CH_3$	pentyl

Branched-Chain Alkanes The straight chain alkanes can also form the basis of branched chains. For example, the molecule at the right is called 3-ethyl-2,4,5-trimethyloctane. The name of the molecule is derived from the length of the longest continuous chain (8 carbon atoms), and the names and locations of the sub-chains that branch off the main chain (one ethyl group off carbon atom 3 and three methyl groups off carbon atoms 2, 4, and 5).

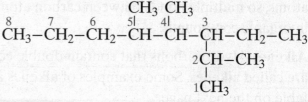

✓ READING CHECK

2. Each carbon atom in an alkane contains _____

single bonds.

Cycloalkanes Alkanes in which the carbon atoms are arranged in a ring, or cyclic structure, are called cycloalkanes. Three different representations of cycloalkanes are demonstrated below. In the third representation, it is understood that a carbon atom is at each corner and that enough hydrogen atoms complete the four covalent bonds to each carbon atom.

$$H-\underset{\underset{H}{|}}{\overset{\overset{H}{|}}{C}}-\underset{\underset{H}{|}}{\overset{\overset{H}{|}}{C}}-H$$
$$H-\underset{\underset{H}{|}}{\overset{\overset{}{|}}{C}}-\underset{\underset{H}{|}}{\overset{\overset{}{|}}{C}}-H$$

cyclobutane
C_4H_8

CH_2
$CH_2 \quad CH_2$
CH_2-CH_2

or

cyclopentane C_5H_{12}

Properties and Uses of Alkanes The carbon-hydrogen bonds of alkanes are nonpolar, so the only forces of attraction are weak London dispersion forces. Methane, ethane, propane, and butane are all gases at room temperature. Natural gas is a fossil fuel composed primarily of these alkanes. Larger alkanes are liquids and make up the main components of gasoline and kerosene. The largest molecules are solids. Paraffin wax is an example of a solid alkane.

Unsaturated Hydrocarbons

Hydrocarbons that do not contain the maximum amount of hydrogen are referred to as unsaturated. They have one or more carbon atoms that have a double or triple bond. Carbon atoms can easily form double and triple bonds to other carbon atoms, so multiple bonds between carbon atoms are common in organic compounds.

Alkenes Hydrocarbons that contain double covalent bonds are called **alkenes**. Some examples of alkenes are given in the table on the next page.

✓ READING CHECK

3. What is the difference between saturated hydrocarbons and unsaturated hydrocarbons?

_____

_____

Structures of Alkenes

	ethene	propene	trans-2-butene	cis-2-butene
Structural formula	$\begin{array}{c} H \quad\quad H \\ C=C \\ H \quad\quad H \end{array}$	$\begin{array}{c} H \quad\quad H \\ C=C \\ CH_3 \quad\quad H \end{array}$	$\begin{array}{c} H \quad\quad CH_3 \\ C=C \\ CH_3 \quad\quad H \end{array}$	$\begin{array}{c} H \quad\quad H \\ C=C \\ CH_3 \quad\quad CH_3 \end{array}$
Ball-and-stick model				

Properties and Uses of Alkenes Alkenes are nonpolar. The smallest alkene, ethene, is a gas commonly called ethylene. Ethene is the hydrocarbon commercially produced in the greatest quantity in the United States. It is used in the synthesis of many plastics and commercially important alcohols. Ethene is also an important plant hormone. Ethene can be used to induce plants to flower or fruit to ripen.

Alkynes Hydrocarbons with triple bonds are called **alkynes.** The simplest alkyne is ethyne, shown below. Compare the structures of the simplest alkane, alkene, and alkyne. Alkynes have four fewer hydrogen atoms than the corresponding alkanes and two fewer hydrogen atoms than the corresponding alkenes.

$$\begin{array}{c} H \quad H \\ | \quad\; | \\ H-C-C-H \\ | \quad\; | \\ H \quad H \\ C_2H_6 \end{array} \qquad \begin{array}{c} H \quad\quad H \\ C=C \\ H \quad\quad H \\ C_2H_4 \end{array} \qquad \begin{array}{c} H-C\equiv C-H \\ \\ C_2H_2 \end{array}$$

Properties and Uses of Alkynes Like all hydrocarbons, alkynes are nonpolar. The combustion of ethyne when it is mixed with pure oxygen produces the intense heat of welding torches. The common name of ethyne is acetylene, and welding torches are commonly called oxyacetylene torches.

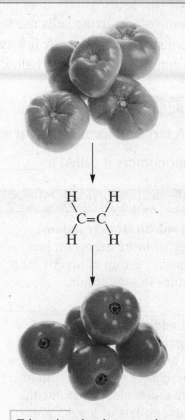

Ethene is a plant hormone that triggers fruit ripening, such as in these tomatoes.

✓ **READING CHECK**

4. What is the main difference between alkanes, alkenes, and alkynes?

_____

_____

Polymers are large molecules made of smaller units.

Polymers are large molecules made of many small units joined together through organic reactions. The small units are called monomers. A polymer can be made from the combination of two or more identical, or different, monomers.

Polymers are all around us. The foods we eat and clothes we wear are made of polymers. Some of the most common natural polymers include starch, cellulose, and proteins. Plastics and some clothing fabrics are artificial polymers.

Organic Reactions

Chemists and living cells use several types of organic reactions to construct polymers. A few types of reactions are summarized in the table below.

 READING CHECK

5. A large molecule made of many small units called

monomers is called a _____.

Organic Reactions	
In **substitution reactions,** one or more atoms replace another group of one or more atoms in a molecule.	H–C–H + Cl–Cl → H–C–Cl + H–Cl methane · chlorine · chloromethane · hydrogen chloride
In **addition reactions,** two parts of a molecule are added to an unsaturated molecule, increasing the saturation of the molecule. The molecule still consists of long chains of carbon atoms, but it contains far fewer double bonds.	$\left(\text{C–C=C–C–C=C–C}\right) + H_2 \xrightarrow{\text{catalyst}} \left(\text{C–C=C–C–C–C–C}\right)$
In **condensation reactions,** two molecules or parts of a molecule combine.	H–N–C–C–OH + H–N–C–C–OH → (dipeptide) + H_2O R R′ amino acid amino acid water
In **elimination reactions,** a simpler molecule, such as water or ammonia, is formed from adjacent carbon atoms of a larger molecule.	H–C–C–H $\xrightarrow[\triangle]{H_2SO_4}$ H–C=C–H + H_2O ethanol ethene water

Macromolecules play important roles in living organisms.

Large organic polymers are called macromolecules. macromolecules play important roles in living systems. Most macromolecules that are essential to life belong to four main classes, three of which we know as nutrients in food.

Proteins

Proteins are important building blocks of all living cells, and are the most complex and varied class of biochemical molecules. A **protein** is an organic biological polymer made up of chains of 50 or more amino acids. Each of the 20 different amino acids is an organic molecule containing an amino group $(-NH_2)$ and a carboxylic acid group $(-COOH)$.

Proteins are the second most common molecules found in the human body, after water, and make up 10%–20% of the mass of a cell. About 9000 different protein molecules are found in cells in the human body. Nitrogen makes up 15% of the mass of a protein molecule. Most proteins also contain sulfur, and others contain iron, zinc, and copper.

Proteins serve many important purposes in the body. Fibrous proteins provide structure and strength. Enzymes, are proteins which act as catalysts for biochemical reactions. Hemoglobin is a protein in blood that carries oxygen to cells. Insulin regulates glucose levels. Antibodies help protect the body from foreign substances.

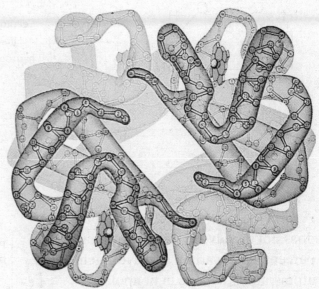

Hemoglobin is a complex protein made of hundreds of amino acids.

✓ READING CHECK

6. Describe the importance of proteins to the human body.

_____

_____

_____

_____

_____

Carbohydrates

Carbohydrates are molecules composed of carbon, hydrogen, and oxygen atoms in a 1:2:1 ratio. They provide nutrients to the cells of living things. Sugars, starches, and cellulose are examples of carbohydrates. Plants build carbohydrates with the help of photosynthesis. Animals must get many of their carbohydrates through eating food.

The basic unit of a carbohydrate is a simple sugar called a monosaccharide. Glucose and fructose are the two most common monosaccharides. Examples of how glucose is linked to form complex carbohydrates are shown below.

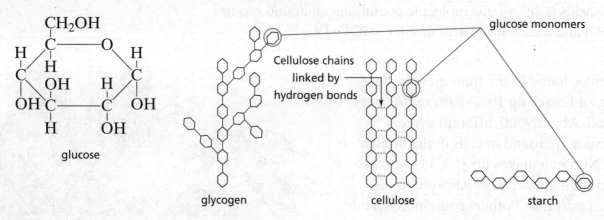

glucose monomers

Cellulose chains linked by hydrogen bonds

glucose

glycogen

cellulose

starch

Lipids

A **lipid** is a type of biochemical that does not dissolve in water, has a high percentage of carbon and hydrogen atoms, and is soluble in nonpolar solvents. Lipids are found in dairy products, grains, meats, and oils. Long-chain fatty acids, phospholipids, steroids, and cholesterol are all lipids. Fats are lipids that are used to store energy.

Polar head

Non-polar tails

Polar

Nonpolar

Polar

Lipids are also the main compounds in cell membranes. They have a polar "head" and a nonpolar "tail." Two layers of lipids form a lipid bilayer that keeps the contents of the cell separated from the outer environment.

✓ READING CHECK

7. What distinguishes lipids from other biological compounds?

Nucleic Acids

Nucleic acids contain all of the genetic information of an organism. They are the means by which a living organism stores and conveys instructions for all of its activities. They are also the means by which organisms reproduce. The two nucleic acids found in organisms are DNA and RNA.

The basic unit of a nucleic acid is a nucleotide. Adenine, guanine, thymine, and cytosine are the four nucleotides that make up DNA. Three of the same four, with uracil in place of thymine, make up RNA. The DNA in each human cell, if it were unwrapped and spliced together, is about 2 m long.

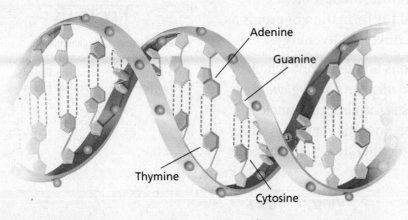

Adenine
Guanine
Thymine
Cytosine

REVIEW

1. Give one example of a use for each of the three types of hydrocarbons.

_____

_____

2. What are two reactions by which polymers can be formed?

_____

3. Describe the four major types of macromolecules that make up the organic compounds in the human body.

_____

_____

_____

_____

TOPIC 4   For more details, see the student edition chapter on
nuclear chemistry.

Nuclear Chemistry

The mass of an atom is slightly less than the mass of its separate neutrons, protons, and electrons. This is not a violation of the law of conservation of mass. Albert Einstein's famous relationship $E = mc^2$ states that energy and matter are two aspects of the same thing. Therefore, the law of conservation of mass is not violated for formation of atoms as long as the missing mass has been converted to energy.

Atomic nuclei are made of protons and neutrons, which are collectively called *nucleons*. The *nuclear binding energy* is the energy released when a nucleus is formed from nucleons. This energy can be thought of as the potential energy of the nuclear bonds that hold the atom together. It is a measure of the stability of the nucleus.

KEY TERMS

nuclear reaction	gamma ray
radioactive decay	half-life
alpha particle	nuclear fission
beta particle	nuclear fusion

The graph shows the binding energy per nucleon versus mass number. The higher the binding energy, the more tightly the nucleons are held together. The graph shows that the elements with intermediate masses have the greatest binding energies and are the most stable. Iron is the element with the most stable nucleus.

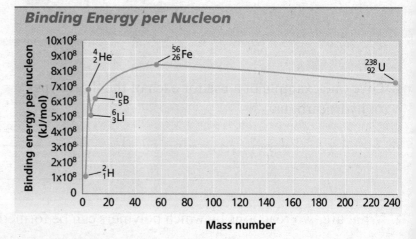

Binding Energy per Nucleon

Unstable nuclei undergo spontaneous changes that alter their composition. They give off large amounts of energy and increase their stability. A **nuclear reaction** is a reaction that changes the nucleus of an atom. In a nuclear reaction, the total atomic number and total mass number is conserved.

✓ READING CHECK

1. How do nuclear reactions and chemical reactions differ?

Radioactive decay leads to more stable nucleons.

Radioactive decay is the spontaneous breakdown of a nucleus into a slightly lighter nucleus, accompanied by the emission of particles, electromagnetic radiation, or both. All of the elements that have an atomic number greater than 83 have unstable nuclei. In nuclei with so many protons, the nuclear binding energy is not strong enough to overcome the repulsive forces of the protons for long periods of time.

Three types of radioactive decay result in the emission of alpha particles, beta particles, and gamma rays. These emissions are summarized in the table at the right.

Radioactive Nuclide Emissions		
Type	Symbol	Charge
Alpha particle	^4_2He	2+
Beta particle	$^0_{-1}\beta$	1-
Positron	$^0_{+1}\beta$	1+
Gamma ray	γ	0

Alpha Emission An **alpha particle** is two protons and two neutrons bound together and emitted from a nucleus. This increases the stability of the nucleus by decreasing its size. Alpha particles are equivalent to the nuclei of helium atoms and have a charge of 2+. The atomic number decreases by two after alpha emission, and the mass number decreases by four.

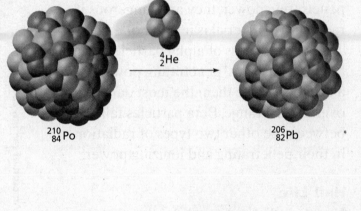

^4_2He

$^{210}_{84}Po$ $^{206}_{82}Pb$

$$^{210}_{84}Po \longrightarrow\ ^{206}_{82}Pb +\ ^4_2He$$

Beta Emission A **beta particle** is an electron emitted from the nucleus, as shown at the right. This occurs when a neutron changes into a proton and an electron. Stability increases as the neutron/proton ratio in the nucleus decreases. The atomic number increases by one and the mass number stays the same.

$$^{14}_6C \longrightarrow\ ^{14}_7N +\ ^0_{-1}\beta$$

Gamma Emission **Gamma rays** are high-energy electromagnetic waves emitted from a nucleus. The nucleus of an atom can exist in excited states in a similar way that electrons can exist in higher than normal electron shells. A nucleus may be excited by alpha or beta emission. The nucleus emits gamma rays as it returns to the ground state.

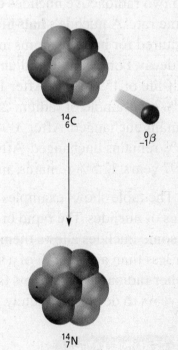

$^{14}_6C$

$^0_{-1}\beta$

$^{14}_7N$

✓ READING CHECK

2. Why does an atomic nucleus undergo radioactive decay?

Nuclear Radiation

Alpha particles, beta particles, and gamma rays are all forms of *nuclear radiation*. The ionizing effects of all types of nuclear radiation can damage living tissue. The diagram at the right shows that different types of radiation have different abilities to penetrate materials. The high energy of gamma rays gives them great penetrating power, and makes them extremely dangerous.

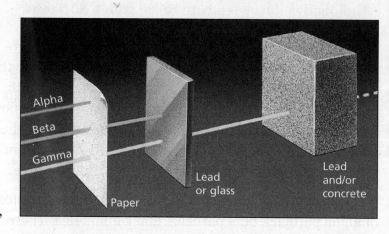

Even though alpha particles have little penetrating power, they are dangerous if radioactive material is inhaled or eaten. The size and mass of alpha particles, which limit the particles' penetrating power over a distance, make them the most dangerous over a short range. Beta particles fall between the other two types of radiation in their penetrating and ionizing power.

Half-Life

No two radioactive nuclides decay at the same rate. A nuclide's **half-life** is the time required for half the atoms in a sample to decay. For example, radium-226 has a half-life of 1599 years. After 1599 years, 50% of a sample of radium-226 will remain unchanged. After 3198 years, 25% remains unchanged. After 4797 years, 12.5% remains, and so on.

The table shows examples of half-lives of nuclides. The rapid breakdown of some nuclides allows them to exist for less than a millionth of a second. Other radioactive elements take billions of years to decay completely.

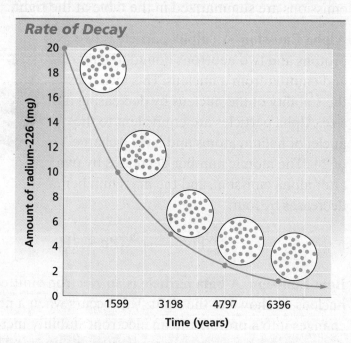

Rate of Decay

Representative Radioactive Nuclides and Their Half-Lives

Nuclide	Half-life	Nuclide	Half-life
$^{3}_{1}\text{H}$	12.32 years	$^{214}_{84}\text{Po}$	163.7 µs
$^{14}_{6}\text{C}$	5715 years	$^{218}_{84}\text{Po}$	3.0 min
$^{32}_{15}\text{P}$	14.28 days	$^{218}_{85}\text{At}$	1.6 s
$^{40}_{19}\text{K}$	1.3×10^9 years	$^{238}_{92}\text{U}$	4.46×10^9 years
$^{60}_{27}\text{Co}$	5.27 years	$^{239}_{94}\text{Pu}$	2.41×10^4 years

✓ READING CHECK

3. Exactly $\frac{1}{16}$ of a given amount of protactinium-234 remains after 26.76 hours. What is the half-life of protactinium-234? _____

Decay Series

One nuclear reaction is not always enough to produce a stable nuclide. A decay series is a series of radioactive nuclides produced by successive radioactive decay until a stable nuclide is reached. The heaviest nuclide of each series is called the parent nuclide. The nuclides produced by the decay of the parent nuclides are called daughter nuclides.

All naturally occurring nuclides with an atomic number greater than 83 belong to one of three natural decay series. The parent nuclides are uranium-238, uranium-235, and thorium-232. The uranium-238 decay series is shown in the chart below. Each step of the decay series is the result of alpha emission or beta emission.

✓ READING CHECK

4. Of the radiaoactive daughter nuclides of uranium-238, which has the longest half-life, and therefore is most likely to be found in nature? _____

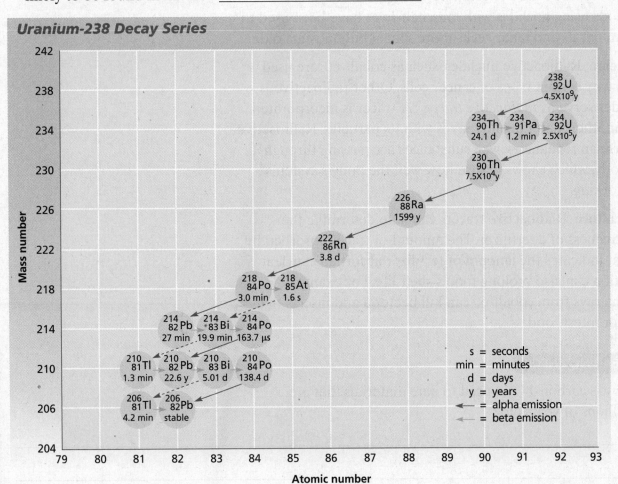

Uranium-238 Decay Series

Applications of Nuclear Radiation

Many applications of nuclear radiation are based on the essential similarity of the physical and chemical properties of stable isotopes and radioactive isotopes of the same elements. A few uses of radioactive nuclides are discussed below.

Radioactive Dating The amount of a certain radioactive nuclide in an object can help determine the object's age. Such an estimate can be made because radioactive substances decay with known half-lives. Age is measured by determining the relative proportion of decayed atoms to undecayed atoms in a sample.

Film badges are used to warn people who work with radioactive materials when radiation levels are rising to dangerous levels.

Carbon-14, which is radioactive, has a half life of approximately 5715 years. It can be used to estimate the age of organic material up to about 50 000 years old. Objects more than 50 000 years old have too little undecayed carbon-14 for this method to be useful. However, nuclides with longer half-lives can be used to estimate the age of older objects. Methods using nuclides with long half-lives have been used to date minerals and lunar rocks more than 4 billion years old.

Medicine Radioactive nuclides, such as cobalt-60, are used to destroy certain types of cancer cells. Other radioactive nuclides serve as *radioactive tracers*. A tracer is incorporated into another material and moves with its particles. Radioactive tracers can reveal how well substances are passing through the body, which shows in turn how well the body's systems are working.

Agriculture Radioactive tracers can help determine the effectiveness of a fertilizer. The amount of tracer absorbed by a plant indicates the amount of fertilizer absorbed. Nuclear radiation can also prolong food's shelf life. For example, gamma rays from cobalt-60 can kill bacteria and insects that spoil or infest food.

✓ READING CHECK

5. Why is carbon-14 not used to date materials that are millions of years old?

_____

_____

In fission, atoms split into nearly equal parts.

In **nuclear fission,** a very heavy nucleus splits into more stable nuclei of intermediate mass. This process releases enormous amounts of energy.

Nuclear fission can occur spontaneously or when nuclei are bombarded by particles. When uranium-235 is bombarded with slow neutrons, a uranium nucleus can capture one of the neutrons, making the nucleus very unstable. It splits into medium-mass nuclei with the emission of more neutrons. The mass of the products is less than the mass of the reactants. The extra mass has been converted into energy.

In a *chain reaction,* the material that starts the reaction is also one of the products and can start another reaction. The diagram below shows how neutrons can start a chain reaction of uranium-235 fission.

✓ READING CHECK

6. Why is nuclear fission a type of nuclear reaction?

_____

_____

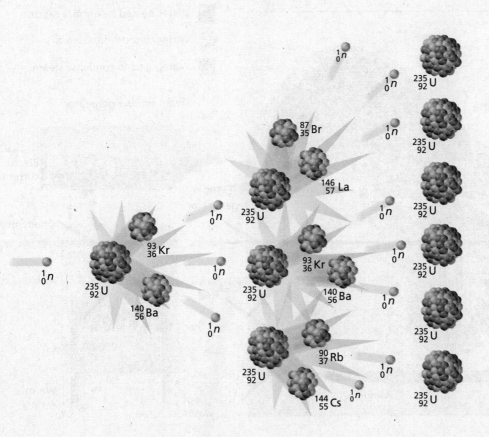

Nuclear Power Plants

Nuclear power plants convert the heat produced by nuclear fission into electrical energy. One design for a nuclear power plant is shown below.

Nuclear power provides competitively priced electricity without emitting pollutants into the atmosphere. However, the use of nuclear fission for power results in the production of nuclear waste. Disposing of this waste, which is radioactive and will last thousands of years, must be considered when using nuclear power. Building safeguards to avoid runaway fission reactions and preventing the radioactive fuels from entering the environment during accidents or equipment failures is another concern.

The use of nuclear power for generating electricity is increasing worldwide. Nuclear power is also used in naval vessels such as submarines and aircraft carriers.

✓ READING CHECK

7. Explain the role of water in producing electricity in a nuclear power plant.

_____

_____

In this model of a nuclear reactor, pressurized water is heated by fission of uranium-235. This water is circulated to a steam generator. The steam drives a turbine to produce electricity. Control rods absorb neutrons, which moderators slow down. Moderators help to control the nuclear reaction to keep it from becoming an uncontrolled chain reaction.

- ■ Water heated by nuclear reactor
- ■ Water converted to steam
- ■ Water used to condense steam

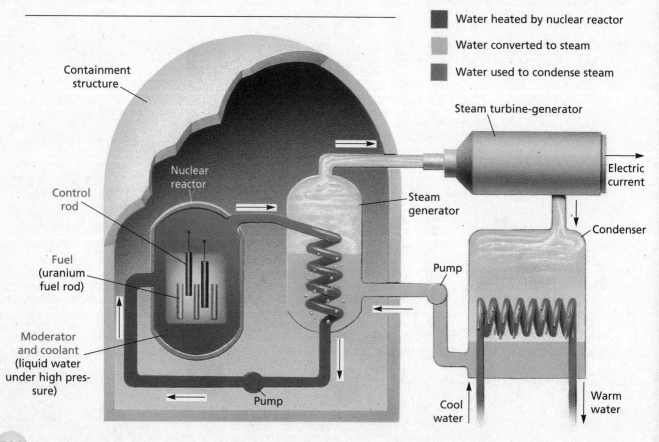

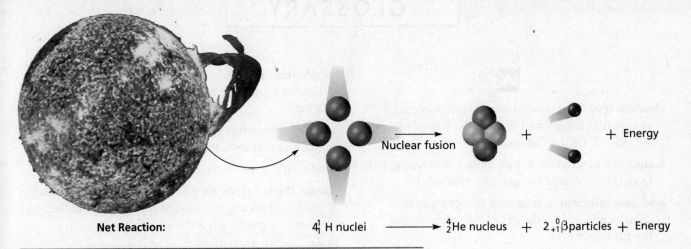

Net Reaction: $4\,^1_1\text{H}$ nuclei $\longrightarrow$ ^4_2He nucleus $+ 2\,^0_{+1}\beta$ particles $+$ Energy

Nuclei combine in nuclear fusion.

In nuclear fission, heavy elements break down into more stable, intermediate elements. The opposite occurs in nuclear fusion. In **nuclear fusion**, low-mass nuclei combine to form a heavier, more stable nucleus. Nuclear fusion releases even more energy per gram of fuel than nuclear fission.

Nuclear fusion is the process that produces energy within stars. Almost all the energy on Earth can be traced back to the fusion of hydrogen atoms into helium in the core of the sun.

Nuclear fusion is not used to generate electric power. Nuclear fusion requires material in the form of a superheated plasma at a temperature of millions of degrees kelvin. A large amount of energy must be used to start a fusion reaction. To date, no artificial process has been developed to generate more energy from nuclear fusion than is used to maintain it.

REVIEW

1. Balance the following nuclear equation: $^9_4\text{Be} + ^4_2\text{He} \longrightarrow$ _____ $+ ^1_0 n$

2. Which of alpha, beta, and gamma emission result in the formation of new nuclides?

_____

3. When does a decay series end?

_____

4. What is the difference between nuclear fission and nuclear fusion?

_____

_____

GLOSSARY

A

absolute zero the temperature at which molecular energy is at a minimum (0 K on the Kelvin scale or −273.15 °C on the Celsius scale)

accuracy a description of how close a measurement is to the true value of the quantity measured

acid-base indicator a substance that changes in color depending on the pH of the solution that the substance is in

actinide any of the series of heavy radioactive elements that extends from thorium (atomic number 90) through lawrencium (atomic number 103) on the periodic table

activation energy the minimum amount of energy required to start a chemical reaction

activity series a series of elements that have similar properties and that are arranged in descending order of chemical activity; examples of activity series include metals and halogens

actual yield the measured amount of a product of a reaction

addition reaction a reaction in which an atom or molecule is added to an unsaturated molecule

alkali metal one of the elements of Group 1 of the periodic table (lithium, sodium, potassium, rubidium, cesium, and francium)

alkaline-earth metal one of the elements of Group 2 of the periodic table (beryllium, magnesium, calcium, strontium, barium, and radium)

alkane a hydrocarbon characterized by a straight or branched carbon chain that contains only single bonds

alkene a hydrocarbon that contains one or more double bonds

alkyne a hydrocarbon that contains one or more triple bonds

alpha particle a positively charged atom that is released in the disintegration of radioactive elements and that consists of two protons and two neutrons

amino acid any one of 20 different organic molecules that contain a carboxyl and an amino group and that combine to form proteins

amorphous solid a solid in which the particles are not arranged with periodicity or order

amphoteric describes a substance, such as water, that has the properties of an acid and the properties of a base

angular momentum quantum number the quantum number that indicates the shape of an orbital

anion an ion that has a negative charge

anode the electrode on whose surface oxidation takes place; anions migrate toward the anode, and electrons leave the system from the anode

Arrhenius acid a substance that increases the concentration of hydronium ions in aqueous solution

Arrhenius base a substance that increases the concentration of hydroxide ions in aqueous solution

artificial transmutation the transformation of atoms of one element into atoms of another element as a result of a nuclear reaction, such as bombardment with neutrons

atmosphere of pressure the pressure of Earth's atmosphere at sea level; exactly equivalent to 760 mm Hg

atom the smallest unit of an element that maintains the chemical properties of that element

atomic number the number of protons in the nucleus of an atom; the atomic number is the same for all atoms of an element

atomic radius one-half the distance between the center of identical atoms that are bonded together

Aufbau principle the principle that states that the structure of each successive element is obtained by adding one proton to the nucleus of the atom and one electron to the lowest-energy orbital that is available

average atomic mass the weighted average of the masses of all naturally occurring isotopes of an element

Avogadro's law the law that states that equal volumes of gases at the same temperature and pressure contain equal numbers of molecules

Avogadro's number 6.022×10^{23}, the number of atoms or molecules in 1 mol

B

barometer an instrument that measures atmospheric pressure

beta particle a charged electron emitted during certain types of radioactive decay, such as beta decay

binary acid an acid that contains only two different elements: hydrogen and one of the more electronegative elements

binary compound a compound composed of two different elements

boiling the conversion of a liquid to a vapor within the liquid as well as at the surface of the liquid at a specific temperature and pressure; occurs when the vapor pressure of the liquid equals the atmospheric pressure

boiling point the temperature and pressure at which a liquid and a gas are in equilibrium

boiling-point elevation the difference between the boiling point of a liquid in pure state and the boiling point of the liquid in solution; the increase depends on the amount of solute particles present

bond energy the energy required to break a chemical bond and form neutral isolated atoms

Boyle's law the law that states that for a fixed amount of gas at a constant temperature, the volume of the gas increases as the pressure of the gas decreases and the volume of the gas decreases as the pressure of the gas increases

Brønsted-Lowry acid a substance that donates a proton to another substance

Brønsted-Lowry acid-base reaction the transfer of protons from one reactant (the acid) to another (the base)

Brønsted-Lowry base a substance that accepts a proton

C

calorimeter a device used to measure the energy as heat absorbed or released in a chemical or physical change

capillary action the attraction of the surface of a liquid to the surface of a solid, which causes the liquid to rise or fall

carbohydrate any organic compound that is made of carbon, hydrogen, and oxygen and that provides nutrients to the cells of living things

catalysis the acceleration of a chemical reaction by a catalyst

catalyst a substance that changes the rate of a chemical reaction without being consumed or changed significantly

cathode the electrode on whose surface reduction takes place

cation an ion that has a positive charge

chain reaction a reaction in which the material that starts the reaction is also one of the products and can start another reaction

change of state the change of a substance from one physical state to another

Charles's law the law that states that for a fixed amount of gas at a constant pressure, the volume of the gas increases as the temperature of the gas increases and the volume of the gas decreases as the temperature of the gas decreases

chemical any substance with a defined composition

chemical bond the attractive force that holds atoms or ions together

chemical change a change that occurs when one or more substances change into entirely new substances with different properties

chemical equation a representation of a chemical reaction that uses symbols to show the relationship between the reactants and the products

chemical equilibrium a state of balance in which the rate of a forward reaction equals the rate of the reverse reaction and the concentrations of products and reactants remain unchanged

chemical formula a combination of chemical symbols and numbers to represent a substance

chemical property a property of matter that describes a substance's ability to participate in chemical reactions

chemical reaction the process by which one or more substances change to produce one or more different substances

chemistry the scientific study of the composition, structure, and properties of matter and the changes that matter undergoes

coefficient a whole number that appears as a factor in front of a formula in a chemical equation

colligative property a property determined by the number of particles in a system that is independent of the properties of the particles themselves

collision theory theory that states that, in order for a chemical reaction to occur, collisions between particles must have sufficient energy and correct orientation

colloid a mixture consisting of tiny particles that are intermediate in size between those in solutions and those in suspensions and that are suspended in a liquid, solid, or gas

combined gas law the relationship between the pressure, volume, and temperature of a fixed amount of gas

combustion reaction the oxidation reaction of an element or compound, in which energy as heat is released

composition stoichiometry calculations involving the mass relationships of elements in compounds

compound a substance made up of atoms of two or more different elements joined by chemical bonds

concentration the amount of a particular substance in a given quantity of a mixture, solution, or ore

condensation the change of state from a gas to a liquid

condensation reaction a chemical reaction in which two or more molecules combine to produce water or another simple molecule

conjugate acid an acid that forms when a base gains a proton

conjugate base a base that forms when an acid loses a proton

continuous spectrum an unbroken sequence of frequencies or wavelengths of electromagnetic radiation, often emitted by an incandescent source

control rod a neutron-absorbing rod that helps control a nuclear reaction by limiting the number of free neutrons

conversion factor a ratio that is derived from the equality of two different units and that can be used to convert from one unit to the other

copolymer a polymer that is made from two different monomers

covalent bond a bond formed when atoms share one or more pairs of electrons

critical mass the minimum mass of a fissionable isotope that provides the number of neutrons needed to sustain a chain reaction

critical point the temperature and pressure at which the gas and liquid states of a substance become identical and form one phase

critical pressure the lowest pressure at which a substance can exist as a liquid at the critical temperature

critical temperature the temperature above which a substance cannot exist in the liquid state

crystal a solid whose atoms, ions, or molecules are arranged in a regular, repeating pattern

crystal structure the arrangement of atoms, ions, or molecules in a regular way to form a crystal

crystalline solid a solid that consists of crystals

cycloalkane a saturated carbon chain that forms a loop or a ring

Dalton's law of partial pressures the law that states that the total pressure of a mixture of gases is equal to the sum of the partial pressures of the component gases

daughter nuclide a nuclide produced by the radioactive decay of another nuclide

decay series a series of radioactive nuclides produced by successive radioactive decay until a stable nuclide is reached

decomposition reaction a reaction in which a single compound breaks down to form two or more simpler substances

density the ratio of the mass of a substance to the volume of the substance; often expressed as grams per cubic centimeter for solids and liquids and as grams per liter for gases

deposition the change of state from a gas directly to a solid

derived unit a unit of measure that is a combination of other measurements

diffusion the movement of particles from regions of higher density to regions of lower density

dimensional analysis a mathematical technique that allows one to use units to solve problems involving measurements

dipole a molecule or a part of a molecule that contains both positively and negatively charged regions

diprotic acid an acid that has two ionizable hydrogen atoms in each molecule, such as sulfuric acid

direct proportion the relationship between two variables whose ratio is a constant value

dissociation the separating of a molecule into simpler molecules, atoms, radicals, or ions

double-displacement reaction a reaction in which the ions of two compounds exchange places in an aqueous solution to form two new compounds

ductility the ability of a substance to be hammered thin or drawn out into a wire

E

effervescence a bubbling of a liquid caused by the rapid escape of a gas rather than by boiling

effusion the passage of a gas under pressure through a tiny opening

elastic collision a collision between ideally elastic bodies in which the final and initial kinetic energies are the same

electrochemistry the branch of chemistry that is the study of the relationship between electric forces and chemical reactions

electrode a conductor used to establish electrical contact with a nonmetallic part of a circuit, such as an electrolyte

electrolysis the process in which an electric current is used to produce a chemical reaction, such as the decomposition of water

electrolyte a substance that dissolves in water to give a solution that conducts an electric current

electrolytic cell an electrochemical device in which electrolysis takes place when an electric current is in the device

electromagnetic radiation the radiation associated with an electric and magnetic field; it varies periodically and travels at the speed of light

electromagnetic spectrum all of the frequencies or wavelengths of electromagnetic radiation

electron affinity the energy change that occurs when an electron is acquired by a neutral atom

electron configuration the arrangement of electrons in an atom

electron-dot notation an electron configuration notation in which only the valence electrons of an atom of a particular element are shown, indicated by dots placed around the element's symbol

electronegativity a measure of the ability of an atom in a chemical compound to attract electrons

electroplating the electrolytic process of plating or coating an object with a metal

element a substance that cannot be separated or broken down into simpler substances by chemical means; all atoms of an element have the same atomic number

elimination reaction a reaction in which a simple molecule, such as water or ammonia, is removed and a new compound is produced

emission-line spectrum a series of specific wavelengths of electromagnetic radiation emitted by electrons as they move from higher to lower energy states

empirical formula a chemical formula that shows the composition of a compound in terms of the relative numbers and kinds of atoms in the simplest ratio

end point the point in a titration at which a marked color change takes place

enthalpy change the amount of energy released or absorbed as heat by a system during a process at constant pressure

enthalpy of combustion the energy released as heat by the complete combustion of a specific amount of a substance at constant pressure or volume

enthalpy of reaction the amount of energy released or absorbed as heat during a chemical reaction

enthalpy of solution the amount of energy released or absorbed as heat when a specific amount of solute dissolves in a solvent

entropy a measure of the randomness or disorder of a system

enzyme a type of protein that acts as a catalyst and speeds up metabolic reactions in plants and animals without being permanently changed or destroyed

equilibrium in chemistry, the state in which a chemical process and the reverse chemical process occur at the same rate such that the concentrations of reactants and products do not change; in physics, the state in which the net force on an object is zero

equilibrium constant a number that relates the concentrations of starting materials and products of a reversible chemical reaction to one another at a given temperature

equilibrium vapor pressure the vapor pressure of a system at equilibrium

equivalence point the point at which the two solutions used in a titration are present in chemically equivalent amounts

ether an organic compound in which two carbon atoms bond to the same oxygen atom

evaporation the change of state from a liquid to a gas

excess reactant the substance that is not used up completely in a reaction

excited state a state in which an atom has more energy than it does at its ground state

extensive property a property that depends on the extent or size of a system

family a vertical column of the periodic table

fatty acid an organic acid that is contained in lipids, such as fats or oils

fluid a nonsolid state of matter in which the atoms or molecules are free to move past each other, as in a gas or liquid

formula equation a representation of the reactants and products of a chemical reaction by their symbols or formulas

formula mass the sum of the average atomic masses of all atoms represented in the formula of any molecule, formula unit, or ion

formula unit the simplest collection of atoms from which an ionic compound's formula can be written

free energy the energy in a system that is available for work; a system's capacity to do useful work

free-energy change the difference between the change in enthalpy, ΔH, and the product of the Kelvin temperature and the entropy change, which is defined as $T\Delta S$, at a constant pressure and temperature

freezing the change of state in which a liquid becomes a solid as energy as heat is removed

freezing point the temperature at which a solid and liquid are in equilibrium at 1 atm pressure; the temperature at which a liquid substance freezes

freezing-point depression the difference between the freezing points of a pure solvent and a solution, which is directly proportional to the amount of solute present

frequency the number of cycles or vibrations per unit of time; *also* the number of waves produced in a given amount of time

functional group the portion of a molecule that is active in a chemical reaction and that determines the properties of many organic compounds

gamma ray the high-energy photon emitted by a nucleus during fission and radioactive decay

gas a form of matter that does not have a definite volume or shape

Gay-Lussac's law the law that states that the volume occupied by a gas at a constant pressure is directly proportional to the absolute temperature

Gay-Lussac's law of combining volumes of gases the law that states that the volumes of gases involved in a chemical change can be represented by a ratio of small whole numbers

Graham's law of effusion the law that states that the rates of effusion of gases at the same temperature and pressure are inversely proportional to the square roots of their molar masses

ground state the lowest energy state of a quantized system

group a vertical column of elements in the periodic table; elements in a group share chemical properties

half-life the time required for half of a sample of a radioactive isotope to break down by radioactive decay to form a daughter isotope

half-reaction the part of a reaction that involves only oxidation or reduction

halogen one of the elements of Group 17 (fluorine, chlorine, bromine, iodine, and astatine); halogens combine with most metals to form salts

heat the energy transferred between objects that are at different temperatures; energy is always transferred from higher-temperature objects to lower-temperature objects until thermal equilibrium is reached

Heisenberg uncertainty principle the principle that states that determining both the position and velocity of an electron or any other particle simultaneously is impossible

Henry's law the law that states that at constant temperature, the solubility of a gas in a liquid is directly proportional to the partial pressure of the gas on the surface of the liquid

Hess's law the overall enthalpy change in a reaction is equal to the sum of the enthalpy changes for the individual steps in the process

heterogeneous composed of dissimilar components

homogeneous describes something that has a uniform structure or composition throughout

Hund's rule the rule that states that for an atom in the ground state, the number of unpaired electrons is the maximum possible and these unpaired electrons have the same spin

hybrid orbitals orbitals of equal energy produced by the combination of two or more orbitals on the same atom

hybridization the mixing of two or more atomic orbitals of the same atom to produce new orbitals; hybridization represents the mixing of higher- and lower-energy orbitals to form orbitals of intermediate energy

hydration the strong affinity of water molecules for particles of dissolved or suspended substances that causes electrolytic dissociation

hydrocarbon an organic compound composed only of carbon and hydrogen

hydrogen bond the intermolecular force occurring when a hydrogen atom that is bonded to a highly electronegative atom of one molecule is attracted to two unshared electrons of another molecule

hydrolysis a chemical reaction between water and another substance to form two or more new substances; a reaction between water and a salt to create an acid or a base

hydronium ion an ion consisting of a proton combined with a molecule of water; H_3O^+

hypothesis an explanation that is based on prior scientific research or observations and that can be tested

I

ideal gas an imaginary gas whose particles are infinitely small and do not interact with each other

ideal gas constant the proportionality constant that appears in the equation of state for 1 mol of an ideal gas; $R = 0.082\ 057\ 84$ (L•atm)/(mol•K)

ideal gas law the law that states the mathematical relationship of pressure (P), volume (V), temperature (T), the gas constant (R), and the number of moles of a gas (n); $PV = nRT$

immiscible describes two or more liquids that do not mix with each other

intensive property a property that does not depend on the amount of matter present, such as pressure, temperature, or density

intermediate a substance that forms in a middle stage of a chemical reaction and is considered a stepping stone between the parent substance and the final product

inverse proportion the relationship between two variables whose product is constant

ion an atom, radical, or molecule that has gained or lost one or more electrons and has a negative or positive charge

ionic bond a force that attracts electrons from one atom to another, which transforms a neutral atom into an ion

ionic compound a compound composed of ions bound together by electrostatic attraction

ionization the process of adding or removing electrons from an atom or molecule, which gives the atom or molecule a net charge

ionization energy the energy required to remove an electron from an atom or ion (abbreviation, IE)

isomer one of two or more compounds that have the same chemical composition but different structures

isotope an atom that has the same number of protons (or the same atomic number) as other atoms of the same element do but that has a different number of neutrons (and thus a different atomic mass)

J

joule the unit used to express energy; equivalent to the amount of work done by a force of 1 N acting through a distance of 1 m in the direction of the force (abbreviation, J)

K

kinetic-molecular theory a theory that explains that the behavior of physical systems depends on the combined actions of the molecules constituting the system

L

lanthanide a member of the rare-earth series of elements, whose atomic numbers range from 58 (cerium) to 71 (lutetium)

lattice energy the energy released when one mole of an ionic crystalline compound is formed from gaseous ions

law of conservation of mass the law that states that mass cannot be created or destroyed in ordinary chemical and physical changes

law of definite proportions the law that states that a chemical compound always contains the same elements in exactly the same proportions by weight or mass

law of multiple proportions the law that states that when two elements combine to form two or more compounds, the mass of one element that combines with a given mass of the other is in the ratio of small whole numbers

Lewis acid an atom, ion, or molecule that accepts a pair of electrons

Lewis acid-base reaction the formation of one or more covalent bonds between an electron-pair donor and an electron-pair acceptor

Lewis base an atom, ion, or molecule that donates a pair of electrons

Lewis structure a structural formula in which electrons are represented by dots; dot pairs or dashes between two atomic symbols represent pairs in covalent bonds

limiting reactant the substance that controls the quantity of product that can form in a chemical reaction

lipid a type of biochemical that does not dissolve in water, including fats and steroids; lipids store energy and make up cell membranes

liquid the state of matter that has a definite volume but not a definite shape

London dispersion force the intermolecular attraction resulting from the uneven distribution of electrons and the creation of temporary dipoles

---

M

magnetic quantum number the quantum number that indicates the orientation of an orbital around the nucleus; symbolized by m

main-group element an element in the s-block or p-block of the periodic table

malleability the ability of a substance to be hammered or beaten into a sheet

mass a measure of the amount of matter in an object

mass defect the difference between the mass of an atom and the sum of the masses of the atom's protons, neutrons, and electrons

mass number the sum of the numbers of protons and neutrons that make up the nucleus of an atom

matter anything that has mass and takes up space

melting the change of state in which a solid becomes a liquid by adding energy as heat or changing pressure

melting point the temperature and pressure at which a solid becomes a liquid

metabolism the sum of all chemical processes that occur in an organism

metal an element that is shiny and that conducts heat and electricity well

metallic bond a bond formed by the attraction between positively charged metal ions and the electrons around them

metalloid an element that has properties of both metals and nonmetals; sometimes referred to as a semiconductor

millimeters of mercury a unit of pressure

miscible describes two or more liquids that can dissolve into each other in various proportions

mixture a combination of two or more substances that are not chemically combined

model a pattern, plan, representation, or description designed to show the structure or workings of an object, system, or concept

moderator a material that slows the velocity of neutrons so that they may be absorbed by the nuclei

molal boiling-point constant a quantity calculated to represent the boiling-point elevation of a 1-molal solution of a nonvolatile, nonelectrolyte solution

molal freezing-point constant a quantity calculated to represent the freezing-point depression of a 1-molal solution of a nonvolatile, nonelectrolyte solute

molality the concentration of a solution expressed in moles of solute per kilogram of solvent

molar enthalpy of formation the amount of energy as heat resulting from the formation of 1 mol of a substance at constant pressure

molar enthalpy of fusion the amount of energy as heat required to change 1 mol of a substance from solid to liquid at constant temperature and pressure

molar enthalpy of vaporization the amount of energy as heat required to evaporate 1 mol of a liquid at constant pressure and temperature

molar mass the mass in grams of 1 mol of a substance

molarity a concentration unit of a solution expressed as moles of solute dissolved per liter of solution

mole the SI base unit used to measure the amount of a substance whose number of particles is the same as the number of atoms of carbon in exactly 12 g of carbon-12

mole ratio a conversion factor that relates the amounts in moles of any two substances involved in a chemical reaction

molecular compound a chemical compound whose simplest units are molecules

molecular formula a chemical formula that shows the number and kinds of atoms in a molecule, but not the arrangement of the atoms

molecule a neutral group of atoms that are held together by covalent bonds

monatomic ion an ion formed from a single atom

monomer a simple molecule that can combine with other like or unlike molecules to make a polymer

monoprotic acid an acid that can donate only one proton to a base

monosaccharide a simple sugar that is the basic subunit of a carbohydrate

multiple bond a bond in which the atoms share more than one pair of electrons, such as a double bond or a triple bond

N

natural gas a mixture of gaseous hydrocarbons located under the surface of Earth

net ionic equation an equation that includes only those compounds and ions that undergo a chemical change in a reaction in an aqueous solution

neutralization the reaction of the ions that characterize acids (hydronium ions) and the ions that characterize bases (hydroxide ions) to form water molecules and a salt

newton the SI unit for force; the force that will increase the speed of a 1 kg mass by 1 m/s each second that the force is applied (abbreviation, N)

noble gas one of the elements of Group 18 of the periodic table (helium, neon, argon, krypton, xenon, and radon); noble gases are unreactive

noble-gas configuration an outer main energy level fully occupied, in most cases, by eight electrons

nomenclature a naming system

nonelectrolyte a substance that dissolves in water to give a solution that does not conduct an electric current

nonmetal an element that conducts heat and electricity poorly and that does not form positive ions in an electrolytic solution

nonpolar-covalent bond a covalent bond in which the bonding electrons are equally attracted to both bonded atoms

nonvolatile substance a substance that has little tendency to become a gas under existing conditions

nuclear binding energy the energy released when a nucleus is formed from nucleons

nuclear fission the splitting of the nucleus of a large atom into two or more fragments; releases additional neutrons and energy

nuclear forces the interaction that binds protons and neutrons, protons and protons, and neutrons and neutrons together in a nucleus

nuclear fusion the combination of the nuclei of small atoms to form a larger nucleus; releases energy

nuclear power plant a facility that uses heat from nuclear reactors to produce electrical energy

nuclear radiation the particles that are released from the nucleus during radioactive decay, such as neutrons, electrons, and photons

nuclear reaction a reaction that affects the nucleus of an atom

nuclear reactor a device that uses controlled nuclear reactions to produce energy or nuclides

nucleic acid an organic compound, either RNA or DNA, whose molecules are made up of one or two chains of nucleotides and carry genetic information

nucleon a proton or neutron

nuclide an atom that is identified by the number of protons and neutrons in its nucleus

orbital a region in an atom where there is a high probability of finding electrons

organic compound a covalently bonded compound that contains carbon, excluding carbonates and oxides

osmosis the diffusion of water or another solvent from a more dilute solution (of a solute) to a more concentrated solution (of the solute) through a membrane that is permeable to the solvent

osmotic pressure the external pressure that must be applied to stop osmosis

oxidation a reaction that removes one or more electrons from a substance such that the substance's valence or oxidation state increases

oxidation number the number of electrons that must be added to or removed from an atom in a combined state to convert the atom into the elemental form

oxidation state the condition of an atom expressed by the number of electrons that the atom needs to reach its elemental form

oxidation-reduction reaction any chemical change in which one species is oxidized (loses electrons) and another species is reduced (gains electrons); also called *redox reaction*

oxidized describes an element that has lost electrons and that has increased its oxidation number

oxidizing agent the substance that gains electrons in an oxidationreduction reaction and that is reduced

oxyacid an acid that is a compound of hydrogen, oxygen, and a third element, usually a nonmetal

oxyanion a polyatomic ion that contains oxygen

parent nuclide a radionuclide that yields a specific daughter nuclide as a later member of a radioactive series

partial pressure the pressure of each gas in a mixture

pascal the SI unit of pressure; equal to the force of 1 N exerted over an area of 1 m^2 (abbreviation, Pa)

Pauli exclusion principle the principle that states that two particles of a certain class cannot be in exactly the same energy state

percentage composition the percentage by mass of each element in a compound

percentage error a qualitative comparison of the average experimental value to the correct or accepted value; it is calculated by subtracting the accepted value from the experimental value, dividing the difference by the accepted value, and then multiplying by 100

percentage yield the ratio of the actual yield to the theoretical yield, multiplied by 100

period in chemistry, a horizontal row of elements in the periodic table

periodic law the law that states that the repeating chemical and physical properties of elements change periodically with the atomic numbers of the elements

periodic table an arrangement of the elements in order of their atomic numbers such that elements with similar properties fall in the same column

petroleum a liquid mixture of complex hydrocarbon compounds; used widely as a fuel source

pH a value that is used to express the acidity or alkalinity (basicity) of a system; each whole number on the scale indicates a tenfold change in acidity; a pH of 7 is neutral, a pH of less than 7 is acidic, and a pH of greater than 7 is basic

pH meter a device used to determine the pH of a solution by measuring the voltage between the two electrodes that are placed in the solution

phase in chemistry, one of the four states or conditions in which a substance can exist: solid, liquid, gas, or plasma; a part of matter that is uniform

phase diagram a graph of the relationship between the physical state of a substance and the temperature and pressure of the substance

photoelectric effect the emission of electrons from a material when light of certain frequencies shines on the surface of the material

photon a unit or quantum of light; a particle of electromagnetic radiation that has zero rest mass and carries a quantum of energy

physical change a change of matter from one form to another without a change in chemical properties

physical property a characteristic of a substance that does not involve a chemical change, such as density, color, or hardness

plasma in physical science, a state of matter that starts as a gas and then becomes ionized; it consists of free-moving ions and electrons and it takes on an electric charge

pOH the negative of the common logarithm of the hydroxide ion concentration of a solution

polar describes a molecule in which the positive and negative charges are separated

polar-covalent bond a covalent bond in which a pair of electrons shared by two atoms is held more closely by one atom

polyatomic ion an ion made of two or more atoms

polymer a large molecule that is formed by more than five monomers, or small units

polyprotic acid an acid that can donate more than one proton per molecule

polysaccharide one of the carbohydrates made up of long chains of simple sugars; polysaccharides include starch, cellulose, and glycogen

precipitate a solid that is produced as a result of a chemical reaction in solution

precision the exactness of a measurement

pressure the amount of force exerted per unit area of a surface

primary standard a highly purified solid compound used to check the concentration of a known solution in a titration

principal quantum number the quantum number that indicates the energy and orbital of an electron in an atom

product a substance that forms in a chemical reaction

protein an organic compound that is made of one or more chains of amino acids and that is a principal component of all cells

pure substance a sample of matter, either a single element or a single compound, that has definite chemical and physical properties

Q

quantity something that has magnitude, size, or amount

quantum the basic unit of electromagnetic energy; it characterizes the wave properties of electrons

quantum number a number that specifies certain properties of electrons

quantum theory the study of the structure and behavior of the atom and of subatomic particles from the view that all energy comes in tiny, indivisible bundles

R

radioactive dating the process by which the approximate age of an object is determined based on the amount of certain radioactive nuclides present

radioactive decay the disintegration of an unstable atomic nucleus into one or more different nuclides, accompanied by the emission of radiation, the nuclear capture or ejection of electrons, or fission

radioactive nuclide a nuclide that contains isotopes that decay and that emit radiation

radioactive tracer a radioactive material that is added to a substance so that its distribution can be detected later

reactant a substance or molecule that participates in a chemical reaction

reaction mechanism the way in which a chemical reaction takes place; expressed in a series of chemical equations

reaction rate the rate at which a chemical reaction takes place; measured by the rate of formation of the product or the rate of disappearance of the reactants

reaction stoichiometry calculations involving the mass relationships between reactants and products in a chemical reaction

real gas a gas that does not behave completely like a hypothetical ideal gas because of the interactions between the gas molecules

redox reaction See *oxidation-reduction reaction*

reduced describes a substance that has gained electrons, lost an oxygen atom, or gained a hydrogen atom

reducing agent a substance that has the potential to reduce another substance

reduction a chemical change in which electrons are gained, either by the removal of oxygen, the addition of hydrogen, or the addition of electrons

reduction potential the decrease in voltage that takes place when a positive ion becomes less positive or neutral or when a neutral atom becomes negative ion

resonance the bonding in molecules or ions that cannot be correctly represented by a single Lewis structure

reversible reaction a chemical reaction in which the products re-form the original reactants

salt an ionic compound that forms when a metal atom or a positive radical replaces the hydrogen of an acid

saturated hydrocarbon an organic compound formed only by carbon and hydrogen linked by single bonds

saturated solution a solution that cannot dissolve any more solute under the given conditions)

scientific method a series of steps followed to solve problems, including collecting data, formulating a hypothesis, testing the hypothesis, and stating conclusions

scientific notation a method of expressing a quantity as a number multiplied by 10 to the appropriate power

self-ionization of water a process in which two water molecules produce a hydronium ion and a hydroxide ion by transfer of a proton

semipermeable membrane a membrane that permits the passage of only certain molecules

SI Le Système International d'Unités, or the International System of Units, which is the measurement system that is accepted worldwide

significant figure a prescribed decimal place that determines the amount of rounding off to be done based on the precision of the measurement

single bond a covalent bond in which two atoms share one pair of electrons

single-displacement reaction a reaction in which one element or radical takes the place of another element or radical in a compound

solid the state of matter in which the volume and shape of a substance are fixed

solubility the ability of one substance to dissolve in another at a given temperature and pressure; expressed in terms of the amount of solute that will dissolve in a given amount of solvent to produce a saturated solution

soluble capable of dissolving in a particular solvent

solute in a solution, the substance that dissolves in the solvent

solution a homogeneous mixture of two or more substances uniformly dispersed throughout a single phase

solution equilibrium the physical state in which the opposing processes of dissolution and crystallization of a solute occur at equal rates

solvated describes a solute molecule that is surrounded by solvent molecules

solvent in a solution, the substance in which the solute dissolves

specific heat the quantity of heat required to raise a unit mass of homogeneous material 1 K or 1°C in a specified way given constant pressure and volume

spectator ions ions that are present in a solution in which a reaction is taking place but that do not participate in the reaction

spin quantum number the quantum number that describes the intrinsic angular momentum of a particle

standard molar volume of a gas a volume of 22.414 10 L at 0°C temperature and 1.00 atm pressure

standard solution a solution of known concentration, expressed in terms of the amount of solute in a given amount of solvent or solution

strong acid an acid that ionizes completely in a solvent

strong electrolyte a compound that completely or largely dissociates in an aqueous solution, such as soluble mineral salts

structural formula a formula that indicates the location of the atoms, groups, or ions relative to one another in a molecule and that indicates the number and location of chemical bonds

sublimation the process in which a solid changes directly into a gas (the term is sometimes also used for the reverse process)

substitution reaction a reaction in which one or more atoms replace another atom or group of atoms in a molecule

supercooled liquid a liquid that is cooled below its normal freezing point without solidifying

supersaturated solution a solution that holds more dissolved solute than is required to reach equilibrium at a given temperature

surface tension the force that acts on the surface of a liquid and that tends to minimize the area of the surface

suspension a mixture in which particles of a material are more or less evenly dispersed throughout a liquid or gas

synthesis reaction a reaction in which two or more substances combine to form a new compound

system a set of particles or interacting components considered to be a distinct physical entity for the purpose of study

T

temperature a measure of how hot (or cold) something is; specifically, a measure of the average kinetic energy of the particles in an object

theoretical yield the maximum amount of product that can be produced from a given amount of reactant

theory an explanation for some phenomenon that is based on observation, experimentation, and reasoning

thermochemical equation an equation that includes the quantity of energy as heat released or absorbed during the reaction as written

thermochemistry the branch of chemistry that is the study of the energy changes that accompany chemical reactions and changes of state

titration a method to determine the concentration of a substance in solution by adding a solution of known volume and concentration until the reaction is completed, which is usually indicated by a change in color

transition element one of the metals that can use the inner shell before using the outer shell to bond

transition interval the range in concentration over which a variation in a chemical indicator can be observed

transmutation the transformation of atoms of one element into atoms of a different element as a result of a nuclear reaction

transuranium element a synthetic element whose an atomic number is greater than that of uranium (atomic number 92)

triple point the temperature and pressure conditions at which the solid, liquid, and gaseous phases of a substance coexist at equilibrium

triprotic acid an acid that has three ionizable protons per molecule, such as phosphoric acid

U

unified atomic mass unit a unit of mass that describes the mass of an atom or molecule; it is exactly 1/12 of the mass of a carbon atom with mass number 12 (abbreviation, u)

unit cell the smallest portion of a crystal lattice that shows the three-dimensional pattern of the entire lattice

unsaturated hydrocarbon a hydrocarbon that has available valence bonds, usually from double or triple bonds with carbon

unsaturated solution a solution that contains less solute than a saturated solution does and that is able to dissolve additional solute

V

valence electron an electron that is found in the outermost shell of an atom and that determines the atom's chemical properties

vaporization the process by which a liquid or solid changes to a gas

volatile liquid a liquid that evaporates readily or at a low temperature

volume a measure of the size of a body or region in three-dimensional space

VSEPR theory a theory that predicts some molecular shapes based on the idea that pairs of valence electrons surrounding an atom repel each other

W

wavelength the distance from any point on a wave to an identical point on the next wave

weak acid an acid that releases few hydrogen ions in aqueous solution

weak electrolyte a compound that dissociates only to a small extent in aqueous solution

weight a measure of the gravitational force exerted on an object; its value can change with the location of the object in the universe

word equation an equation in which the reactants and products in a chemical reaction are represented by words